Fourth Edition

Structured FORTRAN 77 FOR ENGINEERS AND SCIENTISTS

D. M. ETTER

Department of Electrical & Computer Engineering
University of Colorado, Boulder

The Benjamin/Cummings Publishing Company, Inc.
Redwood City, California • Menlo Park, California • Reading, Massachusetts
New York • Don Mills, Ontario • Wokingham, U.K. • Amsterdam • Bonn
Sydney • Singapore • Tokyo • Madrid • San Juan

Sponsoring Editor: Jennifer Young
Production Editor: Jean Lake
Art and Design Manager: Michele Carter
Cover and Text Designer: Don Taka
Cover Photo: Solar dishes © Nadia Mackenzie/TSW.
Photo Editor: Kelli West
Composition and Illustrations: Progressive Typographers
Printing and Binding: R. R. Donnelley and Sons

Library of Congress Cataloging-in-Publication Data

Etter, D. M.
Structured FORTRAN 77 for engineers and scientists / D. M. Etter. --4th ed.
p. cm.
Includes index.
ISBN 0-8053-1775-9
1. FORTRAN 77 (Computer program language) 2. Computer programming. I. Title.
QA76.73.F25E85 1993
005.13'3--dc20 92-35063
CIP

2 3 4 5 6 7 8 9 10—DO—95 94 93

The Benjamin/Cummings Publishing Company, Inc.
390 Bridge Parkway
Redwood City, California 94065

To my family, Amy Marie and Jerry Richard.

Preface

This text was designed with three objectives in mind. The first objective is to introduce engineering and science students to a problem solving technique that they can use in solving engineering problems. Since engineering and science students are faced with solving problems in many of their courses (engineering courses, physics, chemistry, calculus, . . .), it is important that this technique be adaptable to various types of problems. It is also important that the technique be reinforced with many examples, both simple and more complicated. We present a five-step methodology for solving problems in Chapter 1 and then use it throughout the text when we develop programs. Each step is clearly identified to help students focus on the process of breaking a problem into smaller components and then addressing the smaller components.

The second objective is to provide a fundamental understanding of computers and to specifically develop a working knowledge of FORTRAN 77. We do not assume that the students have worked with computers, and Chapter 1 gives an introduction to both computer hardware and computer software. A discussion of computer languages, software tools, and operating systems helps the student understand the capabilities and functions of various kinds of software. Chapters 2 – 9 cover the complete FORTRAN 77 languages, with special emphasis on the control structures and data structures that are commonly used in engineering problem solutions. Chapter 10 introduces several commonly used numerical techniques and then develops solutions using them. Since the new Fortran 90 standard has been accepted, we include information on the new features of this language throughout the text. We also devote Chapter 11 specifically to a discussion of this new standard.

The third objective is to motivate and excite students about engineering; we also want to help them understand the types of problems that engineers solve. To achieve this objective, we have adopted a theme for the text that is based on the ten top engineering achievements that were selected by the National Academy of Engineering. These ten top achievements represent technological breakthroughs during the past 25 years. We use these achievements in a number of ways: Chapter 1 contains a color gallery that discusses each of the achievements; each chapter is opened with another picture related to one of the achievements along with more discussion on the topic; and each chapter contains an application section which contains a problem related to the chapter opening achievement that is then solved using the five-step process and FORTRAN 77. These ten top achievements are also related to a number of the end-of-chapter problems.

New Features

In addition to continuing to include the features in our previous edition, we have added some new features and expanded other features.

Fortran 90 Coverage Although the new Fortran 90 standard has been accepted, it will still be some time before compilers are readily available. However, it is important to make students aware of the new standard and to inform them of the new features that will be available. We incorporate the Fortran 90 coverage in two ways. Throughout Chapters 2 – 10, we include short comments that mention new Fortran 90 statements in the section that covers related statements. These comments are carefully identified so that they cannot be confused with FORTRAN 77 statements. Then, Chapter 11 is a detailed summary of some of the important new features with specific examples.

New Engineering Applications Engineering applications have always been a strength of past editions of this text, and we have added even more to this edition. We added nine new application sections with engineering problems that relate specifically to the top ten engineering achievements. We have also added problems that relate to additional engineering disciplines such as optical engineering, acoustical engineering, biomedical engineering, and genetic engineering.

Expanded Numerical Methods We have expanded the coverage of commonly used numerical methods. In particular, we have focused on developing an intuitive understanding of the methods, using diagrams and plots. The topics covered in detail include linear interpolation, roots of polynomials, least-squares methods, matrix operations, solutions to systems of linear equations, numerical integration, and numerical differentiation.

Expanded Data File Coverage Since data files are used so frequently to store engineering data, we have expanded the coverage of these files. Chapter 4 contains a detailed discussion on reading data files, with emphasis on the different ways that data can be stored. For example, some files will have trailer records, others will have a header record, and others will contain only data. In addition to examples showing how to read the various forms of data files, we also discuss generating data files. Guidelines are given for selecting the type of data file to use when generating a file. Chapter 9 then contains advanced file handling techniques, covering sequential and direct-access data files.

Appendix on Plotting Since graphs are so useful in interpreting engineering data and computational results, an appendix is included that illustrates the steps in plotting information from data files using both MATLAB and Lotus 1-2-3.

Distinguishing Features

A number of features continue to distinguish this text from other FORTRAN texts.

Engineering and Science Applications Over 600 examples and problems represent a wide range of engineering and science applications. The problems are related to the classical engineering disciplines such as electrical engineering, mechanical engineering, aerospace engineering, chemical engineering, civil engineering, power engineering, and petroleum engineering. Problems have also been added to relate to newer engineering disciplines such as biomedical engineering, genetic engineering, environmental engineering, optical engineering, manufacturing engineering, and robotic engineering. The topics addressed include equipment reliability, terrain navigation, water treatment, sensor data, climatology, wind tunnel data analysis, and spacecraft data analysis. Many of the solved problems contain sample data and corresponding output from actual computer runs.

Problem Solving Methodology The five-step problem solving methodology introduced in Chapter 1 is used throughout the text. The five steps are:

1. State the problem clearly.
2. Describe the input and the output.
3. Work the problem by hand (or with a calculator) for a specific set of data.
4. Develop a solution that is general in nature.
5. Test the algorithm with a variety of data sets.

This process is consistently used to develop all complete programs.

Engineering Case Studies The application sections comprise a set of 30 engineering case studies. Each case study includes a detailed development of the problem's solution along with sample data to illustrate testing the algorithm.

Subprograms Algorithms for common techniques are presented and their use is reinforced through a variety of applications. Sort algorithms are provided for selection sorts, insertion sorts, and bubble sorts. Search algorithms for searching both ordered and unordered lists are presented with sequential and binary searches. Algorithms for inserting and deleting with ordered lists are also covered. These algorithms are then developed as functions and subroutines so that students can refer to these common subprograms in other programs. The reuse of existing subprograms is stressed throughout the text.

Structure Charts Structure charts provide a graphical picture of the modular structure of a program. Structure charts are included for all programs that contain subroutines and/or functions. Pseudocode and flowcharts are used to illustrate graphically the logical flow of the steps in an algorithm.

Complete FORTRAN 77 Coverage Complete coverage of FORTRAN 77 makes this book not only suitable for the first-time computer user but also as a valuable reference for the experienced user. In addition, only standard FORTRAN 77 statements and structures are used, so all programs and statements are compatible with any FORTRAN 77 compiler. Another advantage of using only standard FORTRAN 77 is that all programs will work properly in Fortran 90 because the new standard is upward compatible.

Motivational Problems as Chapter Openers Each chapter begins with a discussion of a topic related to one of the top ten engineering achievements. Then, later in the chapter, an application section presents a specific problem related to that achievement and develops a solution to the problem using the five-step process.

Early Programming This book assumes no prior experience with computers; it begins with an introductory chapter that explains many terms associated with computing. A discussion of current computer hardware and software is presented, along with photos of the various types of computers that the student might be using. The presentation of FORTRAN statements begins with Chapter 2. By the end of Chapter 2, complete programs have been written.

Top-Down Design The five-step problem solving methodology that appears throughout the text stresses top-down design techniques. A problem is first decomposed into general steps shown in a block diagram. Then, using stepwise refinement, the steps are translated into a computer language. Both pseudocode and flowcharts contribute to the development of the stepwise refinements so that students become acquainted with both techniques. Structure charts illustrate the modular structure of programs.

Structured Programming Approach To promote simplicity in solutions and reduce the time spent in testing and debugging programs, all problem solutions use structures with one way into the structure and one way out of the structure. All programs are implemented as either While loops or iterative loops (DO loops). GO TO statements are used only to implement While loops.

FORTRAN Statement Summaries Each chapter contains a summary of the FORTRAN statements presented in that chapter. The summary contains the general form of the statement, specific examples of the statement, and a brief discussion of the rules for using the statement.

Self-Tests and Solutions The self-tests in Chapters 2–10 contain completely new problems that allow students to check their understanding of the new material. Students can immediately determine whether they are ready to proceed to the next section by checking their answers to the self-tests against the solutions included at the end of the text.

Style/Technique Guides Each chapter after the introductory chapter contains a style/technique guide to promote good programming habits that stress readability and simplicity. Although entire books are devoted to programming style and technique, this topic is included in each chapter on the premise that developing good style and technique is an integral part of learning the language. In addition to this special section at the end of each chapter, a number of examples in the text have multiple solutions, thereby exposing students to different approaches to solving the same problem. If one of these solutions has better style or technique than the others, it is pointed out in the accompanying discussion.

Debugging Aids Debugging aids are included in Chapters 2–10. This section outlines efficient methods for locating and correcting program errors relevant to the programming techniques described in the chapter. With guidance from this section, students learn consistent methods for spotting and avoiding the common errors associated with each new FORTRAN statement. In addition to debugging aids, a number of examples in the text include an incorrect solution to a problem along with the correct solution. The incorrect solution is used to highlight common errors, thus helping students avoid making the same mistakes.

Key Words and Glossary A list of key words appears at the end of each chapter. For easy reference, the definition of each of the key words is in the glossary at the end of the text.

Large Number of Problems Over 400 problems are included in the self-tests and end-of-chapter problems. These problems vary in degree of difficulty, from simple to more challenging problems. Solutions to all of the self-tests and to many of the end-of-chapter problems are included at the end of the text.

I/O Flexibility List-directed input statements and simple formatted output statements are used throughout the text. This choice provides maximum flexibility in the form in which data is entered and maximum control over the form of output data. We encourage the use of list-directed output for the testing and debugging phases, but we always use formatted output in our final programs.

Use of Color Color is used throughout the text to emphasize important material. Pedagogically, the use of color in emphasizing certain statements within a computer program is especially significant. Without using arrows or lines or distracting symbols, we can clearly stress the use of a new statement or point out the differences in two similar program segments. All pseudocode and flowcharts are highlighted in color for easy reference. End-of-chapter problem numbers appear in color to indicate that the solution is included at the end of the text.

■ Organization

We recommend that Chapters 1 – 7 be covered sequentially because these first seven chapters contain material that provides students with a thorough knowledge of the fundamentals of the language. Then, material can be selected from the last four chapters as time permits. The text is intended for an audience of engineering and science students who have no prior computer background. Calculus is not required, but knowledge of college algebra and trigonometry is assumed.

■ Supplements

Instructor's Guide An instructor's guide is available on request from the publisher. This supplement contains suggested course syllabi for both semester and quarter courses, viewgraphs, additional computer projects, and complete solutions to the end-of-chapter problems.

Test Bank A test bank is also available on request from the publisher. This supplement contains 150 quizzes that are printed one per page to allow simple copying of the pages for use in the classroom. Midterm and final exams are also included for class distribution as actual exams or practice exams. Solutions to the quizzes and exams are included.

Engineering Signals Diskette An engineering signals diskette is included with the instructor's guide. This diskette contains numerous additional data sets from real-world engineering applications, including speech signals, seismic signals, and weather pattern signals. Suggested programming assignments that use these engineering signals are given in the instructor's guide. The diskette also contains all the programs and data sets from the application sections in the text. All the files on the diskette are ASCII files so that they can be uploaded to whatever system is being used.

Acknowledgments

I continue to appreciate the value of suggestions, guidance, and criticism provided by reviewers. I would especially like to thank Professors Jeanine Ingber and W. F. Beckwith for their assistance with this edition. Reviewers of previous editions were Professors Betty J. Barr, Lawrence J. Genalo, John Cowles, Mike Manry, Josann Duane, Ronald Danielson, William Holley, John Goda, Lee Maxwell, John R. Zimmerman, Susanne M. Shelley, Ted Wagstaff, Glen Williams, Edward T. Ordman, Elizabeth Unger, Joe Jefferis, Robert Aiken, Enrique A. Gonzales, and William Harlow. I also want to thank the following people at the Benjamin/Cummings Publishing Company who continue to be as excited and enthusiastic about the capabilities of FORTRAN for engineers and scientists as I am: Jennifer Young, Dan Joraanstad, and Laura Cheu (Editorial), Jean Lake (Production), and Mary Tudor and Liane Shayer (Marketing). I would also like to thank Lisa Moller for initiating this project and supporting it with her enthusiasm and efforts. Special thanks go to my husband Jerry (a mechanical/aerospace engineer), who helped develop some of the new engineering applications and data sets. Finally, I want to express my appreciation to Vena Margo for her assistance in testing the many programs and solutions.

About the Author

Dr. Delores M. Etter, recently elected a Fellow of the IEEE for her contributions to education and technical leadership in digital signal processing, is a professor of electrical and computer engineering at the University of Colorado. She has received a number of teaching awards, including the Distinguished Educator Award and the Outstanding Engineering Professor Award. Her research has been funded by IBM, Sandia National Laboratories, and the National Science Foundation, as well as other corporations and laboratories, and she has published numerous articles in areas such as adaptive echo-cancelling and digital filter design.

Brief Contents

Detailed Contents

Chapters 1 – 10 begin with a discussion of one of the ten outstanding achievements and a reference to an application section that solves a related problem. Chapter 1 also contains a list of references to more information on these outstanding achievements. Each chapter begins with an introduction and ends with a summary. In addition, chapters also include the following:

- keywords
- debugging aids
- style/technique guides
- programming problems
- FORTRAN statement summaries

2 Arithmetic Computations 25

■ 5 Array Processing 203

■ 6 Function Subprograms 259

11 The New Fortran 90 Standard 517

Engineering and Science Applications

Acoustical Engineering

Aerospace Engineering

Biomedical Engineering

Chemical Engineering

Civil Engineering

Electrical Engineering

Electric Circuit Model (Sec. 8–6, p. 407; Probs. 8.11–8.15, p. 414)
Transfer Functions (Probs. 8.20–8.22, p. 415)
Voyager Spacecraft Data Analysis (Sec. 9–4, p. 434; Probs. 9.1–9.5, p. 458)
Power in Frequency Bands (Probs. 10.16–10.17, p. 513)

Environmental Engineering

Timber Regrowth (Sec. 3–8, p. 140; Probs. 3.16–3.20, p. 155)

Genetic Engineering

Protein Molecular Weights (Sec. 8–2, p. 386; Probs. 8.1–8.5, p. 413; Probs. 8.43–8.45, p. 419)

Manufacturing Engineering

Critical Path Analysis (Sec. 4–4, p. 183; Probs. 4.6–4.10, p. 194)
Equipment Maintenance (Prob. 5.32, p. 253)

Mechanical Engineering

Stride Estimation (Sec. 2–9, p. 68; Probs. 2.21–2.25, p. 80)
Cable Car Velocity (Ex. 3–4, p. 109)
Trajectory (Prob. 3.33, p. 157)
Solar Device (Prob. 4.16, p. 195)
Robot Arm Stability (Sec. 6–7, p. 292; Probs. 6.11–6.15, p. 316)
Composite Materials (Sec. 7–5, p. 354; Probs. 7.11–7.15, p. 364)
Temperature Distribution (Sec. 8–4, p. 395; Probs. 8.6–8.10, p. 413; Prob. 8.42, p. 419)
Materials Testing (Probs. 9.23–9.27, p. 461)
Accelerometer Model (Sec. 10–2, p. 471; Probs. 10.1–10.5, p. 512)

Optical Engineering

Light Pipes (Sec. 3–3, p. 113; Probs. 3.1–3.5, p. 154)
Spherical Mirrors (Ex. 8–9, p. 394)
Deformable Mirrors (Sec. 10–5, p. 488; Probs. 10.6–10.10, p. 512)

Petroleum Engineering

Seismic Drilling (Probs. 4.23–4.25, p. 197)
Oil Well Production (Sec. 6–6, p. 286; Probs. 6.6–6.10, p. 316)

Power Engineering

Power Plant Data Analysis (Sec. 5–7, p. 238; Probs. 5.11–5.15, p. 251)
Nuclear Plant Cooling System (Prob. 5.35, p. 255)

Transportation Engineering

Railroad Track Design (Probs. 2.37–2.38, p. 82)
Fuel Consumption (Probs. 4.21–4.22, p. 196; Prob. 8.26, p. 415)

Computer Engineering/Computer Science

Sorting (Prob. 3.25, p. 156; Sec. 5–4, p. 219; Ex. 7–2, p. 327; Ex. 8–7, p. 385, Probs. 8.28–8.29, p. 416; Probs. 8.31–8.35, p. 416; Prob. 8.37, p. 418; Prob. 8.40, p. 419)
Character Editing (Ex. 8–3, p. 379; Ex. 8–4, p. 381; Ex. 8–5, p. 382; Probs. 8.16–8.17, p. 414; Probs. 8.24–8.25, p. 415; Prob. 8.27, p. 416; Probs. 8.30–8.32, p. 416; Probs. 8.34–8.36, p. 417)
Collating Sequences (Ex. 8–6, p. 384)
Printer Plotting (Prob. 8.33, p. 416)
Searching (Sec. 6–8, p. 304; Ex. 6–7, p. 304; Ex. 6–8, p. 308; Ex. 6–9, p. 310)
Inserting and Deleting (Sec. 7–4, p. 344; Ex. 7–3, p. 344; Ex. 7–4, p. 348)
Cryptography (Probs. 8.38–8.39, p. 418)

Archeology

Carbon Dating (Sec. 2–7, p. 63; Probs. 2.11–2.15, p. 79)

Astronomy

Solar Distances (Ex. 8–8, p. 392)

Biology

Bacteria Growth (Sec. 2–6, p. 61; Probs. 2.6–2.10, p. 78; Prob. 3.38, p. 158)
Nutrition Study (Prob. 2.39, p. 82; Ex. 9–4, p. 428; Prob. 4.17, p. 195)
Whooping Crane Migration (Sec. 9–5, p. 441; Probs. 9.6–9.10, p. 458)

Chemistry

Temperature Conversions (Probs. 2.31–2.34, p. 81; Sec. 6–3, p. 265; Probs. 6.1–6.5, p. 315)

Mathematics

Rectangle Properties (Prob. 2.26, p. 81)
Slope of a Line (Prob. 2.28, p. 81)
Circle Properties (Prob. 2.29, p. 81)
Metric Conversions (Prob. 2.30, p. 81)
Coordinate Distances (Prob. 2.41, p. 83)
Triangle Area (Prob. 2.42, p. 83; Prob. 2.48, p. 85; Ex. 6–2, p. 262)
Volume (Prob. 2.45, p. 84; Probs. 6.16–6.20, p. 316)
Polynomial Evaluations (Ex. 3–9, p. 134; Ex. 3–10, p. 135; Ex. 3–11, p. 138)
Factorials (Ex. 3–13, p. 148; Prob. 3.40, p. 159; Prob. 6.31, p. 318)
Quadratic Formula (Prob. 3.34, p. 159; Ex. 8–10, p. 406; Prob. 8.19, p. 415; Prob. 8.41, p. 419)

Function Values (Probs. 3.21 – 3.24, p. 155; Probs. 6.26 – 6.20; p. 317)
Data Tables (Probs. 3.31 – 3.32, p. 156; Probs. 7.22 – 7.25, p. 365)
Infinite Series (Prob. 3.39, p. 159; Probs. 6.33 – 6.35, p. 318; Prob. 8.18, p. 414)
Polar Coordinates (Probs. 4.28 – 4.30, p. 199)
Matrix Operations (Ex. 5 – 7, p. 234; Ex. 10 – 1, p. 478; Ex. 10 – 2, p. 478; Ex. 10 – 3, p. 479; Ex. 10 – 4, p. 481; Ex. 10 – 5, p. 481; Probs. 10.21 – 10.24, p. 515)
Data Analysis (Probs. 5.23 – 5.24, p. 252; Prob. 5.28, p. 252; Prob. 5.30, p. 253; Probs. 6.23 – 6.25, p. 317; Prob. 6.30, p. 317; Prob. 6.32, p. 318; Probs. 7.18, p. 365; Probs. 7.20 – 7.21, p. 365; Prob. 7.27, p. 365)
Airline Reservations (Prob. 5.34, p. 254)
Gregorian – Julian dates (Probs. 5.36 – 5.37, p. 255)
Approximations (Probs. 10.18 – 10.20, p. 514)

Meteorology

Climatology Data (Sec. 4 – 3, p. 178; Probs. 4.1 – 4.5, p. 195; Probs. 4.31 – 4.35, p. 202; Probs. 5.44 – 5.46, p. 256; Probs. 6.42 – 6.45, p. 320)
Yearly Rainfall Analysis (Prob. 5.33, p. 254)

Physics

Gravitation Pull (Probs. 2.35 – 2.36, p. 82)
Rectifier Tube (Prob. 2.44, p. 84)

Sociology

Weight Category (Ex. 3 – 5, p. 111)

Statistics

Averages (Sec. 1 – 6, p. 17; Ex. 3 – 1, p. 99; Ex. 3 – 6, p. 117; Prob. 3.26, p. 156; Ex. 4 – 1, p. 170; Ex. 4 – 2, p. 172; Ex. 4 – 3, p. 175; Prob. 5.29, p. 253; Ex. 6 – 4, p. 278; Prob. 7.19, p. 365)
Labor Force Percentages (Prob. 2.43, p. 84)
Gaussian Density (Probs. 2.46 – 2.47, p. 85)
Maximum, Minimum (Ex. 3 – 2, p. 102; Ex. 3 – 7, p. 120; Prob. 3.26, p. 156; Prob. 5.21 – 5.22, p. 251; Prob. 5.33, p. 254; Ex. 6 – 6, p. 281; Probs. 6.21 – 6.22, p. 317; Probs. 7.16 – 7.17, p. 365; Prob. 7.26, p. 365)
Experimental Sums (Ex. 3 – 8, p. 131; Ex. 3 – 12, p. 146)
Scatter Reduction (Prob. 5.31, p. 253)
Median Values (Ex. 6 – 5, p. 279)
Array Statistics (Ex. 7 – 1, p. 325)
Variance, Standard Deviation (Probs. 7.28 – 7.29, p. 365)
Bias Adjustment (Prob. 7.30, p. 366)

1 An Introduction to Problem Solving with FORTRAN 77

1

APPLICATION

Moon Landing

The moon landing is probably the most complex and ambitious engineering project ever attempted. Major technological breakthroughs occurred in a number of the areas supporting the Saturn/Apollo system. For example, the Apollo spacecraft required a new inertial navigation system. The lunar lander ascent engine had to work correctly because there was no backup. The spacesuits had to be designed to survive a hostile environment and still have flexibility for movement. The Saturn V rocket had to be 15 times as powerful as the rockets available in the early 1960s. Given all these major technical problems to solve, the program was clearly successful. A total of nine spacecraft and 12 astronauts landed on the moon between 1968 and 1972.

Photo courtesy of NASA.

Introduction

In this chapter we introduce you to problem solving by first presenting 10 recent outstanding engineering and scientific achievements. We then discuss some grand challenges—problems yet to be solved. Since the computer is an essential tool in engineering problem solving, we discuss the different types of computers, from notebook computers to supercomputers. We compare computer languages and discuss some of the reasons why there are so many computer languages and software tools. Finally, we present a five-step process that can be applied to solving a wide variety of problems and we give a simple example that uses this five-step process to compute the average of a set of laboratory measurements.

1·1 ■ Engineering and Scientific Achievements

In celebration of its 25-year anniversary, the National Academy of Engineering selected what it considers to be the 10 most important engineering achievements during the past 25 years. Each of these achievements represented a major advance or breakthrough in engineering and a significant contribution to human welfare. These achievements are highlighted in the discussion that follows, in the photograph gallery in this chapter, and in each of the chapter opening applications.

■ Moon Landing

The Saturn/Apollo system consisted of the Apollo spacecraft, the lunar lander, and the three-stage Saturn V rocket. The new inertial navigation system used gyroscopes and accelerometers that sensed change in direction and speed. The lunar lander was the first manned vehicle designed to fly solely in space. One of its most critical parts (which had no backup) was the small ascent engine that was used to return the astronauts to the mother ship. In addition, the final design of the spacesuits consisted of a three-piece suit and backpack, which together weighed 190 pounds. The first piece of the suit was a cooling undergarment of knitted nylon-spandex with a network of plastic tubes filled with circulating water. The next piece was a rubber-coated bladder between a cloth lining and a nylon cover. The final piece was a protective outer garment of 17 layers; 6 of the 17 layers were made of a fireproof fabric of fiberglass threads coated with Teflon.

An individual moon flight required the coordination of more than 450 persons in the launch control center and nearly 7000 others on nine ships, in 54 aircraft, and at stations located around the earth. Clearly, the Apollo program pioneered techniques that remain the model for operating a massive engineering project.

■ Application Satellites

Satellite systems ring the earth today giving weather information, relaying communication signals, mapping uncharted terrain, and providing navigational information. Satellites in geostationary orbit rotate around with the earth 22,300 miles above the equator. At this altitude, they complete one revolution every 24 hours and thus remain stationary relative to the surface of the earth. Other groups of satellites use oblong orbits looping over northern latitudes. These satellites are not geostationary, but can be spaced so that one always rises over a spot before another sets.

Landsat satellites were first launched in 1972 and provide information on the entire earth from near-polar orbits, observing each spot at the same local time every 18 days. Landsats use multispectral sensors that transmit data, which is processed into images that yield information not available in standard images. For example, infrared satellite sensors use thermal information to provide images that show heat differentials. These images can be used to analyze geologic formations, to monitor pollution, and to observe volcanic activity.

Navstar is a Global Positioning System (GPS) that will have 18 satellites plus three spares in orbit when it is complete. Each satellite contains an atomic clock that loses or gains 1 second every 33,000 years. A GPS receiver on the earth receives signals from four satellites, each telling the time it was emitted and the position of the satellite. The receiver calculates how far each signal traveled and uses that information to determine the receiver's location to within 10 meters.

■ Microprocessors

A microprocessor is a tiny computer smaller than your fingernail. Because of its capabilities and size, the range of applications is virtually limitless. They can be programmed to perform specific tasks, such as operating remote television controllers or videocassette recorders (VCRs). If extra memory and input/output devices are added, a microprocessor can also be used as a general-purpose computer in hand-held calculators or personal computers.

Technology continues to provide smaller and yet more powerful microprocessors at lower prices. As a result, applications are being developed that use many microprocessors at once, with each given a specific task that can be performed simultaneously with other tasks. Thus, massively parallel computer systems can be designed to solve problems that could not feasibly be solved with a single computer.

■ Computer-Aided Design and Manufacturing

CAD (computer-aided design) and CAM (computer-aided manufacturing) have brought another industrial revolution to the world by increasing the speed and efficiency of many types of manufacturing processes. CAD typically refers to the use of the computer to generate designs, particularly using computer graphics. CAD programs combine the steps to take an idea through the initial sketch (which can also be done on the computer) to the completed design with schematics, parts lists, and computer simulation results.

CAM uses design parameters (sometimes produced by CAD systems) to automatically control machinery or industrial robots in manufacturing parts, assembling components, and moving them to the desired locations. CAM is especially useful in operations that would be hazardous to humans or that require high precision in tooling or milling.

CAT Scan

A CAT (computerized axial tomography) scanner is a machine that generates three-dimensional images or slices of an object using x-rays. A series of x-rays are generated from many angles, encircling the object or patient. Each x-ray measures a density at its angle, and by combining these density measurements with sophisticated computer algorithms, an image can be reconstructed that gives clear, detailed pictures of the inside of the object. A scan today takes less than 2 seconds as 1000 detectors each record 2000 separate measurements.

CAT scans have been used to identify medical problems such as tumors, infections, bleeding, and blood clots that would not have been identified by regular x-rays or other noninvasive procedures. Brain abnormalities related to schizophrenia, alcoholism, manic-depressive illness, and Alzheimer's disease can be identified from CAT scans. CAT scan machines are available in most hospitals, and the U.S. Army is developing a rugged, lightweight one that can be transported to medical stations in combat zones.

Advanced Composite Materials

Composites consist of a matrix of one material that has been reinforced by the fibers or particles of another material. Examples include using straw in mud bricks to make the bricks stronger and using steel rods in concrete to reinforce bridges and buildings. Advanced composite materials were developed to provide lighter, stronger, and more temperature-resistant materials for aircraft and spacecraft.

The first commercial advanced composite materials appeared in sporting goods. Downhill snow skis use layers of woven Kevlar fibers to increase their strength and reduce weight. Golf club shafts of graphite/epoxy are stronger and lighter than the steel in conventional shafts. Composite materials are now incorporated in new designs of fishing rods, bicycle frames, and race-car chassis.

Jumbo Jets

The origins of the jumbo jet (747, DC-10, L-1011) came from the Air Force C-5A cargo plane, which began operational flights in 1969. Much of the success of the jumbo jets can be attributed to the high-bypass fanjet engine, which allowed the planes to fly farther, with less fuel, and with less noise than previous jet engines. The core of the engine operates like a pure turbojet, in which compressor blades pull air into the engine's combustion chamber. The hot expanding gas thrusts the engine forward and at the same time spins a turbine, which in turn drives the compressor and the large fan on the front of the engine. The spinning fan provides the bulk of the engine's thrust. The turbines in the new engines tolerate burner-exit gas temperatures up to 2800°F. The turbine blades are made from a nickel alloy that is more heat resistant and much stronger than earlier blades.

The jumbo jets also have an increased emphasis on safety. Many systems have multiple backups to provide a wider margin of safety. For example, there are four main landing-gear legs, instead of two, on a 747. A middle spar was added to the wings in the event one is damaged, and redundant hydraulic systems operate the critical system of elevators, stabilizers, and flaps that control the motion of the plane.

■ Lasers

Light waves from a laser have the same frequency and thus create a beam with one characteristic color. More importantly, the light waves travel in phase, forming a narrow beam that can easily be directed and focused. CO_2 lasers can be used to drill holes in materials that range from ceramics to composite materials to rubber. Medical uses of lasers include welding detached retinas, sealing leaky blood vessels, vaporizing brain tumors, removing warts and cysts, and performing delicate inner-ear surgery. Laser light can also be used inside the body through fiber-optic endoscopes to burn fatty deposits out of clogged arteries, pulverize kidney stones, and open blocked fallopian tubes.

Lasers are also used to make three-dimensional pictures called holograms. One part of a laser beam is focused directly onto photographic film while the other part bounces off an object and onto the film. The waves from the two beams interfere with each other in complex patterns that are recorded on the film. When the film is developed, the patterns reflect a slightly different image in slightly different directions, thus giving the three-dimensional image. Hologram images are used to develop tamper-proof seals, bar code readers, and sensitive sensors. Other applications of lasers include fiber-optic cable communications, compact disc recording, and laser radar.

■ Fiber-Optic Communications

An optical fiber (a transparent glass thread) is thinner than a human hair but can carry more information than either radio waves or electric waves in copper telephone wires. In addition, fiber-optic communication signals do not produce electromagnetic waves that cause "cross-talk" noise on communication lines. The TAT-8, the first trans-oceanic fiber-optic cable, was laid across the Atlantic in 1988. It contains four fibers that can handle up to 40,000 calls at once. An undersea fiber-optic cable linking the United States and Japan was activated in 1989.

Other applications for optical fibers include motion sensing in gyroscopes, linking industrial lasers to machining tools, and threading light into the human body for examinations and laser surgery. Current research is aimed at designing optical computers that theoretically would be 1000 times faster than the best modern supercomputers.

■ Genetically Engineered Products

Genetically engineered products are produced by splicing a gene that produces a valuable substance from one organism into another organism that will multiply itself and the foreign gene along with it. Once the new organism has been created, a system has to be designed to produce and process the product in large quantities at a reasonable cost. The first commercial product of genetic engineering was human insulin, which appeared commercially under the trade name Humulin. The human insulin molecule is composed of two parts called A and B chains. The original Humulin process used two versions (one containing a gene producing A chains and the other containing the B chain gene) of the common bacterium *Escherichia coli* (*E. coli*). Each version was grown in a large tank, and the chains were extracted and purified. In a third vessel the chains were combined, purified, and crystallized into human insulin. Current research is investigating the use of genetically altered microbes to clean up toxic waste, degrade pesticides, and turn organic waste into useful products.

Instrumentation used in genetic engineering has had a tremendous impact on the detective work involved. A protein sequencer was developed in 1969 that can identify the sequence of amino acids in a protein molecule. Once the amino acid order is known, biologists can identify the gene that made the protein. A DNA (the genetic material found in cells) synthesizer, developed in 1982, can build small genes or gene fragments out of DNA. It is hoped that some day this research will lead to determination of the entire sequence of human DNA and the mapping of the location of its more than 100,000 genes.

1·2 ■ Engineering and Scientific Challenges

In every field, there are significant engineering and scientific challenges. The Office of Science and Technology Policy in Washington, D.C. recently published a research and development strategy for high-performance computing, which refers to the full range of supercomputing activities and the new generation of large-scale parallel architectures. As part of this strategy, the Office of Science and Technology Policy identified a number of grand challenges — those that would benefit from high-performance computing. These grand challenges are fundamental problems in science or engineering with broad applications. The following is a brief description of some of these grand challenges and the types of benefits that will come with their solution.

■ Prediction of Weather, Climate, and Global Change

In order to make long-range predictions about the coupled atmosphere, ocean, biosphere system, we must understand its behavior with a great amount of detail. This detail includes understanding CO_2 dynamics in the atmosphere and ocean, ozone depletion, and climatological changes due to the releases of chemicals or energy.

■ Speech Recognition and Understanding

Speech research covers a number of areas with incredible potential. Automatic speech understanding by computers could revolutionize our communication systems, but the problems involved are enormous. Speaker-dependent systems have been developed that can understand words from a small vocabulary spoken by a specific person, but to expand these systems to speaker-independent systems that understand large vocabularies is still not feasible. Exciting applications include telephone systems in which one speaker might be speaking Japanese on one phone, and the speech signal would be understood and translated by a computer so that the person on the other end of the connection hears the speech in English.

■ Machine Vision

Human vision and object recognition represents an incredibly powerful and complex sensory process. Adapting this process to machines represents a formidable challenge as well as a significant advancement. Machine vision for computers and robots requires technological advances in many areas, including image signal processing, texture and color modeling, geometric processing and reasoning, object modeling, and advanced sensors.

■ Vehicle Performance

Substantial improvements in vehicle (car, plane, ship, train . . .) performance requires more complex physical modeling in the areas of fluid dynamic behavior for three-dimensional flow fields and flow inside engine turbomachinery and ducts. Turbulence in fluid flows affects the stability and control, thermal characteristics, and fuel performance of aerospace vehicles, and modeling this flow is necessary for the analysis of new configurations. Analysis of the aeroelastic behavior of vehicles also affects new designs. The efficiency of combustion systems is also related, because attaining significant improvements in combustion efficiency requires understanding the relationships between the flows of the various substances and the quantum chemistry that causes the substances to react.

■ Superconductivity

Superconductivity has provided the potential for spectacularly energy-efficient power transmission and the design of ultrasensitive instrumentation. However, the materials currently supporting high-temperature superconductivity are difficult to form, stabilize, and use.

■ Enhanced Oil and Gas Recovery

Dependence on oil and gas dictates that technology be used to locate the estimated 300 billion barrels of oil reserves in the United States. Also, new technology should focus on developing economical and environmentally sound ways of extracting and using these natural resources. Seismic signal processing is a key component of identifying geological formations likely to contain oil.

■ Nuclear Fusion

The development of controlled nuclear fusion would clearly revolutionize energy development. However, the behavior of fully ionized gases at very high temperatures under the influence of strong magnetic fields is not well understood. The behavior must also be analyzed in terms of the complex three-dimensional geometry.

The grand challenges listed here are only a few of the many interesting problems waiting to be solved by engineers and scientists. The solutions to problems of this magnitude will be the result of organized approaches that combine ideas and technologies through logical processes. Therefore, in the next four sections we discuss the capabilities of computers and present a problem solving process for developing computer solutions to engineering problems.

1·3 ■ Computer Hardware

A *computer* is a machine that is designed to perform operations that are specified with a set of instructions called a *program*. Computer *hardware* refers to the computer equipment, and computer *software* refers to the programs that describe the steps we want the computer to perform. In this section we discuss computer hardware and the various components of a computer; in the next section we discuss computer software.

All computers have a common internal organization, shown in the block diagram in Figure 1 – 1. We usually use keyboards to enter information into the computer. Typing information using a keyboard is similar to typing information using a typewriter, but a computer keyboard has additional keys with special functions. We can also enter information using devices such as a mouse, a light pen, and a bar code reader.

The processing unit or *processor* is the part of the computer that controls all the other parts. The processor accepts input values and stores them in the *memory*. It also interprets the instructions in a computer program. If we want to add two values, the processor will retrieve them from the memory and send them to the *arithmetic logic unit* or *ALU*. The ALU performs the desired addition, and the processor then stores the result in the memory. The processing unit and the ALU use a small amount of

Figure 1·1 Block diagram of a computer.

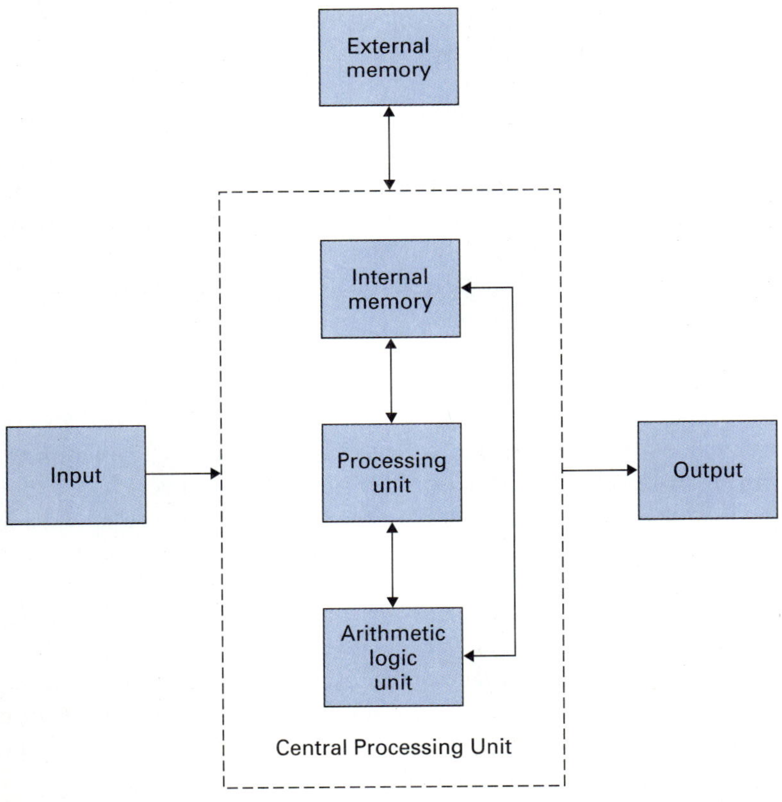

TEN TOP ENGINEERING ACHIEVEMENTS

1.

2.

The moon landing was probably the most complex and ambitious engineering project ever attempted. Several major technological advances occurred in a number of areas that made the Saturn/Apollo system possible. For example, the Apollo spacecraft required a new inertial navigation system; the lunar lander ascent engine had to work perfectly because there was no backup; the space suits had to be designed to protect the astronauts in a hostile environment and still allow flexibility for movement; and the Saturn V rocket had to be 15 times more powerful than the biggest rockets available in the early 1960s. Given all these major technical problems to solve, the program was clearly successful. A total of 9 spacecraft and 12 astronauts landed on the moon between 1968 and 1972.

The National Academy of Engineering recently selected what it considers to be the 10 most important engineering achievements during the past 25 years. This photograph gallery recognizes each of these 10 achievements, beginning with the moon landing and covering a wide range of advances and breakthroughs.

1. **Moon Landing** The lunar lander, photographed from the Apollo 11 Lunar Module as it prepares to descend to the lunar surface, was the first manned vehicle designed to fly solely in space. One of its most critical parts (which had no backup) was the small ascent engine that was used to return the astronauts to the Command Module. (Photo courtesy of NASA.)
2. **Application Satellites** Satellite systems ring the earth today giving weather information, relaying communication signals, mapping uncharted terrain, and providing navigational information. This Tracking and Data Relay satellite was used to communicate with spacecraft in low-earth orbit. (Photo courtesy of NASA.)

3. **Microprocessors** A microprocessor is a tiny computer smaller than your fingernail. With its size and capabilities, the applications range from operating remote television controllers or VCR recorders to providing the computational power in hand-held calculators or personal computers. This microprocessor is used for document image compression. (Photo © Melgar Photography, Inc.)

4. **Jumbo Jet** Much of the success of the jumbo jet (747, DC-10, L-1011) can be attributed to the high-bypass fanjet engine that allowed the planes to fly farther using less fuel and with less noise than previous jet engines. The jumbo jets also have an increased emphasis on safety, with four main landing-gear legs on a 747 instead of two. A middle spar was added to the wings in the event one is damaged, and redundant hydraulic systems operate the critical system of elevators, stabilizers, and flaps that control the motion of the plane. (Photo courtesy of Boeing.)

3.

4.

5. **CAT Scan** A CAT scan (computerized axial tomography scanner) is a machine that generates three-dimensional images or slices of an object using x-rays. A series of x-rays is generated from many angles, encircling the object or patient. Each x-ray measures a density at its angle, and by combining these density measurements with sophisticated computer algorithms, an image can be reconstructed that gives clear detailed pictures of the inside of the object. (Photo © Matthew Borkoski.)
6. **Advanced Composite Materials** Composites consist of a matrix of one material that has been reinforced by the fibers or particles of another material. Examples include using straw in mud bricks to make the bricks stronger and using steel rods in concrete to reinforce bridges and buildings. This composite bicycle wheel is made of epoxy resin reinforced with carbon fiber, Kevlar® aramid fiber, and glass fiber. (Photo courtesy of DuPont.)
7. **CAD/CAM** CAD (computer-aided design) typically refers to the use of the computer to generate designs, particularly using computer graphics. CAM (computer-aided manufacturing) uses design parameters (sometimes produced by CAD systems) to automatically control the machinery or industrial robots in manufacturing the parts assembling components and moving them to the desired locations. These three CAD views show a solid model of a crane lifting mechanism. (Photo courtesy of Aries Technology.)

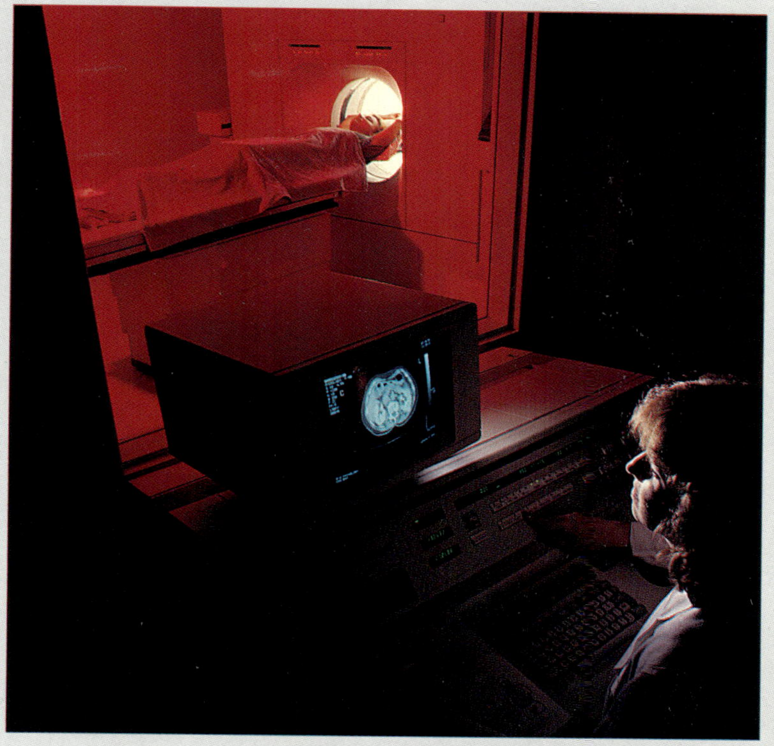

5.

6.

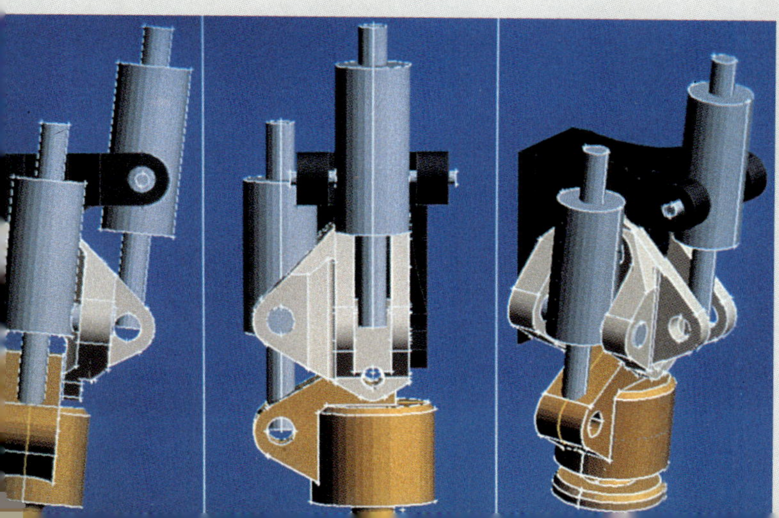

7.

8.

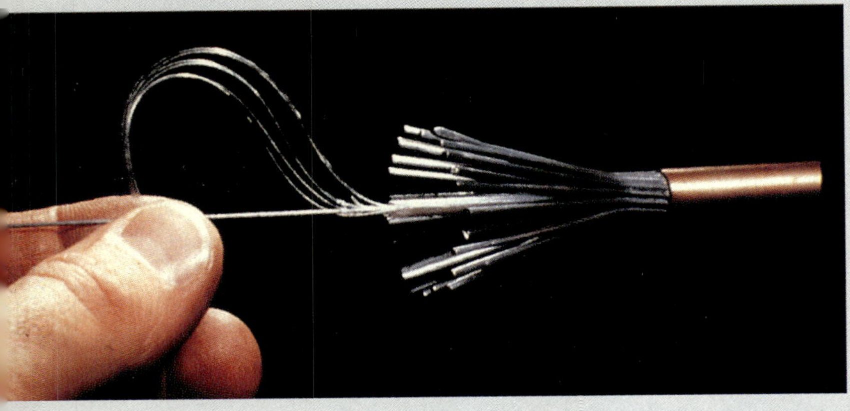

9.

10.

8. **Lasers** Light waves from a laser have the same frequency and thus create a beam with one characteristic color. More importantly, the light waves travel in phase, forming a narrow beam that can easily be directed and focused. CO_2 lasers can be used to drill holes in materials such as ceramics, composite materials, and rubber. Medical uses of lasers include repairing detached retinas, sealing leaky blood vessels, vaporizing brain tumors, removing warts and cysts, and performing delicate inner-ear surgery. This laser beam is being aligned by an optical system. (Photo courtesy of Ball Aerospace Systems Group.)

9. **Fiber-Optic Communications** An optical fiber (a transparent glass thread) is thinner than a human hair but can carry more information than either radio waves or electrical waves in copper telephone wires. In addition, fiber-optic communication signals do not produce electromagnetic waves that cause "cross-talk" noise on communication lines. The first transoceanic fiber-optic cable was laid in 1988 across the Atlantic. It contains four fibers that can handle up to 40,000 calls at one time. This undersea cable contains six optical fibers. (Photo courtesy of AT&T.)

10. **Genetically Engineered Products** Genetically engineered products are created by splicing a gene that produces a valuable substance from one organism into another organism that will multiply itself and the foreign gene along with it. Once the new organism has been created, a system has to be designed to produce and process the product in large quantities at a reasonable cost. The first commercial product of genetic engineering was the production of human insulin, which appeared commercially under the trade name Humulin. The molecules are produced by the genetically engineered bacteria and are then crystallized into human insulin. (Photo courtesy of Eli Lilly & Co.)

Figure 1·2(a) Macintosh Powerbook 170.

Figure 1·2(b) IBM personal computer PS/2.

Figure 1·3(a) IBM minicomputer AS/400.

Figure 1·3(b) IBM mainframe ES/9000.

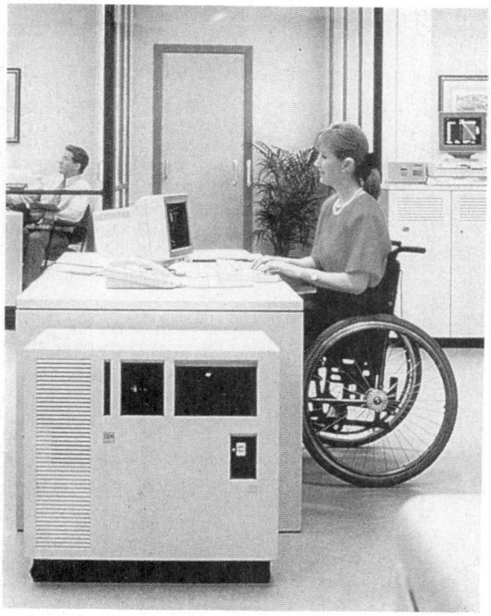

Figure 1-4 Sun workstation SPS10.

memory, the *internal memory*, in their processing; most data is stored in *external memory* or *secondary memory* using hard disk drives or floppy disk drives that are attached to the processor. The processor, internal memory, and ALU are collectively called the *central processing unit* or *CPU*. A *microprocessor* is a CPU contained in a single integrated circuit chip that has thousands of components in an area smaller than your fingernail.

In our computer programs, we usually instruct the computer to print the results of its calculations on a terminal screen, or *CRT* (*cathode ray tube*) screen. The computer output can also be printed on paper if a printer is attached to the computer. Dot matrix printers use a matrix (or grid) of pins to produce the shape of a character on paper, while a laser printer uses a light beam to transfer images to paper. The computer can also write information to diskettes that record the data magnetically. A printed copy of information is called a hard copy; a magnetic copy of information is called an electronic copy.

Computers come in all sizes, shapes, and forms. Figures 1 – 2(a) and (b) contain small personal computers (PCs) or microcomputers. The computers in Figures 1 – 3(a) and (b) are more powerful computers called minicomputers and mainframes. These computers are often used in businesses and laboratories. A workstation is a mainframe computer that is small enough to fit on a desktop or table, as shown in Figure 1 – 4.

Figure 1·5 Cray-2 supercomputer.

Supercomputers are the fastest of all computers and are capable of solving very complex problems that cannot be feasibly solved on other computers. A supercomputer requires special facilities, such as the one shown in Figure 1 – 5, and a specialized staff is also required to run and maintain the computer system.

The type of computer needed to solve a particular problem depends on the application. If the computer is to be a part of a home security system, a microprocessor is sufficient; if the computer is to handle airline reservations for a major airline, a mainframe is required. *Computer networks* interface computers so that they can communicate with each other; computer networks also allow several computers to share the same resource, such as a color printer.

1·4 ■ Computer Software

Computer software contains the instructions or commands that we want the computer to perform. This software can be written in a variety of languages and for a variety of purposes. In this section we first discuss computer languages. We then discuss two important types of software — software tools and operating systems.

■ Computer Languages

Machine language is the language that is understood by the computer hardware. Because computer designs are based on two-state technology (devices with two states, such as open or closed circuits, on or off switches, positive or negative charges), machine language is written using two symbols, which are usually represented using the digits 0 and 1. Therefore, machine language is also a *binary language*, and the instructions are written as sequences of 0's and 1's called binary strings. Machine language (also called a *low-level language*) is closely tied to the design of the computer hardware, and thus the machine language for a Sun computer is different from the machine language for a VAX computer.

Writing programs in machine language is very tedious and error-prone, so *assembly languages* were developed that used terms such as ADD to indicate that we wanted to add two numbers, instead of using a binary code such as 1101 to represent addition. A program (written in binary) called an *assembler* translates the assembly language program into machine language. However, since an assembly language is specific to the particular computer, we cannot run a program written in the assembly language for a Macintosh on an IBM PC. Furthermore, writing in assembly language is still a tedious task even though we are using mnemonic instructions instead of binary.

High-level languages are computer languages that have English-like commands and instructions. Most programmers prefer to write programs in high-level languages because they are easier to learn and easier to use. Originally developed in the 1950s for technical applications, FORTRAN (FORmula TRANslation) was one of the first high-level computer languages. FORTRAN 77 is a specific version of FORTRAN based on a set of standards established in 1977. These new standards greatly improved the language by adding new features and structures that allow us to write powerful yet readable programs. A new standard, Fortran 90, has recently been accepted and provides a number of very powerful additions to the language; Chapter 11 summarizes the new features in Fortran 90. COBOL is a high-level language that was designed to handle business-related problems and file manipulations. BASIC is a high-level language that is commonly used with personal computers. Pascal and C are more recent high-level languages that are called structured languages because special control structures are included in the language. (FORTRAN 77 and Fortran 90 are also structured languages, but the original FORTRAN was not.) Ada is a high-level language designed for the U.S. Department of Defense for use in technical applications.

Example statements from several high-level languages are illustrated in Table 1 – 1. Each section of code represents the calculation of a water bill based on the number of gallons of water used. In order to encourage conservation of water, many communities charge a higher rate per gallon if the usage is over a specified amount. In this example, we will assume that one rate is used if the number of gallons is less than or equal to 5000 and another rate is used for each gallon over 5000. The different names used to represent gallons used, water rates, and total water bill reflect the various rules within the individual languages. Also note the differences in punctuation among the various languages.

Because we have been trained to think in terms of English-like phrases and formulas, we prefer to use high-level languages such as FORTRAN 77 to tell the computer the steps we want it to perform. A special program called a *compiler* is then needed to translate a FORTRAN 77 program into the binary strings that the computer can understand. We will discuss compilers in the next section.

Learning a high-level computer language is similar to learning a foreign language. Each step you want the computer to perform must be described in the specific com-

Table 1·1 Examples of High-Level Languages

Language	Example Statements

FORTRAN 77	`IF (GALLNS.LE.5000.0) THEN`
	`   BILL = GALLNS*RATE1`
	`ELSE`
	`   BILL = 5000.0*RATE1 + (GALLNS - 5000.0)*RATE2`
	`END IF`

Pascal	`IF GALLONS <= 5000.0 THEN`
	`   BILL := GALLONS*RATE1`
	`ELSE`
	`   BILL := 5000.0*RATE1 + (GALLONS - 5000.0)*RATE2;`

C	`IF (GALLONS <= 5000.0)`
	`   BILL = GALLONS*RATE1;`
	`ELSE`
	`   BILL = 5000.0*RATE1 + (GALLONS - 5000.0)*RATE2;`

Ada	`IF GALLONS <= 5000.0 THEN`
	`   BILL := GALLONS*RATE1;`
	`ELSE`
	`   BILL := 5000.0*RATE1 + (GALLONS - 5000.0)*RATE2;`

BASIC	`      IF G > 5000.0 THEN 200`
	`      LET B = G*R1`
	`      GO TO 250`
	`200   LET B = 5000.0*R1 + (G - 5000.0)*R2`
	`250`

COBOL	`IF GALLONS IS LESS THAN 5000.0 OR`
	`   GALLONS IS EQUAL TO 5000.0`
	`      COMPUTE BILL = GALLONS*RATE1`
	`ELSE`
	`      COMPUTE BILL = 5000.0*RATE1 +`
	`                     (GALLONS - 5000.0)*RATE2.`

puter language syntax. Fortunately, computer languages have small vocabularies and no verb conjugations; however, computers are unforgiving in punctuation and spelling. A comma or letter incorrectly placed will cause errors that keep your program from working properly.

Software Tools

Software tools are programs that have been written to perform common operations. For example, *word processors* are programs that have been written to help you enter and format text. Word processors allow you to move sentences and paragraphs easily and often have the capability to check the spelling of the words that you have entered. But the word processor is a program, written in a language such as C, in which the input is your initial text and the output is the formatted report. Very sophisticated word processors allow you to produce well-designed pages that combine elaborate charts and graphics with text and headlines; these word processors use a technology called desktop publishing, which combines a very powerful word processor with a high-quality printer to produce professional-looking documents.

Spreadsheet programs are software tools that make it easy to work with data that can be displayed in a grid of rows and columns. Spreadsheet programs were initially used for financial and accounting applications, but many science and engineering problems can easily be solved using spreadsheets. Most spreadsheet packages include plotting capabilities, so they can be especially useful in analyzing and displaying information using the same software tool.

Another popular group of software tools are *database management programs*. These programs allow you to store a large amount of data and then easily retrieve pieces of the data and format them into reports. Databases are used by large organizations such as banks, hospitals, hotels, and airlines. Scientific databases are also used to analyze large amounts of data. Meteorology data is an example of scientific data that requires large databases for storage and analysis.

Graphics packages are software tools that allow you to create a variety of graphs with your data. These packages allow you to generate XY graphs, bar graphs, three-dimensional graphs, and contour plots. Graphics packages usually include the software to interface to a variety of graphics printers.

There are also many engineering computational tools. Some of these tools have been written to be used in very specific applications. For example, Spice is a software package for designing and analyzing electrical circuits. Other engineering tools are very general in nature. MATLAB and Mathematica are software tools that provide very powerful capabilities for performing computations and generating plots of data.

Operating Systems

An *operating system* is a set of programs that provide the interface between you (the user) and the computer hardware, as shown in Figure 1–6. The operating system provides a convenient and efficient environment in which you can execute application programs, including compilers, assemblers, software tools, and games. (Do not confuse application programs with the engineering applications that relate our programs to real-world examples.) For example, if your computer contains a word processor (such as Microsoft Word), a spreadsheet program (such as Lotus 1-2-3), a FORTRAN 77 language compiler, and a computational tool (such as MATLAB), you interact with the operating system to select the software you want to use.

Operating systems also contain a group of programs called utilities that allow you to perform functions such as printing files, copying files from one diskette to another, and listing the files that you have saved on a diskette. Although these utilities are common to most operating systems, the commands themselves are often different in various operating systems. For example, to list your files using DOS (a disk operating system used mainly with PCs), the command is *dir*; to list your files with UNIX (an operating

Figure 1·6 Operating system interface.

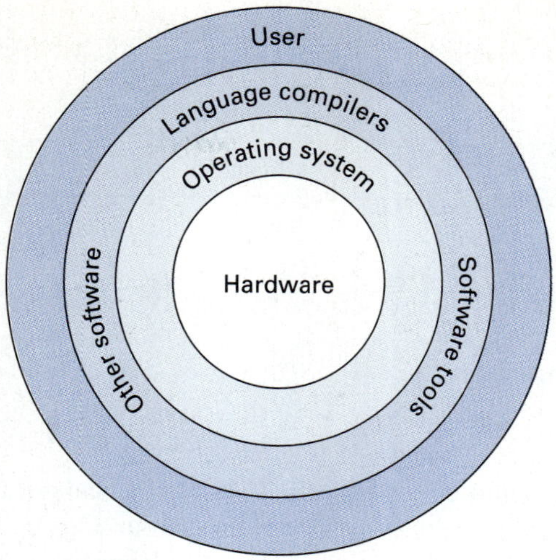

system used mainly with workstations), the command is *ls*. Some operating systems contain programs to simplify the interface with the operating system; examples of user-friendly systems are the Macintosh environment and the Windows environment.

1·5 ■ Executing a Computer Program

In the previous section, we defined a compiler as a program that translates a high-level language to machine language. This *compilation* step is the first step in running a computer program. As the compiler translates statements, it also checks for *syntax errors*. Syntax errors, which are also called compiler errors, are errors in the statements themselves, such as misspellings and punctuation errors. If syntax errors (often referred to as *bugs*) are found, the compiler will print error messages or *diagnostics* for you. After correcting the errors (*debugging*), you must rerun your program, again starting with the compilation step. Once you have compiled your program without errors, a linkage editor program performs the final preparations so that it can be submitted to the *execution* step. It is in the execution step that the statements are actually performed. Errors can also arise in the execution step; these are called *logic errors*, run-time errors, or execution errors. These errors (or bugs) are not in the statement syntax but are errors in the logic of the statements, which are detected only when the computer attempts to execute the statement. For example, the statement

```
X = A/B
```

is a valid FORTRAN 77 statement that directs the computer to divide A by B and call the result X. Suppose, though, that the value of B is zero. Then, as we try to divide A by B, we are attempting to divide by zero, which is an invalid operation; we will get an execution error message. Logic errors do not always generate an error message. For

Figure 1·7 Compiling and executing a program.

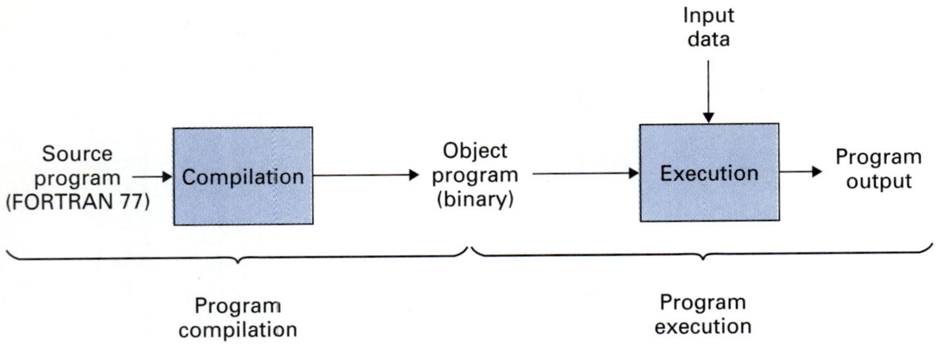

instance, if we were supposed to divide by 0.10 and instead we multiplied by 0.10, no error would be detected by the computer although our answers would be wrong.

A computer program written in a high-level language is often called a *source program*. After it is converted into machine language by a compiler, it is called an *object program*. A diagram of the compilation and execution process is shown in Figure 1–7.

It is uncommon for a program to compile, link, and execute correctly on the first run. Do not become discouraged if it takes several attempts to get your answers. When you do get answers, do not assume they are correct. If possible, check your answers with a calculator, and always ask yourself if the answers make sense. For example, if the answer represents the weight of a jet engine, then 5 pounds is not reasonable and suggests that you have given the computer incorrect data or incorrect logic to execute.

If you are running your programs on a standalone personal computer, the computer compiles and executes the program when you give the appropriate commands. If you are running your programs on terminals that are connected by a network to a mainframe computer, the computer *time-shares* between the requests from the various terminals. That is, the computer does a few steps of a program from one terminal, then a few steps of a program from another terminal, and so on until it is back to the first terminal. The computer then performs another cycle of steps in each program. We usually do not notice the time between cycles because the computer executes statements so quickly. We seem to have the undivided attention of the computer, although we are actually sharing it with many other terminal users.

Most time-sharing systems allot each user a specified amount of memory to be used as a workspace in the computer. This workspace is usually divided into a temporary workspace and a permanent workspace. As you enter programs or data into the temporary workspace you can edit the information, which means you can add to it, delete portions of it, or modify it with the use of an editing program (called an editor). When you have the program in the form you want, you can save it in the permanent workspace. You can then clear the temporary workspace and begin entering new information or you can "log off" the terminal. The next time you "log on," you can load any information that was previously saved in your permanent workspace into your temporary workspace.

1·6 ■ A Five-Step Problem Solving Process

Problem solving is an activity in which we participate every day. Problems range from analyzing our chemistry lab data to finding the quickest route to work. Computers can solve many of our problems if we learn how to communicate with them in computer languages such as FORTRAN 77. Some people believe that if we describe a problem to a computer, it will solve it for us. Programming would be simpler if this were the case; unfortunately, it is not. Computers only perform the steps that we specify in detail. You may wonder, then, why we go to the effort of writing computer programs to solve problems if we have to describe every step carefully. The answer is that computers can perform the tasks extremely accurately and with fantastic speed (millions of arithmetic operations per second). In addition, computers never get bored. Imagine sitting at a desk analyzing laboratory data for 8 hours a day, 5 days a week, year after year. Yet, thousands of laboratory results must be analyzed every day. Once the steps involved in performing a particular analysis (such as computing an average) have been carefully described to a computer, it can analyze data 24 hours a day, with more speed and accuracy than a group of technicians.

We will spend much of this text teaching you the FORTRAN 77 language, but any computer language is useless unless you can break a problem into steps that a computer can perform. The procedure that we use for problem solving has five steps:

1. State the problem clearly.
2. Describe the input and output information.
3. Work the problem by hand (or with a calculator) for a simple set of data.
4. Develop a solution that is general in nature.
5. Test the solution with a variety of data sets.

We now discuss these steps, using the familiar problem of computing an average. This task arises in many applications, such as in summarizing data from a lab experiment.

The **first step** is to state the problem clearly. It is important to give a clear, concise problem statement to avoid any misunderstandings. For this example, the problem statement is the following:

Compute the average of a set of experimental data values.

The **second step** is to describe carefully any information or data needed to solve the problem and then identify the values to be computed. These items represent the input and the output for the problem; collectively, they are called *input/output*, or *I/O*. In this example, the I/O description is the following:

Input — the list of experimental data values
Output — the average of the data values

The **third step** is to work the problem by hand or with a calculator, using a simple set of data. An example of a set of data values and the computed average is the following:

Lab Measurements—4/23/92

Number	Value
1	23.43
2	37.43
3	34.91
4	28.37
5	30.62
	154.76

Average = sum/5 = 30.95

The **fourth step** is to describe, in general terms, the operations you performed by hand. The sequence of operations that solves the problem is called an *algorithm.* The procedure that we use in our algorithm development is called *top-down design* because we start at the top with the original problem and break it down into smaller problems that can be addressed separately. Top-down design uses two techniques: *decomposition* and *stepwise refinement.* Decomposition is a form of "divide and conquer" in which we identify the pieces of the problem that need to be solved sequentially. Stepwise refinement successively refines each smaller piece of the solution using more detail. The refining continues until the solution is specific enough to convert into computer instructions.

Top-down design has several advantages. First, it helps us write programs that are easier to understand because the instructions in the computer program will follow the initial decomposition. Another advantage of top-down design is that we can initially think of the overall steps required without getting lost in the details. Details are introduced only as we begin the refinement of our algorithm. We will show the decomposition in a block diagram to emphasize that we are breaking the solution into a series of sequentially executed steps. To assist us in refining the decomposition into a more specific solution, we use flowcharts, which show the steps in an algorithm in graphic form, or pseudocode, which presents algorithm steps in a series of English-like statements. The details of flowcharts and pseudocode are presented in Chapter 3.

Decomposition

Read the data values and sum them.
Divide the sum by the number of data values.
Print the average.

The refinement of the decomposition for this example uses pseudocode to specify the details or to outline the steps in the algorithm:

Pseudocode

1. Set the sum of the values to zero.
2. Set a count of the values to zero.

3. As long as there are more data values,
   Add the next data value to the sum.
   Add 1 to the count.
4. Divide the sum by the count to get the average.
5. Print the average.

Once the detailed algorithm is described, we are ready to convert it into FORTRAN 77. The statements for solving this problem will not all be presented until Chapter 3, so there are items in the solution that you probably won't understand at this time. We present the solution here so that you can see how similar it is to the decomposition and pseudocode. We assume that a data value of zero is used to indicate that we have reached the end of the data values.

FORTRAN Program

```
*-----------------------------------------------------------------------*
      PROGRAM COMPUT
*
*  This program computes and prints the average
*  of a set of experimental data values.
*
      INTEGER COUNT
      REAL SUM, X, AVERG
*
      SUM = 0.0
      COUNT = 0
*
      READ*, X
    1 IF (X.NE.0.0) THEN
         SUM = SUM + X
         COUNT = COUNT + 1
         READ*, X
         GO TO 1
      END IF
*
      AVERG = SUM/REAL(COUNT)
*
      PRINT 5, AVERG
    5 FORMAT (1X,'THE AVERAGE IS ',F5.2)
*
      END
*-----------------------------------------------------------------------*
```

The **fifth step** in our problem solving process is to test the FORTRAN solution. We first execute the program to be sure the syntax is correct. We then test the program to be sure our logic is correct, and this is more difficult than testing for correct syntax. We test the program with a number of typical sets of data to be sure it works properly. A correct algorithm to average data should work properly for any set of data. If the data from our hand example were used in the FORTRAN program presented here, the output on our terminal screen would be the following:

```
THE AVERAGE IS 30.95
```

Algorithm testing is discussed further in later chapters.

Summary

The description of the top 10 engineering and scientific achievements and the discussion of the grand challenges will hopefully spark your interest in learning more about engineering and scientific disciplines. Because engineering and science are built around problem solving, it is important to begin your investigation with a solid methodology for solving problems and to then teach you how to use the computer to help solve the problems encountered. We discussed the fundamental concepts of computers and computing and the process for converting a problem solution into a form the computer can understand and execute. A five-step procedure for developing problem solutions (algorithms) was presented. The five steps are the following:

1. State the problem clearly.
2. Describe the input and output information.
3. Work the problem by hand (or with a calculator) for a simple set of data.
4. Develop a solution that is general in nature.
5. Test the solution with a variety of data sets.

The solution is developed using top-down design. Decomposition assists in describing the general steps that have to be performed to solve the problem. Stepwise refinement guides us in refining the steps and adding necessary details. FORTRAN 77 will be used to implement these solutions in the chapters that follow because it can easily and efficiently solve engineering and scientific problems.

Key Words

algorithm
arithmetic logic unit (ALU)
assembler
assembly language
binary language
bug
cathode ray tube (CRT)
central processing unit (CPU)
compilation
compiler
computer
computer network
database management program
debug
decomposition
diagnostic
execution
FORTRAN 77
hardware
high-level language
input/output (I/O)
internal memory
logic error
low-level language
machine language
memory
microprocessor
object program
operating system
processor
program
secondary memory
software
software tool
source program
spreadsheet program
stepwise refinement
syntax error
time-sharing
top-down design
word processor

■ References

For further reading on the 10 top engineering and scientific achievements of the last 25 years, we recommend the following references. Many of these references are from the National Academy of Engineering brochure entitled "10 Outstanding Achievements 1964–1989," published in 1989.

Moon Landing

Bilstein, Roger E., "Stages to Saturn: A Technical History of the Apollo/Saturn Launch Vehicles." Washington, D.C.: NASA, 1980.

Brooks, Courtney G., James M. Grimwood, and Lloyd S. Swenson, Jr., "Chariots for Apollo: A History of Manned Lunar Spacecraft." Washington, D.C.: NASA, 1979.

Hallion, Richard P., and Tom D. Crouch, eds. "Apollo: Ten Years Since Tranquility Base." Washington, D.C.: Smithsonian Institution Press, 1979.

Pellegrino, Charles R., and Joshua Stoff. "Chariots for Apollo: The Untold Story Behind the Race to the Moon." New York: Atheneum, 1985.

Stix, Gary, ed. "Moon Lander." Spectrum, Vol. 25, No. 11, 1988, pp. 76–82.

Application Satellites

Badgley, Peter C. "Remote Sensing." McGraw-Hill Encyclopedia of Science & Technology. New York: McGraw-Hill, 1987.

Canby, Thomas Y. "Satellites That Serve Us." National Geographic, September 1983, pp. 281–334.

Heckman, Joanne. "Read, Set, GOES: Weather Eyes for the 21st Century." Space World, July 1987, pp. 23–26.

Rasool, S. I. "Applications Satellites." McGraw-Hill Encyclopedia of Science & Technology. New York: McGraw-Hill, 1987.

Microprocessors

"EDN Microprocessor Issue." EDN, October 27, 1988.

"A Century of Electricals." New York: Institute of Electrical and Electronic Engineers, 1984, pp. 44–45.

Garetz, Mark. "Evolution of the Microprocessor: An Informal History." BYTE, September 1985, pp. 209–215.

Grossblatt, Robert. "A Decade of Change: The Microprocessor." Radio-Electronics, April 1986, pp. 61–65.

Kerr, Douglas A. "It's 16 bits, But Is That Wide or What?" Creative Computing, June 1985, pp. 40–45.

Reid, T. R. "The Chip." Simon & Schuster, 1985.

Toong, Hou-Min D. "Microprocessors." Scientific American, Vol. 237, No. 3, 1977, pp. 146–151.

Computer-Aided Design and Manufacturing

Loeffelholz, Suzanne. "CAD/CAM Comes of Age." Financial World, October 18, 1988, pp. 38–40.

Pond, James B., and Robert E. Harvey. "Dream Factories Leap-Frog the Opposition." Iron Age, November 15, 1985, pp. 26–36.

Mitchell, Larry D. "Computer-Aided Design and Manufacturing." McGraw-Hill Encyclopedia of Science & Technology. New York: McGraw-Hill, 1987.

CAT Scan

Andreasen, Nancy C. "Brain Imaging: Applications in Psychiatry." Science, March 18, 1988, pp. 1381–1388.

Randal, Judith E. "NMR: The Best Thing Since X-Rays?" Technology Review, January 1988, pp. 59–65.

Sochurek, Howard. "Medicine's New Vision." Easton, Pa.: Mack Publishing, 1988.

Sochurek, Howard. "Medicine's New Vision." National Geographic, January 1987, pp. 2–40.

Advanced Composite Materials

Chou, Tsu-Wei, Roy L. McCullough, and R. Byron Pipes, "Composites." Scientific American, October 1986, pp. 192–203.

Office of Technology Assessment, U.S. Congress. "Advanced Materials by Design." Washington, D.C.: U.S. Government Printing Office, 1988.

Rapson, Robert L. "Advanced Composites" (under "Composite Material"). McGraw-Hill Encyclopedia of Science & Technology. New York: McGraw-Hill, 1987.

Steinberg, Morris A. "Materials for Aerospace." Scientific American, October 1986, pp. 67–72.

Jumbo Jets

Aeronautical Staff of Aero Publishers. "DC-10 Jetliner." Fallbrook, Calif: Aero Publishers, 1973.

Ingells, Douglas J. "The L-1011 Tristar and the Lockheed Story." Fallbrook, Calif: Aero Publishers, 1973.

Ingells, Douglas J. "747: Story of the Boeing Super Jet." Fallbrook, Calif: Aero Publishers, 1970.

Stewart, Stanley. "Flying the Big Jets." New York: Arco Publishing, 1985.

Lasers

Ausubel, Jesse H., and H. Dale Langford, eds. "Lasers: Invention to Application." Washington, D.C.: National Academy Press, 1987.

"Lasers Then and Now" (special issue). Physics Today, October 1988.

Lavrakas, Paul. "Laser: The Healing Light of Medicine." Consumers' Research, October 1985, pp. 11–15.

Townes, Charles H. "Harnessing Light." Science 84, November 1984, pp. 153–155.

Fiber-Optic Communications

Bell, Trudy, ed., "Fiber Optics." Spectrum, Vol. 25, No. 11, 1988, pp. 97–102.

Hubbard, W. M. "Optical Communications." McGraw-Hill Encyclopedia of Science & Technology. New York: McGraw-Hill, 1987.

Koepp, Stephen. "Calling London, on a Beam of Light." Time, January 19, 1987, p. 52.
Lucky, Robert W. "Message by Light Wave." Science 85, November 1985, pp. 112–113.
Slutsker, Gary. "Good-Bye Cable TV, Hello Fiber Optics." Forbes, September 19, 1988, pp. 174–179.

Genetically Engineered Products

"DNA: Inherited Wealth." The Economist, April 30, 1988, Biotechnology Survey, pp. 3–18.
Eskow, Dennis. "Here Come the Assembly-Line Genes." Popular Mechanics, March 1983, pp. 92–96.
Hood, Leroy. "Biotechnology and Medicine of the Future." JAMA, March 25, 1988, pp. 1837–1844.
Weaver, Robert F. "Beyond Supermouse: Changing Life's Genetic Blueprint." National Geographic, December 1984, pp. 818–847.

2 Arithmetic Computations

2

APPLICATION

Microprocessors

A microprocessor is a central processing unit (CPU) that has been implemented using integrated circuit technology. With this technology, the microprocessor can be packaged in a small chip that can then be used as a component in the design of other equipment and devices. The computer board in the photo was designed to be inserted in IBM AT-compatible computers and provides the interface between the computer and high-quality speech and stereo music signals. The microprocessor on this board is a TMS320C31 chip that was designed by Texas Instruments specifically for fast digital signal processing (DSP); this chip is near the upper left corner of the photo. The entire board is 8.65 inches by 4.80 inches and approximately 2/3 of the board is shown in the photo. (See Section 2–8 for the solution to a problem related to this application.)

Photo courtesy of Atlanta Signal Processors, Inc.

Introduction

Arithmetic operations (adding, subtracting, multiplying, and dividing) are the most fundamental operations performed by computers. Engineers and scientists also need other routine operations, such as raising a number to a power, taking the logarithm of a number, or computing the sine of an angle. This chapter discusses methods of storing data with FORTRAN 77 and develops the statements for performing arithmetic calculations with that data. We also introduce statements for simple data input and output. With this group of statements, we can write complete FORTRAN 77 programs.

2·1 ■ Constants and Variables

Numbers are introduced into a computer program either directly with the use of *constants* or indirectly with the use of *variables*. Constants are numbers used in FORTRAN 77 statements, such as −7, 3.141593, and 32.0. Constants may contain plus or minus signs and decimal points, but they may not contain commas. Thus, 3147.6 is a valid FORTRAN constant, but 3,147.6 is not. Constants are stored in memory locations but can be accessed only by using the constant value itself.

A variable represents a memory location that is assigned a name. The memory location contains a value; we reference that value with the name assigned to that memory location. We can visualize variables, their names, and their values as shown:

AMOUNT	36.84	VOLUME	183.0
RATE	0.065	TOTAL	486.5
TEMP	17.5	INFO	72

Each memory location to be used in a program is given a name and may be assigned a value using a FORTRAN statement. For example, in the preceding example, the memory location named RATE has been assigned the value 0.065.

■ Variable Names

Each variable must have a different name, which you provide in your program. The names may contain one to six characters consisting of both alphabetic characters and digits; however, the first character of a name must be alphabetic. FORTRAN does not distinguish between uppercase and lowercase characters. We will use uppercase characters for FORTRAN variables and statements in examples. The following are examples of both valid and invalid variable names:

Variable Name	Valid or Invalid
DISTANCE	invalid—too long
TIME	valid
PI	valid

$	invalid—illegal character ($)
TAX-RT	invalid—illegal character (-)
B1	valid
2X	invalid—first character must be alphabetic

In Fortran 90, variable names can contain up to 31 characters and can include alphabetic characters, digits, and the underscore (_). Thus, valid names are ACCELERATION and X_SUM. Fortran 90

Data Types

FORTRAN 77 allows you to use six different types of values, as illustrated in the list below:

Data Type	**Examples**
Integers	32, −7
Real values	−15.45, 0.004
Double-precision values	3.1415926536, 1.000000006
Complex values	1-2*i*, 5*i* (where $i = \sqrt{-1}$)
Character values	'velocity', 'Report 3'
Logical values	.TRUE., .FALSE.

The first four types of values represent numerical values. In this chapter we discuss integers and real values; double-precision and complex values are discussed in Chapter 8. Logical constants and variables are discussed in Chapter 3; character constants and variables are discussed in Chapter 8.

Integer values are those with no fractional portion and no decimal point, such as 16, −7, 186, and 0. On the other hand, *real values* contain a decimal point and may or may not have digits past the decimal point, such as 13.86, 13., 0.0076, −14.1, 36.0, and −3.1; real values are also called floating-point values.

In Fortran 90, the real data type also includes double precision. Fortran 90

A memory location can contain only one type of value. The type of value stored in a variable is specified by two methods: *implicit typing* or *explicit typing*. With implicit typing, the first letter of a variable name determines the value type that can be stored in it. Variable names beginning with the letters I, J, K, L, M, or N are used to store integers. Variable names beginning with one of the other letters, A–H and O–Z, are used to store real values. Thus, with implicit typing, AMOUNT represents a real value and MONEY represents an integer value. An easy way to remember which letters are used for integers is to observe that the range of letters is I – N, the first two letters of the word integer.

With explicit typing, FORTRAN statements are used to specify the variable types. For example, the statements

```
INTEGER WIDTH
REAL ITEM, LENGTH
```

specify that WIDTH is a variable containing an integer value and that ITEM and LENGTH are variables containing real values. These *specification statements* or *type statements* have the following general forms:

INTEGER *variable list*

REAL *variable list*

The variable list contains variable names separated by commas. These statements are *nonexecutable* because they are not translated into machine language. Instead, they are used by the compiler to assign memory locations and to specify the types of values to be stored in the locations.

Fortran 90

In Fortran 90, type statements use two colons to separate the type and the variable name, as in

```
INTEGER :: WIDTH
```

It is helpful to select a variable name that is descriptive of the value being stored. For example, if a value represents a tax rate, name it RATE or TAX. If the implicit typing of the variable name does not match the type of value to be stored in it, then use a REAL or INTEGER statement at the beginning of your program to specify the desired type of value. It is good programming style to list all variables in specification statements, including those correctly typed by the implicit rules. In the example programs used in this book, all variables are included in specification statements.

The PARAMETER statement is a specification statement used to assign names to constants, with the following general form:

PARAMETER *(name1 = expression, name2 = expression, . . .)*

The expression after the equal sign typically is a constant, although it can be an expression consisting of other constants and operations such as those discussed later in this chapter. An example of a PARAMETER statement is

```
PARAMETER (PI=3.141593)
```

Type statements should precede the PARAMETER statement in order to assign the proper type to the constant.

Fortran 90

In Fortran 90, the type statement and the PARAMETER statement can be combined:

```
INTEGER :: PARAMETER :: PI=3.141593
```

Scientific Notation

When a real number is very large or very small, decimal notation does not work satisfactorily. For example, a value that is used frequently in chemistry is Avogadro's constant, whose value to four significant places is 602,300,000,000,000,000,000,000. Obviously, we need a more manageable notation for very large values like Avogadro's constant or for very small values like 0.000000000042. *Scientific notation,* commonly used in science, expresses a value as a number between 1 and 10 multiplied by a power of 10. In scientific notation, Avogadro's constant becomes 6.023×10^{23}. Elements of this form are commonly referred to as the mantissa (6.023) and the exponent (23). The FORTRAN form of scientific notation, called *exponential notation,* expresses a value as a number between 0.1 and 1 multiplied by an appropriate power of 10. Exponential notation uses the letter E to separate the mantissa and the exponent. In exponential form, Avogadro's constant becomes 0.6023E24. Other examples of decimal values in scientific and exponential notation are

Decimal	Scientific	Exponential
3,876,000,000	3.876×10^{9}	0.3876E10
0.0000010053	1.0053×10^{-6}	0.10053E−05
−8,030,000	-8.03×10^{6}	−0.803E07
−0.000157	-1.57×10^{-4}	−0.157E−03

Although FORTRAN uses an exponential form with a mantissa between 0.1 and 1.0, it will accept mantissas outside that range; for instance, the constant 0.16E03 would also be valid in the forms 1.6E02 or 0.016E04.

Magnitude Limitations

There are limitations on the magnitude and precision of values that can be stored in a computer. All limitations on values depend on the specific computer. For instance, π is an irrational number and cannot be written with a finite number of decimal positions; in a computer with seven digits of accuracy, π could be stored as 3.141593. In addition to limits on the number of significant positions in the mantissa, there are also limits on the size of the exponent.

Table 2 – 1 compares the approximate range of integers that can be stored in several computers. The range of values is determined by the design of the CPU. Check a

Table 2-1 Integer Representations in Typical Computers

Computer	Number of Binary Digits (or Bits) Per Data Value	Number of Integers*
Texas Instruments 32020 Microprocessor	16	65,536
Motorola 68020 Microprocessor	32	4.3×10^9
IBM PC	32	4.3×10^9
Macintosh	32	4.3×10^9
VAX 11/780	32	4.3×10^9
Sun Sparc Station 10	32	4.3×10^9
Cray Y MP C90	48	2.8×10^{14}
Cray-2	64	1.8×10^{19}

*Generally, half of the integers will represent negative values, so the maximum integer is usually equal to the number of integers divided by 2.

reference manual to find the ranges of real and integer values for the computer you will be using.

Fortran 90

Fortran 90 allows you to specify the number of decimal digits of precision and the maximum exponent to be used in your program. Of course, these limits cannot exceed the limits of the computer on which you are executing the program.

SELF-TEST 2-1

This self-test allows you to check quickly to see if you have remembered some of the key points from Section 2-1. If you have any problems with the exercises, you should reread this section. The solutions are included at the end of the text.

Problems 1-10 contain both valid and invalid variable names. Explain why the invalid names are unacceptable.

1. SQ.YD
2. MICRON
3. WEIGHT
4. DEGREES
5. NET_WT
6. SIDE-1
7. F(T)
8. 3J6
9. TOTAL
10. FIVE%

In problems 11-16, tell whether or not the pair of real constants represents the same number. If not, explain.

11. 15.7; 0.157E−2
12. −1.7; 1.7E−01
13. 10; 1000.0E−02
14. 0.005; 0.00005E−02
15. 0.899; 89.9E02
16. −0.044; 4.4E−02

2·2 ■ Arithmetic Operations

Computations in FORTRAN may be specified with the *assignment statement* whose general form is

> *variable name = expression*

The simplest form of an expression is a constant. Hence, if the value of π is needed frequently in a program, we might choose to define a variable PI with the value 3.141593. We could then refer to the variable PI each time we needed the constant. An assignment statement that assigns a value to PI is

```
PI = 3.141593
```

The name of the variable receiving a new value must always be on the left-hand side of the equal sign. In FORTRAN, the equal sign can be read as "is assigned the value of." Thus, this statement could be read "PI is assigned the value 3.141593." The term "*initialized*" is often used to refer to the first value assigned to a variable in a program; this statement could also be read "PI is initialized to the value 3.141593."

It is important to recognize that a variable can store only one value at a time. For example, suppose the following statements were executed one after another:

```
WIDTH = 36.7
WIDTH = 105.2
```

The value 36.7 is stored in the variable WIDTH after the first statement is executed. The second statement replaces that value with the new value 105.2, and the first value is lost.

Consider these statements:

```
TEMP1 = -52.6
TEMP2 = TEMP1
```

The first statement stores the value −52.6 in TEMP1. The second statement stores the same value in TEMP2 that is stored in TEMP1. Note that the value in TEMP1 is not lost; both TEMP1 and TEMP2 now contain the value −52.6.

In Fortran 90, variables can be initialized in a type statement, as in Fortran 90

```
INTEGER :: WIDTH = 0
```

■ Simple Arithmetic

Often we want to calculate a new value using arithmetic operations with other variables and constants. For instance, assume that the variable RADIUS has been assigned a value and we want to calculate the area of a circle having that radius. To do so, we must square the radius and then multiply by the value of π. Table 2–2 shows the FORTRAN expressions for the basic arithmetic operations. Note that an asterisk (instead of ×)

Table 2·2 Arithmetic Operations in Algebraic Form and in FORTRAN

Operation	Algebraic Form	FORTRAN
Addition	$A + B$	A+B
Subtraction	$A - B$	A-B
Multiplication	$A \times B$	A*B
Division	$\frac{A}{B}$	A/B
Exponentiation	A^3	A**3

represents multiplication; this avoids confusion because AxB (commonly used in algebra to indicate the product of A and B) represents a variable name in FORTRAN. Division and exponentiation also have different symbols that allow us to write these arithmetic operations on a single line.

Evaluating an Arithmetic Expression

Because several operations can be combined in one *arithmetic expression*, it is important to determine the priorities of the operations (the order in which the operations are performed). For instance, consider the following assignment statement that calculates the area of a circle:

```
AREA = PI*RADIUS**2
```

If the exponentiation is performed first, we compute $PI \times (RADIUS)^2$; if multiplication is performed first, we compute $(PI \times RADIUS)^2$. Note that the two computations yield different results. The order of priorities for computations in FORTRAN is given in Table 2–3 and follows the standard algebraic priorities.

When executing the previous FORTRAN statement, the RADIUS is first squared; then the result is multiplied by PI—correctly determining the area of the circle. Remember that we assume that both PI and RADIUS have been initialized. The following statements also correctly compute the area of the circle:

```
AREA = PI*RADIUS*RADIUS
AREA = 3.141593*RADIUS*RADIUS
```

Table 2·3 Priorities of Arithmetic Operations

Priority	Operation
1	Parentheses
2	Exponentiation
3	Multiplication and division
4	Addition and subtraction

If a minus sign precedes the first variable name in an expression, it is computed on the same priority level as subtraction. For example, −A**2 is computed as if it were −(A**2), −A*B is computed as if it were −(A*B), and −A+B is computed as if it were (−A)+B.

When two operations are on the same priority level, as in addition and subtraction, all operations except exponentiation are performed from left to right. Thus, B − C + D is evaluated as (B − C) + D. If two exponentiations occur sequentially in FORTRAN, as in A**B**C, they are evaluated right to left, as in A**(B**C). Thus, 2**3**2 is 2^9, or 512, as opposed to (2**3)**2, which is 8^2, or 64.

A more complicated example is represented by the following equation for one of the real roots of a quadratic equation:

$$\text{X1} = \frac{-B + \sqrt{B^2 - 4AC}}{2A}$$

Recall that A, B, and C are coefficients of the quadratic equation ($AX^2 + BX + C = 0$). Because computers cannot divide by zero, we will assume for now that A is not equal to zero. The value of X1 can be computed in FORTRAN with the following statement, assuming that the variables A, B, and C have been initialized:

```
X1 = (-B + (B**2 - 4.0*A*C)**0.5)/(2.0*A)
```

To check the order of operations in a long expression, you should start with the operations inside parentheses; that is, find the operation done first, then second, and so on. The following diagram outlines this procedure, using braces to show the steps of operations. Beneath each brace is the value calculated in that step:

```
X1 = (-B + (B**2 - 4.0*A*C)**0.5)/(2.0*A)
```

$$\underbrace{-B}\qquad \underbrace{B^2 - 4AC}\qquad \underbrace{2A}$$

$$\underbrace{-B + \sqrt{B^2 - 4AC}}$$

$$\frac{-B + \sqrt{B^2 - 4AC}}{2A}$$

As shown in the final brace, the desired value is computed by this expression.

Parentheses placement is important. If the outside set of parentheses in the numerator in the previous FORTRAN statement was omitted, our assignment statement would become

```
X1 = -B + (B**2 - 4.0*A*C)**0.5/(2.0*A)
```

$$\underbrace{-B}\qquad \underbrace{B^2 - 4AC}\qquad \underbrace{2A}$$

$$\underbrace{\sqrt{B^2 - 4AC}}$$

$$\underbrace{\frac{\sqrt{B^2 - 4AC}}{2A}}$$

$$-B + \frac{\sqrt{B^2 - 4AC}}{2A}$$

As you can see, omission of the outside set of parentheses causes the wrong value to be calculated as a root of the original quadratic equation. Omission of a different set of parentheses would result in the following expression:

```
X1 = (-B + B**2 - 4.0*A*C**0.5)/(2.0*A)
```

$$\underbrace{-B + B^2 - 4A\sqrt{C}} \qquad \underbrace{2A}$$

$$\frac{-B + B^2 - 4A\sqrt{C}}{2A}$$

Again, the wrong value would be calculated. If all parentheses were omitted, the expression would become

```
X1 = -B + B**2 - 4.0*A*C**0.5/2.0*A
```

$$\underbrace{-B} \quad \underbrace{B^2} \quad \underbrace{\sqrt{C}}$$

$$\frac{4A\sqrt{C}A}{2}$$

$$-B + B^2 - \frac{4A^2\sqrt{C}}{2}$$

Still another incorrect value would be computed.

Omitting necessary parentheses results in incorrect calculations. Using extra parentheses to emphasize the order of calculations is permissible even though they may not be needed. It is advisable to insert extra parentheses in a statement if it makes the statement more readable.

You also may want to break a long statement into several smaller statements. Recall that the expression $B^2 - 4AC$ in the quadratic equation is called the discriminant. Both roots of the solution could be calculated with the following statements after initialization of A, B, and C:

```
DISCR = B**2 - 4.0*A*C
X1 = (-B + DISCR**0.5)/(2.0*A)
X2 = (-B - DISCR**0.5)/(2.0*A)
```

In the preceding statements we assume that the discriminant, DISCR, is positive, enabling us to obtain X1 and X2, the two real roots to the equation. If the discriminant were negative, an execution error would occur when we attempted to take the square root of the negative value. If the value of A were zero, we would get an execution error for attempting to divide by zero. In later chapters we learn techniques for handling these situations.

We often use variables as counters in our FORTRAN programs. We first initialize the counter to a certain value and later, under certain conditions, change it to another value. For example, a counter named COUNTR, which we assume was listed in an INTEGER statement, is incremented by 1 in the following statement:

```
COUNTR = COUNTR + 1
```

This statement may look invalid because, algebraically, COUNTR cannot be equal to COUNTR + 1. But remember, in FORTRAN, this statement means "COUNTR is assigned the value of COUNTR plus 1." Hence, if the old value of COUNTR is 0, the new value of COUNTR after executing this statement is 1.

■ Truncation and Mixed-Mode Operations

When an arithmetic operation is performed using two real numbers, its *intermediate result* is a real value. For example, the circumference of a circle can be calculated using either of the following two statements:

```
CIRCUM = PI*DIAMTR
CIRCUM = 3.141593*DIAMTR
```

In both statements, we have multiplied two real values, giving a real result, which is then stored in the real variable CIRCUM.

Similarly, arithmetic operations between two integers yield an integer. For instance, if I and J represent two integers and if I is less than or equal to J, then the number of integers in the interval [I,J] can be calculated with the following statement:

```
INTERV = J - I + 1
```

Thus, if I = 6 and J = 11, INTERV will be assigned the value 6, the number of integers in the set {6, 7, 8, 9, 10, 11}.

Now consider the statement

```
LENGTH = SIDE*3.5
```

Assume that SIDE represents a real value and that LENGTH represents an integer value. We know that the multiplication between the real value SIDE and the real constant 3.5 yields a real result. In this case, however, the real result is stored in an integer variable. When the computer stores a real number in an integer variable, it ignores the fractional portion and stores only the whole number portion of the real number; this type of rounding is called *truncation.*

Computations with integers can also give unexpected results. Consider the following statement, which computes the average, or mean, of two integers, N1 and N2:

```
MEAN = (N1 + N2)/2
```

If we assume that all the variables in the statement are integers, the result of the expression will be an integer. Thus, if N1 = 2 and N2 = 4, the mean value is the expected value, 3. But if N1 = 2 and N2 = 3, the result of the division of 5 by 2 will be 2 instead of 2.5 because the division involved two integers; hence, the intermediate result must be an integer. At first glance it might seem that we could solve this problem if we called the average by a real variable named AVE (instead of MEAN) and used this statement:

```
AVE = (N1 + N2)/2
```

Unfortunately, this cannot correct our answer. The result of integer arithmetic is still an integer; all we have done is to move the integer result into a real variable. Thus, if N1 = 2 and N2 = 3, then (N1 + N2)/2 = 2 and AVE = 2.0, not 2.5. One way to correct this problem is to declare N1 and N2 to be real values and use the following statement to calculate the average:

```
AVE = (N1 + N2)/2.0
```

Note the difference between *rounding* and truncation. With *rounding,* the result is the integer closest in value to the real number. Truncation, however, causes any decimal portion to be dropped. If we divide the integer 15 by the integer 8, the truncated result is 1, and the rounded result is 2.

The effects of truncation can also be seen in the following statement, which appears to calculate the square root of NUM:

```
ROOT = NUM**(1/2)
```

However, since 1/2 is truncated to 0, we are really raising NUM to the zero power; ROOT will always contain the value 1.0, no matter what value is in NUM.

We have seen that an operation involving only real values yields a real result and an operation involving only integer values yields an integer result. FORTRAN also accepts a *mixed-mode* operation, which is an operation involving an integer value and a real value. The intermediate result is a real value. The final result depends on the type of variable used to store the result of the mixed-mode operation. Consider the following arithmetic statement for computing the perimeter of a square whose sides are real values:

```
PERIM = 4*SIDE
```

The preceding multiplication is a mixed-mode operation between the integer constant 4 and the real variable SIDE. The intermediate result is real and is correctly stored in the real variable PERIM.

Using mixed mode, we can now correctly calculate the square root of the integer NUM, using this statement:

```
ROOT = NUM**0.5
```

The mixed-mode exponentiation yields a real result, which is stored in ROOT.

To compute the area of a square with real sides, we could use either of the following statements:

```
AREA = SIDE**2
AREA = SIDE**2.0
```

The result in both cases is real, but the first form is preferable because exponentiation to an integer power is generally performed internally in the computer with a series of multiplications such as SIDE times SIDE. If an exponent is real, however, the operation is performed by the arithmetic logic unit using logarithms; SIDE**2.0 is actually computed as antilog(2.0 × log(SIDE)). Logarithms can introduce small errors into the calculations; although 5.0**2 is always 25.0, 5.0**2.0 is often computed as 24.99999. Also, note that (−2.0)**2 is a valid operation, but (−2.0)**2.0 is an invalid operation —the logarithm of a negative value does not exist, and an execution error occurs. As a general guide when raising numbers to an integer power, use an integer exponent, even though the base number is real.

Assume that we want to calculate the volume of a sphere with radius R, where R represents a real value. The volume is computed by multiplying 4/3 times π, times the radius cubed. The following mixed-mode statement at first appears correct:

```
VOLUM = (4/3)*3.141593*R**3
```

The expression contains integer and real values, so the result will be a real value. However, the division of 4 by 3 yields the intermediate value of 1, not 1.333333; therefore, the final answer will be incorrect.

Because mixed-mode operations can sometimes give unexpected results, you should try to avoid writing arithmetic expressions that include them. The only time a mixed-mode expression is desirable is in an exponentiation operation in which an integer is raised to a noninteger power.

■ Underflow and Overflow

In a previous section we discussed magnitude limitations for the values stored in variables. Because the maximum and minimum values that can be stored in a variable depend on the computer system itself, a computation may yield a result that can be stored in one computer system but is too large to be stored in another. For example, suppose we execute the following assignment statements:

```
X = 0.25E20
Y = 0.10E30
```

These values are both valid for a computer with an exponent range of −38 through 38. Suppose we now execute the following statement:

```
Z = X*Y
```

The numerical result of this multiplication is .025E50. Clearly this result is too large to store in a computer with a maximum exponent of 38. The error is not a syntax error; the statements themselves are valid FORTRAN 77 statements. The error is an execution error because it occurred during execution of the program, and it is called an exponent *overflow* error because the exponent of the result of an arithmetic operation was too large to store in the computer's memory.

Exponent *underflow* is a similar error caused by the exponent of the result of an arithmetic operation being too small to store in the computer's memory. Using the same computer as we did for the previous example, the following statements would generate an exponent underflow error because the value that is computed for C has an exponent smaller than −38:

```
A = 0.25E-20
B = 0.10E+20
C = A/B
```

If you get exponent underflow or overflow errors when you run your programs, you need to examine the magnitude of the values you are using. If you really need values whose exponents exceed the limits of your computer, the only solution is to switch to a computer that can handle a wider range of exponents. Most of the time, exponent underflow and overflow errors are caused by other errors in a program. For example, if variables are initialized to an incorrect value or the wrong arithmetic operation is specified, exponent underflow or overflow can occur—but the source of the problem is elsewhere.

SELF-TEST 2-2

This self-test allows you to check quickly to see if you have remembered some of the key points from Section 2–2. If you have any problems with the exercises, you should reread this section. The solutions are included at the end of the text.

1. What value is stored in Y after the following statements are executed?

```
REAL X, A, Y
X = 5.0
A = 2.0
Y = X + 3.0/A*5.0
```

2. What value is stored in X after the following statements are executed?

```
REAL X, X1, X2
X1 = 4.0
X2 = 10.0
X = 1.0/(1.0/X1)+(1.0/X2)
```

3. What value is stored in RESULT after the following statements are executed?

```
INTEGER X, Y, B, RESULT
X = 5
Y = -21
B = 16
RESULT = X + Y + B/5
```

2·3 ■ Intrinsic Functions

Algorithms commonly require simple operations such as computing the square root of a value, computing the absolute value of a number, or computing the sine of an angle. Because these operations occur so frequently, built-in computer functions called *intrinsic functions* are available to handle these routine computations. Instead of using the arithmetic expression X**0.5 to compute a square root, we can use the intrinsic function SQRT(X). Similarly, we can refer to the absolute value of B by ABS(B). A list of some commonly used intrinsic functions appears in Table 2–4, and a complete list of FORTRAN 77 intrinsic functions is contained in Appendix A, along with a brief description of each function.

The name of a function is followed by the input to the function, called the *argument* of the function, which is enclosed in parentheses. This argument can be a constant, variable, or expression. For example, suppose we want to compute the cosine of the variable ANGLE and store the result in another variable COSINE. From Table 2–4, we see that the cosine function assumes that its argument is in radians. If the value in ANGLE is in degrees, we must change the degrees to radians (1 degree $= \pi/180$ radians) and then compute the cosine. The statement below performs the degree-to-radian conversion within the function argument; note that the inside set of parentheses is not required but emphasizes the conversion factor.

```
COSINE = COS(ANGLE*(3.141593/180.0))
```

Table 2·4 Common Intrinsic Functions

Function Name and Argument	Function Value	Comments
SQRT(X)	$\sqrt{X}$	Square root of *X*
ABS(X)	$\lvert X \rvert$	Absolute value of *X*
SIN(X)	Sine of angle *X*	*X* must be in radians
COS(X)	Cosine of angle *X*	*X* must be in radians
TAN(X)	Tangent of angle *X*	*X* must be in radians
EXP(X)	e^X	*e* raised to the *X* power
LOG(X)	$\log_e X$	Natural log of *X*
LOG10(X)	$\log_{10} X$	Common log of *X*
INT(X)	Integer part of *X*	Converts a real value to an integer value
REAL(I)	Real value of *I*	Converts an integer value to a real value
MOD(I,J)	Integer remainder of *I*/*J*	Remainder or modulo function

The REAL and INT functions may be used to avoid undesirable mixed-mode arithmetic expressions by explicitly converting variable types. For example, if we are computing the average of a group of real values, we need to divide the real sum of the values by the number of values. We can convert the integer number of values into a real value for the division using the REAL function, as shown in the following statement:

```
AVERG = SUM/REAL(N)
```

If the values were integers, the sum would also be an integer. We would still probably want the average to be represented by a real value, which could be specified by

```
AVERG = REAL(SUM)/REAL(N)
```

It is also acceptable to use one intrinsic function as the argument of another. For example, we can compute the natural logarithm of the absolute value of X with the following statement:

```
XLOG = LOG(ABS(X))
```

When using one function as an argument for another, be sure to enclose the argument of each function in its own set of parentheses. This *nesting* of functions is also called composition of functions.

It is important to observe that an intrinsic function and its argument represent a value. This value can be used in other computations or stored in other memory locations. It does not of itself, however, represent a memory location. A function can never appear on the left-hand side of an equal sign; it must always be on the right-hand side. For example, to compute the square root of X, we can use the statement

```
ROOT = SQRT(X)
```

but we cannot reverse the order and begin the statement with SQRT(X) because SQRT(X) is not a variable name. The intrinsic square root function could be used in the computation of a root of the quadratic equation used in a previous example, as shown:

```
X1 = (-B + SQRT(B**2 - 4.0*A*C))/(2.0*A)
```

Many intrinsic functions are *generic functions*, which means that the value returned is the same type as the input argument. The absolute value function ABS is a generic function. If X is an integer, then ABS(X) is also an integer; if X is a real value, then ABS(X) is also a real value. Some functions specify the type of input and output required. IABS is a function that requires an integer input and returns an integer absolute value from the function. If K is an integer, then ABS(K) and IABS(K) return the same value. Appendix A contains all forms of the intrinsic functions and identifies all generic functions.

Fortran 90

Fortran 90 contains a number of new intrinsic functions. CEILING is a function that returns the smallest integer that is greater than or equal to the argument; FLOOR returns the greatest integer that is less than or equal to the number. Also included are functions to determine the number of significant digits, the maximum exponent, and the largest integer for the computer being used.

SELF-TEST 2-3

This self-test allows you to check quickly to see if you have remembered some of the key points from Section 2–2 and Section 2–3. If you have any problems with the exercises, you should reread these sections. The solutions are included at the end of the text.

In problems 1–6, convert the equations into FORTRAN assignment statements. Assume all variables represent real values.

1. Magnitude:

$$M = \sqrt{x^2 + y^2}$$

2. Velocity addition formula:

$$u = \frac{u + v}{1 + \dfrac{u \cdot v}{c^2}}$$

3. Damped harmonic motion:

$$y = y_0 \cdot e^{-at} \cdot \cos(2\pi f \cdot t)$$

4. Temperature conversion to degrees K:

$$T = \left(\frac{5}{9}(T_f - 32)\right) + 273.15$$

5. Magnetic field around a current-carrying wire:

$$B = k \cdot \frac{I \cdot d \cdot \sin \theta}{r^2}$$

6. Standard error computation:

$$S = \sqrt{\frac{s_1^{\;2}}{n_1} + \frac{s_2^{\;2}}{n^2}}$$

In problems 7–12, convert the FORTRAN statements into algebraic form.

7. Potential energy:

```
PE = -G*ME*M/R
```

8. Electric flux:

```
DF = E*DA*COS(THETA)
```

9. Average velocity:

```
AV = (X2 - X1)/(T2 - T1)
```

10. Centripetal acceleration:

```
PI = 3.141593
CA = 4.0*PI**2*R/(T**2)
```

11. Distance of an accelerating body:

```
DIST = V*TIME + ACC*TIME**2/2.0
```

12. Atmospheric pressure adjusted for elevation:

```
P = P0*EXP(-M*G*X/R*TK)
```

2·4 ■ Simple Input and Output

Before we discuss input and output statements, we outline the proper form for entering FORTRAN statements in a program. We then present several types of I/O statements. A computer can accept input from different sources, but in this chapter we assume that the input is from the keyboard. Similarly, we can direct output to different devices, but in this chapter we assume that the output is directed to a terminal screen or a printer. Input and output using a data file are discussed in Chapter 4.

FORTRAN Statement Format

FORTRAN programs are created using an editor or a word processor to enter the text. Each statement is entered on a new line. We refer to specific positions within the line by column number: the first position in a line is column 1, the second position in a line is column 2, and so on.

Columns 1 through 5 are reserved for *statement numbers* (also called labels), which must be nonzero positive integers. Most statements do not require a statement number, but as you will see in later chapters, some statements need numbers so they can be referenced by other statements.

Column 6 is used to indicate that a statement has been continued from the previous line. Any nonblank character except a zero can be used in column 6 to indicate continuation. A FORTRAN statement may have several *continuation lines* if it is too long to fit on one line.

A FORTRAN statement starts in column 7 and can extend to column 72. In general, blanks can be inserted anywhere in the statement for readability. All information beyond column 72 is ignored. These rules for the general form of a FORTRAN statement are summarized below:

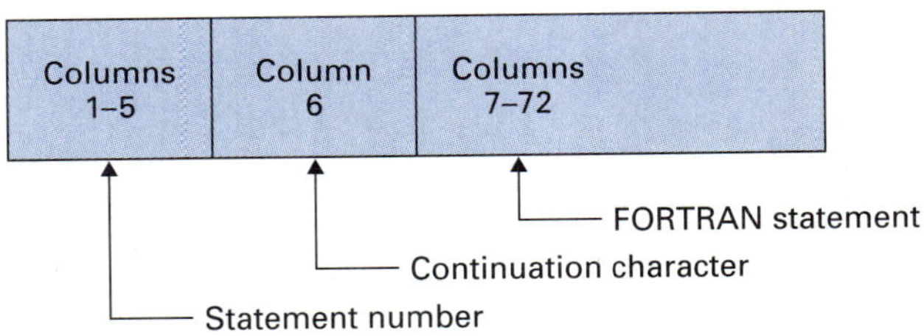

The only exception to the rules for spacing in FORTRAN statements applies to *comment lines*. Comment lines are used for entering general comments about the program, and they are printed in a listing of the program; comment lines are not converted into machine language or used during execution of the program. An asterisk or the letter C in column 1 indicates that a line is a comment line. It is good programming practice to include several comment lines near the beginning of the program to describe its purpose. In fact, you might want to include comments containing the information in step 1 (problem statement) and step 2 (input/output description) of the problem solving process. Blank lines can also be included anywhere in the program.

Some terminal editors require you to number each line. These line numbers are used in editing but cannot be referenced by a FORTRAN statement. If you are using one of these editors, all statements will have a line number, and statements referenced in your program will also need a FORTRAN label.

Fortran 90

In Fortran 90, statements can start in any column, and there can be multiple statements on a line if they are separated by a semicolon. Comments can follow a statement on the same line, and can be indicated by an exclamation point.

List-Directed Output

FORTRAN has two types of statements that allow us to perform I/O operations. *List-directed* input/output statements are easy to use but give us little control over the exact spacing used in the input and output lines. *Formatted* input/output, although more involved, allows us to control the input and output forms with greater detail. In this section, we present list-directed input/output and simple formatted output. For our example programs, we use list-directed input statements and formatted output statements — this allows us to be flexible about the form we use for information we read and, at the same time, allows us to be specific about the form used to display the information computed by our program.

If we wish to print the value stored in a variable, it is necessary to tell the computer the variable's name. The computer can then access the memory location and print its contents. The general form of the list-directed PRINT statement is

`PRINT*,` expression list

The expressions in the list must be separated by commas. The corresponding values are printed in the order in which they are listed in the PRINT statement. The output from each PRINT statement begins on a new line.

In our examples, computer output is shown inside a rounded box, as illustrated in Example 2 – 1.

WEIGHT and VOL . . . . Example 2·1

Print the stored values of the variables WEIGHT and VOL.

Solution

Computer Memory

WEIGHT	35000
VOL	3.15

FORTRAN Statement

```
PRINT*, WEIGHT, VOL
```

Computer Output

```
35000  3.15000
```

The number of decimal positions printed for real values and the spacing between items vary depending on the compiler used. If a value to be printed is very large or very small, many compilers automatically print the value in exponential notation instead of in decimal form, as shown in Example 2-2.

Example 2·2

Density Value

Print the value stored in the variable DENSTY.

Solution

Computer Memory

DENSTY | 0.0000156 |

FORTRAN Statement

```
PRINT*, DENSTY
```

Computer Output

```
0.156000E-04
```

Descriptive information (sometimes called literal information or *literals*) may also be included in the expression list by enclosing the information in single quotation marks or apostrophes. An apostrophe in a literal is represented by two quote marks, as in 'USER''S PROGRAM'. The descriptive information is then printed on the output line along with the values of any variables.

Example 2·3

Literal and Variable Information

Print the variable RATE with a literal that identifies the value as representing a flow rate in gallons per second.

Solution

Computer Memory

RATE | 0.065 |

FORTRAN Statement

```
PRINT*, 'FLOW RATE IS', RATE, 'GALLONS PER SECOND'
```

Computer Output

```
FLOW RATE IS 0.0650000 GALLONS PER SECOND
```

Centrifuge Information

Example 2-4

Print the values stored in the variables RPM and FORCE using descriptive headings.

Solution

Computer Memory

RPM	37.5
FORCE	6.75

FORTRAN Statements

```
PRINT*, 'CENTRIFUGE RPM AND FORCE'
PRINT*, RPM, FORCE
```

Computer Output

```
CENTRIFUGE RPM AND FORCE
37.5000  6.75000
```

In Fortran 90 literals can be enclosed in double quotes (quotation marks).

Fortran 90

List-Directed Input

We frequently want to read information with our programs. The general form of a list-directed READ statement is

```
READ*, variable list
```

The variable names in the list must be separated by commas. The variables receive new values in the order in which they are listed in the READ statement. These values should agree in type (integer or real) with the variables in the list. The system will wait for you to enter the appropriate data values when the READ statement is executed. If more than one value is being read by the statement, the data values can be separated by commas or blanks.

A READ statement will read as many lines as needed to determine values for the variables in its list. Therefore, if a READ statement has four variables on it, it will wait until you have entered four values; the values could be on one line (separated by commas or blanks) or on several lines. Also, each READ statement begins reading from a new line. Thus, if you have executed a READ statement with four variables in its list and you entered five values on one line, the last value will not be read; the next READ statement will assume that a new line is used for entering information.

Example 2-5 Capacitor Charge

Read the beginning and ending charges for a capacitor.

Solution 1

This solution uses one READ statement; thus both values can be entered on the same line.

FORTRAN Statement

```
READ*, BEGIN, ENDING
```

Data Line

```
186.93, 386.21
```

Computer Memory

BEGIN	186.93
ENDING	386.21

The data values in this example could also have been entered on separate lines since the READ statement will read as many lines as needed to find values for the variables in its list.

Solution 2

This solution uses two READ statements; thus the values must be entered on different lines.

FORTRAN Statements

```
READ*, BEGIN
READ*, ENDING
```

Data Lines

```
186.93
386.21
```

Computer Memory

BEGIN	186.93
ENDING	386.21

Formatted Output

To specify the form in which data values are printed and where on the output line they are printed requires formatted statements. The general form of a formatted PRINT statement is

PRINT *k, expression list*

The expression list designates the memory locations whose contents will be printed or arithmetic expressions whose values will be printed. The list of expressions also determines the order in which the values will be printed. The reference *k* refers to a FORMAT statement which will specify the spacing to be used in printing the information. A sample PRINT and FORMAT combination is

```
      PRINT 5, TIME, DISTNC
    5 FORMAT (1X,F5.1,2X,F7.2)
```

Recall that statement labels are entered in columns 1 through 5.

The general form of the FORMAT statement is

k **FORMAT** *(specification list)*

The specification list tells the computer both the vertical and horizontal spacing to be used when printing the output information. The vertical spacing options include printing on the top of a new page (if the output is being printed on paper), the next line (single spacing), double spacing, and no spacing. Horizontal spacing includes indicating how many digits will be used for each value, how many blanks will be between numbers, and how many values are to be printed per line.

To understand the specifications used to describe the vertical and horizontal spacing, we must first examine the output from a printer or terminal, the most common output devices. Other forms of output have similar characteristics.

The line printer prints on continuous computer paper that is on a perforated roll so it is easy to separate the pages; a laser printer uses individual sheets of paper. Typically, 55 to 75 lines of information can be printed per page. The number of characters printed per line depends on the font size, but a typical line contains 60 to 70 characters. The PRINT/FORMAT combination specifically describes where each line is to be printed on the page (vertical spacing) and which positions in the line will contain data (horizontal spacing).

The computer uses the specification list to construct each output line internally in memory before actually printing the line. This internal memory region is called a *buffer*. The buffer is automatically filled with blanks before it is used to construct a line of output. The first character of the buffer is called the *carriage control character;* it determines the vertical spacing for the line. The remaining characters represent the line to be printed, as shown in the following diagram:

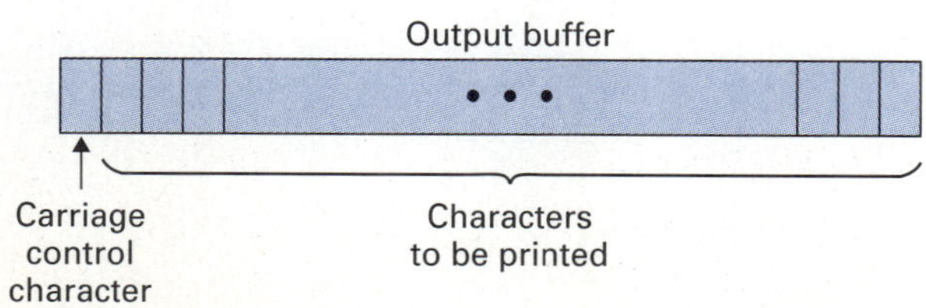

The following list shows some of the valid carriage control characters and the vertical spacing they generate. When needed for clarity in either FORMAT statements or buffer contents, a blank is indicated by the character b placed one-half space below the regular line.

Carriage Control Character	Vertical Spacing
1	New page
blank	Single spacing
0	Double spacing
+	No vertical spacing

Double spacing causes one line to be skipped before the current line of output is printed. When a plus sign is in the carriage control, no spacing occurs and the next line of information will print over the last line printed. On most computers, an invalid carriage control character causes single spacing.

A terminal screen does not have the same capabilities as a printer for spacing; therefore, a 1 in the carriage control usually becomes an invalid control character and causes single spacing. If the terminal I/O does not use carriage control, then the entire contents of the buffer, including the carriage control character, may appear on the terminal screen.

We now examine four FORMAT specifications that describe how to fill the output buffer. Commas are used to separate specifications in the FORMAT statement. Additional FORMAT specifications are included in Section 2–10 and in Appendix B.

Literal Specification The literal specification allows us to put characters directly into the buffer. The characters must be enclosed in single quotation marks or apostrophes. These characters can represent the carriage control character or the characters in a literal. The following examples illustrate use of the literal specification in FORMAT statements.

Example 2-6

Title Heading

Print the title heading TEST RESULTS on the top of a new page, *left-justified* (that is, no blanks to the left of the heading).

Solution

FORTRAN Statements

```
      PRINT 4
    4 FORMAT ('1','TEST RESULTS')
```

Buffer Contents

```
1TEST RESULTS
```

Computer Output

```
       111
123456789012
```

```
TEST RESULTS
```

The buffer is filled according to the FORMAT. No variable names were listed on the PRINT statement; hence, no values were printed. The literal specifications cause the characters 1TEST RESULTS to be put in the buffer, beginning with the first position in the buffer. After filling the buffer, as instructed by the FORMAT, the carriage control is examined to determine vertical spacing. The character 1 in the carriage control position tells the computer to begin a new page. The rest of the buffer is then printed. Notice that the carriage control character is not printed. The row of small numbers above the computer output shows the specific column of the output line: the first T is in column 1, the second T is in column 4, and the third T is in column 11.

Column Headings

Example 2-7

Double space from the last line printed and print column headings 1988 kWh and 1989 kWh, with no blanks on the left-hand side of the line and seven blanks between the two column headings.

Correct Solution

FORTRAN Statements

```
  PRINT 3
3 FORMAT ('0','1988 kWhbbbbbbb1989 kWh')
```

Buffer Contents

```
01988 kWhbbbbbbb1989 kWh
```

Computer Output

```
         11111111112222
12345678901234567890123
```

```
1988 kWh       1989 kWh
```

The line shown is printed after double spacing from the previous line of output.

Incorrect Solution

FORTRAN Statements

```
  FRINT 3
3 FORMAT ('1988 kWhbbbbbbb1989 kWh')
```

Buffer Contents

```
1988 kWhbbbbbbb1989 kWh
```

Computer Output

```
         1111111111222
1234567890123456789012

 988 kWh       1989 kWh
```

In this example we forgot to specify the carriage control. However, the computer does not forget: the first position of the buffer contains a 1, which indicates spacing to a new page. The rest of the buffer is then printed.

X Specification The X specification will insert blanks into the buffer. Its general form is nX, where n represents the number of blanks to be inserted in the buffer. An example using both the X specification and the literal specification follows.

Example 2·8

Centered Heading

Print the heading EXPERIMENT NO. 1 centered at the top of a new page.

Solution

Assume that an output line contains 65 characters. To center the heading we determine the number of characters in the heading (16), subtract that from 65 ($65 - 16 = 49$), and divide that by 2 to put one-half the blanks in front of the heading ($49/2 = 25$).

FORTRAN STATEMENTS

```
   PRINT 35
35 FORMAT ('1',25X,'EXPERIMENT NO. 1')
```

Buffer Contents

```
1bbbbbbbbbbbbbbbbbbbbbbbbbEXPERIMENT NO. 1
```

Computer Output

```
2222333333333344
6789012345678901

EXPERIMENT NO. 1
```

I Specification The literal specification and the X specification allow us to specify carriage control and to print headings. They cannot, however, be used to print variable values. We now examine a specification that prints the contents of integer variables: the specification form is Iw, where w represents the number of positions (width) to be assigned in the buffer for printing the value of an integer variable. The value is always *right-justified* (no blanks to the right of the value) in those positions in the buffer. Extra positions on the left are filled with blanks. Thus, if the value 16 is printed with an I4 specification, the four positions contain two blanks followed by 16. If there are not enough positions to print the value, including a minus sign if the value is negative, the positions are filled with asterisks. Hence, if we print the value 132 or −14 with an I2 specification, the two positions are filled with asterisks. It is important to recognize that the asterisks do not necessarily indicate that there is an error in the value; instead, the asterisks may indicate that you need to assign a larger width in the corresponding output specification.

More than one variable name is often listed in the PRINT statement. When interpreting a PRINT/FORMAT combination, the compiler will match the first variable name to the first specification for printing values, and so on. Therefore, there should be the same number of specifications for printing values as there are variables on the PRINT statement list. (In Section 2–10 we explain what happens if the number of specifications does not match the number of variables.)

Integer Values . . . . Example 2·9

Print the values of the integer variables SUM, MEAN, and N on the same line, single spaced from the previous line.

Solution

Computer Memory

SUM	12
MEAN	−14
N	−146

Fortran Statements

```
      PRINT 30, SUM, MEAN, N
   30 FORMAT (1X,I3,2X,I2,2X,I4)
```

Buffer Contents

```
bb12bb**bb-146
```

Computer Output

```
          1111
 1234567890123

 12  **  -146
```

The computer will print SUM with an I3 specification, MEAN with an I2 specification, and N with an I4 specification. The value of SUM is 12, so the three corresponding positions contain a blank followed by the number 12. The value of MEAN, −14, requires at least three positions, so the two specified positions are filled with asterisks. The value of N fills all four allotted positions. The carriage control character is a blank, thus the line of output is single spaced from the previous line.

Example 2·10

Literal and Variable Information

On separate lines, print the values of MEAN and SUM, along with an indication of the name of each of the integer variables.

Solution

Computer Memory

SUM	12
MEAN	−14

FORTRAN Statements

```
  PRINT 2, MEAN
2 FORMAT (1X,'MEAN = ',I4)
  PRINT 3, SUM
3 FORMAT (1X,'SUM = ',I4)
```

Buffer Contents

```
bMEANb=bb-14
```

```
bSUMb=bbb12
```

Computer Output

```
         11
12345678901

MEAN =  -14
SUM =    12
```

F Specification The F specification is used to print real numbers in a decimal form (for example, 36.21) as opposed to an exponential form (for example, 0.3621E+02). The general form for an F specification is Fw.d, where w represents the total width (number of positions, including the decimal point) to be used and d represents the number of those positions that will represent decimal positions to the right of the decimal point as shown below:

$$\underbrace{\texttt{XX.}\overbrace{\texttt{XXX}}^{\text{decimal portion} = d}}_{\text{total width} = w}$$

If the value to be printed has fewer than d decimal positions, zeros are inserted on the right-hand side of the decimal point. Thus, if the value 21.6 is printed with an F6.3 specification, the output is 21.600. If the value to be printed has more than d decimal positions, only d decimal positions are printed, dropping the rest. Thus, if the value 21.86342 is printed with an F6.3 specification, the output is 21.863. Many compilers will round to the last decimal position printed; in these cases, the value 18.98662 will be printed as 18.987 if an F6.3 specification is used.

If the integer portion of a real value requires fewer positions than allotted in the F specification, the extra positions on the left-hand side of the decimal point are filled with blanks. Thus, if the value 3.123 is printed with an F6.3 specification, the output is a blank followed by 3.123. If the integer portion of a real value, including the minus sign if the value is negative, requires more positions than allotted in the F specification, the entire field is filled with asterisks. Thus, if the value 312.6 is printed with an F6.3 specification, the output is ******.

If a value is between −1 and +1, positions must usually be allowed for both a leading zero to the left of the decimal point and a minus sign if the value is negative. Thus, the smallest F specification that could be used to print −0.127 is F6.3. If a smaller specification width were used, all the positions would be filled with asterisks.

Angle THETA . . . . Example 2·11

Print the value of an angle called THETA. Construct the Greek symbol for θ using a zero with a dash printed over it. The output should be in this form:

$$\theta = \text{XX.XX}$$

Solution

Computer Memory

THETA | 3.184 |

FORTRAN Statements

```
  PRINT 1
1 FORMAT (1X,'0')
  PRINT 2, THETA
2 FORMAT ('+','- = ',F5.2)
```

Buffer Contents

```
b0
```

```
+-b=bb3.18
```

Computer Output

```
123456789
 θ =  3.18
```

The first PRINT statement printed a zero in the first position of the output line after single spacing from the previous line. The second PRINT statement had a plus sign in the carriage control, which caused no vertical spacing. The dash character is therefore printed on top of the character zero, giving the Greek symbol theta. The value of the variable THETA is printed on the same line. (Remember that overprinting will work only if the output device uses carriage control; otherwise all output is single-spaced.)

Example 2·12

Sine and Cosine Computation

Print the values of the sine and cosine of the angle THETA. Assume that THETA is in radians. Use descriptive literals.

Solution

Computer Memory

THETA | 1.26 |

FORTRAN Statements

```
  PRINT 1, THETA, SIN(THETA)
1 FORMAT (1X,'THE SINE OF ',F5.2,' RADIANS = ',F4.2)
  PRINT 2, THETA, COS(THETA)
2 FORMAT (1X,'THE COSINE OF ',F5.2,' RADIANS = ',F4.2)
```

Buffer Contents

```
bTHEbSINEbOFbb1.26bRADIANSb=b0.95
```

```
bTHEbCOSINEbOFbb1.26bRADIANSb=b0.31
```

Computer Output

```
         1111111111222222222233333
1234567890123456789012345678901234

 THE SINE OF  1.26 RADIANS = 0.95
 THE COSINE OF  1.26 RADIANS = 0.31
```

Suppose that the value of THETA was 1.78 radians. Then the computer output for this set of FORTRAN statements would be

Computer Output

```
              1111111111222222222233333
     1234567890123456789012345678901234

     THE SINE OF  1.78 RADIANS = 0.98
     THE COSINE OF  1.78 RADIANS = ****
```

The asterisks were printed instead of the correct value of -0.21 because the correct value requires a total of five positions instead of the four allotted with the specification F4.2. In order to have a solution that will work for all possible values of the sine and cosine functions, we should use an F5.2 format specification in both formats, as shown below:

```
  PRINT 1, THETA, SIN(THETA)
1 FORMAT (1X,'THE SINE OF ',F5.2,' RADIANS = ',F5.2)
  PRINT 2, THETA, COS(THETA)
2 FORMAT (1X,'THE COSINE OF ',F5.2,' RADIANS = ',F5.2)
```

E Specification Real numbers may be printed in an exponential form with the E specification. This specification is used primarily for very small values, or very large values, or when you are uncertain of the magnitude of a number. If you use an F format that is too small for a value, the output field will be filled with asterisks. In contrast, a real number will always fit in an E specification field.

The general format for an E specification is Ew.d. The w again represents the total width or number of positions to be used in printing the value. The d represents the number of positions to the right of the decimal point, assuming that the value is in exponential form, with the decimal point to the left of the first nonzero digit. The framework for printing a real value in an exponential specification with three decimal places is

decimal portion = d

SO.XXXESXX

total width = w

The symbol S indicates that positions must be reserved for both the sign of the value and the sign of the exponent in case they are negative. Note that, with all the extra positions, the total width becomes ten positions. Three of the ten positions are the decimal positions and the other seven are positions that are always needed for an E format. Thus, the total width of an E specification must be at least d+7; otherwise, asterisks will be printed. The specification above is E10.3.

If there are more decimal positions in the specification than are in the exponential form of the value, the extra decimal positions are filled on the right with zeros. If the total width of the E specification is more than 7 plus the decimal positions, the extra positions appear as blanks on the left side of the value.

Example 2·13

TIME in an Exponential Form

Print the value of TIME in an exponential form with four decimal positions.

Solution 1

Computer Memory

TIME | −0.00125 |

FORTRAN Statements

```
   PRINT 10, TIME
10 FORMAT (1X,'TIME = ',E11.4)
```

Buffer Contents

| bTIMEb=b-0.1250E-02 |

Computer Output

```
         111111111
123456789012345678

 TIME = -0.1250E-02
```

Solution 2

Computer Memory

TIME | −0.00125 |

FORTRAN Statements

```
   PRINT 15, TIME
15 FORMAT (1X,'TIME = ',E13.4)
```

Buffer Contents

| bTIMEb=bbb-0.1250E-02 |

Computer Output

```
         11111111112
12345678901234567890

 TIME =   -0.1250E-02
```

Both of these solutions use an exponential format, but the second solution places two additional blanks after the equal sign. ◀

Since the format specifications can be included as a character constant in the PRINT statement in Fortran 90, there is no need for a separate FORMAT statement.

Fortran 90

SELF-TEST 2-4

This self-test allows you to check quickly to see if you have remembered some of the key points from Section 2–4. If you have any problems with the exercises, you should reread this section. The solutions are included at the end of the text.

1. What is printed by the following statements? Show the exact location of any blanks.

```
      REAL X
      X = -27.632
      PRINT 5, X
    5 FORMAT (1X,'X = ',F7.1,' DEGREES')
```

2. What is printed by the following statements? Show the exact location of any blanks.

```
      REAL DIST, VEL
      DIST = 28732.5
      VEL = -2.6
      PRINT 5, DIST, VEL
    5 FORMAT (1X,'DISTANCE = ',E10.3,
     +        5X,'VELOCITY = ',F5.2)
```

2·5 ■ Complete Programs

The PROGRAM statement identifies the beginning of a program and assigns the program name. The general form of this statement is

PROGRAM *program name*

Like a variable name, the program name can be one to six characters, begins with a letter, and contains only letters and digits. Some example PROGRAM statements are

```
PROGRAM TEST
PROGRAM COMPUT
PROGRAM SORT2
```

You may not use a variable in your program that has the same name as the program name. The PROGRAM statement is not required, but we recommend using it to clearly identify the beginning of a program.

The STOP statement signals the computer to terminate execution of the program. It can appear anywhere in the program that makes sense, and it can appear as often as necessary. For example, certain data values may not be valid, and we may want to stop executing the program if they occur. The general form of the STOP statement is

```
STOP
```

The STOP statement is optional in most programs, as explained in the next paragraph.

The END statement identifies the physical end of our FORTRAN program for the compiler. Since the compiler stops translating statements when it reaches the END statement, every FORTRAN program must terminate with the END statement, whose general form is

```
END
```

If a STOP statement does not immediately precede the END statement, the compiler will automatically add one. Therefore, a program may use both a STOP and an END at the end of the program, although the STOP is not necessary. In our programs we will not use the STOP statement when it immediately precedes the END statement.

All nonexecutable statements, including specification statements, must precede *executable statements* in a program. Therefore, FORTRAN programs should have the following general structure:

PROGRAM statement
Nonexecutable statements
Executable statements
END statement

If you look back at the program in Chapter 1, on page 19, you will be able to identify the different groups of statements.

Fortran 90

In Fortran 90, the word PROGRAM and the program name can be added to the END statement, as in

```
END PROGRAM TEST
```

In addition to learning to write correct programs, it is important to learn to write programs with good programming style, that is, to write programs with a simple and consistent form. At the end of this chapter and each of the remaining chapters, we include two special sections. A Debugging Aids section outlines efficient methods for locating and correcting program errors relevant to the new material presented in the chapter. A Style/Technique Guide contains suggestions for building good programming habits that stress readability and simplicity. Some of the style and technique guidelines that we will follow in our example programs are the following:

1. We will mark the beginning and end of each program with a comment line containing a series of dashes. A PROGRAM statement will always be the first FORTRAN statement in a program.
2. A brief discussion of the purpose of the program will follow the PROGRAM statement. This information should be similar to the information in the first two steps of our problem solving process—the problem statement and a description of the input and output.
3. Specification statements will be used to specify the type of all variables used in the program.
4. In longer programs, comment lines containing blanks will be used to separate portions of programs into sections that correspond to the decomposition of the problem solution.
5. Any statement number will be right-justified within the group of columns 1 through 5.

Turn again to the program in Chapter 1 on page 19 and observe how these guidelines were followed.

Convert Kilowatt-Hours to Joules . . . . Example 2·14

Write a program to convert an amount in kWh (kilowatt-hours) to joules. The amount in kWh is to be entered from the terminal. The output should be the number read in kWh and the converted value in joules. (Use the following conversion factor: joules = 3.6E+06 × kWh.)

Solution

The **first step** is to state the problem clearly: Convert a value in kilowatt-hours to joules.

The **second step** is to describe the input and output:

Input—value in kilowatt-hours
Output—corresponding value in joules

The **third step** is to work a simple example by hand. Therefore, let the input value be 5.5 kilowatt-hours. Then the number of joules is 3.6E+06 × 5.5 = 20E+06.

The **fourth step** is to develop an algorithm. We start with the decomposition, and then add more details to obtain the pseudocode. We can usually go directly from the pseudocode to the FORTRAN program.

Decomposition

Read amount in kilowatt-hours.
Convert amount to joules.
Print both amounts.

Pseudocode

Convert: Read kilowatt-hours
joules ← 3.6E+06 × kilowatt-hours
Print kilowatt-hours, joules

FORTRAN Program

```
*-------------------------------------------------------------------*
      PROGRAM CONVRT
*
*  This program reads an input value in kilowatt-hours,
*  and then converts it to joules.  Both values are then printed.
*
      REAL KWH, JOULES
*
      PRINT*, 'ENTER ENERGY IN KILOWATT-HOURS'
      READ*, KWH
*
      JOULES = 3.6E+06*KWH
*
      PRINT 5, KWH, JOULES
    5 FORMAT (1X,F6.2,' KILOWATT-HOURS = ',E9.2,' JOULES')
*
      END
*-------------------------------------------------------------------*
```

The **fifth step** is to test the program. The following computer output illustrates a sample run of the program using the same data that we used in the hand example.

```
ENTER ENERGY IN KILOWATT-HOURS
5.5
  5.50 KILOWATT-HOURS =  0.20E+08 JOULES
```

In the program in Example 2–14, we printed a message to the user that specified the input that the program was expecting. After converting the value in kilowatt-hours to joules, we printed the value of kilowatt-hours along with the converted value in joules. This interaction between the program and the user resembles a conversation and is called *conversational computing*.

Biology

A biology laboratory experiment involves the analysis of a strain of bacteria. Because the growth of bacteria in the colony can be modeled with an exponential equation, we are going to write a computer program to predict how many bacteria will be in the colony after a specified amount of time. Suppose that, for this type of bacteria, the equation to predict growth is

$$y_{new} = y_{old}e^{1.386t}$$

where y_{new} is the new number of bacteria in the colony, y_{old} is the initial number of bacteria in the colony, and t is the elapsed time in hours. Thus, when $t = 0$, we have

$$y_{new} = y_{old}e^{1.386 \cdot 0} = y_{old}$$

1. Problem Statement

Using the equation

$$y_{new} = y_{old}e^{1.386t}$$

predict the number of bacteria (y_{new}) in a bacteria colony given the initial number in the colony (y_{old}) and the time elapsed (t) in hours.

2. Input/Output Description

Input—the initial number of bacteria and the time elapsed

Output—the number of bacteria in the colony after the elapsed time

3. Hand Example

You will need your calculator for these calculations. For $t = 1$ hour and $y_{old} = 1$ bacterium, the new colony contains

$$y_{new} = 1 \cdot e^{1.386 \cdot 1} = 4.00$$

After 6 hours, the size of the colony is

$$y_{new} = 1 \cdot e^{1.386 \cdot 6} = 4088.77$$

If we start with 2 bacteria, after 6 hours the size of the colony is

$$y_{new} = 2 \cdot e^{1.386 \cdot 6} = 8177.54$$

4. Algorithm Development

Decomposition

Read y_{old}, t.
Compute y_{new}.
Print y_{old}, t, y_{new}.

Pseudocode

Growth: Read y_{old}, t
$y_{new} \leftarrow y_{old}e^{1.386t}$
Print y_{old}, t, y_{new}

FORTRAN Program

```
*-----------------------------------------------------------------------*
      PROGRAM GROWTH
*
*  This program reads the initial population and the time elapsed
*  and then computes and prints the predicted population.
*
      REAL YOLD, YNEW, TIME
*
      PRINT*, 'ENTER INITIAL POPULATION'
      READ*, YOLD
      PRINT*, 'ENTER TIME ELAPSED IN HOURS'
      READ*, TIME
*
      YNEW = YOLD*EXP(1.386*TIME)
*
      PRINT 10, YOLD
   10 FORMAT (1X,'INITIAL POPULATION = ',F9.4)
      PRINT 20, TIME
   20 FORMAT (1X,'TIME ELAPSED (HOURS) = ',F9.4)
      PRINT 30, YNEW
   30 FORMAT (1X,'PREDICTED POPULATION = ',F9.4)
*
      END
*-----------------------------------------------------------------------*
```

5. Testing

The program output using data from one of our hand examples is

```
ENTER INITIAL POPULATION
1.0
ENTER TIME ELAPSED IN HOURS
6.0
INITIAL POPULATION =    1.0000
TIME ELAPSED (HOURS) =    6.0000
PREDICTED POPULATION = 4088.7722
```

Try using other values in the program to see if the results appear reasonable. Very large values of TIME will result in an overflow error. Negative values of TIME represent population decreases, but if the population falls below 1 the model is no longer applicable.

2·7 Application ■ Carbon Dating

Archeology

Carbon dating is a method for estimating the age of organic substances such as shells, seeds, and wooden artifacts. The technique compares the amount of carbon 14, a radioactive carbon, contained in the remains of the substance with the amount of carbon 14 that would have been in the object's environment at the time it was alive. The age of the cave paintings in Lascaux, France, has been estimated at 15,500 years using this technique.

Assume that you are working as an assistant to an archeologist on Saturdays. Artifacts from a recent excavation have been sent to a laboratory for carbon analysis. The lab will determine the proportion of carbon 14 that remains in the artifact. The archeologist has shown you the following equation that gives the estimated age of the artifact in years:

$$\text{age} = \frac{-\log_e(\text{carbon 14 proportion remaining})}{0.0001216}$$

Recall that $\log_e X$ is the natural logarithm of the value X.

The archeologist would like you to write a FORTRAN program that will read the proportion of carbon 14 remaining in an artifact and then compute and print its estimated age.

1. Problem Statement

Read the proportion of carbon 14 remaining in an artifact. Then compute its estimated age.

2. Input/Output Description

Input—the proportion of carbon 14 left in the artifact

Output—an estimate in years of the age of the artifact

3. Hand Example

Suppose that no carbon 14 has decayed; then the carbon 14 proportion is 1.0, and the estimated age is

$$\text{age} = \frac{-\log_e(1.0)}{0.0001216} = \frac{0}{0.0001216} = 0$$

This age makes sense because the artifact must be relatively young if no carbon 14 decay has occurred.

Now assume that one-half of the carbon has decayed. Thus, we will use 0.5 as the proportion of carbon 14 left and see how this affects the formula:

$$\text{age} = \frac{-\log_e(0.5)}{0.0001216} = 5700.2 \text{ years}$$

(Reference books give the half-life of carbon 14 as 5700 years, so this is a good check for the equation.)

4. Algorithm Development

Decomposition

Read proportion of carbon 14 remaining.
Compute estimated age.
Print estimated age.

Pseudocode

Age: Read proportion of carbon 14 remaining

$$\text{age} \leftarrow \frac{-\log_e(\text{carbon 14 proportion remaining})}{0.0001216}$$

Print estimated age

To compute the estimated age, we need to compute a natural logarithm. Using Table 2–4, we find that the intrinsic function LOG performs this operation. LOG is a generic function; thus, it will return a real value if its argument is real.

FORTRAN Program

```
*-----------------------------------------------------------------------*
      PROGRAM DATE
*
*  This program estimates and prints the age of an artifact
*  from the proportion of carbon 14 remaining in the artifact.
*
      REAL CARBON, AGE
*
      PRINT*, 'ENTER PROPORTION REMAINING FOR CARBON DATING'
      READ*, CARBON
*
      AGE = (-LOG(CARBON))/0.0001216
*
      PRINT 5, AGE
    5 FORMAT (1X,'ESTIMATED AGE OF ARTIFACT IS ',F6.1,' YEARS')
*
      END
*-----------------------------------------------------------------------*
```

5. Testing

We can test the program with the examples we used in the hand examples. A typical screen display should be

```
ENTER PROPORTION REMAINING FOR CARBON DATING
0.5
ESTIMATED AGE OF ARTIFACT IS 5700.2 YEARS
```

2-8 Application ■ Equipment Reliability

Electrical Engineering

If you have a personal computer or if you have a friend who has one, open the back of the computer system and look at the computer board(s) that contains its circuitry. Each board contains a large number of components. You might wonder how computers can be so reliable when so many different pieces could malfunction. Much of their reliability is due to the quality control maintained during their manufacture. However, before the design of a computer or any complicated piece of instrumentation is actually implemented in hardware, the reliability of the device is analyzed. In this section we look at one way of estimating the reliability of a group of components. The reliability of a single component is generally available from the manufacturer. For example, a company may sell transistors that are guaranteed to be reliable 98 percent of the time. This information tells us how reliable one transistor is, but it does not tell us how reliable a piece of instrumentation may be if it contains 5000 of these transistors.

Equations for analyzing reliability come from the area of mathematics called statistics and probability. However, in order to select the correct equation, we must know something about the design. For example, consider the following diagrams.

Series Design

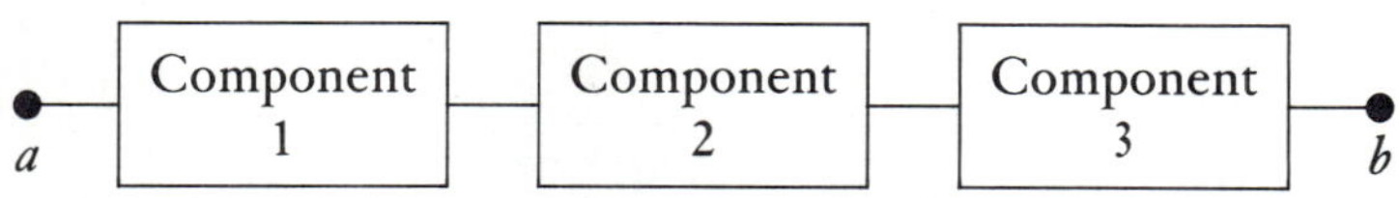

Parallel Design

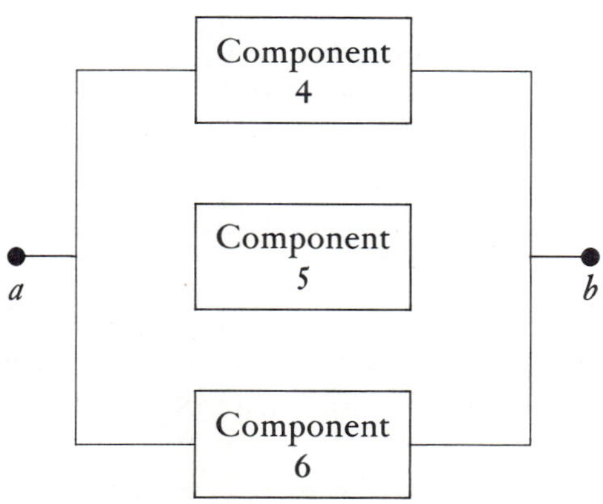

The design on top contains three components connected serially—or in series. In order for information to flow from point a to point b, all three components must work properly. The design on the bottom contains three components connected in parallel. In order for information to flow from point a to point b, only one of the three components must work properly. If all the individual components have the same reliability, we would expect the parallel configuration to have better overall performance. This can also be verified with mathematical equations.

In this section we are going to estimate the reliability of a piece of equipment relative to a specific component that is used in many places in the design. We are going to compute the percentage of the time that all the components will be working properly, so we are looking at a series-type design. This situation can be described using a Bernoulli equation. With this equation we can compute the probability that all the components will work properly. This probability can be expressed as the percentage of time that there will be no component failures. If this percentage is not high, we may not want to perform critical operations with the instrumentation or we may want to request that the instrumentation be redesigned.

Assume that p is the percentage of time that a single component will be good and n is the total number of components connected in series in a piece of equipment. Then the reliability, or percentage of the time that none of the components will fail, is given by the Bernoulli equation below:

$$\text{percentage} = \left(\frac{p}{100.0}\right)^n \cdot 100.0$$

Using the Bernoulli equation, write a program that will read the reliability of a single component and the number of components connected serially in a design. Compute the percentage of time that all the components will work properly.

1. Problem Statement

Compute the reliability of a piece of instrumentation relative to a group of components, using the approximation given by the Bernoulli equation.

2. Input/Output Description

Input—the reliability of a single component and the number of components connected serially in the instrumentation

Output—the overall reliability of the instrumentation relative to the components in series

3. Hand Example

Suppose we are evaluating a piece of instrumentation that contains 20 transistors. Each transistor has a reliability of 96 percent. We are interested in the reliability of the instrument with no transistor failures. The calculation is performed as shown below:

$$n = 20$$

$$p = 96.0$$

$$\text{percentage} = \left(\frac{96.0}{100.0}\right)^{20} \cdot 100.0$$

$$= 44.2$$

where the percentage is the percentage of the time that there will be no transistor failures. This number is probably lower than you expected. Even with 99 percent reliability of an individual component, the reliability of 20 of them at one time is 81.8 percent. Clearly, designers must have ways of improving reliability over that given by serial designs. Designs that use parallel features have greatly increased reliability, and different equations are used for the reliability computations.

4. Algorithm Development

Decomposition

Read reliability of component and number of components.
Compute reliability of group of components.
Print reliability.

Pseudocode

Rely: Read p,n

$$\text{percent} \leftarrow \left(\frac{p}{100.0}\right)^{n} \cdot 100.0$$

Print percent

FORTRAN Program

```
*-----------------------------------------------------------------------*
      PROGRAM RELY
*
*  This program reads the reliability of a single component
*  and the number of components in series in a piece of equipment.
*  It then computes and prints the reliability of the
*  equipment using a Bernoulli equation.
*
      INTEGER N
      REAL P, PERC
*
      PRINT*, 'ENTER RELIABILITY OF SINGLE COMPONENT'
      PRINT*, '(USE PERCENTAGE BETWEEN 0.0 AND 100.0)'
      READ*, P
      PRINT*, 'ENTER NUMBER OF COMPONENTS IN EQUIPMENT'
      READ*, N
*
      PERC = (P/100.0)**N*100.0
*
```

```
      PRINT*, 'PERCENT OF THE TIME THAT THE EQUIPMENT'
      PRINT 5, PERC
    5 FORMAT (1X,'SHOULD WORK WITHOUT FAILURE IS ',F6.2,' %')
*
      END
*-----------------------------------------------------------------------*
```

5. Testing

If we test this program with 20 components, each of which has a reliability of 96 percent, the output is

```
ENTER RELIABILITY OF SINGLE COMPONENT
(USE PERCENTAGE BETWEEN 0.0 AND 100.0)
96.0
ENTER NUMBER OF COMPONENTS IN EQUIPMENT
20
PERCENT OF THE TIME THAT THE EQUIPMENT
SHOULD WORK WITHOUT FAILURE IS  44.20 %
```

If we test this program with 20 components, each of which has a reliability of 99 percent, the output is

```
ENTER RELIABILITY OF SINGLE COMPONENT
(USE PERCENTAGE BETWEEN 0.0 AND 100.0)
99.0
ENTER NUMBER OF COMPONENTS IN EQUIPMENT
20
PERCENT OF THE TIME THAT THE EQUIPMENT
SHOULD WORK WITHOUT FAILURE IS  81.79 %
```

2.9 Application ▪ Stride Estimation

Mechanical Engineering

The physics that govern the motion of a simple pendulum enable us to estimate the time that it takes for a natural stride of a person given only the length of his or her leg. This is done by modeling the leg by a long, thin rod of uniform cross section that pivots about its upper end, as shown in the diagram on next page.

Using this model, a freely swinging rod supported at its upper end will take T seconds to swing from one end to another, and back to its original position, where[1]

$$T = 2 \cdot \pi \sqrt{\frac{2L}{3g}}$$

[1] E. R. Jones and R. L. Childer, "Contemporary College Physics," Reading, Mass.: Addison-Wesley, pp. 392–393, 1990.

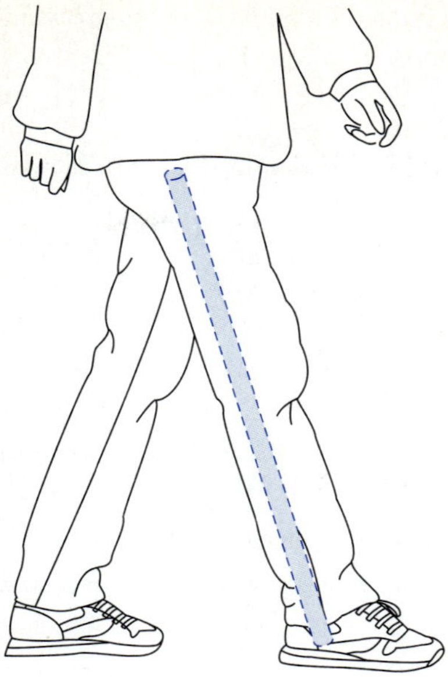

where L is the length of the rod (or leg) in feet and g is the acceleration due to gravity, which is approximately 32 ft/s^2. A stride will take $T/2$ seconds, since a stride is a step with only one leg.

It is interesting to observe that the length of a stride L_s is proportional to L, the length of the leg. Thus, we can express L_s as a product of a constant a and L:

$$L_s = aL$$

If we know the length of a stride and the time it takes to take a stride, we can compute the walking speed, which is the number of feet per second traveled while walking:

$$\begin{aligned}\text{walking speed} &= \frac{L_s}{\frac{T}{2}} \\ &= \frac{aL}{\pi\sqrt{\frac{2L}{3g}}} \\ &= \frac{a}{\pi\sqrt{\frac{2}{3g}}} \cdot \sqrt{L}\end{aligned}$$

Therefore, the walking speed in feet per second is proportional to the square root of the length of the leg. Thus people with longer legs have a faster walking speed, or go farther per second. This model does not work for running because the leg does not swing freely in a running gait.

Write a program that reads the length of a leg in feet, and estimates the time required for a stride.

1. Problem Statement

Compute the time required for a stride.

2. Input/Output Description

Input—the length of the leg
Output—the time required for a stride

3. Hand Example

Let the leg length be 3 feet. Then T_s, the time for a stride, is

$$T_s = \frac{T}{2} = \pi \sqrt{\frac{2L}{3g}} = \pi \sqrt{\frac{6}{96}} = 0.79 \text{ s}$$

Just for fun, measure your leg (from the hip joint to the heel) and use a stopwatch to time your natural walking stride. Compare that to the value computed using the equation above. (It would also be interesting to measure the length of your stride and compute an estimate for the constant *a*. Compare your estimate for *a* with estimates from classmates with a wide range of heights. They should be similar.)

4. Algorithm Development

Decomposition

Read leg length.
Compute stride time.
Print stride time.

Pseudocode

Stride: Read L

$$T_s \leftarrow \pi \sqrt{\frac{2L}{3g}}$$

Print T_s

In the FORTRAN program that follows, note that we defined the constants as separate variables so that the equation for T_s is as close as possible to the original equation. This makes the program easier to read and reduces the possibility of errors in converting the equation into FORTRAN.

FORTRAN Program

```
*-----------------------------------------------------------------------*
      PROGRAM STRIDE
*
*  This program reads the length of a leg, and then
*  computes and prints the time required for a stride.
*
      REAL LEG, PI, G, TIME
      PARAMETER (PI=3.141593, G=32.0)
*
      PRINT*, 'ENTER THE LEG LENGTH IN FEET'
      READ*, LEG
*
      TIME = PI*SQRT(2.0*LEG/(3.0*G))
*
      PRINT*
      PRINT 5, TIME
    5 FORMAT (1X,'THE STRIDE TIME IS ',F5.2,' SECONDS')
      PRINT 6, LEG
    6 FORMAT (1X,'FOR A LEG LENGTH OF ',F5.2,' FEET')
*
      END
*-----------------------------------------------------------------------*
```

5. Testing

If we test this program with the hand example data, the output is the following:

```
ENTER THE LEG LENGTH IN FEET
3

THE STRIDE TIME IS  0.79 SECONDS
FOR A LEG LENGTH OF  3.00 FEET
```

2·10 ■ Additional Formatting Features

In this section we present several useful features of FORMAT statements. We illustrate each feature with examples.

■ Repetition

If we have two identical specifications in a row, we can use a constant in front of the specification (or sets of specifications) to indicate repetition. For instance, I2, I2, I2 can be replaced by 3I2. Often our FORMAT statements can be made shorter with repetition constants. The following pairs of FORMAT statements illustrate the use of repetition constants:

```
10  FORMAT (3X,I2,3X,I2)
10  FORMAT (2(3X,I2))

20  FORMAT (1X,F4.1,F4.1,1X,I3,1X,I3,1X,I3)
20  FORMAT (1X,2F4.1,3(1X,I3))
```

Slash

A slash (/) in a FORMAT statement specifies that the current buffer should be printed and a new one started. The slash is especially useful in inserting blank lines in the output. However, do not assume that a slash will always cause single spacing; the spacing following the line printed by the slash depends on the carriage control character of the next line. The slash character may be enclosed in commas if desired.

The following statements print the heading TEST RESULTS followed by column headings TIME and HEIGHT:

```
  PRINT 5
5 FORMAT (1X,'   TEST RESULTS'/1X,'TIME',5X,'HEIGHT')
```

The columns are separated by five spaces and the heading is centered over the column headings, as shown below:

```
   TEST RESULTS
TIME     HEIGHT
```

If we add another slash in the FORMAT statement, we have these statements:

```
  PRINT 5
5 FORMAT (1X,'   TEST RESULTS'//1X,'TIME',5X,'HEIGHT')
```

The execution of these statements gives a blank line between the two headings:

```
   TEST RESULTS

TIME     HEIGHT
```

Tab Specification

The tab specification Tn allows you to shift directly to a specified position, n, in the output line. The following pairs of FORMAT statements function exactly the same:

```
500  FORMAT (58X,'EXPERIMENT  NO.  1')
500  FORMAT (T59,'EXPERIMENT  NO.  1')

550  FORMAT (1X,'SALES',10X,'PROFIT',10X,'LOSS')
550  FORMAT (1X,'SALES',T17,'PROFIT',T33,'LOSS')

600  FORMAT (F6.1,15X,I7)
600  FORMAT (F6.1,T22,I7)
```

The TLn and TRn specifications tab left or right for n positions from the current position. The following formats are therefore equivalent:

```
85  FORMAT (1X,25X,'HEIGHT',5X,'WEIGHT')
85  FORMAT (T27,'HEIGHT',TR5,'WEIGHT')
```

The tab specifications are especially useful in aligning column headings and data.

■ Number of Specifications

Suppose there are more FORMAT specifications than variables on a PRINT list, as shown:

```
  PRINT 1, SPEED, DIST
1 FORMAT (4F5.2)
```

In these cases, the computer uses as much of the specification list as it needs and ignores the rest. In our example, SPEED and DIST would be matched to the first two specifications; the last two specifications would be ignored.

Suppose there are fewer FORMAT specifications than variables on a PRINT list, as shown:

```
   PRINT 20, TEMP, VOL
20 FORMAT (1X,F6.2)
```

In these cases, we match variables and specifications until we reach the end of the FORMAT. Then, two events occur:

1. We print the current buffer and start a new one.
2. We back up in the FORMAT specification list until we reach a left parenthesis, and we again begin matching the remaining variables to the specifications at that point. If a repetition constant is in front of this left parenthesis, it applies to the FORMAT specifications being reused.

In the previous statements, TEMP would be matched to the F6.2 specification. Because there is no specification for VOL, we do the following:

1. Print the value of TEMP after single spacing.
2. Back up to the beginning of the FORMAT specification list (first left parenthesis) and match the F6.2 to the value of VOL. We then reach the end of the list and single space to print the value of VOL. TEMP and VOL are thus printed on separate lines.

This discussion allows you to understand what happens if the number of specifications is not the same as the number of variables. However, we recommend that you only reference the same FORMAT with more than one PRINT statement when the FORMAT specifications are exactly the same. Write a new FORMAT statement if the number of variables is different; this keeps the program simpler to understand.

SELF-TEST 2-5

This self-test allows you to check quickly to see if you have remembered some of the key points from Section 2–10. If you have any problems with the exercises, you should reread this section. The solutions are included at the end of the text.

In problems 1–3, show the output from the following PRINT statements. Be sure to indicate the vertical as well as the horizontal spacing. Use the following variables and corresponding values:

TIME = 3.5, RESP1 = 178.8, RESP2 = 0.00204

1.
```
   PRINT 5, TIME, RESP1, RESP2
 5 FORMAT (1X,F6.2,T20,2F7.4)
```

2.
```
   PRINT 4, TIME, RESP1, TIME, RESP2
 4 FORMAT (1X,'TIME = ',F5.2,TR5,'RESPONSE 1 = ',E9.2/
  +         1X,'TIME = ',F5.2,TR5,'RESPONSE 2 = ',E9.2)
```

3.
```
   PRINT 1, TIME, RESP1, RESP2
 1 FORMAT (1X,'EXPERIMENT RESULTS'//
  +         1X,'TIME',2X,'RESPONSE 1',2X,'RESPONSE 2'/
  +         1X,F4.2,2F12.3)
```

In problems 4–7, tell how many data lines are printed by the following PRINT statements. Indicate which variables are on each line and which columns are used.

4.
```
   PRINT 4, TIME, DIST, VEL, ACCEL
 4 FORMAT (4(1X,F6.3))
```

5.
```
    PRINT 14, TIME, DIST, VEL, ACCEL
 14 FORMAT (1X,F6.2)
```

6.
```
   PRINT 2, TIME, DIST, VEL, ACCEL
 2 FORMAT (1X,F4.2/1X,F4.1)
```

7.
```
   PRINT 3, TIME, DIST
   PRINT 3, VEL, ACCEL
 3 FORMAT (1X,4F6.3)
```

Summary

In this chapter we learned how to define variables and constants in FORTRAN. We discussed the arithmetic operations and intrinsic functions that allow us to compute new values using these variables and constants. Some of the considerations that are unique to computer computations were discussed with specific examples: magnitude limitations, truncation, mixed-mode operations, underflow, and overflow. Statements for reading information from the terminal and for printing answers were covered. Several complete example programs were developed.

■ Debugging Aids

If a program is not working correctly, you should *echo* the values that you read in the program — that is, immediately after reading them, print them out to be sure that the values you want to give the variables are being used. A common mistake is to enter the data values in the wrong order. For example, instead of entering the initial number of bacteria followed by the elapsed time, you enter the elapsed time followed by the initial number of bacteria.

Assignment Statements These debugging aids are specifically for assignment statements.

1. Double check the placement of parentheses. Add parentheses if you are not sure what order the computer will use to compute the operations involved. Be sure that you always have the same number of left parentheses as right parentheses.
2. Review each variable name on the right-hand side of the assignment statement to be sure you have spelled it exactly as previously used. (Did you use VEL when you should have used VELCTY?)
3. Make sure that all variables on the right-hand side of the assignment statement have been previously initialized.
4. Be sure that arguments of functions are in the correct units. (For example, trigonometric functions use angles in radians, not in degrees.)

I/O Statements These debugging aids are specifically for I/O statements.

1. Check to be sure you have given values to all variables in an output list.
2. If any of your output values contain asterisks instead of numbers, enlarge the width of the corresponding specifications or use an E format.
3. Be sure that the order of variables in the input or output list matches the order you used when writing the format.
4. Check every line of output to ensure that you have correctly specified carriage control unless you are using list-directed output. Look for incorrect spacing between lines or missing first letters or numbers in the output.
5. Be sure that you have as many FORMAT specifications as variable names in the READ or PRINT list. In general, do not try to share FORMAT statements.
6. Be sure you do not have the characters I and 1 or the characters O (letter) and 0 (number) interchanged.
7. Be sure that you have not exceeded column 72 on long statements.
8. Use unformatted statements to print values first. After you determine that the values are correct, change to formatted statements.
9. Be careful splitting a literal specification between two lines. Break the literal into two literals so that unexpected blanks do not appear. For example, consider the following FORMAT statement:

```
 10 FORMAT (1X,'EXPERIMENTAL RESULTS
+           FROM PROJECT 1')
```

Any blanks between the word RESULTS and column 72 of the first line and between the continuation character + and the word FROM will be inserted in the literal. Thus, the heading would appear something like:

```
EXPERIMENTAL RESULTS                                        FROM PROJECT 1
```

A better solution is to split the literal into two literals, which is illustrated in the following FORMAT:

```
10 FORMAT (1X,'EXPERIMENTAL RESULTS ',
 +         'FROM PROJECT 1')
```

The corresponding output is:

```
EXPERIMENTAL RESULTS FROM PROJECT 1
```

If these steps do not help you isolate your error, ask your instructor or a classmate to check the program. If no one is available to check your program and you cannot find the error, start over on a clean sheet of paper. Sometimes it is hard to spot your own errors because you know what you want the statements to do and you read that into the statements when searching for errors.

Style/Technique Guides

A program should be written so that another person who knows FORTRAN can readily understand the statements and interpret the procedures—this is especially important because the person updating a program may not always be the same person who originally wrote it. Writing a clear, easily understood program is challenging and necessitates building good habits. The following guides will help you develop a style and technique that will enable you to meet these requirements.

Assignment Statements These guidelines refer specifically to assignment statements.

1. Use variable names that indicate something about the values being stored in the variable. For instance, represent velocity by VELCTY instead of V or X or something obscure.
2. Use a consistent number of significant digits in constants. Do not use 3.14 as a value for π in the beginning of your program and later use 3.141593. Assure this consistency by using the PARAMETER statement to define constants and their values.
3. Break long expressions into smaller expressions and recombine them in a separate statement. A complicated fraction can be computed by first calculating a numerator, then calculating a denominator, then dividing in a separate statement.
4. Insert extra parentheses for readability. Inserting extra pairs of parentheses is

never wrong as long as they are properly located. Extra parentheses often make arithmetic expressions much more readable.

5. Use the intrinsic functions where possible.
6. Do not mix modes. Use the intrinsic functions REAL and INT to avoid mixing types by explicit conversion.

I/O Statements These guidelines refer specifically to I/O statements.

1. Develop the habit of echo printing values that you have read.
2. Print the physical units that correspond to the numeric values being printed—this information is vital for proper interpretation of results.
3. Be consistent about your placement of FORMAT statements. Either put the FORMAT immediately after the statement that uses it or put the FORMAT just before the END statement in your program.
4. Label FORMAT statements so that the numbers are in ascending order and they fit into the order of other statements in your program. Do not, however, number statements sequentially—you may need to insert additional statements later.
5. Make your carriage control evident. For instance use (1X,F4.1) instead of (F5.1).
6. Label values printed. Use (1X,'X=',F3.1) instead of (1X,F3.1).
7. Use an E format to print values for which you cannot approximate the size. After seeing the answer, you can change the E specification to an F specification that will accommodate the value, if you wish.
8. Do not print more significant digits than you have. For instance, if you compute sums with values that have one decimal position, do not print the result with three decimal positions.
9. Generally, it is best to use the same number of specifications in the FORMAT as there are variable names in the variable list.
10. Do not use extremely long FORMAT statements; use additional statements with separate FORMAT statements.
11. Remember that the slash character should always be followed by carriage control in output statements unless it is followed by another slash.

■ Key Words

argument
arithmetic expression
assignment statement
buffer
carriage control
comment line
constant
continuation line
conversational computing
echo
executable statement
explicit typing
exponential notation
formatted I/O
generic function
implicit typing

initialize
integer value
intermediate result
intrinsic function
left-justified
list-directed I/O
literal
mixed-mode operation
nested function
nonexecutable statement
overflow
real value
right-justified
rounding
scientific notation
specification statement
statement label
truncation
type statement
underflow
variable

Problems

We begin our problem set with modifications to programs given earlier in this chapter. Give the decomposition, pseudocode, and FORTRAN program for each problem.

Problems 1 – 5 modify the energy conversion program CONVRT given on page 60.

1. Modify the energy conversion program so that it converts joules to kilowatt-hours.
2. Modify the energy conversion program so that it converts British thermal units to joules. (1 Btu = 1056 joules.)
3. Modify the energy conversion program so that it converts calories to joules. (1 calorie = 4.19 joules.)
4. Modify the energy conversion program so that it converts joules to British thermal units and to calories.
5. Modify the energy conversion program so that it converts kilowatt-hours to calories.

Problems 6 – 10 modify the bacteria growth program GROWTH given on page 62.

6. Modify the bacteria growth program so that the time elapsed is entered in minutes even though the equation still requires a time in hours.
7. Modify the bacteria growth program so that the time elapsed is entered in days even though the equation still requires a time in hours.
8. Modify the bacteria growth program so that an initial population is read from the terminal. The program should compute and print the percent increase in population as time increases from 2 hours to 3 hours.
9. Modify the bacteria growth program so that the program reads two time values from the terminal, where the first time is less than the second time. Compute and print the amount of growth between the times, assuming an initial population value of 1.
10. Modify the bacteria growth program so that the program reads two time values from the terminal, with no restrictions on which time is larger. Com-

pute and print the amount of growth between the two times, assuming an initial population value of 1. (*Hint:* Review the absolute value function.)

Problems 11–15 modify the carbon-dating program DATE given on page 64.

11. Modify the carbon-dating program so that it truncates the age to the nearest year.
12. Modify the carbon-dating program so that it rounds the age to the nearest year. (*Hint:* Review the NINT function.)
13. Modify the carbon-dating program so that it gives the age in centuries instead of in years. Use two decimal places in the output age.
14. Modify the carbon-dating program so that it gives the age in centuries instead of in years. Truncate the resulting age to the nearest century.
15. Modify the carbon-dating program so that it gives the age in centuries instead of in years. Round the resulting age to the nearest century.

Problems 16–20 modify the equipment reliability program RELY given on page 67. In the modifications, if P1 is the reliability of component 1 and P2 is the reliability of component 2, then the reliability of the components connected in series is

$$\text{percentage} = \frac{\text{P1}}{100.0} \cdot \frac{\text{P2}}{100.0} \cdot 100.0$$

The reliability of two components connected in parallel is

$$\text{percentage} = \left(\frac{\text{P1}}{100.0} + \frac{\text{P2}}{100.0} - \frac{\text{P1}}{100.0} \cdot \frac{\text{P2}}{100.0}\right) \cdot 100.0$$

16. Modify the reliability program so that it reads the reliabilities of two components and then computes the reliability of the two components connected in series, as shown in the following diagram:

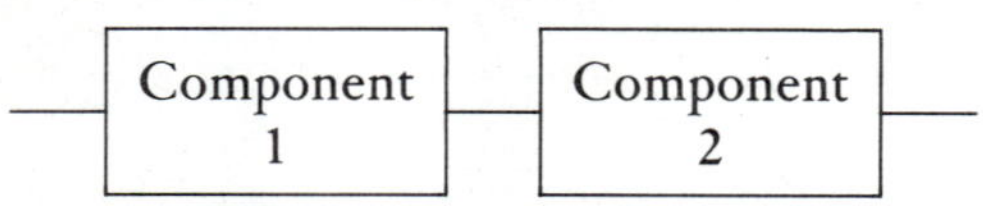

17. Modify the reliability program so that it reads the reliabilities of two components and then computes the reliability of the two components connected in parallel, as shown in the following diagram:

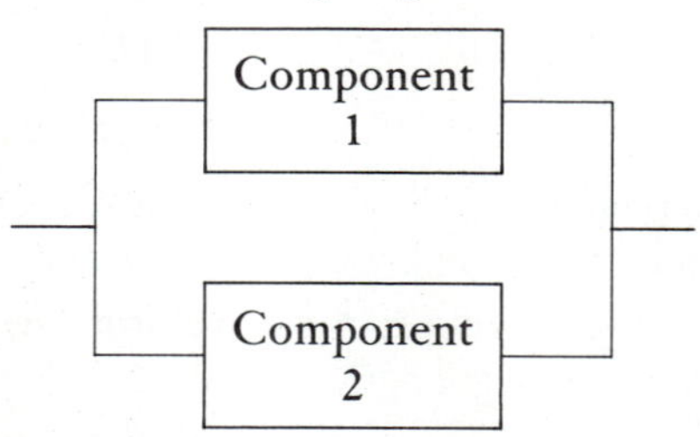

18. Modify the reliability program so that it reads the reliabilities of three components and then computes the reliability of the components connected as shown in the following diagram:

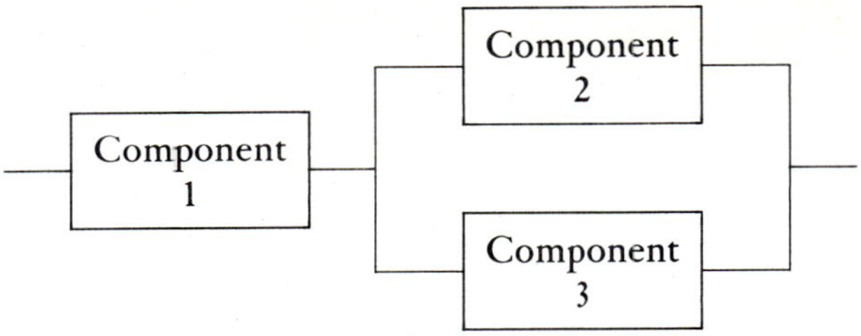

19. Modify the reliability program so that it reads the reliabilities of four components and then computes the reliability of the components connected as shown in the following diagram:

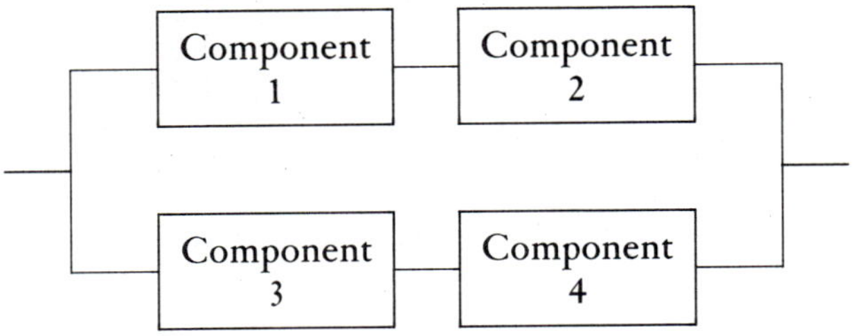

20. Modify the reliability program so that it reads the reliabilities of four components and then computes the reliability of the components connected as shown in the following diagram:

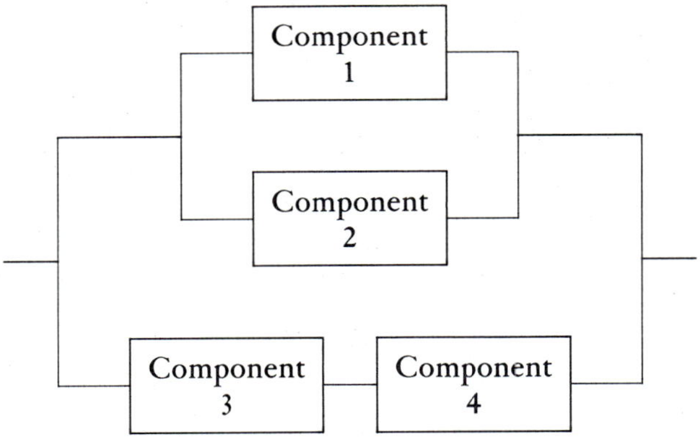

Problems 21 – 25 modify the stride time computation program STRIDE given on page 71.

21. Modify the stride computation program so that it accepts the leg length in meters instead of feet. (Use the gravitation constant 9.807 m/s^2.)
22. Modify the stride computation program so that it accepts the stride time in seconds and computes the leg length in feet.
23. Modify the stride computation program so that it accepts the stride length and the leg length and computes the walking speed in ft/s.
24. Modify the stride computation program so that it computes the length of a stride given the leg length. (Assume that the constant *a* is equal to 0.75.)

25. Experimentally determine a value for the constant a. Then modify the stride computation program so that it accepts the leg length and computes the time required for a stride, the length of a stride, and the walking speed.

Develop programs for problems 26–50. Use the five-phase design process.

26. Write a program to read the length and width of a rectangle and compute and print its perimeter and area.
27. Hot-air balloons act on the principle that heated air is less dense than cool air. The mass of air inside the balloon, for a fixed volume, is less than the mass of an equivalent volume of cooler air outside. This occurs because as the air inside is heated, it expands and some escapes in order to maintain constant atmospheric pressure. Thus, the air inside is less dense than the air outside and the balloon floats. Write a program to determine the mass of air that remains (m_2) after reading the original mass of air (m_1), the original volume (v_1), and the volume after heating (v_2). Use the following equation for computing m_2:

$$m_2 = \frac{v_1}{v_2} m_1$$

28. Write a program to read the coordinates of two points (X_1,Y_1), (X_2,Y_2). Compute the slope of the straight line between these two points where

$$\text{SLOPE} = \frac{Y_2 - Y_1}{X_2 - X_1}$$

Print the points and the slope of the line between the points.
29. Write a program to read the diameter of a circle. Compute the radius, circumference, and area of the circle. Print these new values in the following form:

```
PROPERTIES OF A CIRCLE WITH DIAMETER XXXX.XXX
(1)     RADIUS = XXXX.XXX
(2)     CIRCUMFERENCE = XXXX.XXX
(3)     AREA = XXXX.XXX
```

30. Write a program to read a measurement in meters. Print the value followed by the units, METERS. Convert the measurement to kilometers and print the value on the next line, again with the correct units. Convert the measurement to miles and print the value on the third line, with correct units. (Use 1 mile = 1.609 kilometers.)
31. Write a program to read a temperature in degrees Fahrenheit and convert it to degrees Celsius, degrees Kelvin, and degrees Rankin. Print the temperature in all four degree measurements. The following equations will be helpful in performing the conversions, where we assume that T_F, T_C, T_K, and T_R represent the various temperatures:

$$T_F = T_R - 459.67°R$$

$$T_F = \frac{9}{5} T_C + 32°F$$

$$T_R = \frac{9}{5} T_K$$

32. Using the information from Problem 31, write a program to read a temperature in degrees Celsius and convert it to degrees Kelvin, degrees Rankin, and degrees Fahrenheit. Print the temperature in all four degree measurements.

33. Using the information from Problem 31, write a program to read a temperature in degrees Kelvin and convert it to degrees Rankin, degrees Fahrenheit, and degrees Celsius. Print the temperature in all four degree measurements.

34. Using the information from Problem 31, write a program to read a temperature in degrees Rankin and convert it to degrees Fahrenheit, degrees Celsius, and degrees Kelvin. Print the temperature in all four degree measurements.

35. The escape velocity is defined as the minimum initial upward speed necessary to overcome the gravitational pull of an orbiting body. As the density of a body, such as a star, increases, so does its escape velocity. If a star is very dense, its escape velocity approaches c, the speed of light. Thus, when the escape velocity is equal to c, nothing, not even light, can escape. This condition exists in black holes. As light is not given off by a black hole, properties such as mass (M) must be gathered by observing how other stars in the system respond to the gravitational effects of the black hole. Once this is done, the radius of the black hole can be calculated. Write a program to read the mass of a black hole and then calculate and print the radius R_s using the following equation:

$$R_s = \frac{2\,G \cdot M}{v^2}$$

where G is the universal gravitational constant, 6.673×10^{-11} newton meter^2/kg^2, and v is the escape velocity in m/s. (The speed of light is 299,792,458 m/s.)

36. Use the information in Problem 35 to write a program that reads the mass and radius of a star and then computes its escape velocity.

37. When a train travels over a straight section of track, it exerts a downward force on the rails; but when it rounds a level curve, it also exerts a horizontal force outward on the rails. Both of these forces must be considered when designing the track. The downward force is equivalent to the weight of the train. The horizontal force, called centrifugal force, is a function of the weight of the train, its speed as it rounds the curve, and the radius of the curve. The equation to compute the horizontal force in pounds is

$$\text{force} = \frac{\text{weight} \cdot 2000}{32} \cdot \frac{(\text{mph} \cdot 1.4667)^2}{\text{radius}}$$

where weight is the weight of the train in tons, mph is the speed of the train in miles per hour, and radius is the radius of the curve in feet. Write a program to read values for weight, mph, and radius. Compute and print the corresponding horizontal force generated.

38. Modify the program in Problem 37 so that the speed is entered in kilometers per hour instead of miles per hour. (Recall that 1 mile is equal to 1.609 kilometers.)

39. A research scientist performed nutrition tests using three animals. Data on each animal includes an identification number, the weight of the animal at the

beginning of the experiment, and the weight of the animal at the end of the experiment. Write a program to read this data and print a report. The report is to include the original information plus the percentage increase in weight for each animal.

40. Write a program to read three resistance values (R1, R2, R3) and compute their combined resistance (RC) for the parallel arrangement shown. Print the values of R1, R2, R3, and RC.

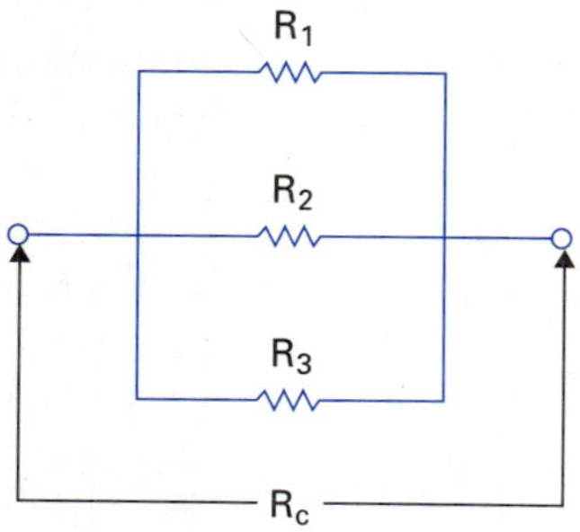

$$RC = \frac{1}{\frac{1}{R1} + \frac{1}{R2} + \frac{1}{R3}}$$

41. The distance between points with coordinates (XA, YA) and (XB,YB) is given by

$$\text{DISTANCE} = \sqrt{(XA - XB)^2 + (YA - YB)^2}$$

You are given the coordinates of three points (X1,Y1), (X2,Y2), (X3,Y3). Write a program to read the coordinates. Next, calculate and print the distance DIST12 between points 1 and 2, the distance DIST13 between points 1 and 3, and the distance DIST23 between points 2 and 3.

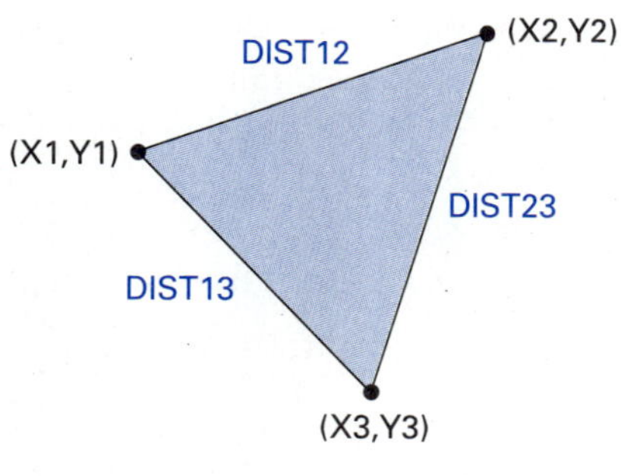

42. The area of a triangle can be computed from the following equation, where A, B, and C represent the sides of the triangle and s is equal to half of the sum of the three sides of the triangle:

$$\text{area} = \sqrt{s(s-A)(s-B)(s-C)}$$

Write a program to read the coordinates of the three vertices of a triangle (X1,Y1), (X2,Y2), (X3,Y3) and then compute and print the corresponding area. (See Problem 41 for helpful information.)

43. Write a program to read the following information from the terminal:

Year
Number of people in the civilian labor force
Number of people in the military labor force

Compute the percentage of the labor force that is civilian and the percentage that is military. Print the following information:

```
LABOR FORCE  - YEAR XXXX
NUMBER OF WORKERS (THOUSANDS) AND PERCENTAGE OF WORKERS
CIVILIAN         XXX.XXX       XXX.XXX
MILITARY         XXX.XXX       XXX.XXX
TOTAL            XXX.XXX       XXX.XXX
```

44. The approximate time for electrons to travel from the cathode to the anode of a rectifier tube is given by

$$\text{TIME} = \sqrt{\frac{2\text{M}}{\text{Q} \cdot \text{V}}} \cdot \text{R1} \cdot \text{Z} \cdot \left(1 + \frac{\text{Z}}{3} - \frac{\text{Z}^2}{10} + \frac{\text{Z}^3}{42} + \frac{\text{Z}^4}{216}\right)$$

where Q = charge of the electron (1.60206E−19 coulombs)
M = mass of the electron (9.1083E−31 kilograms)
V = accelerating voltage in volts
R1 = radius of the inner tube (cathode)
R2 = radius of the outer tube (anode)
Z = natural logarithm of R2/R1

Define the values of Q and M in the constant section of your program. Read values for V, R1, and R2, then calculate Z and TIME. Print the values of V, R1, R2, and TIME.

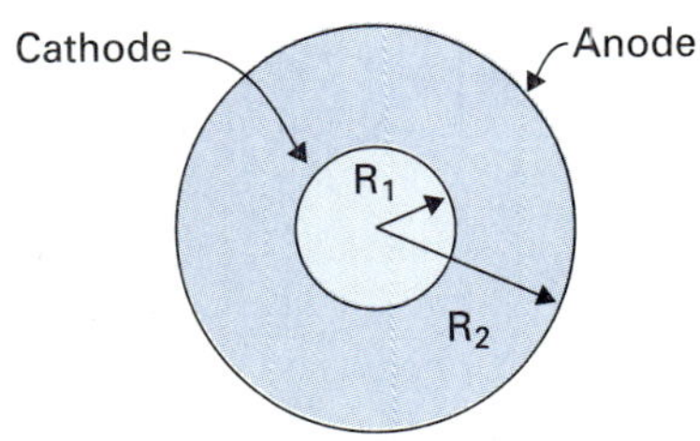

Rectifier tube

45. Write a program to compute the volume of the shell of a hollow ball. Assume that the values for the radius of the ball and for the thickness of the shell are to be read. The volume of a sphere is related to the radius r by

$$\text{VOLUME} = \frac{4}{3}\pi r^3$$

46. The Gaussian density function is commonly used in engineering statistics. This function is defined in the equation that follows:

$$Y = \frac{1}{\sqrt{2\pi}} e^{-0.5x^2}$$

Write a program to read a value of X and compute the corresponding value of Y. Print the values in the following form:

```
THE STANDARD NORMAL DENSITY FUNCTION EVALUATED
AT XXX.XX GIVES A VALUE OF XX.XXXXX
```

47. A Gaussian density function is defined in Problem 46. Write a program to compute and print the change in y between $x = 0.0$ and $x = 1.0$. Also compute and print the change in y between $x = 1.0$ and 2.0 and between $x = 2.0$ and 3.0. Use the following output form:

```
STANDARD GAUSSIAN DENSITY FUNCTION
X:  0.0 TO 1.0    CHANGE IN Y:  XXX.XX
X:  1.0 TO 2.0    CHANGE IN Y:  XXX.XX
X:  2.0 TO 3.0    CHANGE IN Y:  XXX.XX
```

48. Write a program to read the x and y coordinates of three points from the terminal. Then compute the area of the triangle formed from these points using the following equation:

$$\text{AREA} = 0.5\,|X_1Y_2 - X_2Y_1 + X_2Y_3 - X_3Y_2 + X_3Y_1 - X_1Y_3|$$

Print the coordinates and the area in the following form:

```
TRIANGLE VERTICES:
(1)       XXX.X, XXX.X
(2)       XXX.X, XXX.X
(3)       XXX.X, XXX.X

TRIANGLE AREA:
XXX.XX
```

(Be sure to give a descriptive message to the user to describe the form and order for the input values.)

49. The radioactive decay of thorium is given by the equation

$$N = N_0 \cdot e^{\left[-0.693 \frac{t}{1.65 \times 10^{16}}\right]}$$

where N_0 represents the initial amount of thorium and t represents the time elapsed. When $t = 0$, N is equal to N_0 and no decay has occurred. As t increases, the amount of thorium is decreased. Read values for N_0 and t from the terminal, and then compute and print the amount of thorium left after the specified time has elapsed. Use the following output form:

```
INITIAL VALUE OF THORIUM:     XXX.XXX
TIME ELAPSED                  XXX.XXX
REMAINING THORIUM:            XXX.XXX
```

FORTRAN STATEMENT SUMMARY

Assignment Statement:

variable = expression

Examples:

```
PI = 3.141593
AREA = SIDE*SIDE
ROOT = SQRT(X)
```

Discussion:

The left-hand side of the assignment statement must be a variable name. The right-hand side can be any form of an expression, from a simple constant to a complex arithmetic expression involving other variables and intrinsic functions.

END Statement:

```
END
```

Discussion:

This statement must be the last statement in a FORTRAN program. It is a signal to the compiler that there are no further statements to translate. Program execution stops when it reaches the END statement.

FORMAT Statement:

k FORMAT *(format specifications)*

Examples:

```
 5 FORMAT (1X,'TEMPERATURE DATA FROM EXPERIMENT 1')
10 FORMAT (1X,'THE VALUE OF X IS ',F7.3)
15 FORMAT (1X,I3,2X,F7.1)
```

Discussion:

The FORMAT statement must always have a statement label, which is referenced in a formatted statement such as a PRINT statement. The FORMAT statement specifies the exact form of the output that is being requested, including the vertical spacing (how many lines to skip) and the horizontal spacing (how many spaces to skip between values).

■ **INTEGER** Statement:

INTEGER *variable list*

Examples:

```
INTEGER SUM
INTEGER ID, TOTAL, X
```

Discussion:

The INTEGER statement explicitly lists all variables that will store integer values. Listing a variable name in an INTEGER statement overrides its implicit typing.

■ **PARAMETER** Statement:

PARAMETER *(name1=expression, name2=expression, . . .)*

Example:

```
PARAMETER (PI=3.14159, N=20)
```

Discussion:

The PARAMETER statement is used to assign names to constants. It should follow the type specification statements.

■ **PRINT*** Statement:

PRINT*, *expression list*

Examples:

```
PRINT*, 'DISTANCE VERSUS VELOCITY MEASUREMENTS'
PRINT*, 'SLOPE = ', SLOPE
PRINT*, X, Y, X + Y
```

Discussion:

The PRINT* statement is a list-directed output statement. The value of any literals, variables, constants, or expressions in its expression list will be printed in the order in which they are listed. The form of numeric output is predetermined by the compiler.

PRINT *k* Statement:

```
PRINT k, expression list
```

Examples:

```
PRINT 5, ALPHA, BETA
PRINT 50, SLOPE
PRINT 25
```

Discussion:

The PRINT *k* statement is a formatted output statement. The value of any variables or expressions in its expression list will be printed in the order in which they are listed according to the specifications in the FORMAT statement with label *k*.

PROGRAM Statement:

```
PROGRAM program name
```

Examples:

```
PROGRAM CALC
PROGRAM REPORT
```

Discussion:

The PROGRAM statement is optional, but it must be the first statement in a program if it is used. It assigns a name to the program. This name must be unique and cannot be used for a variable in the program.

READ* Statement:

```
READ*, variable list
```

Examples:

```
READ*, TIME
READ*, DIST, VELCTY
```

Discussion:

The READ* statement is a list-directed input statement that reads values for the variables in its list. The values are stored in the order in which the variables are listed. Data values must be separated by blanks or commas, and as many lines as are needed will be read. Each READ* statement will begin searching for values with a new line.

■ **REAL** Statement:

```
REAL variable list
```

Examples:

```
REAL FORCE
REAL TEMP, PRESS, VOL
```

Discussion:

The REAL statement explicitly lists all variables that are to store real values. Listing a variable name in a REAL statement overrides its implicit typing.

■ **STOP** Statement:

```
STOP
```

Discussion:

The STOP statement is an optional statement that stops the execution of a program. Programs may have more than one STOP statement. The END statement also serves to stop program execution if a STOP statement does not immediately precede the END statement.

3 Control Structures

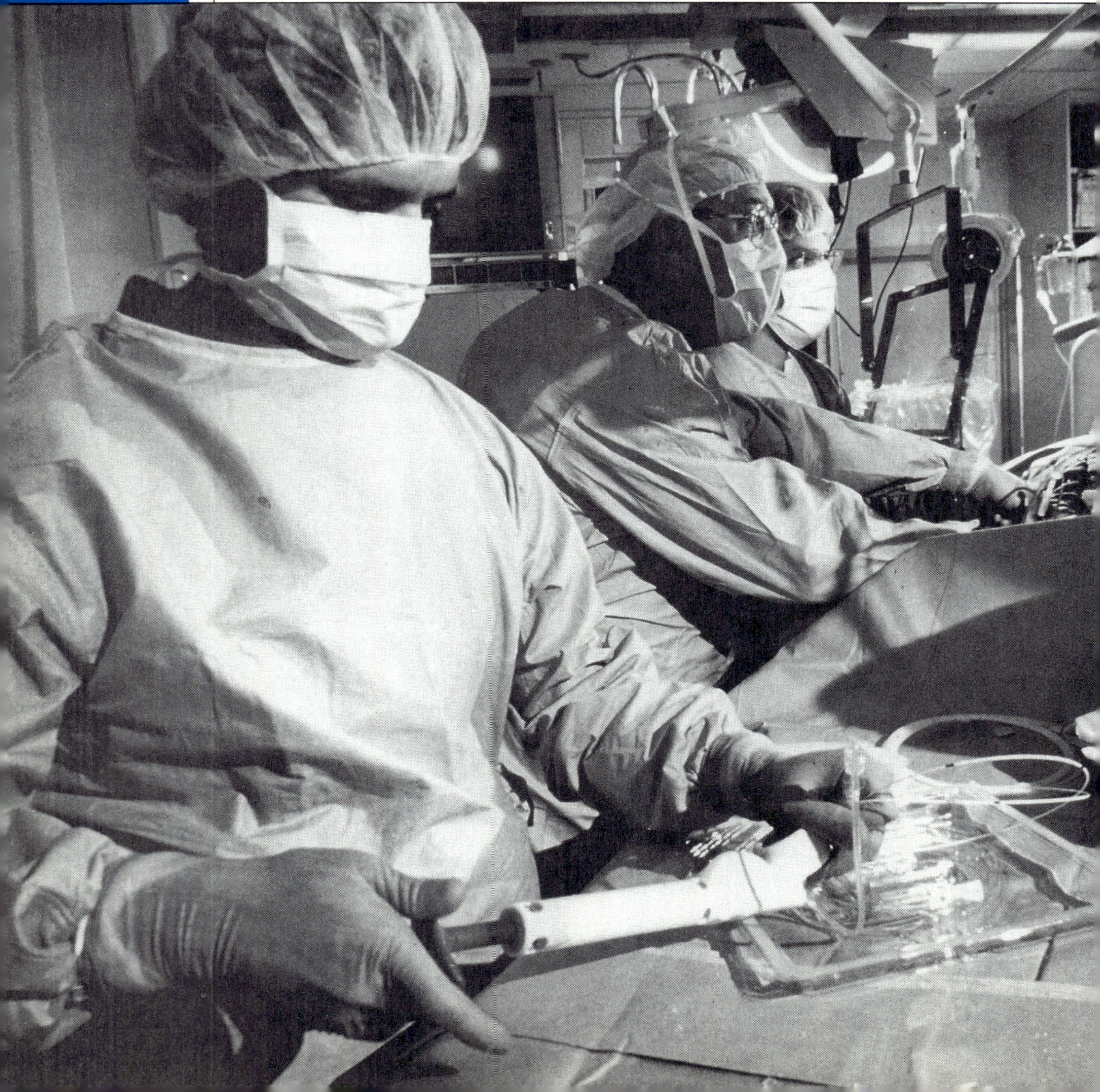

3

APPLICATION

Fiber Optics

Fiber optics can be coupled with lasers to provide a unique technique for identifying and treating medical problems. In the surgical procedure pictured opposite, an optical fiber 1 mm in diameter is inserted into the center of a catheter that is 1½ mm in diameter. This fiber is used to transmit a holmium-YAG laser beam. The catheter carrying the fiber is carefully inserted into the femoral artery of the patient until it comes to the blocked artery in the heart. The exact position of the laser tip is determined using x-rays. The optical fiber is then used to send very brief pulses of light from this cold-tip laser to break up the blood clot in the artery. As the procedure finishes, the surgeons can actually see the blood supply return through the artery to the damaged heart muscle. Biomedical applications that use a combined fiber optic/laser approach include unclogging obstructed arteries, breaking up kidney stones, clearing cataracts, and even altering genetic material. (See Section 3–3 for the solution to a problem related to this application.)

Photo © Howard Sochurek/Medical Images Inc.

Introduction

In Chapter 2 we wrote complete FORTRAN programs, but the steps were all executed sequentially. The programs were composed of reading data, computing new data, and printing the new data. We now introduce FORTRAN statements that allow us to control the sequence of the steps being executed. This control is achieved through statements that allow us to select different paths through our programs and statements that allow us to repeat certain parts of our programs.

3·1 ■ Algorithm Structure

In Chapter 1 we presented a five-step process for developing problem solutions:

1. State the problem clearly.
2. Describe the input and the output.
3. Work the problem by hand (or with a calculator) for a simple set of data.
4. Develop an algorithm that is general in nature.
5. Test the algorithm with a variety of data sets.

To describe algorithms consistently, we use a set of standard forms, or structures. When an algorithm is described in these standard structures, it is a *structured algorithm*. When the algorithm is converted into computer instructions, the corresponding program is a *structured program*. We first discuss pseudocode and flowcharts which will be used to describe the steps in an algorithm; then we discuss organizing the steps in standard structures.

■ Pseudocode and Flowcharts

Each structure for building algorithms can be described in an English-like notation called *pseudocode*. Because pseudocode is not really computer code, it is language independent; that is, pseudocode depends only on the steps needed to solve a problem, not on the computer language that will be used for writing the solution. *Flowcharts* also describe the steps in algorithms, but they are a graphical description, as opposed to a set of English-like steps. Neither pseudocode nor flowcharts are intended to be a formal way of describing the algorithm; they are informal ways of easily describing the steps in the algorithm without worrying about the syntax of a specific computer language. We will include a number of examples of both pseudocode and flowcharts so that you can compare the techniques and choose the one that works best for you.

The basic operations that we perform in algorithms are computations, input, output, and comparisons. Table 3–1 compares examples of pseudocode notation and flowchart symbols for these basic operations, plus the notation and symbols for identifying the beginning and end of an algorithm. Do not worry about whether the names you have chosen are valid FORTRAN names; both pseudocode and flowcharts are describing the operations, and they are independent of the language that will be used to implement the computer solution.

Table 3·1 Pseudocode Notation and Flowchart Symbols

Basic Operation	Pseudocode Notation	Flowchart Symbol
Computations	Average ← $\frac{\text{sum}}{\text{count}}$	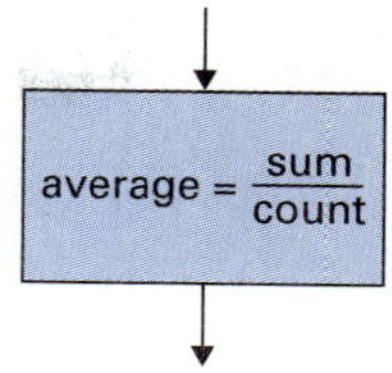
Input	Read A, B	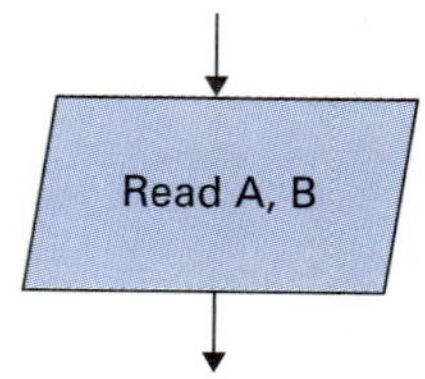
Output	Print A, B	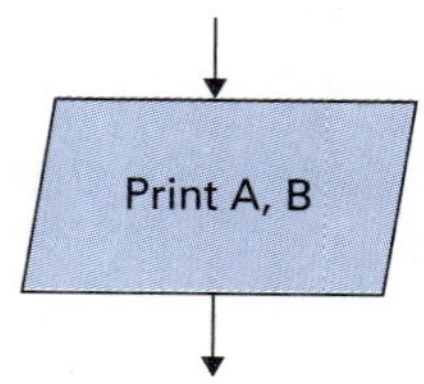
Comparisons	If A > 0.0 then . . .	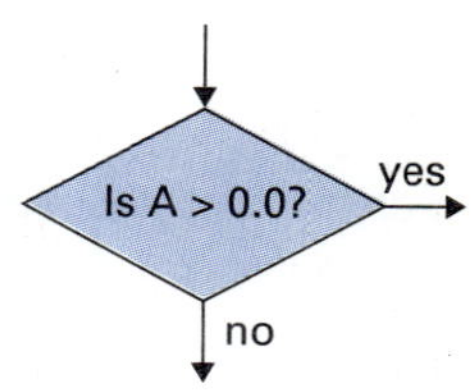
Beginning of algorithm	Report:	
End of algorithm		

In pseudocode, a computation is indicated with an arrow, as shown in the following:

$$\text{average} \leftarrow \frac{\text{sum}}{\text{count}}$$

We read this pseudocode statement as "the average is replaced by the sum divided by the count" or "the sum is divided by the count, giving the average."

A comparison is used to ask a question within an algorithm. Then, depending on the answer to the question, we can perform one set of statements as opposed to another set of statements. The questions that we ask must be answered with yes or no (or true or false). For example, we can determine if a data value A is greater than zero by using the expressions "If A > 0.0, then . . ." or "Is A > 0.0?"

An algorithm defined in pseudocode begins with the name of the algorithm, followed by the first step in the algorithm. Thus, if the first step in an algorithm named Report is to set a sum to zero, the first pseudocode statement is

$$\text{Report: sum} \leftarrow \text{sum} + 1$$

Pseudocode does not need a special statement to signify the end of the algorithm; we assume that the end occurs after the last step described in pseudocode.

General Structures

The steps in an algorithm can be divided into three general structures—sequences, selections, and repetition. A sequence is a set of steps that are performed sequentially, or one after another. A selection structure allows us to compare two values, and then specify a different set of steps to execute, depending on the result of the comparison. The repetition structure is used when we want to repeat a set of steps. We can repeat the steps a specified number of times, or we can repeat the steps as long as a specified condition is true. We now discuss each of these structures separately.

Sequence A *sequence* is a set of steps in an algorithm that are performed sequentially. For example, all of the programs in Chapter 2 were sequential algorithms that contained an input step, a computation step, and an output step. We included sample pseudocode in the development of the programs in Chapter 2; shown opposite is the flowchart for the program RELY from page 67.

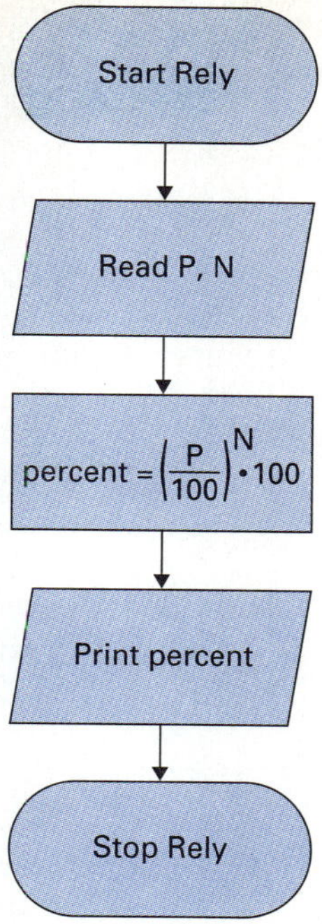

Selection In the *selection* structure, a comparison is performed to determine which steps are to be performed next. The selection structure is commonly described in terms of an If structure that can have several forms.

All forms of the structure include a comparison that tests a *condition* that can be evaluated to be true or false. If the condition is true, then a step or a group of steps is performed. For example, suppose the algorithm that we are developing must count the number of students who are on the honor roll and print their student ID numbers. One step in our algorithm might be "if the grade point average (GPA) is greater than or equal to 3.0, then print the ID and add 1 to the number of students on the honor roll." This step is shown in both pseudocode and a flowchart; note the use of indenting in the pseudocode.

```
If GPA ≥ 3.0 then
    Print ID
    count ← count + 1
```

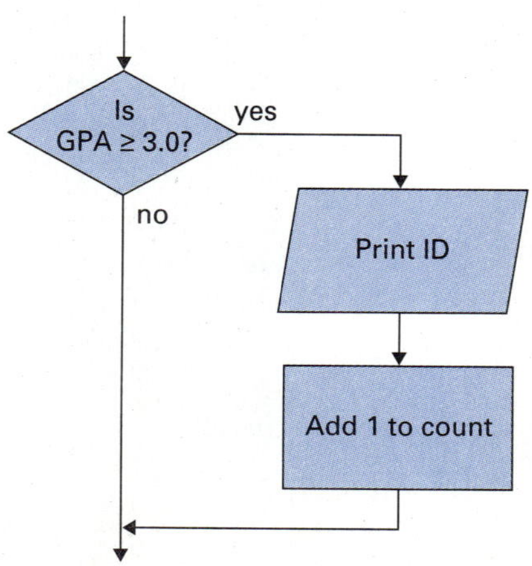

Another form of the If structure contains an additional clause called an Else clause that specifies an alternate set of steps to perform if the condition is false. For example, suppose we want to modify the example so that we print the ID of each student. Then, if the student is on the honor roll, we also print the GPA on the same line beside the student's ID. These steps are described with the following pseudocode and flowchart:

```
If GPA ≥ 3.0 then
        Print ID, GPA
        count ← count + 1
Else
        Print ID
```

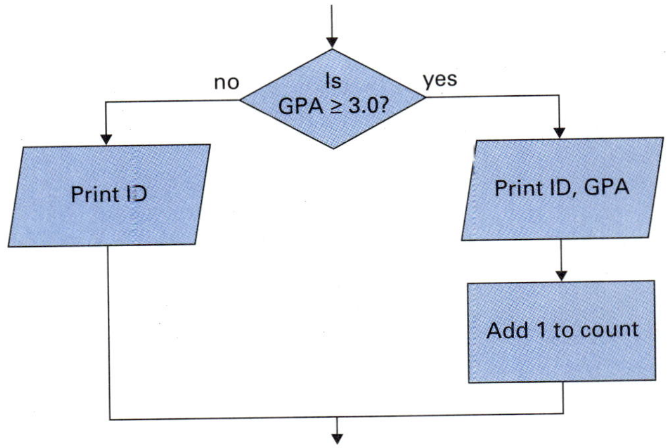

The last form of the If structure contains Else If clauses that allow us to test for multiple conditions. A single Else If clause can be illustrated by extending the honor roll example. Assume that the president's honor roll requires a GPA greater than 3.5 and that the dean's honor roll requires a GPA greater than or equal to 3.0. We want to count the number of students on each honor roll. We also want to print each student's ID and GPA if the GPA is above 3.0; in addition, we want to include an asterisk beside the GPA if it is above 3.5. The following pseudocode and flowchart describe this set of steps:

```
If GPA > 3.5 then
        Print ID, GPA, '*'
        president's count ← president's count + 1
Else If GPA ≥ 3.0 then
        Print ID, GPA
        dean's count ← dean's count + 1
Else
        Print ID
```

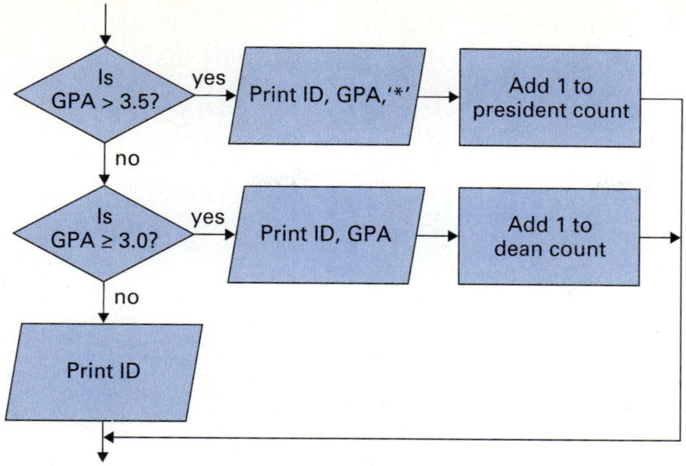

Repetition A *repetition* structure allows us to use *loops*, which are sets of steps in an algorithm that are repeated. One type of loop, called a While loop, repeats the steps as long as a certain condition is true; this was the type of loop used in the example program in Chapter 1 on page 19. Another type of loop, called a *counting loop*, repeats the steps a specified number of times. The steps within a loop can contain sequential steps, selection steps, or other repetition steps.

Suppose that we wish to continue reading data values and adding them to a sum as long as that sum is less than 1000. These steps are described in the following pseudocode and flowchart:

```
While sum < 1000 do
    Read data value
    sum ← sum + data value
```

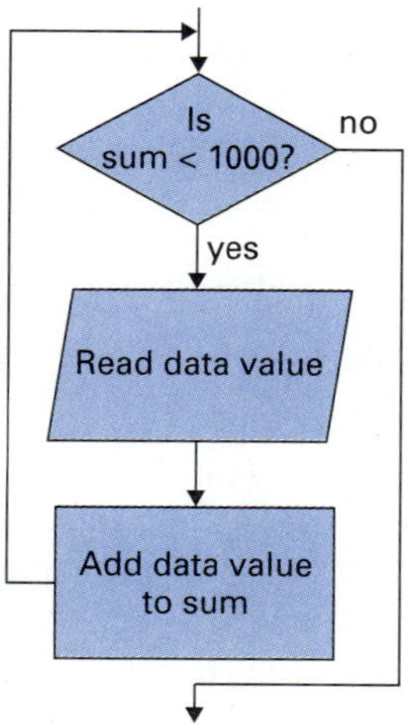

Again, note that the indenting in the pseudocode specifies the steps that are included in the While loop. If we wish to print the value of the sum after exiting the While loop, we can use the following pseudocode and flowchart:

```
While sum < 1000 do
      Read data value
      sum ← sum + data value
Print sum
```

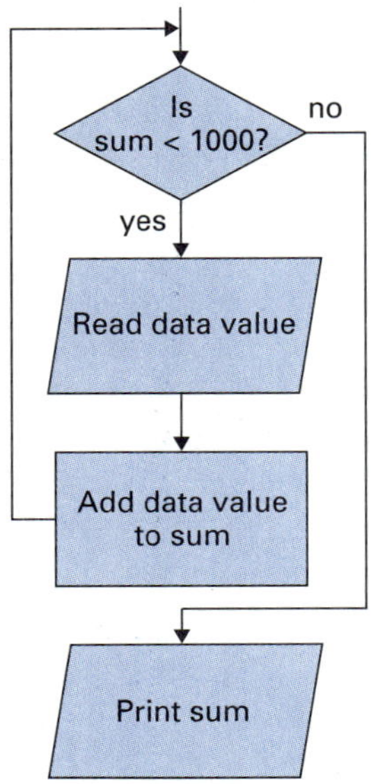

Counting loops repeat a set of steps a specified number of times. For example, suppose we are going to read 10 values from the terminal and perform some calculations with each value. We can describe the steps in a counting loop that is repeated 10 times. However, a counting loop can also be considered a special form of a While loop in which a counter has been introduced. The counter represents the number of times that the loop has been executed. The counter is usually initialized to zero before the loop is executed. Inside the loop, the counter is incremented by one. The loop is then executed "while the value of the counter is less then 10." The pseudocode and flowchart for this counting loop example are the following:

```
count ← 0
While count < 10 do
      read data value
      (process the data)
      count ← count + 1
```

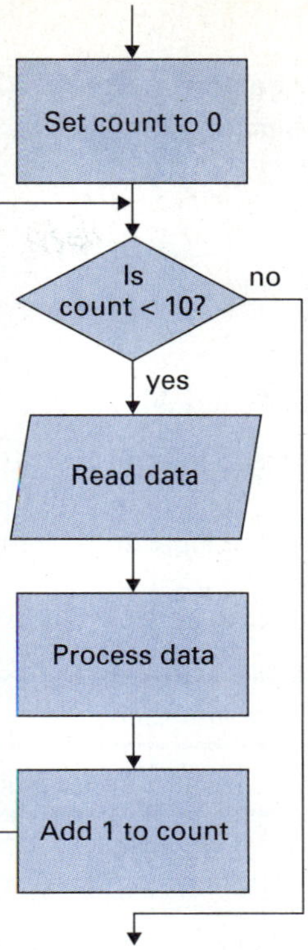

We can describe algorithms for almost any problem using these three structures—sequential steps, selection steps, and repetitive steps. We now present two examples to illustrate the process of developing an algorithm composed of these structures.

Average of a Set of Data Values . . . . Example 3·1

In Chapter 1 we illustrated top-down design with an algorithm to compute the average of a set of data values. We now look at the problem again and develop a flowchart for the solution. Assume that we are reading data values from the terminal. A value of zero indicates that we have reached the end of the data values.

Solution

The **first step** is to state the problem clearly: Compute the average of a set of experimental data values.

The **second step** is to describe the input and output:

Input—the list of experimental data values
Output—the average of the data values

The **third step** is to work a simple example by hand:

Lab Measurements—4/23/92

Number	Value
1	23.43
2	37.43
3	34.91
4	28.37
5	30.62
	154.76

Average = sum/5 = 30.95

The **fourth step** is to develop an algorithm, starting with the decomposition.

Decomposition

Read the data values and sum them.
Divide the sum by the number of data values.
Print the average.

We now take each of the sequential steps in the decomposition and refine it using the structures that we have just discussed: sequential steps, selection steps, and repetition steps. The first step in the decomposition is "read the data values and sum them." This step can be refined by recognizing that it is composed of setting a sum to zero and a loop to read the values and update the sum. We also recognize that we will need the number of data values, so we must also set a count to zero and add one to the count each time that we execute the loop. The loop should be structured as a While loop because we want to stay in the loop as long as (while) the data value is not zero.

We will need to read a data value before entering the While loop because the If structure will immediately compare the data value to zero, and thus we must have already read a data value. We then continue to read values inside the loop. When the data value is equal to zero, we exit the loop and perform the sequential steps to compute the average and print it. We can now describe these refined steps with a flowchart. We will convert the flowchart to FORTRAN and test it later in this chapter.

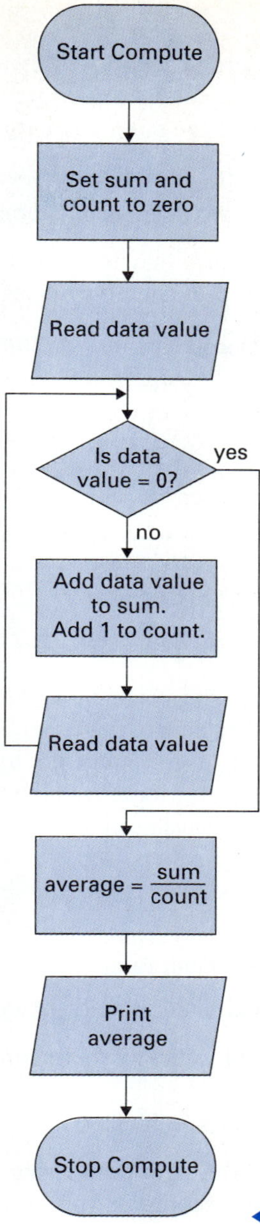

Experimental Data Analysis

Example 3·2

Develop an algorithm to analyze a set of experimental data values, determine the minimum and the maximum values, and compute the range of the data values. Assume that a zero data value indicates that all the data values have been read.

Solution

The **first step** is to state the problem clearly: Determine the minimum and maximum values and the range of values for a set of experimental values.

The **second step** is to describe the input and output:

Input—the list of experimental data values
Output—the minimum, the maximum, the range of values

The **third step** is to work a simple example by hand. Assume that the following lab worksheet contains data from a recent chemistry experiment:

Lab Measurements—9/30/92

40.56
55.92
66.31
58.35
62.88
41.99
49.70
53.21

We begin with the steps to find the maximum value. We look at the first value, compare it to the second value, and denote the larger of the two as the "maximum so far." Now we look at the third value and compare it to our "maximum so far." If the "maximum so far" is larger, we go to the fourth value; but if the third value is larger than our "maximum so far," we update the value in our "maximum so far." Continuing this process with the entire list of data results in the "maximum so far" containing the maximum value from the list. A similar process finds the minimum value. For the preceding data, our results are

$$\text{maximum value} = 66.31$$
$$\text{minimum value} = 40.56$$

Now we can compute the range of values by subtracting the minimum value from the maximum value:

$$\text{range of values} = 66.31 - 40.56 = 25.75$$

The **fourth step** is to develop an algorithm. Using the steps that we performed in the hand example, we can now decompose the problem solution into a series of sequentially executed steps.

Decomposition

Read data values and determine maximum and minimum values.
Subtract minimum value from maximum value to get range.
Print maximum, minimum, range.

For this example, we refine the solution with pseudocode. We take each step of the decomposition and decide which structures (sequential, selection, and repetition) define the step in greater detail. Clearly, our first decomposition step requires the greatest refinement because it includes sequential steps (initializing our maximum and minimum values) plus the repetition step (the loop to read values and update our maximum and minimum values if necessary). The maximum and minimum values are commonly initialized to the first data value, so we read one data value to initialize them. We then read the second data value and enter the While loop. "While the data value is not zero," we update the maximum and minimum values if necessary. Note that we do not need a count of the data values or a sum for this problem. We now describe these refined steps in pseudocode.

Pseudocode

```
Analysis: Read data value
          maximum ← data value
          minimum ← data value
          Read data value
          While the data value is not zero do
                If data value > maximum then
                      maximum ← data value
                If data value < minimum then
                      minimum ← data value
                Read data value
          range ← maximum − minimum
          Print 'MAXIMUM DATA VALUE =', maximum
          Print 'MINIMUM DATA VALUE =', minimum
          Print 'RANGE OF VALUES = ', range
```

This was a simple algorithm; only one refinement was needed. Additional refinements are often necessary for more complex problems. ◀

In the next two sections, we present the FORTRAN statements for the If structure and the While loop. We then return to the two algorithms we have just developed and translate them into complete FORTRAN 77 programs.

3·2 ■ If Structures

In Section 3 – 1 we presented the pseudocode and flowcharts for the three forms of the selection structure. In this section we present the corresponding FORTRAN statements. All three forms used an *If structure* which contains a logical expression that is evaluated to determine which path to take in the structure. Therefore, before we discuss the FORTRAN statements, we discuss logical expressions that are used as the logical expressions to be tested.

Logical Expressions

A *logical expression* is analogous to an arithmetic expression but is always evaluated to either true or false, instead of a number. Logical expressions can be formed using *relational operators*, which are listed:

Relational Operator	Interpretation
EQ.	equal to
.NE.	not equal to
.LT.	less than
.LE.	less than or equal to
.GT.	greater than
.GE.	greater than or equal to

Numeric variables can be used on both sides of the relational operators to yield a logical expression whose value is either true or false. For example, consider the logical expression A.EQ.B where A and B are real values. If the value of A is equal to the value of B, then the logical expression A.EQ.B is true. Otherwise, the expression is false. Similarly, if the value of X is 4.5, then the expression X.GT.3.0 is true.

Fortran 90 In Fortran 90, symbols may also be used as relational operators, as shown below:

==	.EQ.	equal to
/=	.NE.	not equal to
<	.LT.	less than
<=	.LE.	less than or equal to
>	.GT.	greater than
>=	.GE.	greater than or equal to

We can also combine two logical expressions into a *compound logical expression* with the *logical operators* .OR. and .AND.. When two logical expressions are joined by .OR., the entire expression is true if either or both expressions are true; it is false only when both expressions are false. When two logical expressions are joined by .AND., the entire expression is true only if both expressions are true. These logical operators are used only between complete logical expressions. For example, A.LT.B.OR.A.LT.C is a valid compound logical expression because .OR. joins A.LT.B and A.LT.C. However, A.LT.B.OR.C is an invalid compound expression because C is a numeric variable, not a complete logical expression.

Logical expressions can also be preceded by the logical operator NOT. This operator changes the value of the expression to the opposite value; hence, if A.GT.B is true, then .NOT.A.GT.B is false.

A logical expression may contain several logical operators, as in

```
.NOT.(A.LT.15.4).OR.KT.EQ.ISUM
```

The *hierarchy*, from highest to lowest, is .NOT., .AND., and .OR.. In the preceding statement, the logical expression A.LT.15.4 would be evaluated, and its value, true or false, would then be reversed. This resultant value would be used, along with the value of KT.EQ.ISUM, with the logical operator .OR.. For example, if A is 5.0, KT is 5, and ISUM is 5, then the left-hand expression is false and the right-hand expression is true; but these expressions are connected by .OR., thus the entire expression is true.

Another type of variable, a *logical variable*, is also useful in writing the logical expressions that allow us to choose different paths and to repeat parts of our programs. A logical variable can have one of two values: true or false. A logical variable must be defined with a specification statement whose form is

```
LOGICAL variable list
```

Logical constants are .TRUE. and .FALSE.. Therefore, the statements necessary to define a logical variable and give it a value of false are

```
LOGICAL DONE
DONE = .FALSE.
```

Logical variables are generally used to make our programs more readable; thus, they are not usually part of the input or output. In several examples in this chapter, we will compare solutions using logical variables to ones without logical variables.

It is invalid to compare two logical variables with the relation .EQ. or .NE.. Instead, two new relations, .EQV. and .NEQV., are used to represent equivalent and not equivalent. If we want to compare .NOT.DONE to the value .TRUE., we could use this statement:

```
IF (.NOT.DONE.EQV..TRUE.) THEN
```

Table 3-2 summarizes the evaluation of the logical operators for all possible cases.

Whenever arithmetic, relational, and logical operators are in the same expression, the arithmetic operations are performed first; the relational operators are then applied to yield true or false values; and these values are evaluated with the logical operators, whose precedence is .NOT., .AND., and .OR.. The relations .EQV. and .NEQV. are evaluated last.

As an example, assume that ERROR is a logical variable and that A, B, and C are real variables. Consider the following expression:

```
A.GT.B+C.OR.ERROR
```

Table 3-2 Logical Operators

A	B	.NOT.A	A.AND.B	A.OR.B	A.EQV.B	A.NEQV.B
False	False	True	False	False	True	False
False	True	True	False	True	False	True
True	False	False	False	True	False	True
True	True	False	True	True	True	False

Table 3-3 Relational and Arithmetic Operator Precedence

Priority	Operation	Order
1.	Parentheses	Innermost first
2.	Exponentiation	Right to left
3.	Multiplication and division	Left to right
4.	Addition and subtraction	Left to right (unary first, as in −A, then binary, as in A−B)
5.	Relational operators	Left to right
6.	.NOT.	Left to right
7.	.AND.	Left to right
8.	.OR.	Left to right
9.	.EQV., .NEQV.	Left to right

This expression will be true if either A > B+C or ERROR is .TRUE.; the expression will also be true if both A > B+C and ERROR are .TRUE.. Table 3-3 lists the precedence of operators in a logical expression.

Logical IF Statement

FORTRAN implements a logical IF statement and a block IF statement. The logical IF statement is used if a single statement is to be performed if a logical expression is true. The block IF statement is used if we want to perform several statements if a logical expression is true, or if we want to use an ELSE statement, or if we want to use an ELSE IF statement.

The general form of the logical IF statement is

```
IF (logical expression) executable statement
```

Execution of this statement consists of the following steps:

1. If the logical expresssion is true, we execute the statement that is on the same line as the logical expresssion and then go to the next statement in the program.
2. If the logical expression is false, we jump immediately to the next statement in the program.

A typical IF statement is the following:

```
IF (A.LT.B) SUM = SUM + A
```

If the value of A is less than the value of B, then the value of A is added to SUM. If the value of A is greater than or equal to B, then control passes to whatever statement follows the IF statement in the program. Other examples of IF statement are

```
IF (TIME.GT.1.5) READ*, DISTNC
IF (DEN.LE.0.0) PRINT*, DEN
IF (-4.NE.NUM) NUM = NUM + 1
```

The executable statement that follows the logical expression is typically a computation or an input/output statement — it cannot be another IF statement.

Block IF Statement

In many instances we would like to perform more than one statement if a logical expression is true. The form of the IF statement that allows us to perform any number of statements if a logical expression is true uses the words THEN and END IF to identify these steps. The general form is

```
IF (logical expression) THEN
   statement 1
   .
   .
   .
   statement n
END IF
```

Execution of this block of statements consists of the following steps:

1. If the logical expresssion is true, we execute statements 1 through n and then go to the statement following END IF.
2. If the logical expression is false, we jump immediately to the statement following END IF.

Although not required, the statements to be performed when the logical expression is true should be indented to indicate that they are a group of statements within the IF statement.

Zero Divide

Example 3-3

Assume that you have calculated the numerator NUM (explicitly typed REAL) and the denominator DEN of a fraction. Before dividing the two values, you want to see if DEN is zero. If DEN is zero, you want to print an error message and stop the program; if DEN is not zero, you want to compute the result and print it. Write the statements to perform these steps.

Solution

```
IF (DEN.EQ.0.0) THEN
   PRINT*, 'DENOMINATOR IS ZERO'
   STOP
END IF
FRACTN = NUM/DEN
PRINT*, 'FRACTION = ', FRACTN
```

IF statements can also be nested; the following construction includes an IF statement within an IF statement:

```
IF (logical expression 1) THEN
      statement 1
      .
      .
      .
      statement n
      IF (logical expression 2) THEN
            statement n + 1
            .
            .
            .
            statement m
      END IF
      statement m + 1
      .
      .
      .
      statement p
END IF
statement q
```

Again, the indenting of statements within the construction is not required but makes the logic easier to follow. If logical expression 1 is true, we always execute statements 1 through n and statements $m + 1$ through p. If logical expression 2 is also true, we also execute statements $n + 1$ through m. If logical expression 1 is false, we immediately go to statement q.

Consider these statements:

```
IF (GPA.GE.3.0) THEN
   PRINT*, 'HONOR ROLL'
   IF (GPA.GT.3.5)THEN
      PRINT*, 'PRESIDENT''S LIST'
   END IF
END IF
```

If the GPA is less than 3.0, the entire construction is skipped. If the GPA is between 3.0 and 3.5, only HONOR ROLL is printed. If the GPA is greater than 3.5, then HONOR ROLL is printed, followed on the next line by PRESIDENT'S LIST.

ELSE Statement The ELSE statement allows us to execute one set of statements if a logical expression is true and a different set if the logical expression is false. The general form of an IF statement combined with an ELSE statement (an IF-ELSE statement) is shown below. If the logical expression is true, then statements 1 through n are executed. If the logical expression is false, then statements $n + 1$ through m are executed. Any statement can also be another IF or IF-ELSE statement to provide a nested structure.

```
IF (logical expression) THEN
      statement 1
      .
      .
      .
      statement n
ELSE
      statement n + 1
      .
      .
      .
      statement m
END IF
```

Now consider this set of statements which uses a logical variable VALID with the IF structure:

```
READ*, VOLTS
IF (VOLTS.GE.-5.0.AND.VOLTS.LE.5.0) THEN
   VALID = .TRUE.
ELSE
   VALID = .FALSE.
END IF
IF (.NOT.VALID) PRINT*, 'ERROR IN DATA'
```

In these statements, the variable VALID is true if the value in VOLTS is between −5.0 and 5.0; otherwise VALID is false. After determining the value of VALID, it can be used in other places in the program, such as in an IF statement to print an error message if the value is not valid. The advantage of using the logical variable is that we can reference it each time we need to know if the value is valid, instead of repeating the test to see if value in VOLTS is between −5.0 and 5.0.

Velocity Computation . . . . Example 3-4

Give the statements for calculating the velocity VEL of a cable car. The variable DIST contains the distance of the cable car from the nearest tower. Use this equation if the cable car is within 30 feet of the tower:

$$\text{velocity} = 2.425 + 0.00175\ \text{distance}^2\ \text{ft/sec}$$

Use this equation if the cable car is farther than 30 feet from the tower:

$$\text{velocity} = 0.625 + 0.12\ \text{distance} - 0.00025\ \text{distance}^2\ \text{ft/sec}$$

Correct Solution

```
IF (DIST.LE.30.0) THEN
   VEL = 2.425 + 0.00175*DIST*DIST
ELSE
   VEL = 0.625 + 0.12*DIST - 0.00025*DIST*DIST
END IF
```

Incorrect Solution

```
IF (DIST.LE.30.0) VEL = 2.425 + 0.00175*DIST*DIST
VEL = 0.625 + 0.12*DIST - 0.00025*DIST*DIST
```

This incorrect solution points out a common error. Suppose DIST is greater than 30; then the first logical expression is false and we proceed to the next statement to calculate VEL—this part works fine.

Now suppose the logical expression is true—that is, DIST is less than or equal to 30. We execute the assignment statement in the IF statement, correctly calculating VEL when DIST is less than or equal to 30; but the next statement that is executed is the other assignment statement, which replaces the correct value in VEL with an incorrect value.

ELSE IF Statement When we nest several levels of IF-ELSE statements, it may be difficult to determine which logical expressions must be true (or false) to execute a set of statements. In these cases, the ELSE IF statement is often used to clarify the program logic; the general form of this statement is

```
IF (logical expression 1) THEN
      statement 1
      .
      .
      .
      statement m
ELSE IF (logical expression 2) THEN
      statement m + 1
      .
      .
      .
      statement n
ELSE IF (logical expression 3) THEN
      statement n + 1
      .
      .
      .
      statement p
ELSE
      statement p + 1
      .
      .
      .
      statement q
END IF
```

We have shown two ELSE IF statements; there may be more or less in an actual construction. If logical expression 1 is true, then only statements 1 through m are executed. If logical expression 1 is false and logical expression 2 is true, then only statements $m+1$ through n are executed. If logical expressions 1 and 2 are false and logical expression 3 is true, then only statements $n+1$ through p are executed. If more than one logical expression is true, the first true logical expression encountered is the only one executed.

If none of the logical expressions are true, then statements $p+1$ through q are executed. If there is not a final ELSE statement and none of the logical expressions are true, then the entire construction is skipped. The IF-ELSE IF form is also called a CASE structure because a number of cases are tested. Each case is defined by its corresponding logical expression.

Weight Category . . . . Example 3-5

An analysis of a group of weight measurements involves converting a weight value into an integer category number that is determined as follows:

Category	Weight (pounds)
1	weight $\leq$ 50.0
2	50.0 $<$ weight $\leq$ 125.0
3	125.0 $<$ weight $\leq$ 200.0
4	200.0 $<$ weight

Write FORTRAN statements that put the correct value (1, 2, 3, or 4) into CATEGR based on the value of WEIGHT. Assume that CATEGR has been explicitly typed as an integer variable.

Solution 1

This solution uses nested IF-ELSE statements:

```
IF (WEIGHT.LE.50.0)THEN
   CATEGR = 1
ELSE
   IF (WEIGHT.LE.125.0)THEN
      CATEGR = 2
   ELSE
      IF (WEIGHT.LE.200.0)THEN
         CATEGR = 3
      ELSE
         CATEGR = 4
      END IF
   END IF
END IF
```

Solution 2

This solution uses the IF-ELSE IF statement:

```
IF (WEIGHT.LE.50.0) THEN
   CATEGR = 1
ELSE IF (WEIGHT.LE.125.0) THEN
   CATEGR = 2
ELSE IF (WEIGHT.LE.200.0) THEN
   CATEGR = 3
ELSE
   CATEGR = 4
END IF
```

As you can see, Solution 2 is more compact than Solution 1: It combines the ELSE and IF statements into the single statement ELSE IF and eliminates two of the END IF statements.

The order of the logical expressions is important in Solution 2 because the evaluation will stop as soon as a true logical expression has been encountered. Changing the order of the logical expressions and the category assignments can cause the CATEGR value to be set incorrectly.

Fortran 90

Fortran 90 includes a CASE control structure, or construct, that permits selection of a number of different alternative blocks of statements.

SELF-TEST 3-1

This self-test allows you to check quickly to see if you have remembered some of the key points from Section 3–2. If you have any problems with the exercises, you should reread this section. The solutions are included at the end of the text.

For problems 1–8, use the values given to determine whether the following logical expressions are true or false.

A = 2.2 B = −1.2 I = 5 DONE = .TRUE.

1. `A.LT.B`
2. `A - B.GE.6.5`
3. `I.NE.5`
4. `A + B.GE.B`
5. `.NOT.(A.EQ.2*B)`
6. `I.LE.I - 5`
7. `(A.LT.10.0).AND.(B.GT.5.0)`
8. `(ABS(I).GT.2).OR.DONE`

For problems 9–15, give FORTRAN statements that perform the steps indicated.

9. If TIME is greater than 5.0, increment TIME by 0.5.
10. When the square root of POLY is greater than or equal to 8.0, print the value of POLY.
11. If the difference between VOLT1 and VOLT2 is smaller than 6.0, print the values of VOLT1 and VOLT2.
12. If the absolute value of DEN is less than 0.005, print the message 'DENOMINATOR IS TOO SMALL.'
13. If the natural logarithm of X^2 is greater than or equal to 3, set TIME equal to zero and add X to SUM.
14. If DIST is less than 50.0 or TIME is greater than 10.0, increment TIME by 1.0. Otherwise, increment TIME by 0.5.
15. If DIST is greater than or equal to 50.0, increment TIME by 2.0 and print a message 'DISTANCE > 50.0.'
16. If DIST is greater than 100.0, increment TIME by 2.0. If DIST is between 50.0 and 100.0 (including 100.0), increment TIME by 1.0. Otherwise, increment TIME by 0.5.

3-3 Application ▪ Light Pipes

Optical Engineering

If we direct light into one end of a long rod of glass or plastic, the light is totally reflected by the walls, bouncing back and forth until it emerges at the far end of the rod. Light pipes use this interesting optical phenomenon to transmit light, and even images, from one place to another. If we bend a light pipe, the light will follow the shape of the pipe and emerge only at the end, as shown in the diagram below:

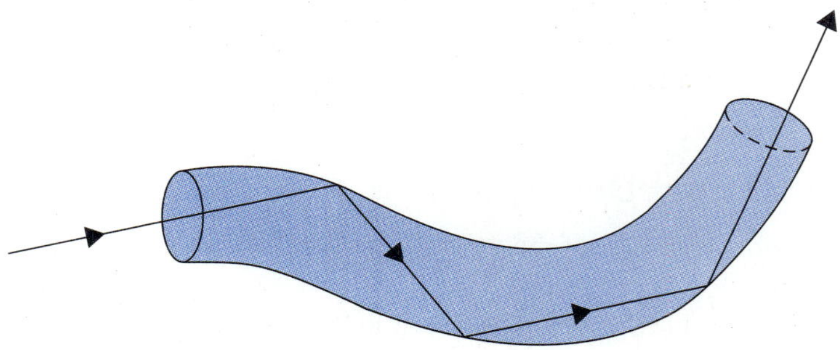

Light pipes made of very thin optical fibers can be grouped into bundles. If the fiber ends are polished and the spatial arrangement is the same at both ends (a coherent bundle), the fiber bundle can be used to transmit an image, and the bundle is called an image conduit. If the fibers do not have the same arrangement at both ends (an incoherent bundle), light is transmitted instead of an image, and the bundle is called a light guide. Because the optical fibers are so flexible, light guides and image conduits are used in instruments designed to permit visual observation of objects or areas that would otherwise be inaccessible. For example, an endoscope is an instrument used by physicians to examine the interior of a patient's body with only a very small incision.

This phenomenon of total internal reflection can be predicted using Snell's law and the indices of refraction of the materials being considered for the light pipe. A light pipe is actually composed of two materials—the material forming the rod or pipe itself and the material that surrounds the pipe. Normally, the material forming the rod is denser than the surrounding medium. When light passes from one material into another material with a different density, the light is bent, or "refracted," at the interface of the two materials. The amount of refraction depends on the indices of refraction of the materials and the angle of incidence of the light. If the light striking the interface comes from within the denser material, it may reflect off the interface rather than pass through it. The angle of incidence where the light will be reflected from the surface, rather than cross it, is called the critical angle θ_c. Since the critical angle depends on the indices of refraction of the two materials, we can compute this angle and determine whether light entering the pipe at a particular angle will stay within the pipe. Assume n_2 is the index of refraction of the surrounding medium and n_1 is the index of refraction of the pipe itself. If n_2 is greater than n_1, the pipe will not transmit light; otherwise, the critical angle can be determined from the following equation:

$$\sin \theta_c = \frac{n_2}{n_1}$$

Write a program that reads the indices of refraction for two materials that form a pipe and the angle at which light enters the pipe. Print a message indicating if the pipe will transmit light or not.

1. Problem Statement

Determine whether a light pipe generated from two materials will transmit light that enters it at a given angle.

2. Input/Output Description

Input—indices of refraction of the two materials and the angle at which light enters the pipe

Output—message indicating whether or not light is transmitted

3. Hand Example

The index of refraction of air is 1.0003 and the index of glass is 1.5. If we form a light pipe of glass surrounded by air, the critical angle θ_c can be computed as follows:

$$\theta_c = \sin^{-1}\left(\frac{n_2}{n_1}\right) = \sin^{-1}\left(\frac{1.0003}{1.5}\right)$$
$$= \sin^{-1}(0.66687) = 41.82°$$

This light pipe will transmit light for all angles of incidence greater than 41.82°.

4. Algorithm Development

Decomposition

Read n_1, n_2, and incidence angle.
Determine appropriate message.

We will need to make sure that n_2 is not greater than n_1 before we compute the critical angle, since the inverse sine function will give an error message if its argument is greater than 1.0.

Pseudocode

Pipe: Read n_1, n_2, and incidence angle
  If $n_2 > n_1$ then
    Print 'Light is not transmitted'
  Else

$$\text{critical angle} \leftarrow \sin^{-1}\left(\frac{n_2}{n_1}\right)$$

    If incidence angle > critical angle then
      Print 'Light is transmitted'
    Else
      Print 'Light is not transmitted'

As we convert the pseudocode into FORTRAN, we need to be sure to remind the user to use the proper units for the angle measurement. The program can be written to accept either radians or degrees, but the equation for computing the critical angle will depend on the units of the input angle.

FORTRAN Program

```
*-----------------------------------------------------------------------*
      PROGRAM PIPE
*
*  This program reads the indices of refraction for two materials
*  forming a light pipe. It also reads the angle of incidence for
*  light striking the pipe and determines if it is transmitted.
*
      REAL N1, N2, ANGLE, CRTCL
*
      PRINT*, 'ENTER INDEX OF REFRACTION FOR ROD'
      READ*, N1
      PRINT*, 'ENTER INDEX OF REFRACTION FOR SURROUNDING MEDIUM'
      READ*, N2
      PRINT*, 'ENTER ANGLE OF TRANSMISSION OF LIGHT IN DEGREES'
      READ*, ANGLE
*
      IF (N2.GT.N1) THEN
         PRINT*, 'LIGHT IS NOT TRANSMITTED'
      ELSE
         CRTCL = ASIN(N2/N1)*(180.0/3.141593)
         IF (ANGLE.GT.CRTCL) THEN
            PRINT*, 'LIGHT IS TRANSMITTED'
         ELSE
            PRINT*, 'LIGHT IS NOT TRANSMITTED'
         END IF
      END IF
*
      END
*-----------------------------------------------------------------------*
```

5. Testing

To test this program with a variety of possible pipes, we now list the index of refraction for some common materials[1].

Material	Index of Refraction
Gases (at atmospheric pressure and 0°C)	
Hydrogen	1.0001
Air	1.0003
Carbon dioxide	1.0005
Liquids (at 20°C)	
Water	1.333
Ethyl alcohol	1.362
Glycerine	1.473
Solids (at room temperature)	
Ice	1.31
Polystyrene	1.59
Crown glass	1.50–1.62
Flint glass	1.57–1.75
Diamond	2.417
Acrylic (polymethylmethacrylate)	1.49

If we use this program to determine whether light with an incidence angle of 45° is transmitted through an acrylic pipe in water, we get the following output:

```
ENTER INDEX OF REFRACTION FOR ROD
1.49
ENTER INDEX OF REFRACTION FOR SURROUNDING MEDIUM
1.333
ENTER ANGLE OF TRANSMISSION OF LIGHT IN DEGREES
45.0
LIGHT IS NOT TRANSMITTED
```

[1] E. R. Jones and R. L. Childers, "Contemporary College Physics," Addison-Wesley, Reading, Mass., 1990.

3-4 ■ While Loop Structure

The *While loop* is an important structure for repeating a set of statements as long as a certain condition is true. In pseudocode, the While loop structure is

```
While condition do
    statement 1
      .
      .
      .
    statement m
statement p
```

While the condition is true, statements 1 through *m* are executed. After the group of statements is executed, the condition is retested. If the condition is still true, the group of statements is reexecuted. When the condition is false, execution continues with the statement following the While loop (statement *p* in our example). The variables modified in the group of statements in the While loop must involve the variables tested in the While loop's condition, or the value of the condition will never change.

Standard FORTRAN 77 does not include a WHILE statement, although many compilers have implemented their own WHILE statement. We will implement the While loop with the IF statement as shown below, so that our programs will be standard and will execute on other FORTRAN 77 compilers without any conversion.

```
n IF (logical expression) THEN
     statement 1
     .
     .
     .
     statement m
     GO TO n
  END IF
```

In this implementation we used an unconditional transfer statement whose general form is

```
GO TO n
```

where *n* is the statement number or label of an executable statement in the program. The execution of the GO TO statement causes the flow of program control to transfer, or *branch*, to statement *n*.

We are now ready to write programs for the algorithms we developed in Section 3 – 1.

Average of a Set of Data Values . . . . Example 3-6

In Example 3 – 1 we developed a flowchart for the algorithm to find the average of a set of data values. This flowchart is repeated here:

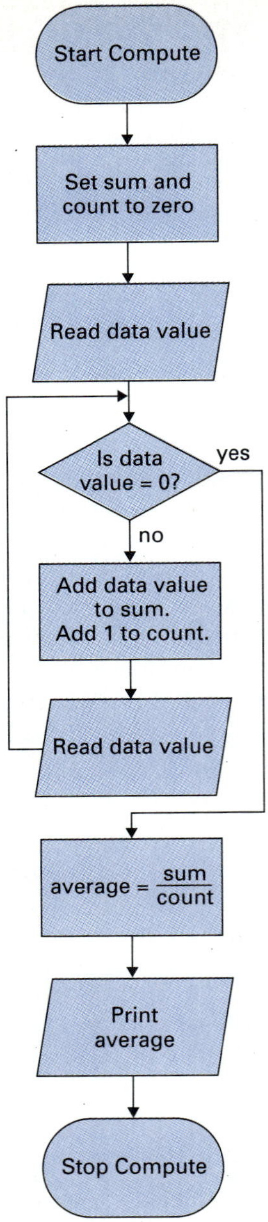

Solution 1

We have covered the FORTRAN statements for the If structures and for the While loop. Using these statements, we can translate each step in the flowchart into FORTRAN.

```
*-----------------------------------------------------------------------*
      PROGRAM COMPUT
*
*  This program computes and prints the average
*  of a set of experimental data values.
*
      INTEGER COUNT
      REAL SUM, X, AVERG
*
      SUM = 0.0
      COUNT = 0
*
      READ*, X
    1 IF (X.NE.0.0) THEN
         SUM = SUM + X
         COUNT = COUNT + 1
         READ*, X
         GO TO 1
      END IF
*
      AVERG = SUM/REAL(COUNT)
*
      PRINT 5, AVERG
    5 FORMAT (1X,'THE AVERAGE IS ',F5.2)
*
      END
*-----------------------------------------------------------------------*
```

This is the program we used in Chapter 1 to illustrate the form and readability of a FORTRAN program. Sample output is shown in Chapter 1 on page 19.

Solution 2

We now present a second solution that uses a logical variable DONE to specify when we have reached the end of the data. In this solution, we initialize the logical variable to the value .FALSE.; when we find the value that indicates the end of the data, we change the value of the logical variable to .TRUE..

```
*-----------------------------------------------------------------------*
      PROGRAM COMPUT
*
*  This program computes the average of
*  a set of experimental data values.
*
      INTEGER COUNT
      REAL SUM, X, AVERG
      LOGICAL DONE
*
      SUM = 0.0
      COUNT = 0
      DONE = .FALSE.
*
```

```
    1 IF (.NOT.DONE) THEN
         READ*, X
         IF (X.EQ.0.0) THEN
            DONE = .TRUE.
         ELSE
            SUM = SUM + X
            COUNT = COUNT + 1
         END IF
         GO TO 1
      END IF
*
      AVERG = SUM/REAL(COUNT)
*
      PRINT 5, AVERG
    5 FORMAT (1X,'THE AVERAGE IS ',F5.2)
*
      END
*-----------------------------------------------------------------------*
```

Example 3-7

Experimental Data Analysis

In Example 3–2 we developed pseudocode for the algorithm to analyze a set of experimental data values and determine the minimum and maximum values and compute the range of data values. This pseudocode is repeated again:

```
Analysis: Read data value
          maximum ← data value
          minimum ← data value
          Read data value
          While the data value is not zero do
              If data value > maximum then
                  maximum ← data value
              If data value < minimum then
                  minimum ← data value
              Read data value
          range ← maximum − minimum
          Print maximum, minimum, range
```

Convert this pseudocode into a FORTRAN program.

Solution

Again, using the statements presented in this chapter for the IF structure and the While loop, we can convert each step of the pseudocode into FORTRAN.

```
*-----------------------------------------------------------------------*
      PROGRAM ANALYZ
*
*  This program determines maximum and minimum values
*  and the range of values for a set of data values.
*
      REAL X, MAX, MIN, RANGE
*
```

```
      READ*, X
      MAX = X
      MIN = X
*
      READ*, X
    1 IF (X.NE.0.0) THEN
         IF (X.GT.MAX) MAX = X
         IF (X.LT.MIN) MIN = X
         READ*, X
         GO TO 1
      END IF
*
      RANGE = MAX - MIN
*
      PRINT 5, MAX, MIN, RANGE
    5 FORMAT (1X,'MAXIMUM DATA VALUE = ',F8.2/
     +        1X,'MINIMUM DATA VALUE = ',F8.2/
     +        1X,'RANGE OF VALUES =    ',F8.2)
*
      END
*----------------------------------------------------------------------*
```

If we use the sample data from Example 3–2, the output is

```
MAXIMUM DATA VALUE =     66.31
MINIMUM DATA VALUE =     40.56
RANGE OF VALUES =        25.75
```

In Fortran 90, the DO WHILE construct can be used to implement While loops. It has the following form: Fortran 90

```
DO WHILE (logical expression)
   .
   .
   .
END DO
```

3-5 Application ■ Rocket Trajectory

Aerospace Engineering

A small rocket is being designed to make wind shear measurements in the vicinity of thunderstorms. Before testing begins, the designers are developing a simulation of the rocket's trajectory. They have derived the following equation, which they believe will predict the performance of their test rocket, where t is the elapsed time in seconds:

$$\text{height} = 60 + 2.13t^2 - 0.0013t^4 + 0.000034t^{4.751}$$

The equation gives the height above ground level at time t. The first term (60) is the height in feet above ground level of the nose of the rocket. To check the predicted performance, the rocket is "flown" on a computer, using the preceding equation.

Develop an algorithm and use it to write a complete program to cover a maximum flight of 100 seconds. Increments in time are to be 2.0 seconds from launch through the ascending and descending portions of the trajectory until the rocket descends to within 50 feet of ground level. Below 50 feet the time increments are to be 0.05 seconds. If the rocket impacts prior to 100 seconds, the program is to stop immediately after impact. The output is to be a table of corresponding time and height values.

As shown in the following diagram, several possible events could occur as we simulate the flight. The height above the ground should increase for a period and then decrease until the rocket impacts. We can test for impact by testing the height for a value equal to or less than zero. It is also possible that the rocket will still be airborne after 100 seconds of flight time. Therefore, we must also test for this condition and stop the program if the value of time becomes greater than 100. In addition, we need to observe the height above ground. As the rocket approaches the ground, we want to monitor its progress more frequently; we will need to reduce our time increment from 2.0 seconds to 0.05 seconds.

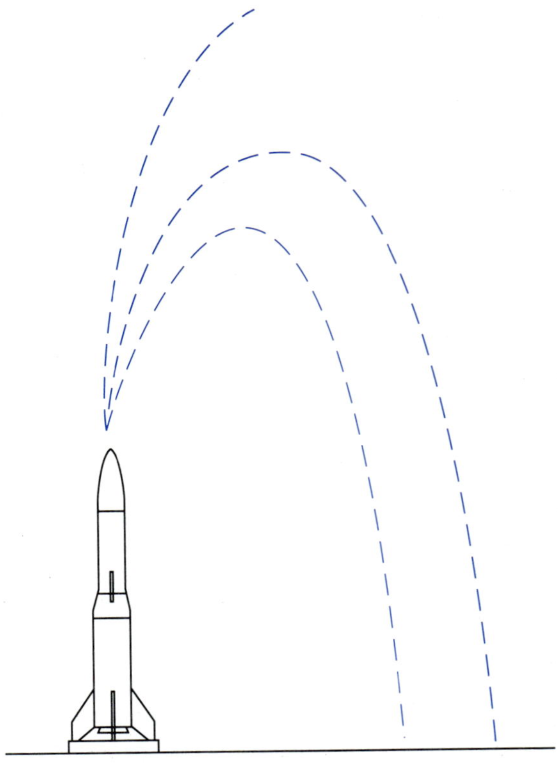

1. Problem Statement

Print a table of time and height values for a rocket trajectory. Start time at zero and increment it by 2.0 seconds until the height is less than 50 feet, then increment time by 0.05 seconds. Stop the program if the rocket impacts or if the total time exceeds 100 seconds.

2. Input/Output Description

Input — none
Output — a table of time and height values

3. Hand Example

Using a calculator, we compute the first three entries in our table as shown:

Time (s)	Height (ft)
0.0000	60.0000
2.0000	68.5001
4.0000	93.7719

We are now ready to develop the algorithm so that the computer can compute the rest of the table for us.

4. Algorithm Development

Decomposition

Set time to zero.
Compute and print times and heights.

We do the refinement in two steps for this problem:

Initial Pseudocode

```
Rocket1: time ← 0
         While above ground and time ≤ 100 do
             Compute height
             Print time, height
             Increment time
```

In our refinement, we replace "Increment time" with the steps that take into account our height above ground. We also replace the condition "above ground" with a specific condition based on our height above ground.

Final Pseudocode

```
Rocket1: time ← 0
         height ← 60
         While height > 0 and time ≤ 100 do
              Compute height
              Print time, height
              If height < 50 then
                   time ← time + 0.05
              Else
                   time ← time + 2.0
```

Notice that the height variable was initialized to 60.0 before entering the While loop. Why? Could it have been initialized after the condition was tested? The height must also be set to a value greater than zero or the While loop would never be executed.

FORTRAN Program 1

```
*-------------------------------------------------------------------*
      PROGRAM RCKET1
*
*  This program simulates a rocket flight for up to 100 seconds.
*  A table contains height values at increments of 2 seconds until
*  the rocket is within 50 feet of the ground. Within 50 feet
*  of the ground, the height values are computed every 0.05 seconds.
*
      REAL TIME, HEIGHT
*
      TIME = 0.0
      HEIGHT = 60.0
*
      PRINT 5
    5 FORMAT (1X,'TIME (S)     HEIGHT(FT)')
      PRINT*
*
   10 IF (HEIGHT.GT.0.0.AND.TIME.LE.100.0) THEN
         HEIGHT = 60.0 + 2.13*TIME**2 - 0.0013*TIME**4
     +            + 0.000034*TIME**4.751
         PRINT 15, TIME, HEIGHT
   15    FORMAT (1X,F7.4,8X,F9.4)
         IF (HEIGHT.LT.50.0) THEN
            TIME = TIME + 0.05
         ELSE
            TIME = TIME + 2.0
         END IF
         GO TO 10
      END IF
*
      END
*-------------------------------------------------------------------*
```

As our programs become longer, we use comment lines with only an asterisk in column 1 to separate groups of statements that have a common function. In the preceding program, the blank comment lines separate steps that initialize variables and print the heading from the While loop.

We now present another solution to this problem that uses logical variables. In this solution, we use a logical variable called DONE. As long as neither of the conditions that indicate that we want to stop the program occurs, the value of this variable remains false. Thus, as long as .NOT.DONE is true, we want to stay in the While loop.

FORTRAN Program 2

```
*-----------------------------------------------------------------------*
      PROGRAM RCKET2
*
*  This program simulates a rocket flight for up to 100 seconds.
*  A table contains height values at increments of 2 seconds until
*  the rocket is within 50 feet of the ground. Within 50 feet
*  of the ground, the height values are computed every 0.05 seconds.
*
      REAL TIME, HEIGHT
      LOGICAL DONE
*
      TIME = 0.0
      HEIGHT = 60.0
      DONE = .FALSE.
*
      PRINT 5
    5 FORMAT (1X,'TIME (S)     HEIGHT (FT)')
      PRINT*
*
   10 IF (.NOT.DONE) THEN
         HEIGHT = 60.0 + 2.13*TIME**2 - 0.0013*TIME**4
     +            + 0.000034*TIME**4.751
         PRINT 15, TIME, HEIGHT
   15    FORMAT (1X,F7.4,8X,F9.4)
         IF (HEIGHT.LT.50.0) THEN
            TIME = TIME + 0.05
         ELSE
            TIME = TIME + 2.0
         END IF
         DONE = HEIGHT.LE.0.0.OR.TIME.GT.100.0
         GO TO 10
      END IF
*
   END
*-----------------------------------------------------------------------*
```

5. Testing

The first few lines and the last few lines of output are shown. The values are in agreement with the hand-worked example.

```
TIME (S)        HEIGHT (FT)
 0.0000            60.0000
 2.0000            68.5001
 4.0000            93.7719
 6.0000           135.1644
 8.0000           191.6590
.
.
.
 54.0000          999.1536
 56.0000          827.4205
 58.0000          633.2993
 60.0000          418.3975
 62.0000          184.8088
 64.0000          -64.8608
```

Can you think of ways to test different parts of the algorithm? We now know that the rocket impacts before 100 seconds of flight time; we could change the cutoff time to 50 seconds to see if this exit from the While loop were working correctly. How could you modify the program to check the change in the increment of the time variable from 2.0 seconds to 0.05 seconds?

3-6 Application ▪ Suture Packaging

Biomedical Engineering

Sutures are strands or fibers used to sew living tissue together after an injury or an operation. Packages of sutures must be sealed carefully before they are shipped to hospitals so that contaminants cannot enter the packages. The object that seals the package is referred to as a sealing die. Generally, sealing dies are heated with an electric heater. For the sealing process to be a success, the sealing die is maintained at an established temperature and must contact the package with a predetermined pressure for an established time period. The time period in which the sealing die contacts the package is called dwell time. We want to develop an algorithm and a FORTRAN program to analyze the data collected on batches of sutures that have been rejected. We assume that we will be given the temperature, pressure, and dwell time for each batch. For the sutures that have been sealed, the following acceptable range of parameters has been established:

Temperature: 150.0 – 170.0°C
Pressure: 60 – 70 psi
Dwell: 2.0 – 2.5 s

All sutures in a batch will be rejected if any of these conditions is not met.

Our program will ask the user to enter the batch code, temperature, pressure, and dwell time for each batch that has been rejected during some time period. (A negative batch code will indicate the end of the data.) We want to collect data on the reasons why the batches were rejected to attempt to find the underlying problem. For example, if most of the rejections were due to temperature problems, then we need to check the electric heater in the sealing die. If most of the rejections were due to pressure problems, then we need to check the pressure in the air cylinder that lowers the die to the package. Or, if most of the rejections were due to dwell time, then the control information in the sealing die may be in error. Clearly, the first step in locating the source of the problem must be to get a good analysis of the data from rejected batches of sutures. The data we will compute in this program will be the percentage of rejections due to temperature, the percentage of rejections due to pressure, and the percentage of rejections due to dwell time. If a batch was rejected for more than one reason, it should be counted in the total for each rejection category.

We now use our five-phase design process to develop an algorithm and a FORTRAN solution to this problem.

1. Problem Statement

Print a report analyzing the information for all batches of sutures that were not properly sealed, where a proper seal requires the following range of parameters:

Temperature: 150.0 – 170.0°C
Pressure: 60 – 70 psi
Dwell: 2.0 – 2.5 s

2. Input/Output Description

Input—four values for each batch that was rejected: the batch number, the temperature, the pressure, and the dwell time

Output—a report giving the percentages of the batches rejected because of temperature problems, pressure problems, and dwell time problems.

3. Hand Example

Assume the following data represents the information on the batches rejected during one day:

Batch Number	Temperature	Pressure	Dwell Time
24551	145.5	62.3	2.13
24582	153.7	63.0	2.52
26553	160.3	58.9	2.51
26623	159.5	58.9	2.01
26624	160.5	61.3	1.98

In this data, batch 24551 was rejected because of temperature, batch 24582 was rejected because of dwell time, batch 26553 was rejected because of pressure and dwell time, batch 26623 was rejected due to pressure, and batch 26624 was rejected due to dwell time. The report summarizing this information is the following:

```
SUMMARY OF BATCH REJECT INFORMATION

20.0 % REJECTED DUE TO TEMPERATURE
40.0 % REJECTED DUE TO PRESSURE
60.0 % REJECTED DUE TO DWELL TIME
```

4. Algorithm Development

Decomposition

Read data and collect information.
Print report.

Using the worked example as a guide, we develop the initial pseudocode for this problem.

Initial Pseudocode

```
Seals: count ← 0
       Read batch, temperature, pressure, dwell
       While batch ≥ 0 do
              Determine reject reason and add to totals
              count ← count + 1
              Read batch, temperature, pressure, dwell
       Convert totals to percentages
       Print report
```

We still need to refine the step further to determine which parameters were not within the specified values and then add to the corresponding totals. This involves three different tests: one for the temperature, one for the pressure, and one for the dwell time. We will call the rejection totals rejctt (for rejections due to temperature), rejctp (for rejections due to pressure), and rejctd (for rejections due to dwell time). The final refinement in pseudocode follows.

Final Pseudocode

```
Seals: count ← 0
       rejctt ← 0
       rejctp ← 0
       rejctd ← 0
       Read batch, temperature, pressure, dwell
```

```
While batch ≥ 0 do
    If temperature out of bounds then
        rejctt ← rejctt + 1
    If pressure out of bounds then
        rejctp ← rejctp + 1
    If dwell out of bounds then
        rejctd ← rejctd + 1
    count ← count + 1
    Read batch, temperature, pressure, dwell
Convert reject totals to percentages
Print report
```

FORTRAN Program

```
*-----------------------------------------------------------------------*
      PROGRAM SEALS
*
*  This program analyzes data on batches of sutures that have
*  not been properly sealed and then prints a report.
*
      INTEGER COUNT, REJCTT, REJCTP, REJCTD, BATCH
      REAL TEMP, PRESSR, DWELL, PERCT, PERCP, PERCD
*
      COUNT = 0
      REJCTT = 0
      REJCTP = 0
      REJCTD = 0
*
      PRINT*, 'ENTER BATCH NUMBER, TEMPERATURE, PRESSURE, DWELL'
      PRINT*, 'FOR BATCHES THAT HAVE BEEN REJECTED'
      PRINT*, '(NEGATIVE BATCH NUMBER TO STOP)'
      READ*, BATCH, TEMP, PRESSR, DWELL
*
    5 IF (BATCH.GE.0) THEN
         IF (TEMP.LT.150.0.OR.TEMP.GT.170.0) REJCTT = REJCTT + 1
         IF (PRESSR.LT.60.0.OR.PRESSR.GT.70.0) REJCTP = REJCTP + 1
         IF (DWELL.LT.2.0.OR.DWELL.GT.2.5) REJCTD = REJCTD + 1
         COUNT = COUNT + 1
         PRINT*, 'ENTER NEXT SET OF DATA'
         READ*, BATCH, TEMP, PRESSR, DWELL
         GO TO 5
      END IF
*
      PERCT = REAL(REJCTT)/REAL(COUNT)*100.0
      PERCP = REAL(REJCTP)/REAL(COUNT)*100.0
      PERCD = REAL(REJCTD)/REAL(COUNT)*100.0
*
      PRINT*
      PRINT*, 'SUMMARY OF BATCH REJECT INFORMATION'
      PRINT*
      PRINT 10, PERCT, PERCP, PERCD
   10 FORMAT (1X,F7.1,' % REJECTED DUE TO TEMPERATURE'/
     +        1X,F7.1,' % REJECTED DUE TO PRESSURE'/
     +        1X,F7.1,' % REJECTED DUE TO DWELL')
*
      END
*-----------------------------------------------------------------------*
```

5. Testing

The output of this program from the data used in the hand example is:

```
ENTER BATCH NUMBER, TEMPERATURE, PRESSURE, DWELL
FOR BATCHES THAT HAVE BEEN REJECTED
(NEGATIVE BATCH NUMBER TO STOP)
24551      145.5          62.3           2.13
ENTER NEXT SET OF DATA
24582      153.7          63.0           2.52
ENTER NEXT SET OF DATA
26553      160.3          58.9           2.51
ENTER NEXT SET OF DATA
26623      159.5          58.9           2.01
ENTER NEXT SET OF DATA
26624      160.5          61.3           1.98
ENTER NEXT SET OF DATA
-1           0.0          0.00           0.0

SUMMARY OF BATCH REJECT INFORMATION

   20.0 % REJECTED DUE TO TEMPERATURE
   40.0 % REJECTED DUE TO PRESSURE
   60.0 % REJECTED DUE TO DWELL TIME
```

3·7 ■ DO Loop

In Section 3–4 we used the IF statement to build While loops. A special form of the While loop is the counting loop, or *iterative loop*. Implementing a counting loop generally involves initializing a counter before entering the loop, modifying the counter within the loop, and exiting the loop when the counter reaches a specified value. Counting loops are executed a specified number of times. The three steps (initialize, modify, and test) can be incorporated in a While loop as we have already seen, but they still require three different statements. A special statement, the DO statement, combines all three steps into one. Using the DO statement to construct a loop results in a construction called a DO loop.

The general form of the DO statement is

DO *k index = initial, limit, increment*

The constant *k* is the number of the statement that represents the end of the loop; *index* is a variable used as the loop counter; initial represents the *initial value* given to the loop counter; *limit* represents the value used to determine when the DO loop has been completed; and *increment* represents the value to be added to the loop counter each time the loop is executed.

The values of initial, limit, and increment are the *parameters* of the DO loop. If the increment is omitted, an increment of 1 is assumed. When the value of the index is greater than the limit, control is passed to the statement following the end of the loop.

The end of the loop is usually indicated by the CONTINUE statement, whose general form is

```
k CONTINUE
```

where k is the statement number referenced by the corresponding DO statement. Before we list the rules for using a DO loop, let's look at a simple example.

Integer Sum . . . . Example 3·8

The sum of the integers 1 through 50 is represented mathematically as

$$\sum_{i=1}^{50} i = 1 + 2 + \cdots + 49 + 50$$

Obviously, we do not want to write one long assignment statement to compute this sum. A better solution is to build a loop that executes 50 times and adds a number to the sum each time, as shown in the following solutions.

While Loop Solution

```
   SUM = 0
   NUMBER = 1
10 IF (NUMBER.LE.50) THEN
      SUM = SUM + NUMBER
      NUMBER = NUMBER + 1
      GO TO 10
   END IF
```

DO Loop Solution

```
   SUM = 0
   DO 10 NUMBER=1,50
      SUM = SUM + NUMBER
10 CONTINUE
```

The DO statement identifies statement 10 as the end of the loop. The index NUMBER is initialized to 1. The loop is repeated until the value of NUMBER is greater than 50. Because the third parameter is omitted, the index NUMBER is incremented automatically by 1 at the end of each loop. Comparing the DO loop solution with the While loop solution, we see that the DO loop solution is shorter but that both compute the same value for SUM. ◀

■ Structure of a DO Loop

We have seen a DO loop in a simple example. We now need to summarize the rules related to its structure.

1. The index of the DO loop must be a variable, but it may be either real or integer.
2. The parameters of the DO loop may be constants, variables, or expressions and can also be real or integer types.
3. The increment can be either positive or negative, but it cannot be zero.
4. A DO loop may end on any executable statement that is not a transfer, an IF statement, or another DO statement. The CONTINUE statement is an executable statement that was designed expressly for closing a DO loop; although

other statements may be used, we strongly encourage the consistent use of the CONTINUE statement to indicate the end of the loop.

5. We will use the following pseudocode for a counting loop:

For index = initial to limit by step do
    set of statements

The "by step" clause is omitted if the increment is 1. The pseudocode for the loop in Example 3–8 is

For number = 1 to 50 do
    sum ← sum + number

6. The flowchart symbol for a DO loop is

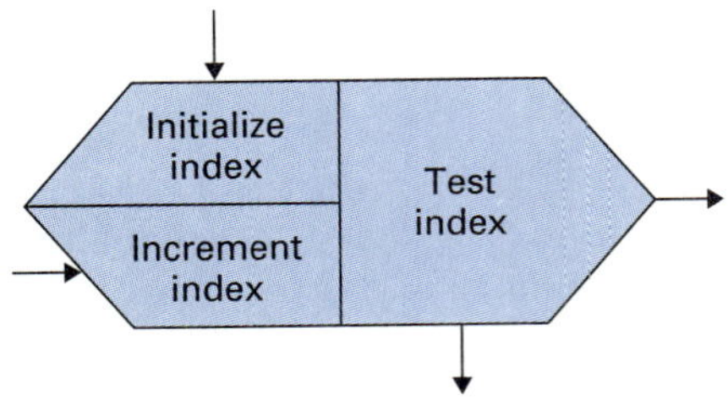

Note that the symbol is divided into three parts, each corresponding to the three steps in building an iterative loop. The flowchart for the iterative loop in Example 3–8 is

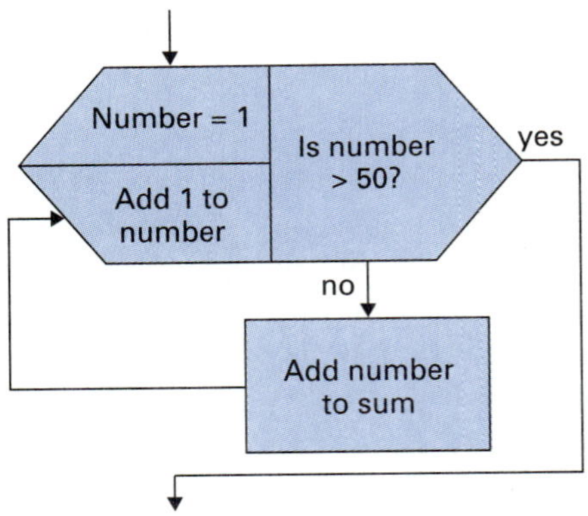

These rules define the structure of the DO loop but do not define the steps in its execution, which is covered next.

■ Execution of a DO Loop

In the following list we present a complete set of rules related to DO loop execution. We suggest that you read through them once and then go through the set of examples that follow the rules. Later, reread these rules. Do not worry about memorizing them; after you have gone through the set of examples most of the rules will seem logical.

1. The test for completion is done at the beginning of the loop, as in a While

loop. If the initial value of the index is greater than the limit and the increment is positive, the loop will not be executed. For instance, the statement

```
DO 10 I=5,2
```

sets up a loop that ends at statement 10. The initial value of the index I is 5, which is greater than the limit 2; therefore, the statements within the loop will be skipped and control passes to the statement following statement 10.

2. The value of the index should not be modified by other statements during the execution of the loop.
3. After the loop begins execution, changing the values of the parameters will have no effect on the loop.
4. If the increment is negative, the exit from the loop will occur when the value of the index is less than the limit.
5. Although it is not recommended, you may branch out of a DO loop before it is completed. The value of the index will be the value just before the branch. (If you need to exit the DO loop before it is completed, you should restructure the loop as a While loop to maintain a structured program.)
6. Upon completion of the DO loop, the index contains the last value that exceeded the limit.
7. Always enter a DO loop through the DO statement so that it will be initiated properly.
8. It is invalid to use a GO TO statement to transfer from outside a DO loop to inside the DO loop.
9. The number of times that a DO loop will be executed can be computed as

$$\left[\frac{\text{limit} - \text{initial}}{\text{increment}}\right] + 1$$

The brackets around the fraction represent the greatest integer value; that is, we drop any fractional portion (truncate) of the quotient. If this value is negative, the loop is not executed. If we had the following DO statement

```
DO 35 K=5,83,4
```

the corresponding DO loop would be executed the following number of times:

$$\left[\frac{83 - 5}{4}\right] + 1 = \left[\frac{78}{4}\right] + 1 = 20$$

The value of the index K would be 5, then 9, then 13, and so on until the final value of 81. The loop would not be executed with the value 85 because it is greater than the limit, 83.

Fortran 90

In Fortran 90, a CYCLE statement causes termination of the execution of one iteration of a DO loop. A sample of this statement is:

```
IF (TIME < 5.0) CYCLE
```

Fortran 90

In Fortran 90, an EXIT statement causes termination of the DO loop. A sample of this statement is:

```
IF (TIME == 0.0) EXIT
```

The next set of examples illustrates both the structure and the execution of the DO loop.

Example 3-9

Polynomial Model with Integer Time

Polynomials are often used to model data and experimental results. Assume that the polynomial $3t^2 + 4.5$ models the results of an experiment where t represents time in seconds. Write a complete program to evaluate this polynomial for the period of time from 1 second to 10 seconds in increments of 1 second (that is, let $t = 1, 2, 3, 4, 5, 6, 7, 8, 9$, and 10). For each value of time, print the time and the polynomial value.

Solution

The **first step** is to state the problem clearly: Print a report to evaluate the polynomial $3t^2 + 4.5$ for a period from 1 second to 10 seconds in increments of 1 second.

The **second step** is to describe the input and output:

Input — none
Output — report containing polynomial values

The **third step** is to work a simple example. Therefore, the first few lines of output should be:

Polynomial Model

Time (S)	Polynomial
1	7.50
2	16.50
3	31.50

The **fourth step** is to develop an algorithm, starting with the decomposition.

Decomposition

Print headings.
Print report.

Pseudocode

```
Poly1: Print headings
       For time = 1 to 10 do
           poly ← 3 time² + 4.5
           Print time, poly
```

FORTRAN Program

```
*-----------------------------------------------------------------------*
      PROGRAM POLY1
*
*  This program prints a table of values for a polynomial
*  starting with time equal to 1 second through 10 seconds
*  in increments of 1 second.
*
      INTEGER TIME
      REAL POLY
*
      PRINT*, 'POLYNOMIAL MODEL'
      PRINT*
      PRINT*, 'TIME   POLYNOMIAL'
      PRINT*, '(S)'
*
      DO 15 TIME=1,10
         POLY = 3.0*REAL(TIME)**2 + 4.5
         PRINT 10, TIME, POLY
   10    FORMAT (1X,I2,5X,F6.2)
   15 CONTINUE
*
      END
*-----------------------------------------------------------------------*
```

The **fifth step** is to test the program. The output from this program is

```
POLYNOMIAL MODEL

TIME   POLYNOMIAL
(S)
 1       7.50
 2      16.50
 3      31.50
 4      52.50
 5      79.50
 6     112.50
 7     151.50
 8     196.50
 9     247.50
10     304.50
```

Polynomial Model with Real Time . . . . Example 3-10

We again assume that the polynomial $3t^2 + 4.5$ models an experiment where t represents time in seconds. Write a program to evaluate this polynomial for time beginning at zero seconds and ending at 5 seconds in increments of 0.5 seconds.

Solution

The **first step** is to state the problem clearly: Print a report to evaluate the polynomial $3t^2 + 4.5$ for a period from 0 seconds through 5 seconds in increments of 0.5 seconds.

The **second step** is to describe the input and output:

Input — none
Output — report containing polynomial values

The **third step** is to work a simple example. Therefore, the first few lines of output should be

Polynomial Model

Time (S)	Polynomial
0.0	4.50
0.5	5.25
1.0	7.50

The **fourth step** is to develop an algorithm, beginning with the decomposition.

Decomposition

Print headings.
Print report.

Pseudocode

```
Poly2: Print headings
       For k = 0 to 50 by 5 do
           time ← 0.1 · k
           poly ← 3 time² + 4.5
           Print time, poly
```

FORTRAN Program

```
*-----------------------------------------------------------------*
      PROGRAM POLY2
*
*  This program prints a table of values for a polynomial
*  starting with time equal to 0 seconds through 5 seconds
*  in increments of 0.5 seconds.
*
      INTEGER K
      REAL TIME, POLY
*
      PRINT*, 'POLYNOMIAL MODEL'
      PRINT*
      PRINT*, 'TIME   POLYNOMIAL'
      PRINT*, '(S)'
*
      DO 15 K=0,50,5
         TIME = 0.1*REAL(K)
         POLY = 3.0*TIME**2 + 4.5
         PRINT 10, TIME, POLY
   10    FORMAT (1X,F4.1,5X,F5.2)
   15 CONTINUE
*
      END
*-----------------------------------------------------------------*
```

Note that the value of TIME is computed from an integer that varies from 0 to 50 in steps of 5. Another possibility would have been to use the following DO statement:

```
DO 15 TIME=0.0,5.0,0.5
```

However, it is wise to avoid DO statements such as this one with real parameters. These statements do not always execute exactly the way we expect because of truncation within the computer. For example, suppose that the value for 0.5 is stored as a value slightly less than 0.5 in our computer system. Each time we add 0.5 to the index, we are adding less than we intend, and the values are not those we intend. Also, in this case, the loop would be executed one more time than we intended because the value of TIME would not exactly equal 5.0 during the execution of the loop.

The **fifth step** is to test the program. The output from this program is

```
POLYNOMIAL MODEL

TIME   POLYNOMIAL
(S)
 0.0      4.50
 0.5      5.25
 1.0      7.50
 1.5     11.25
 2.0     16.50
 2.5     23.25
 3.0     31.50
 3.5     41.25
 4.0     52.50
 4.5     65.25
 5.0     79.50
```

Example 3-11 Polynomial Model with Variable Time

Assume that we want to evaluate the same polynomial $3t^2 + 4.5$, beginning at t equal to zero, in increments of 0.25, for a variable number of seconds. Write a program to read an integer NSEC that represents the number of seconds to be used for evaluating the polynomial. Print the corresponding table.

Solution

The **first step** is to state the problem clearly: Print a report to evaluate the polynomial $3t^2 + 4.5$ for a period from 0 seconds, in increments of 0.25 seconds, for a variable number of seconds.

The **second step** is to determine the input and output:

Input—the number of seconds for evaluating the polynomial
Output—report containing polynomial values

The **third step** is to work a simple example by hand. If we assume that the number of seconds is a number such as 4, then the first few lines of output should be:

Polynomial Model

Time (S)	Polynomial
0.00	4.5000
0.25	4.6875
0.50	5.2500

The **fourth step** is to develop an algorithm, beginning with the decomposition.

Decomposition

Read number of seconds.
Print headings.
Print report.

Pseudocode

```
Poly3: Read nsec
       Print headings
       For k=0 to 100 · nsec by 25 do
           time ← 0.01 · k
           poly ← 3 time² + 4.5
           Print time, poly
```

FORTRAN Program

```
*-----------------------------------------------------------------------*
      PROGRAM POLY3
*
*  This program prints a table of values for a polynomial
*  starting with time equal to 0 seconds, in increments of
*  0.25 seconds, for a variable number of seconds that is
*  entered by the user.
*
      INTEGER NSEC, K
      REAL TIME, POLY
*
      PRINT*, 'ENTER NUMBER OF SECONDS FOR TABLE'
      READ*, NSEC
      PRINT*
      PRINT*, 'POLYNOMIAL MODEL'
      PRINT*
      PRINT*, 'TIME   POLYNOMIAL'
      PRINT*, '(S)'
*
      DO 15 K=0,100*NSEC,25
         TIME = 0.01*REAL(K)
         POLY = 3.0*REAL(TIME)**2 + 4.5
         PRINT 10, TIME, POLY
   10    FORMAT (1X,F5.2,5X,F7.4)
   15 CONTINUE
*
      END
*-----------------------------------------------------------------------*
```

The **fifth step** is to test the program. If we enter the value 4 for the number of seconds, the output from this program is

```
ENTER NUMBER OF SECONDS FOR TABLE
4

POLYNOMIAL MODEL

TIME   POLYNOMIAL
(S)
 0.00      4.5000
 0.25      4.6875
 0.50      5.2500
 0.75      6.1875
 1.00      7.5000
 1.25      9.1875
 1.50     11.2500
 1.75     13.6875
 2.00     16.5000
 2.25     19.6875
 2.50     23.2500
 2.75     27.1875
 3.00     31.5000
 3.25     36.1875
 3.50     41.2500
 3.75     46.6875
 4.00     52.5000
```

SELF-TEST 3-2

This self-test allows you to check quickly to see if you have remembered some of the key points from Section 3–7. If you have any problems with the exercises, you should reread this section. The solutions are included at the end of the text.

In problems 1–6, determine the number of times that the statements in the DO loop will be executed. Assume that the index is an integer variable.

1. `DO 10 NUM=5,14`
2. `DO 10 COUNT=-4,4`
3. `DO 10 K=15,3,-1`
4. `DO 10 TIME=-5,15,3`
5. `DO 10 TIME=50,250,25`
6. `DO 10 INDEX=72,432,4`

For problems 7–11, give the value in COUNT after each of the following loops is executed. Assume that COUNT is an integer variable initialized to zero before each problem.

7.
```
   DO 5 I=1,8
      COUNT = COUNT + 1
 5 CONTINUE
```

8.
```
   DO 5 K=1,5
      COUNT = COUNT + K
 5 CONTINUE
```

9.
```
   DO 5 INDEX=0,7
      COUNT = COUNT - 2
 5 CONTINUE
```

10.
```
   DO 5 NUM=8,0,-1
      COUNT = COUNT + 2
 5 CONTINUE
```

11.
```
   DO 5 M=5,5
      COUNT = COUNT + (-1)**M
 5 CONTINUE
```

3-8 Application ▪ Timber Regrowth

Environmental Engineering

A problem in timber management is to determine how much of an area to leave uncut so that the harvested area is reforested in a certain period of time. It is assumed that reforestation takes place at a known rate per year, depending on climate and soil conditions. A reforestation equation expresses this growth as a function of the amount of timber standing and the reforestation rate. For example, if 100 acres are left standing after harvesting and the reforestation rate is 0.05, then $100 + 0.05 \times 100$, or 105 acres, are forested at the end of the first year. At the end of the second year, the number of acres forested is $105 + 0.05 \times 105$, or 110.25 acres.

Write a program to read the identification number of an area, the total number of acres in the area, the number of acres that are uncut, and the reforestation rate. Print a report that tabulates for 20 years the number of acres reforested and the total number of acres forested at the end of each year.

1. Problem Statement

Compute the number of acres forested at the end of each year for 20 years for a given area.

2. Input/Output Description

Input—the identification number for the area of land, the total acres, the number of acres with trees, and the reforestation rate

Output—a table with a row of data for each of 20 years. Each row of information contains the number of acres reforested during that year and the total number of acres forested at the end of the year.

3. Hand Example

Assume that there are 14,000 acres total with 2500 acres uncut. If the reforestation rate is 0.02, we can compute a few entries as shown:

Year 1 $2500 \times 0.02 = 50$ acres of new growth
original 2500 acres + 50 new acres = 2550 acres forested

Year 2 $2550 \times 0.02 = 51$ acres of new growth
original 2550 acres + 51 new acres = 2601 acres forested

Year 3 $2601 \times 0.02 = 52.02$ acres of new growth
original 2601 acres + 52.02 new acres = 2653.02 acres forested

4. Algorithm Development

The overall structure is a counting loop that is executed 20 times, once for each year. Inside the loop we need to compute the number of acres reforested during that year and add that number to the acres forested at the beginning of the year; this will compute the total number of acres forested at the end of the year. The output statement should be inside the loop because we want to print the number of acres forested at the end of each year.

Decomposition

Read initial information.
Print headings.
Print report.

Initial Pseudocode

```
Timber: Read initial information
        Print headings
        For year = 1 to 20 do
            Compute reforested amount
            Add reforested amount to uncut amount
            Print reforested amount, uncut amount
```

Clearly, an error condition exists if the uncut area exceeds the total area. We will test for this condition and exit after printing an error message if it occurs. It is possible to imagine soil conditions that would result in a zero or negative reforestation rate, so we will not perform any error checking on the rate. However, all the values read will be printed, or echoed, so that the user can recognize an error in an input value. We now add these refinements to our initial pseudocode.

Final Pseudocode

```
Timber: Read identification, total, uncut, rate
        Print identification, total, uncut, rate
        If uncut > total then
            Print error message
        Else
            Print headings
            For year = 1 to 20 do
                refor ← uncut × rate
                uncut ← uncut + refor
                Print year, refor, uncut
```

From the pseudocode, the overall structure of the program is evident. The outer structure is an IF-ELSE structure, with a DO loop in the ELSE portion.

FORTRAN Program

```
*-----------------------------------------------------------------------*
      PROGRAM TIMBER
*
*  This program computes a reforestation summary
*  for an area that has not been completely harvested.
*
      INTEGER ID, YEAR
      REAL TOTAL, UNCUT, RATE, REFOR
*
      PRINT*, 'ENTER LAND IDENTIFICATION (INTEGER)'
      READ*, ID
      PRINT*, 'ENTER TOTAL NUMBER OF ACRES'
      READ*, TOTAL
      PRINT*, 'ENTER NUMBER OF ACRES UNCUT'
      READ*, UNCUT
      PRINT* 'ENTER REFORESTATION RATE'
      READ*, RATE
*
      IF (UNCUT.GT.TOTAL) THEN
         PRINT*, 'UNCUT AREA LARGER THAN ENTIRE AREA'
      ELSE
         PRINT 5, ID, TOTAL, UNCUT, RATE
    5    FORMAT (/'REFORESTATION SUMMARY'//
     +           1X,'IDENTIFICATION NUMBER ',I5/
     +           1X,'TOTAL ACRES = ',F10.2/
     +           1X,'UNCUT ACRES = ',F10.2/
     +           1X,'REFORESTATION RATE = ',F5.3//
     +           1X,'YEAR  REFORESTED  TOTAL REFORESTED')
         DO 15 YEAR = 1,20
            REFOR = UNCUT*RATE
            UNCUT = UNCUT + REFOR
            PRINT 10, YEAR, REFOR, UNCUT
   10       FORMAT (1X,I3,F11.3,F17.3)
   15    CONTINUE
      END IF
*
      END
*-----------------------------------------------------------------------*
```

5. Testing

Using the test data from the hand example, a typical interaction is

```
ENTER LAND IDENTIFICATION (INTEGER)
25563
ENTER TOTAL NUMBER OF ACRES
14000.0
ENTER NUMBER OF ACRES UNCUT
2500.0
ENTER REFORESTATION RATE
0.02

REFORESTATION SUMMARY

IDENTIFICATION NUMBER 25563
TOTAL ACRES =   14000.00
UNCUT ACRES =    2500.00
REFORESTATION RATE = 0.020

YEAR  REFORESTED  TOTAL REFORESTED
  1     50.000         2550.000
  2     51.000         2601.000
  3     52.020         2653.020
  4     53.060         2706.080
  5     54.122         2760.202
  6     55.204         2815.406
  7     56.308         2871.714
  8     57.434         2929.148
  9     58.583         2987.731
 10     59.755         3047.486
 11     60.950         3108.436
 12     62.169         3170.604
 13     63.412         3234.017
 14     64.680         3298.697
 15     65.974         3364.671
 16     67.293         3431.964
 17     68.639         3500.604
 18     70.012         3570.615
 19     71.412         3642.028
 20     72.841         3714.868
```

The numbers match the ones we computed by hand. Try an example to test the error condition by using an uncut area larger than the total area. What happens if the reforestation rate is 0.00 or −0.02? Should there be an upper limit on the reforestation rate? This information is not given in the original problem, so we probably should not set one arbitrarily. What happens if you enter 14,000.0 instead of 14000.0? It might be a good idea to remind the program user not to use commas in numbers. How would you do this?

3·9 ■ Nested DO loops

DO loops can be nested within other DO loops, just as we used IF structures within other IF structures. The following rules apply to writing and executing *nested DO loops:*

1. A nested DO loop cannot use the same index as a loop that contains it.
2. A nested DO loop must be completely within the outer DO loop. For example, if the DO statement is within another DO loop, the CONTINUE statement for the nested loop must also be within the outer loop.
3. DO loops that are independent of each other may use the same index, even if they are all contained within another DO loop.
4. When one loop is nested within another, the inside loop is completely executed each pass through the outer loop.
5. Although nested DO loops can end on the same CONTINUE statement, we recommend that you end each loop with a separate CONTINUE so that the indenting can be consistent.

Listed below are a set of valid loops and a set of invalid loops.

Valid Loops

```
      DO 15 I=1,5
         DO 10 J=1,8
            DO 5 K=2,10,2
               ...
 5          CONTINUE
10       CONTINUE
15    CONTINUE
```

```
      DO 15 I=1,5
         DO 10 K=1,8
            ...
10       CONTINUE
         DO 5 K=2,10,2
            ...
 5       CONTINUE
15    CONTINUE
```

Invalid Loops

```
      DO 15 I=1,5
         DO 10 J=1,8
            DO 5 K=2,10,2
               ...
10       CONTINUE
         ...
 5          CONTINUE
15    CONTINUE
```

(overlapping loops)

```
      DO 20 J=1,5
         DO 10 J=1,8
            ...
10       CONTINUE
         DO 15 K=2,10,2
            ...
15       CONTINUE
20    CONTINUE
```

(same index for dependent loops)

To illustrate the execution of a program with nested loops, consider the following:

```
*-----------------------------------------------------------------------*
      PROGRAM NEST
*
*  This program prints the indices in nested DO loops.
*
      INTEGER I, J
*
      PRINT*, '  I   J'
      PRINT*
```

```
      DO 20 I=1,5
         DO 10 J=3,1,-1
            PRINT 5, I, J
 5          FORMAT (1X,I3,3X,I3)
 10      CONTINUE
         PRINT*, '  END OF PASS'
 20   CONTINUE
*
      END
*-----------------------------------------------------------------*
```

The output is:

```
I      J

1      3
1      2
1      1
END OF PASS
2      3
2      2
2      1
END OF PASS
3      3
3      2
3      1
END OF PASS
4      3
4      2
4      1
END OF PASS
5      3
5      2
5      1
END OF PASS
```

The first time through the outer loop, I is initialized to the value 1. We thus begin executing the inner loop: The variable J is initialized to the value 3. After executing the PRINT 5 statement, we reach the end of the inner loop and J is decremented by 1 to the value 2. Because 2 is still larger than the final value of 1, we repeat the loop. J is decremented by 1 to the value 1, and the loop is repeated again. When J is decremented again, it is less than the final value of 1, so we have completed the inner loop and the message 'END OF PASS' is printed. I is incremented to 2, and we begin the inner loop again. This process is repeated until I is greater than 5.

Example 3-12

Experimental Sums

Write a complete program to read 20 data values. Compute the sum of the first 5 values, the next 5 values, and so on. Print the four sums. Assume that the values are real.

Solution

The **first step** is to state the problem clearly: Read 20 data values and compute the sum of the first five values, the second five values, and so on.

The **second step** is to describe the input and output:

Input—20 data values

Output—sum of the first five values, sum of the second set of five values, and so on for all 20 data values

The **third step** is to work a simple example by hand. Assume we have six values and we want to sum them in groups of two. Then we have three sums to compute, and for each sum we add two values.

values — 4, 6, 1, −2, 7, −2

The corresponding sums are 10, −1, 5

The **fourth step** is to develop an algorithm. Although we will read a total of 20 data values, we need only 5 values at a time; thus, an outer loop is needed to read four sets of data. Each set of data is 5 values; thus, the inner loop reads the 5 values. It is important to initialize to zero the variable being used to store the sum before the inner loop is begun. We then add 5 values, print the sum, and set the sum back to zero before we read the next values.

The decomposition is a single step in this problem; all the other steps are performed inside the overall loop.

Decomposition

Read data, and compute and print sums.

The refinement in pseudocode illustrates the structure of this algorithm, which is a loop within a loop.

Pseudocode

```
Sums: For i = 1 to 4 do
            sums ← 0
            For j = 1 to 5 do
                  Read value
                  sum ← sum + value
            Print sum
```

We can now translate the pseudocode into FORTRAN.

FORTRAN Program

```
*-----------------------------------------------------------------------*
      PROGRAM SUMS
*
*  This program reads 20 values and prints
*  the sum of each group of 5 values.
*
      INTEGER I, J
      REAL SUM, VALUE
*
```

```
      DO 15 I=1,4
         SUM=0.0
*
         DO 5 J=1,5
            READ*, VALUE
            SUM = SUM + VALUE
    5    CONTINUE
*
         PRINT 10, I, SUM
   10    FORMAT(1X,'SUM ',I1,' = ',F6.2)
   15 CONTINUE
*
      END
*-----------------------------------------------------------------------*
```

The **fifth step** is to test the program. Here is a sample of the type of output that would be printed from this program after the 20 values have been entered.

```
SUM 1 =  23.44
SUM 2 =  10.23
SUM 3 =  -5.69
SUM 4 =   1.01
```

Example 3-13

Factorial Computation

Write a complete program to compute the factorial of an integer. A few factorials and their corresponding values are shown (an exclamation point following a number symbolizes a factorial):

$$0! = 1$$
$$1! = 1$$
$$2! = 2 \times 1$$
$$3! = 3 \times 2 \times 1$$
$$4! = 4 \times 3 \times 2 \times 1$$
$$5! = 5 \times 4 \times 3 \times 2 \times 1$$

Compute and print the factorial for four different values that are read from the terminal.

Solution

The **first step** is to state the problem clearly: Compute the factorial of values read from the terminal.

The **second step** is to describe the input and output:

Input — four data values

Output — factorial of each of the four data values

The **third step** is to work a simple example by hand:

$$0! = 1$$
$$1! = 1$$
$$2! = 2 \times 1 = 2$$
$$3! = 3 \times 2 \times 1 = 6$$
$$4! = 4 \times 3 \times 2 \times 1 = 24$$
$$5! = 5 \times 4 \times 3 \times 2 \times 1 = 120$$

The **fourth step** is to develop an algorithm. Because the factorial of a negative number is not defined, we should include an error check in our algorithm for this condition. In computing a factorial, we use a counting loop to perform the successive multiplications. Because the overall structure of this problem solution is a loop, the decomposition is again a single step.

Decomposition

Read values, and compute and print factorials.

As you read the following pseudocode, notice that the overall structure of the algorithm is a counting loop. Within the counting loop are an input statement and an IF-ELSE structure. Within the ELSE portion is another counting loop.

Pseudocode

```
Fact: For i = 1 to 4 do
          Read n
          If n < 0 then
              Print error message
          Else
              nfact ← 1
              If n > 1 then
                  For k = 1 to n do
                      nfact ← nfact × k
              Print n, nfact
```

FORTRAN Program

```
*-----------------------------------------------------------------------*
      PROGRAM FACT
*
*  This program computes the factorial
*  of four values read from the terminal.
*
      INTEGER I, N, NFACT, K
*
      DO 20 I=1,4
         PRINT*, 'ENTER N'
         READ*, N
*
         IF (N.LT.0) THEN
*
            PRINT 5, N
    5       FORMAT (1X,'INVALID N = ',I7)
*
         ELSE
*
            NFACT = 1
            IF (N.GT.1) THEN
               DO 10 K=1,N
                  NFACT = NFACT*K
   10          CONTINUE
            END IF
            PRINT 15, N, NFACT
   15       FORMAT (1X,I4,'! = ',I8)
*
         END IF
   20 CONTINUE
*
      END
*-----------------------------------------------------------------------*
```

The **fifth step** is to test the program. The output from a sample run of this program is

```
ENTER N
3
   3! =        6
ENTER N
-2
INVALID N =      -2
ENTER N
11
  11! = 39916800
ENTER N
0
   0! =        1
```

SELF-TEST 3-3

This self-test allows you to check quickly to see if you have remembered some of the key points from Section 3–9. If you have any problems with the exercises, you should reread this section. The solutions are included at the end of the text.

For problems 1–3, give the value in COUNT after each of the following loops is executed. Assume that COUNT is initialized to zero before starting each problem.

1.
```
      DO 10 IN=5,15
         DO 5 K=2,0,-1
            COUNT = 100 + 1
    5    CONTINUE
   10 CONTINUE
```

2.
```
      DO 10 K=0,5
         DO 5 J=5,-5,-2
            COUNT = COUNT + 1
    5    CONTINUE
   10 CONTINUE
```

3.
```
      DO 10 I=5,14,2
         DO 5 K=4,0
            COUNT = COUNT + 1
    5    CONTINUE
         COUNT = COUNT + 1
   10 CONTINUE
```

Summary

This chapter greatly expanded the types of problems we can solve in FORTRAN with use of IF statements: We can now control the order in which statements are executed. An important property of these statements is that they are entered only at the top of the structure and that they have only one exit; with only one entrance and one exit, this type of flow promotes the writing of simpler programs. We also learned to use both While loops and DO loops to implement repetition steps—most of the programs in the rest of the text will use either one or the other of these loop structures.

Debugging Aids

The most helpful debugging tool is the PRINT* statement. Just knowing that your program is working incorrectly does not tell you where to begin looking for errors. If you have the computer print the values of key variables at different points in your program, however, it becomes easier to isolate the parts of the program that are not working correctly. The locations of these checkpoints, or places to write the values of key variables, depend on the program; some of the obvious places are after reading new values for variables and after completing loops and computations.

It is also a good idea to number the checkpoints and then print the checkpoint number along with the other values. For instance, if you print the values of X and Y at several checkpoints, it may not be obvious which set of X and Y values have been printed. However, the following output is clear:

```
CHECKPOINT 3: X = 14.76  Y = -3.82
```

If you have narrowed the problem to an IF statement, then first check the condition. Did you use .LT. when you needed .LE.? Be careful when not using .NOT. in an expression because the relationships can get complex. For example, .NOT.((A.EQ.1.0).OR.(B.EQ.2.0)) is also equal to (A.NE.1.0).AND.(B.NE.2.0).

Another possible error with IF statements can be traced to values being close to, but not exactly equal to, the desired value. For instance, suppose that the result of a mathematical computation should have a real value of 5.0. Because computers have limitations on the number of digits of accuracy, the result might be 4.999 or 5.001; if you check only for 5.0, you may not realize that you really have the correct value. One way to address this problem is to use the IF statement to look for values close to 5.0. For instance, if

$$|X - 5.0| < .001$$

then X is between 4.999 and 5.001. If this is close enough for the problem being solved, then replace the statement

```
IF (X.EQ.5.0) SUM = SUM + 1
```

with this statement

```
IF (ABS(X-5.0).LE.001) SUM = SUM + 1
```

If you believe that a programming error is within a While loop, print the values of key variables at the beginning of the loop; this information will be printed each time the loop is executed, so you should be able to locate the trouble spot.

Most errors in a DO loop involve the loop parameters. When a program error seems to involve a DO loop, print the value of the index or count variable immediately within the loop. After executing the loop with this output statement, you can answer the following questions:

1. Did the index start with the correct value?
2. Did the index increment by the proper amount?
3. Did the index have the correct value during the last execution of the loop?

If the answer to any of these questions is no, check the DO statement itself; you probably have an error in the variables or expressions that you specified.

If the error is not in your original specification of the DO statement, print the values of the index at both the beginning and the end of the loop statements. After executing the loop with these two output statements, you will be able to determine if the value of the index is changed by the statements inside the loop. If the index is modified, either you have used the index inadvertently, which can be corrected, or you should replace the DO loop with a While loop.

Another common error associated with DO loops occurs when a similar variable name is used instead of the index. For instance, if the index of the DO loop is INDEX, use INDEX and not I inside the loop when you intend to use the index value.

Style/Technique Guides

The larger a program grows in size, the more apparent becomes the programmer's style—not only does bad style/technique become more obvious, it also becomes harder to correct. Practicing good style/technique in your small programs builds habits that will carry over into all your programming.

One of the best guides to good style is to use the While loop and the DO loop consistently. With a little practice, you will find that all loops fit easily into one of these two forms. As we pointed out in the summary, these types of loops have only one entrance and one exit—enhancing readability and adding simplicity to your program.

Another characteristic of good style is the use of indenting to emphasize the statements in If structures and loops. You can convince yourself of the importance of indenting if you try to follow a program written by someone else who has not indented statements within control structures. If loops are nested, indent each nested loop from the previous one.

Use the CONTINUE statement consistently to define the end of each DO loop. Although other statements are valid, the CONTINUE statement becomes an important part of the structure definition. Do not close more than one loop with the same CONTINUE statement.

Comment lines are yet another sign of good style; however, the use of comment lines can become excessive. Use only as many lines as are needed to show the program's organization and enhance its readability. Comment lines should be easy to distinguish from FORTRAN statements. We use blank lines before and after our comments and also use lowercase letters within the comment itself. You should always use initial comments to describe the purpose of the program. If needed, comments may be used throughout the program to identify processes, values, variables, and so on. You will also find that blank comment lines can be effective in separating different steps within a program—this technique is often used in our example programs.

A program that exhibits good style will save time in the long run because it is easier to debug. Programmers who may need to modify your programs in future projects will also appreciate your good style. Changing a few lines of FORTRAN code to achieve this will be time well spent.

Key Words

branch
compound logical expression
condition
control structure
counting loop
DO loop
flowchart
IF structure
increment value
index
initial value
iterative loop
limit value
logical expression
logical operator
logical value
loop
nested loop
parameter
pseudocode
relational operator
repetition
selection
sequence
structured programming
While loop

■ Problems

We begin our problem set with modifications to programs given earlier in this chapter. Give the decomposition, refined pseudocode or flowchart, and FORTRAN program for each problem.

Problems 1 – 5 modify the light pipe program PIPE, given on page 115.

1. Modify the light pipe program so that the user enters the incidence angle in radians instead of degrees.
2. Modify the light pipe program so that it reads the index of refraction for two materials and then prints the range of angles of incidence (between 0° and 90°) necessary for the pipe to transmit light.
3. Modify the light pipe program so that it contains a DO loop that allows the user to enter 5 sets of data.
4. Modify the light pipe program so that it contains a While loop that allows the user to keep entering data until a refraction index of 0.0 is read.
5. Modify the light pipe program so that it reads the refraction index for the rod material. Then, for an incidence angle of 45°, give the range of refraction indices for materials that will create light pipes.

Problems 6 – 10 modify the rocket trajectory program RCKET1, given on page 124.

6. Modify the rocket trajectory program so that it stops if the rocket impacts or the total time exceeds 50 seconds.
7. Modify the rocket trajectory program so that it starts time at zero seconds and increments it by 1 second until the height is less than 50 feet; then increment time by 0.25 seconds.
8. Modify the rocket trajectory program so that it starts time at zero seconds and increments it by 0.5 seconds until the height is less than 80 feet; then increment time by 0.25 seconds.
9. Modify the rocket trajectory program so that it reads two values, INCR1 and INCR2. Start time at zero seconds and increment it by INCR1 seconds until the distance is less than 50 feet; then increment time by INCR2 seconds.
10. Modify the rocket trajectory program so that it does not print a table but instead prints two values. The first value is the time at which the rocket begins falling back to the ground and the second value is the time at which the rocket impacts. Start time at zero and increment it by 0.01 seconds.

Problems 11 – 15 modify the suture packaging program SEALS, given on page 129.

11. Modify the suture packaging program so that it also writes the total number of batches rejected.
12. Modify the suture packaging program so that it also writes the number of batches in each rejection category.
13. Modify the suture packaging program so that it prints an error message if the information is entered for a batch that should not have been rejected. Do not count this batch in the overall count of rejected batches.

14. Modify the suture packaging program so that it also counts and writes the total number of batches with ranges out of bounds on more than one of the parameters.
15. Modify the suture packaging program so that it counts and prints the total number of batches with ranges out of bounds on all three parameters.

Problems 16–20 modify the timber management program TIMBER, given on page 143.

16. Modify the timber management program so that a value N is read from the terminal, where N represents the number of years that are to be used in printing the table.
17. Modify the timber management program so that it computes information for 20 years but only prints information for every other year (second year, fourth year, and so on). (Hint: Review the MOD function.)
18. Modify the timber management program so that a value of M is read from the terminal, where M represents the number of years that should be between lines in the output table. (Problem 17 is a special case where M = 2.)
19. Modify the timber management program so that instead of printing data for 20 years, it prints yearly information until at least 10 percent of the cut area has been reforested.
20. Modify the timber management program so that it prints only the final line of data after 20 years and then allows the user to input a different reforestation rate. The program should then print the final line of data after 20 years with this new reforestation rate and again allow the user to input a different reforestation rate. The program should end when a reforestation rate of 0.00 is entered. Thus, the user can compare the results of several reforestation rates over the same 20 years.

For problems 21–24, write complete FORTRAN programs to print tables showing the values of the input variables and the function shown using DO loops to control the loops.

21. Print a table of values for K where

$$K = 2M - M^2$$

for values of $M = 1, 2, \ldots, 10$.

22. Print a table of values for K where

$$K = |J - 3J + \sqrt{J}|$$

for values of $J = 0, 1, 2, \ldots, N$, where N is read from the terminal.

23. Print a table of values for Y where

$$Y = \cos X$$

for values of $X = 0.0, 10.0, \ldots, 350.0$ where the units of X are in degrees.

24. Print a table of values for F where

$$F = XY - 1$$

for values of $X = 1, 2, \ldots, 9$ and values of $Y = 0.5, 0.75, 1.0, \ldots, 2.5$.

Develop new programs in problems 25–41. Use the five-phase design process.

25. Write a program to read three integers I, J, K. Then, determine if the integers are in ascending order ($I \leq J \leq K$), or if the integers are in descending order ($I \geq J \geq K$), or if they are in neither order. Print an appropriate message.
26. A set of 20 temperatures has been recorded during an experiment. We want to compute and print the average temperature, and we also want to determine if a new record low or record high temperature occurred during this particular experiment. Therefore, on one line we enter the previous low temperature and the previous high temperature. The remaining 20 temperatures are entered one per line. Read this information and print the average. If a new record low or high occurred, print an appropriate message.
27. The sine function is a function of angle. However, if the sine is written such that the angle is represented by ωt, where ω is an angular frequency in radians per second and t is time in seconds, then we call the function a sinusoid. Therefore, a sinusoid has the following form:

$$s(t) = A\ sin(\omega t + \phi)$$

where A is the amplitude of the sinusoid, ω is the angular frequency, and ϕ is the phase angle. Write a program that reads A, ω, and ϕ and then prints a table containing values of t and $s(t)$ for times from 0.0 to 10.0 in increments of 0.5.
28. Modify the program in problem 27 such that the frequency f is read in Hz (cycles per second), where $f = \omega/2\pi$.
29. Modify the program in problem 27 such that the user also enters the starting time, the ending time, and the increment.
30. The period of a sinusoid is equal to $1/f$ where f is the frequency in Hz. Also, $f = \omega/2\pi$. Modify the program in problem 27 such that the program computes the period of the sinusoid and then prints 100 lines of the table of t and $s(t)$ covering one period of the sinusoid beginning with $t = 0.0$.
31. Write a program to print a table of consecutive even integers and their square values, beginning with 2 and continuing through 200. Use the following output format:

```
I AND I*I

2     4
4    16
.
.
.
```

32. Write a program to read a value FINAL. Print a table that contains values of X and $X \times X$, starting with X equal to zero and incrementing by 0.5, until X is greater than FINAL. Use the following output format:

```
X                    X SQUARED

0.0                  0.00
0.5                  0.25
.
.
.
```

33. Consider the trajectory of a stone which is hurled into the air with an initial velocity v at an angle to the horizontal of θ. Neglecting drag due to friction with the atmosphere, the following equations describe the stone's distance (d) from the initial spot and the height (h) of the stone at time t:

$$d = v \cdot t \cos \theta$$

$$h = v \cdot t \sin \theta - \frac{1}{2} g \cdot t^2$$

where g is the acceleration due to gravity (9.8 m/s² or 32 ft/s²). Write a program to read the initial velocity and angle and then print a table of distance and height values. Use intervals of 0.25 seconds between values and stop when the height becomes negative.

34. Write a program to read the coefficients A, B, C of a quadratic equation:

$$Ax^2 + Bx + C = 0$$

If the roots are positive or zero, print the values. If the roots are complex, compute the real and imaginary parts as two real numbers and print these values with appropriate literals.

35. Write a program that will read circuit inspection data from the terminal. Each line should contain a circuit ID number and the number of inspections successfully completed. If the number of inspections successfully completed is between 0 and 11, the inspection is in-progress; if the number of inspections successfully completed is 12, the inspection is complete and the circuit passes inspection; and if the number of inspections is -1, the inspection is complete but the circuit has failed the inspection. Thus, the classification of a circuit is based on the following table:

Classification	**Test Completed**
In-progress	0–11
Passed	12
Failed	−1

The program should print a report similar to the following, with a line of output for each circuit:

```
INSPECTION REPORT

CIRCUIT ID AND CLASSIFICATION
XXXXX - XXXXXXXXXXX
.
.
.
```

An ID of 999 will indicate the end of the data.

36. Modify problem 35 so that a final summary report follows the inspection report and has the following form:

```
INSPECTION SUMMARY

IN-PROGRESS                XXXX
PASSED                     XXXX
FAILED                     XXXX

TOTAL CIRCUITS                 XXXXX
```

37. A rocket is being designed to test a retrorocket that is intended to permit softer landings. The designers have derived the following equations that they believe will predict the performance of the test rocket, where t represents the elapsed time in seconds:

$$\text{ACCELERATION} = 4.25 - 0.015t^2$$

$$\text{VELOCITY} = 4.25t - 0.005t^3$$

$$\text{DISTANCE} = 90 + 2.125t^2 - 0.00125t^4$$

The distance equation gives the height above ground level at time t. Thus, the first term (90) is the height in feet above ground level of the nose of the rocket launch. To check the predicted performance, the rocket will be "flown" on a computer, using the derived equations. Write a program to print the time, height, velocity, and acceleration for the rocket from a time of zero seconds through 50 seconds, in increments of 1 second. Use the following report form:

```
                     ROCKET FLIGHT SIMULATION

TIME           ACCELERATION        VELOCITY        DISTANCE
(SEC)          (FT/SEC*SEC)        (FT/SEC)        (FT)

XXX.XX            XXXX.XX           XXXX.XX        XXXX.XX
  .
  .
  .
```

38. A biologist, after discovering the omega bacterium, has spent 5 years determining its characteristics. She has found that the bacterium has a constant growth rate. If 10 cells are present with a growth factor of 0.1, the next generation will have $10 + 10(0.1) = 11$ cells. Write a program that will report with the following format:

```
                       OMEGA BACTERIA GROWTH

                   NUMBER OF CELLS   PETRI DISH        GROWTH
CULTURE NUMBER     INITIALLY         DIAMETER (CM)     RATE

    XXXX           XXXX              XXX               XX.XX

GENERATION  NUMBER OF CELLS   % AREA OF PETRI DISH COVERED
    1           XXXX.X                 XXX.XX
    .
    .
    .
    5
```

Ten cells occupy 1 square millimeter. Use the following input data for four cultures:

```
                              OMEGA BACTERIA GROWTH

                       NUMBER OF CELLS    PETRI DISH          GROWTH
   CULTURE NUMBER      INITIALLY          DIAMETER (M)        RATE

        1984               100              10 cm              0.50
        1776              1300               5 cm              0.16
        1812               600              15 cm              0.55
        1056               700               8 cm              0.80
```

39. The square of the sine function can be represented by the following:

$$\sin^2 x = x^2 - \frac{2^3x^4}{4!} + \frac{2^5x^6}{6!} - \cdots = \sum_{n=1}^{\infty} \frac{(-1)^{n+1}2^{2n-1}x^{2n}}{(2n)!}$$

Write a program to evaluate this series for an input value, x, printing the results after 2, 4, 6, 8, . . . , 14 terms and comparing each sum to the true solution. Note that the term for $n = 1$ is x^2 and that all consecutive terms can be obtained by multiplying the previous term by

$$\frac{-(2x)^2}{2n(2n-1)}$$

The output should have the following form:

```
             COMPARISION OF VALUES OF SINE SQUARED

   NUMBER      SERIES         INTRINSIC     ABSOLUTE
   OF TERMS    SUMMATION      FUNCTION      DIFFERENCE

       2       XX.XXXX        XX.XXXX       XX.XXXX
       4       XX.XXXX        XX.XXXX       XX.XXXX
       .
       .
       .
      14
```

40. When N is an integer greater than or equal to zero, the expression $N!$ (called N factorial) represents the product of all integers from 1 through N. We define 0! to be equal to 1. The following are a few factorials and their corresponding values:

$$0! = 1$$

$$1! = 1$$

$$2! = 1 \times 2 = 2$$

$$3! = 1 \times 2 \times 3 = 6$$

An approximation to $N!$ can be computed using Stirling's formula

$$N! = \sqrt{2\pi N}\left(\frac{N}{e}\right)^N$$

where $e = 2.718282$. Write a program that reads a value of N from the terminal and then computes an approximation of $N!$ using Stirling's formula.

Print the following message before you read the value of N:

```
ENTER N WHERE N IS BETWEEN 1 AND 10
```

Limiting the size of N is necessary to ensure that the value of $N!$ will fit within our limits of integers on most computers. The output of the program should be in this form:

```
XX! IS APPROXIMATELY XXXXXXX
```

Continue reading values of N and computing an approximation to $N!$ until a negative value is read. If a value greater than 10 is read, print a message that the input is out of the specified range and ask the user to enter a new value.

41. The current-voltage relationship in an ideal *p-n* junction diode is described by the equation

$$I = I_s \left(e^{QV/kT} - 1\right)$$

where I = current through diode, amps
V = voltage across diode, volts
I_s = saturation current, amps
Q = electron charge, 1.6E−19 coulomb
k = Boltzmann's constant, 1.38E−23 joule/degree K
T = junction temperature, K

Write a program that calculates I as V varies from −0.250 V to 0.500 V in increments of 0.125 V, for junction temperatures of 32, 100, and 212 degrees Fahrenheit. (Use the following equation to convert degrees Fahrenheit to degrees Kelvin: K = (F − 32)×(5/9) + 273.16.) Saturation current is 1 microamp in all three cases. Your output should be in the following form:

```
JUNCTION TEMPERATURE = XXX.XX  F = XXX.XX K

VOLTAGE ACROSS DIODE          CURRENT THROUGH DIODE
       -0.250 V                   SO.XXXXESXX A
       -0.125 V                   SO.XXXXESXX A
         .
         .
         .
        0.500 V                   SO.XXXXESXX A
```

FORTRAN STATEMENT SUMMARY

CONTINUE Statement:

```
k CONTINUE
```

Example:

```
10 CONTINUE
```

Discussion:

The CONTINUE statement is used to define the end of a DO loop. The statement number of the CONTINUE statement is also referenced in the DO statement.

DO Statement

```
DO k index=initial,limit,increment
```

Examples:

```
DO 10 I=1,20
DO 20 TIME=1,200,5
DO 30 K=10,0,-1
DO 40 K=1,NUMBER
```

Discussion:

The DO statement defines an iterative loop where *k* is the statement number of the statement that represents the end of the loop; index is a variable used as the loop counter; initial represents the initial value given to the loop counter; limit represents the value used to determine when the DO loop has been completed; and increment represents the value to be added to the loop counter each time that the loop is executed. If the increment is omitted, an increment of 1 is assumed.

GO TO Statement:

```
GO TO n
```

Example:

```
GO TO 25
```

Discussion:

The GO TO statement is an unconditional branch to the executable statement with label *n*. It should be used only to implement the While loop.

Logical IF Statement:

IF *(condition) statement*

Examples:

```
IF (A.GT.15.5) COUNT = COUNT + 1

IF (X.LE.0.0) PRINT*, 'DATA ERROR'
```

Discussion:

The logical IF statement is used to execute a single statement if the condition is true. The statement on the same line as the condition may not be another IF statement.

Block IF Statement:

IF *(condition)* THEN
    set of statements
END IF

Example:

```
   IF (MIN.GE.60.0) THEN
      HOURS = HOURS + 1
      MIN = MIN - 60.0
      PRINT 5, HOURS
5     FORMAT (1X,I6,' HOURS')
   END IF
```

Discussion:

If the condition is true, then all the statements between the THEN and the corresponding END IF statement are executed. This statement differs from the IF statement in that it can execute more than one statement if the condition is true.

IF-ELSE Statement

IF *(condition)* THEN
    set of statements
ELSE
    set of statements
END IF

Example:

```
IF (TIME.GE.LAUNCH) THEN
   VELCTY = ACCEL*TIME
ELSE
   VELCTY = 0.0
END IF
```

Discussion:

The IF-ELSE statement allows you to execute one set of statements if the condition is true and a different set of statements if the condition is false.

■ **IF-ELSE IF** Statement

```
IF (condition 1) THEN
    set of statements
ELSE IF (condition 2) THEN
    set of statements
ELSE
    set of statements
END IF
```

Example:

```
      IF (TEMP.GE.65.0.AND.TEMP.LE.70.0) THEN
         PRINT 5
5        FORMAT (1X,'NORMAL TEMPERATURE')
      ELSE IF (TEMP.LT.65.0) THEN
         PRINT 6
6        FORMAT (1X,'LOW TEMPERATURE')
      ELSE
         PRINT 7
7        FORMAT (1X,'HIGH TEMPERATURE')
      END IF
```

Discussion:

The IF-ELSE IF statement includes several conditions. The conditions are tested in the order in which they appear in the statement. When a true condition is encountered, the set of statements following that condition is executed; control then passes to the statement following the END IF. If none of the conditions are true, the set of statements following the ELSE statement is executed. The ELSE statement at the end of the IF-ELSE IF statement is optional.

■ **LOGICAL** Statement

```
LOGICAL variable list
```

Examples:

```
LOGICAL DONE

LOGICAL SORTED, ERROR
```

Discussion:

The LOGICAL statement explicitly lists all variables that are to store logical values. These variables may have values of either true or false.

4 Engineering and Scientific Data Files

4

APPLICATION

Weather Satellites

Meteorology is the science that deals with the atmosphere and its phenomena, and especially with weather and weather forecasting. Technology has aided meteorologists in the prediction of weather with satellites that collect images worldwide and with remote sensing stations that constantly relay weather information. In addition, technology has developed new tools such as Doppler radar, which measures wind speed and direction. A great deal of information about the weather can also be learned from analyzing past and present data to observe the conditions that lead to extreme weather events such as tornadoes, hurricanes, typhoons, and microbursts. (See Section 4–3 for the solution to a problem related to this application.)

Photo of typhoon Pat, © Weatherstock/NASA.

Introduction

Engineers and scientists must frequently analyze large amounts of data. It is not reasonable to enter all this data into the computer by hand each time it is needed. We can enter the data once into a data file; then each time that the data is needed, we can read it from the data file. In addition to printing data for a report, we can write it into a data file; other programs can then easily access the data. In this chapter, we learn how to read information from existing data files and how to generate new data files.

4-1 ■ I/O Statements

In our programs in the previous chapters, we used READ statements when we needed information entered during the execution of the program. For small amounts of data, this interaction through the keyboard is satisfactory. However, for large amounts of data it is not feasible to enter the data every time we need to run the program. A *data file* is a file that contains data that can be read by a program. A data file can be built in two ways — it can be generated by another program, or it can be generated using a word processor or an editor. Each line of the data file is a *record*. A record in a FORTRAN 77 program file contains a computer language instruction, while a record in a data file contains data values. Once a file is generated, it can be listed or updated using an editor or a word processor. For now, our data files will contain only numbers, but in Chapter 8 we learn how to work with character information.

To use data files with our programs, we must use some new statements and some extensions of old statements. Each of these statements references the filename that is assigned when a file is built. If you build a data file with a word processor or an editor, you assign the filename when you enter the data. If you build a data file with a program, you include a statement in the program that gives the file a name.

If a file is going to be used in a program, it must be opened before any processing can be done with the file. The OPEN statement gives the program several important pieces of information about the file, including the name of the file and whether the file is an input file or an output file. In addition, the OPEN statement connects the file to the program using a unit number that corresponds to the file. Then, within the program, whenever we want to refer to the file, we use the unit number. Since there may be several files used in the same program, the unit number gives us a method for uniquely specifying a file. The general form of the OPEN statement that we use in this chapter is the following:

```
OPEN (UNIT=integer expression, FILE=filename, STATUS=literal)
```

The integer expression designates the unit number assigned to the file, the filename refers to the name given to the file when it was built, and the STATUS literal tells the computer whether the file is an input file or an output file. If the file is an input file, it is specified with STATUS='OLD'; if the file is an output file, it is specified with STATUS='NEW'.

The OPEN statement must precede any READ or WRITE statements that use the file. Also, the OPEN statement should be executed only once; therefore, it should not be inside a loop. Some systems require a REWIND statement after opening an input file to position the file at its beginning. The REWIND statement and additional advanced information on building and accessing data files are presented in Chapter 9.

To read from a data file, we use an extension of the list-directed READ statement that has the following form:

READ *(unit number,*) variable list*

Formatted READ statements are not commonly used with data files, so we have included the discussion on them in Chapter 9. To write information to a data file, we use a new statement—a WRITE statement. Just like the PRINT statement, the WRITE statement can be used with list-directed output or formatted output. The list-directed WRITE statement has the following form:

WRITE *(unit number,*) expression list*

The formatted WRITE statement has the following general form:

WRITE *(unit number, k) expression list*

where *k* is the statement number of the corresponding FORMAT statement. In all of these general forms, the unit number corresponds to the unit number assigned in the OPEN statement. The asterisk following the unit number specifies that we are using list-directed input or output.

Most computer systems have several input or output devices attached to them. Each device is assigned a unit number. For example, if a laser printer has been assigned unit number 8, then the following statement would write the values of X and Y using the laser printer:

```
WRITE (8,*) X, Y
```

Many systems assign the standard input device (typically the terminal keyboard) to unit number 5 and the standard output device (typically the terminal screen) to unit number 6; these devices are used when your program executes READ* or PRINT* statements. Avoid using preassigned unit numbers with your data files; if your computer system assigns unit numbers 5 and 6 as previously defined, do not use them with your data files. Otherwise, errors could result if your program assigned a data file to unit 6 and the program then executed a PRINT* statement. The name of the file is determined when the file is built, but we may choose any unit number to refer to the file as long as the number is not preassigned by our computer system. Thus, in one program, we could use unit 10 to refer to a file of experimental velocity measurements, and then in another program, we could use unit 12 to refer to the same file.

When we finish executing a program that has used files, the files are automatically closed before the program terminates. Occasionally there are situations in which you would like to specifically close, or disconnect a file from your program. The FORTRAN statement to close a file has the following general form:

```
CLOSE (UNIT=integer expression)
```

In Chapter 9, we present additional options for the CLOSE statements.

We now summarize some important rules to remember when reading data from data files.

1. Each READ statement will start with a new line of data. If there are values left on the previous line that were not read, they will be skipped.
2. If a line does not contain enough values to match to the list of variables on the READ statement, another data line will automatically be read to acquire more values. Additional data lines will be read until values have been acquired for all the variables listed on the READ statement.
3. A READ statement does not have to read all the values on the data line; however, it does have to read all the values on the line prior to the values that you want. For example, if a file has 5 values per line and you are interested in the third and fourth values, you must read the first and second values to get to the third and fourth values, but you do not need to read the fifth value.

In order to use the correct READ statement, you must know how the values were entered in the data file. For example, assume that a data file contains two numbers per line, representing a time and a temperature measurement. Also assume that the first three lines of the file contain the following information:

line 1:	0.0	89.5
line 2:	0.1	90.3
line 3:	0.2	90.8

The following statement will correctly read a time and temperature value from the data file:

```
READ (10,*) TIME, TEMP
```

However, it would be incorrect to use the following two statements in place of the previous statement:

```
READ (10,*) TIME
READ (10,*) TEMP
```

The execution of these two statements reads two lines from the data file, not one. For example, if the two statements are the first READ statements to be executed using this file, the value of TIME will be 0.0 and the value of TEMP will be 0.1. Not only will we have the wrong values in our variables, but also there will not be an error message to let us know that something is wrong. This example illustrates the importance of carefully testing our programs with known data before we use them with other data files.

SELF-TEST 4-1

This self-test allows you to check quickly to see if you have remembered some of the key points from Section 4–1. If you have any problems with the exercises, you should reread this section. The solutions are included at the end of the text.

The data file LAB1 contains the following information, which represents a time and temperature for each line:

line 1:	0.0	86.3
line 2:	0.5	93.5
line 3:	1.0	95.5
line 4:	1.5	97.8
line 5:	2.0	98.2
line 6:	2.5	99.1

Give the values of the variables after executing these statements. For each problem, assume that the data file has been opened but no previous READ statements have been executed.

1. `READ (10,*) TIME, TEMP`

2.
```
READ (10,*) TIME
READ (10,*) TEMP
```

3. `READ (10,*) TIME1, TEMP1, TIME2, TEMP2`

4.
```
READ (10,*) TIME1, TEMP1
READ (10,*) TIME2, TEMP2
```

5.
```
READ (10,*) TIME1
READ (10,*) TEMP1
READ (10,*) TIME2
READ (10,*) TEMP2
```

6.
```
READ (10,*) TIME1, TIME2
READ (10,*) TEMP1, TEMP2
```

4·2 ■ Techniques for Reading Data Files

To read information from a data file, we must first know some information about the file. In addition to the name of the file, we must know what information is stored in the file. This information must be very specific, such as the number of values entered per line and the units of the values. In addition, we need to know if there is any special information in the file that will be useful in deciding how many records are in the file, or how to determine when we have read the last record. This information is important because if we execute a READ statement after we have already read the last record in the file, we will get an execution error and the program will quit. We can avoid an execution error by using the information that we have about the file to decide what kind of loop we should use in the program. For example, if we know that there are 200 records in the file, then we can use a DO loop that is executed 200 times, and each time through the loop we read a record and perform the desired computations with the information. Often, we do not know ahead of time how many records are in the data file, but we know that the last record contains special values so that our program can test for them. For example, if a file contained time and temperature measurements, the last record could contain values of −999 for both measurements to signal that it is the last record. Then, we could exit a While loop when the time and temperature values are −999. Finally, a third situation arises when we do not know ahead of time how many records are in a file, and there is not a special value at the end of the file. A special option in the READ statement allows us to handle this situation.

We now discuss each of these three cases separately. For each case we use the same example so that you can compare the solutions.

Specified Number of Records

The first case we consider is the one in which we know or we can ascertain the number of records in the data file. If we know the exact number of records, a DO loop can be used to process the data. Sometimes, we generate files with special information, such as the number of valid data records, in the first record in the data file. Then, each time that we update the data file, we update the number in the first record. To process this file, we read the number at the beginning of the file using a variable, such as COUNT. Then we can execute a DO loop with COUNT as part of the DO statement. The following example illustrates reading a data file with a record count in the first record.

Example 4-1 ▶ **Average of Laboratory Data**

Assume that we have a data file named RESULTS1 that contains information collected from a laboratory experiment. Each line of the data file, except the first line, contains two numbers—a time value in seconds and a temperature measurement in degrees Fahrenheit. Read the data and compute the average temperature value. Print the number of data values and the average value.

Solution

The **first step** is to state the problem clearly: Compute and print the average of a set of temperature measurements.

The **second step** is to describe the input and output:

Input—time and temperature values in a data file named RESULTS1

Output—the average of the temperature values and a count of the temperature values

The **third step** is to work a simple example by hand. Assume that the data file contains the following information:

```
4
0.0      120
0.5      132
1.0      144
1.5      163
```

For this data, the total number of values is 4, and the average temperature is (120+132+144+163)/4, or 139.75° Fahrenheit.

The **fourth step** is to develop an algorithm, starting with the decomposition.

Decomposition

Read and compute a sum of temperature values.
Compute the average temperature.
Print the count and the average temperature.

When we convert the decomposition to pseudocode, we add the details that relate to the specific information in the data file.

Pseudocode

```
Soln1: sum ← 0
       Read count
       If count < 1 then
             Print error message
       Else
             For j=1 to count do
                   Read time, temperature
                   sum ← sum + temperature
             average ← sum / count
             Print count, average
```

FORTRAN Program

```
*----------------------------------------------------------------------*
      PROGRAM SOLN1
*
*  This program computes the average temperature using a set of times
*  and temperatures stored in a data file.  The first line of the data
*  file contains the number of actual data records that follow.
*
      INTEGER COUNT, J
      REAL SUM, TIME, TEMP
*
      OPEN (UNIT=10,FILE='RESULTS1',STATUS='OLD')
*
      READ (10,*) COUNT
```

```
      IF (COUNT.LT.1) THEN
*
         PRINT*, 'NO DATA ACCORDING TO RECORD COUNT'
*
      ELSE
*
         SUM = 0.0
         DO 20 J=1,COUNT
            READ (10,*) TIME, TEMP
            SUM = SUM + TEMP
   20    CONTINUE
         AVE = SUM/REAL(COUNT)
         PRINT 25, COUNT, AVE
   25    FORMAT (1X,'COUNT = ',I3,5X,'AVERAGE = ',F8.2,' DEGREES F')
*
      END IF
*
      END
*-----------------------------------------------------------------------*
```

The **fifth step** is to test the program. If we test this program using the hand example, the following information is printed:

```
COUNT =   4     AVERAGE =    139.75 DEGREES F
```

Trailer or Sentinel Signals

Special data values that are used to signal the last record of a file are called *trailer*, or *sentinel, signals*. When we generate the file, we add the special data values in the last record. Then, if we add or delete records from the file, we do not need to update a count; we only need to be sure that the last record still contains the special data values. When using a file with a trailer signal, we need to be careful that our program does not treat the information on the trailer line as regular data. For example, if we are counting the number of valid lines of data in the file, we want to be sure that we do not count the trailer line. Also, it is important to include the same number of data values on the trailer line as are on the rest of the lines in the data file. Since the trailer line is read with the statement that reads the other lines, it will try to read the line after the trailer line if there are not enough values on the trailer line; this will cause an execution error.

The following example illustrates reading a data file with a trailer record.

Example 4-2

Average of Laboratory Data

Assume that we have a data file named RESULTS2 that contains information collected from a laboratory experiment. Each line of the data file contains two numbers — a time value in seconds and a temperature measurement in degrees Fahrenheit. However, the last line of the file is a trailer signal that contains −999.0 for the time value and temperature values. Read the data and compute the average value. Print the number of data values and the average value.

Solution

The **first step** is to state the problem clearly: Compute and print the average of a set of temperature measurements.

The **second step** is to describe the input and output:

Input—time and temperature values in a data file named RESULTS2
Output—the average of the temperature values and a count of the temperature values

The **third step** is to work a simple example. Assume that the data file contains the following information:

```
0.0       120
0.5       132
1.0       144
1.5       163
-999.0    -999.0
```

For this data, the total number of values is 4, and the average temperature is (120+132+144+163)/4, or 139.75° Fahrenheit.

The **fourth step** is to develop an algorithm, starting with the decomposition.

Decomposition

Read and compute a sum of the temperature values.
Compute the average temperature.
Print the count and the average temperature.

Pseudocode

Soln2: sum ← 0
    count ← 0
    Read time, temperature
    While time ≠ −999.0 then
        sum ← sum + temperature
        count ← count + 1
        Read time, temperature
    If count = 0 then
        Print error message
    Else
        $\text{average} \leftarrow \dfrac{\text{sum}}{\text{count}}$
        Print count, average

FORTRAN Program

```
*-----------------------------------------------------------------------*
      PROGRAM SOLN2
*
*  This program computes the average temperature using a set of times
*  and temperatures stored in a data file.  The data file contains
*  a trailer line containing -999.0 for time and temperature.
*
      INTEGER COUNT
      REAL TIME, TEMP, SUM
*
      OPEN (UNIT=10,FILE='RESULTS2',STATUS='OLD')
*
      SUM = 0.0
      COUNT = 0
*
      READ (10,*) TIME, TEMP
    5 IF (TIME.NE.-999.0) THEN
         SUM = SUM + TEMP
         COUNT = COUNT + 1
         READ (10,*) TIME, TEMP
         GO TO 5
      END IF
*
      IF (COUNT.EQ.0) THEN
         PRINT*, 'NO DATA VALUES IN THIS FILE'
      ELSE
         AVE = SUM/REAL(COUNT)
         PRINT 25, COUNT, AVE
   25    FORMAT (1X,'COUNT = ',I3,5X,'AVERAGE = ',F8.2,' DEGREES F')
      END IF
*
      END
*-----------------------------------------------------------------------*
```

The **fifth step** is to test the program. If we test this program using the hand example, the following information is printed:

```
COUNT =   4     AVERAGE =    139.75 DEGREES F
```

■ END Option

If we do not know the number of data lines in a file, and if there is not a trailer signal at the end, we must use a different technique. In pseudocode, we want to perform these steps:

While there is more data do
  Read variables
  Process variables

To implement this in FORTRAN, we use an option available with the READ statement. This option tests for the end of the data and branches to a specified statement if the end is detected. A list-directed READ statement that uses this option has the following general form:

```
READ (unit number,*,END=n) variable list
```

As long as there is data to read in the data file, this statement executes exactly like this statement:

```
READ (unit number,*) variable list
```

However, if the last line of the data file has already been read and we execute the READ statement with the *END option*, then instead of getting an execution error, control is passed to the statement referenced in the END option. If the READ statement is executed a second time after the end of the data has been reached, an execution error will occur.

A READ statement with the END option is actually a special form of the While loop. When using it in a program, use the same indenting style as used in the While loop. A GO TO statement is also needed to complete the While loop, as shown:

```
 5 READ (10,*,END=15) TIME, TEMP
      SUM = SUM + TEMP
      COUNT = COUNT + 1
      GO TO 5
15 PRINT*
```

This special implementation of the While loop should be used only when you do not know the number of data lines to be read and there is no trailer signal at the end of the file. If you have a trailer value, test for that value to exit the loop instead of using the END option. The choice of the correct technique for reading data from a data file depends on the information in the data file. We now solve the problem of computing an average of laboratory data for a file with no trailer signal and no way to determine the number of records in the file before running the program.

Average of Laboratory Data . . . . Example 4-3

Assume that we have a data file named RESULTS3 that contains information collected from a laboratory experiment. Each line of the data file contains two numbers — a time value in seconds and a temperature measurement in degrees Fahrenheit. There is no special information in the first record containing the number of lines in the file, and there is no trailer signal. Read the data and compute the average value. Print the number of data values and the average value.

Solution

The **first step** is to state the problem clearly: Compute and print the average of a set of temperature measurements.

The **second step** is to describe the input and output:

Input — time and temperature values in a data file named RESULTS3
Output — the average of the temperature values and a count of the temperature values

The **third step** is to work a simple example by hand. Assume that the data file contains the following information:

```
0.0     120
0.5     132
1.0     144
1.5     163
```

For this data, the total number of values is 4, and the average temperature is $(120+132+144+163)/4$, or $139.75°$ Fahrenheit.

The **fourth step** is to develop an algorithm, beginning with the decomposition.

Decomposition

Read and compute a sum of the temperature values.
Compute the average temperature.
Print the count and the average temperature.

Pseudocode

Soln3: sum ← 0
    count ← 0
    While more data do
        Read time, temperature
        sum ← sum + temperature
        count ← count + 1
    If count = 0 then
        Print error message
    Else
        $\text{average} \leftarrow \dfrac{\text{sum}}{\text{count}}$
        Print count, average

FORTRAN Program

```
*--------------------------------------------------------------------*
      PROGRAM SOLN3
*
*  This program computes the average temperature using a set of times
*  and temperatures stored in a data file.  The data file contains
*  only the time and temperature values.
*
      INTEGER COUNT
      REAL SUM, TIME, TEMP
*
      OPEN (UNIT=10,FILE='RESULTS3',STATUS='OLD')
```

```
*
      SUM = 0.0
      COUNT = 0
*
    5 READ (10,*,END=15) TIME, TEMP
         SUM = SUM + TEMP
         COUNT = COUNT + 1
         GO TO 5
*
   15 IF (COUNT.EQ.0) THEN
         PRINT* 'NO DATA VALUES IN THE FILE'
      ELSE
         AVE = SUM/REAL(COUNT)
         PRINT 25, COUNT, AVE
   25    FORMAT (1X,'COUNT = ',I3,5X,'AVERAGE = ',F8.2,' DEGREES F')
      END IF
*
      END
*-----------------------------------------------------------------------*
```

The **fifth step** is to test the program. If we test this program using the hand example, the following information is printed:

```
COUNT =   4     AVERAGE =    139.75 DEGREES F
```

SELF-TEST 4-2

This self-test allows you to check quickly to see if you have remembered some of the key points from Section 4-2. If you have any problems with the exercises, you should reread this section. The solutions are included at the end of the text.

Assume that a data file contains time and altitude measurements from a rocket trajectory. Each line of the data file contains a corresponding time and altitude measurement. A trailer signal with a time equal to −99. 0 is used to signal the end of the data file. Assume that the program contains the following statements:

```
     READ (10,*) TIME, ALT
   5 IF (TIME.NE.-99.0) THEN
        PRINT*, TIME, ALT
        READ (10,*) TIME, ALT
        GO TO 5
     END IF
```

For each of the following data lines, indicate if the line would work properly as the trailer line. If the line would not work properly, explain why it would not work.

1. -99.0 -99.0
2. -99.0 100.0
3. 100.0 -99.0
4. -99.0
5. -99.0 100.0 15.7

4-3 Application ▪ Climatology Data

Meteorology

A number of national agencies are interested in weather information. NOAA (National Oceanic and Atmospheric Administration) is a research-oriented organization that studies the oceans and the atmosphere. It also funds environmental research in data analysis, modeling, and experimental work relative to global changes. The National Environmental Satellite, Data, and Information Service collects and distributes information relative to the weather. The National Climatic Data Center collects and compiles climatology information from National Weather Service offices across the country. It is also the National Weather Service offices that interact with state and local weather forecasters to keep the general public aware of current weather information.

The National Climatic Data Center in North Carolina is responsible for maintaining climatological data from National Weather Service offices. This data is available in many forms, including local climatology data by month, data by state, and data for the world. It also maintains historical climatology data beginning with 1931. Figure 4–1 contains a monthly summary of local climatology data that was collected by the National Weather Service office at Stapleton International Airport in Denver, Colorado for the month of December 1990. The summary contains 23 different pieces of weather information collected for each day, including maximum and minimum temperatures, amount of precipitation, peak wind gusts, and minutes of sunshine. This data is then analyzed to generate the monthly summary information at the bottom of the form, which includes average temperature, total rainfall, total snowfall, and number of days that were partly cloudy.

Assume that the weather information for Stapleton International Airport for December 1990 is stored in a data file named DEC90. Each record or line of information corresponds to the complete information collected for one day. Although the National Weather Service table shows 23 different fields, there are actually more than 23 pieces of data for each day in Figure 4–1. The degree-day information is labeled as 7A and 7B and will require two different values. The weather types category can contain several numbers for a day. For example, July 9, 1990 had heavy fog, thunderstorms, hail, and haze. Since there are nine different weather types, we use nine fields to store the weather types. If a field contains a zero, the weather type did not occur; if a field contains a one, then the weather type did occur. Thus, a total of 32 different values is needed for each line of the file.

In a few of the columns in Figure 4–1 the letter T is used to indicate a trace amount. In order to avoid using characters in the data file, the T is replaced with 0.001. For wind direction, the following table was used to convert wind direction to an integer:

Direction	Code
N	1
NE	2
E	3

Direction	Code
SE	4
S	5
SW	6
W	7
NW	8

Using the data in DEC90, determine the information needed to complete the entries in the following table:

Maximum Temperature Distribution
for December 1990

Temperature	Days
Below 0	xx
0–32	xx
33–50	xx
51–60	xx
61–70	xx
Over 70	xx

1. Problem Statement

Generate a table that gives the number of days with maximum temperatures in a group of specified ranges.

2. Input/Output Description

Input—date and temperature values from a data file DEC90

Output—a maximum temperature distribution table

3. Hand Example

Using the data from Figure 4–1, we can complete this table for December 1990:

Maximum Temperature Distribution
for December 1990

Temperature	Days
Below 0	3
0–32	5
33–50	13
51–60	5
61–70	5
Over 70	0

DEC 1990
DENVER, CO
NAT'L WEA SER OFC
10230 SMITH ROAD

ISSN 0198-7690

LOCAL CLIMATOLOGICAL DATA

Monthly Summary

STAPLETON INTERNATIONAL AP

LATITUDE 39° 45'N LONGITUDE 104° 52'W ELEVATION (GROUND) 5282 FEET TIME ZONE MOUNTAIN 23062

DEC 1990
DENVER, CO

DATE	TEMPERATURE °F: MAXIMUM	MINIMUM	AVERAGE	DEPARTURE FROM NORMAL	AVERAGE DEW POINT	DEGREE DAYS BASE 65°F: HEATING (SEASON BEGINS WITH JUL)	COOLING (SEASON BEGINS WITH JAN)	WEATHER TYPES (1 FOG, 2 HEAVY FOG, 3 THUNDERSTORM, 4 ICE PELLETS, 5 HAIL, 6 GLAZE, 7 DUSTSTORM, 8 SMOKE, HAZE, 9 BLOWING SNOW)	SNOW ICE PELLETS OR ICE ON GROUND AT 0500 INCHES	PRECIPITATION: WATER EQUIVALENT (INCHES)	SNOW, ICE PELLETS (INCHES)	AVERAGE STATION PRESSURE IN INCHES ELEV. 5332 FEET ABOVE M.S.L.	WIND (M.P.H.): RESULTANT DIR.	RESULTANT SPEED	AVERAGE SPEED	PEAK GUST: SPEED	PEAK GUST: DIRECTION	FASTEST 1-MIN: SPEED	FASTEST 1-MIN: DIRECTION	SUNSHINE: MINUTES	PERCENT OF TOTAL POSSIBLE	SKY COVER (TENTHS): SUNRISE TO SUNSET	MIDNIGHT TO MIDNIGHT
1	2	3	4	5	6	7A	7B	8	9	10	11	12	13	14	15	16	17	18	19	20	21	22	23
01	40	21	31	-4	22	34	0		0	0.00	0.0	24.760	33	3.8	6.3	23	NW	17	30	532	93	1	1
02	37	16	27	-8	8	38	0		0	0.00	0.0	24.630	31	6.8	8.7	48	W	28	29	342	60	6	3
03	41	13	27	-7	4	38	0		0	0.00	0.0	24.890	16	4.9	6.1	17	S	14	19	570	100	0	0
04	66	29	48	14	14	17	0		0	0.00	0.0	24.780	18	6.7	8.8	20	S	14	18	521	91	8	6
05	55	27	41	7	16	24	0		0	0.01	0.1	24.740	10	4.9	7.4	26	N	16	10	227	40	8	8
06	37	19	28	-6	18	37	0		1	0.04	0.7	24.940	17	2.4	4.6	14	N	12	01	547	96	1	4
07	60	23	42	8	17	23	0		0	0.00	0.0	24.830	18	5.5	6.7	18	S	13	18	499	88	4	2
08	64	22	43	9	15	22	0		0	0.00	0.0	24.820	17	2.9	4.4	14	S	9	19	526	93	0	0
09	62	28	45	11	17	20	0		0	0.00	0.0	24.870	18	5.6	6.0	14	S	9	19	531	94	0	0
10	68	35	52	18	17	13	0		0	0.00	0.0	24.730	18	7.1	7.7	17	S	15	20	542	96	0	0
11	68*	37	53*	20	14	12	0		0	0.00	0.0	24.510	26	6.3	10.2	24	W	18	31	544	96	0	1
12	52	32	42	9	24	23	0		0	T	T	24.640	11	7.3	8.6	28	E'	15	08	440	78	8	7
13	39	24	32	-1	27	33	0	1 8	0	0.00	0.0	24.610	34	4.3	6.4	15	NW	9	34	361	64	7	8
14	44	21	33	0	9	32	0	2 8	0	T	T	24.440	29	13.6	15.1	51	W	33	29	463	82	4	4
15	50	18	34	1	0	31	0		0	0.00	0.0	24.620	24	0.7	5.0	31	NW	18	27	532	94	1	1
16	50	22	36	3	10	29	0		0	0.00	0.0	24.475	03	1.8	3.3	16	NE	7	04	411	73	6	8
17	37	24	31	-2	21	34	0		T	0.06	0.6	24.450	19	1.2	5.4	17	SE	8	19	460	82	6	5
18	46	25	36	4	12	29	0		0	0.00	0.0	24.260	26	3.4	11.0	40	W	28	28	412	73	6	6
19	28	-3	13	-19	5	52	0	1	0	0.05	1.5	24.360	04	7.6	9.2	22	N	18	01	26	5	10	8
20	-3	-16	-10	-42	-16	75	0	2 8	1	0.06	1.0	24.460	04	8.4	9.8	18	N	15	01	0	0	10	10
21	-7	-21	-14	-46	-22	79	0		2	0.01	0.2	24.540	07	3.9	4.8	13	E	9	05	279	50	4	5
22	-3	-25*	-14*	-46	-20	79	0	1 8	2	0.00	0.0	24.510	36	0.6	3.2	10	SW	7	35	456	81	1	1
23	21	-17	2	-30	-11	63	0	1	2	0.00	0.0	24.720	17	4.0	5.7	18	S	14	19	536	96	0	0
24	37	6	22	-9	1	43	0		2	0.00	0.0	24.640	18	2.2	6.0	20	S	15	18	499	89	7	4
25	18	2	10	-21	4	55	0		1	0.00	0.0	24.680	28	1.3	4.7	14	NW	9	33	455	81	7	5
26	29	1	15	-16	5	50	0		1	0.00	0.0	24.670	14	1.2	3.6	13	E	8	13	452	80	7	5
27	53	4	29	-2	8	36	0		1	0.00	0.0	24.440	20	3.9	5.9	22	S	14	19	542	96	4	3
28	36	2	19	-12	9	46	0	1	T	0.01	0.1	24.310	07	5.5	7.1	23	NE	15	05	442	79	5	6
29	2	-7	-3	-34	-8	68	0	1	T	0.03	0.5	24.530	05	5.1	7.8	17	NE	12	05	123	22	9	10
30	41	-8	17	-13	3	48	0		T	0.00	0.0	24.640	13	0.9	6.4	23	SE	14	33	549	97	2	1
31	57	16	37	7	10	28	0		T	0.00	0.0	24.740	23	3.1	8.0	29	NW	16	31	542	96	2	2
	SUM	SUM				TOTAL	TOTAL	NUMBER OF DAYS		TOTAL	TOTAL	FOR THE MONTH:								TOTAL	% FOR MONTH	SUM	SUM
	1225	370				1211	0			0.27	4.7	24.620	17	0.6	6.9	51	W	33	29	13361		134	124
	AVG.	AVG.	AVG.	DEP.	AVG.	DEP.	DEP.	PRECIPITATION		DEP.						DATE:14		DATE: 14		POSSIBLE		AVG.	AVG.
	39.5	11.9	25.7	-6.9	7.3	207	0	≥ .01 INCH.	8	-0.28										17505	76	4.3	4.0

NUMBER OF DAYS				SEASON TO DATE	
MAXIMUM TEMP.		MINIMUM TEMP.		TOTAL	TOTAL
≥ 90°	≤ 32°	≤ 32°	≤ 0°	2301	782
				DEP.	DEP.
0	8	29	7	-41	102

NUMBER OF DAYS	
SNOW, ICE PELLETS ≥ 1.0 INCH	2
THUNDERSTORMS	0
HEAVY FOG	2

CLEAR 12 PARTLY CLOUDY 13 CLOUDY 6

GREATEST IN 24 HOURS AND DATES			
PRECIPITATION		SNOW, ICE PELLETS	
0.09	19-20	1.8	19-20

GREATEST DEPTH ON GROUND OF SNOW, ICE PELLETS OR ICE AND DATE	
2	24+

* EXTREME FOR THE MONTH - LAST OCCURRENCE IF MORE THAN ONE.
T TRACE AMOUNT.
\+ ALSO ON EARLIER DATE(S).
HEAVY FOG: VISIBILITY 1/4 MILE OR LESS.
BLANK ENTRIES DENOTE MISSING OR UNREPORTED DATA.

DATA IN COLS 6 AND 12-15 ARE BASED ON 21 OR MORE OBSERVATIONS AT HOURLY INTERVALS. RESULTANT WIND IS THE VECTOR SUM OF WIND SPEEDS AND DIRECTIONS DIVIDED BY THE NUMBER OF OBSERVATIONS. COLS 16 & 17: PEAK GUST - HIGHEST INSTANTANEOUS WIND SPEED. ONE OF TWO WIND SPEEDS IS GIVEN UNDER COLS 18 & 19: FASTEST MILE - HIGHEST RECORDED SPEED FOR WHICH A MILE OF WIND PASSES STATION (DIRECTION IN COMPASS POINTS). FASTEST OBSERVED ONE MINUTE WIND - HIGHEST ONE MINUTE SPEED (DIRECTION IN TENS OF DEGREES). ERRORS WILL BE CORRECTED IN SUBSEQUENT PUBLICATIONS.

I CERTIFY THAT THIS IS AN OFFICIAL PUBLICATION OF THE NATIONAL OCEANIC AND ATMOSPHERIC ADMINISTRATION, AND IS COMPILED FROM RECORDS ON FILE AT THE NATIONAL CLIMATIC DATA CENTER

Kenneth D Hadeen
DIRECTOR
NATIONAL CLIMATIC DATA CENTER

noaa

NATIONAL OCEANIC AND ATMOSPHERIC ADMINISTRATION

NATIONAL ENVIRONMENTAL SATELLITE, DATA AND INFORMATION SERVICE

NATIONAL CLIMATIC DATA CENTER ASHEVILLE NORTH CAROLINA

Figure 4-1 Climatological data.

4. Algorithm Development

Decomposition

Set sums to zero.
Read the data and increment sums.
Print report.

Before we refine the decomposition into pseudocode, we must decide which of the three techniques for reading data files fit this situation. There is not an initial line in the file giving the number of lines that follow, and there is not a trailer signal. However, since the file contains information for each day of December, we know there are 31 lines in the file, so we can use a simple DO loop to read the data.

Pseudocode

```
Temp: Set five sums to zero
      For day = 1 to 31 do
          Read date, max
          Increment corresponding sum
      Print report
```

FORTRAN Program

```
*-----------------------------------------------------------------------*
      PROGRAM TEMP
*
*  This program determines the number of days with maximum temperature
*  in a group of intervals, using the information in a data file
*  for December 1990 at Stapleton International Airport.
*
      INTEGER SUMLOW, SUM32, SUM50, SUM60, SUM70, SUMHI, K, DATE, MAXTMP
*
      OPEN (UNIT=15,FILE='DEC90',STATUS='OLD')
*
      SUMLOW = 0
      SUM32 = 0
      SUM50 = 0
      SUM60 = 0
      SUM70 = 0
      SUMHI = 0
*
```

```
      DO 10 K=1,31
         READ (15,*) DATE, MAXTMP
         IF (MAXTMP.LT.0) THEN
            SUMLOW = SUMLOW + 1
         ELSE IF (MAXTMP.LE.32) THEN
            SUM32 = SUM32 + 1
         ELSE IF (MAXTMP.LE.50) THEN
            SUM50 = SUM50 + 1
         ELSE IF (MAXTMP.LE.60) THEN
            SUM60 = SUM60 + 1
         ELSE IF (MAXTMP.LE.70) THEN
            SUM70 = SUM70 + 1
         ELSE
            SUMHI = SUMHI + 1
         END IF
   10 CONTINUE
*
      PRINT 20
   20 FORMAT (1X,'Maximum Temperature Distribution',/,
     +        1X,'for December 1990',//,
     +        1X,'Temperature',6X,'Days',/)
      PRINT 30, SUMLOW, SUM32, SUM50, SUM60, SUM70, SUMHI
   30 FORMAT (1X,'Below 0 ',9X,I2,/,1X,'0-32    ',9X,I2,/,
     +        1X,'33-50   ',9X,I2,/,1X,'51-60   ',9X,I2,/,
     +        1X,'61-70   ',9X,I2,/,1X,'OVER 70 ',9X,I2,/)
*
      END
*-----------------------------------------------------------------------*
```

5. Testing

Using the data in the file DEC90, the output from this program is the following:

```
Maximum Temperature Distribution
for December 1990

Temperature       Days

Below 0             3
0-32                5
33-50              13
51-60               5
61-70               5
Over 70             0
```

4-4 Application ▪ Critical Path Analysis

Manufacturing Engineering

A critical path analysis is a technique used to determine the time schedule for a project. This information is important in the planning stages before a project is begun, and it is also useful to evaluate the progress of a project that is partially completed. One method for this analysis starts by breaking a project into sequential events, then breaking each event into various tasks. Although one event must be completed before the next one is started, various tasks within an event can occur simultaneously. The time it takes to complete an event, therefore, depends on the number of days required to finish its longest task. Similarly, the total time it takes to finish a project is the sum of the times it takes to finish the individual events.

Assume that the critical path information for a major construction project has been stored in a data file in the computer. You have been asked to analyze this information so that your company can develop a bid on the project. Specifically, the management would like a summary report that lists each event along with the number of days for the shortest task in the event and the number of days for the longest task in that event. In addition they would like the total project length computed in days and converted to weeks (five days per week).

The data file named PROJECT contains three integers per line. The first number is the event number, the second number is the task number, and the third number is the number of days required to complete the task. The data has been stored such that all the task data for event 1 is followed by all the task data for event 2, and so on. The task data for a particular event is also in order. You do not know ahead of time how many entries are in the file, but there is an upper limit of 98 total events, so a trailer signal is used to indicate the last line in the data file. The last line will contain a value of 99 for the event number and zeros for the corresponding task and days.

1. Problem Statement

Determine and print a project completion timetable.

2. Input/Output Description

Input — a data file named PROJECT that contains the critical path information for the events in the project

Output — a report

3. Hand Example

Use the following set of project data for the hand example:

Event Number	Task Number	Days
1	1	5
1	2	4
2	1	3
2	2	7
2	3	4
3	1	6
99	0	0

The corresponding report based on this data is shown next:

```
PROJECT COMPLETION TIMETABLE
EVENT NUMBER      TASK MINIMUM      TASK MAXIMUM
     1                 4                 5
     2                 3                 7
     3                 6                 6
TOTAL PROJECT LENGTH = 18 DAYS
                     = 3 WEEKS 3 DAYS
```

4. Algorithm Development

Decomposition

Read project event data and print event information
Print summary information

To develop an algorithm, we look at the way we compiled the data in the hand example. Because all the data for the first event is together, we scan down the list of data for event 1 and keep track of the minimum number of days and maximum number of days. When we reach the task for event 2, we print the information related to event 1 and then repeat the process for event 2. We continue until we reach event 99, which is a signal that we do not have any more data. We print the information for the last event and then print the summary information using a total in which we accumulated the total maximum number of days for all the events.

Initial Pseudocode

```
Path: total ← 0
      Read event, task, days
      number ← event
      min ← days
      max ← days
```

```
While not done do
      If same event then
            Update min and max
      Else
            Print number, min, max
            total ← total + max
            number ← event
            min ← days
            max ← days
      Read event, task, days
Print number, min, max for last event
Print total
```

As we refine the pseudocode, we need to be more specific about how we determine if we are done. We also need to add more details to the update for the minimum and maximum days for an event. Finally, when we print the total, we also need to compute and print the number of weeks.

Final Pseudocode

```
Path: total ← 0
      Read event, task, days
      number ← event
      min ← days
      max ← days
      If event = 99 then
            done ← true
      Else
            done ← false
      While not done do
            If event = number then
                  If days < min then
                        min ← days
                  If days > max then
                        max ← days
            Else
                  Print number, min, max
                  total ← total + max
                  number ← event
                  min ← days
                  max ← days
            Read event, task, days
            If event = 99 then
                  done ← true
      Print number, min, max for last event
      weeks ← total/5
      plus ← total − weeks × 5
      Print total, weeks, plus
```

Note that we will need to do the computation for WEEKS so that the result is an integer instead of a real value.

FORTRAN Program

```
*-------------------------------------------------------------------------*
      PROGRAM PATH
*
* This program determines the critical path
* information from project data stored in a data file.
*
      INTEGER TOTAL, EVENT, TASK, DAYS, NUMBER, MIN, MAX, WEEKS, PLUS
      LOGICAL DONE
*
      OPEN (UNIT=8,FILE='PROJECT',STATUS='OLD')
*
      PRINT*, 'PROJECT COMPLETION TIMETABLE'
      PRINT*
      PRINT*, 'EVENT NUMBER     TASK MINIMUM     TASK MAXIMUM'
*
      TOTAL = 0
*
      READ (8,*) EVENT, TASK, DAYS
      NUMBER = EVENT
      MIN = DAYS
      MAX = DAYS
*
      IF (EVENT.EQ.99) THEN
         DONE = .TRUE.
      ELSE
         DONE = .FALSE.
      END IF
*
    5 IF (.NOT.DONE) THEN
         IF (EVENT.EQ.NUMBER) THEN
*
            IF (DAYS.LT.MIN) THEN
               MIN = DAYS
            ELSE IF (DAYS.GT.MAX) THEN
               MAX = DAYS
            END IF
*
         ELSE
*
            PRINT 10, NUMBER, MIN, MAX
   10       FORMAT (1X,I6,11X,I6,11X,I6)
            TOTAL = TOTAL + MAX
            NUMBER = EVENT
            MIN = DAYS
            MAX = DAYS
*
         END IF
         READ(8,*) EVENT, TASK, DAYS
         IF(EVENT.EQ.99) DONE = .TRUE.
         GO TO 5
      END IF
*
      PRINT 10, NUMBER, MIN, MAX
      TOTAL = TOTAL + MAX
*
```

```
      WEEKS = TOTAL/5
      PLUS = TOTAL - WEEKS*5
      PRINT 15, TOTAL
   15 FORMAT (/,1X,'TOTAL PROJECT LENGTH = ',I2,' DAYS')
      PRINT 20, WEEKS, PLUS
   20 FORMAT (1X,20X,' = ',I2,' WEEKS',I2,' DAYS')
*
      END
*-----------------------------------------------------------------------*
```

Note that the days remaining after subtracting the number of days in the full weeks could also have been computed using the MOD function, as shown here:

```
PLUS = MOD(TOTAL,5)
```

5. Testing

If we use the sample set of data from the hand example with this program, the following report is printed:

```
PROJECT COMPLETION TIMETABLE

EVENT NUMBER      TASK MINIMUM      TASK MAXIMUM
     1                 4                 5
     2                 3                 7
     3                 6                 6

TOTAL PROJECT LENGTH = 18 DAYS
                     =  3 WEEKS 3 DAYS
```

4-5 ■ Generating Data Files

To generate a data file we use the OPEN statement and the WRITE statement. However, before we start to write FORTRAN statements, a little planning is important. In Section 4–2, we covered three different techniques for reading data files. These techniques depended on whether the data file had a trailer signal, or whether we knew something about how many records were in the file. Therefore, the way that you generate a data file will determine the techniques that have to be used to read the file in other programs, so you want to carefully select the form that you choose for generating a data file.

A data file with a trailer signal is probably the simplest form of data file. You can add and delete records without updating any counters—you just have to be sure that the trailer record does not get deleted. Choosing a value for the trailer signal must be done carefully. For example, if the first field in the records in the data file is a temperature value, then you must be sure that the trailer signal is a value that can never be an actual data value. For example, suppose the trailer signal contained −9 as a temperature. Also suppose that a valid line of data in the file also contained a temperature of −9 degrees. The program would assume that the valid line of data was actually the trailer signal, and it would exit the loop without processing the rest of the data. Not only would your results be incorrect, but there would be no indication that an error occurred.

Using the first record in the data file to give the number of lines of actual valid data that follow in the data file makes reading the data file contents simple. However, every time information is added or deleted from the file, the number of valid records in the first line must be updated. If this number is not correct, your program will read fewer records than it should or it will try to read more records than exist in the file and an execution error will result.

If you decide to generate the file so that it contains nothing except valid data, then the file will need to be read using the END option with the READ statement. This is the simplest file to maintain—you don't have to worry about updating a count or choosing trailer information.

All three forms of data files are commonly used in engineering and scientific applications. Therefore, when you are working with a data file, do not automatically assume information about it. Check carefully so that you are using the appropriate technique for reading the file in order to have correct results. Similarly, when you generate a data file, make sure that the information on using the file is available with the file. Also make sure that the documentation in your program describes how the data file is being generated.

SELF-TEST 4-3

This self-test allows you to check quickly to see if you have remembered some of the key points from Section 4–5. If you have any problems with the exercises, you should reread this section. The solutions are included at the end of the text.

The following information contains the year and Richter scale readings of major earthquakes to hit California this century:

Year	Richter Scale	Year	Richter Scale
1906	8.3	1980	7.0
1911	6.6	1980	6.6
1923	7.2	1983	6.5
1925	6.3	1984	6.2
1926	6.1	1986	6.0
1927	7.7	1987	5.9
1933	6.3	1989	7.1
1940	6.7	1991	7.1
1952	7.8	1991	5.8
1968	6.4	1991	6.1
1971	6.4	1992	6.1
1979	6.4	1992	6.9

1. Assume this information is going to be stored in a data file using a trailer line. Determine a reasonable trailer line, and show the first 3 lines of the file and the last 3 lines of the file.
2. Assume this information is going to be stored in a data file in which the first line will contain a count of the valid data lines that follow. Show the first 3 lines of the file and the last 3 lines of the file.
3. Assume this information is going to be stored in a data file containing only valid information. Show the first 3 lines of the file and the last 3 lines of the file.
4. Of the three different ways of storing this data, which do you think is most appropriate for this data? Why?

4-6 Application ■ Sonar Signals

Acoustical Engineering

The study of sonar (SOund Navigation And Ranging) includes the generation, transmission, and reception of sound energy in water. Oceanological applications include ocean topography, geological mapping, and biological signal measurements; industrial sonar applications include fish finding, oil and mineral exploration, and acoustic beacon navigation; naval sonar applications include submarine navigation and submarine tracking. An active sonar system transmits a signal that often is a sinusoid with a known frequency. The reflections or echoes of the signal are then received and analyzed to provide information about the surroundings. A passive sonar system does not transmit signals but collects signals from sensors and analyzes them based on their frequency content.

To test algorithms that analyze sonar signals, engineers and scientists would first work with simple simulated sonar signals instead of actual sonar signals. A simple sonar signal can be represented by the following equation:[1]

$$x(t) = \sqrt{\frac{2E}{PD}}\cos(2\pi f_c t), \qquad 0 \le t \le PD$$

$$= 0, \qquad \text{elsewhere}$$

where E = the transmitted energy
PD = the pulse duration in seconds
f_c = the frequency in Hz

Durations of a sonar signal can range from a fraction of a millisecond to several seconds, and frequencies can range from a few hundred Hz to tens of kHz (kilohertz) depending on the sonar system and its desired operating range.

Write a program in which the user inputs the values for E, PD, and f_c. Then generate a data file called SONAR that contains samples of this sonar signal. The

[1] A. B. Baggeroer, Sonar signal processing, Chapter 6 of "Applications of Digital Signal Processing," Prentice-Hall, Englewood Cliffs, N.J., 1978.

sampling of the signal should cover the pulse duration and be such that there are 10 samples for every period of $x(t)$, where a period is equal to $1/f_c$ seconds. The data file should contain two values for every line: a time value (starting at zero) and the corresponding value of the sonar signal.

1. Problem Statement

Generate a sonar signal that contains 10 samples from each period of a specified sinusoid, covering a given time duration.

2. Input/Output Description

Input—the values of E (transmitted energy in joules), PD (pulse duration in seconds), and f_c (frequency in Hz)

Output—a data file named SONAR that contains time and signal values for the sonar pulse duration

3. Hand Example

For a hand example, we use the following values:

$$E = 500 \text{ joules}$$
$$PD = 0.5 \text{ milliseconds (ms)}$$
$$f_c = 3.5 \text{ kHz}$$

The period of the sinusoid is 1/3500, or approximately 0.3 ms. Thus, to have 10 samples per period, the sampling interval must be approximately 0.03 ms. The pulse duration is 0.5 ms, and thus we need 17 samples of the following signal:

$$\begin{aligned} x(t) &= \sqrt{\frac{2E}{PD}} \cos(2\pi f_c t) \\ &= \sqrt{\frac{1000}{0.0005}} \cos(2\pi(3500)t) \\ &= 1414.2 \cos(2\pi \; 3500 \; t) \end{aligned}$$

The values for the sonar signal are:

t (ms)	$x(t)$
0.0	1414.2
0.03	1117.4
0.06	351.7
0.09	−561.6
0.12	−1239.3
0.15	−1396.8

t (ms)	$x(t)$
0.18	−968.1
0.21	−133.1
0.24	757.77
0.27	1330.6
0.30	1345.0
0.33	794.9
0.36	−88.8
0.39	−935.2
0.42	−1389.2
0.45	−1260.1
0.48	−602.1

4. Algorithm Development

Decomposition

Read energy, pulse duration, frequency.
Compute amplitude, sampling time, number of points.
Generate file containing time values and sinusoid values.

The problem description did not specify using a trailer signal or an initial record with the number of lines in the data file; therefore, we will generate a data file with only valid data lines.

Pseudocode

Pulse: Read energy (E), pulse duration (PD), frequency

$$A \leftarrow \sqrt{\frac{2E}{PD}}$$

$$\text{period} \leftarrow \frac{1}{\text{frequency}}$$

$$\text{sample interval} \leftarrow \frac{\text{period}}{10}$$

$$\text{number of samples} \leftarrow \frac{PD}{\text{sample interval}}$$

For $k = 0$ to (number of samples − 1) do
    time ← k · (sample interval)
    signal ← A cos(2π frequency · time)
    Write time and signal to data file

FORTRAN Program

```
*-----------------------------------------------------------------------*
      PROGRAM PULSE
*
*  This program generates a sonar signal.
*
      INTEGER NUMBER, K
      REAL E, PD, FREQ, A, PERIOD, T, PI, TIME, SIGNAL
*
      OPEN (UNIT=10,FILE='SONAR',STATUS='NEW')
*
      PRINT*, 'ENTER TRANSMITTED ENERGY IN JOULES'
      READ*, E
      PRINT*, 'ENTER PULSE DURATION IN SECONDS'
      READ*, PD
      PRINT*, 'ENTER SINUSOID FREQUENCY IN HERTZ'
      READ*, FREQ
*
      A = SQRT(2.0*E/PD)
      PERIOD = 1.0/FREQ
      T = PERIOD/10.0
      NUMBER = NINT(PD/T)
      PI = 3.141593
*
      DO 10 K=0,NUMBER-1
         TIME = REAL(K)*T
         SIGNAL = A*COS(2.0*PI*FREQ*TIME)
         WRITE (10,*) TIME, SIGNAL
   10 CONTINUE
*
      END
*-----------------------------------------------------------------------*
```

The nearest integer function (NINT) was used in the computation of the number of samples to round the answer.

5. Testing

The terminal screen interaction and a plot of the SONAR file generated by MATLAB follow for a sample interaction:

Computer Output

```
ENTER TRANSMITTED ENERGY IN JOULES
500.0
ENTER PULSE DURATION IN SECONDS
0.005
ENTER SINUSOID FREQUENCY IN HERTZ
3500.0
```

Plot of the file SONAR

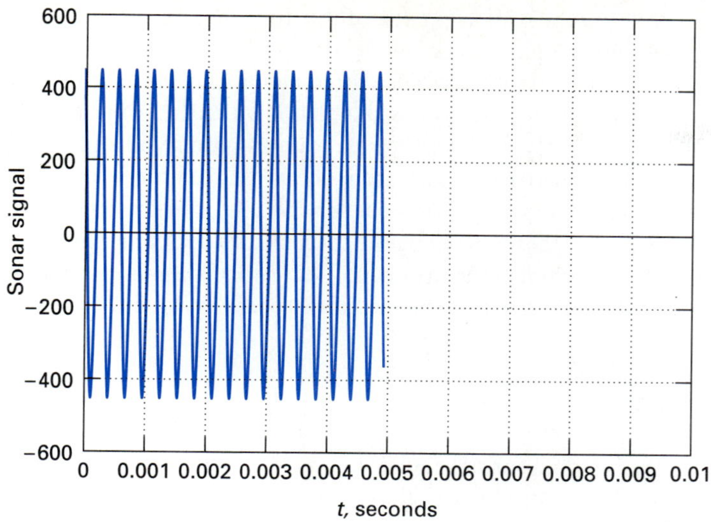

Summary

Data files are necessary in engineering and scientific applications involving large amounts of data. We presented the I/O statements for working with data files. We also discussed how to read information from data files. In particular, we discussed three techniques for reading data files that depend on whether there is a trailer signal or an initial line in the data file that contains the number of valid data records that follow it. We also discussed how to generate a data file. We will use data files frequently throughout this text.

Debugging Aids

When debugging a program with a data file, it is very important to be sure that your I/O statements are working properly. The following suggestions will help you identify errors in the data file I/O.

Input Data Files Test your program initially with a small data file so that you can print each line of the file as you read it. Check carefully to be sure that you are not skipping any data lines or data values that should be read. If the file has a trailer signal, print it out after you exit the loop reading the data. If the file has an initial count in the first record, print the count after reading it.

Output Data Files After you have generated a data file, list the contents of the data file. This is a good test to see if the data file is structured the way that you intended. Be especially careful that the number of values that you intend to be on the same line really are on the same line in the data file.

■ Style/Technique Guides

Almost all data files can be read using one of the three techniques that we presented in this chapter. Use these techniques as a model instead of writing them from scratch each time you read a data file. If you use these three models, including the loop structures and as many of the variable names as possible, there will be less opportunity for errors. Since you will be using only three structures, your programs will also be easier to read.

Be sure to include the basic information about the data file in the program documentation. This helps you remember what type of I/O is necessary to work with the data file. It is also a good idea to print on the screen or in a printed report the number of data records read or written in the program. This information is useful to the user and can be helpful in keeping track of the quantity of data in the file.

■ Key Words

data file
END option
record
sentinel signal
trailer signal

■ Problems

We begin our problem set with modifications to programs developed earlier in this chapter. Give the decomposition, pseudocode or flowchart, and FORTRAN program for each problem.

Problems 1–5 modify the climatology data program TEMP given on page 181.

1. Modify the climatology data program so that it computes the percentage of time that the maximum temperature fell in each of the categories.
2. Modify the climatology data program so that it prints the maximum and minimum temperatures and the first days of the month on which they occurred.
3. Modify the climatology data program so that it prints the maximum rainfall and the last day on which it occurred.
4. Modify the climatology data program so that it computes the average temperature for days with fog.
5. Modify the climatology data program so that it determines the date with the largest difference between the maximum temperature and the minimum temperature. Print the date, both temperatures, and the difference.

Problems 6–10 modify the critical path analysis program PATH, given on page 186.

6. Modify the critical path analysis program so that it prints the event number and task number for the task that requires the maximum amount of time.
7. Modify the critical path analysis program so that it prints the event number for the event that requires the maximum amount of time.

8. Modify the critical path analysis program so that it prints the average amount of time required for the tasks.
9. Modify the critical path analysis program so that it prints the event and task number for all tasks requiring more than five days.
10. Modify the critical path analysis program so that it prints a list of the events and the number of tasks in each event.

Problems 11 – 15 modify the sonar program PULSE, given on page 192.

11. Modify the sonar program so that the pulse duration is entered in milliseconds.
12. Modify the sonar program so that the user can specify the number of samples per period for sampling the sinusoid. (The program currently samples the sinusoid 10 times per period.)
13. Modify the sonar program so that the output data file has a trailer signal with −99.0 as the first number on the trailer line.
14. Modify the sonar program so that it prints a first line in the data file that contains the number of valid data lines that follow.
15. Modify the sonar program so that it scales the sinusoid so that its maximum absolute value is 1.0.

In problems 16-35 develop programs using the five-step process.

16. As a practicing engineer, you have been collecting data on the performance of a new solar device. You have been measuring the sun's intensity and the voltage produced by a photovoltaic cell exposed to the sun. These measurements have been taken every 30 minutes during daylight hours for 2 months. Because the sun sets at a different time each day, the number of measurements taken each day may vary.

    Each line of valid data contains the sun's intensity (integer), the time (24-hours, where 1430 represents 2:30 PM), and the voltage (real). A trailer signal contains 9999 for the sun's intensity. Write a complete program to read this data and compute and print the total number of measurements, the average intensity of the sun, and the average voltage value.
17. Write a program for a nutrition study that will read the value of N from the first line in a data file called WEIGHTS. If N is zero or negative, stop the program; otherwise, use N to specify the number of data lines remaining in the data file, where each data line contains an identification number (integer), the initial weight, and the final weight of a participant in the study. Print a table containing this original data and the percentage increase in weight for each participant. Number the lines. Use the following report form:

```
                         NUTRITION STUDY

           ID        INITIAL WT    FINAL WT      PERCENT INCREASE
     1.    XXX         XXX.X        XXX.X            XXX.XX
```

18. Write a program for analyzing pressure data. Read 20 lines of data with three

integer numbers per line from a data file called RESULTS. Each line represents pressure measurements made in three different chambers. Find the maximum pressure in each chamber and print the following:

```
MAXIMUM PRESSURE IN CHAMBER 1 = XXXX
MAXIMUM PRESSURE IN CHAMBER 2 = XXXX
MAXIMUM PRESSURE IN CHAMBER 3 = XXXX
```

19. Twenty-four temperature measurements for two compounds have been taken at 20-minute intervals over a period of time. Each pair of temperatures is entered in a data file TEMP in the order in which the measurements were made. Write a program to read the data and print it in the following manner:

```
TEMPERATURE MEASUREMENTS

TIME ELAPSED
HOURS AND MINUTES          COMPOUND 1         COMPOUND 2

0          0                 XXXXX              XXXXX
0         20                 XXXXX              XXXXX
0         40                 XXXXX              XXXXX
1         00                 XXXXX              XXXXX
1         20                 XXXXX              XXXXX
1         40                 XXXXX              XXXXX
2          0                 XXXXX              XXXXX
```

20. Modify problem 19 so that the following output lines are printed after the temperature measurements.

```
MINIMUM TEMPERATURE AND TIME ELAPSED (HOURS AND MINUTES)
      COMPOUND 1      XXXXX                 XX  XX
      COMPOUND 2      XXXXX                 XX  XX
```

21. Write a program to compute fuel cost information for an automobile. The input data is stored in a data file called MILES. The first line in the file contains the initial mileage (odometer reading). Each following data line contains information collected as the automobile was refueled and includes the new mileage reading, the cost of the fuel, and the number of gallons of fuel. The last line of the file contains a negative value and two zeros, instead of the refueling information. The output of the program should compute the cost per mile and the number of miles per gallon for each line of input data. Use the report format shown:

```
                  FUEL COST INFORMATION

MILES     GALLONS     COST     COST/MILE     MILES/GALLON
XXX.X     XX.X        XX.XX    X.XX          XX.X
```

22. Add the following summary information at the end of the report printed in problem 21:

```
          SUMMARY INFORMATION

    TOTAL MILES                XXXX.X
    TOTAL COST               XXXXX.XX
    TOTAL GALLONS              XXXX.X
    AVERAGE COST/MILE            X.XX
    AVERAGE MILES/GALLON         XX.X
```

23. Oil exploration and recovery is an important concern of large petroleum companies. Profitable oil recovery requires careful testing by drilling seismic holes and blasting with specific amounts of dynamite. For optimum seismic readings, a specific ratio between the amount of dynamite and the depth of the hole is required. Assume that each stick of dynamite is 2.5 feet long and weighs 5 pounds. The ideal powder charge requires a dynamite to depth-of-hole ratio of 1:3. Thus, a 60-foot hole would require 20 feet of dynamite, which is equal to 8 sticks, or 40 pounds. The actual powder charge is not always equal to ideal powder charge because the ideal powder charge may not be in 5-pound increments; in these cases, the actual powder charge should be rounded down to the nearest 5-pound increment. (You cannot cut or break the dynamite into shorter lengths for field operations.) The following example should clarify this process:

Hole depth = 85 feet
Ideal charge = 85/3 = 28.33333 feet
= 11.33333 sticks
= 56.666666 pounds
Actual charge = 55 pounds
= 11 sticks

Information on the depths of the holes to be tested each day is stored in a data file called DRILL. The first line contains the number of sites to be tested that day. Each following line contains integer information for a specified site that gives the site identification number and the depth of the hole in feet. Write a complete program to read this information and print the report in the following format:

```
                         DAILY DRILLING REPORT

SITE      DEPTH     IDEAL POWDER      ACTUAL POWDER      STICKS
ID        (FT)      CHARGE (LBS)      CHARGE (LBS)
12980     85         56.6666              55               11
```

24. Modify the program in problem 23 so that a final summary report follows the drilling report and has the form

```
TOTAL POWDER USED = XXXXX LBS   (XXXX STICKS)
TOTAL DRILLING FOOTAGE = XXXXXX FT
```

25. Modify the program in problem 24 so that it takes into consideration a special situation: If the depth of the hole is less than 30 feet, the hole is too shallow for blasting. Instead of printing the charge values for such a hole, print the site identification number, the depth, and the message HOLE TOO SHALLOW FOR BLASTING. The summary report should not include data for these shallow holes. Add a line to the summary report that contains the number of holes too shallow for blasting.

26. Beam analysis is an important part of the structural analysis conducted before construction of a building begins. A frequently used type of beam is a cantilever beam, which is fixed on one end and free on the other. The amount of deflection when a load is applied to this type of beam can be computed with

the following equation:

$$\text{deflection} = \frac{L \cdot a^2}{2E \cdot I}\left(\text{length} - \frac{a}{3.0}\right)$$

where L = applied load in pounds
a = length from fixed end to applied load in feet
E = elasticity of material (wood, steel, . . .)
I = moment of inertia of the beam, which can be computed with the following equation:

$$I = \frac{\text{base} \cdot \text{height}^3}{12}$$

Assume that we have information on five different beams in a data file BEAM. The data for each beam is given in the following five real values, which are stored in one data line in the proper units for the equations above:

Beam length
Beam base
Beam height
Elasticity constant
Applied load

Write a program to read the information for each beam and print a report that places the applied load at 1-foot intervals starting at 1 foot from the fixed end and moving down the length of the beam. The output for a beam should contain the following information:

```
BEAM NO.1    TOTAL LENGTH = XXX.XX FT

        DISTANCE OF LOAD FROM FIXED END        DEFLECTION
                    1.0                          XXX.XX
                    2.0                          XXX.XX
```

27. Modify the program in problem 26 so that the deflections for each beam are printed only as long as they are less than 5 percent of the beam length. When the beam deflection is greater than or equal to 5 percent, the program should stop computing values for that beam and go on to the next. If the deflection distance of 5 percent is never reached, the program should print an appropriate message. The header line for each beam should also contain the 5 percent length computation. An example of this output is

```
BEAM NO.  1          TOTAL LENGTH = 10.00 FT
                             5% OF LENGTH = 0.50 FT

        DISTANCE FROM FIXED END         DEFLECTION
              1.00                                   0.15
              2.00                                   0.38
              3.00                                   0.48
```

```
BEAM NO.  2              TOTAL LENGTH = 3.00 FT
                              5% OF LENGTH = 0.15 FT

          DISTANCE FROM FIXED END           DEFLECTION
                1.00                              0.04
                2.00                              0.09
                3.00                              0.12

                 DEFLECTION OF 5% OF LENGTH NOT REACHED
```

28. Assume that a data file called DATAXY contains a set of data coordinates that are to be used by several different programs. The first line of the file contains the number of data coordinates in the file, and each of the remaining lines contains the x and y coordinates for one of the data points. Since some of the programs need polar coordinates, we will generate a second data file that has each point in polar form, which is a radius and an angle in radians. Then, no matter how many programs use the data, it only has to be converted to polar coordinates once, and each program can then reference the appropriate file. Write a program to generate a new file called POLAR that contains the coordinates in polar form instead of rectangular form. The following equations convert a coordinate in rectangular form to polar form:

$$r = \sqrt{x^2 + y^2}$$

$$\theta = \arctan\left(\frac{y}{x}\right)$$

(Be sure that the first line of the new data file specifies the number of data coordinates.)

29. Rewrite the program from problem 28, assuming that the original file is POLAR and that it contains data coordinates in polar form. The new output file should be called DATAXY and should contain data coordinates in rectangular form. The equations for converting polar coordinates to rectangular coordinates are

$$x = r\cos(\theta)$$

$$y = r\sin(\theta)$$

30. Rewrite the program from problem 28 such that it creates a data file called POINTS. The first line of data should still contain the number of coordinates in the data file. Each following line of the data file should contain four values. The first two values represent the rectangular coordinates (x and y), and the next two values represent the corresponding polar coordinates (r and θ) for the data point.

The following set of problems refer to data files that contain the climatology data for one year, from May 1990 to April 1991, for Stapleton International Airport. Each file contains one month of data, stored in the same format as the data for December 1990 that was discussed on page 178. The file name contains the three-letter abbreviation for the month, plus the year; the file named SEP90 contains the data for September 1990.

31. Use the climatology data to determine and print the maximum temperature over the period June through August 1990.
32. Use the climatology data to determine and print the average rainfall for the period January through April 1991.
33. Use the climatology data to determine and print the maximum peak wind gust for each month in the period January through April 1991.
34. Use the climatology data to print a table giving the average temperature for each day in the first week of the months of November and December. Use the following format:

```
First Week Average Temperatures
           Nov           Dec
Day 1 xxx           xxx
.
.
.
Day 7
```

35. Use the climatology data to determine the maximum and minimum temperatures of the 12-month period covered by the data files. Print the temperatures and the last time they occurred in the files.

FORTRAN STATEMENT SUMMARY

OPEN Statement:

OPEN (UNIT=*integer expression*,FILE=*filename*,STATUS=*literal*)

Examples:

```
OPEN (UNIT=15,FILE='EXAMS',STATUS='OLD')
OPEN (UNIT=10,FILE='VELOCITY',STATUS='NEW')
```

Discussion:

The OPEN statement is used to connect a particular data file to a program. All I/O statements refer to the unit number in the OPEN statement. If the file is an input file, then its status is 'OLD'; if the file is an output file, then its status is 'NEW'.

■ READ * Statement:

READ *(unit number,*,*END=*n) variable list*

Examples:

```
READ (10,*) X, Y
READ (15,*,END=50) TIME, TEMP
```

Discussion:

This form of the READ statement is used with data files. The data file is referenced by the unit number, which must correspond to a unit number assigned to a file by an OPEN statement. The asterisk specifies that the statement is a list-directed input statement. The END clause is optional and will cause control to be passed to the statement with statement number *n* if the READ statement is executed after the last line of data has been read.

■ WRITE * Statement:

WRITE *(unit number,*) variable list*

Examples:

```
WRITE (13,*) A, B, C
WRITE (10,*) X
```

Discussion:

This WRITE statement is a list-directed output statement that writes information into a data file specified by the unit number. The unit number must correspond to the unit number of a file that has been assigned in an OPEN statement.

■ WRITE *k* Statement

WRITE *(unit number, k) variable list*

Examples:

```
WRITE (10,5) A, B, C
WRITE (15,15) X
```

Discussion:

The WRITE statement is a formatted output statement that writes information into a data file specified by the unit number. The unit number must correspond to the unit number of a file that has been assigned in an OPEN statement. The format statement is referenced by *k*.

5 Array Processing

5

APPLICATION

Jet Aerodynamics

To measure aerodynamic data for a new aircraft shape, an accurate scale model of the aircraft is mounted on a force-measuring support in a wind tunnel test chamber. The wind tunnel is then operated to generate a certain wind speed, or Mach number (which is the wind speed divided by the speed of sound), and measurements of the forces on the model are made at many different angles of the model relative to the wind direction. The Mach number is then adjusted to a new value, and another data set is collected. At the end of the tests, many sets of data have been collected and can be used to determine the lift, drag, and other aerodynamic performance characteristics of the new aircraft at its various operating speeds and positions. The model in the photo is larger than it seems — note the man standing next to one of the supports. (See Section 5 – 3 for the solution to a problem related to this application.)

Photo courtesy of NASA – Ames Research Center

Introduction

This chapter develops a method for storing groups of values without explicitly giving each value a different name—each group (called an array) has a common name, but individual values have a unique index or subscript. This technique allows us to analyze the data using loops, where the common name remains the same but the index or subscript becomes a variable that changes with each pass through the loop. Because the data values are stored in separate memory locations, we can also access the data as often as needed without rereading it.

5·1 ■ One-Dimensional Arrays

An *array* is a group of storage locations that have the same name. Individual members of an array are called *elements* and are distinguished by using the common name followed by a *subscript* or an index in parentheses. Subscripts are represented by consecutive integers, usually beginning with the integer 1. A *one-dimensional array* can be visualized as either one column of data or one row of data. The storage locations and associated names for a one-dimensional integer array J of 5 elements and a one-dimensional real array DIST with 4 elements are shown:

J(1)	2
J(2)	−5
J(3)	14
J(4)	80
J(5)	−12

1.2	−0.8	36.9	−0.07
DIST(1)	DIST(2)	DIST(3)	DIST(4)

■ Storage and Initialization

The DIMENSION statement, a nonexecutable statement, is used to reserve memory space or storage for an array. In its general form, a list of array names and their corresponding sizes follows the word DIMENSION, as shown:

```
DIMENSION array1(size), array2(size), . . .
```

Array sizes must be specified with constants, not variables. A DIMENSION statement that reserves storage for the two arrays previously mentioned is

```
DIMENSION J(5), DIST(4)
```

The number in parentheses after the array name gives the total number of values that can be stored in that array. Two separate DIMENSION statements, with one array listed in each statement, would also be valid but not preferable because it would require an extra statement. All DIMENSION statements must be placed before any executable statements in your program because they are specification statements.

The type of values stored in an array can be specified implicitly through the choice of array name or explicitly with a type specification statement. The following statement specifies that AREA is an array of 15 elements that contains integer values:

```
INTEGER AREA(15)
```

The typing of an array, whether implicit or explicit, applies to all elements of the array; hence, an array cannot contain both real values and integer values. Explicitly typed array names do not appear in DIMENSION statements because the array size has also been specified in the type statement. Because explicit typing is desirable, we will use explicit typing statements instead of DIMENSION statements for defining the arrays in our examples.

The range of subscripts associated with an array can be specified with a beginning subscript number and an ending subscript number. Both numbers must be integers separated by a colon and must follow the array name in the DIMENSION statement or the type statement. The following statements reserve storage for a real array TAX whose elements are TAX(0), TAX(1), TAX(2), TAX(3), TAX(4), and TAX(5) and an integer array INCOME whose elements are INCOME(−3), INCOME(−2), INCOME(−1), INCOME(0), INCOME(1), INCOME(2), and INCOME(3):

```
REAL TAX(0:5)
INTEGER INCOME(-3:3)
```

Also note that the following declarations are equivalent:

```
INTEGER AREA(1:15)
INTEGER AREA(15)
```

Unless otherwise stated, we will assume in our text that all array subscripts begin with the integer 1. However, there are situations in which the range of the subscripts logically starts with an integer other than 1. For example, if we have a set of population values for the years 1880–1980, it might be convenient to use the year to specify the corresponding population. We could specify such an array with the following statement:

```
INTEGER POPUL(1880:1980)
```

Then, if we wish to refer to the population for 1885, we use the reference POPUL(1885).

In Fortran 90, an array can be defined without specifying a size. During the execution of the program a size can be specified with the ALLOCATE statement. The memory used by the array can be released using the DEALLOCATE statement. Fortran 90

Values are assigned to array elements in the same way that values are assigned to regular variables. The following are valid assignment statements:

```
J(1) = 0
J(5) = NUM*COUNT
DIST(2) = 46.2 + SIN(X)
```

It is not valid to use an array name without a subscript in an assignment statement.

It is also extremely helpful to use variables and expressions, instead of constants, as subscripts. The following loop initializes all elements of the array J to the value 10. Observe that the variable I is used as a subscript and also as the DO loop index:

```
   DO 20 I=1,5
      J(I) = 10
20 CONTINUE
```

The next loop initializes the array J to the values shown:

```
   DO 30 I=1,5
      J(I) = I
30 CONTINUE
```

J(1)	J(2)	J(3)	J(4)	J(5)
1	2	3	4	5

The values of the array DIST are initialized to real values with this set of statements:

```
  DO 5 K=1,4
     DIST(K) = REAL(K)*1.5
5 CONTINUE
```

DIST(1)	DIST(2)	DIST(3)	DIST(4)
1.5	3.0	4.5	6.0

The previous examples illustrate that a subscript can be an integer constant or an integer variable. Subscripts can also be integer expressions, as indicated in the following statements:

```
J(2*I) = 3
R(J) = R(J-1)
B = TR(2*I) + TR(2*I+1)
```

Whenever an expression is used as a subscript, be sure the value of the expression is between the starting and ending subscript value. If a subscript is outside the proper range, the program will not work correctly. With some compilers, a logic error message is given if a subscript is out of bounds; other compilers use an incorrect value for the invalid array reference, causing serious errors that are difficult to detect.

Fortran 90

In Fortran 90, the contents of one array can be moved to another array of the same size with a single statement. Also, sections of an array (such as a column or row) can be specified for arithmetic operations using a single statement.

Input and Output

To read data into an array from a terminal or from a data file, we use the READ statement. If we wish to read an entire array, we can use the name of the array without subscripts. We can also specify specific elements in a READ statement. If the array A contains 3 elements, then the following two READ statements are equivalent; if the array A contains 8 elements, then the first READ statement reads values for all 8 elements and the second READ statement reads values for only the first 3 elements:

```
READ*, A
READ*, A(1), A(2), A(3)
```

Array values may also be read using an *implied DO loop.* Implied Do loops use the indexing feature of the DO statement and may be used only in input and output statements and in the DATA statement presented in Section 5–2. For example, if we wish to read the first 10 elements of the array R, we can use the following implied DO loop in the READ statement:

```
READ*, (R(I),I=1,10)
```

Further examples illustrate the use of these techniques for reading data into an array.

Temperature Measurements . . . . Example 5·1

A set of 50 temperature measurements has been entered into a data file, 1 value per line. The file is accessed with unit number 9. Give a set of statements to read this data into an array:

TEMP(l) ← line 1 of data file
TEMP(2) ← line 2 of data file
.
.
.
TEMP(50) ← line 50 of data file

Solution 1

The READ statement in this solution reads 1 value, but it is in a loop that is executed 50 times and reads the entire array:

```
   REAL TEMP(50)
   .
   .
   .
   DO 10 I=1,50
      READ (9,*) TEMP(I)
10 CONTINUE
```

Solution 2

The READ statement in this solution contains no subscript; thus, it reads the entire array:

```
REAL TEMP(50)
.
.
.
READ (9,*) TEMP
```

Solution 3

The READ statement in this solution contains an implied loop and is equivalent to a READ statement that listed TEMP(l), TEMP(2), . . ., TEMP(50):

```
REAL TEMP(50)
.
.
.
READ (9,*) (TEMP(I),I=1,50)
```

Note that Solution 2 and Solution 3 are exactly the same as far as the computer is concerned; they both represent one READ statement with 50 variables. Solution 1 is the same as 50 READ statements with 1 variable per READ statement. If the data file contains 50 lines, each with 1 temperature measurement, all three solutions store the same data in the array TEMP.

However, suppose that each of the 50 lines in the data file has two numbers: a temperature measurement and a humidity measurement. Solution 1 will read a new data line for each temperature measurement because it is the equivalent of 50 READ statements. But, because Solutions 2 and 3 are the equivalent of one READ statement with 50 variables listed, they will go to a new line only when they run out of data. Thus, the data is stored as shown:

TEMP(l) ← first temperature
TEMP(2) ← first humidity
TEMP(3) ← second temperature
TEMP(4) ← second humidity
.
.
.

This is a subtle, but important, distinction: the computer does not recognize that an error has occurred in the last example shown. It has data for the array and continues processing, assuming it has the correct data.

Example 5-2

Rainfall Data

A set of 28 daily rainfall measurements is stored in a data file, with 1 week of data per line. The unit number is again assumed to be 9. Give statements to read this data into an array called RAIN:

RAIN(1)	RAIN(2)	...	RAIN(7)	← line 1 of data file
RAIN(8)	RAIN(9)	...	RAIN(14)	← line 2 of data file
RAIN(15)	RAIN(16)	...	RAIN(21)	← line 3 of data file
RAIN(22)	RAIN(23)	...	RAIN(28)	← line 4 of data file

Correct Solution

The READ statement in this solution contains no subscript and thus reads the entire array. Because each line contains 7 data values, 4 lines of data are required:

```
REAL RAIN(28)
.
.
.
READ (9,*) RAIN
```

Incorrect Solution

The READ statement in this solution reads 1 value, and the READ statement is in a loop executed 28 times; thus, 28 lines of data are required. Because the data file contains only 4 lines of data, an execution error occurs:

```
      REAL RAIN(28)
      .
      .
      .
      DO 10 I=1,28
         READ (9,*) RAIN(I)
   10 CONTINUE
```

Techniques to print values in an array are similar to those used to read values into an array. The following examples illustrate the use of DO loops and implied loops for arrays in PRINT statements.

Mass Measurements . . . . Example 5·3

A group of 30 mass measurements is stored in a real array MASS. Print the values in the following tabulation:

```
MASS( 1) = XXX.X KG
MASS( 2) = XXX.X KG
.
.
.
MASS(30) = XXX.X KG
```

Solution

For each output line, we need to reference 1 value in the array. The values of the subscript can be generated with a DO statement that has an index of 1 – 30. The output form of this solution is important; go through it carefully to be sure you understand the placement of the literals in the FORMAT statement:

```
      REAL MASS(30)
      .
      .
      .
      DO 20 I=1,30
         PRINT 15, I, MASS(I)
   15    FORMAT (1X,'MASS(',I2,') = ',F5.1,' KG')
   20 CONTINUE
```

Example 5-4

Distance, Velocity, Acceleration

Arrays DIS, VEL, and ACC each contain 50 values: the first value in each array represents the distance, velocity, and acceleration, respectively, of a test rocket at time equal to 1 second. The second set of values represents data for time equal to 2 seconds, and so on. Print the data in the following tabulation:

```
TIME    DISTANCE    VELOCITY    ACCELERATION
(SEC)   (M)         (M/SEC)     (M/(SEC*SEC))
XXX     XXX.XX      XXX.XX      XXX.XX
```

Correct Solution

The index of the DO loop is used as a subscript for each array reference. This solution is the equivalent of 50 PRINT statements, each with 4 output variables:

```
      REAL DIS(50), VEL(50), ACC(50)
      .
      .
      .
      PRINT
    5 FORMAT (1X,'TIME   DISTANCE   VELOCITY   ACCELERATION')
      PRINT 6
    6 FORMAT (1X,'(SEC)  (M)        (M/SEC)    (M/(SEC*SEC))')
      DO 10 I=1,50
         PRINT 7, I, DIS(I), VEL(I), ACC(I)
    7    FORMAT (1X,I3,4X,F6.2,5X,F6.2,5X,F6.2)
   10 CONTINUE
```

Incorrect Solution

This solution is incorrect because, each time through the loop, we are printing the index I, the entire DIS array (50 values), the entire VEL array (50 values), and the entire ACC array (50 values)—thus, each time through the loop, we print 151 values.

```
      REAL DIS(50), VEL(50), ACC(50)
      .
      .
      .
      PRINT 5
    5 FORMAT (1X,'TIME   DISTANCE   VELOCITY   ACCELERATION')
      PRINT 6
    6 FORMAT (1X,'(SEC)  (M)        (M/SEC)    (M/(SEC*SEC))')
      DO 10 I=1,50
         PRINT 7, I, DIS, VEL, ACC
    7    FORMAT (1X,I3,4X,F6.2,5X,F6.2,5X,F6.2)
   10 CONTINUE
```

SELF-TEST 5-1

This self-test allows you to check quickly to see if you have remembered some of the key points from Section 5 – 1. If you have any problems with the exercises, you should reread this section. The solutions are included at the end of the text.

Problems 1 – 3 contain statements that initialize and print one-dimensional arrays. Show the output from each set of statements. Assume that each set of statements is independent of the others.

1.
```
      INTEGER I, M(10)
      DO 5 I=1,10
         M(I) = 11 - I
    5 CONTINUE
      PRINT*, 'ARRAY VALUES:'
      DO 15 I=1,10
         PRINT 10, I, M(I)
   10    FORMAT (1X,'M(',I2,') = ',I4)
   15 CONTINUE
```

2.
```
      INTEGER K, LIST(8)
      DO 5 K=1,8
         LIST(K) = K**2 - 4
    5 CONTINUE
      PRINT 10, LIST
   10 FORMAT (1X,8I4)
```

3.
```
      INTEGER J
      REAL TIME(20)
      TIME(1) = 3.0
      DO 5 J=2,20
         TIME(J) = TIME(J-1) + 0.5
    5 CONTINUE
      PRINT 10, (J,TIME(J),J=1,20,4)
   10 FORMAT (1X,'TIME ',I2,' = ',F5.2)
```

5-2 ■ DATA Statement

The DATA statement is a specification statement and is therefore nonexecutable; it is useful in initializing both simple variables and arrays. The general form of the DATA statement is

DATA *list of variable names/list of constants/*

An example of a DATA statement to initialize simple variables is

```
DATA SUM, VEL, VOLT, LENGTH /0.0,32.75,-2.5,10/
```

The number of data values must match the number of variable names. The data values should also be of the correct type so that the computer does not have to convert them. The preceding DATA statement initializes the following variables:

SUM	0.0
VEL	32.75
VOLT	−2.5
LENGTH	10

Because the DATA statement is a specification statement, it should precede any executable statements; it is therefore located near the beginning of your program, along with the REAL, INTEGER, LOGICAL, and DIMENSION statements. It follows these other statements because the specification of the types of variables or the declaration of an array should precede values given to the corresponding memory locations.

Caution should be exercised when using the DATA statement because it initializes values only at the beginning of program execution; this means that the DATA statement cannot be used in a loop to reinitialize variables. If it is necessary to reinitialize variables, you must use assignment statements.

If a number of values are to be repeated in the list of values, a constant followed by an asterisk indicates a repetition. The following statement initializes all 4 variables to zero:

```
DATA A, B, C, D /4*0.0/
```

The next statement initializes the variables I, J, and K to 1 and X, Y, and Z to 0.5:

```
DATA I, J, K, X, Y, Z /3*1,3*0.5/
```

A DATA statement can also be used to initialize one or more elements of an array:

```
INTEGER J(5)
REAL TIME(4)
DATA J, TIME /5*C,1.0,2.0,3.0,4.0/
```

J	0	0	0	0	0

TIME	1.0	2.0	3.0	4.0

```
REAL HOURS(5)
DATA HOURS(1) /60.0/
```

HOURS	60.0	?	?	?	?

The question marks indicate that some array elements were not initialized by the DATA statement. A syntax error would have occurred if the subscript was left off the array reference HOURS(1) because the number of variables would then not match the number of data values; that is, HOURS represents 5 variables, but HOURS(1) represents only 1 variable.

An implied loop can also be used in a DATA statement to initialize all or part of an array, as in

```
INTEGER YEAR(100)
DATA (YEAR(I),I=1,50) /50*0/
```

The first 50 elements of the array are initialized to zero, and the last 50 are not initialized. You must therefore make no assumptions about the contents of the last 50 values in the array.

5·3 Application ▪ Wind Tunnels

Aerospace Engineering

Wind tunnels are used to collect very accurate measurements of the lift and drag forces generated by a moving air stream on an aerodynamic body. When the data are subsequently used in engineering analyses, linear interpolation is frequently used to estimate values between the measured data points. Therefore, in this section, we discuss linear interpolation, and then we use linear interpolation in the analysis of the data from the wind tunnel.

Linear Interpolation

Interpolation is a numerical technique that is used to estimate unknown values of a function by using known values of the function at specific points. The simplest and probably the most popular interpolation method is linear interpolation. Essentially, all that is involved is connecting the data points with straight line segments and then interpolating for unknown values of the function on the straight line segments which connect adjacent data points. For example, consider the following graph that contains two values of a function at $x=1$ and at $x=3$. These two points have been connected with a straight line:

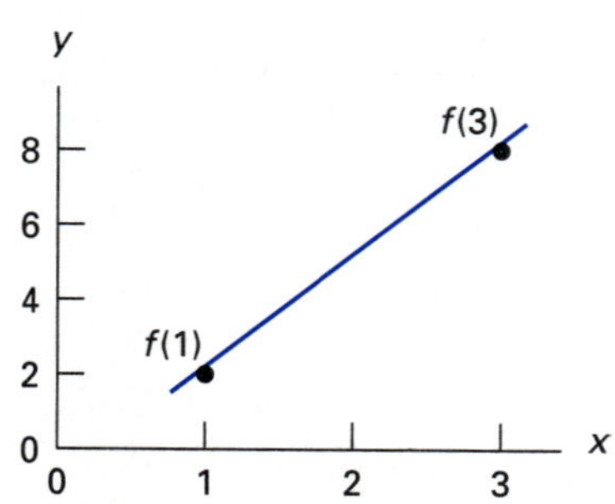

We can use linear interpolation to estimate the value of the function at $x=1.5$ using similar triangles, as shown in the following graph:

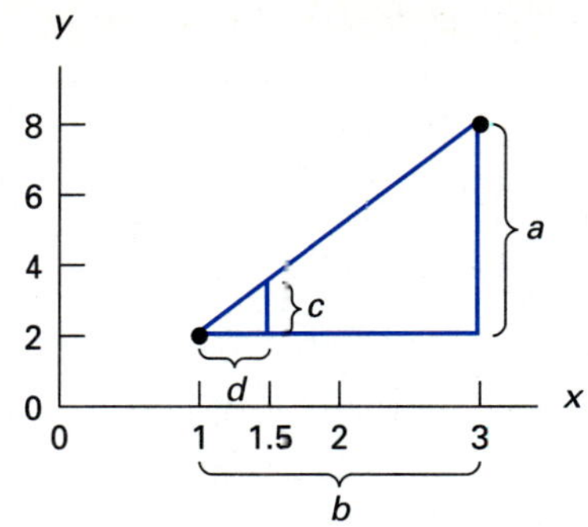

Thus,

$$\frac{a}{b} = \frac{c}{d}$$

or

$$\frac{f(3) - f(1)}{3 - 1} = \frac{f(1.5) - f(1)}{1.5 - 1}$$

If we solve this equation for $f(1.5)$, we have:

$$f(1.5) - f(1) = \frac{(1.5 - 1) \cdot (f(3) - f(1))}{3 - 1}$$

or

$$\begin{aligned} f(1.5) &= f(1) + \frac{(1.5 - 1) \cdot (f(3) - f(1))}{3 - 1} \\ &= 2 + \frac{(0.5) \cdot (8 - 2)}{2} \\ &= 3.5 \end{aligned}$$

We can develop a general linear interpolation formula for finding a function value $f(x)$ when x is between a and b and when the values of $f(a)$ and $f(b)$ are known. This formula is essentially the formula used in the previous example. It calculates the portion of the difference between the values on the x axis and then adds the corresponding portion of the difference between the values on the y axis to the leftmost function value:

$$f(x) = f(a) + \frac{(x - a)}{(b - a)} (f(b) - f(a))$$

This general formula works for linear interpolation of straight lines with either positive or negative slopes.

Computation of Lift and Drag Forces

In this section, we use a set of lift data on an aircraft wing. The 17 points in the data file are tabulated and plotted opposite to show the "coefficient of lift," C_L, at various flight path angles of the wing for a Mach number of 0.3. It is easy to judge from the appearance of the data that linear interpolation provides a reasonably accurate method of estimating the lift coefficient at points between the data points, even in the region where the function is curved.

Flight Path Angle	Coefficient of Lift
−4	−0.202
−2	−0.050
0	0.108
2	0.264
4	0.421
6	0.573
8	0.727
10	0.880
12	1.027
14	1.150
15	1.195
16	1.225
17	1.244
18	1.250
19	1.245
20	1.221
21	1.177

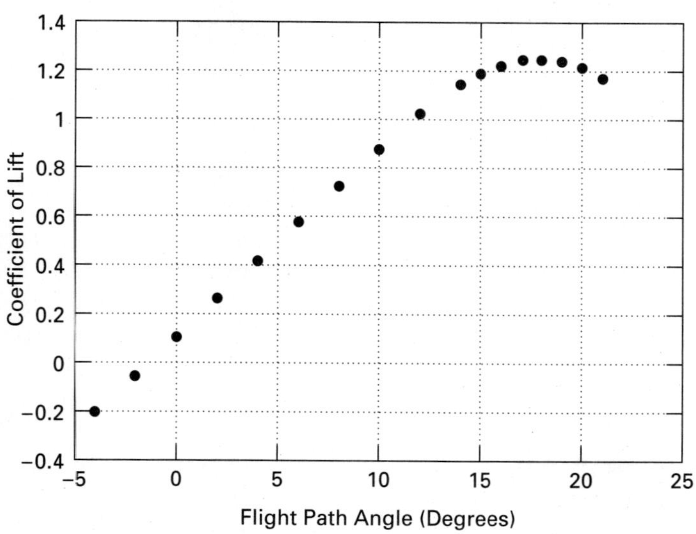

Write a program to read the data from a data file called LIFT. The first line in the data file contains the number of data pairs. Each successive line in the data file contains two numbers, where the first value represents alpha, the flight path angle in degrees, and the second value contains C_L, the coefficient of lift measured during the wind tunnel test for the corresponding angle. Assume that the data pairs contained in the data file are in ascending order based on alpha, with the smallest value of alpha first and the largest value of alpha last.

The program should then read a value of alpha entered from the keyboard for which we need to know the interpolated value of C_L. Using the algorithm shown earlier in this section, the program should interpolate for the lift coefficient, print the value of alpha and the corresponding estimate of C_L, and then prompt us for a new value of alpha. If we enter a value of alpha that is outside the range of the data, the program should print a message that the requested value is not within the interpolation region. The program terminates when we enter a value of 999.0 for alpha.

1. Problem Statement

Using linear interpolation with a wind tunnel data file, compute the lift coefficients that correspond to specified flight path angles.

2. Input/Output Description

Input—the wind tunnel data file and the values of alpha for which we need the interpolated value of C_L

Output—a list of the input values of alpha and the corresponding values of C_L

3. Hand Example

The data file that we use for testing contains the 17 data points given at the beginning of this section. Assume that we want to estimate the value of C_L that corresponds to alpha = 6.3. Using this data file and the linear interpolation formula from the previous section, the estimated value of C_L is

$$\begin{aligned} C_L &= 0.573 + \frac{6.3-6}{8-6}(0.727-0.573) \\ &= 0.573 + 0.15(0.154) \\ &= 0.596 \end{aligned}$$

4. Algorithm Development

Decomposition

Read data file.
Read angles and interpolate coefficients.

As we refine these steps, remember that we need to determine if the input value of alpha is within the interpolation region. We can do this by checking to see if alpha is between the first flight path angle and the last flight path angle in the data file. If the input value of alpha is not within this allowable interpolation region, we print a message. We also need to check for an input alpha value of 999.0 so that we can terminate the program.

Pseudocode

Wind: Read N, the number of data pairs
    Read data file into arrays A and C
    Read input angle alpha
    While alpha $\neq$ 999.0 do
        If $A(1) \leq \text{alpha} \leq A(N)$ then
            Find k such that $A(k-1) \leq \text{alpha} \leq A(k)$
            Interpolate for C_L

$$C_L \leftarrow C(k-1) + \frac{\text{alpha} - A(k-1)}{A(k) - A(k-1)} \cdot (C(k) - C(k-1))$$

            Print alpha, C_L
        Else
            Print message that alpha is out of range
        Read new input angle alpha

FORTRAN Program

```
*-----------------------------------------------------------------------*
      PROGRAM WIND
*
*  This program reads a file of wind tunnel test data and then
*  uses linear interpolation to compute lift coefficients for
*  additional flight angles.
*
      INTEGER N, K
      REAL A(500), C(500), ALPHA, CL
*
      OPEN (UNIT=10,FILE='LIFT',STATUS='OLD')
      READ (10,*) N
      DO 5 K=1,N
         READ (10,*) A(K), C(K)
    5 CONTINUE
*
      PRINT*, 'ENTER FLIGHT PATH ANGLE IN DEGREES'
      READ*, ALPHA
   10 IF (ALPHA.NE.999.0) THEN
*
         IF (A(1).LE.ALPHA.AND.ALPHA.LE.A(N)) THEN
*
            IF (ALPHA.EQ.A(1)) THEN
               K = 2
            ELSE
               K = 1
   15          IF (A(K).LT.ALPHA) THEN
                  K = K + 1
                  GO TO 15
               END IF
            END IF
            CL = C(K-1) + (ALPHA - A(K-1))/(A(K) - A(K-1))
     +                  *(C(K) - C(K-1))
            PRINT 20, ALPHA, CL
   20       FORMAT (1X,'FLIGHT ANGLE = ',F7.2/
     +              1X,'CORRESPONDING COEFFICIENT OF LIFT = ',F7.3)
*
         ELSE
*
            PRINT*,'ANGLE OUT OF RANGE FOR DATA FILE'
*
         END IF
*
         PRINT*
         PRINT*, 'ENTER FLIGHT PATH ANGLE IN DEGREES'
         PRINT*, '(999.0 TO QUIT)'
         READ*, ALPHA
         GO TO 10
      END IF
*
      END
*-----------------------------------------------------------------------*
```

5. Testing

We specified 500 values for arrays A and C, but these can be increased if we expect to need more values. Using the data file given at the beginning of this section, we tested the program with several values of alpha, including values outside the range of the data file. The interaction with the program is shown below:

```
ENTER FLIGHT PATH ANGLE IN DEGREES
6.3
FLIGHT ANGLE =    6.30
CORRESPONDING COEFFICIENT OF LIFT =   0.596

ENTER FLIGHT PATH ANGLE IN DEGREES
(999.0 TO QUIT)
20.5
FLIGHT ANGLE =   20.50
CORRESPONDING COEFFICIENT OF LIFT =   1.199

ENTER FLIGHT PATH ANGLE IN DEGREES
(999.0 TO QUIT)
-5
ANGLE OUT OF RANGE FOR DATA FILE

ENTER FLIGHT PATH ANGLE IN DEGREES
(999.0 TO QUIT)
22.5
ANGLE OUT OF RANGE FOR DATA FILE

ENTER FLIGHT PATH ANGLE IN DEGREES
(999.0 TO QUIT)
-4
FLIGHT ANGLE =   -4.00
CORRESPONDING COEFFICIENT OF LIFT =  -0.202

ENTER FLIGHT PATH ANGLE IN DEGREES
(999.0 TO QUIT)
21
FLIGHT ANGLE =   21.00
CORRESPONDING COEFFICIENT OF LIFT =   1.177

ENTER FLIGHT PATH ANGLE IN DEGREES
(999.0 TO QUIT)
10
FLIGHT ANGLE =   10.00
CORRESPONDING COEFFICIENT OF LIFT =   0.880

ENTER FLIGHT PATH ANGLE IN DEGREES
(999.0 TO QUIT)
999.0
```

Note that the first value computed by the program is the same value that we computed in the hand example. Also note that we tested all the special cases, including values of alpha that are out of range, values at the endpoints, and values at a data point.

5·4 ■ Sorting Algorithms

In this section we develop algorithms to *sort* or reorder a one-dimensional array or list in *ascending,* or low-to-high, order. (With minor alterations, the algorithm can be changed to one that sorts in *descending*, high-to-low, order. We will also see in Chapter 8 that these sort algorithms can be used to alphabetize character data.) The topic of sorting techniques is the subject of entire textbooks and courses; therefore, this text will not attempt to present all the important aspects of sorting. Instead, we present three common sorting techniques and develop pseudocode and FORTRAN solutions for all three so that you can compare the different techniques.

A *selection sort* is a simple sort that is based on finding the minimum value and placing it first in the list, finding the next smallest value and placing it second in the list, and so on. A *bubble sort* is based on interchanging adjacent values in the array until all the values are in the proper position. This sort is sometimes called a multipass sort. An *insertion sort* starts at the beginning of the list, comparing adjacent elements. If an element is out of order, it is continually exchanged with the value below it in the list until it is in its proper place. The sort then continues with the next element out of order.

No one sort algorithm is the best to use for all situations. In order to choose a good algorithm, you need to know something about the expected order of the data. For example, if your data is already very close to being in the correct order, both the insertion sort and the version of the bubble sort presented in this section are good choices. If your data is in a random order or close to the opposite order desired, then the insertion sort and the selection sort are good choices. None of these sorts is efficient if you are sorting a very large set of data. You should consult texts that cover other types of sorts in order to choose a good sort algorithm for a large set of data.

In the three sort algorithms presented in this section, we will use only one array. If you need to keep the original order of the data as well as the sorted data, copy the original data into a second array and sort it. Since the actual number of values in the array may be less than the maximum number of values that could be stored in it, we will assume that the variable COUNT specifies the actual number of data values to be sorted.

Selection Sort

We begin the discussion of the selection sort with a hand example. Consider the list of data values below:

Original List	
	4.1
	7.3
	1.7
	5.2
	1.3

In this algorithm, we first find the minimum value. Scanning down the list, we find that the last value, 1.3, is the minimum. We now want to put the value 1.3 in the first position of the array, but we do not want to lose the value 4.1 that is currently in the first position. Therefore, we will exchange the values. The switch of two values requires three steps, not two as you might imagine. Consider these statements:

```
X(I) = X(J)
X(J) = X(I)
```

Suppose X(I) contained the value 3.0 and X(J) contained the value −1.0. The first statement will change the contents of X(I) from the value 3.0 to the value −1.0. The second statement will move the value in X(I) to X(J), so that both locations contain −1.0. These steps are shown next, along with the changes in the corresponding memory locations:

	X(I)	X(J)
	3.0	−1.0
`X(I) = X(J)`	−1.0	−1.0
`X(J) = X(I)`	−1.0	−1.0

A correct way to switch the two values is shown here, along with the changes in the corresponding memory locations:

	X(I)	X(J)	HOLD
	3.0	−1.0	?
`HOLD = X(I)`	3.0	−1.0	3.0
`X(I) = X(J)`	−1.0	−1.0	3.0
`X(J) = HOLD`	−1.0	3.0	3.0

Once we have switched the first value in the array with the value that has the minimum value, we search the values in the array from the second value to the last value for the minimum in that list. We then switch the second value with the minimum. We continue this until we are looking at the next-to-last and last values. If they are out of order, we switch them. At this point, the entire array will be sorted into an ascending order, as shown in the diagram below:

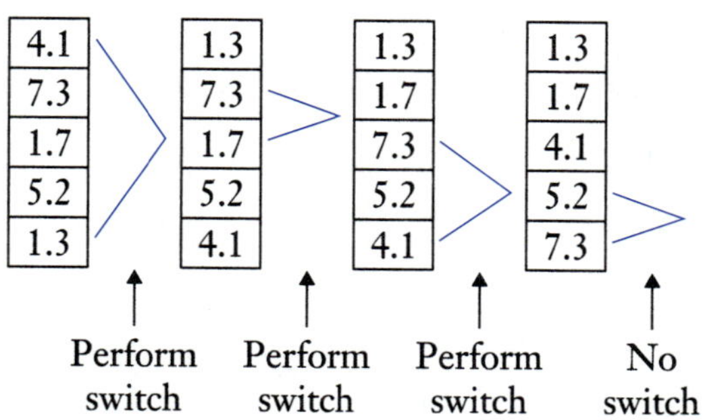

We now develop the pseudocode and FORTRAN statements for this selection sort.

Decomposition

Sort list of data values into ascending order.

In the refinement below, notice that we do not keep track of the minimum value itself; instead, we are interested in keeping track of the subscript or location of the minimum value. We need the subscript in order to be able to switch positions with another element in the array. Since the portion of the array that we search for the next minimum gets smaller, we use two variables, FIRST and LAST, to keep track of this array portion. FIRST will start at 2 and increment by one each time we do a switch.

LAST will always be equal to COUNT since we search to the bottom of the list of valid values each time.

Pseudocode

```
(Assumes: the values are already stored in the array X; and a variable COUNT
specifies the number of valid data values in the array.)

Selection: last ← count
        For j = 1 to count − 1 do
            ptr ← j
            first ← j + 1
            For k = first to last do
                If x(k) < x(ptr) then
                    ptr ← k
            Switch values in x(j) and x(ptr)
```

FORTRAN Statements

```
*
*  These statements sort the values in the array X
*  using a selection sort.  The variable COUNT
*  contains the number of valid data values in X.
*
      LAST = COUNT
      DO 10 J=1,COUNT-1
         PTR = J
         FIRST = J + 1
*
         DO 5 K=FIRST,LAST
            IF (X(K).LT.X(PTR)) PTR = K
    5    CONTINUE
*
         HOLD = X(J)
         X(J) = X(PTR)
         X(PTR) = HOLD
   10 CONTINUE
*
```

■ Bubble Sort

The basic step to the bubble sort algorithm is a single pass through the array, comparing adjacent elements. If a pair of adjacent elements is in the correct order (that is, the first value is less than or equal to the second value), we go to the next pair. If the pair is out of order, we switch the values and then go to the next pair.

The single pass through the array can be performed in a counting loop with index J. Each pair of adjacent values will be referred to by the subscripts J and J + 1. If the number of valid data elements in the array is stored in COUNT, we will make COUNT − 1 comparisons of adjacent values in a single pass through the array.

A single pass through a one-dimensional array, switching adjacent elements that are out of order, is not guaranteed to sort the values. Consider a single pass through the following array:

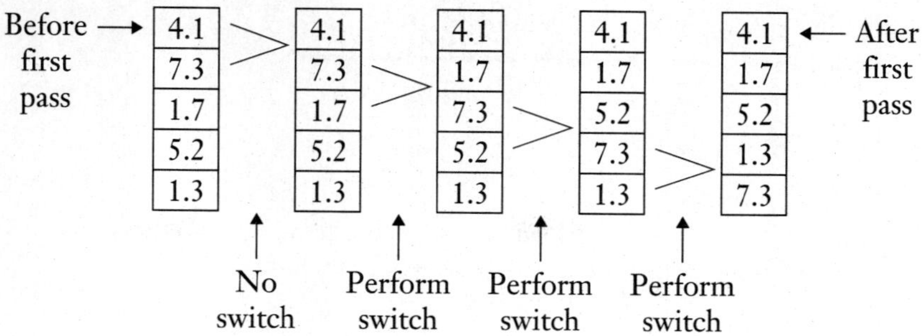

It will take two more complete passes before the array is sorted into ascending order, as shown in the following diagram:

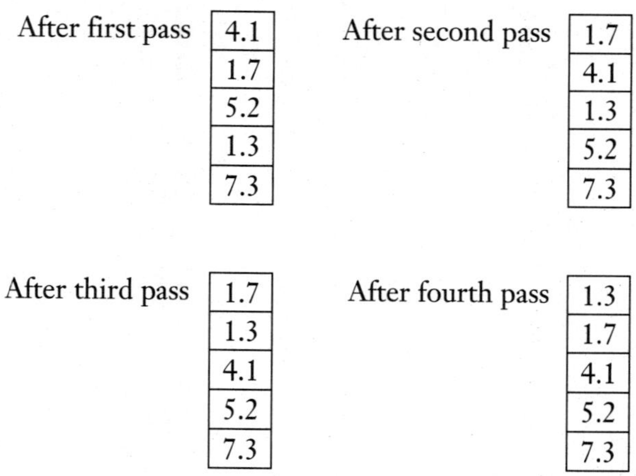

A maximum of COUNT-1 passes may be necessary to sort an array with this technique. If no switches are made during a single pass through the array, however, it is in ascending order. Thus, our algorithm for sorting a one-dimensional array will be to perform single passes through the array making switches until no elements are out of order. In developing the pseudocode we use a logical variable SORTED that is initialized to true at the beginning of each pass through the data array. If any adjacent values are out of order, we switch the values and then change the value of SORTED to false because at least one pair of values was out of order on the pass. At the end of a pass through the data, if the value of SORTED is still true, the array is in ascending order.

We will make one more addition to the algorithm. Observe that during the first pass through the array we switch any adjacent pairs that are out of order. Although this does not necessarily sort the entire array, it is guaranteed to move the largest value to the bottom of the list. During the second pass, the next-largest value will be moved to the next-to-the-last position. Therefore, when we make each pass through the array, we must start at the first position, but we do not need to check values all the way to the end. In fact, with each pass we can reduce the number of positions that we check by one.

We now develop the pseudocode and FORTRAN statements for this bubble sort.

Decomposition

Sort list of data values into ascending order.

Pseudocode

(Assumes: the values are already stored in the array X; and a variable COUNT specifies the number of valid data values in the array.)

```
Bubble: sorted ← false
        first ← 1
        last ← count − 1
        While not sorted do
            sorted ← true
            For j = first to last do
                If x(j) > x(j + 1) then
                    Switch values
                    sorted ← false
            last ← last − 1
```

FORTRAN Statements

```
*
*  These statements sort the values in the array X
*  using a bubble sort.  The variable COUNT
*  contains the number of valid data values in X.
*
      SORTED = .FALSE.
      FIRST = 1
      LAST = COUNT - 1
    5 IF (.NOT.SORTED) THEN
         SORTED = .TRUE.
*
         DO 10 J=FIRST,LAST
            IF (X(J).GT.X(J+1)) THEN
               HOLD = X(J)
               X(J) = X(J+1)
               X(J+1) = HOLD
               SORTED = .FALSE.
            END IF
   10    CONTINUE
*
         LAST = LAST - 1
         GO TO 5
      END IF
*
```

■ Insertion Sort

The insertion sort starts at the beginning of the list, comparing adjacent elements. If an element is out of order, we switch it with the previous element and check to see if it is now in its proper place. If not, we switch it with the new previous element, and again check. We continue moving the element up in the array until it is in its proper position.

We then return to the position in the list where we located the element out of order and pick up at that point, comparing the next pair of adjacent elements. When we reach the end of the list, it will be in order because each element that we found out of order was inserted in its proper position before we continued. The following diagram shows these steps with our sample array.

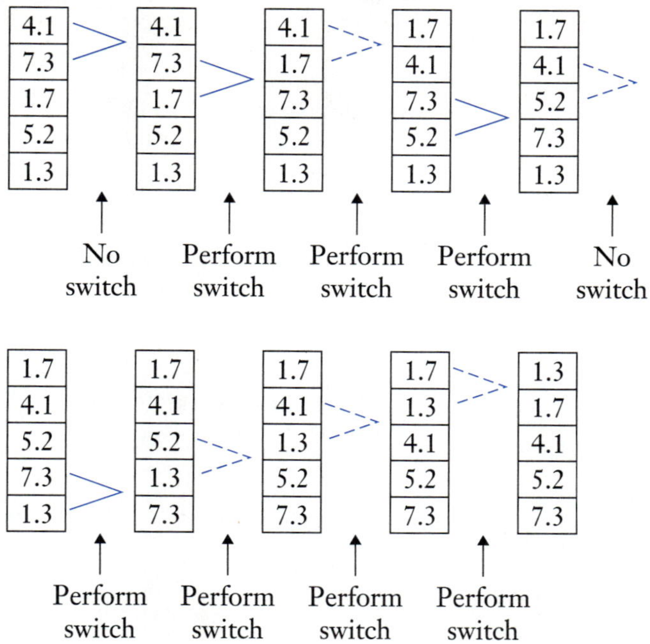

We now develop the pseudocode and FORTRAN statements for this insertion sort.

Decomposition

Sort list of data values into ascending order.

In the following refinement, notice that we use the subscript j of the counting loop to point to our position before we begin backing up in the array to find the proper position for the element out of order. After putting the element in the correct spot, we can jump back to the next pair of elements in the list that we need to compare, since the value of the subscript j has not been changed.

Pseudocode

(Assumes: the values are already stored in the array X; and a variable COUNT specifies the number of valid data values in the array.)

```
Insert: For j = 1 to count − 1 do
            If x(j) > x(j+1) then
                  done ← false
                  k ← j
                  While not done do
                        Switch x(k) with x(k+1)
                        If (k = 1) or (x(k) ≥ x(k − 1)) then
                              done ← true
                        Else
                              k ← k − 1
```

FORTRAN Statements

```
*
*  These statements sort the values in the array X
*  using an insertion sort.  The variable COUNT
*  contains the number of valid data values in X.
*
      DO 10 J=1,COUNT-1
*
         IF (X(J).GT.X(J+1)) THEN
*
            DONE = .FALSE.
            K = J
*
    5       IF (.NOT.DONE) THEN
               HOLD = X(K)
               X(K) = X(K+1)
               X(K+1) = HOLD
               IF (K.EQ.1) THEN
                  DONE = .TRUE.
               ELSE IF (X(K).GE.X(K-1)) THEN
                  DONE = .TRUE.
               ELSE
                  K = K - 1
               END IF
               GO TO 5
            END IF
*
         END IF
*
   10 CONTINUE
*
```

The final condition was separated into two separate conditions in the FORTRAN statements because it would be invalid to examine X(K−1) if K has the value 1.

SELF-TEST 5-2

This self-test allows you to check quickly to see if you have remembered certain key points from Section 5–4. If you have any problems with the exercises, you should reread this section. The solutions are included at the end of the text. Consider the following list with six elements in it:

31
24
63
16
21
8

1. Show the sequence of changes that occur in the list if it is sorted using the selection sort algorithm.
2. Show the sequence of changes that occur in the list if it is sorted using the bubble sort algorithm.
3. Show the sequence of changes that occur in the list if it is sorted using the insertion sort algorithm.

5-5 Application ■ Earthquake Measurements

Civil Engineering

In this application we analyze data that might be collected in a field laboratory that monitors seismic (earthquake) activity. This data is collected by instruments called seismometers that are located around the world. Suppose that a location in California has been the site of earthquake activity for a number of years. The magnitude of each event has been recorded using the Richter scale. This data is stored in a data file MOTION in the chronological order in which the earthquakes occurred. Write a program to read this information, sort it into ascending order based on magnitude, and print the data in this new order.

The initial line of the data file contains a five-digit integer that represents the location number for the laboratory. When new earthquakes occur, the information is added to the end of the file. Therefore, you do not know ahead of time how many data values are in the file. You can, however, assume an upper limit of 200 data values.

1. Problem Statement

Sort a group of earthquake measurements into ascending order.

2. Input/Output Description

Input—the earthquake measurements from a data file MOTION
Output—a listing of the earthquake measurements in ascending order

3. Hand Example

Using the following example test file data, we sort the data into ascending order and print it.

Data File MOTION

```
17758
2.5810
1.5000
1.6200
3.7800
4.2500
1.7330
```

Output List

```
1.5000
1.6200
1.7330
2.5810
3.7800
4.2500
```

4. Algorithm Development

In Section 5–4 we presented three different sort techniques. Any of the three techniques could be used in this example. We have selected the first sort algorithm, the selection sort. You may want to review the selection sort algorithm before continuing with this development. The decomposition of this problem solution breaks into the following steps:

```
      PRINT 22, LOCATE, N
   22 FORMAT (1X,'LOCATION = ',I5,'; N = ',I4)
      PRINT 23
   23 FORMAT (1X,'QUAKE DATA:')
      PRINT 24, (QUAKE(I),I=1,N)
   24 FORMAT (1X,5F5.2)
      STOP
```

To test the sort portion, use a small data set so that you are not overwhelmed with data. Insert the PRINT statements previously used to print the QUAKE array before statement 40; this will print the data values after each pass through the array. Notice how these pieces that we test individually correspond to the overall steps in the initial decomposition.

When you have the algorithm working, be sure to use a variety of test data sets. Use sets that are already in order and sets that are in reverse order, in addition to sequences in random order. The output from a sample set of data would be in this form:

Data File MOTION

```
17758
2.5810
1.5000
1.6200
3.7800
4.2500
1.7330
```

Computer Output

```
LOCATION NUMBER:  17758
  1.    1.5000
  2.    1.6200
  3.    1.7330
  4.    2.5810
  5.    3.7800
  6.    4.2500
```

After sorting the array QUAKE, we changed the order of the values from one that was sequential in time to one that is in ascending order. In so doing, we lost the original order within our program. The data file is still in the original order, but our program has the data only in ascending order. If the program also needed the original data, we could copy the original data into a second array after it was read but before it was sorted. Then, after sorting, we would have two arrays of data—one in the original order and one in ascending order.

5·6 ■ Two-Dimensional Arrays

If we visualize a one-dimensional array as a single column of data, we can visualize a *two-dimensional* array as a group of columns, as illustrated:

	column 1	column 2	column 3	column 4	column 5	column 6
row 1 →	2	4	7	6	–1	0
row 2 →	13	19	18	17	1	2
row 3 →	0	–2	2	8	6	9
row 4 →	3	2	1	4	86	–3

Two-dimensional array with 4 rows and 6 columns

The diagram depicts an integer array with 24 elements. As in one-dimensional arrays, each of the 24 elements has the same array name. However, one subscript is not sufficient to specify an element in a two-dimensional array. For instance, if the array's name is M, it is not clear whether M(3) should be the third element in the first row or the third element in the first column. To avoid ambiguity, elements in a two-dimensional array are referenced with two subscripts: the first subscript references the row and the second subscript references the column. Thus, M(2,3) refers to the number in the second row, third column. In our diagram, M(2,3) contains the value 18.

■ Storage and Initialization

Two-dimensional arrays must be specified with a DIMENSION statement or a type statement—but not both. The following type statements reserve storage for a one-dimensional real array B of 10 elements, a two-dimensional real array C with 3 rows and 5 columns, a two-dimensional real array NUM with 5 rows and 2 columns, and a two-dimensional integer array J with 7 rows and 4 columns:

```
REAL B(10), C(3,5), NUM(5,2)
INTEGER J(7,4)
```

This next statement reserves storage for a two-dimensional array with three rows and three columns:

```
REAL R(0:2,-1:1)
```

Two-dimensional arrays can be initialized with assignment statements, with input statements, and with the DATA statement. A two-dimensional array name can be used without subscripts in input statements, DATA statements, and output statements; if the name of the array is used in one of these statements without subscripts, the array is accessed in column order. We will always explicitly use subscripts with two-dimensional arrays in order to be clear whether we are referencing the array elements in row order or in column order. It is common notation to use I for the row subscript and J for the column subscript.

Array Initialization, AREA

Example 5·5

Define an array AREA with 5 rows and 4 columns. Fill it with the values shown:

1.0	1.0	2.0	2.0
1.0	1.0	2.0	2.0
1.0	1.0	2.0	2.0
1.0	1.0	2.0	2.0
1.0	1.0	2.0	2.0

Solution 1

```
      REAL AREA(5,4)
      .
      .
      .
      DO 10 I=1,5
         AREA(I,1) = 1.0
         AREA(I,2) = 1.0
         AREA(I,3) = 2.0
         AREA(I,4) = 2.0
   10 CONTINUE
```

Solution 2

```
      REAL AREA(5,4)
      DATA ((AREA(I,J),I=1,5),J=1,4) /10*1.0,10*2.0/
```

Array Initialization, SUM

Example 5·6

Define and fill the integer array SUM as shown:

1	1	1
2	2	2
3	3	3
4	4	4

Solution 1

If we observe that each element of the array contains its corresponding row number, then the following solution can be used:

```
      INTEGER SUM(4,3)
      .
      .
      .
      DO 10 I=1,4
         DO 5 J=1,3
            SUM(I,J) = I
    5    CONTINUE
   10 CONTINUE
```

Solution 2

The following DATA statements also initialize the array correctly:

```
INTEGER SUM(4,3)
DATA ((SUM(I,J),I=1,4),J=1,3) /3*(1,2,3,4)/
```

or

```
INTEGER SUM(4,3)
DATA ((SUM(I,J),J=1,3),I=1,4) /3*1,3*2,3*3,3*4/
```

Example 5·7

Identity Matrix

A matrix is a structure used to store data that can be represented as a rectangular grid of numbers. Therefore, a matrix looks very similar to a two-dimensional array, except that a matrix has brackets on the sides while a two-dimensional array is shown inside a grid. When a matrix is used in a FORTRAN program, we store it in a two-dimensional array. When using matrix operations to solve engineering and science problems, we frequently use a matrix called an *identity matrix*. This matrix has the same number of rows as columns, so it is also called a *square matrix*. The identity matrix contains all 0's except for the main diagonal elements, which are 1's. (The main diagonal is composed of elements that have the same value for row number and for column number.) An identity matrix with 5 rows and 5 columns is shown.

$$\begin{bmatrix} 1 & 0 & 0 & 0 & 0 \\ 0 & 1 & 0 & 0 & 0 \\ 0 & 0 & 1 & 0 & 0 \\ 0 & 0 & 0 & 1 & 0 \\ 0 & 0 & 0 & 0 & 1 \end{bmatrix}$$

Define and fill a real array with these values.

Solution

Because the value 1 appears at different positions in each row of the array, we cannot use the same type of solution we used in Example 5–6. If we list the elements that contain the value 1.0, we find that they are positions (1,1), (2,2), (3,3), (4,4), and (5,5); thus, the row and the column number are the same value. Recognizing this pattern, we can initialize the array as follows:

```
      REAL IDEN(5,5)
      .
      .
      .
      DO 10 I=1,5
         DO 5 J=1,5
            IF (I.EQ.J) THEN
               IDEN(I,J) = 1.0
            ELSE
               IDEN(I,J) = 0.0
            END IF
 5       CONTINUE
10    CONTINUE
```

Input and Output

The main difference between using values from a one-dimensional array and using values from a two-dimensional array is that the latter requires two subscripts. Most loops used in the reading or printing of two-dimensional arrays are therefore nested loops. You can also use implied loops with two-dimensional array I/O. Avoid using only the array name on I/O statements with two-dimensional arrays; using the array name with no subscripts is equivalent to listing all the values in the array, but in an order that goes down the columns instead of across the rows.

Reading Array Values from a Data File . . . . **Example 5·8**

Suppose that a data file contained temperature measurements taken at five times during an experiment. For each time, temperatures are taken at three locations in the jet engine being tested and stored on the same line in a data file. Read this data and store it in a real array TEMPS that has been dimensioned with five rows and three columns. Assume that the data file has already been opened.

Correct Solution 1

This solution uses a single DO loop and lists the variable names for each row on the READ statement.

```
      DO 10 I=1,5
         READ (10,*) TEMPS(I,1), TEMPS (I,2), TEMPS (I,3)
   10 CONTINUE
```

Correct Solution 2

This solution executes exactly like solution 1 because the implied DO loop on the READ is equivalent to listing the variables.

```
      DO 10 I=1,5
         READ (10,*) (TEMPS(I,J),J=1,3)
   10 CONTINUE
```

Incorrect Solution 1

This solution is the equivalent of 15 READ statements. Since each READ statement reads a new line in the data file, this solution tries to read each value from a new data line. Thus, the first number on line 1 will be read into TEMPS(1,1), the first number on line 2 will be read into TEMPS(1,2), and so on. The values are being stored in the wrong locations, and an execution error will occur when the program tries to read past the end of the data file.

```
      DO 10 I=1,5
         DO 5 J=1,3
            READ (10,*) TEMP(I,J)
    5    CONTINUE
   10 CONTINUE
```

Incorrect Solution 2

This solution is equivalent to one READ statement with all 15 variables written on it, but the variables are in column order, as in TEMPS(1,1), TEMPS(2,1), TEMPS(3,1), TEMPS(4,1), TEMPS(5,1), TEMPS(1,2). . . . . Since the order of the values in the data file is in row order, not column order, the values will be read into the wrong locations. Unfortunately, no error is detected by the computer, so we may not detect this error unless we carefully test our program.

```
READ (10,*) TEMPS
```

Example 5-9

Print Array Values

In this example, we assume that we have correctly read the temperature data from the data file described in Example 5 – 8. We now want to print the data.

Correct Solution 1

This solution uses a single DO loop and lists the variable names for each row on the PRINT statement. Five lines of output will be printed with three values per line, using a list-directed format.

```
      DO 10 I=1,5
         PRINT*, TEMPS(I,1), TEMPS (I,2), TEMPS (I,3)
   10 CONTINUE
```

Correct Solution 2

This solution also prints three values per line using the specified format instead of the list-directed format.

```
      DO 10 I=1,5
         PRINT 3, TEMPS(I,1), TEMPS (I,2), TEMPS (I,3)
    3    FORMAT (1X,3(F5.2,2X))
   10 CONTINUE
```

Incorrect Solution

This solution prints one value per line instead of three because the format contains only one specification. Recall that when we run out of format specification, we print the current buffer and then back up in the format list to get a specification.

```
      DO 10 I=1,5
         PRINT 3, TEMPS(I,1), TEMPS (I,2), TEMPS (I,3)
    3    FORMAT (1X,F5.2)
   10 CONTINUE
```

Example 5-10

Medical Data

The analysis of a medical experiment requires the use of a set of data containing the weight of 100 participants at the beginning and at the end of an experiment. The integer data values have been stored in a data file and are accessed using unit number 13. Each line in the file contains the initial weight and the final weight of a participant.

Give statements to store the data in an array WEIGHT which has been defined to have 100 rows and 2 columns.

Solution 1

```
      DO 10 I=1,100
         READ (13,*) WEIGHT(I,1), WEIGHT(I,2)
   10 CONTINUE
```

Solution 2

```
      READ (13,*) (WEIGHT(I,1),WEIGHT(I,2),I=1,100)
```

Terminal Inventory

Example 5·11

A large technical firm keeps an inventory of the locations of its computer terminals in a data file. Assume that this data has already been read into a two-dimensional array called INVEN with 20 rows and 4 columns. There are 4 types of terminals, represented by the 4 columns, and 20 laboratories using the terminals, represented by the 20 rows of the array. Print the data in a form similar to the following:

```
TERMINAL INVENTORY
--------------------------------------
TYPE              1     2     3     4
--------------------------------------
LAB       1      XX    XX    XX    XX
LAB       2      XX    XX    XX    XX
.
.
.
LAB      20      XX    XX    XX    XX
```

Solution

This solution uses the index of a DO loop as the row subscript. The index of an implied loop in the PRINT statement supplies the column subscript. Thus, each time the PRINT statement is executed, one row of data is printed.

```
      PRINT 5
    5 FORMAT (1X,'TERMINAL INVENTORY')
      PRINT 10
   10 FORMAT (1X,'- - - - - - - - - - - - - - - - - -')
      PRINT 15
   15 FORMAT (1X,'TYPE           1     2     3     4')
      PRINT 20
   20 FORMAT (1X,'- - - - - - - - - - - - - - - - - -')
      DO 200 I=1,20
         PRINT 30, I, (INVEN(I,J),J=1,4)
   30    FORMAT (1X,'LAB',I4,4(3X,I2))
  200 CONTINUE
```

This self-test allows you to check quickly to see if you have remembered some of the key points from Section 5–6. If you have any problems with the exercises, you should reread this section. The solutions are included at the end of the text.

SELF-TEST 5-3

Problems 1–3 contain statements that initialize and print two-dimensional arrays. Draw the array and indicate the contents of each position in the array. Then, show the output from each set of statements. Assume that each set of statements is independent of the others.

1.
```
      INTEGER I, J, CH(5,4)
      DO 10 I=1,5
         DO 5 J=1,4
            CH(I,J) = 2*(I + J)
    5    CONTINUE
   10 CONTINUE
      PRINT 15, (CH(5,J),J=1,4)
   15 FORMAT (1X,4I5)
```

2.
```
      INTEGER I, J, K(3,3)
      DO 20 I=1,3
         K(I,1) = I
         K(I,2) = K(I,1) + 1
         K(I,3) = K(I,1) - 1
   20 CONTINUE
      DO 35 I=1,3
         PRINT 30, K(I,1), K(I,2), K(I,3)
   30    FORMAT (1X,3I4)
   35 CONTINUE
```

3.
```
      INTEGER I, J
      REAL DIST(2,3), SUM
      SUM = 10.0
      DO 10 J=1,3
         DO 5 I=1,2
            SUM = SUM + 1.5
            DIST(I,J) = SUM
    5    CONTINUE
   10 CONTINUE
      DO 20 I=1,2
         PRINT 15, (DIST(I,J),J=1,3)
   15    FORMAT (1X,3F5.1)
   20 CONTINUE
```

5-7 Application ■ Power Plant Data Analysis

Power Engineering

The following table of data represents typical power outputs in megawatts from a power plant over a period of 8 weeks. Each row represents 1 week's data; each column represents data taken on the same day of the week. The data is stored 1 row per data line in a data file called PLANT.

	Day 1	Day 2	Day 3	Day 4	Day 5	Day 6	Day 7
Week 1	207	301	222	302	22	167	125
Week 2	367	60	120	111	301	499	434
Week 3	211	62	441	192	21	293	316
Week 4	401	340	161	297	441	117	206
Week 5	448	111	370	220	264	444	207
Week 6	21	313	204	222	446	401	337
Week 7	213	208	444	321	320	335	313
Week 8	162	137	265	44	370	315	322

A program is needed to read the data, analyze it, and print the results in the following composite report:

```
                    COMPOSITE INFORMATION
AVERAGE DAILY POWER OUTPUT = XXX.X MEGAWATTS
NUMBER OF DAYS WITH GREATER THAN AVERAGE POWER OUTPUT = XX
DAY(S) WITH MINIMUM POWER OUTPUT:
     WEEK X      DAY X
     .
     .
     .
```

1. Problem Statement

Analyze a set of data from a power plant to determine its average daily power output, the number of days with greater-than-average output, and the day or days that had minimum power output.

2. Input/Output Description

Input—8 weeks of daily power output stored in a data file

Output—a report summarizing the power output for the 8 weeks

3. Hand Example

For the hand example, we use a smaller set of data, but one that still maintains the two-dimensional array form. Consider this set of data:

	Day 1	Day 2
Week 1	311	405
Week 2	210	264
Week 3	361	210

First, we must sum all the values and divide by 6 to determine the average, which yields 1761/6, or 293.5 megawatts. Second, we compare each value to the average to determine how many values were greater than the average. In our small set of data, 3 values were greater than the average. Third, we must determine the number of days with minimum power output, which involves two steps: going through the data again to determine the minimum value, and going back through the data to find the day or days with the minimum power value, then printing its/their position(s) in the array. Using the small set of data, we find that the minimum value is 210 and that it occurred on two days. Thus, the output from our hand-worked example is

```
                    COMPOSITE INFORMATION
AVERAGE DAILY POWER OUTPUT = 293.5 MEGAWATTS
NUMBER OF DAYS WITH GREATER THAN AVERAGE POWER OUTPUT = 3
DAY(S) WITH MINIMUM POWER OUTPUT:
      WEEK 2      DAY 1
      WEEK 3      DAY 2
```

4. Algorithm Development

Before we decompose the problem solution, it is important to spend some time considering the best way to store the data that we need for the program. Unfortunately, once we become comfortable with arrays, we tend to overuse them. Using an array complicates our programs because of the subscript handling. We should always ask ourselves, "should we really use an array for this data?"

If the individual data values will be needed more than once, an array is probably required. An array is also necessary if the data is not in the order needed. In general, arrays are helpful when we must read all the data before we can go back and begin processing it. However, if an average of a group of data values is all that is to be computed, we probably do not need an array; as we read the values, we can add them to a total and read the next value into the same memory location as the previous value. The individual values are not needed again because all the information required is now in the total.

Now, let us look at our specific problem and determine whether or not we need to use an array. First, we need to compute an average daily power output. Then, we need to count the number of days with output greater than average, which requires that we compare each output value to the average. For this application, we need to store all the data in an array, and a two-dimensional array is the best choice of data structure.

When we performed the solution by hand, we made several passes through the data to obtain different pieces of information. As we begin to develop the computer solution, we would like to minimize the number of passes through the data. We can compute the sum of the data points in the same loop in which we determine the minimum data value. However, we must make a separate pass through the data to determine how many values are greater than the average. Because the number of days with greater-than-average output is printed before we print the specific day or days that has/have minimum output, we need separate loops for these operations. For this solution, we need three loops (passes) through the array.

Decomposition

Read data.
Compute information.
Print information.

Initial Pseudocode

```
Powerplant: Read data
            Compute average power and minimum power
            Print average power
            Count days with above-average power
            Print count of days
            Print days with minimum power
```

Final Pseudocode

```
Powerplant: Read data
            Compute average and minimum value
            Print heading, average
            count ← 0
            For each data value do
                If data value > average then
                    count ← count + 1
            Print count
            For each data value do
                If data value = minimum then
                    print row and column positions
```

FORTRAN Program

```
*-----------------------------------------------------------------------*
      PROGRAM PWRPLT
*
*   This program computes and prints a composite report
*   summarizing eight weeks of power plant data.
*
      INTEGER TOTAL, COUNT, I, J, POWER(8,7), MIN
      REAL AVE
*
      DATA TOTAL, COUNT /0,0/
*
```

```
      OPEN (UNIT=12,FILE='PLANT',STATUS='OLD')
      DO 5 I=1,8
         READ (12,*) (POWER(I,J),J=1,7)
    5 CONTINUE
*
      MIN = POWER(1,1)
      DO 15 I=1,8
         DO 10 J=1,7
            TOTAL = TOTAL + POWER(I,J)
            IF (POWER(I,J).LT.MIN) MIN = POWER(I,J)
   10    CONTINUE
   15 CONTINUE
      AVE = REAL(TOTAL)/56.0
*
      DO 25 I=1,8
         DO 20 J=1,7
           IF (POWER(I,J).GT.AVE) COUNT = COUNT + 1
   20    CONTINUE
   25 CONTINUE
*
      PRINT 30, AVE, COUNT
   30 FORMAT (1X,15X,'COMPOSITE INFORMATION'/
     +        1X,'AVERAGE DAILY POWER OUTPUT = ',F5.1,' MEGAWATTS'/
     +        1X,'NUMBER OF DAYS WITH GREATER THAN ',
     +        'AVERAGE POWER OUTPUT = ',I2)
*
      PRINT 45
   45 FORMAT (1X,'DAY(S) WITH MINIMUM POWER OUTPUT:')
      DO 60 I=1,8
         DO 55 J=1,7
            IF (POWER(I,J).EQ.MIN) PRINT 50, I, J
   50          FORMAT (1X,12X,'WEEK ',I2,'   DAY ',I2)
   55    CONTINUE
   60 CONTINUE
*
      END
*-------------------------------------------------------------------*
```

5. Testing

This program should be tested in stages; again, the decomposition gives a good idea of the overall steps involved and can thus be used to identify the steps that should be tested individually. Remember that one of the most useful tools for debugging is the PRINT statement—use it to print the values of key variables in loops that may contain errors.

The output from this program using the data file given at the beginning of this section is

```
                 COMPOSITE INFORMATION
AVERAGE DAILY POWER OUTPUT = 259.2 MEGAWATTS
NUMBER OF DAYS WITH GREATER THAN AVERAGE POWER OUTPUT = 30
DAY(S) WITH MINIMUM POWER OUTPUT:
             WEEK  3   DAY  5
             WEEK  6   DAY  1
```

5-8 Application ■ Terrain Navigation

Aerospace Engineering

The study of terrain navigation has become popular with the advent of remotely piloted vehicles such as planes, missiles, and tanks. The systems that guide these vehicles must be tested over a variety of land formations and topologies. Elevation information for large grids of land is available in computer databases. One way of measuring the "difficulty" of a land grid with respect to terrain navigation is to determine the number of peaks in the grid. (A peak is a point that has lower elevations all around it.)

The program we develop in this application will read the elevation information for a set of grids. Then we will determine the number of peaks for each grid.

We assume that the file that contains the elevation information is called ELEVTN. The first line for each grid contains an identification number. The second line contains the number of points along the side of the grid and the number of points along the top of the grid. The elevation data for that grid then begins on the next line, with the data for the top row first, then the second row, and so on. If the data for the first row does not fit on one line, as many lines as are needed will be used. However, each new row of data will begin on a new line. The last line in the data file contains an identification number of 99999. You can assume that the maximum size grid will be 100 points by 100 points. For each grid, print the identification number, the total number of points in the grid, and the number of peaks in the grid.

1. Problem Statement

Determine the number of peaks in a grid of elevation values, where a peak is defined by a point that is higher than all four of its surrounding points.

2. Input/Output Description

Input—elevation information for a group of grids in a data file named ELEVTN

Output—a report that lists each grid identification number, the total number of points in the grid, and the number of peaks within the grid

3. Hand Example

Assume that the following data represents the elevations for a grid that has 6 points along the side and 8 points along the top. We have circled peaks within the data.

```
92547
6   8
25    59    63    23    21    34    21    50
32    45    43    30   (37)   32    30    27
34    38    38    39    36    28    28    35
40   (45)   42   (48)   32    30    27    25
39    39    40    42    48   (49)   25    30
31    31    31    32    32    33    44    35
```

The output for this grid is

IDENTIFICATION	NUMBER OF POINTS	NUMBER OF PEAKS
92547	48	4

4. Algorithm Development

You probably realized that the search for peaks need only consider interior points in the grid. A point along the edge cannot be counted as a peak because we do not know the elevation on one of its sides. If we are considering a point at location MAP(I,J), then the four adjacent points are at positions MAP(I-1,J), MAP(I+1,J), MAP(I,J−1), and MAP(I,J+1), as shown:

	MAP(I−1,J)	
MAP(I,J−1)	MAP(I,J)	MAP(I,J+1)
	MAP(I+1,J)	

Thus, for MAP(I,J) to be a peak, the following must be true:

$$
\begin{aligned}
MAP(I,J-1) &< MAP(I,J)\\
MAP(I,J+1) &< MAP(I,J)\\
MAP(I-1,J) &< MAP(I,J)\\
MAP(I+1,J) &< MAP(I,J)
\end{aligned}
$$

If all of these conditions are met for a point MAP(I,J), it represents a peak.

Decomposition

Print heading.
Read map information and generate report.

Pseudocode

```
Navigate: Print heading
          Read ID
          While ID not = 99999 do
                Read NROW, NCOL
                Read array MAP
                count ← 0
                For each interior point do
                      If interior point > all adjacent points then
                            increment count
                Print ID, number of peaks
                Read ID
```

FORTRAN Program

```
*-----------------------------------------------------------------------*
      PROGRAM NAVIG
*
*  This program reads the elevation data for a set of land
*  grids and determines the number of peaks in each grid.
*
      INTEGER MAP(100,100), I, J, ID, NROWS, NCOLS, COUNT
*
      OPEN (UNIT=15,FILE='ELEVTN',STATUS='OLD')
*
      PRINT 5
    5 FORMAT (1X,'SUMMARY OF LAND GRID ANALYSIS'/
     +         1X,'IDENTIFICATION   NUMBER OF POINTS   NUMBER OF PEAKS')
*
      READ (15,*) ID
   15 IF (ID.NE.99999) THEN
*
         READ (15,*) NROWS, NCOLS
         DO 20 I=1,NROWS
            READ (15,*) (MAP(I,J),J=1,NCOLS)
   20    CONTINUE
*
         COUNT = 0
         DO 30 I=2,NROWS-1
            DO 25 J=2,NCOLS-1
               IF ((MAP(I-1,J).LT.MAP(I,J)).AND.
     +             (MAP(I+1,J).LT.MAP(I,J)).AND.
     +             (MAP(I,J-1).LT.MAP(I,J)).AND.
     +             (MAP(I,J+1).LT.MAP(I,J))) THEN
                  COUNT = COUNT + 1
               END IF
   25       CONTINUE
   30    CONTINUE
*
         PRINT 35, ID, NROWS*NCOLS, COUNT
   35    FORMAT (1X,3X,I7,10X,I7,10X,I7)
*
         READ (15,*) ID
         GO TO 15
      END IF
*
      END
*-----------------------------------------------------------------------*
```

5. Testing

Using the data from the hand-worked example, our output is

```
SUMMARY OF LAND GRID ANALYSIS
IDENTIFICATION   NUMBER OF POINTS   NUMBER OF PEAKS
     92547               48                 4
```

As you try to think of any special cases that might cause problems for this program, you can probably think of some unique grid shapes, such as grids with 1 or 2 rows or 1 or 2 columns. If we look at our program, we see that the DO loops used in counting peaks are

```
DO 30 I=2,NROWS-1
   DO 25 J=2,NCOLS-1
```

If we substitute 2 for NROWS and NCOLS, we have the following loops:

```
DO 30 I=2,1
   DO 25 J=2,1
```

These loops would not be executed, and because the number of peaks was initialized to zero, the number of peaks would remain at zero. Thus, the program can handle these unique grid cases correctly. If the values of NROWS and NCOLS were less than 1 or greater than 100, then the program would not work correctly. It might be a good idea to test NROWS and NCOLS after they are read and print an appropriate error message if they are out of bounds.

Note: This program will locate individual peaks, but it will not locate a ridge where two or more adjacent peaks are at the same elevation. Our algorithm would need to be modified if we were interested in this type of formation.

5·9 ■ Multidimensional Arrays

FORTRAN allows as many as seven dimensions for arrays. We can easily visualize a three-dimensional array such as a cube. We are also familiar with using three coordinates, *X*, *Y*, and *Z*, to locate points. This idea extends into subscripts. The following three-dimensional array could be defined with this statement:

```
REAL T(3,4,4)
```

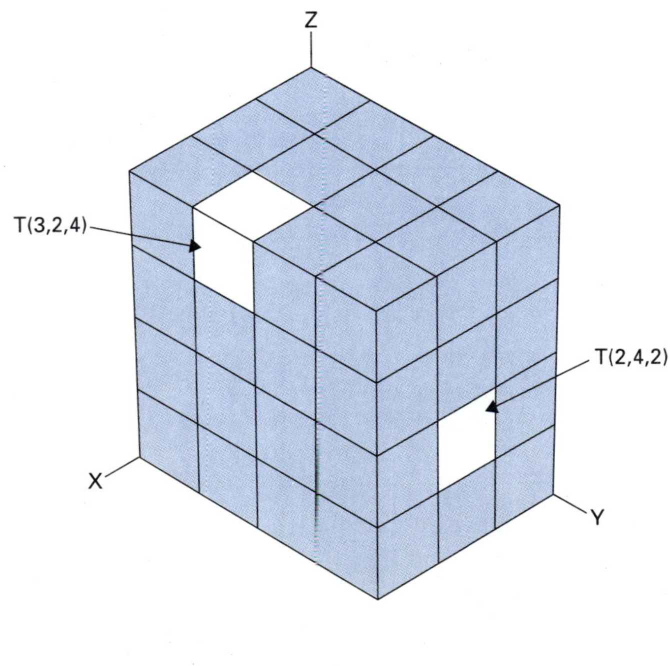

If we use the three-dimensional array name without subscripts, we access the array with the first subscript changing fastest, the second subscript changing second fastest, and the third subscript changing slowest. Thus, using the array T from the previous diagram, these two statements are equivalent:

```
READ *, T
READ *, (((T(I,J,K),I=1,3),J=1,4),K=1,4)
```

It should be evident that three levels of nesting in DO loops are often needed to access a three-dimensional array.

Most applications do not use arrays with more than three dimensions, probably because visualizing more than three dimensions seems too abstract. However, we now present a simple scheme that may help you to picture even a seven-dimensional array.

A *four-dimensional array* can be visualized as a row of three-dimensional arrays. The first subscript specifies a unique three-dimensional array. The other three subscripts specify a unique position in that array.

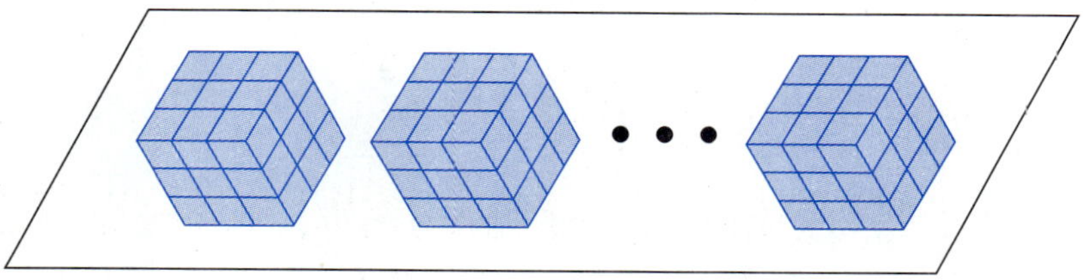

A *five-dimensional array* can be visualized as a block or grid of three-dimensional arrays. The first two subscripts specify a unique three-dimensional array. The other three subscripts specify a unique position in that array.

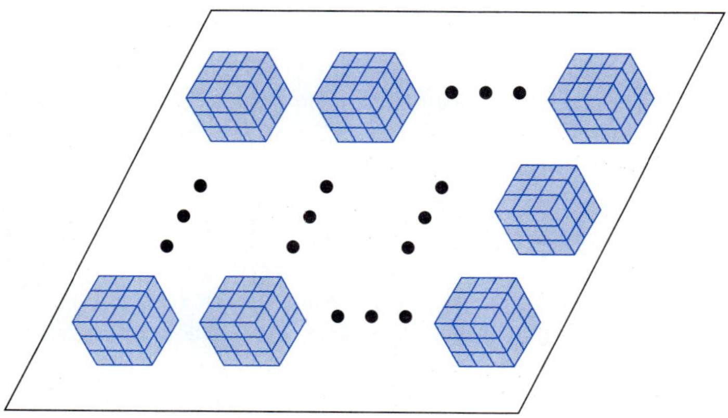

A *six-dimensional array* can be visualized as a row of blocks or grids. One subscript specifies the grid. The other five subscripts specify the unique position in the grid.

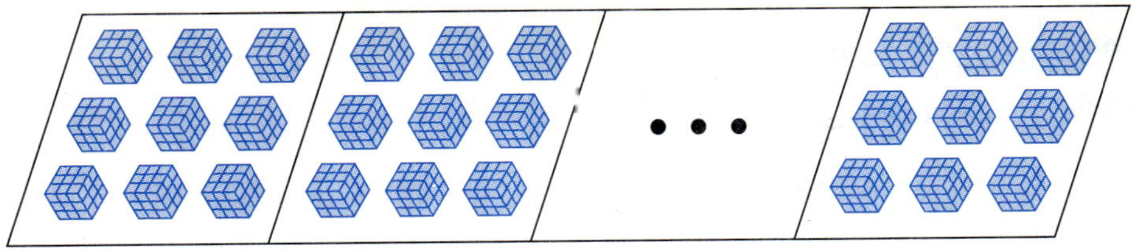

A *seven-dimensional array* can be visualized as a grid of grids or a grid of blocks. Two subscripts specify the grid. The other five subscripts specify the unique position in the grid.

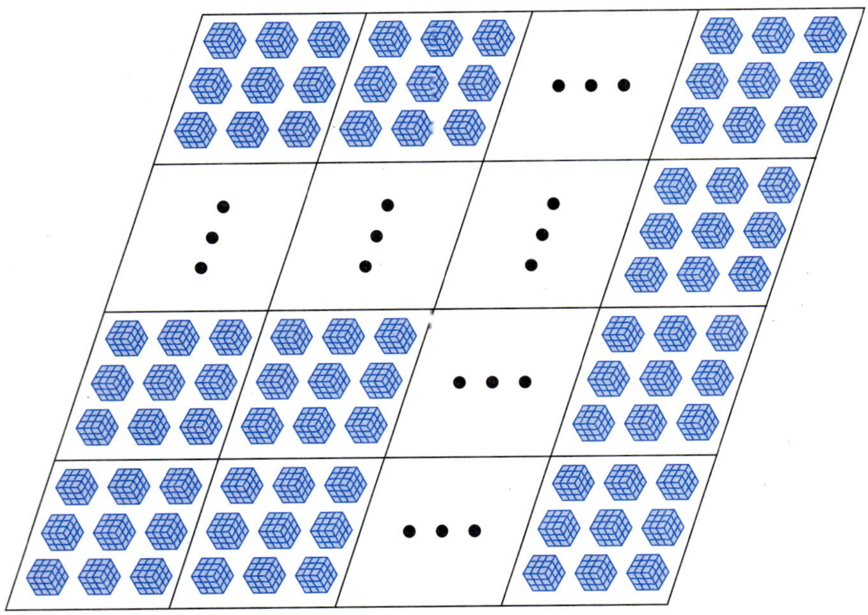

Now that you can visualize *multidimensional arrays,* a natural question is, "what dimension array do I use for solving a problem?" There is no single answer. A problem that can be solved with a two-dimensional array of 4 rows and 3 columns can also be solved with four one-dimensional arrays of 3 elements each. Usually the data fits one array form better than another; you should choose the form that is the easiest for you to work with in your program. For example, if you have census data from 10 countries over the period 1950–1980, you would probably use an array with 10 rows and 31 columns, or 31 rows and 10 columns. If the data represents the populations of 5 cities from each of 10 countries for the period 1950–1980, a three-dimensional array would be most appropriate; the three subscripts would represent year, country, and city.

Summary

In this chapter we learned how to use an array—a group of storage locations that all have a common name but are distinguished by one or more subscripts. Arrays are one of the most powerful elements in FORTRAN because they allow us to keep large amounts of data easily accessible to our programs. The remaining chapters in this text rely heavily on arrays for storing and manipulating data. Also presented were three sort algorithms.

Debugging Aids

Because arrays are so convenient for handling large amounts of data, a natural tendency is to overuse them—and, unfortunately, arrays can also introduce new errors. As you debug programs that use arrays, consider the decision to use each array: ask yourself, "will I need this data more than once?" and "must this data be stored before I can use it?" If the answers to both questions are "no," you should eliminate the array and replace it with simple variables. You will also probably be eliminating some loops and statements involving subscripts; these changes may not only reduce the number of errors in your program but also reduce its overall complexity.

If arrays are necessary, then consider each of the following items if your program is working incorrectly:

Size—The array specification must specify the maximum number of elements that is to be stored in the array. Although you do not have to use all the elements of an array, you can never use more elements than originally specified.

Subscript—Check each subscript to be sure it represents an integer that falls within the proper range of values. Particularly check for subscript values that are one value too small or one value too large.

DO Loop—If you are using the index of a DO loop as a subscript, be sure you have used the same variable identifier in your statements. That is, if the DO loop index is K, did you use I instead of K as a subscript?

Reverse Subscripts—When you are working with multidimensional arrays, be sure you have the subscripts in the proper order. Do you want B(K,L) or B(L,K)?

Style/Technique Guides

As mentioned in Debugging Aids, be sure that you really need an array before implementing an algorithm with an array. If you need arrays to solve your problem, take some time to decide the optimum size. Depending on the application, you may find that a two-dimensional array with 10 rows and 2 columns is more direct and understandable than two separate arrays of 10 elements each. Choose the array structure that best suits the data.

Be consistent in your choice of subscript names. Common practice is to use the variable I for the first subscript, J for the second subscript, and K for the third subscript.

If you follow the same pattern or a similar pattern, it is much easier to decide the nesting of loops and the values of DO loop indexes that are also used as subscripts.

Key Words

array	multidimensional array
ascending order	multipass sort
bubble sort	one-dimensional array
descending order	selection sort
element	sort
implied DO loop	subscript
insertion sort	two-dimensional array

Problems

We begin our problem set with modifications to programs developed in this chapter. Give the decomposition, pseudocode or flowchart, and FORTRAN program for each problem. Problems 1–5 modify the wind tunnel analysis program WIND given on page 218.

1. Modify the wind tunnel analysis program so that it prints a message to the user giving the range of angles that are covered in the data file.
2. Modify the wind tunnel analysis program so that it prints the two flight path angles between which the maximum coefficient of lift occurs.
3. Modify the wind tunnel analysis program so that it computes the range of angles that are covered in the data file and prints this range in both degrees and radians.
4. Modify the wind tunnel analysis program so that it asks the user to enter the flight path angle in radians and then converts the angle to degrees to match the data file in the computations.
5. Modify the wind tunnel analysis program so that it asks the user to enter the flight path angle in degrees, but assume that the data file contains the angle in radians.

Problems 6–10 modify the earthquake measurement program EARTH given on page 230.

6. Modify the earthquake measurement program so that it sorts the data values into descending order.
7. Modify the earthquake measurement program so that it prints the average earthquake value.
8. Modify the earthquake measurement program so that it prints the maximum earthquake value.
9. Modify the earthquake measurement program so that it prints the median earthquake value.

10. Modify the earthquake measurement program so that it computes and prints the number of earthquake values that are in the same position in the list both before and after the ascending sort.

Problems 11–15 modify the power plant data analysis program PWRPLT given on page 241.

11. Modify the power plant data analysis program so that it prints the minimum power output, in addition to printing the days on which it occurred.
12. Modify the power plant data analysis program so that it prints both the minimum and maximum power outputs.
13. Modify the power plant data analysis program so that it reads a value N that determines the number of weeks that will be used for the report. Assume that N will never be more than 20.
14. Modify the power plant data analysis program so that it prints a count of the number of days with the minimum power output instead of printing the specific days.
15. Modify the power plant data analysis program so that it prints the average daily power output for each week of data.

Problems 16–20 modify the terrain navigation program NAVIG given on page 245.

16. Modify the terrain navigation program so that it prints a count of the number of land grids analyzed.
17. Modify the terrain navigation program so that it prints the location (row and column subscripts) of the peaks in each land grid.
18. Modify the terrain navigation program so that it computes and prints the percentage of points in each grid that are peaks.
19. Modify the terrain navigation program so that it prints the maximum and minimum elevations for each land grid.
20. Modify the terrain navigation program so that it computes and prints the average elevation for each land grid.

For problems 21–24, assume that K, a one-dimensional array of 50 integer values, has already been filled with data.

21. Give FORTRAN statements to find and print the maximum value of K in the following form:

```
MAXIMUM VALUE IS XXXXX
```

22. Give FORTRAN statements to find and print the minimum value of K and its position or positions in the array in the following form:

```
MINIMUM VALUE OF K IS
K(XX) = XXXXX
```

23. Give FORTRAN statements to count the number of positive values, zero values, and negative values in K. The output form should be

```
XXX POSITIVE VALUES
XXX ZERO VALUES
XXX NEGATIVE VALUES
```

24. Give FORTRAN statements to replace each value of K with its absolute value, then print the array K with two values per line.

Develop these programs and program segments. Use the five-step process for all complete programs.

25. An array TIME contains 30 integers. Give statements that will print every other value, beginning with the second value, in this form:

```
TIME( 2) CONTAINS XXXX SECONDS
TIME( 4) CONTAINS XXXX SECONDS
.
.
.
TIME(30) CONTAINS XXXX SECONDS
```

26. An array WIND of 70 integer values represents the average daily wind velocities in Chicago over a 10-week period. Assume the array with 10 rows and 7 columns has been filled. Give FORTRAN statements to print the data so that each week is on a separate line. Use a heading as shown:

```
        CHICAGO WIND VELOCITY (MILES/HOUR)

XXX    XXX    XXX    XXX    XXX    XXX    XXX
```

27. Give FORTRAN statements to print the last 10 elements of a real array M of size N. For instance, if M contains 25 elements, the output form is

```
M(  16) = XXX.X
M(  17) = XXX.X
.
.
.
M(  25) = XXX.X
```

28. Give FORTRAN statements to interchange the first and one-hundredth elements, the second and ninety-ninth elements, and so on, of the array NUM that contains 100 integer values. See the diagram that follows:

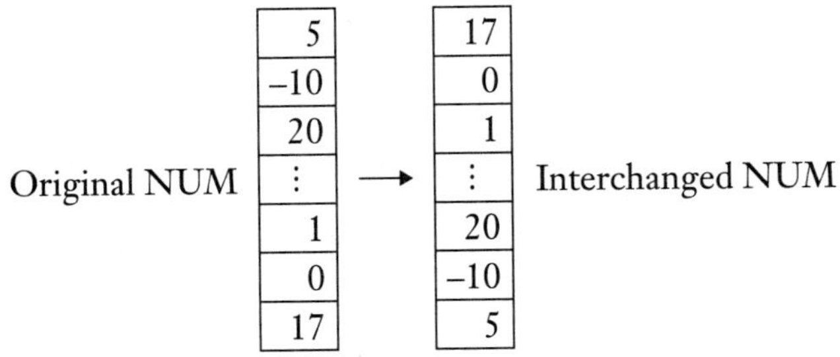

(*Hint:* You will need a temporary storage when you switch values.)

29. An array TREMOR contains integer counts of the number of daily earth tremors detected for 100 days following a major earthquake. Give the FORTRAN statements necessary to find the average of the first 50 days and the second 50 days. Print the following:

```
                    AVERAGES
     FIRST 50 TREMORS       SECOND 50 TREMORS
          XXX.XX                 XXX.XX
```

30. Write a complete program that will read as many as 20 integers from a file NUMBER, one integer per line. The last line will contain 9999. Write the data in the reverse order from which it was read; thus, the value 9999 will be the first value printed.

31. When a plot is made from experimental data, sometimes the scatter of the data points is such that it is difficult to select a "best representative line" for the plot. In such a case, the data can be adjusted to reduce the scatter by using a "moving average" mathematical method of finding the average of three points in succession and replacing the middle value with this average.

    Write a complete program to read an array Y of 20 real values from a file EXPR where the values are entered one per line. Build an array Z of 20 values where Z is the array of adjusted values. That is, Z(2) is the average of Y(1), Y(2), and Y(3); Z(3) is the average of Y(2), Y(3), and Y(4); and so on. Notice that the first and last values of Y cannot be adjusted and should be moved to Z without being changed. Do not destroy the original values in Y. Print the original and the adjusted values next to each other in a table.

32. A truck leasing company owns 12 delivery vans that are leased to several operators. Maintenance hours for each truck are allocated using a maintenance rate multiplied by the total number of hours accumulated by the entire fleet. The maintenance rate for each truck is determined from its percentage of the total fleet hours and the following table:

Percent of Hours	Maintenance Rate
0.00–9.99	0.02
10.00–24.99	0.04
25.00–100.00	0.06

A vehicle identification number and the monthly hours of use are entered in a data file HOURS. Write a complete program to read the data, convert each truck's hours to a percentage of the total fleet hours, and compute its maintenance hours using the maintenance rate. Round the calculated maintenance hours to the nearest hour, and ensure that each truck is allotted a minimum of one hour of maintenance each month. Print the following report:

```
MONTHLY MAINTENANCE REPORT
ID          HOURS        PERCENT        MAINTENANCE HOURS
XXX         XXXX         XXX.X          XXX
 .
 .
 .
TOTALS      XXXXX        XXX.X          XXXX
```

Test your program with the following input data:

ID	Hours
002	61
009	83
012	101
016	55
025	410
036	97
037	66
040	70
043	122
044	136
045	23
046	142

33. Write a complete program that will read a two-dimensional array called RAIN containing 12 rows (one for each month) and 5 columns (one for each year 1978—1982). Each row of real values is entered on a data line in a file WATER. Determine and print the following table of information:

```
AVERAGE YEARLY RAINFALL
1978 - XXX.XX
1979 - XXX.XX
1980 - XXX.XX
1981 - XXX.XX
1982 - XXX.XX

MAXIMUM RAINFALL
MONTH XX YEAR XXXX

MINIMUM RAINFALL
MONTH XX YEAR XXXX
```

34. Assume that the reservations for an airplane flight have been stored in a file called FLIGHT. The plane contains 38 rows with 6 seats in each row. The seats in each row are numbered 1-6 as follows:

1 Window seat, left side
2 Center seat, left side
3 Aisle seat, left side
4 Aisle seat, right side
5 Center seat, right side
6 Window seat, right side

The file FLIGHT contains 38 lines of information corresponding to the 38 rows. Each line contains 6 values corresponding to the 6 seats. The value for any seat is either 0 or 1, representing either an empty or an occupied seat.

Write a complete program to read the FLIGHT information into a two-dimensional array called SEAT. Find and print all pairs of adjacent seats that are empty. Adjacent aisle seats should not be printed. If all three seats on one side of the plane are empty, then two pairs of adjacent seats should be printed. Print this information in the following manner:

```
AVAILABLE SEAT PAIRS
    ROW         SEATS
    XX          X,X
    .
    .
    .
    XX          X,X
```

If no pairs of seats are available, print an appropriate message.

35. The horsepower needed to pump water through a nuclear plant's cooling system is a function of the length of the pipe and the volume flowrate of the water. The following table shows the horsepower required for six different flowrates through five different cooling loops.

		Flowrate					
		1	2	3	4	5	6
	1	2.1	4.0	8.7	15.2	21.0	34.8
	2	2.7	4.2	9.1	18.0	30.0	41.5
Loop	3	4.0	12.9	27.3	52.6	94.4	131.8
	4	3.3	10.0	22.7	44.7	80.9	11.2
	5	1.8	4.1	8.5	15.3	27.2	46.4

Write a program that uses a DATA statement to initialize an array called POWER for storing the data above for the various combinations of flowrates and pipeline loops. The array's columns represent the six different flowrates in gallons per second and the rows represent the five cooling loops. The horsepower needed to pump J gallons per second through cooling loop I is stored in POWER(I,J). For example, POWER(3,2) contains 12.9, so the horsepower required to pump two gallons per second through cooling loop 3 is 12.9.

The program should ask the user to enter the flowrate in gallons per second for each loop. After rounding the flowrate to the nearest integer, find the corresponding horsepower needed for that cooling loop. If the flowrate is over 6.5 gallons per second or less than 0.5 gallons per second, print an error message. Print the horsepower needed for each loop and the total horsepower needed for the entire cooling system.

36. Engineering data files often contain the dates on which information was recorded along with the information itself. If the data file is large, the date is often stored in a Julian date form, which is the year followed by the number of the day in the year (1 to 365), since the Julian date will need only five digits, while a Gregorian date (month-day-year) requires six digits. For example, 010982 is a Gregorian date that converts to 82009 in Julian form. Write a complete program to convert a Gregorian date to a Julian date. Be sure to take leap years into account. (*Hint:* Use an array to store the number of days in each month.)

37. In problem 36 we saw that engineering data files sometimes contain Julian

dates to minimize storage. However, when the information in the files is printed in reports we want to convert the Julian dates to the more common Gregorian dates. Write a complete program to convert a Julian date to a Gregorian date.

38. A communication system often uses multiple lines, or channels, for sending information. Assume that a communication system has five channels for sending information. There is always a background noise signal on the channel, and the average noise value is monitored because it can indicate the quality of the channel for transmitting information. Assume that background noise for the five channels has been collected in a data file. The data file contains 200 lines of information, with five numbers per line that represent the noise level of the five channels at a specific time. Write a program to read the information into a two-dimensional array. Then compute and print the average noise value for each channel and the percent of time that the noise is above average for each channel.

39. In a file named DATA1, each line of data contains a time value in seconds and a temperature value in degrees Fahrenheit. The first line of the data file contains an integer that gives the number of data lines that follow. Read this data, and sort the temperature values in ascending order. Print the sorted temperature values such that there are 10 values per line. Assume that there are not more than 200 lines of data in the file.

40. In a file named DATA2, each line of data contains a time value in seconds and a temperature value in degrees Fahrenheit. The last line of the file is a trailer line that contains the value −999.0 for both time and temperature. Read this data and sort the temperature values in descending order. Print a list of the sorted temperature values in degrees Centigrade. Print 10 values per line. Assume that there are not more than 200 lines of data in the file.

41. In a file named DATA3, each line of data contains a time value in seconds and a temperature value in degrees Fahrenheit. There is no special header line or trailer line in the file. Read this data and print the number of temperature values, the average temperature values, and the number of temperatures that were greater than the average. Assume that there are not more than 200 lines of data in the file.

42. In a file named DATA3, each line of data contains a time value in seconds and a temperature value in degrees Fahrenheit. There is no special header line or trailer line in the file. Read this data and print the number of temperature values and the maximum temperature value. Also print each time that the maximum temperature value occurred. Assume that there are not more than 200 lines of data in the file.

43. In a file named DATA3, each line of data contains a time value in seconds and a temperature value in degrees Fahrenheit. There is no special header line or trailer line in the file. Read this data and generate a new data file called DATA3S that contains the information sorted in ascending order by temperatures. Be careful to keep the correct time with the temperatures. Assume that there are not more than 200 lines of data in the file.

44. Assume that the file DEC 90 contains weather information for Stapleton International Airport. (See Section 4–3 on page 178 for a description of the

data files.) Write a program to read the data and print a report that gives the maximum temperatures in descending order. Print one temperature per line, along with its corresponding date.

45. Assume that the file DEC 90 contains weather information for Stapleton International Airport. (See Section 4–3 on page 178 for a description of the data files.) Write a program to print a report that lists the temperatures from −20° to 50°. Beside each temperature value print the number of days with that minimum temperature.

46. Assume that the file DEC 90 contains weather information for Stapleton International Airport. (See Section 4–3 on page 178 for a description of the data files.) Write a program to print a report that prints a temperature distribution that begins with −40° and gives the number of maximum temperatures during the month of December 1990 that were in 10-degree intervals. Thus, the first category would include temperatures from −40° to −31°, and so on, through the category containing the maximum temperature.

FORTRAN STATEMENT SUMMARY

■ DATA Statement:

DATA *list of variable names /list of values/*

Example:

```
DATA X, Y, COUNTR /1.0,15.78,0.0/
```

Discussion:

The DATA statement is used to initialize variables at the beginning of your program. It is a specification statement and thus should be positioned before any executable statements.

■ DIMENSION Statement:

DIMENSION *array1(size), array2(size), . . .*

Example:

```
DIMENSION LIST(50), GRID(5,8)
```

Discussion:

The DIMENSION statement is used to define arrays and their corresponding sizes. Elements in an array are referenced using a common name plus a subscript that specifies a unique element of the array. When arrays are defined with the DIMENSION statement, the array type is implicitly specified depending on the first letter of the array name. Because this statement is a specification statement, it should be positioned before any executable statements.

6 Function Subprograms

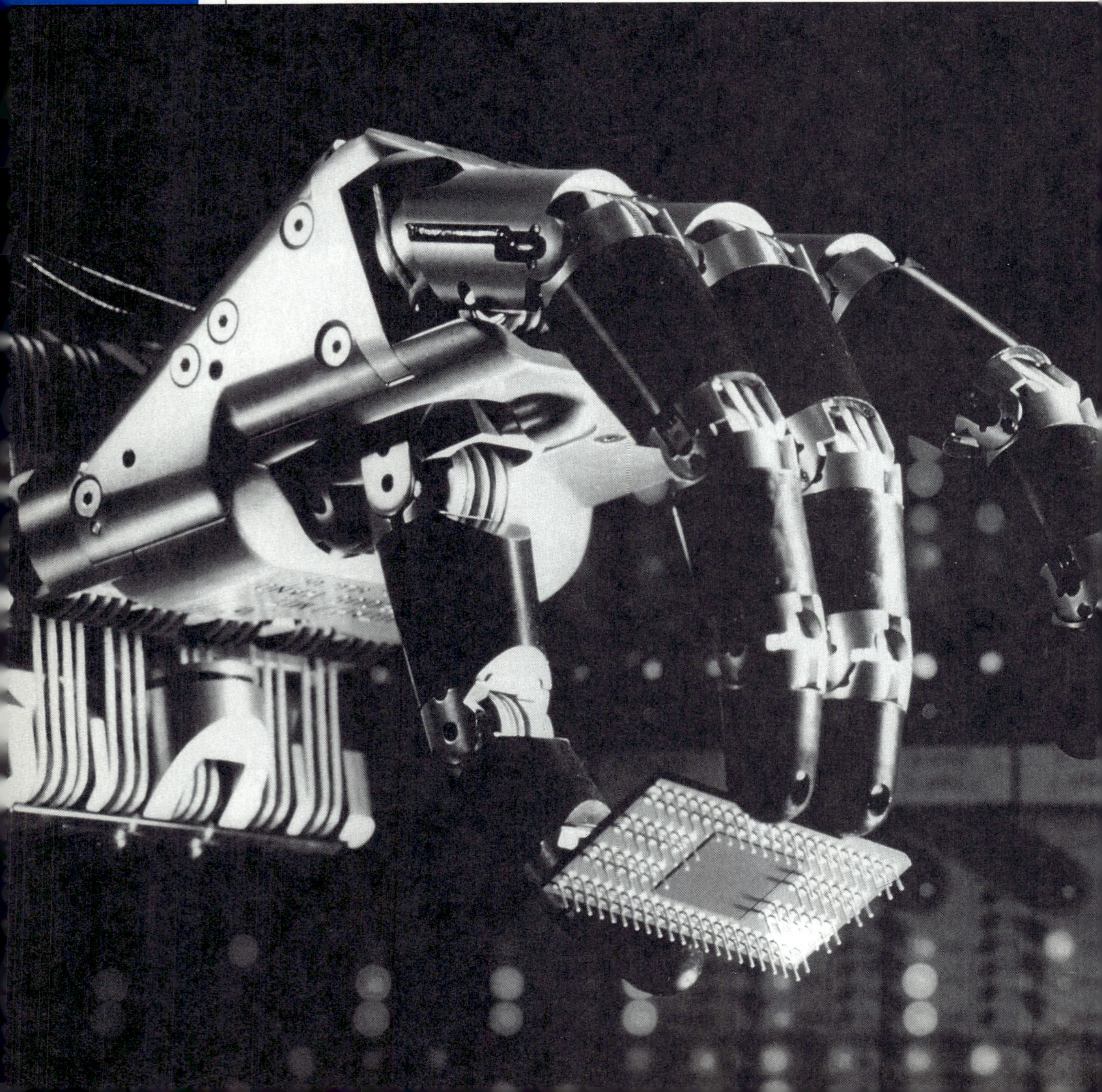

6

APPLICATION

Industrial Robots

Industrial robots are an important part of computer-aided manufacturing (CAM). Some of the tasks that are currently being performed by robots include machine tending, material transfer, spot welding, arc welding, spray painting/coating, routing, drilling, grinding, and electronics assembly. Field robots perform jobs that are dangerous for humans to perform, such as inspecting and repairing nuclear power plants, disposing of bombs, inspecting oil rigs for undersea exploration, and cleaning up chemical accidents. The design of a robot involves the use of mechanisms, sensors, actuators, and computers to synthesize some aspects of human functions. The area of robotics is often split into four major areas: mechanical manipulation, locomotion, computer vision, and artificial intelligence. (See Section 6–7 for the solution to a problem related to this application.)

Photo © John Madere/The Stock Market

Introduction

As our programs become longer and more complicated, we find it harder to maintain program readability and simplicity. We also find that we frequently need to perform the same set of operations at more than one location in our programs. These problems can be solved with *subprograms,* which are groups of statements that are defined separately and then referenced when we need them in our programs. FORTRAN has two types of subprograms: functions and subroutines. In this chapter we review the intrinsic function (such as the square root function and the logarithm function) and learn how to write our own functions to perform computations unique to our applications. The function is quite useful in solving engineering and science problems because many of our solutions involve arithmetic computations. In the next chapter we concentrate on subroutines which are subprograms that allow us to return many values as opposed to a single function value. Subroutines can also be used to read data files and print reports.

6·1 ■ Intrinsic Functions

A *function* computes a single value, such as the square root of a number or the average of an array. You have already used functions in the form of *intrinsic functions* such as SQRT and SIN. These intrinsic functions are in the compiler and are accessible directly from your program. The intrinsic functions (or *library functions*) available in FORTRAN 77 are listed in Appendix A. You should read through the list so that you are aware of the types of operations that can be performed with intrinsic functions. When you need to use one of these operations, you can refer to Appendix A for details on how to use that specific function. Although we introduced intrinsic functions in Chapter 2, we can summarize the main components of these functions:

1. The function name and its input values (or *arguments*) collectively represent a single value.
2. A function can never be used on the left-hand side of an equal sign in an assignment statement.
3. The name of the intrinsic function typically determines the type of output from the function. (For example, if the name begins with one of the letters I through N, its value is an integer.)
4. The arguments of a function are generally of the same type as the function itself. For a few exceptions, refer to the list of intrinsic functions in Appendix A.
5. The arguments of a function must be enclosed in parentheses.
6. The arguments of a function may be constants, variables, expressions, or other functions.

Generic functions accept arguments of any allowable type and return a value of the same type as the argument. Thus, the generic function ABS will return an integer absolute value if its argument is an integer, but it will return a real absolute value if its argument is real. The table in Appendix A identifies generic functions.

Fortran 90 contains new intrinsic functions to perform bit operations (operations on the individual binary digits in a memory location). New intrinsic functions also allow you to perform operations on arrays, such as determining the maximum and minimum and computing the sum or product of elements in the array.

Fortran 90

Odd and Even Values

Example 6·1

Read an integer and then print the word ODD or EVEN, depending on the value read.

Solution

In this solution we use the intrinsic function MOD. This function has two integer arguments, I and J. The function returns the integer remainder in the division of I by J. This operation is also called modulo division—hence, the function is called a MOD function. Some example values for I, J, and MOD(I,J) are

I	J	MOD(I,J)
3	2	1
4	2	0
6	4	2
10	4	2
88	3	1

If a number K is even, it is a multiple of 2, and MOD(K,2) is zero. If K is odd, then MOD(K,2) is 1. The statements that determine if an integer is odd or even using this function are

```
   PRINT*, 'ENTER AN INTEGER'
   READ*, K
   IF (MOD(K,2).EQ.0) THEN
      PRINT 5, K
5     FORMAT (1X,I5,' IS EVEN')
   ELSE
      PRINT 6, K
6     FORMAT (1X,I5,' IS ODD')
   END IF
```

The MOD function can also be used to determine if a number is a multiple of another number. For instance, if MOD(M,5) is zero, then M is a multiple of 5.

6·2 ■ Statement Functions

Engineering and science applications often require a function that is not included in the intrinsic function list. If the computation is needed frequently or requires several steps, we should implement it as a function instead of listing all the computations each time we need them. FORTRAN allows us to write our own functions in two ways: as a *statement function* or as a function subprogram. If the computation can be written in a single assignment statement, we can use the statement function that will be discussed in this section; otherwise, we must use the function subprogram that will be discussed in Section 6 – 5.

The general form for this statement is

function name (argument list) = expression

The following rules apply to writing and using a statement function:

1. The statement function is defined at the beginning of your program, along with your type statements and array definitions. It is a nonexecutable statement; thus, it should precede any executable statement.
2. The definition of the statement function contains the name of the function, followed by its arguments in parentheses, on the left-hand side of an equal sign; the expression for computing the function value is on the right-hand side of the equal sign.
3. The function name should be included in a type statement; otherwise, implicit typing will determine the function type.

Example 6 – 2 illustrates the use of the statement function in a complete program.

Example 6·2

Triangle Area

The area of a triangle can be computed from the lengths of two sides and the angle between them:

```
AREA = 0.5*SIDE1*SIDE2*SIN(ANGLE)
```

Write a program that reads the lengths of the three sides of a triangle and the angles opposite each side.

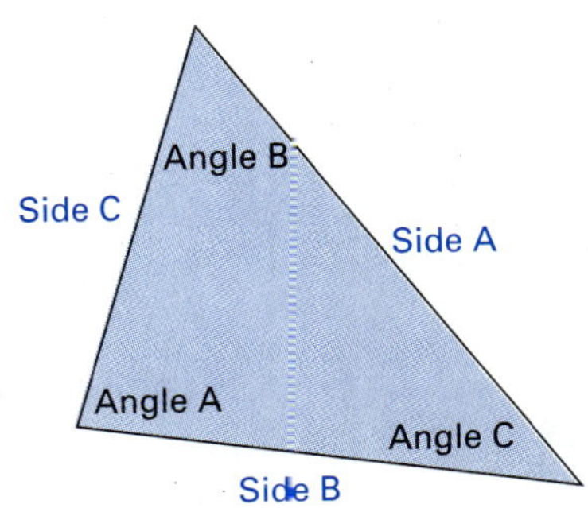

Compute and print the area of the triangle using one pair of sides and its corresponding angle. Then compute and print the area using another pair of sides and its corresponding angle. Finally, compute and print the area using the last pair of sides and its corresponding angle. Use a statement function to compute these areas.

Solution

The **first step** is to state the problem clearly: Compute the area of a triangle. The **second step** is to describe the input and output:

Input—lengths of the three sides *a*, *b*, *c*, and angles *a*, *b*, *c*
Output—areas computed from the sides and angles

The **third step** is to work a simple example. We choose a triangle with sides equal to 1.0, 1.0, $\sqrt{2}$ and angles 45°, 45°, and 90°. (The sides with length 1.0 are opposite the 45° angles.) Using this information, the three areas are:

$$\text{area } 1 = 0.5 \cdot 1.0 \cdot 1.0 \cdot \sin(90°) = 0.5$$
$$\text{area } 2 = 0.5 \cdot 1.0 \cdot \sqrt{2} \cdot \sin(45°) = 0.5$$
$$\text{area } 3 = 0.5 \cdot 1.0 \cdot \sqrt{2} \cdot \sin(45°) = 0.5$$

The **fourth step** is to develop an algorithm, beginning with the decomposition.

Decomposition

Read the sides and angles of a triangle.
Compute the area in three ways.
Print the three areas.

Pseudocode

```
Triangle: Read sides a, b, c and angles a, b, c
          Compute area using side b, side c, and angle a
          Compute area using side a, side c, and angle b
          Compute area using side a, side b, and angle c
          Print three areas
```

FORTRAN Program

```
*-----------------------------------------------------------------------*
      PROGRAM TRIANG
*
*  This program reads the lengths of the sides of a triangle
*  along with the corresponding angles in radians. It then
*  computes and prints the area of the triangle using three
*  different sets of information.
*
      REAL SIDEA, SIDEB, SIDEC, A, B, C, AREA,
     +     AREAA, AREAB, AREAC, SIDE1, SIDE2, ANGLE
*
      AREA(SIDE1,SIDE2,ANGLE) = 0.5*SIDE1*SIDE2*SIN(ANGLE)
*
```

```
      PRINT*, 'ENTER THE LENGTHS OF THE THREE SIDES OF A'
      PRINT*, 'TRIANGLE IN THE FOLLOWING ORDER:'
      PRINT*, 'SIDE A   SIDE B   SIDE C'
      READ*, SIDEA, SIDEB, SIDEC
*
      PRINT*
      PRINT*, 'ENTER THE ANGLE OPPOSITE SIDE A,'
      PRINT*, 'THEN THE ANGLE OPPOSITE SIDE B,'
      PRINT*, 'AND THEN THE ANGLE OPPOSITE SIDE C.'
      PRINT*, '(IN RADIANS)'
      READ*, A, B, C
*
      AREAA = AREA(SIDEB,SIDEC,A)
      AREAB = AREA(SIDEC,SIDEA,B)
      AREAC = AREA(SIDEA,SIDEB,C)
*
      PRINT*
      PRINT*, 'THE THREE AREA COMPUTATIONS YIELD:'
      PRINT 5, AREAA, AREAB, AREAC
    5 FORMAT (1X,3F7.2)
*
      END
*----------------------------------------------------------------------*
```

The **fifth step** is to test the program. The following output represents a typical user interaction with this program:

```
ENTER THE LENGTHS OF THE THREE SIDES OF A
TRIANGLE IN THE FOLLOWING ORDER:
SIDE A   SIDE B   SIDE C
1.0   1.0   1.414

ENTER THE ANGLE OPPOSITE SIDE A,
THEN THE ANGLE OPPOSITE SIDE B,
AND THEN THE ANGLE OPPOSITE SIDE C.
(IN RADIANS)
0.785   0.785   1.571

THE THREE AREA COMPUTATIONS YIELD:
   0.50   0.50   0.50
```

Note that the arguments in the statement function definition are SIDEl, SIDE2, and ANGLE. These arguments do not represent variables used in our program; they tell the compiler that the statement function has three real arguments. When we referenced the function AREA to compute AREAA, note that the variable SIDEB corresponded to the argument SIDEl, the variable SIDEC corresponded to the argument SIDE2, and the variable C corresponded to the argument ANGLE. When we referenced the function AREA to compute AREAB and AREAC, different variables corresponded to the arguments SIDEl, SIDE2, and ANGLE.

Suppose that you forgot to define the statement function AREA. The first statement in your program that uses the function is

```
AREAA = AREA(SIDEB,SIDEC,A)
```

Many compilers assume that AREA is an array that you forgot to define, and they print an error message related to undefined arrays, instead of undefined statement functions.

As a result, you may look in the wrong place in your program to correct this error. When you use statement functions, be aware that the compiler may confuse an undefined statement function with an undefined array; similarly, the compiler may diagnose an undefined array as an undefined statement function.

If you want to enter the angles in degrees, you can convert the degrees to radians in an assignment statement such as

```
A = A*(PI/180.0)
```

You can also perform the degree-to-radian conversion within the statement function, as shown:

```
      AREA(SIDE1,SIDE2,ANGLE) = 0.5*SIDE1*SIDE2*
     +                          SIN(ANGLE*3.14159/180.0)
```

The constant (3.14159/180.0) could be replaced by 0.0175, but leaving it as a division documents the computation for anyone else looking at the program. ◀

SELF-TEST 6-1

This self-test allows you to check quickly to see if you have remembered some of the key points from Section 6–2. If you have any problems with the exercises, you should reread this section. The solutions are included at the end of the text.

For each of the following, give the statement function required to perform the computation.

1. Area of a square: $A = \text{side}^2$
2. Area of a rectangle: $A = \text{side1} \cdot \text{side2}$
3. Area of a parallelogram: $A = \text{base} \cdot \text{height}$
4. Area of a trapezoid: $A = \frac{1}{2} \cdot \text{base} \cdot (\text{height1} + \text{height 2})$
5. Area of a triangle: $A = \frac{1}{2} \cdot \text{base} \cdot \text{height}$

6-3 Application ▪ Temperature Conversions

Chemistry

In this application, we develop a program to print a temperature conversion table. To be flexible, we will let the program user specify the type of conversion (Fahrenheit to Centigrade or Centigrade to Fahrenheit), the starting temperature, the change in temperature for each line, and the ending temperature. The output headings should reflect the correct temperature units. The two equations that we need are

$$\text{degrees C} = (\text{degrees F} - 32) \cdot \frac{5}{9}$$

$$\text{degrees F} = \text{degrees C} \cdot \frac{9}{5} + 32$$

Each of these computations requires only a single statement; thus, we can implement them as statement functions.

1. Problem Statement

Print a conversion table for temperatures in Fahrenheit and Centigrade degrees.

2. Input/Output Description

Input—the temperature unit for the input values, the initial temperature value, the change in temperature from one line to the next, and the final temperature value

Output—a temperature conversion table

3. Hand Example

Assume that we want to convert degrees Fahrenheit to degrees Centigrade. Start the table at zero degrees, increment each line by 10 degrees, and stop when the last line in the table is 50 degrees. Using the preceding equation for converting Fahrenheit to Centigrade, we obtain the following table:

TEMPERATURE CONVERSION TABLE

Degrees, Fahrenheit	Degrees, Centigrade
0.00	−17.78
10.00	−12.22
20.00	−6.67
30.00	−1.11
40.00	4.44
50.00	10.00

4. Algorithm Development

Decomposition

Read input specifications.
Print table.

As we refine these steps, we see that reading the input specifications is a series of sequential steps that print messages to the user requesting the necessary data and then reading the data. Printing the table involves a While loop that is repeated until we have printed all the lines requested in the table. If we use NEXT to represent the next temperature to be converted, we want to remain in the While loop "while NEXT is less than or equal to the final temperature value." These steps are detailed in the following flowchart.

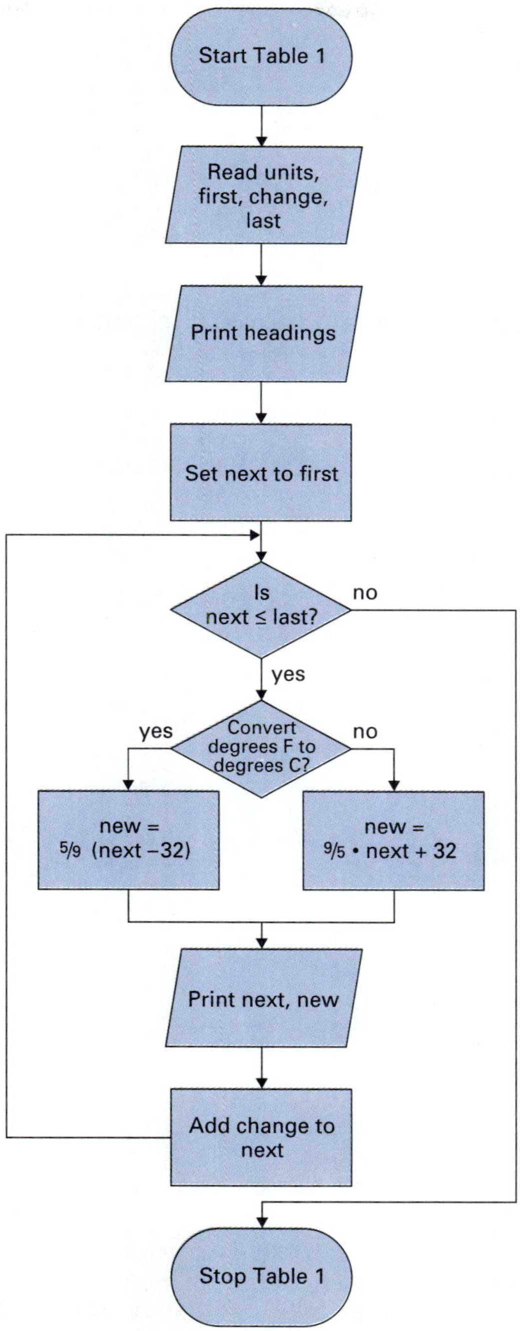

The flowchart is detailed enough to translate the steps into FORTRAN. Note the emphasis in the program on clearly specifying to the user exactly what form to use for entering data.

FORTRAN Program 1

```
*--------------------------------------------------------------------*
      PROGRAM TABLE1
*
*  This program generates a temperature conversion table
*  for temperatures in degrees Fahrenheit and degrees Centigrade.
*
      INTEGER UNITS
      REAL CENT, TEMP, FAHREN, FIRST, CHANGE, LAST, NEXT, NEW
*
      CENT(TEMP) = (TEMP - 32.0)*0.5555556
      FAHREN(TEMP) = 1.8*TEMP + 32.0
*
      PRINT*, 'ENTER 1 TO CONVERT FAHRENHEIT TO CENTIGRADE'
      PRINT*, 'ENTER 2 TO CONVERT CENTIGRADE TO FAHRENHEIT'
      READ*, UNITS
      PRINT*, 'ENTER NUMBER OF DEGREES FOR FIRST LINE'
      READ*, FIRST
      PRINT*, 'ENTER CHANGE IN DEGREES BETWEEN LINES'
      READ*, CHANGE
      PRINT*, 'ENTER NUMBER OF DEGREES FOR LAST LINE'
      READ*, LAST
*
      PRINT 5
    5 FORMAT (1X,6X,'TEMPERATURE CONVERSION TABLE')
      IF (UNITS.EQ.1) THEN
         PRINT 10
   10    FORMAT (1X,'DEGREES, FAHRENHEIT',8X,'DEGREES, CENTIGRADE')
      ELSE
         PRINT 15
   15    FORMAT (1X,'DEGREES, CENTIGRADE',8X,'DEGREES, FAHRENHEIT')
      END IF
*
      NEXT = FIRST
   20 IF (NEXT.LE.LAST) THEN
*
         IF (UNITS.EQ.1) THEN
            NEW = CENT(NEXT)
         ELSE
            NEW = FAHREN(NEXT)
         END IF
*
         PRINT 25, NEXT, NEW
   25    FORMAT (1X,3X,F9.2,17X,F9.2)
*
         NEXT = NEXT + CHANGE
         GO TO 20
      END IF
*
      END
*--------------------------------------------------------------------*
```

Although this solution works correctly and is readable, there are often many ways to solve the same problem. For example, in this solution, we observe that the two equations for converting temperatures are similar. The following steps rewrite the two equations into linear equations with different slopes and different y-intercepts:

$$\text{degrees C} = (\text{degrees F} - 32) \cdot \frac{5}{9}$$

$$= \text{degrees F} \cdot \frac{5}{9} - 32 \cdot \frac{5}{9}$$

$$= 0.5555556 \cdot \text{degrees F} - 17.77778$$

$$\text{degrees F} = \text{degrees C} \cdot \frac{9}{5} + 32$$

$$= 1.8 \cdot \text{degrees C} + 32$$

If NEXT contains the temperature that we are going to convert and NEW is to contain this new value, then both equations can be written in this form:

```
NEW = SLOPE*NEXT + INTERC
```

Thus, instead of using two statement functions, we can use one statement function with three arguments as shown in the following program.

FORTRAN Program 2

```
*-----------------------------------------------------------------------*
      PROGRAM TABLE2
*
*  This program generates a temperature conversion table
*  for temperatures in degrees Fahrenheit and degrees Centigrade.
*
      INTEGER UNITS
      REAL CONV, TEMP, A, B, FIRST, CHANGE, LAST, NEXT, NEW,
     +     SLOPE, INTERC
*
      CONV(TEMP,A,B) = A*TEMP + B
*
      PRINT*, 'ENTER 1 TO CONVERT FAHRENHEIT TO CENTIGRADE'
      PRINT*, 'ENTER 2 TO CONVERT CENTIGRADE TO FAHRENHEIT'
      READ*, UNITS
      PRINT*, 'ENTER NUMBER OF DEGREES FOR FIRST LINE'
      READ*, FIRST
      PRINT*, 'ENTER CHANGE IN DEGREES BETWEEN LINES'
      READ*, CHANGE
      PRINT*, 'ENTER NUMBER OF DEGREES FOR LAST LINE'
      READ*, LAST
*
      PRINT 5
    5 FORMAT (1X,6X,'TEMPERATURE CONVERSION TABLE')
*
      IF (UNITS.EQ.1) THEN
         PRINT 10
   10    FORMAT (1X,'DEGREES, FAHRENHEIT',8X,'DEGREES, CENTIGRADE')
         SLOPE = 0.5555556
         INTERC = -17.77778
      ELSE
         PRINT 15
   15    FORMAT (1X,'DEGREES, CENTIGRADE',8X,'DEGREES, FAHRENHEIT')
         SLOPE = 1.8
         INTERC = 32.0
      END IF
*
```

```
      NEXT = FIRST
   20 IF (NEXT.LE.LAST) THEN
         NEW = CONV(NEXT,SLOPE,INTERC)
         PRINT 25, NEXT, NEW
   25    FORMAT (1X,3X,F9.2,17X,F9.2)
         NEXT = NEXT + CHANGE
         GO TO 20
      END IF
*
      END
*-----------------------------------------------------------------------*
```

5. Testing

If we test either of the programs with our hand example data, the following output is

```
ENTER 1 TO CONVERT FAHRENHEIT TO CENTIGRADE
ENTER 2 TO CONVERT CENTIGRADE TO FAHRENHEIT
1
ENTER NUMBER OF DEGREES FOR FIRST LINE
0.0
ENTER CHANGE IN DEGREES BETWEEN LINES
10.0
ENTER NUMBER OF DEGREES FOR LAST LINE
50.0
      TEMPERATURE CONVERSION TABLE
DEGREES, FAHRENHEIT          DEGREES, CENTIGRADE
        0.00                      -17.78
       10.00                      -12.22
       20.00                       -6.67
       30.00                       -1.11
       40.00                        4.44
       50.00                       10.00
```

In this application we did not error check the input values. What would happen if the last temperature value entered was less than the first temperature value entered? The first time that the While condition was executed, it would be false; thus, the While loop would never be executed. The program would end without an error, but only the headings would be printed.

What would happen if the starting temperature and the change were such that the next temperature was never equal to the last temperature? For example, suppose FIRST was specified to be 0.0, CHANGE was specified to be 2.0, and LAST was specified to be 9.0. Output lines would be printed for values 0.0, 2.0, 4.0, 6.0, and 8.0. When the temperature was incremented to 10.0, it would exceed the last value, and we would exit the While loop.

6-4 ■ Modular Programming

In previous chapters we stressed the importance of using While loops, DO loops, and IF structures as essential ingredients in writing structured programs. Another key element in structuring program logic is the use of *modules*. These modules or procedures allow us to write programs composed of nearly independent segments or routines. There are modules that are part of the language, such as intrinsic functions, and there are user-defined modules. In FORTRAN, user-defined modules are implemented as functions or subroutines. Functions and subroutines are also called *subprograms;* they look very much like programs except that they begin with a FUNCTION statement or a SUBROUTINE statement instead of a PROGRAM statement.

When we decompose a problem solution into a series of sequentially executed steps, we are decomposing the problem into steps that probably could be easily structured into functions and subroutines. The following are some important advantages to breaking programs into modules:

1. You can write and test each module separately from the rest of the program.
2. Debugging is easier because you are working with smaller sections of the program.
3. Modules can be used in other programs without rewriting or retesting.
4. Programs are more readable and thus more easily understood because of the modular structure.
5. Several programmers can work on different modules of a large program relatively independent of one another.
6. Individual parts of the program become shorter and therefore simpler.
7. A module can be used several times by the same program.

Since modules are so important in writing readable, well-structured programs, we are going to devote this chapter to functions and the next chapter to subroutines.

We have used the decomposition diagram to show the sequential steps necessary to solve a problem. Another type of diagram, the *structure chart,* is also very useful as we decompose our problem solution into smaller problems. While the decomposition diagram outlines the sequential operations needed, the structure chart outlines the modules but does not indicate the order in which they are to be executed.

The diagram below contains a structure chart for a program that we will be developing in Section 6–6. In the program we are reading oil well production data from a data file. For each oil well, we read the daily production in barrels, compute a daily average for the week, and print this information in the report. In addition, we keep summary information for all the wells and print it at the end of the report. A function subprogram is used to compute the average daily production for each oil well.

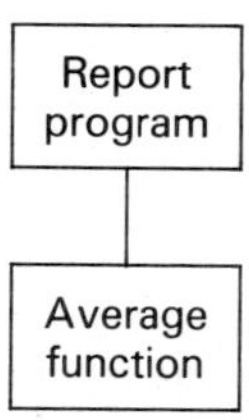

The next structure chart is from a program that we develop in Chapter 10 that uses the Gauss elimination technique to solve a system of linear equations. This solution uses three subroutines.

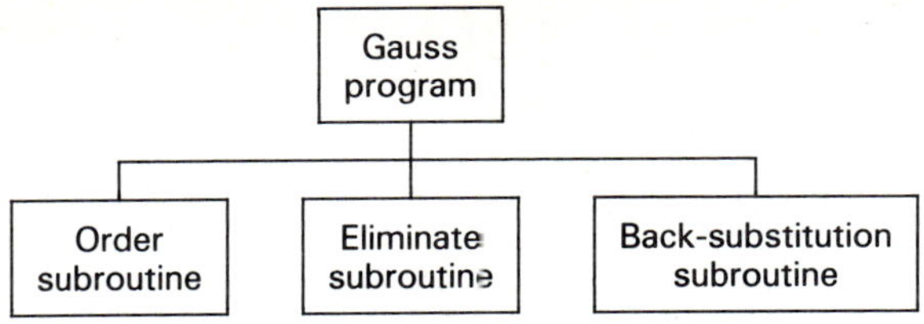

It is important to distinguish between a decomposition diagram and the structure chart. The decomposition diagram shows the sequential order of the steps of the solution; it does not identify any of the steps as modules. The structure chart, on the other hand, clearly defines the module definitions for the program but does not show the order in which the modules are used. Thus, both charts are useful in describing the algorithm that is being developed for the problem solution because they represent different information about the solution.

6·5 ■ User-Defined Functions

Because intrinsic functions are contained in a library that is part of the compiler, you may find that a function in one computer manufacturer's compiler may not be available in another's. You may also find that you would like to use a function that is not a standard FORTRAN 77 intrinsic function. These problems can be solved by writing your own function.

A function subprogram, which is a program itself, is separate from the *main program*. It begins with a nonexecutable statement that identifies the function with a name and an argument list, as shown in the general form

FUNCTION *name (argument list)*

Because a function is separate from the main program, it must end with an END statement. The function should also contain a RETURN statement, which returns control to the statement that referenced the function, although the END statement will also generate a return. The general form of the RETURN statement is

```
RETURN
```

The rules for choosing a function name are the same as those for choosing a program name. In addition, the first letter of the function name specifies the type of value returned unless it is included in a specification statement. The following statements illustrate a simple example with a structure chart, a main program, and a function subprogram.

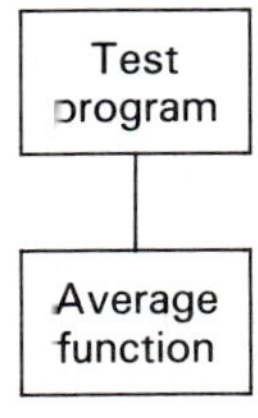

Main Program

```
*----------------------------------------------------------------*
      PROGRAM TEST
*
*  This is a sample main program.
*
      REAL TEST1, TEST2, TEST3, AVE
*
      READ*, TEST1, TEST2, TEST3
      PRINT 5, AVE(TEST1,TEST2,TEST3)
    5 FORMAT (1X,'AVERAGE = ',F5.2)
*
      END
*----------------------------------------------------------------*
```

Function Subprogram

```
      REAL FUNCTION AVE(X,Y,Z)
*
*     This is a sample function.
*
      REAL X, Y, Z
      AVE = (X + Y + Z)/3.0
*
      RETURN
      END
*----------------------------------------------------------------*
```

Several rules must be observed in writing a function subprogram.

1. The function arguments referenced in the main program are the *actual arguments.* They must match in type, number, and order the *dummy arguments* used in the FUNCTION statement. In the preceding example, the actual arguments are TEST1, TEST2, TEST3; the dummy arguments are X, Y, Z. TESTl corresponds to X, TEST2 corresponds to Y, and TEST3 corresponds to Z.
2. If one of the arguments is an array, its dimensions must be specified in both the main program and the function subprogram.
3. The value to be returned to the main program is stored in the function name using an assignment statement.
4. When the function is ready to return control to the statement in the main program that referenced it, a RETURN statement is executed. A function may contain more than one RETURN statement.
5. A function can contain references to other functions, but it cannot contain a reference to itself.
6. A function subprogram is usually placed immediately after the main program, but it also may appear before the main program. If you have more than one function, the order of the functions does not matter as long as each function is completely separate from the other functions.
7. A main program and its subprograms can be stored in the same program file or in separate files. If they are stored in separate files, it is necessary to link them before the main program can be executed. The statements required to perform the linking depend on the compiler and the operating system.
8. The same statement numbers may be used in both a function and the main program. No confusion occurs as to which statement is referenced because the function and the main program are completely separate. Similarly, a function

and a main program can use the same variable name, such as SUM, to store different sums as long as the variable SUM is not an argument of the function.

9. The name of the function should appear in a type statement in the main program as well as in the function statement itself. The following statements illustrate the definition of an integer function AVE that computes an integer average. Compare this main program and function to the previous example that computes a real average.

```
*-----------------------------------------------------------------*
      PROGRAM TEST
*
*  This is a sample main program.
*
      INTEGER TEST1, TEST2, TEST3, AVE
*
      READ*, TEST1, TEST2, TEST3
      PRINT 5, AVE(TEST1,TEST2,TEST3)
    5 FORMAT (1X,AVERAGE = ',I5)
*
      END
*-----------------------------------------------------------------*
      INTEGER FUNCTION AVE(I,J,K)
*
*  This is a sample function.
*
      INTEGER I, J, K
*
      AVE = (I + J + K)/3
*
      RETURN
      END
*-----------------------------------------------------------------*
```

10. Do not change the values of the dummy arguments. Some compilers return the new values to the main program; others do not. If you need to return more than the function value itself, use a subroutine (discussed in Chapter 7) instead of a function.

Fortran 90

In Fortran 90, a function can contain a statement that is a function reference to itself. This type of function is a recursive function, and it is very useful in solving some problems.

We now present a series of examples to illustrate the use of these rules in writing and using user-defined functions. Because a function subprogram is a program separate from the main program, you should approach function design and implementation much as you would a complete program. Follow the same guidelines for developing a decomposition diagram, then refine it using pseudocode or flowcharts until it is detailed enough to convert into FORTRAN. Because the function receives values through the argument list, the pseudocode or flowchart should begin with the name of the function and the variables that are the dummy arguments to the function.

Sales Bonus

Example 6-3

A local company has a number of computer programs that are used in maintaining its accounts and preparing payrolls. Several of the programs need to compute the bonus earned by salespeople who work for the company. Instead of recomputing the sales bonus in each program, subprograms are used. This bonus is computed from the total sales of the salesperson, using the following table:

Total Sales	Bonus Percent
sales < \$1000	1%
\$1000 ≤ sales < \$2000	2%
\$2000 ≤ sales < \$2500	3%
\$2500 ≤ sales	5%

The function is to be called BONUS and has one argument, the total sales for the salesperson.

Solution

The **first step** is to state the problem clearly: Write a function subprogram to compute the sales bonus.

The **second step** is to describe the input and output:

Input—total sales for the salesperson
Output—sales bonus

The **third step** is to work a simple example by hand. If the total sales is \$2100, then the bonus is 0.03 × \$2100 = \$63.00.

The **fourth step** is to develop an algorithm, beginning with the decomposition.

Decomposition

Compute bonus based on sales.
Return.

Flowchart

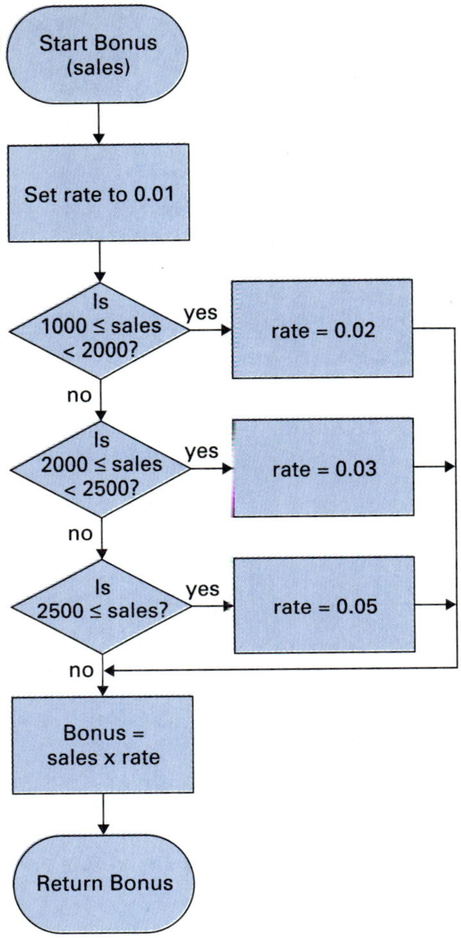

Correct Solution 1

```
*-----------------------------------------------------------------------*
      REAL FUNCTION BONUS(SALES)
*
*  This function computes a bonus based on sales.
*
      REAL SALES, RATE
*
      RATE = 0.01
      IF (SALES.GE.1000.0.AND.SALES.LT.2000.0) RATE = 0.02
      IF (SALES.GE.2000.0.AND.SALES.LT.2500.0) RATE = 0.03
      IF (SALES.GE.2500.0) RATE = 0.05
      BONUS = SALES*RATE
*
      RETURN
      END
*-----------------------------------------------------------------------*
```

Correct Solution 2

```
*----------------------------------------------------------------------*
      REAL FUNCTION BONUS(SALES)
*
*  This function computes a bonus based on sales.
*
      REAL SALES, RATE
*
      IF (SALES.LT.1000.0) THEN
         RATE = 0.01
      ELSE IF (SALES.LT.2000.0) THEN
         RATE = 0.02
      ELSE IF (SALES.LT.2500.0) THEN
         RATE = 0.03
      ELSE
         RATE = 0.05
      END IF
      BONUS = SALES*RATE
*
      RETURN
      END
*----------------------------------------------------------------------*
```

Incorrect Solution

The following function is similar to the function in the previous solution, but this one does not work correctly. See if you can spot the error before reading the explanation.

```
*----------------------------------------------------------------------*
      REAL FUNCTION BONUS(SALES)
*
*  This function computes a bonus based on sales.
*
      REAL SALES, RATE
*
      IF (SALES.GT.2500.0) THEN
         RATE = 0.05
      ELSE IF (SALES.LT.2500.0) THEN
         RATE = 0.03
      ELSE IF (SALES.LT.2000.0) THEN
         RATE = 0.02
      ELSE IF (SALES.LT.1000.0) THEN
         RATE = 0.01
      END IF
      BONUS = SALES*RATE
*
      RETURN
      END
*----------------------------------------------------------------------*
```

The key to understanding the problem with this solution is to remember the manner in which an IF-ELSE IF statement is executed. As soon as a true condition is encountered, the appropriate steps are executed and control passes to the END IF at the end of the structure; even if two conditions are true, the first one encountered is the only one tested. Suppose that the SALES amount is $900. The commission rate should be 1%; however, because SALES is less than 2500.0, the rate is computed to be 3% and control is passed to the END IF and then to the computation for BONUS.

The **fifth step** is to test the program. A main program that uses either of the correct functions might include a statement such as the following, which reads the sales for one of the salespersons and then prints the sales and bonus:

```
      READ*, ID, SALES
      PRINT 5, ID, SALES, BONUS(SALES)
    5 FORMAT (1X,'SALESPERSON:',I5,3X,'SALES:',F8.2,3X,
     +        'BONUS:',F7.2)
```

As stated earlier, when arrays are used as arguments in a function, they must be dimensioned in the function subprogram as well as in the main program. Generally, the array should have the same size in the function as it does in the main program; however, when the size of an array is an argument to the subprogram, we use a technique called *variable dimensioning*. This technique allows us to specify an array of variable size in the subprogram. The argument value then sets the size of the array when the subprogram is executed. We illustrate the use of an array with a fixed size in Example 6–4 and with a variable size in Example 6–5. (Note that variable dimensioning refers to dimensioning of an array used as a dummy argument in a subprogram. Any array that is not a dummy argument, but that is defined and used in a subprogram, must be dimensioned in the subprogram with a constant because it is not dimensioned in the main program.)

Example 6-4

Array Average, Fixed Array Size

Write a function that receives an array of 20 real values. Compute the average of the array and return it as the function value.

Solution

The **first step** is to state the problem clearly: Write a function that computes the average of an array.

The **second step** is to describe the input and output:

Input — array of 20 real values
Output — array average

The **third step** is to work a simple example by hand. Let the input array contain the following values:

$$-2, 36, 24, -3, 19, 21, 8, 2, 5, 38, 16, -4, 2, 7, 17, 24, 9, -3, 6, 0$$

The average is then $\frac{222}{20} = 11.1$.

The **fourth step** is to develop an algorithm, starting with the decomposition.

Decomposition

Compute average of array x.
Return.

Pseudocode

```
Average(x): sum ← 0.0
            For i = 1 to 20
                sum ← sum + x(i)
            average ← sum/20.0
            Return
```

FORTRAN Function

```
*-----------------------------------------------------------------------*
      REAL FUNCTION AVE(X)
*
*  This function computes the average of a real
*  array with twenty values.
*
      INTEGER I
      REAL X(20), SUM
*
      SUM = 0.0
      DO 10 I=1,20
         SUM = SUM + X(I)
   10 CONTINUE
      AVE = SUM/20.0
*
      RETURN
      END
*-----------------------------------------------------------------------*
```

The **fifth step** is to test the program. A portion of a main program that might use this function is

```
      INTEGER ID, I
      REAL SCORES(20), HWAVE, AVE
*
      READ*, ID
      READ*, (SCORES(I),I=1,20)
*
      HWAVE = AVE(SCORES)
```

Median Value, Variable Array Size

Example 6-5

The median of a list of sorted numbers is defined as the number in the middle. If the list has an even number of values, the median is defined as the average of the 2 middle values. Write a function called MEDIAN that has 2 dummy arguments: a real array and an integer that specifies the number of values in the array. The function should assume that the elements of the array have already been sorted. Return the median value of the array as the function value.

Solution

The **first step** is to state the problem clearly: Write a function to determine the median value of an array.

The **second step** is to describe the input and output:

Input—a real array and an integer that specifies the number of values in the array
Output—median of the array

The **third step** is to work a simple example by hand. In the list—5, 2, 7, 36, and 42, the median is the number 7. In the list—5, 2, 7, 36, 42, and 82, the median is (7 + 36)/2, or 21.5.

The **fourth step** is to develop an algorithm, starting with the decomposition.

Decomposition

Determine median of array x.
Return.

In Section 6-1, we used the MOD function to determine if an integer was odd or even. We can use the same technique to determine if the number of elements (n) in the array is odd or even. If n is odd, we must decide which subscript refers to the middle value. For example, if $n = 5$, we want the median to refer to the third value, which is referenced by $(n/2) + 1$. Recall that we are dividing 2 integers, and the result will be truncated to another integer. If n is even, we want to refer to the 2 middle values and compute their average. If $n = 6$, we want to use the third and fourth values, which can be referenced by $(n/2)$ and $(n/2) + 1$.

Pseudocode

Median(x,n): If n is odd, then

$$\text{median} \leftarrow x\left(\frac{n}{2} + 1\right)$$

Else

$$\text{median} \leftarrow \frac{x(n/2) + x(n/2 + 1)}{2}$$

Return

As we convert the pseudocode into FORTRAN, we must remember to specify that the function MEDIAN is a real function. (The default will be an integer.)

FORTRAN Function

```
*-----------------------------------------------------------------------*
      REAL FUNCTION MEDIAN(X,N)
*
*  This function determines the median value in a sorted
*  list of real numbers.
*
      INTEGER N
      REAL X(N)
*
```

```
      IF (MOD(N,2).NE.0) THEN
         MEDIAN = X(N/2+1)
      ELSE
         MEDIAN = (X(N/2) + X(N/2+1))/2.0
      END IF
*
      RETURN
      END
*-----------------------------------------------------------------------*
```

The **fifth step** is to test the program. This function could be tested by a program with the following structure chart and statements:

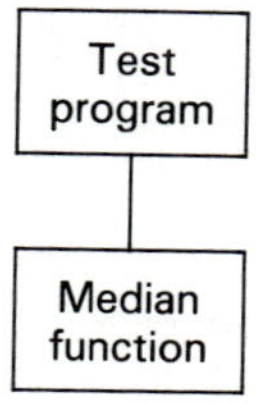

FORTRAN Program

```
*-----------------------------------------------------------------------*
      PROGRAM TEST
*
*  This program is written to test the median function.
*
      INTEGER N,I
      REAL X(10), MEDIAN
*
      PRINT*, 'ENTER NUMBER OF VALUES FOR ARRAY (<11)'
      READ*, N
      PRINT*, 'NOW ENTER SORTED ARRAY VALUES'
      READ*, (X(I),I=1,N)
      PRINT 5, MEDIAN(X,N)
    5 FORMAT (1X,'MEDIAN = ',F7.2)
*
      END
*-----------------------------------------------------------------------*
                          MEDIAN function goes here
*-----------------------------------------------------------------------*
```

Two-Dimensional Array Maximum

Example 6-6

Write a function that will receive an array of integers with 5 rows and 7 columns. The function should return the maximum value in the array.

Solution

The **first step** is to state the problem clearly: Write a function that determines the maximum of a two-dimensional array.

The **second step** is to describe the input and output:

Input — array with 5 rows and 7 columns
Output — maximum of input array

The **third step** is to work a simple example by hand. Let the array be the following:

$$\begin{bmatrix} 2 & 5 & 3 & 1 & 6 & 2 & 19 \\ 20 & 32 & -4 & 2 & 7 & 13 & 2 \\ 8 & 25 & -5 & -4 & 18 & 4 & 9 \\ 28 & -4 & 2 & 6 & 7 & 2 & 5 \\ 3 & 8 & 13 & 23 & 5 & 3 & 9 \end{bmatrix}$$

The maximum value is 32.

The **fourth step** is to develop an algorithm, starting with the decomposition.

Decomposition

Determine maximum of array k.
Return.

To find the maximum value in the array, we initialize the maximum to the first value in the array; then we compare the rest of the elements in the array to the maximum, replacing the maximum value with any larger value that we find.

Pseudocode

```
Maxvalue(k): maxvalue ← k(1,1)
             For i = 1,5 do
                  For j = 1,7 do
                       If k(i,j) > maxvalue then
                            maxvalue ← k(i,j)
             Return
```

FORTRAN Function

```
*-----------------------------------------------------------------------*
      INTEGER FUNCTION MAXVAL(K)
*
*  This function determines the maximum value in an
*  integer array with 5 rows and 7 columns.
*
      INTEGER K(5,7), I, J
*
      MAXVAL = K(1,1)
      DO 10 I=1,5
         DO 5 J=1,7
            IF (K(I,J).GT.MAXVAL) MAXVAL = K(I,J)
    5    CONTINUE
   10 CONTINUE
*
      RETURN
      END
*-----------------------------------------------------------------------*
```

The **fifth step** is to test the program. A statement that might use the function in the main program, after filling an array NUMBER that has 5 rows and 7 columns, is shown in the following group of statements:

```
      INTEGER NUMBER(5,7), MAXVAL
      .
      .
      .
      PRINT 5, MAXVAL(NUMBER)
    5 FORMAT (1X,'MAXIMUM NUMBER IS ',I5)
```

Problems can arise when you use variable dimensioning with arrays that have more than one dimension. The following is an example. First, we modify the MAXVAL function from Example 6-6 so that the number of rows and the number of columns are dummy arguments.

FORTRAN Function

```
*-----------------------------------------------------------------*
      INTEGER FUNCTION MAXVAL(K,NR,NC)
*
*  This example is used to show problems that can occur
*  when using variable dimensioning with 2-D arrays.
*
      INTEGER NR, NC, K(NR,NC), I, J
*
      MAXVAL = K(1,1)
      DO 10 I=1,NR
         DO 5 J=1,NC
            IF (K(I,J).GT.MAXVAL) MAXVAL = K(I,J)
    5    CONTINUE
   10 CONTINUE
*
      RETURN
      END
*-----------------------------------------------------------------*
```

If we modify the function reference to the one shown, the correct maximum value is printed:

```
      INTEGER NUMBER(5,7), MAXVAL
      .
      .
      .
      PRINT 5, MAXVAL(NUMBER,5,7)
    5 FORMAT (1X,'MAXIMUM NUMBER IS ',I5)
```

Suppose we want to determine the maximum value using only the first 2 rows and the first 2 columns of the array NUMBER, as shown in the diagram:

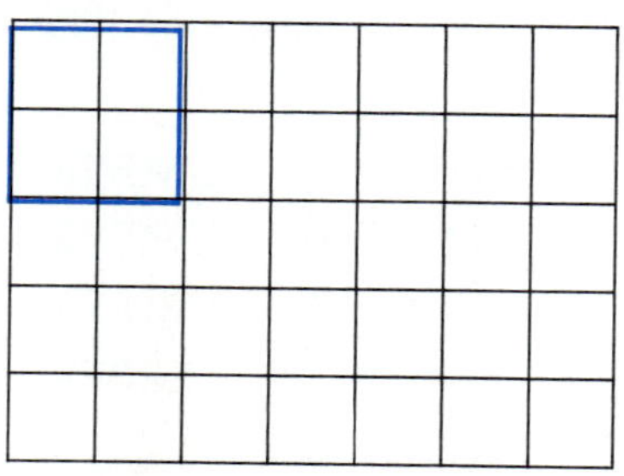

The following statements seem reasonable, but they are incorrect:

```
      INTEGER NUMBER(5,7), MAXVAL
      .
      .
      .
      PRINT 5, MAXVAL(NUMBER,2,2)
    5 FORMAT (1X,'MAXIMUM NUMBER IS ',I5)
```

These statements are incorrect because FORTRAN stores a two-dimensional array by columns. The array NUMBER is actually stored in memory as shown in the following diagram:

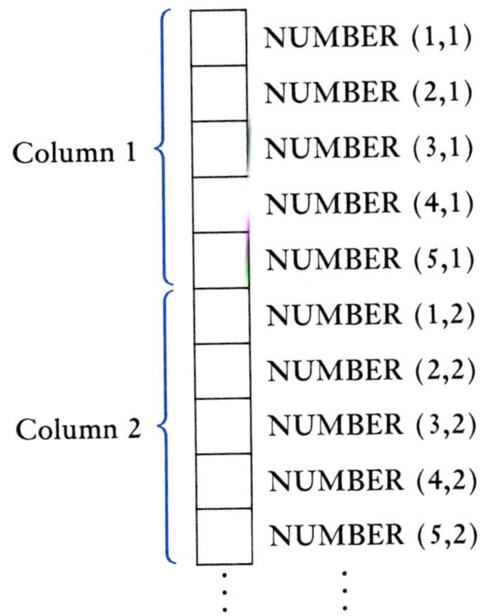

When we reference the array NUMBER in our function and specify that it has 2 rows and 2 columns, FORTRAN assumes that the values in NUMBER are stored in the following order:

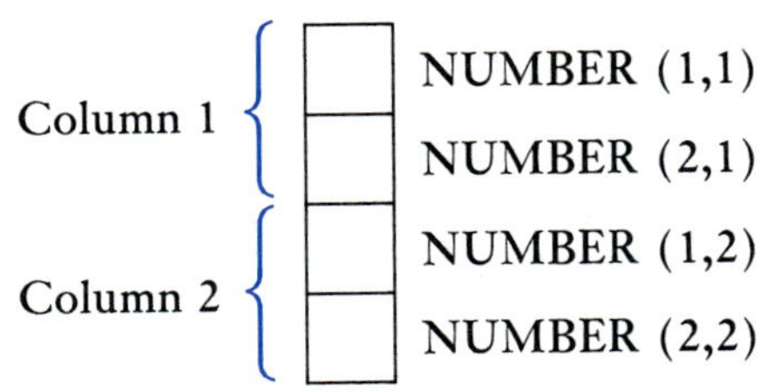

When we put the preceding two diagrams side-by-side, we can see that the array elements do not completely match:

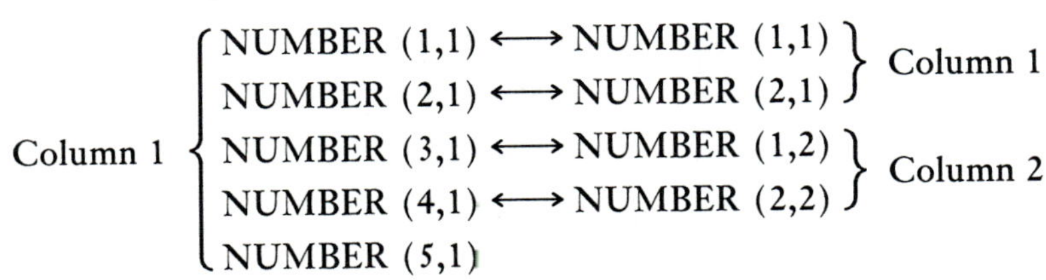

In fact, if we reference an array with 2 rows and 2 columns using the array NUMBER, the elements we are actually going to use are outlined in the following diagram:

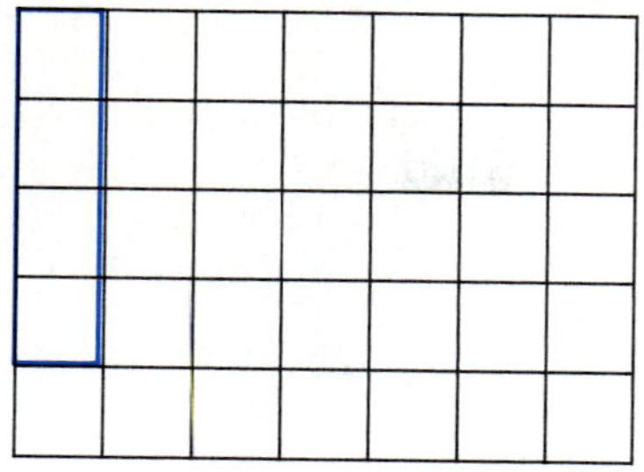

This problem does not result in a compiler error, but the values used by the function are not those that we intend it to use, which can present a difficult error to find in a program. In general, you should not use variable dimensions with arrays that have more than one dimension. If you have an application that requires variable dimensioning with two-dimensional arrays, include arguments that specify an operational size and a dimensional size, where the operational size specifies the part of the array you are actually going to use and the dimensional size specifies the size used in the array specification statement in the main program. We will use NR and NC for the size of the array we are going to use in the function and DR and DC for the dimensions used in the specification statement. These dummy arguments are used in the following function.

```
*-----------------------------------------------------------------*
      INTEGER FUNCTION MAXVAL(K,NR,NC,DR,DC)
*
*     This function determines the maximum value in an integer
*     array with NR rows and NC columns (original size DR by DC).
*
      INTEGER NR, NC, DR, DC, K(DR,DC), I, J
*
      MAXVAL = K(1,1)
      DO 10 I=1,NR
         DO 5 J=1,NC
            IF (K(I,J).GT.MAXVAL) MAXVAL = K(I,J)
    5    CONTINUE
   10 CONTINUE
*
      RETURN
      END
*-----------------------------------------------------------------*
```

SELF-TEST 6-2

This self-test allows you to check quickly to see if you have remembered some of the key points from Section 6–5. If you have any problems with the exercises, you should reread this section. The solutions are included at the end of the text.

For the following problems, give the value of S assuming that A = 8.9, B = 3.1, C = 0.2, and D = −5.5. The function TEST is the following:

```
*-----------------------------------------------------------------*
      REAL FUNCTION TEST(X,Y,Z)
*
*  This function returns either X+Y, X-Y, or X+Z
*  depending on the values of X, Y, Z.
*
      REAL X, Y, Z
*
      IF (X.GT.10.0) THEN
         TEST = X + Y
      ELSE IF (X.GT.Y) THEN
         TEST = X - Y
      ELSE
         TEST = X + Z
      END IF
*
      RETURN
      END
*-----------------------------------------------------------------*
```

1. `S = TEST(A,B,C)`
2. `S = TEST(B,C,D)`
3. `S = TEST(ABS(D),C,D)`
4. `S = TEST(12.0,C,D*D)`

6-6 Application ▪ Oil Well Production

Petroleum Engineering

The daily production of oil from a group of wells is entered into a data file each week for analysis. One of the reports that uses this data file computes the average production from each well and prints a summary of the overall production from this group of wells.

Write a FORTRAN program that will read the information from the data file and generate this report. Assume that the first line of the data file contains a date (month, day, and year of the first day of the week that corresponds to the production data). Each following line in the data file contains an integer identification number for the well and 7 real numbers that represent the well's production for the week. The number of wells to be analyzed varies from week to week, so a trailer line is included at the end of the file; this trailer contains the integer 99999, followed by seven zeros. You may assume that no well will have this integer as its identification number.

The report generated should have the following format:

```
OIL WELL PRODUCTION
WEEK OF XX-XX-XX

WELL ID          AVERAGE PRODUCTION
                 (IN BARRELS)
XXXXX            XXX.XX
```

Include a final line at the end of the report that gives the total number of oil wells plus their overall average.

Use the following set of data (stored in a file called WELLS) for testing the program:

```
05 06 92
52     87   136  0    54   60   82   51
63     54   73   88   105  20   21   105
24     67   98   177  35   65   98   0
8      23   34   52   67   180  80   3
64     33   55   79   108  118  130  20
66     40   44   63   89   36   54   36
67     20   35   76   87   154  98   80
55     10   13   34   23   43   12   0
3      34   56   187  34   202  23   34
2      98   98   87   34   54   100  20
25     29   43   54   65   12   15   17
18     45   65   202  205  100  99   98
14     36   34   98   34   43   23   9
13     0    9    8    4    3    2    10
36     23   88   99   65   77   45   35
38     23   100  134  122  111  211  0
81     23   34   54   98   5    93   82
89     29   58   39   20   50   30   47
99     100  12   43   98   34   23   9
45     23   93   75   93   2    34   8
88     23   301  23   83   23   9    20
77     28   12   43   43   92   83   98
39     98   43   12   23   54   23   98
12     43   54   92   84   75   72   91
48     83   138  189  73   27   49   10
99999  0    0    0    0    0    0    0
```

1. Problem Statement

Generate a report on oil well production from daily production data. Give the average production for individual wells and the overall average.

2. Input/Output Description

Input—a data file with daily production data for a group of oil wells

Output—a report summarizing the oil production

3. Hand Example

For the hand example, we use the first 5 lines of the data file given at the beginning of this application, along with the trailer line:

```
05 06 92
52       87   136   0    54   60   82   51
63       54   73    88   105  20   21   105
24       67   98    177  35   65   98   0
8        23   34    52   67   180  80   3
99999    0    0     0    0    0    0    0
```

We use the date in the first line of the data file in our heading. Each individual data line in the report contains the well identification (the first value in each line) followed by the average. We compute the average from the 7 daily values that follow the identification. We continue computing the individual averages until we reach the trailer signal 99999. At this point, we average the individual wells and print a final summary line:

```
OIL WELL PRODUCTION
WEEK OF 5- 6-92
WELL ID                AVERAGE PRODUCTION
                       (IN BARRELS)
  52                         67.14
  63                         66.57
  24                         77.14
   8                         62.71
OVERALL AVERAGE FOR 4 WELLS IS 68.39
```

4. Algorithm Development

Before we consider the steps in the algorithm, we should first decide the best way to store the data. For instance, do we want to store it in a two-dimensional array, or do we want to store the individual oil production amounts in a one-dimensional array, or can we avoid arrays altogether?

We answer these questions by looking at the way in which we need to use the data. To compute the individual well average, we need a sum of the individual production amounts. Because all 7 values are entered in the same data line, we must read them at the same time—we need an array to store the 7 daily production amounts for an individual well. To compute the overall average, we need a sum of the individual averages and a count of the number of wells—we do not need to keep the individual averages from each well.

In summary, we need a one-dimensional array to store the individual production values, and we do not need a two-dimensional array to store all the data.

We now decompose the algorithm into a sequence of steps. At the same time, we need to decide which operations or steps should be written as functions. Experience is the best guide to selecting which operations to define as functions. By studying how functions are used in the example programs, you will become more proficient at making these decisions. Remember that there are often several ways in which functions can be used in a program.

Decomposition

Generate report.
Print summary line.

Initial Pseudocode

```
Report: Read date
        Read ID, oil production
        While ID ≠ 99999 do
            Determine individual average
            Print individual average
            Update overall average and well count
            Read next ID, oil production
        Print summary information
```

After completing the decomposition and the initial refinement, we can determine if any of the operations should be written as functions. Computations that are repeated in an algorithm and steps that involve long computations are good candidates for functions. Program readability suffers when the details of some of the steps become long and tedious. Even though the steps may be performed only once, placing them in a function may make the program simpler.

For the oil well production problem, a function can be used to compute the individual oil well averages. This operation is needed only once in the main loop, but it involves several steps. The main program will be more readable if the steps are moved to a function subprogram. The function to compute the individual averages is also one that would be useful in other programs that compute averages. To be flexible, we write the function assuming that the data is in an array whose size is one of the function arguments.

Final Pseudocode

```
Report: Read date
        number of wells ← 0
        total oil ← 0.0
        Read ID, oil production
        While ID ≠ 99999 do
            Compute individual average
            Print individual average
            Increment number of wells by 1
            Add individual well average to total oil
            Read next ID, production data
        Print summary information

Average(oil, n): sum ← 0.0
                 For i = 1 to n
                     sum ← sum + oil(i)
                 average ← sum/n
                 Return
```

Structure Chart

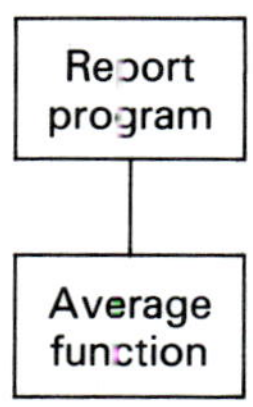

FORTRAN Program

```
*--------------------------------------------------------------------*
      PROGRAM REPORT
*
*  This program generates a report from the daily
*  production information for a set of oil wells.
*
      INTEGER MO, DA, YR, ID, N, I
      REAL OIL(7), TOTAL, AVE, INDAVE
*
      DATA N, TOTAL /0,0.0/
*
      OPEN (UNIT=12,FILE='WELLS',STATUS='OLD')
*
      READ (12,*) MO, DA, YR
      PRINT*, 'OIL WELL PRODUCTION'
      PRINT 5, MO, DA, YR
    5 FORMAT (1X,'WEEK OF ',I2,'-',I2,'-',I2)
```

```
      PRINT*
      PRINT*, 'WELL ID          AVERAGE PRODUCTION'
      PRINT*, '                 (IN BARRELS)'
*
      READ (12,*) ID, (OIL(I),I=1,7)
   10 IF (ID.NE.99999) THEN
         INDAVE = AVE(OIL,7)
         PRINT 15, ID, INDAVE
   15    FORMAT (1X,I5,12X,F6.2)
         N = N + 1
         TOTAL = TOTAL + INDAVE
         READ (12,*) ID, (OIL(I),I=1,7)
         GO TO 10
      END IF
*
      PRINT*
      PRINT 20, N, TOTAL/REAL(N)
   20 FORMAT (1X,'OVERALL AVERAGE FOR ',I3,' WELLS IS ',F6.2)
*
      END
*-----------------------------------------------------------------------*
      REAL FUNCTION AVE(X,N)
*
*  This function computes the average of a real
*  array with N values.
*
      INTEGER N, I
      REAL X(N), SUM
*
      SUM = 0.0
      DO 10 I=1,N
         SUM = SUM + X(I)
   10 CONTINUE
*
      AVE = SUM/REAL(N)
*
      RETURN
      END
*-----------------------------------------------------------------------*
```

Could the variable SUM have been initialized in the function with a DATA statement? (The answer is no. Why?)

5. Testing

Begin testing this program using a small data set such as the one in the hand-worked example. The output from this program using the data file given at the beginning of this application is

```
OIL WELL PRODUCTION
WEEK OF  5- 6-92

WELL ID         AVERAGE PRODUCTION
                (IN BARRELS)
   52              67.14
   63              66.57
   24              77.14
    8              62.71
   64              77.57
   66              51.71
   67              78.57
   55              19.29
    3              81.43
    2              70.14
   25              33.57
   18             116.29
   14              39.57
   13               5.14
   36              61.71
   38             100.14
   81              55.57
   89              39.00
   99              45.57
   45              46.86
   88              68.86
   77              57.00
   39              50.14
   12              73.00
   48              81.29

OVERALL AVERAGE FOR  25 WELLS IS  61.04
```

Could the last line of the data file contain only the trailer identification value 99999? (Are the seven zeros necessary in the last line of the data file?) If you try running the program without these last seven zeros, you will find that an execution error occurs because the program has run out of data. Because the identification number and the well production values are on the same line, we must read them with one READ statement. Each time the READ statement is executed, it reads 8 values before control passes to the next statement. When the READ statement reaches the last line in the data file, it needs 7 values in addition to the 99999 value before it can test for the trailer value.

6-7 Application ▪ Stability Analysis

Robotic Engineering

The design of a control system for a robot arm involves a careful analysis of the stability of the design. One step in the stability analysis uses the roots of polynomials that are used in the control system. Examples of other applications where we need to find roots of equations include designing springs and shock absorbers for an automobile, analyzing the response of a motor, and analyzing the stability of an electric circuit.

Roots of Equations

Suppose that we have a cubic (third-degree) polynomial equation:

$$y = f(x)$$
$$= x^3 - 5x^2 + 2x + 8$$

which is plotted below:

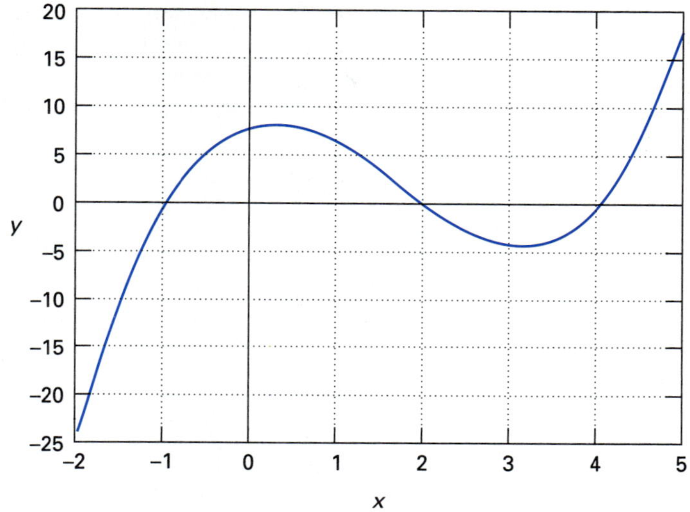

A root of an equation $y = f(x)$ is a value of x that corresponds to a function value of zero. From the previous plot, we see that at the points $x = -1$, $x = 2$, and $x = 4$, the value of y is zero; substituting any one of these values of x into the equation also gives a value of zero for y. Thus, the roots of an equation are found by setting y equal to zero and solving for all the values of x that satisfy the resulting equation. For our cubic polynomial, the equation we need to solve is

$$x^3 - 5x^2 + 2x + 8 = 0$$

If we factor this equation, we have

$$(x+1)(x-2)(x-4) = 0$$

We now see immediately that the values of x which will satisfy this equation, and thus are the roots of the equation, are -1, 2, and 4. Hence, we are able to determine the roots from a plot of the function or from factoring the equation.

An example of a quadratic equation having a multiple root is the following:

$$x^2 + 4x + 4 = 0$$

Factoring this polynomial gives

$$(x+2)(x+2) = 0$$

showing that there is a multiple root at $x = -2$.

Some quadratic equations are not easily factored, so we use the quadratic formula to compute the roots. For example, the equation

$$x^2 + 2x + 2 = 0$$

has complex roots $x = -1 + i$ and $x = -1 - i$. These roots are called a complex conjugate pair because they differ only in the sign of the imaginary term. If a polynomial has only real coefficients, any complex roots it may have will result from quadratic factors such as the one above and will therefore always be conjugate pairs. That is, if $x = a + bi$ is a root, then $x = a - bi$ will also be a root. Polynomial equations that represent the physical systems or processes encountered in engineering and science will have real coefficients.

As illustrated in these examples, we are able in some cases to factor an expression or use a formula, such as the quadratic formula, to find the roots. More often, however, no simple algebraic methods are applicable, so we turn to computers and programs that use numerical methods to obtain an estimate of the roots. In this section, we present techniques to locate real roots.

Incremental-Search Method

One of the simplest, yet most reliable methods for finding roots of an equation is the incremental-search method. A search region of x values is first selected and divided into intervals, as shown here:

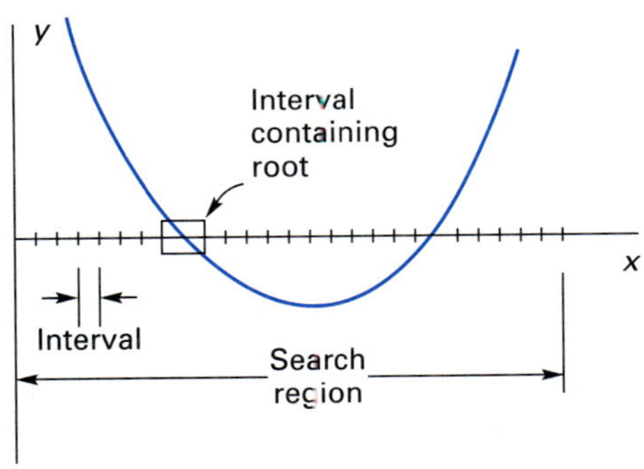

The intervals are chosen to be small enough that it is unlikely there will be more than one root in any interval. Proceeding from left to right, we search for the intervals that contain roots by looking for the places where the function curve crosses the x-axis, as it does in the small box drawn in the figure. We identify these intervals containing a root by computing the values of the function at the endpoints of the interval and checking the signs. If the signs of the function values at the endpoints are different, we know the curve has crossed the x-axis and that there is at least one root in the interval.

As shown in the next figure, the interval containing the root has been further divided into subintervals, and the search process begins again from the left end of the interval until the subinterval containing the root is similarly located.

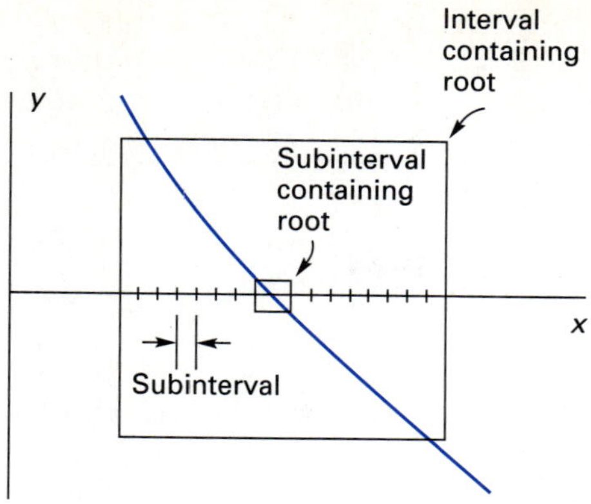

The process of subdividing and searching is repeated until the root has been determined with sufficient accuracy. Once a root has been located, we move to the next interval and continue the search for any remaining roots.

The incremental-search method will only detect places where the curve crosses the x-axis and the function values change sign. Therefore, it will not be able to find complex roots or multiple roots, since the function value does not change signs at those locations. Nevertheless, it is a useful method for finding single real roots. It can also be used to provide a search algorithm for the bisection method, which is discussed next.

Bisection Method

The bisection method begins with an interval that is already known to contain a root. Unlike the incremental-search method, which divides the interval into many subintervals before searching again, the bisection method simply bisects, or divides the interval in half, and then determines which half contains the root. The bisection process is continued until the root is found to the desired accuracy. In most cases, the bisection method converges to the root much quicker than the incremental-search method.

To explain the bisection method in more detail, we look at a simple curve represented by $y = f(x)$:

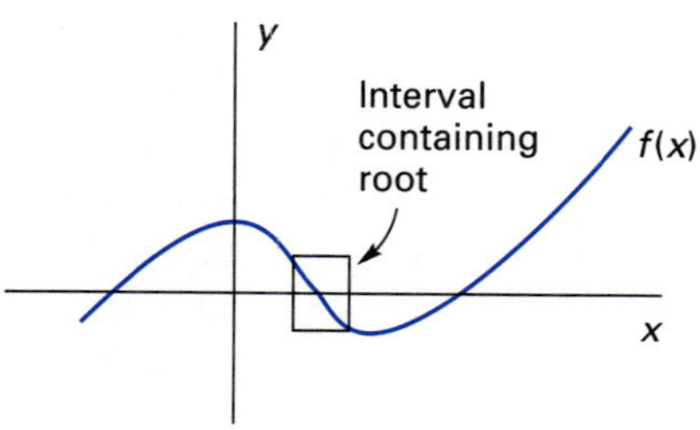

Suppose we evaluated the function at $x = a$ and at $x = b$ and determined that $f(a) \cdot f(b)$ is negative.

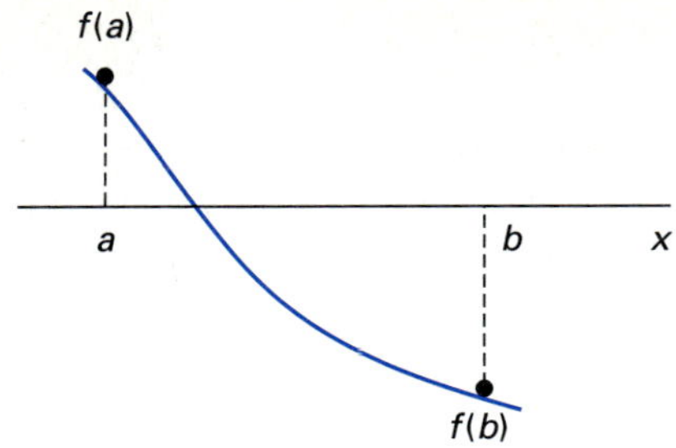

We know from the previous discussion that there is at least 1 real root in the interval between a and b, because the curve must have crossed the x-axis for the product of $f(a)$ and $f(b)$ to be negative. There could also be 3 roots, or another odd number of roots, in the interval between a and b.

We now want to reduce the size of the interval containing the root. If the function is evaluated at m, the midpoint of the interval, there are three possible outcomes: If $f(a) \cdot f(m)$ is zero, then m is a root; if $f(a) \cdot f(m)$ is negative, then the root falls in the interval between a and m; and if $f(a) \cdot f(m)$ is positive, a root falls in the interval between m and b. Thus, either we have found the root or we have halved (or bisected) the interval within which the root must lie. We now perform the steps again, bisecting the new interval known to contain the root. In the graph below, the new interval containing the root is $[a,m]$.

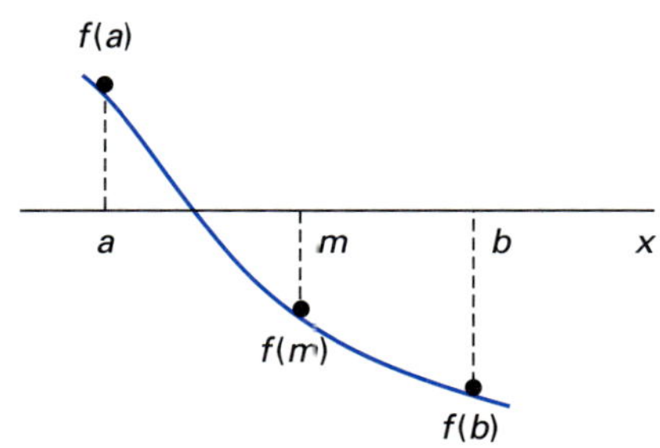

At some point, we need to stop the iterative process, since finding the exact root is seldom practical or necessary. Most often, we will iterate until we find a root to within some tolerance or accuracy which we specify. For example, we might want to continue the process until $|f(m)| < 0.01$. We could also stop the process at some maximum number of iterations; for example, once we find an interval containing a root, we could perform a maximum of five iterations and use the estimate of the root at that point.

Recall that at the beginning of this discussion on the bisection method, we assumed that we begin with an interval that is already known to contain a root. There are various methods that we can use to find the intervals with roots. One suggestion would be to plot enough points of the curve such that intervals containing the x-axis crossings can be determined. Perhaps the easiest way to find the intervals is to use the first part of the incremental-search method. Specifically, we select a search region of x values and divide that region into small intervals. We then search for the intervals where the product of the function values at the endpoints is negative. When we find such an interval, we use the bisection method to find the root.

It is important to remember that the bisection method, like the incremental-search method, can only find single, real roots; multiple roots and complex roots will not be located.

Robot Stability

We are now ready to develop a program that assists in determining the stability of a design for a robot arm. Specifically, we want to develop a program to estimate the roots of a fourth-order polynomial over the interval $[-5,5]$, using a combination of the incremental-search method and the bisection method.

1. Problem Statement

Write a program to determine the roots of a polynomial within the interval $[-5,5]$, where y has the following form:

$$\begin{aligned} y &= f(x) \\ &= a_0x^4 + a_1x^3 + a_2x^2 + a_3x + a_4 \end{aligned}$$

2. Input/Output Description

Input—polynomial coefficients a_0, a_1, a_2, a_3, and a_4
Output—roots of the polynomial in $[-5,5]$

3. Hand Example

We use small intervals of 0.25 in the incremental-search method. For this test case, assume that the polynomial is

$$f(x) = 3x - 2.5$$

This is a linear equation, but it is also a special case of a quartic polynomial with the following coefficients:

$$a_0 = 0, \quad a_1 = 0, \quad a_2 = 0, \quad a_3 = 3, \quad a_4 = -2.5$$

We begin by evaluating $f(x)$ at the endpoints of the following intervals:

$$[-5.0,-4.75], [-4.75,-4.5], \ldots, [4.75, 5.0]$$

When the value of the polynomial at the left endpoint, $f(\text{left})$, has a different sign than the value of the polynomial at the right endpoint, $f(\text{right})$, there is a root in the interval. We also need to check to see if the value of the polynomial at the endpoints is zero in case an endpoint is a root. For this specific example, the endpoints of the intervals have negative function values until we reach the interval

[0.75,1.00], where $f(0.75) = -0.25$ and $f(1.0) = 0.5$. The following steps halve the interval, determine which half contains the root, halve the new interval, and so on, until the root is found or the interval is less than 0.01:

Interval [0.75,1.0]

$f(0.75) = -0.25, f(1.0) = 0.5$
midpoint: $f(0.875) = 0.125$

Iteration 1: Interval [0.75,0.875]

$f(0.75) = -0.25, f(0.875) = 0.125$
midpoint: $f(0.8125) = -0.0625$

Iteration 2: Interval [0.8125,0.875]

$f(0.8125) = -0.0625, f(0.875) = 0.125$
midpoint: $f(0.8438) = 0.0314$

Iteration 3: Interval [0.8125,0.8438]

$f(0.8125) = -0.0625, f(0.8438) = 0.0314$
midpoint: $f(0.8282) = -0.0154$

Iteration 4: Interval [0.8282,0.8438]

$f(0.8282) = -0.0154, f(0.8438) = 0.0314$
midpoint: $f(0.836) = 0.008$

Iteration 5: Interval [0.8282, 0.836]

This interval is less than 0.01; thus, our estimate of the root is the midpoint of this interval, or 0.8321. The polynomial value, $f(x)$, at this point is -0.0037.

4. Algorithm Development

Decomposition

Read coefficients.
Use incremental search to find intervals with roots, and use bisection to locate roots within the intervals.

Pseudocode

```
Roots: Read coefficients
        count ← 0
        For left = −5.0 to 4.75 in steps of 0.25 do
            right ← left + 0.25
            If f(left) = 0.0 then
                Print left
                count ← count + 1
            Else if f(left) · f(right) < 0.0 then
                Iterate for root
                Print root
                count ← count + 1
        left ← 5.0
        If f(left) = 0.0 then
            Print left
            count ← count + 1
        If count = 0 then
            Print 'no roots in interval'
```

We must further refine the iteration step since it contains the bisection method. We will continue the bisection process until the root is found, or until the width of the interval is less than 0.01. We will assume that the root is found when the absolute value of the function is less than or equal to 0.001.

Pseudocode for Iteration

```
Iteration: done ← false
           size ← right − left
           While size > 0.01 and not done do
               mid ← (left + right)/2
               If |f(mid)| ≤ 0.001 then
                   done ← true
               Else if f(mid) · f(left) < 0.0 then
                   right ← mid
               Else
                   left ← mid
               size ← right − left
           If size > 0.01 then
               root ← mid
           Else
               root ← (left + right)/2
```

We are now ready to convert the pseudocode into FORTRAN. The evaluation of the polynomial is implemented as a function. It needs an array A of the coefficients and the value of x for evaluating the polynomial; thus, the reference should be F(A,X).

The structure chart for this program is

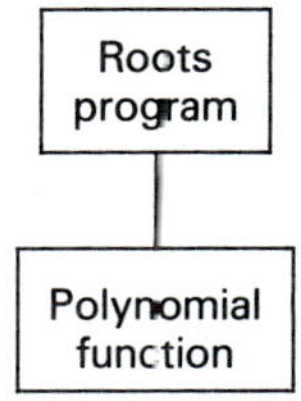

FORTRAN Program

```
*-----------------------------------------------------------------------------*
      PROGRAM ROOTS
*
*  This program determines the roots in the interval [-5,5]
*  for a quartic polynomial using incremental search and
*  the bisection method.
*
      INTEGER COUNT, I
      REAL A(0:4), LEFT, RIGHT, F, MID
      LOGICAL DONE
*
      PRINT*, 'ENTER COEFFICIENTS A0,A1,A2,A3,A4'
      READ*, A
*
      PRINT 5, A
    5 FORMAT (/,' POLYNOMIAL:'/
     +        1X,9X,'4',11X,'3',11X,'2'/
     +        1X,4(F7.3,' X + '),F7.3/)
*
      COUNT = 0
      DO 40 I=1,40
         LEFT = -5.0 + REAL(I-1)*0.25
         RIGHT = LEFT + 0.25
*
         IF (ABS(F(A,LEFT)).LT.0.001) THEN
*
            PRINT 15, LEFT, F(A,LEFT)
   15       FORMAT (1X,'ROOT = ',F7.3,3X,
     +              'F(ROOT) = ',F7.3)
            COUNT = COUNT + 1
*
         ELSE IF (F(A,LEFT)*F(A,RIGHT).LT.0.0) THEN
*
```

```
         DONE = .FALSE.
         SIZE = RIGHT - LEFT
   20    IF (SIZE.GT.0.01.AND..NOT.DONE) THEN
            MID = (LEFT + RIGHT)/2.0
            IF (ABS(F(A,MID)).LT.0.001) THEN
               DONE = .TRUE.
            ELSE IF (F(A,MID)*F(A,LEFT).LT.0.0) THEN
               RIGHT = MID
            ELSE
               LEFT = MID
            END IF
            SIZE = RIGHT - LEFT
            GO TO 20
         END IF
*
         IF (SIZE.GT.0.01) THEN
            ROOT = MID
         ELSE
            ROOT = (LEFT + RIGHT)/2.0
         END IF
*
         PRINT 15, ROOT, F(A,ROOT)
         COUNT = COUNT + 1
*
      END IF
   40 CONTINUE
*
      LEFT = 5.0
      IF (ABS(F(A,LEFT)).LT.0.001) THEN
         PRINT 15, LEFT, F(A,LEFT)
         COUNT = COUNT + 1
      END IF
      IF (COUNT.EQ.0) THEN
         PRINT*, 'NO ROOTS IN INTERVAL [-5,5]'
      END IF
*
      END
*-----------------------------------------------------------------------*
      REAL FUNCTION F(A,X)
*
*  This function evaluates a quartic polynomial at X.
*
      REAL A(0:4), X
*
      F = A(0)*X**4 + A(1)*X**3 + A(2)*X**2 + A(3)*X + A(4)
*
      RETURN
      END
*-----------------------------------------------------------------------*
```

5. Testing

Five different polynomials were used as test data. The output from the program is shown for each polynomial, along with a MATLAB plot (see Appendix C) of the function so that you can see the zero crossings. Explain why the first example found the root at 5.0 twice.

```
ENTER COEFFICIENTS A0,A1,A2,A3,A4
0. 1. -2.125 -25. 53.125

POLYNOMIAL:
        4            3            2
 0.000 X +   1.000 X +  -2.125 X + -25.000 X +  53.125

ROOT =  -5.000    F(ROOT) =   0.000
ROOT =   2.125    F(ROOT) =   0.000
ROOT =   4.996    F(ROOT) =  -0.112
ROOT =   5.000    F(ROOT) =   0.000
```

(See Figure 6–1a.)

```
ENTER COEFFICIENTS A0,A1,A2,A3,A4
0. 0. 1. 14. 3.

POLYNOMIAL:
        4            3            2
 0.000 X +   0.000 X +   1.000 X +  14.000 X +   3.000

ROOT =  -0.215    F(ROOT) =   0.038
```

(See Figure 6–1b.)

```
ENTER COEFFICIENTS A0,A1,A2,A3,A4
3. -12.4 -26.29 29.766 0.

POLYNOMIAL:
        4            3            2
 3.000 X + -12.400 X + -26.290 X +  29.766 X +   0.000

ROOT =  -2.137    F(ROOT) =  -0.131
ROOT =   0.000    F(ROOT) =   0.000
ROOT =   0.855    F(ROOT) =   0.068
```

(See Figure 6–1c.)

```
ENTER COEFFICIENTS A0,A1,A2,A3,A4
0. 0. 1.234 -1.2 10.44

POLYNOMIAL:
        4            3            2
 0.000 X +   0.000 X +   1.234 X +  -1.200 X +  10.440

NO ROOTS IN INTERVAL [-5,5]
```

(See Figure 6–1d.)

```
ENTER COEFFICIENTS A0,A1,A2,A3,A4
0. 0. 0. 3. -2.5

POLYNOMIAL:
          4            3            2
  0.000 X +    0.000 X +    0.000 X +    3.000 X +  -2.500

ROOT =    0.832    F(ROOT) =   -0.004
```

(See Figure 6–1e.)

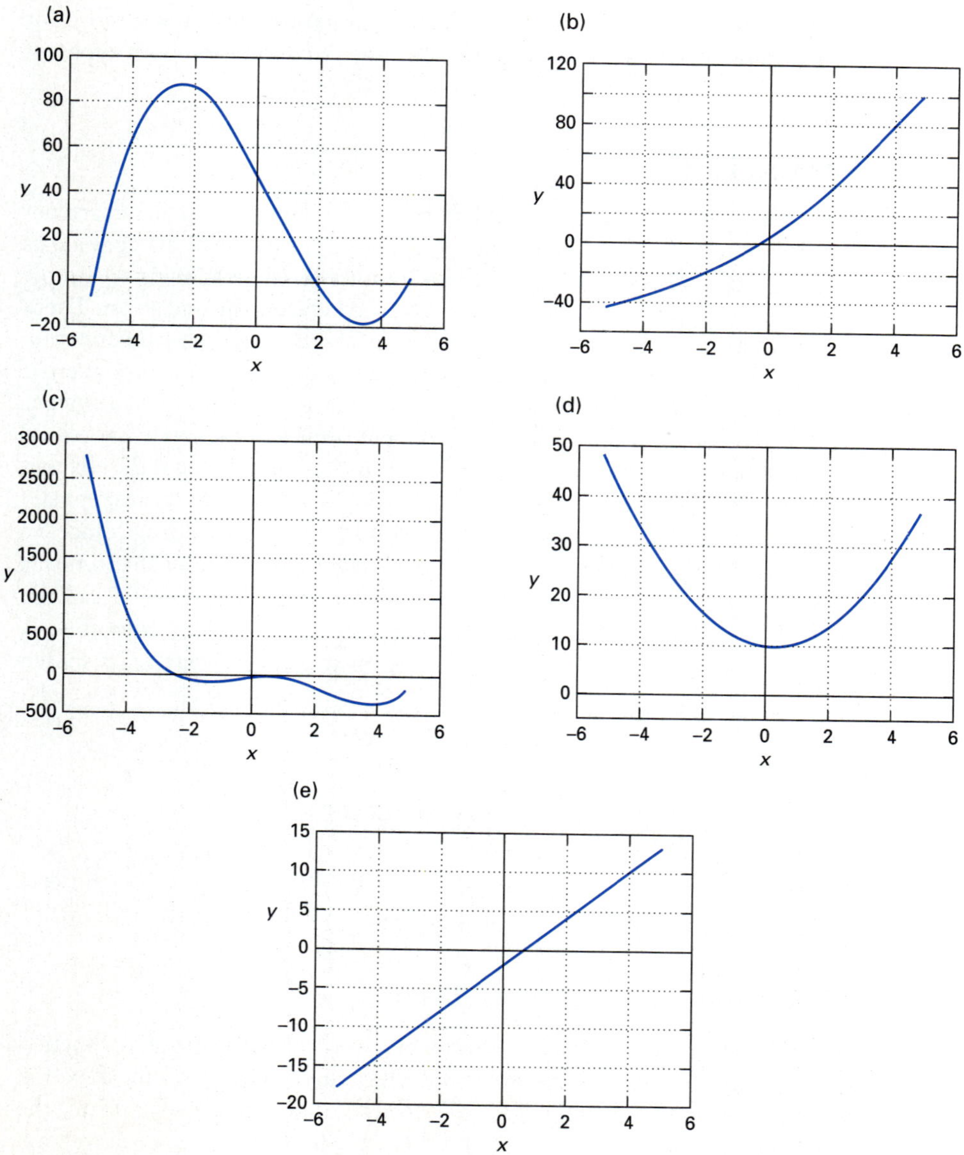

Figure 6•1 Polynomial plots

6·8 ■ Functions for Search Algorithms

Solutions to different problems often include some of the same steps, such as computing the average of a set of values or finding the maximum of a set of values. Once we have written a function, such as one to compute the average of the values in an array, we can often reuse a function in another program with little or no modification to the function. Another very common operation performed with arrays is searching the array for a specific value. We may want to know if a particular value is in the array, how many times it occurs in the array, or where it first occurs in the array. All these forms of searches determine a single value and thus are good candidates for functions. *Searching algorithms* fall into two groups: those for searching an unordered list and those for searching an ordered list. In this section we develop functions for both types of searches.

■ Unordered List

We first consider searching an unordered list; thus we assume the elements are not necessarily sorted into an ascending numerical order or any other order that may aid us in searching the array. The algorithm to search an unordered array is just a simple sequential search: check the first element, check the second element, and so on. There are several ways that we could implement this function. We could develop the function as an integer function that returns the position of the desired value in the array or zero if the desired value is not in the array. We could develop the function as an integer function that returns the number of times the element occurs in the array. We could also develop the function as a logical function that returns a value of true if the element is in the array or false if the element is not in the array. All these ideas represent valid functions, and we could think of programs that would use each of these forms. Since we have already written functions that return an integer value and functions that return a real value, we will implement this function as a logical function. We will call the function FOUND in order to make references to the function read smoothly. A reference to the function FOUND, as it might appear in a main program, is shown next.

```
IF (FOUND(X,COUNT,KEY)) THEN
   PRINT*, 'ITEM IS IN STOCK'
ELSE
   PRINT*, 'ITEM IS NOT IN STOCK'
END IF
```

Note that the function has three arguments, the array (X), the number of valid data values in the array (COUNT), and the value for which we are searching (KEY).

Example 6·7 ▶ **Search Function for Unordered List**

Write a logical function to search an unordered list for a specific value. The function should return a value of true if the specific value is found; otherwise, the function should return a value of false. The function will need three arguments — the array, the number of valid data entries in the array, and the value for which we are searching. Assume that all these values are integers.

Solution

The **first step** is to state the problem clearly: Write a function to search an unordered list.

The **second step** is to describe the input and output:

Input—an array, the number of valid data entries in the array, and the value for which we are searching

Output—a logical value that indicates if we found the value

The **third step** is to work a simple example by hand. Suppose that the array contains the following values:

−7
21
14
8
52
77
15

If the value for which we are searching is 52, we look down the list and determine that the function should return a value of .TRUE.. If the value for which we are searching is 53, then the function should return a value of .FALSE..

The **fourth step** is to develop an algorithm. In the development of the function, we assume that the values are already stored in the array X, a variable COUNT specifies the number of valid data values in the array, and the variable KEY contains the value for which we are searching.

Decomposition

Search an unordered list for a specific value.

Pseudocode

```
Found(x,count,key): If count > 0 then
                        done ← false
                        i ← 1
                    Else
                        done ← true
                        found ← false
                    While not done do
                        If x(i) = key then
                            done ← true
                            found ← true
                        Else
                            i ← i + 1
                        If i > count then
                            done ← true
                            found ← false
                    Return
```

FORTRAN Function

```
*-----------------------------------------------------------------------*
      LOGICAL FUNCTION FOUND(X,COUNT,KEY)
*
*  This function determines whether or not the key value
*  is in an unordered array.
*
      INTEGER COUNT, X(COUNT), KEY, I
      LOGICAL DONE
*
      IF (COUNT.GT.0) THEN
         DONE = .FALSE.
         I = 1
      ELSE
         DONE = .TRUE.
         FOUND = .FALSE.
      END IF
*
    5 IF (.NOT.DONE) THEN
*
         IF (X(I).EQ.KEY) THEN
            DONE = .TRUE.
            FOUND = .TRUE.
         ELSE
            I = I + 1
         END IF
*
         IF (I.GT.COUNT) THEN
            DONE = .TRUE.
            FOUND = .FALSE.
         END IF
*
         GO TO 5
      END IF
*
      RETURN
      END
*-----------------------------------------------------------------------*
```

The **fifth step** is to test the program. We now present a program that could be used to test the search function. The program will ask the user to enter a set of data to be stored in the array. It will then ask the user to enter a specific value to be used in searching the array. The program will use the function to do the search; the program will then print a message giving the result of the search.

Structure Chart

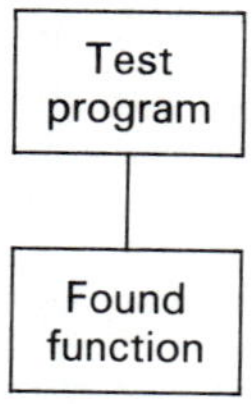

FORTRAN Program

```
*-----------------------------------------------------------------------*
      PROGRAM TEST
*
*  This program tests the search program.
*
      INTEGER X(10), COUNT, KEY, J
      LOGICAL FOUND
*
      PRINT*, 'ENTER COUNT (<11) OF VALUES FOR LIST'
      READ*, COUNT
      PRINT*, 'ENTER VALUES'
      READ*, (X(J),J=1,COUNT)
      PRINT*, 'ENTER VALUE FOR SEARCH'
      READ*, KEY
*
      IF (FOUND(X,COUNT,KEY)) THEN
         PRINT*, KEY,' FOUND IN THE LIST'
      ELSE
         PRINT*, KEY,' NOT FOUND IN THE LIST'
      END IF
*
      END
*-----------------------------------------------------------------------*
                          FOUND function goes here
*-----------------------------------------------------------------------*
```

An example of a test of the function FOUND using this program is shown below:

```
ENTER COUNT (<11) OF VALUES FOR LIST
3
ENTER VALUES
26 -3 7
ENTER VALUE FOR SEARCH
15
   15 NOT FOUND IN THE LIST
```

■ Ordered List

We present two common algorithms for searching an ordered list. The first searches sequentially until we either find the item or recognize that we have passed the position where it would have been in the list. The second algorithm first checks the middle of the array and decides if the item for which we are searching is in the first half of the array or the second half of the array. If it is in the first half, we then check the middle of the first half and decide whether the item is in the first fourth of the array or the second fourth of the array. The process of dividing the array into smaller and smaller pieces continues until we find the element or find the position where it should have been. Since this technique continually divides the part of the array that we are searching in half, it is sometimes called a *binary search.*

Example 6-8

Search Function for Ordered List

Write a logical function to sequentially search an ordered list for a specific value. The function should return a value of true if the specific value is found; otherwise, the function should return a value of false. The function will need three arguments—the array, the number of valid data entries in the array, and the value for which we are searching. Assume that all these values are integers.

Solution

The **first step** is to state the problem clearly: Write a function to search an ordered list.

The **second step** is to describe the input and output:

Input—an array, the number of valid data entries in the array, and the value for which we are searching

Output—a logical value that indicates if we found the value

The **third step** is to work a simple example by hand. Consider the list of ordered values below and assume that we are searching for the value 25:

−7
2
14
38
52
77
105

As soon as you reached the value 38, you knew that 25 was not in the list because you knew that the list was ordered. Therefore, we do not have to search the entire list, as we would have to do for an unordered list; we only need to search past the point where the key value should have been located. If the list is in ascending order, we search until the current value in the array is larger than the key; if the list is in descending order, we search until the current value in the array is smaller than the key value.

The **fourth step** is to develop an algorithm. In the development of the function, we assume that the sorted values are already stored in the array X, a variable COUNT specifies the number of valid data values in the array, and the variable KEY contains the value for which we are searching.

Decomposition

Search ordered list for a specific value.

Pseudocode

```
Found(x,count,key): If count > 0 then
                         done ← false
                         i ← 1
                    Else
                         done ← true
                         found ← false
                    While not done do
                         If x(i) = key then
                              done ← true
                              found ← true
                         Else if x(i) > key then
                              done ← true
                              found ← false
                         Else
                              i ← i + 1
                         If i > count then
                              done ← true
                              found ← false
                    Return
```

FORTRAN Function

```
*-----------------------------------------------------------------------*
      LOGICAL FUNCTION FOUND(X,COUNT,KEY)
*
*  This function determines whether or not the key value
*  is in an ordered array using a sequential search.
*
      INTEGER COUNT, X(COUNT), KEY, I
      LOGICAL DONE
*
      IF (COUNT.GT.0) THEN
         DONE = .FALSE.
         I = 1
      ELSE
         DONE = .TRUE.
         FOUND = .FALSE.
      END IF
*
```

```
    5 IF (.NOT.DONE) THEN
*
         IF (X(I).EQ.KEY) THEN
            DONE = .TRUE.
            FOUND = .TRUE.
         ELSE IF (X(I).GT.KEY) THEN
            DONE = .TRUE.
            FOUND = .FALSE.
         ELSE
            I = I + 1
         END IF
*
         IF (I.GT.COUNT) THEN
            DONE = .TRUE.
            FOUND = .FALSE.
         END IF
*
         GO TO 5
      END IF
*
      RETURN
      END
*----------------------------------------------------------------------*
```

The **fifth step** is to test the program. The program used to test the search function from Example 6–7 can also be used to test this function if the array entered through the keyboard is in ascending order.

Example 6·9

Binary Search Function for Ordered List

In this example, we implement the search function using a binary search algorithm. The only steps that are different from the previous example are the hand example and the algorithm development.

For a hand example, we first illustrate the binary search algorithm with the list used in the previous example in which we were searching sequentially for the value 25.

−7
2
14
38
52
77
105

There are seven values, the first referenced by a subscript value of 1 and the last referenced by a subscript value of 7. In a binary search, we compute the middle position by adding the first position number to the last position number and dividing by two. This should be done as an integer division. In our case, 7 plus 1 equals 8, and 8 divided by 2 is 4. Thus, we check the fourth position and compare its value to the value for which we are searching. The fourth value is 38, which is larger than 25, so we can narrow our search to the top half of the array. Our first position is still 1, and our last position is changed to the position above the middle position, or 3. We now divide that part of the array in half and compute the new midpoint to be $(1 + 3)/2$, or 2. The second value is 2, which is smaller than 25, so we can narrow our search to the second quarter of the array. Our first position is now one past the middle position, or 3, and our last position is 3. When the first and last positions are the same, we have narrowed in on the position where the value should be. Thus, we can exit the search algorithm. This specific example is illustrated in the following diagram. Follow through each step to be sure that you understand the sequence of steps needed.

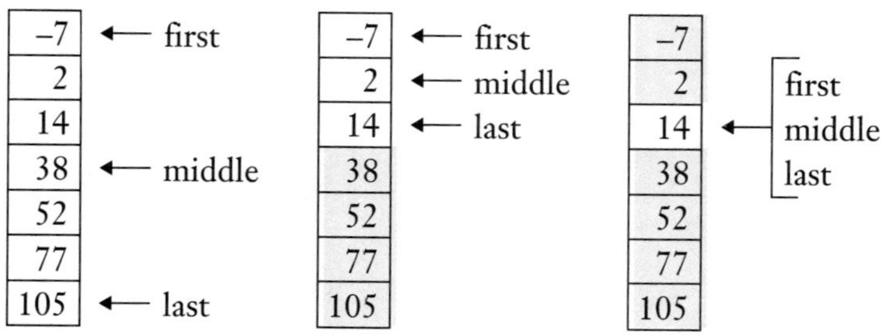

$38 > 25$ so choose top half

$2 < 25$ so choose bottom half

$14 \neq 25$ and first = last so 25 is not in the list

When the number of elements in the array is even, it is possible for the position of the first element to be greater than the position of the last element if the desired value is not in the list. Therefore, if the position of the first element is equal to or greater than the position of the last element, then the key value is not in the list.

The next step is to develop an algorithm. In the development of the function, we assume that the values are already stored in the array X, a variable COUNT specifies the number of valid data values in the array, and the variable KEY contains the value for which we are searching.

Decomposition

Search an ordered list for a specific value.

Pseudocode

```
Found(x,count,key): If count ≤ 0 then
                        found ← false
                    Else if x(1)>key or x(count)<key then
                        found ← false
                    Else
                        done ← false
                        found ← false
                        first ← 1
                        last ← count
                        While not done do
                            middle ← (first + last)/2
                            If x(middle) = key then
                                found ← true
                                done ← true
                            If not done then
                                If first ≥ last then
                                    done ← true
                                Else if x(middle) > key then
                                    last ← middle − 1
                                Else
                                    first ← middle + 1
                    Return
```

FORTRAN Function

```
*-----------------------------------------------------------------------*
      LOGICAL FUNCTION FOUND(X,COUNT,KEY)
*
*  This function determines whether or not the key value
*  is in an ordered array using a binary search.
*
      INTEGER COUNT, X(COUNT), KEY, FIRST, LAST, MIDDLE
      LOGICAL DONE
*
      IF (COUNT.LE.0) THEN
*
         FOUND = .FALSE.
      ELSE IF (X(1).GT.KEY.OR.X(COUNT).LT.KEY) THEN
         FOUND = .FALSE.
*
      ELSE
*
         DONE = .FALSE.
         FOUND = .FALSE.
         FIRST = 1
         LAST = COUNT
*
    5    IF (.NOT.DONE) THEN
*
            MIDDLE = (FIRST + LAST)/2
*
            IF (X(MIDDLE).EQ.KEY) THEN
               FOUND = .TRUE.
               DONE = .TRUE.
            END IF
*
            IF (.NOT.DONE) THEN
               IF (FIRST.GE.LAST) THEN
                  DONE = .TRUE.
               ELSE IF (X(MIDDLE).GT.KEY) THEN
                  LAST = MIDDLE - 1
               ELSE
                  FIRST = MIDDLE + 1
               END IF
            END IF
*
            GO TO 5
         END IF
*
      END IF
*
      RETURN
      END
*-----------------------------------------------------------------------*
```

While both the sequential sort and the binary search correctly search for an item in an ordered list, the sequential sort is more efficient for small lists and the binary search is more efficient for large lists. ◀

Summary

A function is a module that represents a single value. FORTRAN contains many intrinsic functions that compute values such as trigonometric functions and logarithms. We can also write our own functions. The statement function is a specification statement that defines a function within our program. A statement function can be used only when the function can be defined in a single assignment statement. A function subprogram is an independent module that is used to define functions that require more than a single assignment statement. All three forms of functions are useful in engineering and science applications because they simplify the computations in our programs. Several forms of functions for searching an array were also presented.

Debugging Aids

Testing a function should be approached much like testing a complete program. You will also need a simple program, called a *driver*, to initialize the input to the function that you are testing. This driver program should print the output of the function so that you can determine if it is returning the proper value. If it is not returning the proper value, the following list of checks may help you locate the problem.

1. Be sure that the function is returning the proper type of value. The easiest way to ensure this is to use explicit typing with the function.
2. Be sure that each path to a RETURN provides a value for the function.
3. Be sure that the actual arguments listed in the main program match the dummy arguments listed in the function subprogram. Check the corresponding variables for correct type and order.
4. Print the values of all actual variables just before using the function and just after returning from the function as you debug it.
5. Include PRINT statements in the function just as you do in a main program to help isolate trouble spots.
6. Remember that variables should not be initialized within the function with a DATA statement because these are not initialized with each use of the function. The DATA statement initializes variables only when the program is first begun.

Style/Technique Guides

Using statement functions and function subprograms to replace computations within a main program greatly improves program structure and readability. The structure of a function subprogram should receive the same attention as the structure of a main program. If a function becomes long and difficult to read, perhaps additional functions should be used. Function subprograms can reference intrinsic functions and even other function subprograms. Once you have decided which operations will be written as functions, follow these three style suggestions:

1. Choose descriptive names for your functions.
2. Use comments in the functions as you would in the main program. In particular, use comments at the beginning of a function to describe its purpose and to define its arguments, if necessary. Use blank lines to help separate key steps.
3. For clarity, use the same variables in the dummy argument list and in the actual argument list when possible. If the function is needed several times with different actual arguments, choose completely different dummy argument names to avoid confusion with main program variables.

Key Words

actual argument	module
binary search	search algorithm
driver	statement function
dummy argument	structure chart
function	subprogram
library function	variable dimensioning
main program	

Problems

We begin our problem set with modifications to programs developed earlier in this chapter. Give the decomposition, pseudocode or flowchart, and FORTRAN solution for each problem.

Problems 1 – 5 modify the temperature conversion program TABLEl given on page 268.

1. Modify the temperature conversion program so that it reads a variable specifying the number of lines in the table instead of a number of degrees for the last line.
2. Modify the temperature conversion program so that the statement functions convert temperatures using units in Centigrade and in Kelvin. Both conversion equations can be derived from the following equation that converts degrees Kelvin to degrees Centigrade:

$$\text{degrees C} = \text{degrees K} - 273.15$$

3. Modify the temperature conversion program so that the statement functions convert temperatures using units in Rankin and in Fahrenheit. Both conversion equations can be derived from the following equation that converts degrees Fahrenheit to degrees Rankin:

$$\text{degrees R} = \text{degrees F} + 459.67$$

4. Modify the temperature conversion program so that the statement functions convert temperatures using units in Rankin and in Kelvin. Both conversion

equations can be derived from the following equation that converts degrees Kelvin to degrees Rankin:

$$\text{degrees R} = 1.8 \times \text{degrees K}$$

5. Modify the temperature conversion program so that it contains statement functions to convert temperatures from any of the units Fahrenheit, Centigrade, Kelvin, and Rankin to any of the other units.

Problems 6–10 modify the oil well production program REPORT given on page 290.

6. Modify the oil production program so that it asks the user to enter the current date and then prints this date in the upper right-hand corner of the first page of the report. Thus, the report will show the date that the report was run in addition to the date of the time period for which the data was collected.
7. Modify the oil production program so that the maximum weekly production is determined and printed after the summary line.
8. Using an additional function, modify the oil production program so that it determines the maximum daily production for each oil well. Print this value in addition to the well average.
9. Using an additional function, modify the oil production program so that it determines the total production for each oil well. Print this value in addition to the well average.
10. Modify the oil production program so that it determines the average oil production for an oil well based on nonzero production days. Thus, if a well produced 0 barrels of oil one day of the week, the average would be based on 6 days instead of 7.

Problems 11–15 modify the root-finding program ROOTS given on page 300.

11. Modify the root-finding program so that it allows the user to enter the interval endpoints instead of using [−5,5].
12. Modify the root-finding program so that it allows the user to enter the size of the small intervals to use in the incremental search portion.
13. Modify the root-finding program so that it prints the maximum and minimum polynomial values computed during the incremental-search portion.
14. Modify the root-finding program so that it prints the number of iterations performed to find the root.
15. Modify the root-finding program so that it continues halving the interval in the bisection portion until the absolute value of the function is less than 0.01.

For problems 16–20, write the statement function whose return value is described.

16. Volume of a rectangular parallelepiped:

$$V = \text{length} \cdot \text{width} \cdot \text{height}$$

17. Volume of a right circular cylinder:

$$V = \pi \cdot \text{radius}^2 \cdot \text{height}$$

18. Volume of a right circular cone:

$$V = \frac{1}{3} \cdot \pi \cdot \text{radius}^2 \cdot \text{height}$$

19. Volume of a pyramid:

$$V = \frac{1}{3} \cdot \text{area of the base} \cdot \text{height}$$

20. Volume of a sphere:

$$V = \frac{4}{3} \cdot \pi \cdot \text{radius}^3$$

For problems 21–25, write the function subprogram whose return value is described. The input to the function is an integer array K of 100 elements.

21. MAXI(K), the maximum value of the array K.
22. MINI(K), the minimum value of the array K.
23. NPOS(K), the number of values greater than or equal to zero in the array K.
24. NNEG(K), the number of values less than zero in the array K.
25. NZERO(K), the number of values equal to zero in the array K.

For problems 26–29, assume that you have a function subprogram DENOM, with input value x, to compute the following expression:

$$x^2 + \sqrt{1 + 2x + 3x^2}$$

Give the main program statements that use this function to compute and print each of the following expressions:

26. $\text{ALPHA} = \dfrac{6.9 + y}{y^2 + \sqrt{1 + 2y + 3y^2}}$

27. $\text{BETA} = \dfrac{\sin y}{y^4 + \sqrt{1 + 2y^2 + 3y^4}}$

28. $\text{GAMMA} = \dfrac{2.3z + z^4}{z^2 + \sqrt{1 + 2z + 3z^2}}$

29. $\text{DELTA} = \dfrac{1}{\sin^2 y + \sqrt{1 + 2\sin y + 3\sin^2 y}}$

In problems 30–45, develop these programs and functions. Use the five-step process.

30. Write a function whose input is a 2-digit integer. The function is to return a 2-digit number whose digits are reversed from the input number. Thus, if 17 is the input to the function, 71 is the output.

31. Write a function FACT that receives an integer value and returns the factorial of the value. Recall that the definition of a factorial is

$$0! = 1$$
$$n! = n(n-1)(n-2) \cdots 1$$

If $n < 0$, the function should return a value of zero.

32. Write a function TOTAL that will convert three arguments representing hours, minutes, and seconds to all seconds. For example, TOTAL(3,2,5) should return the integer value 10,925.

33. The cosine of an angle may be computed from this series, where x is measured in radians:

$$\cos x = 1 - \frac{x^2}{2!} + \frac{x^4}{4!} - \frac{x^6}{6!} + \cdots$$

Write a function COSX whose input is an angle in radians. The function should compute the first 10 terms of the series and return that approximation of the cosine. Use the factorial function developed in problem 31. (Hint: The alternating sign can be obtained by computing $(-1)^K$. When K is even, $(-1)^K$ is equal to $+1$; when K is odd, $(-1)^K$ is equal to -1.)

34. Rewrite the function in problem 33 such that it computes the cosine with only as many terms of the series as are necessary to ensure that the absolute value of the last term is less than 0.000001.

35. Write a main program that will produce a table with three columns. The first column (x) should contain angles from 0.0 to 3.1 radians in increments of 0.1 radians. The second column should contain the cosines of the angles as computed by the intrinsic function. The third column should contain the cosines as computed by the function in problem 33. Print the cosine values with an F10.7 format.

36. Engineering programs often utilize experimental data that has been collected and then stored in tabular form. The programs read the data and use it to generate plots, displays, or additional data. Examples of such data include wind tunnel force data on a new aircraft design, rocket motor thrust data, or automobile engine horsepower and torque data. The table of data below gives the thrust output of a new rocket motor as a function of time from ignition.

Time	Thrust
0.0	0.0
1.0	630.0
2.0	915.0
5.0	870.0
8.0	860.0
12.0	885.0
13.0	890.0
15.0	895.0
20.0	888.0

Time	Thrust
22.0	860.0
23.0	872.0
26.0	810.0
30.0	730.0
32.0	574.0
33.0	217.0
34.0	0.0

Write a function called THRUST that computes the motor thrust for a rocket flight simulation program. The function should estimate the thrust for a specified time value using data from the table above. If the specified time value is not one of the times in the table, then the new data value can be determined from the tabulated values by using linear interpolation, which is also called linear proportional scaling. For example, the estimated thrust at $T = 2.2$ seconds would be computed in the following manner:

$$\text{THRUST} = 915.0 + \frac{2.2 - 2.0}{5.0 - 2.0} \times (870.0 - 915.0)$$

$$= 912.0$$

Assume that the function has two arguments: the two-dimensional real array with 35 rows and two columns, and the new value of time. If the time matches a time entry in the table, then the function should return the corresponding thrust value. If the time value does not match a time entry in the table, then the function should interpolate for a corresponding thrust value. Assume that the function will not be referenced if the time is less than zero or greater than 34.0.

37. Assume that each line of a data file DATA1 contains a time value in seconds and a temperature value in degrees Fahrenheit. The first line of the data file contains an integer that gives the number of data lines that follow. Write a program that reads this data and prints the average temperature. Use a function to compute the average temperature. Assume that there are not more than 200 lines of data in the file.
38. Modify the program developed in problem 37 so that it prints the maximum temperature. Use a function to compute the temperature.
39. Modify the program developed in problem 37 so that it prints the number of temperatures that were above the minimum. Use a function to count the temperatures.
40. Modify the program developed in problem 37 so that it prints the minimum amount of time between the temperature measurements. Use a function to determine the minimum time.
41. Modify the program developed in problem 37 so that it prints the number of seconds covered by the data from the data file. Use a function to determine this range.

42. Assume that a file name DEC90 contains weather information from Stapleton International Airport. (See Section 4–3 on page 178 for a description of the data file.) Write a program to read the daily maximum and minimum temperatures for December 1990 into two arrays. Then print the average maximum temperature for the month. Use a function to compute this value.

43. Modify the program developed in problem 42 so that it prints the number of days with minimum temperature under 32°. Use a function to determine the number of days.

44. Modify the program developed in problem 42 so that it prints the maximum range of temperatures for one day. Use a function to determine this range.

45. Modify the program develped in problem 42 so that it prints the number of days with the minimum temperature. Use a function to determine this count.

FORTRAN STATEMENT SUMMARY

■ **FUNCTION** Statement:

`FUNCTION` *name (argument list)*

Examples:

```
      FUNCTION SUM(X,N)
REAL FUNCTION AVE(TESTS)
```

Discussion:

The FUNCTION statement assigns a name to a function and lists the arguments that represent the input to the function. The value returned by the function is assigned to the name of the function. We recommend explicit typing of the function to clearly specify the type of value that is being returned by the function.

■ **Statement** Function:

name (argument list) = expression

Example:

```
AREA(SIDE) = SIDE*SIDE
```

Discussion:

A statement function is a function that can be computed with a single assignment statement. It is defined at the beginning of the program instead of in a separate subprogram definition.

7 Subroutine Subprograms

7

APPLICATION

Composite Materials

Composites contain materials that are bonded together such that one material is reinforced by the fibers or particles of another material. For example, straw is used in mud bricks to make stronger bricks, and steel rods are used in concrete to reinforce bridges and buildings. Advanced composite materials were developed to provide lighter, stronger, and more temperature-resistant materials for aircraft and spacecraft. These advanced composite materials are also finding many other applications. For example, in the photo opposite, the man is petting a goat using artificial arms made from composites. Composites are also used in sporting equipment. Downhill snow skis use layers of woven Kevlar fibers to increase their strength and reduce weight. Golf club shafts of graphite/epoxy are stronger and lighter than the steel in conventional shafts. Composite materials are also incorporated in new designs of fishing rods, bicycle frames, and race-car chassis. (See Section 7-5 for the solution to a problem related to this application.)

Photo © Chuck O'Rear/Westlight.

Introduction

FORTRAN supports two types of subprograms: functions and subroutines. In Chapter 6 we developed programs using intrinsic functions, statement functions, and user-defined functions. Whereas a function is restricted to representing a single value subroutines can compute more than one value and they are not limited to computing values. In this chapter we learn how to write subroutines, and we develop solutions to several applications using subroutines. Both functions and subroutines will be used frequently in the remainder of this text to illustrate their importance in making programs simpler and more readable.

7·1 User-Defined Subroutines

Subroutines are modules written to perform operations that cannot be performed by a function. For example, if several values need to be returned from a module, a subroutine is used. A subroutine is also used for operations that do not compute values, such as reading the values in a data file. All subroutines in FORTRAN 77 are user-defined subroutines; there are no intrinsic subroutines.

Many of the rules for writing and using subroutines are similar to those for functions. The following list of rules outlines the differences between subroutines and functions.

1. A subroutine does not represent a value; thus, its name should be chosen for documentation purposes and not to specify a real or integer value.
2. A subroutine is referenced with an executable statement whose general form is

   `CALL` *subroutine name (argument list)*

3. The first line in a subroutine identifies it as a subroutine and includes the name of the subroutine and the argument list, as shown in this general form:

   `SUBROUTINE` *name (argument list)*

4. A subroutine uses the argument list not only for inputs to the subroutine but also for all values returned to the calling program. The subroutine arguments used in the CALL statement are the actual arguments, and the arguments used in the SUBROUTINE statement are the dummy arguments. The arguments in the CALL statement must match in type, number, and order those used in the subroutine definition.
5. A subroutine may return one value, many values, or no value. Similarly, a subroutine may have one input value, many input values, or no input value.
6. Because the subroutine is a separate program, the arguments are the only link

between the main program and the subroutine. Thus, the choice of subroutine statement numbers and variable names is independent of those in the main program. The variables used in the subroutine that are not subroutine arguments are local variables, and their values are not accessible from the main program.

7. Be especially careful using multidimensional arrays in subroutines. It is generally advisable to pass both the dimensioned size and the operational size for arrays with two or more dimensions. You may want to review the discussion of this topic on page 285 in Chapter 6.
8. The subroutine, like the function, requires a RETURN statement to return control to the main program or to the subprogram that called it. It also requires an END statement because it is a complete program module.
9. In a flowchart, the following special symbol is used to show that the operations indicated are performed in a subroutine:

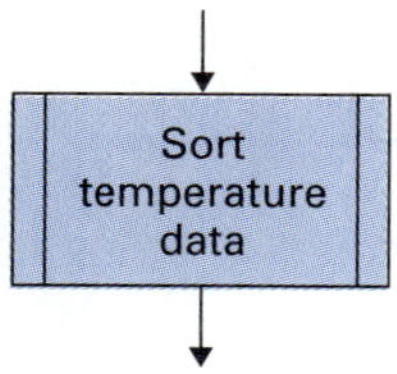

10. A subroutine may reference other functions or call other subroutines, but it cannot call itself.

Fortran 90

Fortran 90 includes intrinsic subroutines for obtaining the date and time information and generating random numbers. Fortran 90 also allows recursive subroutines which can call themselves.

We now present two examples that develop subroutines.

Array Statistics

Example 7-1

Information commonly needed from a set of data includes the average, the minimum value, and the maximum value. These values can be computed using three functions; however, if all three are required, it is more efficient to compute them in one subprogram. Write a subroutine that is called with the statement

```
CALL STAT(X,N,XAVE,XMIN,XMAX)
```

where N is the number of valid elements in the real array X.

Solution

The **first step** is to state the problem clearly: Write a subroutine to determine the average, minimum, and maximum of an array of values.

The **second step** is to describe the input and output:

Input—an array of real values and the number of valid entries in the array
Output—the average, minimum, and maximum values from the array

The **third step** is to work a simple example by hand. However, these operations are all ones that we have used in examples before so we do not repeat the hand examples here.

The **fourth step** is to develop an algorithm. Since we have already developed algorithms for determining averages, minimums, and maximums, the steps for the subroutine are straightforward.

Decomposition

Determine xmin, xmax, xsum.
Compute xave.
Return.

Pseudocode

```
Stat(x,n,xave,xmin,xmax):
    sum ← x(1)
    xmin ← x(1)
    xmax ← x(1)
    For i=2 to n do
        sum ← sum + x(i)
        If x(i) < xmin then xmin ← x(i)
        If x(i) > xmax then xmax ← x(i)
    xave ← sum/n
    Return
```

FORTRAN Subroutine

```
*-----------------------------------------------------------------------*
      SUBROUTINE STAT(X,N,XAVE,XMIN,XMAX)
*
*  This subroutine computes the average, minimum, and
*  maximum of a real array with N values.
*
      INTEGER N, I
      REAL X(N), XAVE, XMIN, XMAX, SUM
*
      SUM = X(1)
      XMIN = X(1)
      XMAX = X(1)
*
```

```
      DO 10 I=2,N
         SUM = SUM + X(I)
         IF (X(I).LT.XMIN) XMIN = X(I)
         IF (X(I).GT.XMAX) XMAX = X(I)
   10 CONTINUE
*
      XAVE = SUM/REAL(N)
*
      RETURN
      END
*-----------------------------------------------------------------------*
```

The **fifth step** is to test the subroutine. We use a program that reads a set of exam scores and then calls the subroutine STAT to compute some statistics from the scores.

FORTRAN Program

```
*-----------------------------------------------------------------------*
      PROGRAM SCORES
*
*  This program reads a set of test scores and then uses a subroutine
*  to determine the average, minimum, and maximum.
*
      INTEGER N, I
      REAL TESTS(100), AVE, MIN, MAX
*
      PRINT*, 'ENTER NUMBER OF TESTS (<101)'
      READ*, N
      PRINT*, 'ENTER TEST SCORES'
      READ*, (TESTS(I),I=1,N)
*
      CALL STAT(TESTS,N,AVE,MIN,MAX)
*
      PRINT 5, AVE
    5 FORMAT (1X,'AVERAGE TEST SCORE = ',F6.2)
      PRINT 10, MIN, MAX
   10 FORMAT (1X,'MINIMUM SCORE = ',F6.2,5X,'MAXIMUM SCORE = ',F6.2)
*
      END
*-----------------------------------------------------------------------*
                     STAT subroutine goes here
*-----------------------------------------------------------------------*
```

Sort Subroutine

Example 7·2

In Chapter 5, we wrote a program that included the steps to sort a one-dimensional array. This operation is used so frequently that we will rewrite it in the form of a subroutine, using the bubble sort algorithm. To make it flexible, we use a variable in the argument list to specify the number of elements in the array. We suggest that you store this subroutine where it can be accessed easily.

Solution

The **first step** is to state the problem clearly: Write a subroutine to sort an array of data.

The **second step** is to describe the input and output:

Input — an array of real values and the number of valid entries in the array
Output — an array of the reordered data

The **third step** is to work a simple example by hand. Since we worked a hand example in Chapter 5 for the bubble sort algorithm, we refer you to page 222 if you need to review it.

The **fourth step** is to develop an algorithm. Since we developed this algorithm in Chapter 5, we need only add the steps so that the solution is implemented as a subroutine.

FORTRAN Subroutine

```
*-----------------------------------------------------------------------*
      SUBROUTINE SORT(X,Y,N)
*
*  This subroutine sorts an array X into an array Y in
*  ascending order.  Both arrays have N values.
*
      INTEGER N, I, FIRST, LAST
      REAL X(N), Y(N), TEMP
      LOGICAL SORTED
*
      DO 10 I=1,N
         Y(I) = X(I)
   10 CONTINUE
*
      SORTED = .FALSE.
      FIRST = 1
      LAST = N - 1
   15 IF (.NOT.SORTED) THEN
         SORTED = .TRUE.
         DO 20 I=FIRST,LAST
            IF (Y(I).GT.Y(I+1)) THEN
               TEMP = Y(I)
               Y(I) = Y(I+1)
               Y(I+1) = TEMP
               SORTED = .FALSE.
            END IF
   20    CONTINUE
         LAST = LAST - 1
         GO TO 15
      END IF
*
      RETURN
      END
*-----------------------------------------------------------------------*
```

The **fifth step** is to test the subroutine. We use the following program that reads a list of data, uses the subroutine to sort them, and then prints the data in the new order.

FORTRAN Program

```
*-----------------------------------------------------------------------*
      PROGRAM LIST
*
*  This program reads a list of real values, sorts them into ascending
*  order using a subroutine, and then prints the reordered values.
*
      INTEGER N, I
      REAL X(25), Y(25)
*
      PRINT*, 'ENTER THE NUMBER OF VALUES TO SORT'
      PRINT*, '(MAXIMUM 25)'
      READ*, N
      PRINT*, 'ENTER THE VALUES'
      READ*, (X(I),I=1,N)
*
      CALL SORT(X,Y,N)
*
      PRINT*, 'VALUES IN ASCENDING ORDER:'
      DO 10 I=1,N
         PRINT 5, Y(I)
    5    FORMAT (1X,F5.2)
   10 CONTINUE
*
      END
*-----------------------------------------------------------------------*
                         SORT subroutine goes here
*-----------------------------------------------------------------------*
```

In the main program, we specified that the list of values to be sorted had a maximum of 25 values (because we dimensioned our arrays to 25 values). Thus, we can use 25 values or less but not more than 25. The subroutine itself does not have any maximum on the array size; it can sort any number of values as long as the values are part of an array that has been properly defined in the main program.

If you do not wish to use two arrays with the sort subroutine, you can use this CALL statement:

```
CALL SORT(X,X,N)
```

Remember, however, that the original order of the values is lost with this reference.

SELF-TEST 7-1

This self-test allows you to check quickly to see if you have remembered some of the key points from Section 7–1. If you have any problems with these exercises, you should reread this section. The solutions are included at the end of the text.

Questions 1 and 2 refer to the following program and subroutine. The program generates an array of 10 numbers containing the integers 1–10. The subroutine modifies these numbers.

```
*-----------------------------------------------------------------*
      PROGRAM QUIZ
*
*  This program tests your understanding of subroutines.
*
      INTEGER K(10), I
*
      DO 10 I=1,10
         K(I) = I
   10 CONTINUE
*
      CALL MODIFY(K,10)
*
      PRINT*, 'NEW VALUES OF K ARE:'
      PRINT 15, (K(I),I=1,10)
   15 FORMAT (1X,5I5)
*
      END
*-----------------------------------------------------------------*
      SUBROUTINE MODIFY(K,N)
*
*  This subroutine modifies elements in K.
*
      INTEGER N, K(N), I
*
      DO 5 I=1,N
         K(I) = MOD(K(I),4)
    5 CONTINUE
*
      RETURN
      END
*-----------------------------------------------------------------*
```

1. What is the program output?
2. What is the program output if the reference to the subroutine is replaced with the following statement?

```
CALL MODIFY(K,8)
```

7.2 Application ▪ Simulation Data

Electrical Engineering

A routine to generate random numbers is useful in many engineering and science applications. Most game programs use randomly generated numbers to make the program appear to have a mind of its own—it chooses different actions each time the game is played. Programs that simulate something, such as tosses of a coin or the number of people at a bank window, also use random number generators.

In this application we use a random number generator to simulate (or model) noise, such as static, that might occur in a piece of instrumentation. The routine that we present generates numbers between 0.0 and 1.0. The numbers are uniformly distributed across the interval between 0.0 and 1.0, which means that we are just as likely to get 0.4455 as we are to get 0.0090. This random number generator requires an argument that is a seed to the computation. When we give the routine a different seed, it returns a different random number. To generate a sequence of random numbers, we initialize the seed once and we do not modify it again. The random number generator modifies the seed itself from one call of the routine to the next and thus must be implemented as a subroutine since it has two outputs. The details of the following random number generator[1] are beyond the scope of this text. It essentially causes the computer to compute integers that are too large to store. The portion of the number that can be stored is a random sequence that is used to determine the random number.

FORTRAN Subroutine

```
*-----------------------------------------------------------------------*
      SUBROUTINE RANDOM(SEED,RANDX)
*
*  This subroutine generates a random number between 0.0 and 1.0.
*  An integer seed is used to initialize the sequence.
*
      INTEGER SEED
      REAL RANDX
*
      SEED = 2045*SEED + 1
      SEED = SEED - (SEED/1048576)*1048576
      RANDX = REAL(SEED + 1)/1048577.0
*
      RETURN
      END
*-----------------------------------------------------------------------*
```

We now present a main program that allows you to enter a seed; the program then prints the first 10 random numbers generated with that seed. Try the program with different seeds and observe that you get different numbers. An example output is shown for a seed of 12357.

[1]S. D. Stearns, "A Portable Random Number Generator for Use in Signal Processing," Sandia National Laboratory Technical Report (1981).

FORTRAN Program

```
*-------------------------------------------------------------------*
      PROGRAM TEST
*
*  This program tests the random number generator.
*
      INTEGER I, SEED
      REAL X
*
      PRINT*, 'ENTER A POSITIVE INTEGER SEED VALUE'
      READ*, SEED
      PRINT*, 'RANDOM NUMBERS:'
      DO 10 I=1,10
         CALL RANDOM(SEED,X)
         PRINT 5, X
    5    FORMAT (1X,F8.6)
   10 CONTINUE
*
      END
*-------------------------------------------------------------------*
                    RANDOM subroutine goes here
*-------------------------------------------------------------------*
```

Sample Output

```
ENTER A POSITIVE INTEGER SEED VALUE
12357
RANDOM NUMBERS:
0.099414
0.299419
0.310731
0.442812
0.548521
0.725532
0.712078
0.199705
0.395030
0.834445
```

We are now ready to discuss the application problem. We want to develop a program that generates a data file containing a sine wave plus noise. The program will use both the intrinsic sine function and the subroutine to generate random numbers. The data file will contain values of this signal

$$f(t) = 2\ \sin(2\pi t) + \text{noise}$$

for $t = 0.0, 0.01, \ldots, 1.00$. Each value of the sine function is added to a random number produced by the random number generator. Since the sine wave can vary from -2 to $+2$ and the random number generator can vary from 0 to 1, we expect this experimental signal to vary from -2 to 3. The signal should be stored in a data file called SIGNAL, where each line of the data file contains the value of t and the corresponding signal value.

1. Problem Statement

Generate a data file that contains samples of the function 2 sin($2\pi t$), with uniform random noise between 0.0 and 1.0 added to it. The data points are to be evaluated with $t = 0.0, 0.01, \ldots, 1.00$.

2. Input/Output Description

Input—the seed to start the random number generator
Output—a data file named SIGNAL

3. Hand Example

In our discussion of the random number generator, we illustrated the first 10 random numbers generated with seed 12357. Using these random numbers, the first 10 data points of the file SIGNAL are

$$f(0.00) = 2 \cdot \sin(2\pi \cdot 0.00) + 0.099414 = 0.0994144$$
$$f(0.01) = 2 \cdot \sin(2\pi \cdot 0.01) + 0.299419 = 0.4250000$$
$$f(0.02) = 2 \cdot \sin(2\pi \cdot 0.02) + 0.310731 = 0.5613975$$
$$f(0.03) = 2 \cdot \sin(2\pi \cdot 0.03) + 0.442812 = 0.8175746$$
$$f(0.04) = 2 \cdot \sin(2\pi \cdot 0.04) + 0.548521 = 1.0459008$$
$$f(0.05) = 2 \cdot \sin(2\pi \cdot 0.05) + 0.725532 = 1.3435660$$
$$f(0.06) = 2 \cdot \sin(2\pi \cdot 0.06) + 0.712078 = 1.4483271$$
$$f(0.07) = 2 \cdot \sin(2\pi \cdot 0.07) + 0.199705 = 1.0512636$$
$$f(0.08) = 2 \cdot \sin(2\pi \cdot 0.08) + 0.395030 = 1.3585374$$
$$f(0.09) = 2 \cdot \sin(2\pi \cdot 0.09) + 0.834445 = 1.9060986$$

4. Algorithm Development

The only input is the random seed. The program then generates the signal values and writes them in a data file. We do not need arrays because each data value is needed only once.

Decomposition

Read random number seed.
Generate data values and write them to the file.

Flowchart

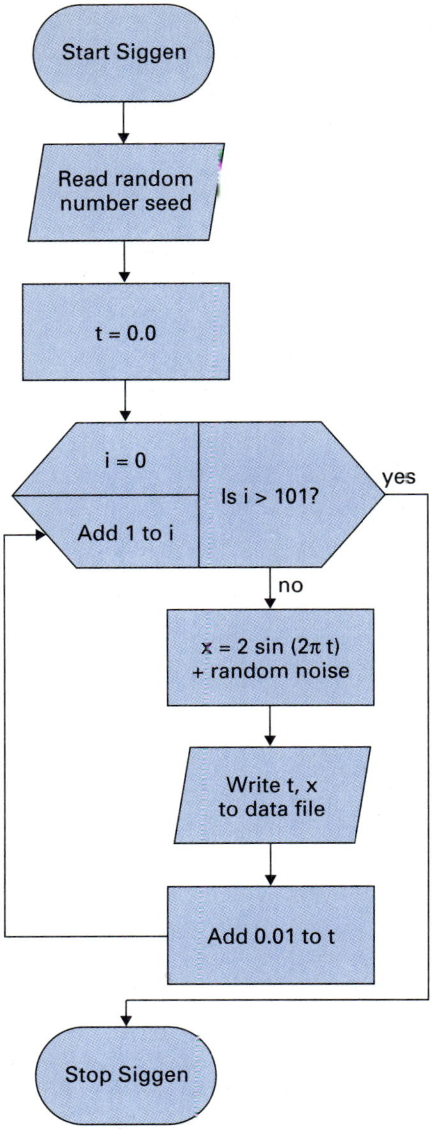

The structure chart for this program is the following:

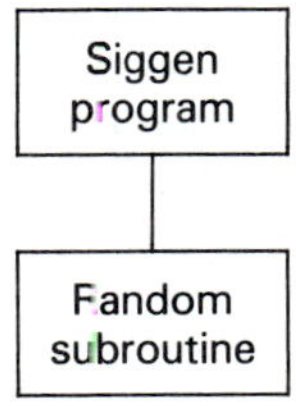

FORTRAN Program

```
*-----------------------------------------------------------------*
      PROGRAM SIGGEN
*
*  This program generates a data file that contains a
*  signal composed of a sine wave plus random noise. The
*  user enters a seed to initialize the random noise signal.
*
      INTEGER SEED, I
      REAL PI, T, NOISE, X
*
      PARAMETER (PI=3.141593)
*
      OPEN (UNIT=15,FILE='SIGNAL',STATUS='NEW')
*
      PRINT*, 'ENTER A POSITIVE INTEGER SEED VALUE'
      READ*, SEED
*
      T = 0.0
      DO 10 I=1,101
         CALL RANDOM(SEED,NOISE)
         X = 2.0*SIN(2.0*PI*T) + NOISE
         WRITE (15,*) T, X
         T = T + 0.01
   10 CONTINUE
*
      END
*-----------------------------------------------------------------*
                  RANDOM subroutine goes here
*-----------------------------------------------------------------*
```

5. Testing

Use the random number generator seed that we used in the hand-worked example. Check the first 10 values of the data signal in the data file; if these match, we can be certain that our random number generator is working. It is difficult to test a program with random values thoroughly because we cannot expect (and should not get) the same values if we change the seed for the random number generator. However, the trend of the data should be the same. For example, in this problem we should be able to see the sine wave in the data even though we use different random numbers for the noise. A plotting routine is helpful here. (In Chapter 8, problem 33 discusses a simple plot routine that can be used to plot data on your terminal screen.) Some plots of the data from program SIGGEN are shown. The first plot shows the sine wave with no noise; the next two plots are plots of the data file using different random seeds. These plots were generated using MATLAB.

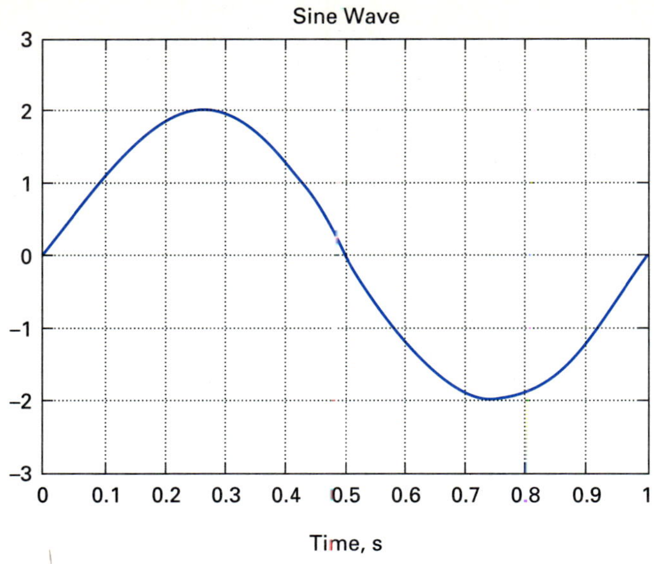
Sine Wave
3
2
1
0
–1
–2
–3
0
0.1
0.2
0.3
0.4
0.5
0.6
0.7
0.8
0.9
1
Time, s

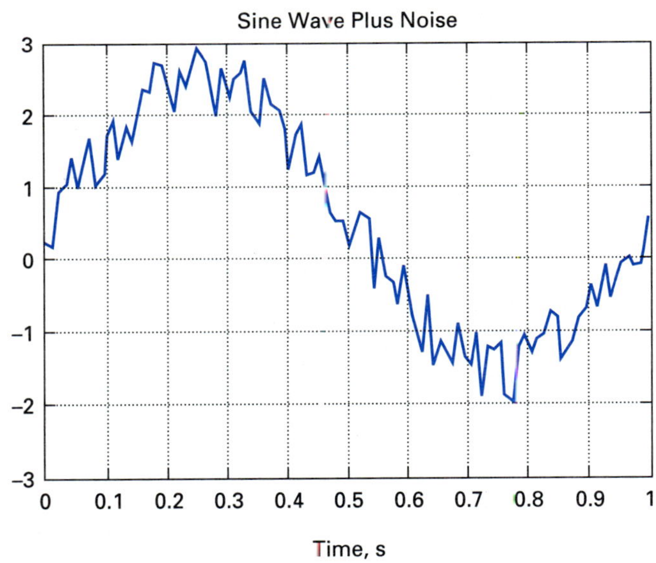
Sine Wave Plus Noise
3
2
1
0
–1
–2
–3
0
0.1
0.2
0.3
0.4
0.5
0.6
0.7
0.8
0.9
1
Time, s

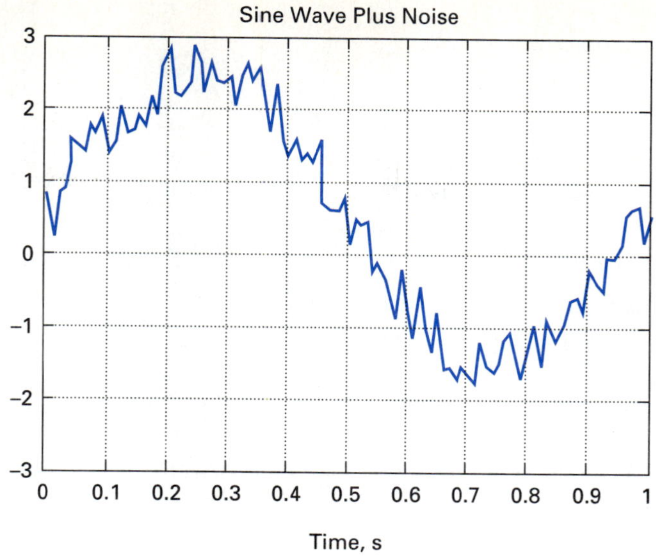

7-3 Application ■ Waste Water Treatment

Chemical Engineering

Organic material in waste water from industrial plants decomposes through chemical and bacterial action. Oxygen is consumed in this process as carbon dioxide and water are produced. As the oxygen is consumed, the waste water is deoxygenated. A standard procedure for determining the rate of deoxygenation begins by diluting a waste water sample with fresh water containing a known amount of dissolved oxygen. The combined sample is held at 20°C for 5 days and then checked for the amount of final oxygen. A biological oxygen demand (BOD) is then calculated from the initial and final oxygen levels. The biological oxygen demand for a 20-day test (at 20°C) is called the first-stage demand. It can be calculated using the five-day (BOD) measurements.

Although oxygen is consumed from the stream when waste water is discharged, oxygen is also continuously being absorbed into the stream from the air. These two processes, deoxygenation and reoxygenation, take place at different rates. The rate of each depends on the oxygen level in the combined mixture of waste water and stream water. Initially, the rate of deoxygenation is rapid as there is a large amount of oxygen in the mixture. For the same reason the rate of reoxygenation is slow. As oxygen is consumed in decomposing the organic material, the oxygen level of the mixture drops. The lower oxygen level in the mixture causes the deoxygenation rate to decrease. It also causes the reoxygenation rate to increase. Hence, the dissolved oxygen level in the mixture decreases with time, reaches a minimum, and then increases. As the dissolved oxygen level decreases below the normal oxygen level of the stream, an oxygen deficit in the mixture is said to occur. The oxygen deficit of the mixture can be calculated in the following manner.

First, calculate the biological oxygen demand for the mixture of the stream and the waste water discharge:

$$bodmix = \frac{bods \cdot qs + bodd \cdot qd}{qs + qd}$$

where *bods* is the biological oxygen demand of the stream
bodd is the biological oxygen demand of the discharge
qs is the stream flow rate in million gallons/day
qd is the discharge flow rate in million gallons/day

Next, estimate the first stage demand (*fsmix*) at the mixture temperature (*tmix*) in degrees centigrade, using the following formula:

$$fsmix = \frac{bodmix}{0.68} \cdot [(0.02 \cdot tmix) + 0.6]$$

Finally, calculate the oxygen deficit as a function of time with the equation

$$defct = \left\{ \frac{kd \cdot fsmix}{kr - kd} \cdot [10^{-kd \cdot t} - 10^{-kr \cdot t}] \right\} + [doxygn \cdot 10^{-kr \cdot t}]$$

where *kd* is the coefficient of deoxygenation
kr is the coefficient of reoxygenation
doxygn is the initial oxygen deficit
t is the elapsed time in days

Also, *kd* can be estimated by

$$kd = 0.1 \cdot 1.047^{(tmix-20)}$$

Assume that you have been hired as a private consultant to a new water analysis laboratory, Clear View Unlimited. Your contract is to write a FORTRAN program to calculate the oxygen deficit as a function of time for several streams being analyzed. The information for the streams is stored in a file called STREAMS. The value in the first data line contains the number of streams in the file. Then each subsequent data line contains the information for one stream in the following order: *qd, qs, bodd, bods, tmix, kr,* and *doxygn.* (All these data values are in the units mentioned in the earlier discussion.) Your program should calculate the oxygen deficit for each stream in the file over a time period using 0.1-day increments. It should find the maximum deficit and when it occurred for each stream. The time period for the analysis will be entered by the user when the program is run.

1. Problem Statement

Write a program to determine the maximum oxygen deficit for each stream in a data file over a time period using 0.1-day increments.

2. Input/Output Description

Input—a data file containing the stream information and a time period for the analysis that will be entered by the user

Output—a report analyzing the oxygen deficit of the streams in the data file

3. Hand Example

For a hand example, we use the following values for the equations:

$$qd = 2.5$$
$$qs = 65.0$$
$$bodd = 0.1$$
$$bods = 15.0$$
$$tmix = 17.6$$
$$kr = 0.45$$
$$doxygn = 7.3$$

The following table lists the days in increments of 0.1 for one day and the corresponding deficits:

Days	Deficits
0.1	6.974
0.2	6.671
0.3	6.391
0.4	6.131
0.5	5.888
0.6	5.662
0.7	5.451
0.8	5.254
0.9	5.070
1.0	4.896

If we were analyzing this stream over one day, the maximum deficit of 6.974 occurred at day 0.1.

4. Algorithm Development

The decomposition for this problem is the following:

Decomposition

Print header.
Compute and print the maximum deficit and the day that it occurred for each stream.

As we refine the steps in the decomposition, we want to consider steps that might be written as functions and subroutines. In this problem, we read a set of parameters for each stream and then use them to compute two values, the maximum deficit and the day that it occurred. Since the computations involved are rather long, a subroutine would be a good way to implement the computations of these two values. (A function is not appropriate since there are two values that need to be returned to the main program.) We now develop a flowchart for the main program and a separate flowchart for the subroutine to calculate the maximum deficit and the day that it occurred.

Main Program Flowchart

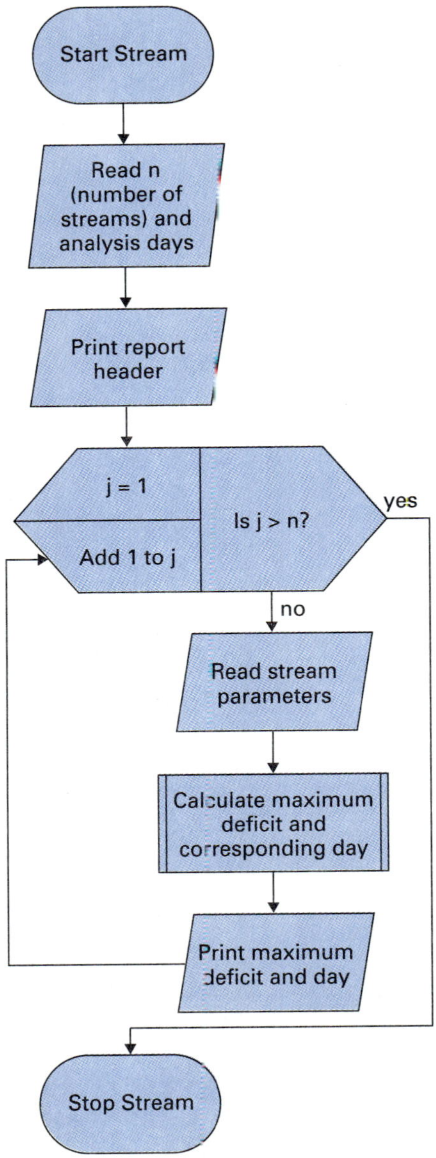

Subroutine Flowchart

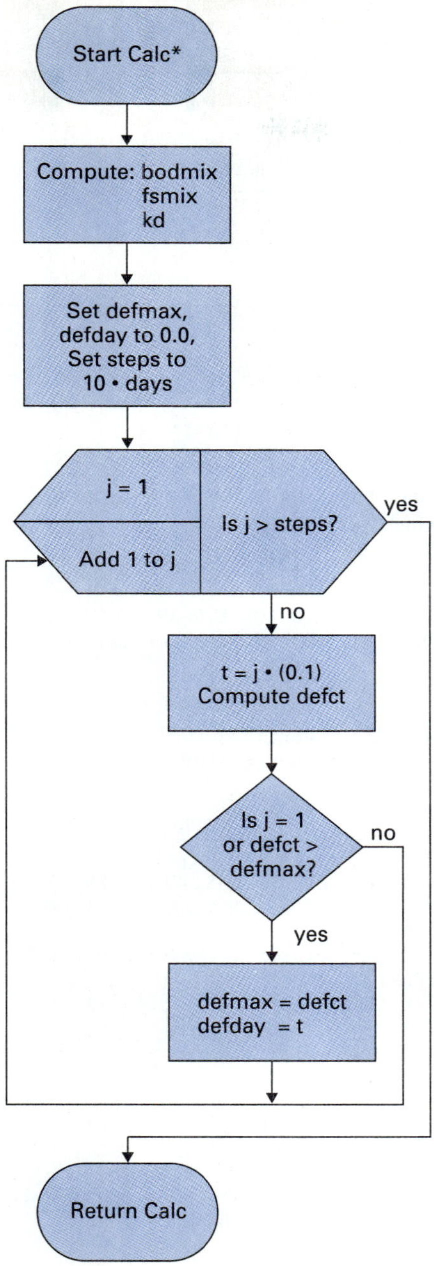

* Subroutine arguments are qd, qs, bodd, bods, tmix, kr, doxygn, days, defmax, defday.

The structure chart for this solution is

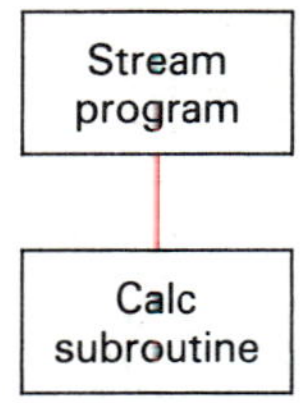

FORTRAN Program

```
*----------------------------------------------------------------------*
      PROGRAM STREAM
*
*  This program computes the maximum oxygen deficit for a
*  group of waste water discharge streams.  The user enters
*  the time period to use for the analysis.
*
      INTEGER N, J
      REAL DAYS, QD, QS, BODD, BODS, TMIX, KR, DOXYGN,
     +     DEFMAX, DEFDAY
*
      OPEN (UNIT=10,FILE='STREAMS',STATUS='OLD')
*
      PRINT*, 'ENTER TIME PERIOD FOR STREAM ANALYSIS'
      PRINT*, '(USE TIME IN TENTHS OF DAYS XX.X)'
      READ*, DAYS
*
      PRINT*
      PRINT*, 'OXYGEN DEFICIT ANALYSIS OF ',
     +        'WASTE WATER DISCHARGE STREAMS'
      PRINT*
*
      READ (10,*) N
      DO 30 J=1,N
         READ (10,*) QD, QS, BODD, BODS, TMIX, KR, DOXYGN
         CALL CALC(QD,QS,BODD,BODS,TMIX,KR,DOXYGN,DAYS,DEFMAX,DEFDAY)
         PRINT 10, J, DEFMAX
   10    FORMAT (1X,'STREAM ',I3,':',' MAXIMUM DEFICIT = ',F6.3)
         PRINT 20, DEFDAY
   20    FORMAT (1X,12X,'OCCURRED AT DAY ',F4.1/)
   30 CONTINUE
*
      END
*----------------------------------------------------------------------*
      SUBROUTINE CALC(QD,QS,BODD,BODS,TMIX,KR,DOXYGN,
     +                DAYS,DEFMAX,DEFDAY)
*
*  This subroutine calculates the maximum oxygen deficit for a
*  stream along with the day that it occurred.
*
      INTEGER STEPS, J
      REAL QD, QS, BODD, BODS, TMIX, KR, DOXYGN, FSMIX, KD, BODMIX,
     +     DEFCT, DAYS, DEFMAX, DEFDAY, T, TEMP1, TEMP2, TEMP3
*
      BODMIX = ((BODS*QS) + (BODD*QD))/(QS + QD)
      FSMIX = BODMIX*(0.02*TMIX + 0.6)/0.68
      KD = 0.1*(1.047**(TMIX - 20.0))
*
```

```
      DEFMAX = 0.0
      DEFDAY = 0.0
      STEPS = INT(DAYS*10.0)
*
      DO 10 J=1,STEPS
         T = REAL(J)*0.1
         TEMP1 = (KD*FSMIX)/(KR - KD)
         TEMP2 = 10.0**(-KD*T) - 10.0**(-KR*T)
         TEMP3 = DOXYGN*(10.0**(-KR*T))
         DEFCT = (TEMP1*TEMP2) + TEMP3
         IF (J.EQ.1.OR.DEFCT.GT.DEFMAX) THEN
            DEFMAX = DEFCT
            DEFDAY = T
         END IF
   10 CONTINUE
*
      RETURN
      END
*-----------------------------------------------------------------------*
```

5. Testing

A sample data file and its corresponding output are shown below:

Data File Streams

```
   4
 2.5    65.0   0.1    15.0   17.6   0.45   7.3
 5.0   108.0   2.5    23.0   12.5   1.85   2.5
23.9     3.5   0.0   145.0   17.6   0.20   1.3
 5.0   108.0   2.5     0.5   20.5   0.20   2.3
```

Computer Output

```
ENTER TIME PERIOD FOR STREAM ANALYSIS
(USE TIME IN TENTHS OF DAYS XX.X)
4.0

OXYGEN DEFICIT ANALYSIS OF WASTE WATER DISCHARGE STREAMS

STREAM   1: MAXIMUM DEFICIT =  6.974
            OCCURRED AT DAY  0.1

STREAM   2: MAXIMUM DEFICIT =  1.997
            OCCURRED AT DAY  0.1

STREAM   3: MAXIMUM DEFICIT =  6.374
            OCCURRED AT DAY  2.9

STREAM   4: MAXIMUM DEFICIT =  2.216
            OCCURRED AT DAY  0.1
```

When you are testing this program, it would be a good idea to put a PRINT statement inside the loop that is computing the deficit for each increment of a day. By checking the set of values computed each time through the DO loop in the subroutine, you can be sure that the steps to determine the maximum deficit are working properly.

7-4 ■ Subroutines for Inserting and Deleting

In the previous chapter we presented a number of common techniques that we implemented with functions. In this section we develop subroutines for *inserting* and *deleting* elements in a list. These techniques are also commonly used in engineering and scientific programs and, like the functions from Chapter 6, will be useful in a variety of programs. The common techniques discussed in the last couple of chapters are often called *software tools* because they are used so frequently. You may want to store these functions and subroutines so they will be convenient to add to programs as you need them.

■ Inserting in an Ordered List

We now consider the steps to insert or delete an element in an ordered list. We assume that the list is ordered in an array and that the value in a variable COUNT will specify how many of the elements in the array represent actual data values.

Example 7-3

Subroutine for Inserting in an Ordered List

Write a subroutine to insert a value in an ordered list of integers. The arguments of the subroutine include the array X, a variable COUNT that specifies the number of valid data values in the array, the variable LIMIT that contains the defined size of the array, and the variable NEW that contains the value to be inserted in the array. Write the subroutine so that it will add a new value to the array even if it is already in the array. If a new element is added to a full array, the last value in the array will be lost.

Solution

The **first step** is to state the problem clearly: Write a subroutine to insert a value in an array.

The **second step** is to describe the input and output:

Input—an integer array, the number of valid elements in the array, the defined size of the array, and the new value to insert

Output—the updated array and the updated number of valid elements in the array

The **third step** is to work a simple example by hand. Consider the following list:

Original List	
	123
	247
	253
	496

There are four valid entries in the array, although we assume that the size of the array might be much larger. Suppose we want to insert the value 147. Think through the steps as you perform them. You scan down the array until you find a value larger than 147, you then move all the rest of the array elements down one position in the array, and finally you insert the new value in the position left open after moving the rest of the array down. (We use the term "up one position in the array" to mean toward the top of the array, or the top of the page. "Down one position in the array" means toward the bottom of the array, or the bottom of the page.) The number of valid elements in the array has now been increased by one. The new contents of the array are the following:

Modified List
123
147
247
253
496

Suppose we now want to insert the value 512. As we scan down the list, we find that we reach the end and the value to be inserted is greater than the last value in the list. We add the new value at the end of the list and increment the count.

Modified List
123
147
247
253
496
512

Are there any special cases that can occur when inserting values in an ordered list? What happens if the value to be inserted is already in the list? If we are updating the list of valid users for a computer system, we don't want to list the identification for a person more than once, so we would not insert the value again if it is already there; on the other hand, if the list represents bank transactions on a specific account, there could be multiple transactions on the same account, so we would want to add the additional information. As another special case, suppose the count equals the defined size of the array; that is, the array is full. To know how to handle this situation requires knowing more about the problem being solved. In some cases we would want to print an error message stating that the array was full and the value could not be added; in other cases we would want to insert the new value and move the rest of the elements down in the array until we reached the end of the array—thus losing the last value in the array.

The **fourth step** is to develop an algorithm, starting with the decomposition.

Decomposition

Insert new item in an ordered list.

Initial Pseudocode

```
Insert(limit,new,count,x):
    If count = limit then
        Print message that last value will be lost
    done ← false
    j ← 1
    While (j ≤ count) and (not done) do
        If x(j) < new value then
            j ← j + 1
        Else
            done ← true
    If j > count then
        Update count
        Add new value at end of list
    Else
        Update count
        Insert new value at this point
    Return
```

We still need to refine a couple of these steps. When we exit the While loop, the If structure tests to see if J is greater than COUNT. If the condition is true, the new element goes at the end of the values. Therefore, if the array is not full, we increment the count and add the new value at the end of the list of valid values; however, if the array is already full, we do nothing because the new value would belong at the end of the list of valid values and there is no room there.

When the new value belongs within the list, we must insert it carefully. First we go to the end of the valid data and move the last value down one position. Then we can move the next-to-the-last value to the position vacated. We continue to move values down until we have moved the value in the position where the new value is to be inserted; we can then insert the new value. If the array is full when we perform the insertion, the value in the last position will be lost. The final pseudocode refinement details these steps.

Final Pseudocode

```
Insert(limit,new,count,x):
    If count = limit then
        Print message that last value will be lost
    done ← false
    j ← 1
    While (j ≤ count) and (not done) do
        If x(j) < new value then
            j ← j + 1
        Else
            done ← true
    If j > count then
        If count < limit then
            count ← count + 1
            x(count) ← new value
    Else
        If count < limit then
            count ← count + 1
        For k = count to j + 1 by −1 do
            x(k) ← x(k − 1)
        x(j) ← new value
    Return
```

Before we convert this to FORTRAN, consider the situation of inserting a value in an empty list—that is, a list which has no valid data values in it and thus has a count of zero. Look at the pseudocode and see if it will handle this situation. (It does, but be sure that you are convinced.) Converting this final refinement to FORTRAN yields the following:

FORTRAN Subroutine

```
*----------------------------------------------------------------------*
      SUBROUTINE INSERT(LIMIT,NEW,COUNT,X)
*
*  This subroutine inserts an element in an ordered list.
*
      INTEGER LIMIT, NEW, COUNT, X(LIMIT), J, K
      LOGICAL DONE
*
      IF (COUNT.EQ.LIMIT) THEN
         PRINT*, 'ARRAY IS FULL'
         PRINT*, 'LAST VALUE WILL BE LOST'
      END IF
*
      DONE = .FALSE.
      J = 1
```

```
    5 IF ((J.LE.COUNT).AND.(.NOT.DONE)) THEN
         IF (X(J).LT.NEW) THEN
            J = J + 1
         ELSE
            DONE = .TRUE.
         END IF
         GO TO 5
      END IF
*
      IF (J.GT.COUNT) THEN
         IF (COUNT.LT.LIMIT) THEN
            COUNT = COUNT + 1
            X(COUNT) = NEW
         END IF
      ELSE
         IF (COUNT.LT.LIMIT) COUNT = COUNT + 1
         DO 10 K=COUNT,J+1,-1
            X(K) = X(K-1)
   10    CONTINUE
         X(J) = NEW
      END IF
*
      RETURN
      END
*-----------------------------------------------------------------------*
```

This insertion subroutine is not trivial. It requires a thorough understanding of arrays and subscript handling. Go through the pseudocode and corresponding FORTRAN statements until you understand the steps.

The **fifth step** is to test the subroutine. After we develop the subroutine for deleting an element from an ordered list, we present a program for testing both the insertion and the deletion subroutines. ◀

■ Deleting from an Ordered List

After you master the insertion technique, you will find the deletion technique easier because there are many similarities. We again assume that the list is ordered in an array and that the value in a variable COUNT will specify how many of the elements in the array represent actual data values.

Example 7-4 ▶

Subroutine for Deleting from an Ordered List . . . .

Write a subroutine to delete a value from an ordered list. The arguments of the subroutine include the array X, a variable COUNT that specifies the number of valid data values in the array, and the variable OLD that contains the value to be deleted from the array.

Solution

The **first step** is to state the problem clearly: Write a subroutine to delete a value in an array.

The **second step** is to describe the input and output:

Input — an integer array, the number of valid elements in the array, and the value to be deleted from the array

Output — the updated array and the updated number of valid elements in the array

The **third step** is to work a simple example by hand. We begin with the following list of values:

Original List	
	123
	247
	253
	496

As before, there are four valid entries in the original array, but we still assume that the actual size of the array could be larger. Suppose we want to delete value 253. Think through the steps as you perform them: you scan down the array until you find the value, you remove the value, and you move the rest of the array values up one position in the array. The number of valid elements in the array has now been decreased by one. The new contents of the array are the following:

Modified List	
	123
	247
	496

Are there any special cases that can occur when deleting values in an ordered list? What happens if the value to be deleted is not in the list? In this situation we probably want to print a message to the user. What happens if we delete the only element in the list? In this situation the count will be decremented to the value zero and we will have an empty list.

The **fourth step** is to develop an algorithm, starting with the decomposition.

Decomposition

Delete item from an ordered list.

Initial Pseudocode

```
Delete(old,count,x):
    done ← false
    j ← 1
    While (j ≤ count) and (not done) do
        If x(j) < old then
            j ← j + 1
        Else
            done ← true
    If (j > count) or (x(j) > old) then
        Write message that value is not in the list
    Else
        Update count
        Delete old value from list
```

Will this pseudocode handle the situation in which the array is empty? Since COUNT will be equal to zero, the condition in the While loop will be false the first time it is tested, because the value of J is 1. A message will be printed that the value is not in the list, which handles the situation properly.

We still need to refine a couple of the steps in the pseudocode. When we exit the While loop, the If structure tests to see if the element was actually in the loop. If we searched until we reached the end of the loop (j > count) or until we passed the position where the element should have been (x(j) > old), we write a message indicating that the element was not in the list. If the element was in the list, we need to subtract one from the count and "delete old value from list." However, we really do not explicitly delete the old value. Instead, we move the value below the old value up one position in the array, the value below that one up one position in the array, and so on until we have moved all the values below the one to be deleted up one position in the array. The final pseudocode refinement details these steps.

Final Pseudocode

```
Delete(old,count,x):
    done ← false
    j ← 1
    While (j ≤ count) and (not done) do
        If x(j) < old then
            j ← j + 1
        Else
            done ← true
    If (j > count) or (x(j) > old) then
        Write message that value is not in the list
    Else
        count ← count − 1
        For k = j to count do
            x(k) ← x(k + 1)
```

Converting this final pseudocode to FORTRAN yields the following statements:

FORTRAN Subroutine

```
*-----------------------------------------------------------------------*
      SUBROUTINE DELETE(OLD,COUNT,X)
*
*  This subroutine deletes an element from an ordered list.
*
      INTEGER OLD, COUNT, X(COUNT), J, K
      LOGICAL DONE
*
      DONE = .FALSE.
      J = 1
    5 IF ((J.LE.COUNT).AND.(.NOT.DONE)) THEN
         IF (X(J).LT.OLD) THEN
            J = J + 1
         ELSE
            DONE = .TRUE.
         END IF
         GO TO 5
      END IF
*
      IF ((J.GT.COUNT).OR.(X(J).GT.OLD)) THEN
         PRINT*, 'VALUE TO DELETE IS NOT IN LIST'
      ELSE
         COUNT = COUNT - 1
         DO 10 K=J,COUNT
            X(K) = X(K+1)
   10    CONTINUE
      END IF
*
      RETURN
      END
*-----------------------------------------------------------------------*
```

The **fifth step** is to test this subroutine. We will perform the testing of the deletion routine along with the testing of the insertion routine using a driver program that allows us to test modules independently of a specific program. In the driver program, the user is asked to enter a list of ordered values. The values are stored; then the user is allowed to perform both deletions and insertions. The program has the following structure chart:

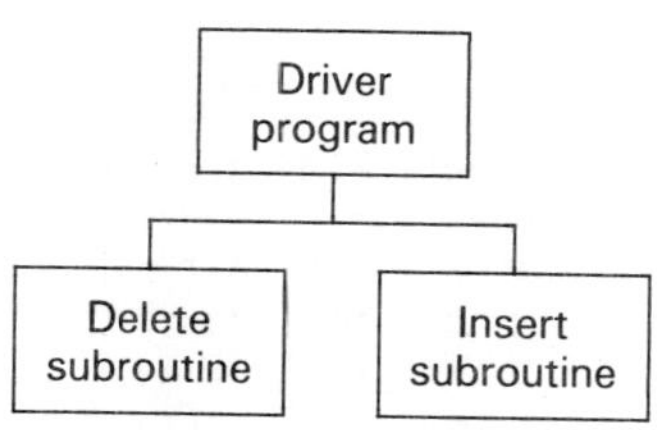

FORTRAN Program

```
*-----------------------------------------------------------------------*
      PROGRAM DRIVER
*
*  This driver tests both the insertion and deletion routines.
*
      INTEGER X(10), COUNT, I, CODE, NEW, OLD, LIMIT
      LOGICAL DONE
*
      DATA LIMIT /10/
*
      PRINT*, 'ENTER COUNT (<11) OF VALUES FOR LIST'
      READ*, COUNT
      PRINT*, 'ENTER VALUES IN ASCENDING ORDER'
      READ*, (X(I),I=1,COUNT)
*
      DONE = .FALSE.
    5 IF (.NOT.DONE) THEN
*
         PRINT*, 'ENTER -1 FOR DELETE, 1 TO INSERT, ',
     +           '9 TO QUIT'
         READ*, CODE
*
         IF (CODE.EQ.-1) THEN
            PRINT*, 'ENTER VALUE TO DELETE'
            READ*, OLD
            CALL DELETE(OLD,COUNT,X)
         ELSE IF (CODE.EQ.1) THEN
            PRINT*, 'ENTER VALUE TO INSERT'
            READ*, NEW
            CALL INSERT(LIMIT,NEW,COUNT,X)
         END IF
*
         IF (CODE.EQ.9) THEN
            DONE = .TRUE.
         ELSE
            PRINT*, 'NEW LIST:'
            DO 10 I=1,COUNT
               PRINT 8, X(I)
    8          FORMAT (1X,I8)
   10       CONTINUE
         END IF
*
         GO TO 5
      END IF
*
      END
*-----------------------------------------------------------------------*
                      DELETE subroutine goes here
*-----------------------------------------------------------------------*
                      INSERT subroutine goes here
*-----------------------------------------------------------------------*
```

The order of the routines is not important; they could be interchanged with no effect on the program.

An example of a test of the insert and delete subroutines using this driver follows:

```
ENTER COUNT (<11) OF VALUES FOR LIST
3
ENTER VALUES IN ASCENDING ORDER
5      13      17
ENTER -1 FOR DELETE, 1 TO INSERT, 9 TO QUIT
1
ENTER VALUE TO INSERT
8
NEW LIST:
        5
        8
       13
       17
ENTER -1 FOR DELETE, 1 TO INSERT, 9 TO QUIT
-1
ENTER VALUE TO DELETE
15
VALUE TO DELETE IS NOT IN LIST
NEW LIST:
        5
        8
       13
       17
ENTER -1 FOR DELETE, 1 TO INSERT, 9 TO QUIT
9
```

If you did not want to require that the user enter data that had already been sorted, you could add a short subroutine such as the one that we developed in Example 7 – 2 on page 328. The new structure chart for the program would then be the one shown below:

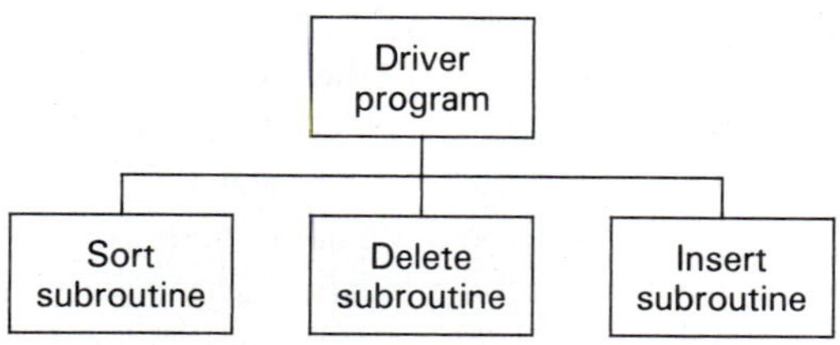

The steps in the driver program that prompt the user to enter the data would then be replaced by the following:

```
PRINT*, 'ENTER COUNT (<11) OF VALUES FOR LIST'
READ*, COUNT
PRINT*, 'ENTER VALUES'
READ*, (X(I),I=1,COUNT)
CALL SORT(X,X,COUNT)
```

SELF-TEST 7-2

This self-test allows you to check quickly to see if you have remembered some of the key points from Section 7–4. If you have any problems with this exercise, reread this section. The solutions are included at the end of the text.

Using the insert and delete routines developed in this section, answer the following questions.

1. Given a specific set of new values to insert, does the order of the insertions affect the results? Explain.
2. If an insertion value matches a value already in the list, does the new value get inserted above or below the existing duplicate value?
3. What happens if two new values to insert are duplicates?
4. Give specific examples showing how the order of a set of insertions and deletions could affect the results.

7·5 Application ▪ Composite Materials

Mechanical Engineering

A large aircraft manufacturer uses a variety of composite materials. Some of the materials will be used on the frame of the aircraft, and some will be used in instrumentation and avionics (the electronics used in the airplane). Assume that a computerized database of the composites used in the current production airplanes is used by a variety of programs, including some computer-aided design and manufacturing programs. Assume that, in addition to the database containing detailed information on each composite, we also keep a file containing the identification number for each composite currently used and the location of the warehouse in which it is stored. This data file is named MATERIAL and contains the composite identification numbers in ascending order. In addition to the identification number, each line of the file contains a warehouse location number. The last line in the file contains values 99999 and 99999.

We want to develop a program that will allow new materials to be added to this list of composites. In developing the program, we must be concerned about the *user interface*—the part of the program that interfaces the user to the steps in the program itself. The user interface should be designed to be easy to use so that users will make fewer errors when entering the information. (Programs that are easy to use are also called *user-friendly* programs.) We will assume that the user will be entering five-digit material identification numbers and three-digit warehouse locations from the keyboard. We will allow the information to be entered in any order; that is, we will not assume that the identification numbers to be inserted are in any particular order.

Because we are inserting elements in a materials list, it does not make sense to insert an element already in the list, unless we assume that composites could be stored in several places. However, assume that we do not want to store the same material in multiple locations. Therefore, we must modify the insertion subroutine from the previous section so that a message is printed if the element is already in the list. Similarly, if the list is full we do not want to insert another element because we would lose the last element in the list. Therefore, before referencing the insert subroutine we will check to see if the list is full and, if so, print a message to the user. Finally, we must also be sure to properly update the warehouse location.

1. Problem Statement

Write a program to update a composite materials list.

2. Input/Output Description

Input — a data file containing material identification numbers and warehouse location numbers for the composite materials and a set of insertions for the data file

Output — a new updated data file and error messages if the materials to be added are already in the file

3. Hand Example

Assume that the following composite identification numbers and materials represent the current composites in the warehouse:

Composite ID	Composite Material	Warehouse Location
20329	Kevlar	52
28912	Graphite/epoxy	16
31933	Silicon-carbide/aluminum	87
45012	Boron/epoxy	52

The updates to this list include the following insertions:

Composite ID	Composite Material	Warehouse Location
12289	Boron/aluminum	52
24444	Resin/glass	16
59595	Aluminum-oxide/aluminum	87
28912	Graphite/epoxy	18

After updating the list, the new composite information list should contain the following:

Composite ID	Warehouse Location
12289	52
20329	52
24444	16
28912	16
31933	87
45012	52
59595	87

4. Algorithm Development

The decomposition of this problem solution is

Decomposition

Read material information from the old file.
Perform insertions to the list.
Write updated list to the new file.

We could store the information from the file in two one-dimensional arrays or in a two-dimensional array. We choose to use two one-dimensional arrays, using an ID array for the composite numbers and a separate LOC array for the warehouse location numbers. We need to be very careful that the items in the two arrays stay in corresponding orders. Otherwise, the locations of the composites will be incorrect.

We now refine the decomposition steps into pseudocode.

Pseudocode

```
Update: Read id and location data from file into arrays
        Set count to number of entries in the arrays
        done ← false
        While not done do
              Print message asking for new data
              Read new id and new location
              If count = limit then
                    Print message that list is full
              Else
                    Insert new id and new location
        Write updated arrays to the new file
```

We now develop the pseudocode for the insertion routine. Some modifications are needed in the insertion routine because we do not want to insert a duplicate number in the list. Instead, we will print a message that the number is already in the list. Since the file includes a trailer signal of 99999, any insertions will be before that value, so we can omit the test for inserting at the end of the list. Since the insertion routine is modified for the program, we use variable names to match those in the main program.

The pseudocode for the insertion routine assumes that the ID values are already in an ascending order in the array ID with the corresponding location values in the array LOC, a variable COUNT specifies the number of data values (including the trailer signal) in the arrays, a variable LIMIT contains the defined size of the arrays, and the variables NEWID and NEWLOC contain the values to be inserted in the arrays.

Pseudocode

```
Insert(limit,newid,newloc,count,id,loc):
    done ← false
    j ← 1
    While id(j) < newid do
        j ← j + 1
    If x(j) = newid then
        Print message that item is already in list
    Else
        count ← count + 1
        For k = count to j+1 by −1 do
            id(k) ← id(k − 1)
            loc(k) ← loc(k − 1)
        id(j) ← newid
        loc(j) ← newloc
    Return
```

The structure chart for the solution is the following:

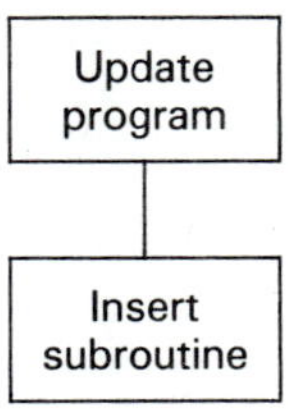

FORTRAN Program

```
*-----------------------------------------------------------------------*
      PROGRAM UPDATE
*
*  This program updates a composite materials information list by
*  adding new composite materials along with their warehouse locations.
*
      INTEGER LIMIT, J, ID(500), LOC(500), COUNT, NEWID, NEWLOC
      LOGICAL DONE
*
      PARAMETER (LIMIT=500)
*
      OPEN (UNIT=8,FILE='COMPIN',STATUS='OLD')
*
      DONE = .FALSE.
      J = 1
```

```
    5 IF (.NOT.DONE) THEN
         READ (8,*) ID(J), LOC(J)
         IF (ID(J).EQ.99999) THEN
            DONE = .TRUE.
         ELSE
            J = J + 1
         END IF
         GO TO 5
      END IF
      COUNT = J
      DONE = .FALSE.
*
   10 IF (.NOT.DONE) THEN
         PRINT*, 'ENTER NEW ID AND LOCATION NUMBER'
         PRINT*, '(NEGATIVE VALUES TO QUIT)'
         READ*, NEWID, NEWLOC
         IF (NEWID.GE.0) THEN
            IF (COUNT.EQ.LIMIT) THEN
               PRINT*, 'LIST IS FULL'
            ELSE
               CALL INSERT(LIMIT,NEWID,NEWLOC,COUNT,ID,LOC)
            END IF
         ELSE
            DONE = .TRUE.
         END IF
         GO TO 10
      END IF
*
      OPEN (UNIT=9,FILE='COMPOUT',STATUS='NEW')
*
      DO 15 J=1,COUNT
         WRITE (9,*) ID(J), LOC(J)
   15 CONTINUE
*
      END
*-----------------------------------------------------------------------*
      SUBROUTINE INSERT(LIMIT,NEWID,NEWLOC,COUNT,ID,LOC)
*
*  This subroutine inserts an element in an ordered list.
*
      INTEGER LIMIT, NEWID, NEWLOC, COUNT, ID(LIMIT), LOC(LIMIT), J, K
*
      J = 1
    5 IF (ID(J).LT.NEWID) THEN
         J = J + 1
         GO TO 5
      END IF
*
      IF (ID(J).EQ.NEWID) THEN
         PRINT*, 'ID ALREADY IN FILE'
      ELSE
         COUNT = COUNT + 1
         DO 10 K=COUNT,J+1,-1
            ID(K) = ID(K-1)
            LOC(K) = LOC(K-1)
   10    CONTINUE
         ID(J) = NEWID
         LOC(J)= NEWLOC
      END IF
*
      RETURN
      END
*-----------------------------------------------------------------------*
```

5. Testing

It might seem that testing this program will be simpler since we modified a procedure that had already been tested independently. However, if we make even small changes in a subprogram, we must go through a thorough testing procedure to be sure that it is correct.

The terminal screen interaction and the input and output file contents from the hand example follow:

Data File COMPIN

```
20329         52
28912         16
31933         87
45012         52
99999      99999
```

Computer Output

```
ENTER NEW ID AND LOCATION NUMBER
(NEGATIVE VALUES TO QUIT)
12289 52
ENTER NEW ID AND LOCATION NUMBER
(NEGATIVE VALUES TO QUIT)
24444 16
ENTER NEW ID AND LOCATION NUMBER
(NEGATIVE VALUES TO QUIT)
59595 87
ENTER NEW ID AND LOCATION NUMBER
(NEGATIVE VALUES TO QUIT)
28912 18
ID ALREADY IN FILE
ENTER NEW ID AND LOCATION NUMBER
(NEGATIVE VALUES TO QUIT)
-1    -1
```

Data File COMPOUT

```
12289         52
20329         52
24444         16
28912         16
31933         87
45012         52
59595         87
99999      99999
```

Note that the trailer signal was kept in the array along with the identification numbers. This was convenient because we always are inserting values within the array, instead of at the end of the array, since all ID values would be less than 99999. Also, by including it in the list of values, it is automatically written to the data file at the end of the program.

7·6 ■ Common Blocks

As you modularize your programs, you will find that the argument lists can become lengthy as you pass more and more data to functions and subroutines. FORTRAN allows you to set up a block of memory that is accessible, or common, to the main program and to all its subprograms—a *common block*. The variables in this block of memory do not have to be passed through argument lists and cannot be used as arguments in subprograms.

FORTRAN allows two types of common blocks: *blank common* and *named common*. Blank common is set up with the specification statement shown:

```
COMMON variable list
```

Each subprogram that uses data in this common block must also contain a COMMON statement. Although the data names do not have to match in every subprogram, the type and order of the names are important. Consider these COMMON statements from a main program and a subprogram, respectively:

```
PROGRAM TEST1
INTEGER J
REAL A, B, X, Y
COMMON A, J, B
.
.
.
CALL ANSWR(X,Y)
.
.
.
END
SUBROUTINE ANSWR(X,Y)
INTEGER KTOT
REAL TEMP, SUM, X, Y
COMMON TEMP, KTOT, SUM
.
.
.
END
```

In these statements, the main program communicates with the subroutine using two arguments, X and Y. In addition, the main program and the subroutine share a memory area. A and TEMP represent the same memory location, J and KTOT represent the same memory location, and B and SUM represent the same memory location, as shown in the following diagram:

Common Memory Area

A	57.63	TEMP
J	−25	KTOT
B	0.007	SUM

Named common, also referred to as *labeled common,* is established if the list of variable names in the COMMON statement is preceded by a name enclosed in slashes:

> COMMON */name/variable list*

The purpose of establishing different blocks of common with unique names is to allow subprograms to refer to the named common block with which they wish to share data without listing all the other variables in the other common blocks.

For example, one group of variables may be used in a set of computations, and another group of variables may be used in generating data files that will be plotted. The first group of variables could comprise one common area named CALC, and the other group of variables could comprise another common area named GRAPH. Both named COMMON statements appear in the main program; then individual subprograms include either or both named COMMON statements depending on the variables they need to access. The argument lists for the individual subprograms include other input and output variables that are not in the common areas. A variable cannot appear in more than one block of named common, and thus a variable could not appear in both the CALC and GRAPH common blocks; if the variable is needed in the computations and the graphics, it should be passed through the argument list of the subprograms or in a third named common block.

Arrays may be included in the COMMON statement. The COMMON statement can be used to define the storage for these arrays as shown:

```
COMMON X(50), INCOME(4)
```

An array size can be specified in the COMMON statement, as shown in the previous statement, or it can be specified in an explicit type statement as in

```
INTEGER SUM
REAL TIME(25), DIST(25)
COMMON SUM, TIME, DIST
```

The size of an array cannot be specified in both a type statement and a COMMON statement.

Variables in blank common cannot be initialized with DATA statements. They can be initialized with READ statements or assignment statements. Variables in named common can be initialized with READ statements, assignment statements, or with a special subprogram called a *BLOCK DATA subprogram.* This subprogram is nonexecutable and serves only to assign initial values to variables in a named common block. An example of a BLOCK DATA subprogram to initialize two named common blocks is

```
BLOCK DATA
COMMON /EXPER1/ TEMP(100)
COMMON /EXPER2/ TIME, DIST, VEL(10)
DATA TEMP, TIME, DIST, VEL /100*0.0, 50.5, 0.5, 10*0.0/
END
```

Both of the COMMON statements must be in the main program. Either or both of the statements also appear in any subprogram that uses variables in these common blocks of memory.

Unless extremely large amounts of data must be passed to subprograms, the use of common blocks is discouraged because it weakens the independence of modules; the module can be affected not only by its arguments but also by variables in common. If you do use common blocks, pay attention to the order of the variables on all COMMON statements. Also look for omitted variables; if a variable is left out of a COMMON statement in a subprogram, incorrect values are used for all variables following it in the COMMON statement. These errors can cause problems that are difficult to locate.

Fortran 90

In Fortran 90, a new program unit called a module provides a way of sharing constants, variables, type definitions, and procedures. A module also provides a means for packaging procedures in a library for different programs to access.

Summary

The subroutine is a subprogram that allows us to return multiple values to the main program, such as when we want to sort an array, or to return no values to the main program, such as when we want to print an error message. Functions and other subroutines can also call a subroutine, in addition to the main program. The subroutine, along with the function, allows us to structure our programs by breaking them into modules that can be written and tested independently of each other. Not only do programs become simpler, but the same module can also be used in other programs without retesting. In this chapter we developed subroutines that are useful in many applications — a sort routine, an insert routine, and a delete routine.

Debugging Aids

Subroutine testing, like function testing, is the same as program testing: it generally involves writing a special main program or driver to initialize values and call the subroutine. The specific guides that we enumerate refer to the argument list, which is the link between the subroutine and the main program:

1. In general, use the argument list to pass information back and forth between the program and the subroutine, as opposed to using common blocks.
2. Be sure that the variables or expressions listed in the argument list of the CALL statement match in type and in order the argument list in the SUBROUTINE statement.
3. Include all variables in the subroutine in type statements to avoid incorrect default typing.
4. Use PRINT statements in the subroutine for debugging, just as you do in the main program.

5. Test each subroutine separately before combining it in a program with other subprograms.
6. Test each of the subroutines with several sets of data to check any special conditions.

■ Style/Technique Guides

Separating a long program into modules that transfer control smoothly from one to another becomes easier with practice. Although different sets of subprograms may solve the same problem, some choices are more logical and readable than others; these are the solutions that you want to develop. Once you have selected a segment that is to be made into a subroutine, you must decide what arguments are needed. Listed are a few style suggestions to keep in mind as you make these decisions:

1. Choose descriptive names for your subroutines.
2. Use comments in the subroutines as you would in the program. In particular, use comments at the beginning of a subroutine to describe its purpose and to define its arguments, if necessary.
3. For clarity, use the same variables in the argument list of the subroutine as those used in the main program, if possible. If the subroutine is called several times with different arguments, choose completely different variable names in the subroutine to avoid confusion with variables in the main program.
4. List input parameters before output parameters in the argument list.

■ Key Words

blank common
BLOCK DATA subprogram
common block
deletion
insertion
named common
subroutine
user-friendly
user interface

■ Problems

We begin our problem set with modifications to programs developed earlier in this chapter. Give the decomposition, refined pseudocode or flowchart, and FORTRAN solution for each problem.

Problems 1 – 5 modify the program SIGGEN given on page 335, which generated a data file composed of a sine wave plus random noise.

1. Modify the signal generating program so that it increments the time by 0.25 instead of 0.01.

2. Modify the signal generating program so that it reads the time increment from the terminal.
3. Modify the signal generating program so that it reads the number of data points that are to be generated from the terminal, instead of generating 101 points.
4. Modify the signal generating program so that it multiplies the noise value generated by the random number generator by a constant that is read from the terminal.
5. Modify the signal generating program so that it adds the noise value to a cosine, instead of a sine wave.

For problems 6–10 modify the program STREAM given on page 342, which determines the maximum oxygen deficit for each stream in a data file.

6. Modify the oxygen deficit program so that it determines the minimum oxygen deficit for each stream in a data file.
7. Modify the oxygen deficit program so that it determines the maximum oxygen deficit for each stream in a data file using 0.25-day increments.
8. Modify the oxygen deficit program so that it determines the maximum oxygen deficit for each stream in a data file using a daily increment that is entered from the terminal.
9. Modify the oxygen deficit program so that it determines the overall maximum oxygen deficit for the group of streams in a data file and prints this maximum at the end of the summary.
10. Modify the oxygen deficit program so that it determines the maximum oxygen deficit for each stream in a data file and prints the day on which it occurred as an integer, instead of a real number. Thus, if the maximum deficit occurred on day 2.8, the program would indicate that it occurred on day 2.

For problems 11–15 modify the program UPDATE given on page 357, which updates a composite material ID list.

11. Modify the update program so that it writes the number of additions performed by the program on the terminal screen before exiting the program.
12. Modify the update program so that it writes the number of composite materials in the ID file on the terminal screen before exiting the program.
13. Modify the update program so that it writes the number of composite materials on the terminal screen before beginning the update process.
14. Modify the update program so that it assumes that the ID file is in descending order instead of ascending order and has a trailer value of zero.
15. Modify the update program so that it prints a report that lists all the composite material ID numbers and their locations after the ID list is updated.

For problems 16–21, assume that TIME, a one-dimensional array of 100 real values, has already been filled with data.

16. Write a subroutine to determine the maximum value in the array TIME and to subtract that value from each value in the array.

17. Write a subroutine to determine the minimum value in the array TIME and to add that value to each value in the array.

18. Write a subroutine to replace each negative value in the array TIME with 0.0.

19. Write a subroutine to determine the average of the values in the array TIME. Add 1.0 to all values above the average; subtract 1.0 from all values below the average.

20. Write a subroutine to replace all values in the array TIME with the absolute value of the corresponding value.

21. Write a subroutine to return a logical value of true if all the values in the array TIME are zero; otherwise, the value returned should be false.

For problems 22–25, assume that Z, a two-dimensional array with 5 rows and 4 columns of real values, has already been filled with data.

22. Write a subroutine that fills an array W (the same size as Z) with the absolute value of the corresponding element in Z.

23. Write a subroutine that fills an array W (the same size as Z) with a value based on the corresponding element in Z, where

$$\begin{aligned} W(I,J) &= \ \ 0.0 \qquad \text{if } Z(I,J) = O \\ W(I,J) &= -1.0 \qquad \text{if } Z(I,J) < O \\ W(I,J) &= \ \ 1.0 \qquad \text{if } Z(I,J) > O \end{aligned}$$

24. Write a subroutine that fills an array W (the same size as Z) in the following manner: W should contain the same values of Z unless the corresponding values in Z are greater than the average value of Z. In these cases, the corresponding value of W should contain the average value of Z.

25. Write a subroutine that fills an array W (the same size as Z) with numbers such that each element of W is the corresponding value of Z rounded up to the next multiple of 10. Thus, 10.76 rounds to 20.0, 18.7 rounds to 20.0, 0.05 rounds to 10.0, 10.0 rounds to 10.0, and −5.76 rounds to 0.0.

Develop these programs and subroutines. Use the five-step design process.

26. Write a subroutine called RANGE that receives an integer array with 50 elements and returns the maximum and minimum values.

27. Write a subroutine that reads a group of test measurements from a data file until it finds a negative measurement. The subroutine should return the number of test measurements read before the negative value was encountered and the average of those test measurements. Assume that the data file has been opened and assigned to unit 12.

28. Write a subroutine that computes the average, the variance, and the standard deviation of an array X of 100 data values. Use the following formulas:

Average: $$\bar{X} = \frac{\sum_{i=1}^{100} X_i}{100}$$

Variance: $$\sigma^2 = \frac{\sum_{i=1}^{100} (\bar{X} - X_i)^2}{99}$$

Standard deviation: $$\sigma = \sqrt{\sigma^2}$$

29. Rewrite the subroutine in problem 28 so that it computes the average, variance, and standard deviation for an array with 500 values. Assume that N contains the number of actual values in the array. The denominator of the expression for the average should be N; the denominator of the expression for the variance should then be N−1.

30. Write a subroutine called BIAS that is called with the following statement:

```
CALL BIAS(X,Y,N)
```

where X is an input array of 200 real values, N is an integer that specifies how many of the values represent actual data values, and Y is an output array the same size as X whose values should be the values of X with the minimum value of the X array subtracted from each one. For example, if

X = | 10 | 2 | 36 | 8 |
|---|---|---|---|

then

Y = | 8 | 0 | 34 | 6 |
|---|---|---|---|

Thus, the minimum value of Y is always zero. (This operation is referred to as removing the bias in X or adjusting for bias in X.)

31. Write a subroutine that receives a two-dimensional real array X with 50 rows and 2 columns and returns the same array with the data reordered. Sort the data such that the values in each column are in descending order.

32. Write a subroutine that receives a two-dimensional real array X with 50 rows and 2 columns and returns the same array with the data reordered. Sort the data such that the values in the second column are in ascending order. The values in the first column should correspond to the values in the second column. That is, the same values should be on a row together in both the original order and the new order, but the ordering of the rows may change.

33. Write a subroutine that receives a two-dimensional real array X with 50 rows and 4 columns and returns the same array with the data reordered. Sort the data such that the values in each row are in ascending order.

34. Write a subroutine that receives a two-dimensional real array X with 50 rows and 4 columns and returns the same array with the data reordered. An additional argument J is used to select a column that is to be sorted in descending order. The other values are not to be changed.

35. Write a subroutine that receives a two-dimensional real array X with 50 rows and 4 columns and returns the same array with the data reordered. An additional argument J is used to select a column that is to be sorted in descending order. The other values are to be changed so that values on the same row stay together in the new reordering.

FORTRAN STATEMENT SUMMARY

■ **BLOCK DATA** Statement:

```
BLOCK DATA
```

Discussion:

The BLOCK DATA statement is the first statement in a BLOCK DATA subprogram. This subprogram contains only DATA statements and is used to initialize variables in named common blocks.

■ **CALL** Statement:

CALL *subroutine name (argument list)*

Examples:

```
CALL MERGE(X,Y)

CALL ERROR
```

Discussion:

The CALL statement is used to transfer control to a subroutine. The inputs and outputs to the subroutine must be listed in the argument list and must match in type and in number those used in the SUBROUTINE statement.

■ **Blank COMMON** Statement:

COMMON *variable list*

Example:

```
COMMON A, B, X(100)
```

Discussion:

The blank COMMON statement defines variables that are stored in a block of memory accessible to all subprograms that also contain the COMMON statement, without the variables being listed as arguments in the subprograms.

■ **Named COMMON** Statement:

`COMMON` */name/ variable list*

Example:

```
COMMON /REPORT/ DATE, PAGENO, TOTAL
```

Discussion:

The named COMMON statement allows us to define several blocks of memory available to subprograms. The subprogram must include the named COMMON statement that contains the variables to be used in that subprogram. The main program must include all named COMMON statements.

■ **SUBROUTINE** Statement:

`SUBROUTINE` *name (argument list)*

Examples:

```
SUBROUTINE SORT(A,B,N)
SUBROUTINE HEADING
```

Discussion:

The SUBROUTINE statement assigns a name to a subroutine and lists the arguments that represent the input and output for the subroutine. This statement must be the first statement in a subroutine subprogram.

8 Additional Data Types

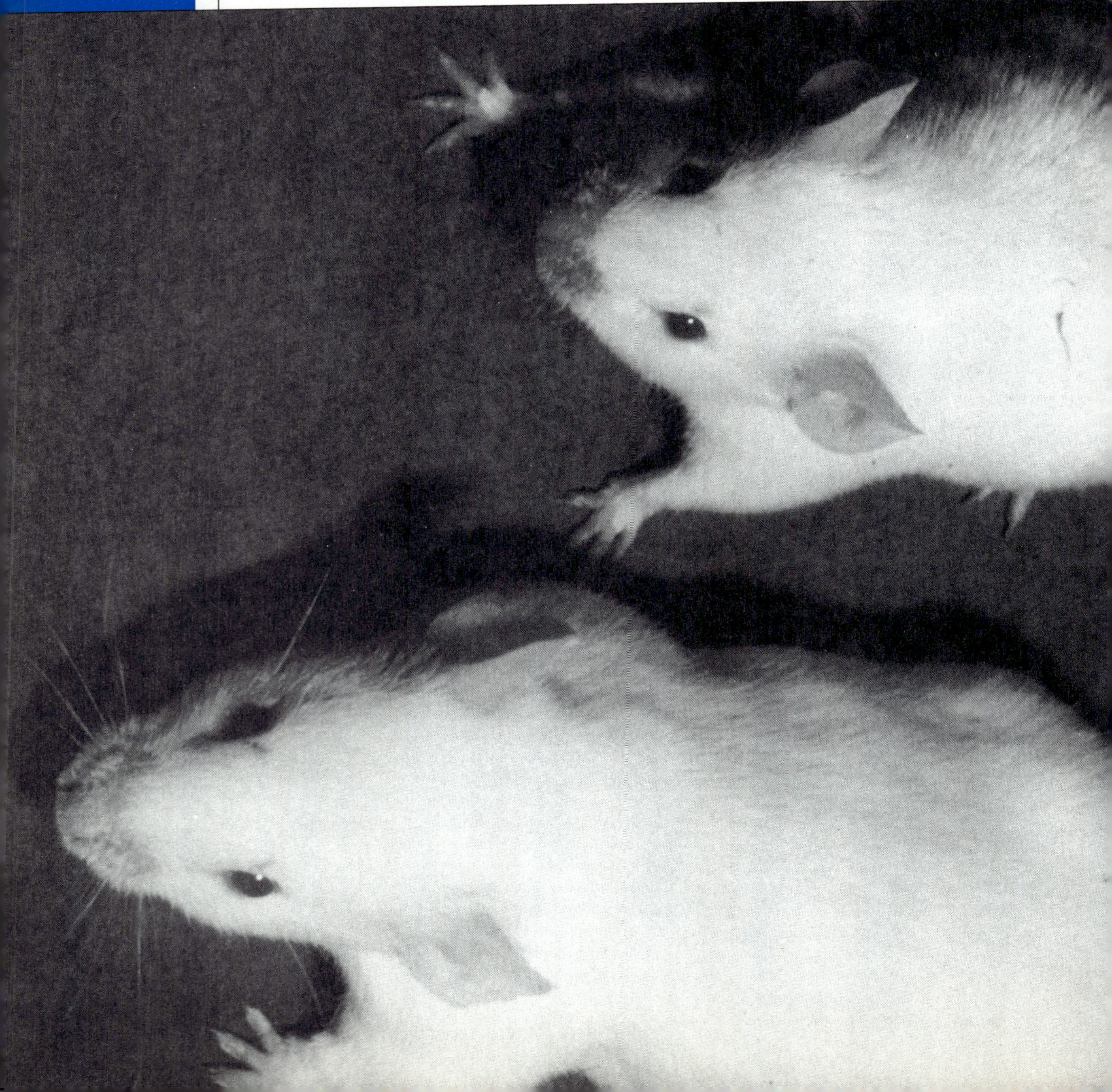

8

APPLICATION

Genetic Engineering

Growth hormone is a protein hormone produced in the pituitary gland. This hormone stimulates most body cells to increase in size and divide, and its major targets are bones and skeletal muscles. Growth hormone deficiency in children results in slowed long bone growth and can result in a maximum height of less than 4 feet. However, when this deficiency in children is diagnosed before puberty, growth hormone replacement therapy can result in nearly normal growth. Genetic engineers have developed a strain of genetically altered bacteria that is used to produce artificial growth hormone, which has been available commercially since 1985. The photo shows the dramatic results that can occur with the use of artificial growth hormone in mice. (See Section 8.2 for the solution to a problem related to this application.)

Photo © Institut Pasteur/Phototake.

Introduction

This chapter presents three data types: character, double precision, and complex. The character data type allows us to read and analyze character data such as chemical formulas. With double-precision data, we can process numeric data more precisely than we could using previously discussed data types. With complex data, we can represent data as numbers that have a real portion and an imaginary portion. Although we do not use these data types routinely, they are special features of FORTRAN that help make it a powerful language for engineering and scientific applications.

8·1 ■ Character Data

In Chapter 1 we learned that computers internally use a binary language that is composed of 0's and 1's. Integers and real numbers are converted to binary numbers when they are used in a computer. If you study computer hardware or computer architecture, you learn how to convert values such as 56 and −13.25 to binary numbers—to use FORTRAN, however, it is not necessary to learn this conversion.

Characters also must be converted into binary form to be used in the computer; they are converted to *binary strings,* which are also sequences of 0's and 1's. Several codes convert character information to binary strings, but most computers use *EBCDIC* (Extended Binary Coded Decimal Interchange Code) or *ASCII* (American Standard Code for Information Interchange). In these codes, each character is represented by a binary string. Table 8–1 contains a few characters and their EBCDIC and ASCII equivalents.

You do not need to use binary codes to use the characters in your FORTRAN programs. However, you must be aware that the computer stores characters differently than the numbers used in arithmetic computations; that is, the integer number 5 and the character 5 are not stored in the same way. Thus, it is not possible to use arithmetic operations with character data even if the characters represent numbers.

We often refer to character data as *character strings* because we usually refer to groups or lists of characters that go together. For example, a chemical formula is usually given one variable name instead of a variable name for each character in the formula.

Table 8·1 Binary Character Codes

Character	ASCII	EBCDIC
A	1000001	11000001
H	1001000	11001000
Y	1011001	11101000
3	0110011	11110011
+	0101011	01001110
$	0100100	01011011
=	0111101	01111110

For example, we might use the name WATER for the string 'H2O'. We can have character string constants that always represent the same information. Character string variables have names and represent character strings that may remain constant or may change. Generally, these character string constants and variables contain characters from the *FORTRAN character set*, which is composed of the 26 alphabetic letters, the 10 numeric digits, a blank, and the following 12 symbols:

```
+   -   *   /   =   (   )   ,   .   '   $   :
```

If other symbols are used, a program may not execute the same way on one computer as it does on another.

Fortran 90

Fortran 90 allows the inclusion of additional character sets, such as chemistry symbols, mathematical symbols, Cyrillic symbols (for Russian and other Slavic languages), and character sets for Hindi, Japanese, and Chinese. The inclusion of these special character sets is optional and will be system dependent.

Character constants are always enclosed in apostrophes. These apostrophes are not counted when determining the length or number of characters in a constant. If two consecutive apostrophes (not a double quotation mark) are encountered within a character constant, they represent a single apostrophe. For example, the character constant for the word LET'S is `'LET''S'`. The following list gives several examples of character constants and their corresponding lengths:

Constant	Length
`'SENSOR 23'`	9 characters
`'TIME AND DISTANCE'`	17 characters
`' $ AMT.'`	7 characters
`'  '`	2 characters
`'08:40-13:25'`	11 characters
`''''''`	2 characters

A character string variable is defined with a specification statement whose general form is

```
CHARACTER*n variable list
```

where *n* represents the number of characters in each character string. For instance, the statement

```
CHARACTER*8 CODE, NAME
```

identifies CODE and NAME as variables containing 8 characters each. Unlike numeric variable names, there is no significance to the first letter of a character variable's name. A variation of the CHARACTER statement allows you to specify character strings of different lengths in the same statement, as shown:

```
CHARACTER TITLE*10, STATE*2
```

An array that contains character strings can be defined using either of the following statements:

```
CHARACTER*4 NAME(50)
CHARACTER NAME(50)*4
```

The preceding specifications reserve memory for 50 elements in the array NAME, where each element contains 4 characters. A reference to NAME(18) references a character string with 4 characters that is the eighteenth element of the array.

Character strings can also be used as arguments in subprograms. The character string must be specified in a CHARACTER statement in both the main program and the subprogram. A subprogram can specify a character string without giving a specific length, as shown:

```
CHARACTER*(*) STRING
```

This technique is similar to specifying the length of an array with an integer variable, as in

```
INTEGER SSN(N)
```

It is also possible to define in a subprogram an array of *N* variables, each of which contains a character string. To make the character string more flexible, its length does not have to be specified in the CHARACTER statement. We use the following statement in the subprogram to accomplish this flexibility:

```
CHARACTER*(*) NAME(N)
```

We discuss special operations and intrinsic functions for character strings later in this section. First, we illustrate how to use character strings in input and output statements.

Character I/O

When a character string is used in a list-directed output statement, the entire character string is printed. Blanks are automatically inserted around the character string to separate it from other output on the same line. When a character string variable is used in a list-directed input statement, the corresponding data value must be enclosed in apostrophes. If the character string within the apostrophes is longer than the defined length of the character string variable, any extra characters on the right are ignored; if the character string within the apostrophes is shorter than the length of the character string variable, the extra positions to the right are automatically filled with blanks. To print a character string in a formatted output statement, use A as the corresponding format specification to print the entire string.

Character I/O

Example 8·1

Write a complete FORTRAN program to read an item description from the terminal and then print the description. Assume that the length of the description is no more than 20 characters.

Solution

We start with the decomposition:

Decomposition

Read description.
Print description.

The following refinement indicates the conversation with the user.

Pseudocode

```
Output: Print message to user to enter description
        Read description
        Print description
```

Translating these steps into FORTRAN results in the following program:

FORTRAN Program

```
*-----------------------------------------------------------------------*
      PROGRAM OUTPUT
*
*  This program reads and prints an item description.
*
      CHARACTER*20 ITEM
*
      PRINT*, 'ENTER ITEM DESCRIPTION IN APOSTROPHES'
      READ*, ITEM
*
      PRINT 5, ITEM
    5 FORMAT (1X,'ITEM DESCRIPTION IS ',A)
*
      END
*-----------------------------------------------------------------------*
```

A sample interaction with this program is

```
ENTER ITEM DESCRIPTION IN APOSTROPHES
'COMPUTER MODEM'
ITEM DESCRIPTION IS COMPUTER MODEM
```

Note that the data entered was not 20 characters long. In this example, the padding of blanks on the end is not noticeable with the output; however, if the output FORMAT had been

```
FORMAT(1X,A,' IS THE ITEM DESCRIPTION')
```

the interaction would have the following appearance:

```
ENTER ITEM DESCRIPTION IN APOSTROPHES
'COMPUTER MODEM'
COMPUTER MODEM       IS THE ITEM DESCRIPTION
```

Another interaction that could come from the original program is

```
ENTER ITEM DESCRIPTION IN APOSTROPHES
'DIGITAL OSCILLOSCOPE WITH MEMORY'
ITEM DESCRIPTION IS DIGITAL OSCILLOSCOPE
```

In this case, the name exceeded the maximum number of characters specified for the description, so part of the data was lost. To avoid this situation, carefully choose the length of your character variables based on the maximum length you expect. You can also tell the program user what length you are expecting. In this example, you could use the following pair of PRINT statements:

```
PRINT*, 'ENTER ITEM DESCRIPTION IN APOSTROPHES'
PRINT*, '(MAXIMUM OF 20 CHARACTERS)'
```

Character Operations

Although character strings cannot be used in arithmetic computations, we can assign values to character strings, compare two character strings, extract a substring of a character string, and combine two character strings into one longer character string.

Assign Values Values can be assigned to character variables with the assignment statement and a character constant. The following statements initialize a character string array RANK with the five abbreviations for freshman, sophomore, junior, senior, and graduate:

```
CHARACTER*2 RANK(5)
RANK(1) = 'FR'
RANK(2) = 'SO'
RANK(3) = 'JR'
RANK(4) = 'SR'
RANK(5) = 'GR'
```

If a character constant in an assignment statement is shorter in length than the character variable, blanks are added to the right of the constant. If the following statement was executed, RANK(1) would contain the letter F followed by a blank:

```
RANK(1) = 'F'
```

If a character constant in an assignment statement is longer than the character variable, the excess characters on the right are ignored. Thus, the following statement,

```
RANK(1) = 'FRESHMAN'
```

would store the letters FR in the character array element RANK(1). These examples emphasize the importance of using character strings that are the same length as the variables used to store them; otherwise, the statements would be misleading.

One character string variable can also be used to initialize another character string variable, as shown:

```
CHARACTER*4 GRADE1, GRADE2
GRADE1 = 'GOOD'
GRADE2 = GRADE1
```

Both variables, GRADE1 and GRADE2, contain the character string 'GOOD'.

Character strings can be initialized with DATA statements. The preceding examples can be performed with a DATA statement, as shown:

```
      CHARACTER RANK(5)*2, GRADE1*4, GRADE2*4
      DATA RANK, GRADE1, GRADE2 /'FR', 'SO', 'JR', 'SR',
     +               'GR', 2*'GOOD'/
```

Compare Values An If statement can be used to compare character strings. Assuming that the variable DEPT and the array CH are character strings, the following are valid statements:

```
IF (DEPT.EQ.'EECE') KT = KT + 1

IF (CH(I).GT.CH(I+1)) THEN
   CALL SWITCH(I,CH)
   CALL PRINT(CH)
END IF
```

To evaluate a logical expression using character strings, first look at the length of the two strings. If one string is shorter than the other, add blanks to the right of the shorter string so that you can proceed with the evaluation using strings of equal length.

The comparison of two character strings of the same length is made from left to right, one character at a time. Two strings must have exactly the same characters in the same order to be equal.

A *collating sequence* lists characters from the lowest to the highest value. Partial collating sequences for EBCDIC and ASCII are given in Table 8–2. Although the ordering is not exactly the same, some similarities include

1. Capital letters are in order from A to Z.
2. Digits are in order from 0 to 9.
3. Capital letters and digits do not overlap; either digits precede letters or letters precede digits.
4. The blank character is less than any letter or number. When necessary for clarity, we use $_b$ to represent a blank.

Table 8-2 Partial Collating Sequences for Characters

ASCII

b " # $ % & ( ) * + , - . /
0 1 2 3 4 5 6 7 8 9
: ; = ? @
A B C D E F G H I J K L M N O P Q R S T U V W X Y Z

EBCDIC

b . (+ & $ *) ; - / , % ? : # @ = "
A B C D E F G H I J K L M N O P Q R S T U V W X Y Z
0 1 2 3 4 5 6 7 8 9

Several pairs of character strings are now listed, along with their correct relationships:

```
    'A1' < 'A2'
  'JOHN' < 'JOHNSTON'
   '176' < '177'
 'THREE' < 'TWO'
     '$' < 'DOLLAR'
```

If character strings contain only letters, their ordering from low to high is alphabetical, which is also called a *lexicographic ordering*.

Extract Substrings A *substring* of a character string is any string that represents a subset of the original string and maintains the original order. The following list contains all substrings of the string 'FORTRAN':

```
'F'   'FO'   'FOR'   'FORT'   'FORTR'   'FORTRA'   'FORTRAN'
'O'   'OR'   'ORT'   'ORTR'   'ORTRA'   'ORTRAN'
'R'   'RT'   'RTR'   'RTRA'   'RTRAN'
'T'   'TR'   'TRA'   'TRAN'
'R'   'RA'   'RAN'
'A'   'AN'
'N'
```

Substrings are referenced by using the name of the character string, followed by two integer expressions in parentheses, separated by a colon. The first expression in parentheses gives the position in the original string of the beginning of the substring; the second expression gives the position of the end of the substring. If the string 'FORTRAN' is stored in a variable LANG, some of its substring references are as shown:

Reference	**Substring**
LANG(1:1)	'F'
LANG(1:7)	'FORTRAN'
LANG(2:3)	'OR'
LANG(7:7)	'N'

If the first expression in parentheses is omitted, the substring begins at the beginning of the string; thus, LANG(:4) refers to the substring 'FORT'. If the second expression in parentheses is omitted, the substring ends at the end of the string; thus, LANG(5:) refers to the substring 'RAN'.

The substring operation cannot operate correctly if the beginning and ending positions are not integers, are negative, or contain values greater than the number of characters in the substring. The ending position must also be greater than or equal to the beginning position of the substring.

The substring operator is a powerful tool, as the next two examples illustrate.

Propane-Heated Balloons . . . . Example 8·2

All aircraft including hot air balloons are assigned registration numbers by the Federal Aviation Agency. A new registration system for balloons has been proposed in which the registration number is a character string of 7 characters. The fifth character specifies balloon type: P, for propane heated; S, for solar heated; and H, for helium or hydrogen filled. Write a segment of FORTRAN code that counts the number of propane-heated hot air balloons using a character array of 500 registration numbers.

Solution

We need a loop to step through the array, checking each balloon registration number. We increment our count if the fifth character in the registration number is the letter P:

```
      CHARACTER*7 REGNUM(500)
      INTEGER COUNT, I
      DATA COUNT /0/
      .
      .
      .
      DO 10 I=1,500
         IF (REGNUM(I)(5:5).EQ.'P') COUNT = COUNT + 1
   10 CONTINUE
```

Character Count . . . . Example 8·3

A string of 50 characters contains encoded information. The number of occurrences of the letter S represents a special piece of information. Write a loop that counts the number of occurrences of the letter S.

Solution

The loop index is used with the substring operator to allow us to test each character in the string:

```
      CHARACTER*50 CODE
      INTEGER COUNT, I
      DATA COUNT /0/
      .
      .
      .
      DO 20 I=1,50
         IF (CODE(I:I).EQ.'S') COUNT = COUNT + 1
   20 CONTINUE
```

A reference to a substring can be used anywhere that a string can be used. For instance, if LANG contains the character string 'FORTRAN', the following statement changes the value of LANG to 'FORMATS':

```
LANG(4:7) = 'MATS'
```

If LANG contains 'FORMATS', the following statement changes the value of LANG to 'FORMATT':

```
LANG(7:7) = LANG(6:6)
```

When modifying a substring of a character string with a substring of the same character string, the substrings must not overlap—that is, do not use LANG(2:4) to replace LANG(3:5). Also, recall that if a substring is being moved into a smaller string, only as many characters as are needed to replace the smaller string are moved from left to right; if the substring is being moved into a larger string, the extra positions on the right are filled with blanks.

Combine Strings *Concatenation* is the operation of combining two or more character strings into one character string. It is indicated by two slashes between the character strings to be combined. The following expression concatenates the constants 'WORK' and 'ED' into one string constant 'WORKED':

```
'WORK'//'ED'
```

The next statement combines the contents of three character string variables MO, DA, and YR into one character string and then moves the combined string into a variable called DATE:

```
DATE = MO//DA//YR
```

If MO = '05', DA = '15', and YR = '86', then DATE = '051586'. Because concatenation represents an operation, it cannot appear on the left-hand side of an equal sign.

■ Character Intrinsic Functions

A number of intrinsic functions are designed for use with character strings:

INDEX locates specific substrings within a given character string.

LEN determines the length of a string and is used primarily in subroutines and functions that have character string arguments.

CHAR and ICHAR determine the position of a character in the collating sequence of the computer.

LGE, LGT, LLE, and LLT allow comparisons to be made based on the ASCII collating sequence, regardless of the collating sequence of the computer.

INDEX The INDEX function has two arguments, both of which are character strings. The function returns an integer value giving the position in the first string of the second string. Thus, if STRGA contains the phrase 'TO BE OR NOT TO BE', INDEX(STRGA,'BE') returns the value 4, which points to the first occurrence of the string 'BE'. To find the second occurrence of the string, we can use the following statements:

```
CHARACTER*18 STRGA
.
.
.
K = INDEX(STRGA,'BE')
J = INDEX(STRGA(K+1:),'BE') + K
```

After executing these statements, K would contain the value 4 and J would contain the value 17. (Note that we had to add K to the second reference of INDEX because the second use referred to the substring 'E OR NOT TO BE', and thus the second INDEX reference returns a value of 13, not 17.) The value of INDEX(STRGA,'AND') would be 0 because the second string 'AND' does not occur in the first string STRGA.

LEN The input to the function LEN is a character string; the output is an integer that contains the length of the character string. This function is useful in a subprogram that accepts character strings of any length but needs the actual length within the subprogram. The statement in the subprogram that allows a character string to be defined without specifying its length is

```
CHARACTER*(*) A, B, STRGA
```

This form can be used only in subprograms. Example 8 – 4 uses both the LEN function and a variable string length in a subprogram.

Frequency of Blanks

Example 8-4

Write a function subprogram that accepts a character string and returns a count of the number of blanks in the string.

Solution

To make this function flexible, we write it so that it can be used with any size character string.

```
*-----------------------------------------------------------------------*
      INTEGER FUNCTION BLANKS(X)
*
*  This function counts the number of blanks in a
*  character string X.
*
      INTEGER I
      CHARACTER*(*) X
*
      BLANKS = 0
      DO 10 I=1,LEN(X)
         IF (X(I:I).EQ.' ') BLANKS = BLANKS + 1
   10 CONTINUE
*
      RETURN
      END
*-----------------------------------------------------------------------*
```

Character strings may also be used in user-written subroutines. In Example 8 – 5, we write a subroutine that combines input character strings into an output character string.

Example 8-5

Name Editing

Write a subroutine that receives 3 character strings, FIRST, MIDDLE, and LAST, each containing 15 characters. The output of the subroutine is a character string 35 characters long that contains the first name followed by 1 blank, the middle initial followed by a period and 1 blank, and the last name. Assume that FIRST, MIDDLE, and LAST have no leading blanks and no embedded blanks. Thus, if

```
FIRST = 'JOSEPH         '
MIDDLE = 'CHARLES        '
LAST = 'LAWTON         '
```

then the edited name would be:

```
JOSEPH C. LAWTON                   '
```

Solution

The solution to this problem is simplified by the use of the substring operation that allows us to look at individual characters and the INDEX function that is used to find the end of the first name. We move to NAME the characters in FIRST, then a blank, the middle initial, a period, another blank, and the last name. As you go through the solution, observe the use of the concatenation operation. Also, note that the move of the first name fills the rest of the character string NAME with blanks because FIRST is shorter than the field to which it is moved:

```
*-----------------------------------------------------------------------*
      SUBROUTINE EDIT(FIRST,MIDDLE,LAST,NAME)
*
*  This subroutine edits a name to the form
*  first, middle initial, last.
*
      INTEGER L
      CHARACTER*15 FIRST, MIDDLE, LAST
      CHARACTER*35 NAME
*
*  MOVE FIRST NAME
*
      NAME = FIRST
*
*  MOVE MIDDLE INITIAL
*
      L = INDEX(NAME,' ')
      NAME(L:L+3) = ' '//MIDDLE(1:1)//'. '
*
*  MOVE LAST NAME
*
      NAME(L+4:) = LAST
*
      RETURN
      END
*-----------------------------------------------------------------------*
```

CHAR, ICHAR These functions refer to the collating sequence used in the computer. If a computer has 50 characters in its collating sequence, these characters are numbered from 0 to 49. For example, assume that the letter A corresponds to position number 12. The function CHAR uses an integer argument that specifies the position of a desired character in the collating sequence, and the function returns the character in the specified position. The following statements print the character A:

```
N = 12
PRINT*, CHAR(N)
```

The ICHAR function is the inverse of the CHAR function. The argument to the ICHAR function is a character variable that contains one character. The function returns an integer that gives the position of the character in the collating sequence. Thus, the output of the following statements is the number 12:

```
CHARACTER*1 INFO
INFO = 'A'
PRINT*, ICHAR(INFO)
```

Because different computers have different collating sequences, these functions can be used to determine the position of certain characters in the collating sequence.

Example 8-6

Collating Sequence

Print each character in the FORTRAN character set along with its position in the collating sequence on your computer. The FORTRAN character set is given on page 373.

Solution

Note the use of the substring operator in initializing the character set:

```
*-----------------------------------------------------------------------*
      PROGRAM SEQNCE
*
*  This program prints the position in the collating sequence
*  of each FORTRAN character.
*
      CHARACTER*49 SET
*
      SET(1:26) = 'ABCDEFGHIJKLMNOPQRSTUVWXYZ'
      SET(27:36) = '0123456789'
      SET(37:49) = ' +-*/=(),.''$:'
*
      DO 10 I=1,49
         PRINT*, SET(I:I), ICHAR(SET(I:I))
   10 CONTINUE
*
      END
*-----------------------------------------------------------------------*
```

Why did we put two apostrophes in the assignment for SET(37:49)? Remember that two apostrophes are converted into a single apostrophe when they are in a literal. If you have several computers available, run this program on each of them to see if they all use the same collating sequence for the FORTRAN character set.

LGE, LGT, LLE, LLT This set of functions allows you to compare character strings based on the ASCII collating sequence. These functions become useful if a program is going to be used on a number of different computers and is using character comparisons or character sorts. The functions represent a logical value, true or false. Each function has two character string arguments, STRG1 and STRG2. The function reference LGE(STRG1,STRG2) is true if STRG1 is lexically greater than or equal to STRG2; thus, if STRG1 comes after STRG2 in an alphabetical sort, this function reference is true. Remember, these functions are based on an ASCII collating sequence regardless of the sequence being used on the computer. The functions LGT, LLE, and LLT perform comparisons "lexically greater than," "lexically less than or equal to," and "lexically less than."

Fortran 90 includes several new intrinsic functions that work with character strings. ADJUSTL and ADJUSTR are functions that adjust a character string left or right by removing leading or trailing blanks, respectively; the overall length of the character string is not changed. The TRIM function removes trailing blanks and correspondingly reduces the length of the string

Fortran 90

ASCII Sort

Example 8·7

In a sort based on the collating sequence in a computer, we perform the following steps, where STRG represents a character array:

```
IF (STRG(I).GT.STRG(I+1)) THEN
   TEMP = STRG(I)
   STRG(I) = STRG(I+1)
   STRG(I+1) = TEMP
   SORTED = .FALSE.
END IF
```

Rewrite this loop so the switch of character strings occurs based on an ASCII collating sequence even if the computer does not use an ASCII code.

Solution

The solution involves replacing the character comparison with the character intrinsic function LGT:

```
IF (LGT(STRG(I),STRG(I+1))) THEN
   TEMP = STRG(I)
   STRG(I) = STRG(I+1)
   STRG(I+1) = TEMP
   SORTED = .FALSE.
END IF
```

SELF-TEST 8-1

This self-test allows you to check quickly to see if you have remembered some of the key points from Section 8–1. If you have any problems with the exercises, you should reread this section. The solutions are included at the end of the text.

For problems 1–10, give the substring referred to in each reference. Assume that a character string of length 35 called TITLE has been initialized with the statements

```
CHARACTER*35 TITLE
TITLE = 'TEN TOP ENGINEERING ACHIEVEMENTS'
```

1. `TITLE(1:20)`
2. `TITLE(1:8)`
3. `TITLE(9:19)`
4. `TITLE(21:21)`
5. `TITLE(9:)`
6. `TITLE(:8)`
7. `TITLE(:)`
8. `TITLE(1:4)//TITLE(21:)`
9. `TITLE(5:8)//TITLE(1:3)`
10. `TITLE(9:16)//TITLE(32:32)//''' '//TITLE(21:)`

In problems 11–16, WORD is a character string of length 6. What is stored in WORD after each of the following statements?

11. `WORD = 'LASER'`
12. `WORD = 'FIBER OPTICS'`
13. `WORD = 'CAD'//'CAM'`
14. `WORD = ''''''''`
15. `WORD = '  12.48'`
16. `WORD = 'GENETIC ENGINEERING'`

8-2 Application ▪ Protein Molecular Weights

Genetic Engineering

Genetic engineering begins with a gene that produces a valuable substance such as the human growth hormone that was discussed in the chapter-opening application. Enzymes are used to dissolve bonds to the neighboring genes, thus separating the valuable gene out of the DNA. This gene is then inserted into another organism, such as a bacterium, that will multiply itself along with the foreign gene.

One step in discovering a valuable gene is identifying the sequence of amino acids in the protein that it produces. A protein sequencer is a sophisticated piece of

Table 8·3 Amino Acids

Amino Acid	Reference	Molecular Weight
Glycine	Gly	75
Alanine	Ala	89
Valine	Val	117
Leucine	Leu	131
Isoleucine	Ile	131
Serine	Ser	105
Threonine	Thr	119
Tyrosine	Tyr	181
Phenylalanine	Phe	165
Tryptophan	Trp	203
Aspartic	Asp	132
Glutamic	Glu	146
Lysine	Lys	147
Arginine	Arg	175
Histidine	His	156
Cysteine	Cys	121
Methionine	Met	149
Asparagine	Asn	132
Glutamine	Gln	146
Proline	Pro	116

equipment that can determine the order of amino acids making up a chainlike protein molecule, thus uncovering the identity of the gene that made it. Although there are only 20 different amino acids, protein molecules have hundreds of amino acids linked in a specific order.

In this problem, we assume that the sequence of amino acids in a protein molecule has been identified and that we want to compute the molecular weight of the protein molecule. Table 8 – 3 lists the amino acids, their three-letter reference, and their molecular weights. A data file named AMINO contains 20 lines of data; each line of the data file contains a three-letter reference (enclosed in quotation marks) and the corresponding molecular weight.

Assume that another data file contains the protein molecule characterizations in amino acids. The first line in the file contains the number of protein molecules in the file, and each following line contains a character string in quotes that contains the amino acid sequence. The maximum number of amino acids in a character string is 50. The program should determine and print the corresponding molecular weight for each protein. Print an error message if an incorrect protein string is detected.

1. Problem Statement

Write a program that will determine the molecular weight of a group of protein molecules containing only amino acids.

2. Input/Output Description

Input—a data file containing the information on amino acids and a different data file containing the protein molecules

Output—the molecular weights of the protein molecules

3. Hand Example

Suppose that the protein molecule is the following:

LysGluMetAspSerGlu

The corresponding molecular weights for the amino acids are

147,146,149,132,105,146

Therefore, the protein molecular weight is 825.

4. Algorithm Development

We start the algorithm development with the decomposition:

Decomposition

Read and store amino acid data in arrays.
Read protein molecules and compute and print the molecular weight.

Pseudocode

```
Weight: Read amino strings and weights into arrays
        Read the number of proteins, n
        For k = 1 to n do
            sum ← 0
            Read protein string
            For each amino acid in the protein string
                Add corresponding weight to the sum
            Print protein string and sum
```

The step to add the weight for each amino acid to the molecular weight sum requires comparing each amino acid string to the reference strings and then selecting the corresponding weight. We will implement this step in a subroutine in order to keep the main program easy to read. Since there is only a small number of amino acids to test, we use a DO loop. If the amino acid is found, the corresponding weight will be moved to a variable named WEIGHT; if the amino acid is not found, a value of zero will be returned in WEIGHT.

```
MWT (ref,mw,string,weight):
    weight ← 0
    For k=1 to 20 do
        if ref(k) = string then
            weight ← mw(k)
    Return
```

FORTRAN Program

```
*-------------------------------------------------------------------*
      PROGRAM WEIGHT
*
*  This program reads character strings containing amino acids
*  from large protein molecules and computes the molecular weights.
*

      INTEGER K, MW(20), N, J, BLNK, NCHAR, AMNUM, SUM, START, AMWT
      CHARACTER*3 REF(20)
      CHARACTER*150 PROTN
      LOGICAL ERROR
*
      OPEN (UNIT=9,FILE='AMINO',STATUS='OLD')
      DO 10 K=1,20
         READ(9,*) REF(K), MW(K)
   10 CONTINUE
*
      OPEN (UNIT=10,FILE='PROTEIN',STATUS='OLD')
      READ(10,*) N
*
      DO 30 J=1,N
*
         READ(10,*) PROTN
         BLNK = INDEX(PROTN,' ')
         NCHAR = BLNK - 1
         AMNUM = NCHAR/3
         SUM = 0
*
         IF (MOD(NCHAR,3).NE.0) THEN
*
            PRINT*, 'LENGTH ERROR IN PROTEIN ', J
            PRINT*, PROTN(:BLNK)
            PRINT*
*
         ELSE
*
            ERROR = .FALSE.
            DO 20 K=1,AMNUM
               START = (K-1)*3 + 1
               CALL MWT(REF,MW,PROTN(START:START+2),AMWT)
               IF (AMWT.NE.0) THEN
                  SUM = SUM + AMWT
               ELSE
                  PRINT*, 'ERROR IN AMINO ', K, ' PROTEIN ', J
                  ERROR = .TRUE.
               END IF
   20       CONTINUE
            IF (.NOT.ERROR) THEN
               PRINT 15, PROTN(:BLNK), SUM
   15          FORMAT (1X,'PROTEIN:  ',A/1X,'MOLECULAR WEIGHT:',I9/)
            ELSE
               PRINT*, PROTN(:BLNK)
               PRINT*
            END IF
*
         END IF
*
   30 CONTINUE
*
      END
*-------------------------------------------------------------------*
```

```
      SUBROUTINE MWT(REF,MW,STRING,WEIGHT)
*
*  This subroutine receives arrays containing the character references
*  and molecular weights for amino acids. It uses these arrays to
*  determine if an input string is an amino acid and, if so, returns
*  the molecular weight of the amino acid; otherwise zero is returned.
*
      INTEGER MW(20), WEIGHT, K
      CHARACTER*3 REF(20), STRING
*
      WEIGHT = 0
      DO 10 K=1,20
         IF (STRING.EQ.REF(K)) WEIGHT = MW(K)
   10 CONTINUE
*
      RETURN
      END
*-----------------------------------------------------------------------*
```

There are several things to note about this program. For example, we used the INDEX function to determine the first blank in the protein string. This allowed us to determine the number of amino acids and also to print only the nonblank characters; otherwise, PROTN would require 150 output characters. Also, note that if we find an error in an amino acid, we contine evaluating the protein string. This allows us to catch all the errors at once, instead of catching only one error per protein at a time.

5. Testing

The following PROTEIN file was used for testing:

```
5
'GlyIle'
'AspHisProGln'
'ThrTbrSerTrpLys'
'AlaValLeuValMet'
'LysGluMetAspSerGlu'
```

The output for the test file was the following:

```
PROTEIN:  GlyIle
MOLECULAR WEIGHT:       206

PROTEIN:  AspHisProGln
MOLECULAR WEIGHT:       550

ERROR IN AMINO    2  PROTEIN    3
ThrTbrSerTrpLys

PROTEIN:  AlaValLeuValMet
MOLECULAR WEIGHT:       603

PROTEIN:  LysGluMetAspSerGlu
MOLECULAR WEIGHT:       825
```

8-3 ■ Double-Precision Data

Double-precision variables are necessary any time we want to keep more significant digits than are stored in real variables. Assume that a real variable can store 7 significant digits; this means that the real variable will keep 7 digits of accuracy, beginning with the first nonzero digit, in addition to remembering where the decimal point goes. A *double-precision* value can store more digits, with the exact number of digits dependent on the computer. For this discussion, assume that double-precision variables store 14 digits. The following table compares values that can be stored in real values (also called single-precision values) and in double-precision values.

Value to be Stored	Single Precision	Double Precision
37.6892718	37.68927	37.689271800000
−1.60003	−1.600030	−1.6000300000000
820000000487.	820000000000.	820000000487.00
18268296.300405079	18268290.	18268296.300405

Note that we are doubling the precision of our values, but we are not doubling the range of numbers that can be stored. The same range of numbers applies to both single- and double-precision values, but double-precision values store those numbers with more digits of precision.

Many science and engineering applications use double-precision values to increase accuracy. For example, the study of solar systems, galaxies, and stars requires storing immense distances with as much precision as possible. Even economic models often need double precision. A model for predicting the gross national debt must handle numbers exceeding $1 trillion. With single precision, you cannot store the values with an accuracy to the nearest dollar. With double precision, amounts up to 100 trillion can be used and still have significant digits for all dollar amounts.

A double-precision constant is written in an exponential form, with a D in place of the E. Some examples of double-precision constants are

```
0.378926542D+04
1.4762D-02
0.25D+00
```

Always use the exponential form with the letter D for double-precision constants, even if the constant uses 7 or fewer digits of accuracy; otherwise, you may lose some accuracy because a fractional value that can be expressed exactly in decimal notation may not be expressed exactly in binary notation.

Double-precision variables are specified with a specification statement whose general form is

`DOUBLE PRECISION` *variable list*

A double-precision array is specified as

```
DOUBLE PRECISION DTEMP(50)
```

Double-Precision I/O

Double-precision variables can be used in list-directed output in the same manner that we list real values. The only distinction is that more digits of accuracy can be stored in a double-precision value; therefore, more digits of accuracy can be written from a double-precision value.

In formatted input and output, double-precision values may be referenced with the F or E format specifications. Another specification, Dw.d, may also be used. Dw.d functions essentially like the E specification, but the D emphasizes that it is being used with a double-precision value. In output, the value in this exponential form is printed with a D instead of an E. Thus, if the following statements were executed,

```
   DOUBLE PRECISION DX
   .
   .
   .
   DX = 1.66587514521D+00
   PRINT 10, DX
10 FORMAT (1X,'DX = ',D17.10)
```

the output would be

```
 DX =  0.1665875145D+01
```

Example 8-8

Solar Distances

Assume that a character array has been filled with the names of planets, moons, and other celestial bodies. A corresponding array has been filled with the distances of these objects from the sun in millions of miles. Both arrays have been defined to hold 200 values, and an integer *N* specifies how many elements are actually stored in the arrays. The array NAME is an array of character strings of length 20, and the array DIST is a double-precision array. Give the statements to print these names and distances.

Solution

Before printing the data in the arrays, we print a heading for the data. Next, a loop is executed *N* times and is used to print the object name and its corresponding distance from the sun in millions of miles. We use a D format for the output because the set of distances may cover a large range of values. The CHARACTER statement and the DOUBLE PRECISION statement are included with the statements to print the data:

```
   CHARACTER*20 NAME(200)
   DOUBLE PRECISION DIST(200)
   .
   .
   .
   PRINT*, 'SOLAR OBJECTS AND DISTANCES FROM THE SUN'
   PRINT*, '                     (MILLIONS OF MILES)'
   PRINT*
   DO 10 I=1,N
      PRINT 5, NAME(I), DIST(I)
 5    FORMAT (1X,A,2X,D15.8)
10 CONTINUE
```

A sample output from these statements is

```
SOLAR OBJECTS AND DISTANCES FROM THE SUN
                     (MILLIONS OF MILES)

JUPITER                 0.43863717D+03
MARS                    0.14151751D+03
SATURN                  0.88674065D+03
VENUS                   0.67235696D+02
PLUTO                   0.36662718D+04
URANUS                  0.17834237D+04
MERCURY                 0.35979176D+02
NEPTUNE                 0.27944448D+04
EARTH                   0.92961739D+02
```

Double-Precision Operations

When an arithmetic operation is performed with two double-precision values, the result is double precision. If an operation involves a double-precision value and a single-precision value or an integer, the result is a double-precision result. In such a mixed-mode operation, do not assume that the other value is converted to double precision; instead, think of the other value as being extended in length with zeros. To illustrate, the first two assignment statements that follow yield exactly the same values; the third assignment statement, however, adds a double-precision constant to DX and yields the most accurate result of the three statements:

```
DOUBLE PRECISION DX, DY1, DY2, DY3
.
.
.
DY1 = DX + 0.3872
DY2 = DX + 0.3872000000000
DY3 = DX + 0.3872D+00
```

The most accurate way to obtain a constant that cannot be written in a fixed number of decimal places is to perform a double-precision operation that yields the desired value. For instance, to obtain the double-precision constant one-third, use the following expression:

```
1.0D+00/3.0D+00
```

Using double-precision values increases the precision of our results, but there is a price for this additional precision — the execution time for computations is longer and more memory is required.

Double-Precision Intrinsic Functions

If a double-precision argument is used in a generic function, the function value is also double precision. Many of the common intrinsic functions for real numbers can be converted to double-precision functions by preceding the function name with the letter D. For instance, DSQRT, DABS, DMOD, DSIN, DEXP, DLOG, and

DLOG10 all require double-precision arguments and yield double-precision values. Since the generic function and double-precision function perform the same operation with double-precision arguments, we recommend using the generic function name for consistency. Double-precision functions can also be used to compute constants with double-precision accuracy. For instance, the following statements compute π with double-precision accuracy:

```
DOUBLE PRECISION DPI
.
.
.
DPI = 4.0D+00*ATAN(1.0D+00)
```

(Recall that $\pi/4$ is equal to the arctangent of 1.0.)

Although Appendix A contains a complete list of the functions that relate to double-precision values, two functions, DBLE and DPROD, are specifically designed for use with double-precision variables. DBLE converts a REAL argument to a double-precision value by adding zeros. DPROD has two real arguments and returns the double-precision product of the two arguments.

Example 8-9

Spherical Mirror Sag

The alignment of curved mirrors in a laser system is an extremely precise operation. The calculations may include computing the sag of the spherical mirror surface, which is calculated with the following equation, assuming that r is the radius of the spherical mirror and s is the distance from the center of the spherical mirror to its tangent plane:

$$\text{Sag} = \frac{rs^2}{1 + \sqrt{1 - r^2s^2}}$$

Assume that DR and DS represent double-precision values in the proper units for the radius (*DR*) of a spherical mirror and the distance (*DS*) from the center of the spherical mirror to its tangent plane. These two values have already been computed in a program. Give the statement to compute the sag to at least 10 digits of accuracy (assuming real values have 7 digits of accuracy).

Solution

```
DOUBLE PRECISION DR, DS, DSAG
.
.
.
DSAG = DR*DS*DS/(1.0D+00 + SQRT(1.0D+00 - DR*DR*DS*DS))
```

SELF-TEST 8-2

This self-test allows you to check quickly to see if you have remembered some of the key points from Section 8–3. If you have any problems with the exercises, you should reread this section. The solutions are included at the end of the text.

In problems 1–6, show how to represent these constants as double-precision constants.

1. 0.75
2. 1.3
3. 1/9
4. 5/6
5. −10.5
6. 3.0

In problems 7–9, show the output of the following PRINT statements if DX = 0.00786924379, where DX is a double-precision variable.

7.
```
  PRINT 4, DX
4 FORMAT (1X,D14.5)
```
8.
```
  PRINT 5, DX
5 FORMAT (1X,D12.3)
```
9.
```
  PRINT 6, DX
6 FORMAT (1X,F12.7)
```

8-4 Application ▪ Temperature Distribution

Mechanical Engineering

In this application, we consider the temperature distribution in a thin metal plate as it reaches a point of thermal equilibrium. The plate is constructed so that each edge is isothermal (maintained at a constant temperature). The temperature of an interior point on the plate is a function of the temperature of the surrounding material. If we consider the plate to be similar to a grid, then a two-dimensional array could be used to store the temperatures of the corresponding points on the plate. The following diagram contains an array that is used to store the temperatures of a plate that is being analyzed with 5 temperature measurements along the sides and 10 temperature measurements along the top and bottom. A total of 50 temperature values is stored.

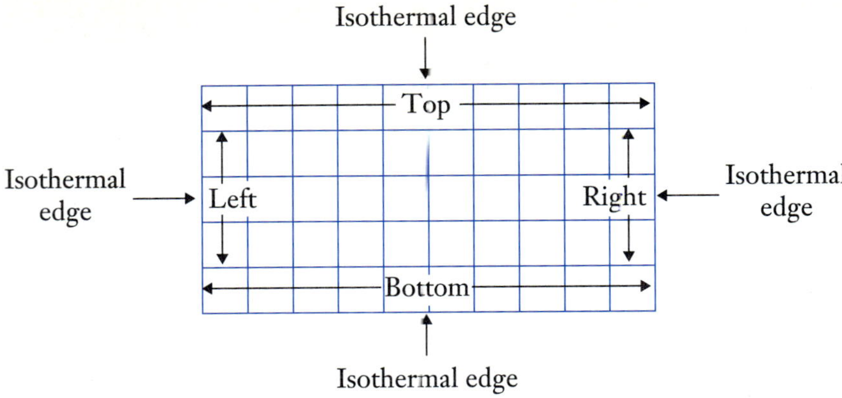

The isothermal temperatures at the top, bottom, left, and right would be given as inputs. The interior points are initially set to some arbitrary temperature, usually zero. The new temperature of each interior point is calculated as the average of its four surrounding points, as shown in the diagram.

$$T_0 = \frac{T_1 + T_2 + T_3 + T_4}{4}$$

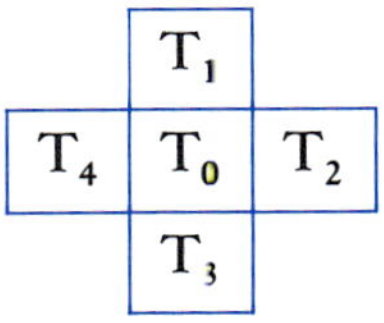

After computing the new temperature for an interior point, the difference between the old temperature and the new temperature is computed. If the magnitude of a temperature change is greater than some specified tolerance value, the plate is not yet in thermal equilibrium and the entire process is repeated.

We use two arrays for the temperatures, one for the old temperatures and one for the new temperatures. We need two arrays because we assume that the temperature changes for all the points are occurring simultaneously, even though we compute them one at a time. If we used only one array, we would be updating information before we were through with the old information. For example, suppose that we are computing the new temperature at position (3,3). The new value would be the average of temperatures in positions (2,3), (3,2), (3,4), and (4,3). When we move on to compute the new temperature at position (3,4), we again compute an average, but we want to use the old value in position (3,3), not its updated value.

Thus, we use a two-dimensional array of old temperatures to compute a two-dimensional array of new temperatures and, at the same time, to check if any of the temperature changes exceed the tolerance. We then move the new temperatures to the old array. When none of the temperature changes exceed the tolerance, we assume that equilibrium has been reached and we print the final temperatures. We use double-precision values so that the equilibrium values can be determined accurately.

1. Problem Statement

Determine the equilibrium values for a metal plate.

2. Input/Output Description

Input—the number of rows and the number of columns in the temperature grid, the top temperature, the bottom temperature, the left temperature, the right temperature, and the tolerance value

Output—a grid of values representing the final temperature values when they have reached equilibrium

3. Hand Example

To be sure that we understand the process, we examine a simple case, studying each iteration. Assume that the array contains 4 rows and 4 columns. The isothermal edge temperatures are

top ← 100.0
bottom ← 200.0
left side ← 100.0
right side ← 200.0

The internal points are initialized to zero, and the tolerance value is 5.0.

100.0	100.0	100.0	100.0
100.0	0.0	0.0	200.0
100.0	0.0	0.0	200.0
200.0	200.0	200.0	200.0

Initial temperatures

100.0	100.0	100.0	100.0
100.0	50.0	75.0	200.0
100.0	75.0	100.0	200.0
200.0	200.0	200.0	200.0

First iteration

100.0	100.0	100.0	100.0
100.0	87.5	112.5	200.0
100.0	112.5	137.5	200.0
200.0	200.0	200.0	200.0

Second iteration

100.0	100.0	100.0	100.0
100.0	106.25	131.25	200.0
100.0	131.25	156.25	200.0
200.0	200.0	200.0	200.0

Third iteration

100.0	100.0	100.0	100.0
100.0	115.63	140.63	200.0
100.0	140.63	165.63	200.0
200.0	200.0	200.0	200.0

Fourth iteration

100.0	100.0	100.0	100.0
100.0	120.31	145.31	200.0
100.0	145.31	170.31	200.0
200.0	200.0	200.0	200.0

Equilibrium

4. Algorithm Development

The general decomposition of the steps in solving this problem is given.

Decomposition

Read isothermal edge temperatures and tolerance.
Update temperatures until equilibrium is reached.
Print equilibrium temperatures.

The first refinement of these steps is illustrated in the following general flowchart:

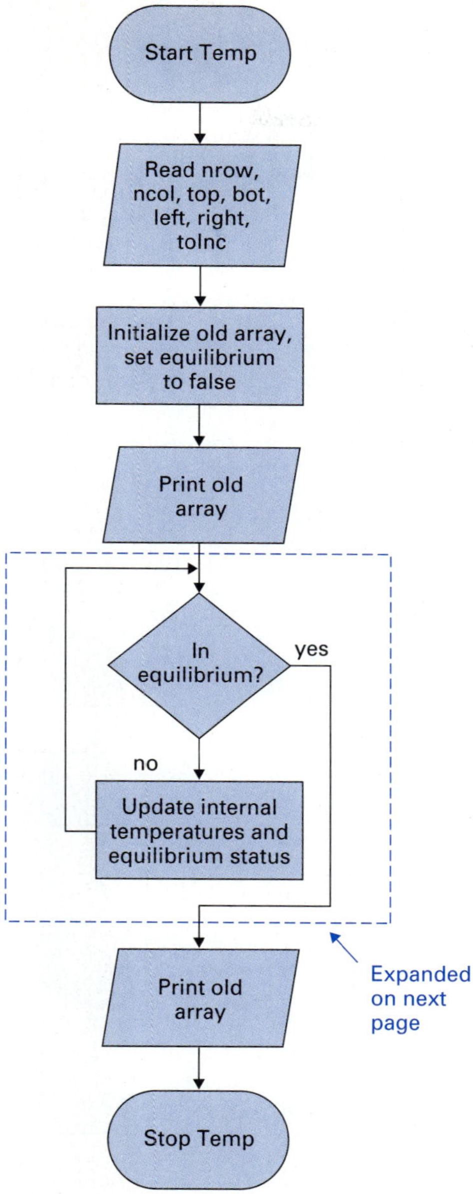

The portion of this flowchart that needs refinement before we can convert the solution into FORTRAN is the step "perform update of internal temperatures." It is in this step that we must compute the updated temperatures, determine if we have reached equilibrium, and move the new temperatures to the array of old temperatures. The refined portion of the flowchart follows:

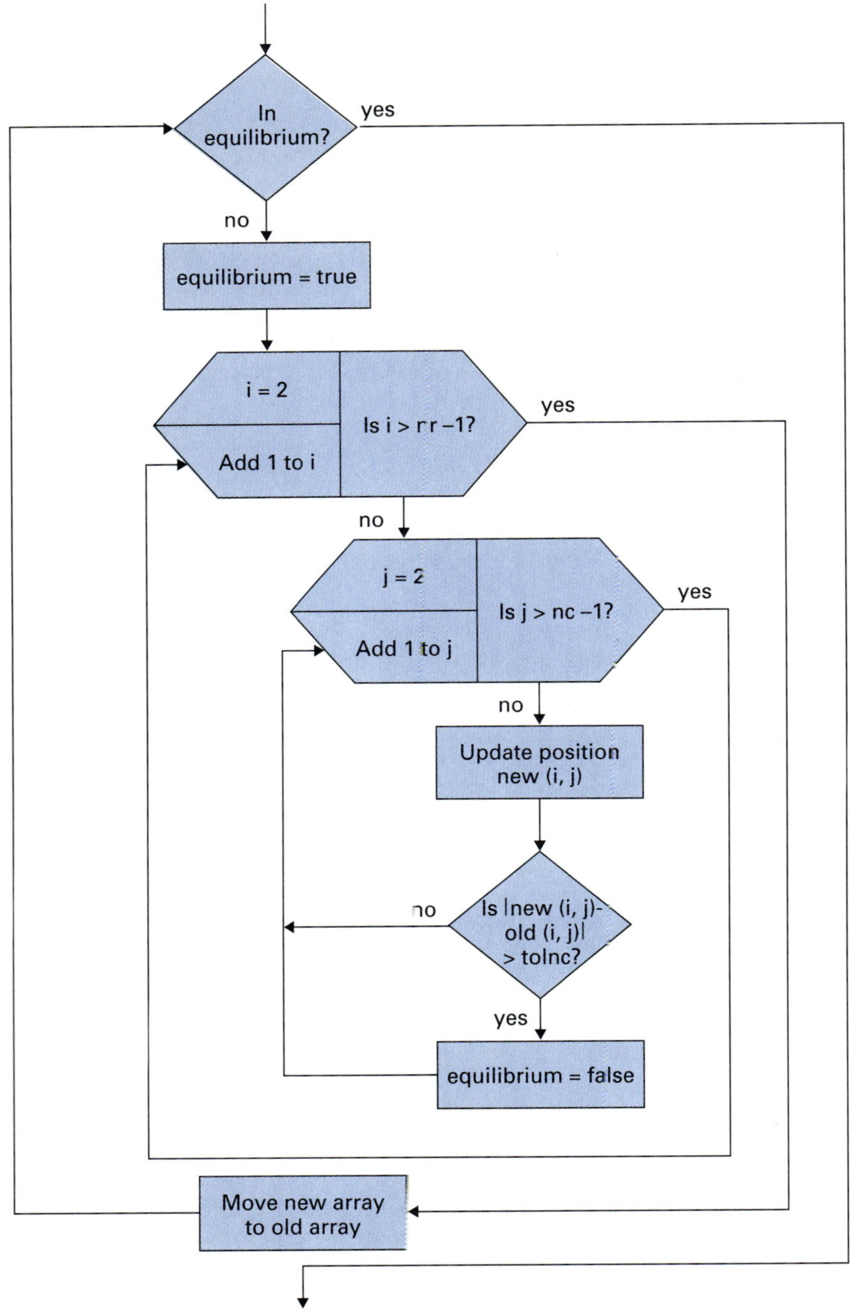

Before we convert the flowchart steps into FORTRAN, we consider data structures and subprograms. Clearly, the data that we are using is best represented by a two-dimensional array. We use a double-precision array to be able to work with tolerances that might be much smaller than the actual temperatures themselves. The arrays need to be defined with a maximum size, and we assume that 10 rows and 10 columns represent this maximum size.

The second issue we need to address is subprograms. As we developed the flowchart for this algorithm, there was no set of operations that needed to be performed in several places in the program. However, if we consider the overall program, it is getting lengthy, and long programs are harder to follow, even if they are properly structured. Therefore, you should look for operations that can easily be written in a subprogram, making your main programs more readable. In this program, the loop to move the new temperatures to the old temperature array is written as a subroutine. In addition, we write a subroutine to print the new temperatures. Even though the problem statement specifies that the temperatures are written only once, we definitely want to print them more often in the debugging stages; thus, it is useful to have a subroutine for printing out the temperatures at intermediate stages. In fact, we will print the initial set of temperatures in this program in order to be sure that the proper data was entered by the user.

The structure chart for this program is

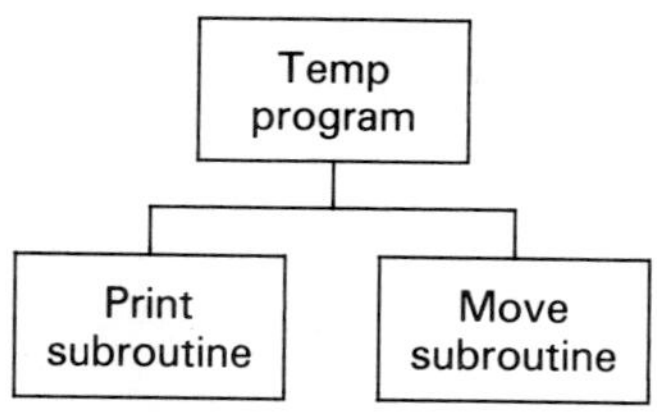

FORTRAN Program

```
*-----------------------------------------------------------------------*
      PROGRAM TEMP
*
*  This program initializes the temperatures in a metal plate
*  and determines the equilibrium temperatures based on a
*  tolerance value.
*
      INTEGER NROW, NCOL, I, J
      LOGICAL EQUILB
      DOUBLE PRECISION OLD(10,10), NEW(10,10), TOLNC,
     +                 TOP, BOT, LEFT, RIGHT
*
      PRINT*, 'ENTER TEMPERATURE GRID SIZE:'
      PRINT*, 'ROWS, COLUMNS (MAXIMUM 10,10)'
      READ*, NROW, NCOL
      PRINT*, 'ENTER ISOTHERMAL EDGE TEMPERATURES:'
      PRINT*, 'TOP, BOTTOM, LEFT, RIGHT'
      READ*, TOP, BOT, LEFT, RIGHT
      PRINT*, 'ENTER EQUILIBRIUM TOLERANCE VALUE'
      READ*, TOLNC
*
*  Initialize temperature array.
*
```

```
      DO 5 J=1,NCOL
         OLD(1,J) = TOP
         OLD(NROW,J) = BOT
    5 CONTINUE
      DO 15 I=2,NROW-1
         OLD(I,1) = LEFT
         DO 10 J=2,NCOL-1
            OLD(I,J) = 0.0D+00
   10    CONTINUE
         OLD(I,NCOL) = RIGHT
   15 CONTINUE
*
*  Print initial temperature array.
*
      PRINT*
      PRINT*, 'INITIAL TEMPERATURES'
      PRINT*
      CALL PRINT(OLD,NROW,NCOL)
      CALL MOVE(OLD,NROW,NCOL,NEW)
*
*  Update temperatures until equilibrium.
*
      EQUILB = .FALSE.
   20 IF (.NOT.EQUILB) THEN
         EQUILB = .TRUE.
         DO 30 I=2,NROW-1
            DO 25 J=2,NCOL-1
               NEW(I,J) = (OLD(I-1,J) + OLD(I+1,J) +
     +                     OLD(I,J-1) + OLD(I,J+1))/4.0D+00
               IF (ABS(NEW(I,J) - OLD(I,J)).GT.TOLNC)
     +                     EQUILB = .FALSE.
   25       CONTINUE
   30    CONTINUE
         CALL MOVE(NEW,NROW,NCOL,OLD)
         GO TO 20
      END IF
*
*  Print equilibrium temperature array.
*
      PRINT*
      PRINT*, 'EQUILIBRIUM TEMPERATURES'
      PRINT*
      CALL PRINT(OLD,NROW,NCOL)
*
      END
*-----------------------------------------------------------------------*
      SUBROUTINE PRINT(OLD,NROW,NCOL)
*
*  This subroutine prints a double-precision array.
*
      INTEGER NROW, NCOL, I, J
      DOUBLE PRECISION  OLD(10,10)
*
      DO 10 I=1,NROW
         PRINT 5, (OLD(I,J),J=1,NCOL)
    5    FORMAT(1X,10(D12.5,1X))
   10 CONTINUE
*
      RETURN
      END
*-----------------------------------------------------------------------*
```

```
      SUBROUTINE MOVE(NEW,NROW,NCOL,OLD)
*
*  This subroutine moves the values in the new array into
*  the old array.
*
      INTEGER NROW, NCOL, I, J
      DOUBLE PRECISION OLD(10,10), NEW(10,10)
*
      DO 10 I=1,NROW
         DO 5 J=1,NCOL
            OLD(I,J) = NEW(I,J)
    5    CONTINUE
   10 CONTINUE
*
      RETURN
      END
*-----------------------------------------------------------------------*
```

5. Testing

Testing this program is easier because of the subroutine that prints the values in the OLD array. You can call this subroutine just after the new temperatures are moved to the old temperatures (just before GO TO 20), which allows you to check the values after each update loop.

Note that the two subroutines used the variables NROW and NCOL as DO loop parameters but not as array dimensions. Remember that it is easy to cause problems with two-dimensional arrays when you use variable dimensioning; thus, we recommend that you use the maximum array size in all subprogram array definitions, as we did in this example. Then use variables to control the portion of the array that you actually use.

After entering the data from our hand-worked example in this program, the output is

```
INITIAL TEMPERATURES

 0.10000D+03  0.10000D+03  0.10000D+03  0.10000D+03
 0.10000D+03  0.00000D+00  0.00000D+00  0.20000D+03
 0.10000D+03  0.00000D+00  0.00000D+00  0.20000D+03
 0.20000D+03  0.20000D+03  0.20000D+03  0.20000D+03

EQUILIBRIUM TEMPERATURES

 0.10000D+03  0.10000D+03  0.10000D+03  0.10000D+03
 0.10000D+03  0.12031D+03  0.14531D+03  0.20000D+03
 0.10000D+03  0.14531D+03  0.17031D+03  0.20000D+03
 0.20000D+03  0.20000D+03  0.20000D+03  0.20000D+03
```

8·5 ■ Complex Data

Complex numbers are needed to solve many problems in science and engineering, particularly in physics and electrical engineering. Therefore, FORTRAN includes a special data type for complex variables and constants. (Recall that complex numbers have the form $a + bi$, where i is $\sqrt{-1}$ and a and b are real numbers. Thus, the real part of the number is represented by a, and the imaginary part of the number is represented by b.) These *complex values* are stored as an ordered pair of real values that represents the real and the imaginary portions of the value.

A complex constant is specified by two real constants separated by a comma and enclosed in parentheses. The first constant represents the real part of the complex value; the second constant represents the imaginary part of the complex value. Thus, the complex constant $3.0 + 1.5i$ is written in FORTRAN as the complex constant (3.0, 1.5).

Complex variables are specified with a specification statement, whose general form is

```
COMPLEX variable list
```

A complex array is specified as

```
COMPLEX CX(100)
```

■ Complex I/O

A complex value in list-directed output is printed as two real values separated by a comma and enclosed in parentheses. Two real values are read for each complex value in a list-directed input statement.

For formatted output, a complex value is printed with two real specifications. The real part of the complex value is printed before the imaginary portion. It is good practice to enclose the two parts printed in parentheses and separate them by a comma or print them in the $a + bi$ form. Both forms are illustrated in the following statements:

```
      COMPLEX CX, CY
      .
      .
      .
      CX = (1.5, 4.0)
      CY = (0.0, 2.4)
      PRINT 5, CX, CY
    5 FORMAT (1X,'(',F4.1,',',F4.1,')'/1X,F4.1,' + ',F4.1,' i')
```

The output from the PRINT statement is

```
( 1.5, 4.0)
 0.0 +  2.4 i
```

■ Complex Operations

When an arithmetic operation is performed between two complex values, the result is also a complex value. In an expression containing a complex value and a real or integer value, the real or integer value is converted to a complex value whose imaginary part is zero. Expressions containing both complex values and double-precision values are not allowed.

The rules for complex arithmetic are not as familiar as those for integers or real values. Table 8–4 lists the results of basic operations on two complex numbers C_1 and C_2, where $C_1 = a_1 + b_1 i$ and $C_2 = a_2 + b_2 i$:

■ Complex Intrinsic Functions

If a complex value is used in one of the generic functions, such as SQRT, ABS, SIN, COS, EXP, or LOG, the function value is also complex. The functions CSQRT, CABS, CSIN, CCOS, CEXP, and CLOG are all intrinsic functions with complex arguments. These function names begin with the letter C to emphasize that they are complex functions.

Although Appendix A contains a complete list of the functions that relate to complex values, four functions, REAL, AIMAG, CONJG, and CMPLX, are specifically designed for use with complex variables: REAL yields the real part of its complex argument; AIMAG yields the imaginary part of its complex argument; CONJG converts a complex number to its conjugate, where the conjugate of $(a + bi)$ is $(a - bi)$; COMPLX converts two real arguments, a and b, into a complex value $(a + bi)$. Note that, while (2.0,1.0) is equal to the complex constant $2.0 + 1.0i$, we must use the expression CMPLX(A,B) to specify the complex variable $A + Bi$; the expression (A,B) by itself does not represent a complex variable in FORTRAN 77.

Table 8-4 Complex Arithmetic Operations

Operation	Result
$C_1 + C_2$	$(a_1 + a_2) + i\,(b_1 + b_2)$
$C_1 - C_2$	$(a_1 - a_2) + i\,(b_1 - b_2)$
$C_1 \cdot C_2$	$(a_1a_2 - b_1b_2) + i\,(a_1b_2 + a_2b_1)$
$\frac{C_1}{C_2}$	$\left(\frac{a_1a_2 + b_1b_2}{a_2^2 + b_2^2}\right) + i\left(\frac{a_2b_1 - b_2a_1}{a_2^2 + b_2^2}\right)$
$\lvert C_1 \rvert$	$\sqrt{a_1^2 + b_1^2}$
e^{C_1}	$e^{a_1} \cos b_1 + i\, e^{a_1} \sin b_1$
$\sin C_1$	$C_1 - \frac{C_1^3}{3!} + \frac{C_1^5}{5!} - \frac{C_1^7}{7!} + \cdots$

(Note that $C_1 = a_1 + ib_1$ and $C_2 = a_2 + ib_2$.)

Example 8-10

Quadratic Formula

The roots of a quadratic equation with real coefficients may be complex. Give the statements to compute and print the two roots of a quadratic equation, given the coefficients A, B, and C as shown:

$$AX^2 + BX + C = 0$$

$$X_1 = \frac{-B + \sqrt{B^2 - 4AC}}{2A} \qquad X_2 = \frac{-B - \sqrt{B^2 - 4AC}}{2A}$$

Solution

```
      COMPLEX DISCR, ROOT1, ROOT2
      .
      .
      .
      DISCR = CMPLX(B*B - 4.0*A*C,0.0)
      ROOT1 = (-B + SQRT(DISCR))/(2.0*A)
      ROOT2 = (-B - SQRT(DISCR))/(2.0*A)
      PRINT*, 'ROOTS TO THE QUADRATIC EQUATION ARE:'
      PRINT 5, ROOT1, ROOT2
    5 FORMAT (1X,F5.2,' + ',F5.2,' i',4X,F5.2,' + ',F5.2,' i')
```

Two sets of sample output are shown, one in which both roots are real and one in which both roots are complex:

```
ROOTS TO THE QUADRATIC EQUATION ARE:
 1.56 +  0.00 i      2.00 +  0.00 i

ROOTS TO THE QUADRATIC EQUATION ARE:
 2.36 +  2.45 i      2.36 + -2.45 i
```

SELF-TEST 8-3

This self-test allows you to check quickly to see if you have remembered some of the key points from Section 8–5. If you have any problems with the exercises, you should reread this section. The solutions are included at the end of the text.

In problems 1–6, compute the value stored in CX if CY $= 2-i$ and CZ $= -1+2i$. Assume that CX, CY, and CZ are complex variables.

1. `CX = CY + 2.CZ`
2. `CX = CZ - CY`
3. `CX = CONJG(CY)`
4. `CX = REAL(CZ) + AIMAG(CY)`
5. `CX = CMPLX(3.5,-1.5)`
6. `CX = ABS(CY + CZ)`

In problems 7 and 8, show the output of the following PRINT statements. Assume that CX $= 2-i$.

7.
```
   PRINT 5, CX
 5 FORMAT (1X,F5.1,'+',F5.1,' i')
```

8.
```
   PRINT 6, CX
 6 FORMAT (1X,'(',F6.2,',',F6.2,')')
```

8-6 Application ▪ Electric Circuit Model

Electrical Engineering

In the analysis of an electric circuit, we are often interested in the transfer function of the circuit. This transfer function can be used to determine the effect of the circuit on a sine function, in terms of magnitude changes and phase changes. The magnitude (absolute value) of the transfer function evaluated at the frequency ω of the sine wave ($\sin \omega t$) is multiplied by the magnitude (or amplitude) of the sine function to give the output magnitude. The phase (arctangent of the imaginary part divided by the real part) of the transfer function evaluated at the frequency of the sine wave is added to the phase of the sine function to give the output phase. For example, consider the following circuit that contains a capacitor C and a resistor R.

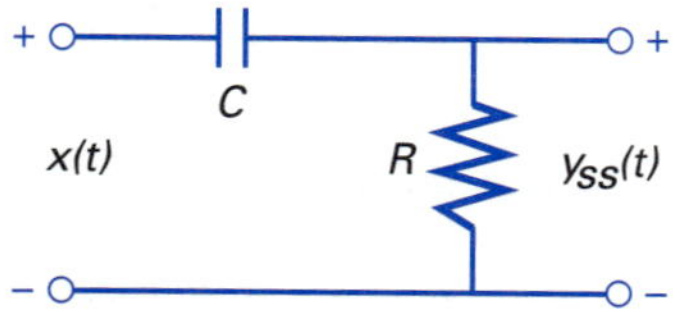

Kirchhoff's voltage law can be used to derive the transfer function for this system:

$$H(\omega) = \frac{\omega RCi}{1 + \omega RCi}$$

where ω represents frequency in radians per second and i represents $\sqrt{-1}$. Write a program that determines the magnitude and phase changes caused by this circuit when a sine wave of a given frequency passes through the circuit.

1. Problem Statement

Write a program that determines the magnitude and phase changes of a sine wave after it passes through the given electric circuit.

2. Input/Output Description

Input—the resistance R in ohms, the capacitance C in farads, and the frequency of the input sine wave

Output—the magnitude and phase of the transfer function evaluated at the input frequency

3. Hand Example

Assume that the input to the circuit is sine $100t$. The frequency of this sine wave is 100 radians per second. Also assume that R is equal to 10,000 ohms and that C is equal to 2.0 microfarads (or 0.000002 farads). The transfer function with these parameters is

$$H(100) = \frac{(100)(10000)(0.000002)i}{1 + (100)(10000)(0.000002)i} = \frac{2i}{1 + 2i}$$

$$= \frac{2i(1 - 2i)}{(1 + 2i)(1 - 2i)} = \frac{4 + 2i}{1 + 4} = 0.8 + 0.4i$$

The magnitude of $(0.8 + 0.4i)$ is .89, and the phase is 0.46 radians. Thus, a sine wave with a frequency of 100 radians per second has its magnitude multiplied by 0.89 and its phase changed by 0.46 radians when it passes through the circuit in this example.

4. Algorithm Development

The decomposition of this problem solution involves reading the input values and then computing the corresponding transfer function magnitude and phase.

Decomposition

Read R, C, and ω.
Compute magnitude and phase.
Print ω, magnitude, and phase.

The refinement of this algorithm involves substituting the equations in the computation step.

Pseudocode

Elect1: Read R, C, and ω
Compute $H(\omega)$
Determine magnitude of $H(\omega)$
Determine phase of $H(\omega)$
Print ω, magnitude, and phase

FORTRAN Program

```
*-----------------------------------------------------------------------*
      PROGRAM ELECT1
*
*  This program determines the magnitude and phase effects of
*  an RC circuit on a sine wave.
*
      REAL R, C, W, MAGN, PHASE
      COMPLEX I, HW
*
      I = (0.0, 1.0)
*
      PRINT*, 'ENTER RESISTANCE IN OHMS'
      READ*, R
      PRINT*, 'ENTER CAPACITANCE IN FARADS'
      READ*, C
      PRINT*, 'ENTER THE SINE FREQUENCY IN RADIANS PER SEC'
      READ*, W
*
      HW = (W*R*C*I)/(1.0 + W*R*C*I)
      MAGN = ABS(HW)
      PHASE = ATAN2(AIMAG(HW),REAL(HW))
*
      PRINT 5, MAGN, PHASE
    5 FORMAT (1X,'MAGNITUDE EFFECT: ',F5.2,3X,
     +        'PHASE EFFECT: ',F5.2)
*
      END
*-----------------------------------------------------------------------*
```

5. Testing

If we use the frequency from our hand-worked example to test this program, our output is

```
ENTER RESISTANCE IN OHMS
10000.
ENTER CAPACITANCE IN FARADS
0.000002
ENTER THE SINE FREQUENCY IN RADIANS PER SEC
100.0
MAGNITUDE EFFECT:  0.89   PHASE EFFECT:  0.46
```

An interesting modification to this program involves looking at the magnitude changes of the circuit over an interval of frequencies as opposed to a specific frequency. For example, some circuits are called low-pass circuits, which means that they pass frequencies below a certain frequency and reject frequencies above a certain frequency. When the magnitude effect is near 1.0, a frequency is being passed; when the magnitude effect is near 0.0, the frequency is being rejected. Other types of circuits are high-pass circuits, band-pass circuits, and band-reject circuits.

If we modify our program to read the starting and ending frequencies for an interval of frequencies, we can look at the magnitude effect over that interval and determine the type of circuit being analyzed. In this program, we print 20 values over the frequency interval. The modified program and a sample output are given.

FORTRAN Program

```
*--------------------------------------------------------------------*
      PROGRAM ELECT2
*
*  This program determines the magnitude effect of an RC circuit
*  over a frequency interval.
*
      INTEGER K
      REAL W, R, C, WS, WE, STEP, MAGN
      COMPLEX I, H, HW
*
      H(W) = (W*R*C*I)/(1.0 + W*R*C*I)
*
      I = (0.0, 1.0)
*
      PRINT*, 'ENTER RESISTANCE IN OHMS'
      READ*, R
      PRINT*, 'ENTER CAPACITANCE IN FARADS'
      READ*, C
      PRINT*, 'ENTER THE STARTING AND ENDING FREQUENCIES'
      PRINT*, '(RADIANS PER SEC)'
      READ*, WS, WE
*
      PRINT*
      PRINT*, 'FREQUENCY AND MAGNITUDE'
      STEP = (WE - WS)/20.0
      DO 20 K=1,20
         W = (K - 1)*STEP + WS
         HW = H(W)
         MAGN = ABS(HW)
         PRINT 10, W, MAGN
   10    FORMAT (1X,F6.2,5X,F5.2)
   20 CONTINUE
*
      END
*--------------------------------------------------------------------*
```

```
ENTER RESISTANCE IN OHMS
10000.
ENTER CAPACITANCE IN FARADS
0.000002
ENTER THE STARTING AND ENDING FREQUENCIES
(RADIANS PER SEC)
0.0 200.0

FREQUENCY AND MAGNITUDE
  0.00        0.00
 10.00        0.20
 20.00        0.37
 30.00        0.51
 40.00        0.62
 50.00        0.71
 60.00        0.77
 70.00        0.81
 80.00        0.85
 90.00        0.87
100.00        0.89
110.00        0.91
120.00        0.92
130.00        0.93
140.00        0.94
150.00        0.95
160.00        0.95
170.00        0.96
180.00        0.96
190.00        0.97
```

Note that this circuit rejects frequencies near zero and passes frequencies with little magnitude distortion when the frequency is between 150 and 190 radians per second.

Summary

With the data types presented in this chapter, we now have a number of choices for defining our variables and constants. For numeric data, we can select integers, real values, or double-precision values. We have character data for information that is not going to be used in numeric computations. For special applications, we have complex variables. In addition to being able to choose the proper data type for our data, we also have special intrinsic functions and operations for simplifying our work with the data.

Debugging Aids

Many errors in character string manipulations occur because the character string is used incorrectly with numeric data. Some typical examples are:

Arithmetic expressions — Even if a character string contains numeric digits, it cannot be used in arithmetic operations.

Comparisons — Character strings should always be compared to other character strings and not to a numeric constant or variable.

Subprogram arguments—A character string used as an argument to a subprogram must be identified in CHARACTER statements in both the main program and the subprogram.

Another source of errors may be introduced when moving or comparing strings of unequal length. For comparisons, the shorter string will be compared as if it had enough blanks on the right to be equal in length to the longer string. Character strings are always moved character by character from left to right until the receiving string is filled. If there are too few characters in the sending string, blanks are moved into the rightmost characters of the receiving string.

A final caution about the substring operation: invalid results occur if the beginning or ending positions of the substring reference are outside the original string itself.

The primary debugging tool for double-precision and complex values is the PRINT statement. If an error is related to a double-precision value, print it out with an E21.14 format (assumes 14 digits of accuracy) each time it is used to be sure that you are not losing the extra accuracy. Also, be sure that you are not moving the value into a single-precision variable in an intermediate step in the program.

If your program errors relate to complex values, write the values of the complex numbers as soon as they are initialized and after each modification. Remember that if you move a complex value into a real variable, the imaginary portion is lost.

■ Style/Technique Guides

A programmer who is comfortable and proficient with character string manipulations will find them extremely useful. The ability to display information clearly and simply is valuable in communication, and the use of character strings adds a new dimension to the method of both reading and displaying information.

Some guides for using character strings in your programs are

1. Use character strings of the same length where possible.
2. Use the function INDEX instead of writing your own routines to find substrings in a string.
3. Become proficient with the substring and concatenation operators; these are powerful tools in manipulating and analyzing character strings.

Finally, when you use a feature of FORTRAN (such as double-precision or complex variables) that is not commonly used, good documentation is important. More comment lines may be necessary to clarify your code. If a computation uses complex numbers, explain the computations in more detail than in regular arithmetic computations. Part of good documentation also includes choosing descriptive names.

Key Words

ASCII code
character string
collating sequence
complex value
concatenation
double-precision value
EBCDIC code
FORTRAN character set
lexicographic order
substring

Problems

We begin our problem set with modifications to programs developed earlier in this chapter. Give the decomposition, refined pseudocode or flowchart, and FORTRAN solution for each problem.

Problems 1 – 5 modify the program WEIGHT, given on page 389, which computes the molecular weight of a large protein molecule.

1. Modify the molecular weight program so that it includes a subroutine that is used to print the contents of the AMINO file at the beginning of the program.
2. Modify the molecular weight program so that it prints a final line with the maximum and minimum protein molecular weights.
3. Modify the molecular weight program so that it prints a final line with the average protein molecular weight.
4. Modify the molecular weight program so that it prints the number of amino acids in each protein molecule.
5. Modify the molecular weight program so that it prints the maximum and minimum number of amino acids in the protein molecules.

Problems 6 – 10 modify the program TEMP, given on page 401, which determines an equilibrium temperature distribution in a metal plate.

6. Modify the temperature distribution program so that it counts the number of iterations needed for the plate to reach equilibrium. Print this value after the final grid.
7. Modify the temperature distribution program so that the initialization of the temperature array is performed in a subroutine.
8. Modify the temperature distribution program so that the computation of the new temperature values is performed in a subroutine.
9. Modify the temperature distribution program so that the temperature iteration continues until equilibrium has been reached or until 10 iterations have been performed.
10. Modify the print subroutine so that it also prints the maximum and minimum temperatures and their positions in the temperature array.

Problems 11–15 modify the program ELECT1, given on page 409, which determines the magnitude and phase effects of an RC circuit on a sine wave.

11. Modify the program ELECT1 so that it prints the phase effect in degrees instead of radians.
12. Modify the program ELECT1 so that it reads the resistance in units of thousands of ohms.
13. Modify the program ELECT1 so that it reads the capacitance in units of microfarads. (One microfarad = 0.000001 farad.)
14. Modify the program ELECT1 so that it reads the sine frequency in hertz (or cycles per second) instead of radians per second. (1 hertz = 2π radians per second.)
15. Add a loop to the program ELECT1 so it continues computing magnitude and phase effects until a negative value is entered for the sine frequency.

In problems 16–45, develop programs and modules using the five-step design process.

16. Write a complete program that reads a data file ADDR containing 50 names and addresses. The first line for each person contains the first name (10 characters), the middle name (6 characters), and the last name (21 characters). The second line contains the address (25 characters), the city (10 characters), the state abbreviation (2 characters), and the zip code (5 characters). Each character string is enclosed in quotes in the file. Print the information in the following label form:

```
First Initial. Middle Initial. Last Name
Address
City, State Zip
```

Skip four lines between labels. The city should not contain any blanks before the comma that follows it. A typical label might be

```
J. D. Doe
117 Main St.
Taos, NM 87166
```

For simplicity, assume there are no embedded blanks in the individual data values. For example, San Jose would be entered as SanJose and printed in the same manner.

17. Write a subroutine CNDNS that receives a character array of 50 characters and returns a character array OUT, also of 50 characters, which has no adjacent blanks except at the end of the string. Thus, if IN was composed of 'HELLO THERE' followed by blanks, then the output array OUT should contain 'HELLOTHERE' followed by blanks.
18. Write a complete program to read a double-precision value from the terminal. Compute the sine of the value using the following series:

$$\sin X = X - \frac{X^3}{3!} + \frac{X^5}{5!} - \frac{X^7}{7!} + \cdots$$

Continue using terms until the absolute value of a term is less than 1.OD−09. Print the computed sine and the value obtained from the sine function for comparison.

19. Write a program that reads the coefficients A, B, and C of a quadratic equation from a data line. Compute and print the two roots of the equation. If the roots are real values, use an F format to print them. If the roots are complex, use the $a + bi$ form for output. If the value of A is zero, print a message stating that the equation is linear and not quadratic.

20. Write a program that reads the complex coefficients A, B, C, D, and E for a general transfer function with the following equation:

$$H(\omega) = \frac{A \cdot \omega^2 + B \cdot \omega + C}{\omega^2 + D \cdot \omega + E}$$

Read an input frequency ω and determine the magnitude and phase effects of this transfer function on a sinusoid with frequency ω.

21. Modify the program in problem 20 to read a beginning and ending frequency from the terminal. Compute and print the magnitude effects for 20 frequency points spaced evenly over the interval.

22. Modify the program in problem 20 to read a beginning and ending frequency from the terminal. Also read the number of points desired in the frequency interval. Print the magnitude effects for these frequency points spaced evenly over the interval.

23. Write a program that prints a table of values for exp(x) where x varies from 0.1 to 2.0 in increments of 0.1. Print 3 columns: x, exp(x) using the single-precision intrinsic function, and exp(x) using the double-precision intrinsic function.

24. Write a subroutine DELETE that has an argument list composed of a character array TEXT of 100 characters and a pointer PTR. The subroutine should delete the character in position PTR. The characters in the positions following PTR should be moved one position to the left. A blank should be added at the end of TEXT to keep the length of TEXT at 100 characters.

25. Write a subroutine INSERT that has an argument list composed of a character string TEXT of 100 characters, a pointer PTR, and a single character CHARl. The subroutine should insert CHARl in the position pointed to by PTR. The rest of the characters should be moved one position to the right, with the last character truncated to keep the length of TEXT at 100 characters.

26. A data file called CARS contains the license plate number for each car in a particular region and the number of gallons of gas required to fill the car's gas tank. The license plate is composed of 3 characters, followed by a space, and then 3 digits. Each line in the file contains a license number and a real number that gives the corresponding gallons of gas. The last line in the file has a license number of ZZZ 999 and is not a valid data line. Write a complete program that helps analyze the feasibility of gas rationing based on whether

the license plate number is odd or even. The data to be computed and printed is the following:

```
SUM OF GAS FOR ODD CARS         XXXXX GALLONS       XX.X%
SUM OF GAS FOR EVEN CARS        XXXXX GALLONS       XX.X%
```

27. A palindrome is a word or piece of text that is spelled the same forward and backward. The word 'RADAR' is an example of a palindrome, but ' RADAR' is not a palindrome because of the unmatched blank. 'ABLE ELBA' is another palindrome. Write a logical function PALIND that receives a character variable X of length 20. The function should be true if the character array is a palindrome; otherwise, it should be false.
28. Write a subroutine ALPHA that receives an array of 50 letters. The subroutine should alphabetize the list of letters.
29. Modify the subroutine in problem 28 to remove duplicate letters and to add blanks at the end of the array for the letters removed.
30. Write a subroutine whose input is a character array of length 50. Change all punctuation marks (commas, periods, exclamation points, and question marks) to blanks. Assume that the program calls the subroutine with the following statement:

```
CALL EDIT(STRING)
```

31. Write a subroutine that receives a piece of text called PROSE that contains 200 characters. The subprogram should print the text in lines of 30 characters each. Do not split words between two lines. Do not print any lines that are completely blank.
32. Write a function CONSNT that receives a character array of 100 alphabetic letters. Count the number of consonants and return that number to the main program. (It might be easiest to count the number of vowels and subtract that number from 100.)
33. Write a subroutine that receives an array of N real values (maximum value of N is 200) and generates a printer plot. Use an output line of 101 characters. Scale the line from the minimum value to the maximum value. The first line of output should be 101 periods representing the Y-axis. All the following lines should contain a period in the column representing $X = 0$ (if this point is included in the graph), and the letter X in the position of each data point, as shown in the following diagram. (In this diagram, the minimum and the maximum values have the same absolute value.)

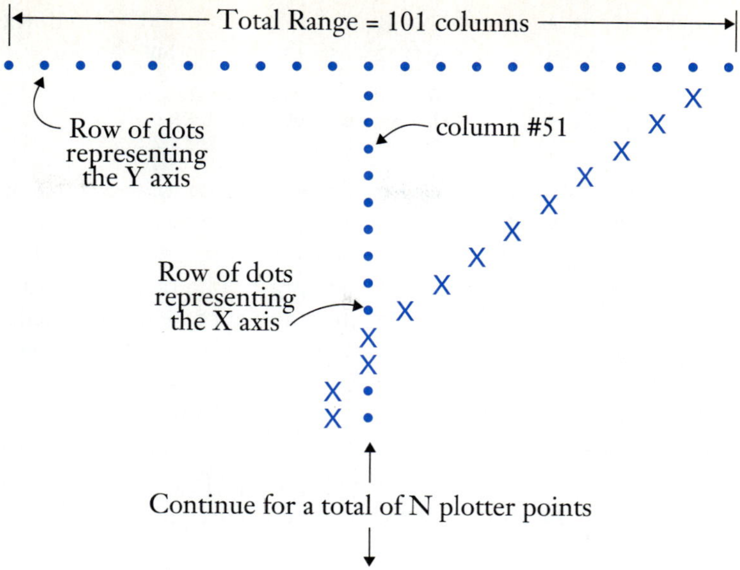

34. Write a complete program that reads and stores the following two-dimensional array of characters:

```
ATIDEB
LENGTH
ECPLOT
DDUEFS
OUTPUT
CGDAER
HIRXJI
KATIMN
BHPARG
```

Now read the 11 strings that follow and find the same strings in the preceding array. Print the positions of characters of these hidden words that may appear forward, backward, up, down, or diagonally. For instance, the word EDIT is located in positions (1,5), (1,4), (1,3), and (1,2).

Hidden Words

PLOT	STRING
CODE	TEXT
EDIT	READ
LENGTH	GRAPH
INPUT	BAR
OUTPUT	

35. Modify the subprogram of problem 31 such that the length of the output line is an argument of the subroutine. Distribute any blanks between words on a line such that every line begins and ends with a nonblank character. Thus, if

the character string PROSE contained a portion of the Gettysburg Address and the line length is 23, the first three lines of output should be

```
FOUR  SCORE  AND  SEVEN
YEARS  AGO, OUR FATHERS
BROUGHT FORTH UPON THIS
```

36. Text material is sometimes analyzed very carefully to determine quantities such as average word length. Such a quantity can be used to recommend the level of reading ability necessary to read the text. Average word length can even be used to help determine authorship of a literary work; it has been applied to the works of Shakespeare in an attempt to indicate whether Sir Frances Bacon authored some of the plays attributed to Shakespeare. Write a function that receives a character string and returns the average word length of the string. Assume that all words are separated from adjacent words by at least one blank. The first and last characters may or may not be blanks.
37. Write a subroutine that sorts a complex array of N values into a descending order based on the absolute value of the complex values. Assume that the subroutine is called with the statement

```
CALL ORDER(CDATA,N)
```

where CDATA is an array of N complex values.
38. Write a subroutine ENCODE that receives a character string KEY containing 26 characters and a character string MESSGE of an unspecified size. The subroutine should encode MESSGE, using a substitution code where the first letter in KEY is substituted for the letter A in MESSGE, the second letter in KEY is substituted for the letter B in MESSGE, and so on. Thus, if KEY contained the character string

```
'YXAZKLMBJOCFDVSWTREGHNIPUQ'
```

and MESSGE contained the character string

```
'MEET AT AIRPORT SATURDAY'
```

then the encoded character string would be

```
'DKKG YG YJRWSRG EYGHRZYU'
```

The encoded character string should be stored in a character string called SECRET. The subroutine is called with the following statement:

```
CALL ENCODE(KEY,MESSGE,SECRET)
```

39. Write a subroutine DECODE that receives a character string KEY containing 26 characters and a character string SECRET of an unspecified size. The subroutine should decode SECRET, which has been encoded with a substitution key where the first letter in KEY was substituted for the letter A, the second letter in KEY was substituted for the letter B, and so on. Blanks were not changed in the coding process. Thus, if KEY contained the character string

```
'YXAZKLMBJOCFDVSWTREGHNIPUQ'
```

and SECRET contained the character string

```
'DKKG YG YJRWSRG EYGHRZYU'
```

then the decoded character string would be

```
'MEET AT AIRPORT SATURDAY'
```

The decoded character string should be stored in a character string called MESSGE. The subroutine is called with the statement

```
CALL DECODE(KEY,SECRET,MESSGE)
```

40. Write a subroutine to sort a character string array into alphabetical order. Assume that each character string in the array contains 4 characters. Remove any leading blanks from the character strings before sorting. The input is a character array with *N* values. The output is the same array, but with the character strings reordered into alphabetical order and the leading blanks removed. Use the following statement to call the subroutine:

```
CALL ALPHA(NAME,N)
```

The following example illustrates the reason for removing leading blanks:

Original Order	Alphabetical Order with Blanks	Alphabetical Order without Blanks
SAMb	bbED	ALbb
bbED	bALb	AMYb
bSUE	bSUE	BEVb
MARY	AMYb	EDbb
JOSE	BEVb	JOHN
JOHN	JOHN	JOSE
AMYb	JOSE	LISA
bALb	LISA	MARY
LISA	MARY	SAMb
BEVb	SAMb	SUEb

41. Write a subroutine to compute and return the roots of a quadratic equation. Remember that the roots may be complex values.

42. Modify the temperature distribution program such that it has a constant heat source inside the metal plate instead of at the edges of the metal plate. Assume that the metal plate is a square represented by an even number of grid values on each side. The constant heat source is the four grid values in the center of the metal plate. Assume that all other grid values begin at zero. The program should determine the equilibrium point using the same temperature update scheme as in the program on page 401.

43. Table 8 – 5 contains the 20 amino acids in proteins, along with the number of molecules of oxygen (O), carbon (C), nitrogen (N), sulfur (S), and hydrogen (H). Generate a data file contining this information, and then use double-

Table 8·5 Amino Acid Molecules

Amino Acid	O	C	N	S	H
Glycine	2	2	1	0	5
Alanine	2	3	1	0	7
Valine	2	5	1	0	11
Leucine	2	6	1	0	13
Isoleucine	2	6	1	0	13
Serine	3	3	1	0	7
Threonine	3	4	1	0	9
Tyrosine	3	9	1	0	11
Phenylalanine	2	9	1	0	11
Tryptophan	2	11	2	0	11
Aspartic	4	4	1	0	6
Glutamic	4	5	1	0	8
Lysine	2	6	2	0	15
Arginine	2	6	4	0	15
Histidine	2	6	3	0	10
Cysteine	2	3	1	1	7
Methionine	2	5	1	1	11
Asparagine	3	4	2	0	8
Glutamine	3	5	2	0	10
Proline	2	5	1	0	10

precision variables to compute the molecular weights of the amino acids using these more accurate molecular weights:

Oxygen	15.9994
Carbon	12.011
Nitrogen	14.00674
Sulfur	32.066
Hydrogen	1.00794

44. Use the information generated in problem 43 to generate a data file named AMINODP that contains the double-precision molecular weights instead of the integer molecular weights. Use the AMINO file to obtain the 3-character references.
45. Using the AMINO file and the AMINODP file from problem 44, print the average amino acid molecular weight for integer weights and for double-precision weights.

FORTRAN STATEMENT SUMMARY

■ **CHARACTER** Statement:

```
CHARACTER variable list
```

Examples:

```
CHARACTER*5 NAME, DESC(10)
CHARACTER CITY*20, LOCATION*35
```

Discussion:

The CHARACTER statement defines variables that store character information. It also specifies the number of characters in the variable.

■ **COMPLEX** Statement:

```
COMPLEX variable list
```

Example:

```
COMPLEX I, CX, Z(10)
```

Discussion:

The COMPLEX statement defines variables that represent complex values. Each complex variable consists of two real values, the first representing the real part of the complex value and the second representing the imaginary part of the complex value. When a complex value is read or printed, two real values correspond to the complex value.

■ **DOUBLE PRECISION** Statement:

```
DOUBLE PRECISION variable list
```

Example:

```
DOUBLE PRECISION X, Y, ACCEL(25)
```

Discussion:

The DOUBLE PRECISION statement defines variables that have more significant digits of accuracy than real variables. The exact number of significant digits of accuracy in a double-precision variable depends on the computer system. Typically, a real value contains 7 digits of accuracy and a double-precision value contains 14 digits of accuracy.

9 Additional File Handling

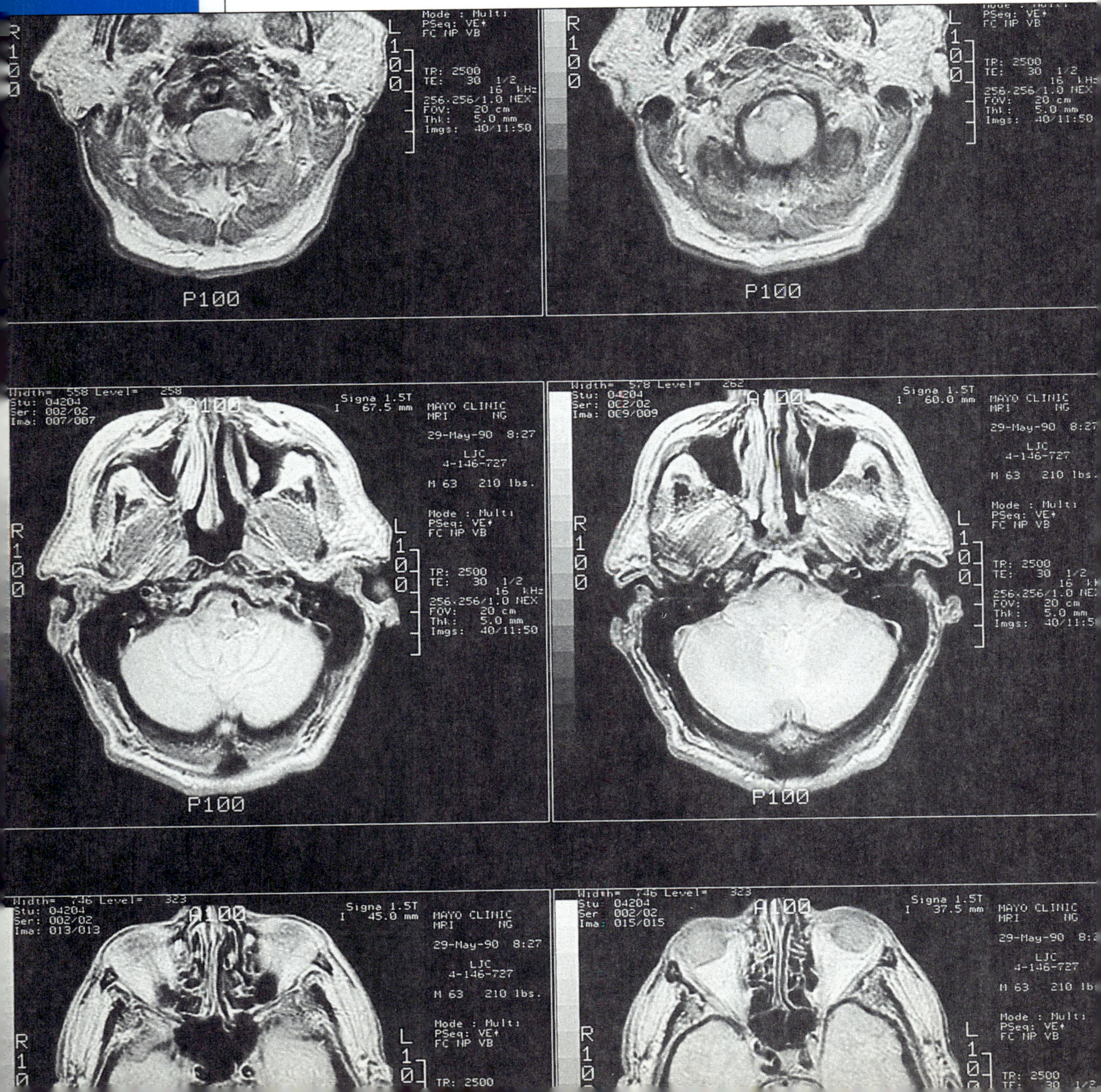

9

APPLICATION

Computerized Axial Tomography

Computerized axial tomography (CAT) is an imaging technique that uses x-rays combined with sophisticated computer algorithms. The CAT scanning machine is a doughnut-shaped machine with an x-ray tube that rotates around the patient and sends beams from all directions to a specific "slice" of the patient's body. For multiple images or slices, the patient is moved slowly through the machine. The computer algorithms translate the x-ray information into a detailed cross-sectional picture of each of the body regions scanned. The clarity of the CAT scan images has eliminated most exploratory surgery, and the images are used for evaluating problems that affect the brain, as well as abdominal problems and certain skeletal problems. (See Section 9-7 for the solution to a problem related to this application.)

Introduction

In previous chapters, we used files extensively. For example, READ* and PRINT* statements referred to input and output files connected to a terminal screen (or a line printer). Using the OPEN statement introduced in Chapter 4, we also connected other data files called *external files* because they are external to the memory area reserved by our program.

In this chapter we discuss additional techniques and FORTRAN statements for working with data files. In most of these techniques, formatted input statements are desirable, so we first discuss formatted READ statements. We then present three new types of files—internal files, sequential files, and direct-access files.

Internal files are really character strings that can be read as if they were data contained in a data file. Sequential files and direct-access files are additional types of external files that are connected to devices such as magnetic tape drives or magnetic disk drives; on these devices, files have special properties that determine the types of statements used to process them. We use the term *record* to describe a unit of information in the file; in a data file, one line represents a record. Each record contains *fields* of information. For instance, a payroll file contains individual payroll records, and each record could contain fields such as a name, hours worked, and hourly rate.

Sequential access of a file involves processing records from the physical beginning of the file. Throughout this text, we have used this type of access. We read the first data line, then the second data line, and so on. In *direct access*, information is not necessarily accessed in its physical order. We may reference the tenth record, then the last record, and then the second record, all without reading the records in between. This type of access is also called *random access* because we can access the records in random order.

External files are often used because they are *portable*—they can be used not only on another computer of the same manufacturer but also on computers made by different manufacturers. For example, a magnetic tape file created on a Digital Equipment Corporation VAX computer can be read on a Sun computer. But for these files to be portable, standard procedures must be observed when creating and using them; for example, because list-directed input and output are system dependent with regard to the formats used, all input and output stored on external devices must use formats to guarantee consistency from one computer to another.

9·1 Formatted READ Statements

To specify the columns to be used in reading data from a data file (specified by a unit number), we use a formatted READ statement. The general form is

READ *(unit number,k) variable list*

The variable list determines the order in which new values are stored, and *k* is a format reference number that refers to the FORMAT statement that describes the positions to be read. A typical READ/FORMAT combination to read information from a data file is

```
   READ (10,5) X, Y
 5 FORMAT (F5.1,2X,F6.1)
```

The form of the FORMAT appears the same as that used with PRINT statements; even the specifications look familiar. There are, however, differences between the specifications used for reading data values and those used for writing data values. Also, no carriage control is needed with READ statements. Each READ statement begins reading at column 1 of a new data line. The new values must agree in type with the variables in the list.

We now look at several specifications individually, as we did for the PRINT statement specifications. The D format is not discussed separately since it is so similar to the E format.

■ X Specification

The X specification skips positions on the data line. Its general form is nX, where n represents the number of positions to skip; thus, we can skip over unnecessary values without storing them in variables.

■ I Specification

The I specification is required when reading a value into an integer variable. The form of this specification is Iw, where w represents the number of positions to use from the data line. Any blanks in the w positions will be interpreted as zeros. Any characters besides numbers, plus or minus signs, and blanks will cause an execution error. Thus, 5.0 cannot be read with an I3 specification; but $_{bb}$5 will be read correctly with an I3 specification.

MEAN and NORM ◀ Example 9-1

Read the values of the variables MEAN and NORM from a data line. MEAN is in columns 1–4 and NORM is in columns 10 and 11.

Correct Solution

FORTRAN Statements

```
   READ (10,1) MEAN, NORM
 1 FORMAT (I4,5X,I2)
```

Data Line

$_b123_{bbbbb}10_b$

Computer Memory

MEAN [123]

NORM [10]

The first four columns, b123, are used to assign a value to MEAN. The first blank is interpreted as a zero; thus 0123 is stored in MEAN. We then skip the next five columns. From columns 10 and 11, we pick up the value 10 for NORM.

Incorrect Solution

FORTRAN Statements

```
READ (10,2) MEAN, NORM
2 FORMAT (1X,I4,5X,I2)
```

Data Line

b123bbbbb10b

Computer Memory

MEAN [1230]

NORM [0]

If carriage control is used with READ statements, incorrect values may be stored in memory. In this example, we skip the first column and use the next four columns for determining the value of MEAN. These columns contain 123_b, which is interpreted as 1230. We then skip five columns, and use the next two columns for determining the value of NORM. The contents 0_b will be interpreted as 0. ◀

■ F Specification

The F specification is used to read a value for a real variable. The form of this specification is Fw.d, where w represents the total number of positions to use from the data line and d represents the number of decimal positions. As with the I specification, any blanks in the w positions will be interpreted as zeros. If a decimal point is included in the w positions, the value will be stored as it was entered, regardless of what value has been given to d. Thus, if a real value DIST is read with an F4.1 specification and the four characters are 1.26, the value of DIST is 1.26. If there is no decimal point within the specified positions, the value of d is used to position a decimal place before storing the value. Thus, if the characters 1246 are read with an F4.1 specification, the value stored is 124.6, a value with one decimal position. Note that printing this value would require an F5.1 specification; the same specification will therefore not always work for both input and output.

TIME and TEMP

Example 9-2

Read two variables, TIME and TEMP. TIME will be in columns 10–13, with two decimal positions, and TEMP will be in columns 16–18, with one decimal position.

Solution

FORTRAN Statements

```
    READ (8,200) TIME, TEMP
200 FORMAT (9X,F4.2,2X,F3.1)
```

Data Line

```
bbbbbbbbb4.66bb125
```

Computer Memory

TIME	4.66
TEMP	12.5

Because there was no decimal point in the TEMP field, which was read with F3.1, one was positioned in the three numbers so that one position was a decimal position.

E Specification

The E specification is used in a READ/FORMAT combination when a variable is entered in an E format, or exponential form. The general form is Ew.d, where w represents the total number of positions that are being considered and d represents the number of decimal positions when the value is expressed in exponential form. If a decimal point is included, its placement will override the value of d. If no decimal point is included, one is located, according to d, before storing the value. It is not necessary that the width be at least seven positions greater than the number of decimal positions (as is necessary for output with an E format).

For READ statements, the E format will accept many forms of input. The following list shows some of the different ways in which the value 1.26 can be entered in a field read with E9.2. Note that the data can even be in an F specification form.

Data Line	Value Stored
0.126Eb01	1.26
1.26bEb00	1.26
1.26bbbbb	1.26
12.60E-01	1.26
bbb.126E1	1.26
bbbbbb126	1.26

Remember that the system will use two positions for the exponent if they are available. Thus `bbb.126E1` will be interpreted as 1.26, but `bb.126E1b` will be interpreted as `bb.126E10`, or 0.126×10^{10}.

Example 9-3

Job Number and Computer Time

Read two values. The first value, in columns 2–6, represents an integer job number assigned to a computer run. The second value, in columns 10–16, represents the number of computer seconds used to run the program. This computer time will be entered in an exponential form, with two decimal places.

Solution

FORTRAN Statements

```
   READ (7,10) NUM, CTIME
10 FORMAT (1X,I5,3X,E7.2)
```

Data Line

```
b13034bbb.36E-02
```

Computer Memory

NUM	13034
CTIME	0.0036

A Specification

The A specification is used to read character information. Its general form is Aw, where w represents the number of positions to read. The character information should not be enclosed in quote marks, as was required for list-directed character input.

Example 9-4

Nutrition Research Results

A research scientist performed nutrition tests using three animals. Data on each animal includes an identification number, the weight of the animal at the beginning of the experiment, and the weight of the animal at the end of the experiment. This data is stored in a data file called TEST1, and the data values for each animal are on a separate line: the integer identification number in columns 1–5, the initial weight in columns 10–14, and the final weight in columns 15–18. Both weights have one decimal position. Write a complete program to read this information and print a report. The report is to include both the original information and the percentage increase in weight for each test animal.

Solution

The decomposition is only a single step.

Decomposition

Generate report.

In the refinement, the report generation step becomes a loop that reads the data for each animal, then computes and prints the corresponding data line.

Pseudocode

```
Resrch: Print headers
        For i=1 to 3 do
            Read ID, initial weight, final weight
            percent increase ← (final − initial)/initial · 100
            Print ID, initial, final, percent increase
```

Converting the pseudocode into a FORTRAN program gives the following:

FORTRAN Program

```
*-----------------------------------------------------------------------*
      PROGRAM RESRCH
*
*  This program prints a report on the results of
*  an experiment involving three test animals.
*
      INTEGER I, ID
      REAL IWT, FWT, PERC
*
      OPEN (UNIT=10,FILE='TEST1',STATUS='OLD')
*
      PRINT 5
    5 FORMAT (1X,'TEST RESULTS'//,
     +        1X,'NUMBER INITIAL WT  FINAL WT  PERCENTAGE INCREASE')
*
      DO 25 I=1,3
*
         READ (10,15) ID, IWT, FWT
   15    FORMAT (I5,4X,F5.1,F5.1)
*
         PERC = (FWT - IWT)/IWT*100.0
*
         PRINT 20, ID, IWT, FWT, PERC
   20    FORMAT (1X,I4,5X,F5.1,6X,F5.1,6X,F10.5)
*
   25 CONTINUE
*
      END
*-----------------------------------------------------------------
```

A sample data file and its corresponding output are:

Data File

```
bbb10bbbbbb5.3bb6.2

bbb11bbbbbb5.2bb5.2

bbb12bbbbbb5.3bb5.1
```

Computer Output

```
TEST RESULTS

NUMBER INITIAL WT  FINAL WT  PERCENTAGE INCREASE
  10        5.3        6.2         16.98112
  11        5.2        5.2          0.00000
  12        5.3        5.1         -3.77359
```

9·2 ■ Internal Files

When the unit number in an input or output statement is the name of a character variable, the statement transfers data from one internal storage area to another. These storage areas are called *internal files*. For instance, we can read data from a character string instead of a data line; the input and output statements function exactly as if the contents of the character string were actually entered in a data line, as shown:

```
CHARACTER*13 DATA1
DATA1 = '127 65  42.17'
READ (DATA1,*) I, J, X
```

After execution, the value of I is 127, the value of J is 65, and the value of X is 42.17.

The internal file feature is useful if you want to perform some type of editing on the data before using it. For example, suppose you are reading information from a data file that contains amounts entered with dollar signs to the left of the amounts. If the fields are read directly into real variables, execution errors occur. Using internal files, you can read the data into a character string, edit the data by changing all dollar signs to blanks, and then read the number values from the modified character string. The following statements read a character string from a data line, change a leading dollar sign to a blank, and then read the value into a real variable.

```
  INTEGER PTR
  REAL AMOUNT
  CHARACTER*10 TEMP
  .
  .
  .
  READ (12,5) TEMP
5 FORMAT (A10)
  IF (INDEX(TEMP,'$').NE.0) THEN
     PTR = INDEX(TEMP,'$')
     TEMP(PTR:PTR) = ' '
  END IF
  READ (TEMP,*) AMOUNT
```

A similar use of internal files is beneficial if you want to edit lines of an output report before printing. For example, you might want to insert dollar signs next to real values to be printed; with internal files, you can insert the dollar sign next to the digits, as in `bbb$146.21`, instead of next to the output field, as in `$bbb146.21`.

9·3 ■ Sequential Files

Sequential files are typically built by one program and then accessed by other programs. Once a sequential file is created, individual records cannot be updated. When changes need to be made to the information, the updating is usually done by reading the information in a record, updating it if desired, and then writing the information to an output record. The process is repeated for each record in the file. Sometimes this technique is referred to as *father-son updating.* (The original file is the father file, and the updated file is the son.)

When we use sequential files, the same READ and WRITE statements are used, but other statements may also be needed: an extended form of the OPEN statement and statements to close the file, to reposition the record pointer to the first record in the file, to backspace one record in the file, and to add an end-of-file indicator to a new file.

■ Open Statement

The OPEN statement connects an external file to a program. The OPEN statement is executable but typically is placed at the beginning of the program because it should generally be executed only once. A simplified form of the OPEN statement was introduced in Chapter 4. The complete form of the OPEN statement is

```
OPEN (UNIT=integer expression,
      FILE=character expression,
      ACCESS=character expression,
      STATUS=character expression,
      FORM=character expression,
      IOSTAT=integer variable,
      RECL=integer expression,
      BLANK=character expression,
      ERR=integer statement reference)
```

UNIT Number The integer expression in this specification is usually a constant. This value is used in READ or WRITE statements to specify the file to be used. The following example illustrates the use of unit number 13 to open the file DIST and write information into it with a WRITE statement:

```
   OPEN (UNIT=13,FILE='DIST',STATUS='NEW')
   WRITE (13,10) X, Y
10 FORMAT (F8.3,F5.1)
```

FILE The character expression in this file specification is the name of the file; all references to the file must use the same name. Filenames typically consist of 1–6

alphabetic letters or numbers, with an alphabetic letter as the first character, and may include a file extension, as in EXPER1.DAT.

ACCESS The character string in this specification must be either 'SEQUENTIAL' or 'DIRECT'. If this specification is omitted, 'SEQUENTIAL' is assumed.

STATUS The character string in this specification must be 'NEW', 'OLD', or 'SCRATCH'. 'NEW' specifies that the file is being created with WRITE statements. 'OLD' specifies that the file is already built and its records are accessed with READ statements. 'SCRATCH' specifies that the file is an output file that is not being used after the program has been executed; hence, it will be deleted.

FORM The character string in this specification must be either 'FORMATTED' or 'UNFORMATTED'. A FORMATTED file uses either formatted READ and WRITE statements or list-directed input/output statements. All examples used in this text have been formatted. UNFORMATTED input/output is used for transfer of data with no data conversion; the data is transferred as binary strings, not as numbers or characters. One of the main uses of UNFORMATTED input/output is to transfer tape or disk data to another tape or disk file. If this specification is omitted, the default is 'FORMATTED' for sequential files and 'UNFORMATTED' for direct files.

IOSTAT The IOSTAT specification is not required but can be used to provide error recovery. If no errors occur in attaching the specified file to the program, the value of the integer variable is zero. If an error occurs, such as when an input file with the proper name is not found, a value specified by the computer system is stored in the variable. You can test this variable in your program and specify what action is to be taken if it is nonzero. In this next example, an error in opening the file causes IERR to be nonzero. An error message can be printed, and execution then continues. If the IOSTAT specification were not used and an error occurred in opening the file, execution would be terminated with an execution error.

```
OPEN (UNIT=15,FILE='XYDATA',STATUS='OLD',IOSTAT=IERR)
IF (IERR.NE.0) PRINT*, IERR
```

The IOSTAT specification can also be used with READ and WRITE statements.

RECL The RECL specification is required for direct-access files and specifies the record length. It is not used with sequential-access files. This specification is discussed further in Section 9–6.

BLANK The character string in this specification must be either 'NULL' or 'ZERO' and cannot be used with unformatted files. If the specification is 'NULL', blanks are usually ignored in numeric fields, but this is system dependent; if the specification is 'ZERO', blanks are assumed to be zeros in numeric fields. If the specification is omitted, 'NULL' is assumed.

ERR This specification is optional and provides error recovery. If an error occurs during execution of a statement that contains this ERR specification, control passes to the statement referenced by this specification instead of causing an execution error. The ERR specification can also be used with READ and WRITE statements.

■ Close Statement

The CLOSE statement is an executable statement that disconnects a file from a program. Its general form is

```
CLOSE (UNIT=integer expression,
       STATUS=character expression,
       IOSTAT=integer variable,
       ERR=integer statement reference)
```

The CLOSE statement is optional because all files are closed automatically upon termination of a program. The STATUS, IOSTAT, and ERR specifications are also optional. The STATUS specification options for the CLOSE statement are not the same as for the OPEN statement. When a file is closed, the default option is 'KEEP', which indicates that the file is to be kept. The option 'DELETE' may be chosen to indicate that the file is no longer needed and should be deleted.

■ Rewind Statement

The REWIND statement is an executable statement that repositions a sequential file at the first record of the file. Its general form is

```
REWIND (UNIT=integer expression,
        IOSTAT=integer variable,
        ERR=integer statement reference)
```

Some systems require a REWIND statement before reading an input file.

■ Backspace Statement

The BACKSPACE statement is an executable statement that repositions a sequential file to the last record read; thus, it backs up one record in the file. Its general form is

```
BACKSPACE (UNIT=integer expression,
           IOSTAT=integer variable,
           ERR=integer statement reference)
```

■ Endfile Statement

When a sequential file is being built, a special end-of-file record must be written to specify the end of the file. This special record is written when the ENDFILE statement is executed. The general form of the executable ENDFILE statement is

```
ENDFILE (UNIT=integer expression,
         IOSTAT=integer variable,
         ERR=integer statement reference)
```

The CLOSE statement automatically performs this function on most systems.

SELF-TEST 9-1

This self-test allows you to check quickly to see if you have remembered some of the key points from Section 9–3. If you have any problems with the exercise, you should reread this section. The solution is included at the end of the text.

1. Write a program to count and print the number of records in files DATA1 and DATA2. Assume that each file is sequential and each record contains two real values in the following format:

   ```
   FORMAT (F6.2,1X,F6.2)
   ```

   If an error occurs in opening either file, print an error message instead of the number of records.

9-4 Application ▪ Voyager Spacecraft Data Analysis

Electrical Engineering

The pictures of Saturn sent back by Voyager II were spectacular. However, these pictures were not discernible by the human eye because they were transmitted as a long string of numbers or digital intensities that had to be processed and reassembled to compose the pictures that we saw. In this application we will write a program to perform a simple type of digital image processing called edge detection, where an edge detector distinguishes between the different surfaces in a two-dimensional image.

In the program, we will assume that we have a data file similar to that which might have been sent by Voyager II. Although it takes a very sophisticated procedure to recreate the original image, you can often determine the major features of the image by locating major differences in the digital intensities. If a large difference occurs between the intensities represented by the data points, an edge has been encountered. The actual calculation to determine if an edge has been encountered is performed as follows (assuming that we are trying to determine if point P5 is part of an edge):

P1	P2	P3
P4	P5	P6
P7	P8	P9

$$\text{DIF} = \frac{|P5 - P2| + |P5 - P4| + |P5 - P6| + |P5 - P8|}{4}$$

If DIF (which is the average difference between P5 and its neighboring intensities) is greater than some specified threshold, such as 1.25, you may have detected an edge. The threshold may be changed depending on the amount of detail you wish to have in your reconstructed image.

Assume that the image intensities are represented by integers from 0 to 9, with 0 representing white and 9 representing black and the integers in between representing shades of gray. Furthermore, assume that the spacecraft camera converts its images into two-dimensional information with a maximum of 50 values per line and a maximum of 40 lines. The number of values per line and the number of lines per image depend on the resolution desired for the particular image. The data is sent back to earth in streams of integers that are stored one row per line in a data file. Each image is preceded by a line that gives an identification number for the image and the number of rows and the number of columns in that image. In order to store the information efficiently, no blanks or commas are used between the integers that represent the intensities, or shades of gray, in the image; therefore, this information will need to be read with a formatted READ statement. A trailer line in the file will contain an identification number of 9999 followed by two zero values.

The output from your program is to be a picture of the edges in a specified image. Thus, at each point in the image that corresponds to an edge, print the symbol #; at each point in the image that is not an edge, print a period. Allow the user to enter the threshold for edge detection.

The program should ask the user for the name of the data file to be used by the program. Since there might be many images stored in the same data file, the program should first scan the file and print the identification and size of all images in the file. Because there might be many images, it is not feasible to store them all in memory as you read them; only print the identification and size of the images. Then, ask the user which image is to be analyzed and the threshold to be used. After reading this information from the terminal, rewind the file and locate the desired image. Read the image data into an array and perform the edge analysis using the threshold specified by the user.

1. Problem Statement

Write a program to read a two-dimensional image from a data file. The program should determine the location of edges in the file and print the edge image.

2. Input/Output Description

Input—the name of the data file with the images will be entered by the user, along with the identification number of the image to be used

Output—a list of the identification numbers and sizes of all images in the file, and an edge image from the image selected by the user

3. Hand Example

We will use a small image for our example. Consider the following two-dimensional array of intensities:

3	7	8	8	8	7
4	5	7	8	8	6
4	5	5	5	5	6
4	4	4	5	6	6

In general, we assume that points on the top, bottom, and sides of the array are not edges because we do not have complete data on these points. Therefore, we consider only "interior" points in our analysis. Call the array *P*. Then for the point in *P*(2,2) we compute the difference DIF to be the following:

$$\text{DIF} = (|5 - 7| + |5 - 4| + |5 - 7| + |5 - 5|) /4 = 1.25$$

If our threshold is 1.25 or below, *P*(2,2) corresponds to an edge; otherwise, it is not an edge. If we generate an image with the symbol #, using a threshold of 0.9, our image is the following:

```
.  .  .  .  .  .
.  #  #  #  #  .
.  .  .  .  #  .
.  .  .  .  .  .
```

4. Algorithm Development

Decomposition

Read file name.
Read desired intensity data.
Determine and print edge information.

Pseudocode

```
Voyage: Read filename
        Print a list of all images in file
        Read desired intensity data
        Read threshold
        Determine edge information
        Print edge information
```

The step to produce the list of images in the file will require reading and printing the identification and size of an image, reading past its image data, reading and printing the identification and size of the next image, and so on until we reach the identification number of 9999. Since we know that each line of an image starts on a new line in the file, we have to read only the first value of the line as we skim through the file looking for the next image. We need the complete data only for the image that we are going to analyze.

As we convert the pseudocode to FORTRAN, we want to ask ourselves if any of the steps involved should be implemented as functions or subroutines. The step to determine the edge information is one that is a good candidate for a subroutine because it involves a number of steps that will make our program longer and harder to read if we include them in the main program. The structure chart for this program is

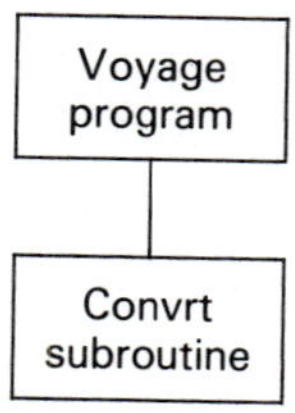

FORTRAN Program

```
*-----------------------------------------------------------------------*
      PROGRAM VOYAGE
*
*  This program opens a user-specified file and prints information
*  on the images in the file.  The user selects an image, and the
*  program prints an edge image for a specified tolerance.
*
      INTEGER ID, NR, NC, I, IMAGE(40,50), J, NEWID
      REAL LIMIT
      CHARACTER FILENM*6, EDGE(40)*50
      LOGICAL DONE
*
      PRINT*, 'ENTER NAME OF IMAGE FILE ENCLOSED IN QUOTES'
      READ*, FILENM
      OPEN (UNIT=8,FILE=FILENM,STATUS='OLD')
*
      PRINT*
      PRINT*,'IMAGES IN THIS FILE'
      READ (8,*) ID, NR, NC
*
```

```
    5 IF (ID.NE.9999) THEN
*
         PRINT 10, ID, NR, NC
   10    FORMAT (1X,'ID = ',I4,' SIZE = (',I2,',',I2,')')
*
         DO 20 I=1,NR
            READ (8,15) IMAGE(I,1)
   15       FORMAT (50I1)
   20    CONTINUE
*
         READ (8,*) ID, NR, NC
         GO TO 5
*
      END IF
*
      PRINT*
      PRINT*, 'ENTER ID OF IMAGE TO BE ANALYZED'
      READ*, NEWID
      PRINT*, 'ENTER THRESHOLD FOR EDGE DETECTION'
      READ*, LIMIT
*
      REWIND (UNIT=8)
      READ (8,*) ID, NR, NC
      DONE = .FALSE.
*
   25 IF (.NOT.DONE) THEN
*
         IF (ID.EQ.NEWID) THEN
*
            DO 30 I=1,NR
               READ (8,15) (IMAGE(I,J),J=1,NC)
   30       CONTINUE
            CALL CONVRT(LIMIT,IMAGE,EDGE,NR,NC)
            PRINT 35, LIMIT
   35       FORMAT (/1X,'THRESHOLD VALUE = ',F5.2/)
            DO 45 I=1,NR
               PRINT 40, EDGE(I)(1:NC)
   40          FORMAT (1X,A)
   45       CONTINUE
            DONE = .TRUE.
*
         ELSE IF (ID.EQ.9999) THEN
*
            DONE = .TRUE.
            PRINT*, 'IMAGE NOT FOUND'
*
         ELSE
*
            DO 50 I=1,NR
               READ (8,15) IMAGE(I,1)
   50       CONTINUE
            READ (8,*) ID, NR, NC
*
         END IF
         GO TO 25
*
      END IF
*
      END
*-----------------------------------------------------------------------------*
```

```
      SUBROUTINE CONVRT(LIMIT,IMAGE,EDGE,NR,NC)
*
*  This subroutine converts a two-dimensional image to a
*  character array containing edge information.
*
      INTEGER IMAGE(40,50), I, J, NR, NC
      REAL LIMIT, DIF
      CHARACTER EDGE(40)*50
*
      DO 5 J=1,NC
         EDGE(1)(J:J) = '.'
    5 CONTINUE
*
      DO 20 I=2,NR-1
         EDGE(I)(1:1) = '.'
         DO 15 J=2,NC-1
            DIF = (ABS(IMAGE(I-1,J)-IMAGE(I,J)) +
     +             ABS(IMAGE(I,J-1)-IMAGE(I,J)) +
     +             ABS(IMAGE(I,J+1)-IMAGE(I,J)) +
     +             ABS(IMAGE(I+1,J)-IMAGE(I,J)))/4.0
            IF (DIF.GT.LIMIT) THEN
               EDGE(I)(J:J) = '#'
            ELSE
               EDGE(I)(J:J) = '.'
            END IF
   15    CONTINUE
         EDGE(I)(NC:NC) = '.'
   20 CONTINUE
*
      DO 25 J=1,NC
         EDGE(NR)(J:J) = '.'
   25 CONTINUE
*
      RETURN
      END
*-----------------------------------------------------------------*
```

Note that the first DO loop in the subroutine fills the top row of the image with periods and that the last DO loop in the subroutine fills the bottom row of the image with periods. The first statement of the DO 20 loop fills the left side of the other rows with a period, and the last statement of the DO 20 loop fills the right side of the other rows with a period.

5. Testing

The following data file called IMAGES was used to test the edge detection program.

```
87 4 6
378887
457886
455556
444566
25 12 28
1111111111111111311111111331
1333111111111111131111111311
1111311111111111113311111131
1111131111111111111133111113
1111131111111111111111311111
1111113111111111111111411111
1111114111111111111111311111
1111111311111111111111131111
1111111311111111111111113111
1111111131111111111111111311
1111111113111111111111113111
1111111113111111111111111111
34 5 5
22435
22444
23334
24244
24333
9999 0 0
```

The output from the program is shown below:

```
ENTER NAME OF IMAGE FILE ENCLOSED IN QUOTES
'IMAGES'

IMAGES IN THIS FILE
ID =    87 SIZE = ( 4, 6)
ID =    25 SIZE = (12,28)
ID =    34 SIZE = ( 5, 5)

ENTER ID OF IMAGE TO BE ANALYZED
25
ENTER THRESHOLD FOR EDGE DETECTION
1.0

THRESHOLD VALUE =  1.00

............................
.#.#.............#.......##.
....#.............##......#.
.....#..............##......
.....#................#.....
......#...............#.....
......##..............#.....
......##...............#....
.......#................#...
........#...............##..
.........#..............#...
............................
```

Biology

Several operations are commonly encountered as we process data. For instance, we have seen a number of applications that use sorting algorithms. Other operations frequently used include finding the minimum value or maximum value in a set of data, computing the average value in a set of data, inserting or deleting values in a list, and searching for a value in a list.

In this application, we use the *merge* operation, which is the combining of an ordered list (the current whooping crane migration information) with another list that preserves the same order (the new sightings information). We assume that we are merging only two lists.

Assume that arrays A and B have each been sorted into ascending order, as shown:

Array A
1
5
8
25
92

Array B
7
15
19
106

If these arrays are merged into an array C, the result is

Array C
1
5
7
8
15
19
25
92
106

Note that array C is larger than either array A or B; in fact, if array A contains N elements and array B contains M elements, array C should contain $N + M$ elements.

Data to be merged must have some order, such as ascending or descending. Alphabetical data can also be merged. In either case, what should you do about items that appear in both lists? Should the duplicate item appear once or twice in the merged list?

The answer depends on the application. If the merged data represents an alphabetical mailing list that has been put together from several sources, we would not want to duplicate a name on both lists. However, if we are merging bank transactions that are received in the mail with transactions processed at the teller windows, we would want to keep transactions with the same account number because they represent different transactions. Therefore, a specific requirement on how to handle duplicates must be included in the problem statement for a problem that includes a merging operation.

In this application, we want to print this information in the order of the sightings, which requires merging the master file with new sightings information received by the Wildlife Service. Assume that each sighting record contains the following information:

Sighting date (month, day, year)
Sighting time (time using a 24-hour clock)
Grid location (2 integer coordinates)
Number of birds

We assume that the data in the master file CRANES is stored as a series of integers (month, day, year, time, gridl, grid2, and birds) with the following format:

```
FORMAT (3I2,1X,I4,1X,2I2,1X,I4)
```

The new sightings information in the file SIGHTS is stored in the same format.

1. Problem Statement

Write a program to merge data in two files: the current whooping crane migration information file with the new sightings information file.

2. Input/Output Description

Input — a data file CRANES that contains the sightings information in ascending order by date and time, and a data file SIGHTS that has new information

Output — an updated CRANES file and an ordered listing of the sightings information

3. Hand Example

For a hand-worked example, we use the following data for the master file and the file of new sightings information:

Master File CRANES

Date	Time	Grid	Number of Birds
040392	0920	21 07	5
040892	0830	21 07	4
050192	1805	22 08	4
051092	0915	22 09	4
051592	0730	23 07	5

Update File SIGHTS

040592	0815	21 09	4
051092	0800	22 09	4

If we merge these files by the date and time, the migration file CRANES and the corresponding report should contain the following information:

```
WHOOPING CRANE MIGRATION

CURRENT SIGHTINGS

04-03-92     0920
     GRID LOCATION:  21  7
     NUMBER OF BIRDS      5

04-05-92     0815
     GRID LOCATION:  21  9
     NUMBER OF BIRDS      4

04-08-92     0830
     GRID LOCATION:  21  7
     NUMBER OF BIRDS      4

05-01-92     1805
     GRID LOCATION:  22  8
     NUMBER OF BIRDS      4

05-10-92     0800
     GRID LOCATION:  22  9
     NUMBER OF BIRDS      4

05-10-92     0915
     GRID LOCATION:  22  9
     NUMBER OF BIRDS      4

05-15-92     0730
     GRID LOCATION:  23  7
     NUMBER OF BIRDS      5
```

Note that we may need to use part or all of the values for year, month, day, and time to order the sightings correctly.

4. Algorithm Development

The general steps in the algorithm are simple to list. We want to merge the two data files, generate a new master file, and print the contents of the master file.

Decomposition

Merge sightings file and master file into new master file.
Print the data in the new master file.

We now need to develop an algorithm for merging two lists. One algorithm might be to move one list (with M elements) into the first part of a larger array with $M + N$ elements and then move the other array (with N elements) into the last part of the larger array. We could sort the large array and have the data items in the desired order. This idea could be extended to three or more lists. However, there are two reasons why this is not a good algorithm. It is inefficient because each individual array or list is already sorted, and it requires that all the data to be merged reside in memory at one time, which is impractical with large files.

If we reexamine the hand-worked example, we see that we need only the next value on each list to determine which record should be moved to the output file: the record with the smaller date is moved to the output file, and the next record of that file is read. A trailer signal simplifies the algorithm's logic development because we do not need to worry about what to do when we reach the end of a data file while there are still records left in the other file. When we read a trailer record with 999999 as the date, it is larger than the other valid dates and thus forces the rest of the records to be moved to the output file until we are positioned at the trailer signal of each file. We then write a trailer signal to the output file.

We now try some simple data with this algorithm. Assume that we want to merge File 1 and File 2. Both files contain a trailer signal 999. The arrows point to the current record (the one we have just read for the input files or the one we have just written for output files).

File 1	File 2	Output File
→ 5	→ 2	
10	51	
82	999	
107		
999		

File 1	File 2	Output File
→ 5	2	→ 2
10	→ 51	
82	999	
107		
999		

File 1	File 2	Output File
5	2	2
→ 10	→ 51	→ 5
82	999	
107		
999		

File 1	File 2	Output File
5	2	2
10	→ 51	5
→ 82	999	→ 10
107		
999		

File 1	File 2	Output File
5	2	2
10	51	5
→ 82	→ 999	10
107		→ 51
999		

File 1	File 2	Output File
5	2	2
10	51	5
82	→ 999	10
→ 107		51
999		→ 82

File 1	File 2	Output File
5	2	2
10	51	5
82	→ 999	10
107		51
→ 999		82
		→ 107

File 1	File 2	Output File
5	2	2
10	51	5
82	→ 999	10
107		51
→ 999		82
		107
		→ 999

We develop the pseudocode for the merge separately and then add it to the pseudocode for the whooping crane migration algorithm. We assume that a merge of two files is always sufficient. If you have three files to merge, merge two of them and then merge the combined file with the third file. If you have more than three files, continue merging two at a time until you have combined them all.

Merge Pseudocode

```
Merge: Read first record in both files
       While more data do
             Write information from file with smaller code
             Read new information from file with smaller code
       Write trailer signal
```

We now return to our whooping crane migration problem and include the steps for the merge.

Pseudocode

```
Migrat: Read first master record
        Read first update record
        While more data do
              If update date < master date then
                    Write update record
                    Read new update record
              else
                    Write master record
                    Read new master record
        Write trailer signal
        Copy merged file to master file and print report
```

Because we are reading data that represents the same types of information from both files, we would like to choose names that indicate which file contained the data. Thus, for the day from the file CRANES, we use the variable CDA; for the day from the file SIGHTS, we use the variable SDA. When we copy the output file back into the file CRANES, we use the variable DA because it is not being compared to other variables.

Before we convert the refined pseudocode into FORTRAN, we need to discuss one more item in the algorithm. We compare the date from one record with the date in another record to determine which date occurred first. This comparison first involves comparing the years. If the years are equal, we compare the months. If the months are equal, we compare the days. If the days are equal, we compare the times. This process is easy to understand, but it is cumbersome to translate into FORTRAN. Thus, we use a statement function to recombine the month, day, year, and time into a number that can make all the comparisons simultaneously; for example, if month = 09, day = 25, year = 92, and time = 0845, we create a number equal to the value 9209250845. If we compare another date in this new form, we need only one comparison to determine which date occurred first. This new number that we compute cannot be an integer because its value is typically greater than the maximum integer in many computers (approximately 2 billion for a VAX computer). We also cannot use a real number because we need 10 digits of precision. Thus, we must use a double-precision number to store the number that combines the year, month, day, and time information.

FORTRAN Program

```
*-----------------------------------------------------------------------*
      PROGRAM MIGRAT
*
*  This program merges new sighting information into the
*  master file of migration information on whooping cranes.
*
      INTEGER M,D,Y,T,MO,DA,YR,TIME,GRID1,GRID2,BIRDS,
     +        SMO,SDA,SYR,STIME,SGRID1,SGRID2,SBIRDS,
     +        CMO,CDA,CYR,CTIME,CGRID1,CGRID2,CBIRDS
      LOGICAL DONE
      DOUBLE PRECISION DATE, CDATE, SDATE
*
      DATE(M,D,Y,T) = DBLE(REAL(Y)*1.0D08) +
     +                DBLE(REAL(M)*1.0D06) +
     +                DBLE(REAL(D)*1.0D04) +
     +                DBLE(REAL(T))
*
      OPEN (UNIT=10,FILE='SIGHTS',STATUS='OLD')
      OPEN (UNIT=11,FILE='CRANES',STATUS='OLD')
      OPEN (UNIT=12,FILE='TEMP',STATUS='NEW')
*
      READ (10,5) SMO,SDA,SYR,STIME,SGRID1,SGRID2,SBIRDS
    5 FORMAT (3I2,1X,I4,1X,2I2,1X,I4)
      READ (11,5) CMO,CDA,CYR,CTIME,CGRID1,CGRID2,CBIRDS
*
      SDATE = DATE(SMO,SDA,SYR,STIME)
      CDATE = DATE(CMO,CDA,CYR,CTIME)
      IF (SMO.EQ.99.AND.CMO.EQ.99) THEN
         DONE = .TRUE.
      ELSE
         DONE = .FALSE.
      END IF
*
   10 IF (.NOT.DONE) THEN
*
         IF (CDATE.LT.SDATE) THEN
*
            WRITE (12,5) CMO,CDA,CYR,CTIME,CGRID1,CGRID2,CBIRDS
            READ (11,5) CMO,CDA,CYR,CTIME,CGRID1,CGRID2,CBIRDS
            CDATE = DATE(CMO,CDA,CYR,CTIME)
*
         ELSE
*
            WRITE (12,5) SMO,SDA,SYR,STIME,SGRID1,SGRID2,SBIRDS
            READ (10,5) SMO,SDA,SYR,STIME,SGRID1,SGRID2,SBIRDS
            SDATE = DATE(SMO,SDA,SYR,STIME)
*
         END IF
*
         IF (SMO.EQ.99.AND.CMO.EQ.99) DONE = .TRUE.
*
         GO TO 10
      END IF
*
      WRITE (12,5) SMO,SDA,SYR,STIME,SGRID1,SGRID2,SBIRDS
      CLOSE (UNIT=11,STATUS='DELETE')
      CLOSE (UNIT=12)
*
      OPEN (UNIT=11,FILE='CRANES',STATUS='NEW')
      OPEN (UNIT=12,FILE='TEMP',STATUS='OLD')
```

```
      PRINT*, 'WHOOPING CRANE MIGRATION'
      PRINT*
      PRINT*, 'CURRENT SIGHTINGS'
      PRINT*
*
   15 READ (12,5,END=50) MO,DA,YR,TIME,GRID1,GRID2,BIRDS
         IF (MO.NE.99) THEN
            PRINT 20, MO,DA,YR,TIME
   20       FORMAT (1X,I2,'-',I2,'-',I2,4X,I4)
            PRINT 25, GRID1,GRID2
   25       FORMAT (1X,5X,'GRID LOCATION: ',2I3)
            PRINT 30, BIRDS
   30       FORMAT (1X,5X,'NUMBER OF BIRDS',1X,I5)
         END IF
         WRITE (11,5) MO,DA,YR,TIME,GRID1,GRID2,BIRDS
         GO TO 15
*
   50 STOP
      END
*-----------------------------------------------------------------------*
```

5. TESTING

If we use the data from the hand-worked example in this program, the output from our program is

```
WHOOPING CRANE MIGRATION

CURRENT SIGHTINGS

 4- 3-92     920
      GRID LOCATION:  21  7
      NUMBER OF BIRDS      5

 4- 5-92     815
      GRID LOCATION:  21  9
      NUMBER OF BIRDS      4

 4- 8-92     830
      GRID LOCATION:  21  7
      NUMBER OF BIRDS      4

 5- 1-92    1805
      GRID LOCATION:  22  8
      NUMBER OF BIRDS      4

 5-10-92     800
      GRID LOCATION:  22  9
      NUMBER OF BIRDS      4

 5-10-92     915
      GRID LOCATION:  22  9
      NUMBER OF BIRDS      4

 5-15-92     730
      GRID LOCATION:  23  7
      NUMBER OF BIRDS      5
```

Throughout this text, we have emphasized the importance of carefully selecting test data. If you look at the updates in this set of test data, you see that it includes data in an order that causes insertions to be made at two different points in the file. Also, the program is not thoroughly tested until the test data includes insertions that occur both at the beginning and at the end of the master file. Finally, because the date and time are involved in determining the correct order of the sightings, we include some sightings with the same date but different times to test this part of the program.

9·6 ■ Direct-Access Files

Records in direct-access files are not accessed sequentially; they are accessed in the order specified. You specify that you want to read the tenth record, then the second record, and so forth. (However, you could read them sequentially by specifying that you want to read the first record, then the second record, and so on.)

When a direct file is opened, the ACCESS specification in the OPEN statement must be set to 'DIRECT' and a record length must be given with the RECL specifier. The READ and WRITE statements must include a REC specification to give the record number of the record to be addressed. The general form of a direct-access READ or WRITE is

`READ` *(unit number,format reference,*`REC=`*integer expression) variable list*

`WRITE` *(unit number,format reference,*`REC=`*integer expression) variable list*

The integer expression on the REC specification is evaluated to give the record number to be accessed. The ERR and IOSTAT specifications may also be used with the direct-access READ or WRITE statement. The END option may be used only with the READ statement.

Applications that use direct files usually have an account number or identification number that is part of each record, which can be used as the record number. For example, student identification numbers in a university often start at 00001 and increase in steps of 1; thus, the information for student number 00210 could be stored in record 210. Sometimes a numerical computation is performed on a field in the record to yield its record number. Suppose an inventory file contains records for items with stock numbers 500 through 1000. If 499 is subtracted from the stock number, we have the record number for the record that stores information about that stock item. When the steps to convert a value into a record number for a direct file reference become more complicated, the steps are called a *hash code* and the value computed as the record number is often called a *key*.

A direct file is usually built by loading the information into the file sequentially, with the record number starting at 1 and increasing by 1 each time a new record is written. The file can be accessed in a sequential order by varying the record number from 1 through the total number of records. However, the real power of a direct file is apparent when we want to update information in some of its records. Instead of reading each record sequentially, looking for the one we want to update, we specify the record number and that record is accessed automatically. Once we have updated the information in that record, we can write that new information back into the record. Note that this is not father-son updating — we are actually updating information in the direct file itself, which can be considered a *master file*, because it contains all the updated information. If we specify a record number in a READ statement for a record that does not exist, an error occurs. To recover, the ERR specification can be included in the READ statement to provide a controlling branch to an error routine. These concepts are illustrated in Section 9-7.

SELF-TEST 9-2

This self-test allows you to check quickly to see if you have remembered some of the key points from Section 9-6. If you have any problems with the exercise, you should reread this section. The solution is included at the end of the text.

1. A direct-access file called STORES contains 100 records. Each record contains an item number that varies from 1 through 100 and is used as the record key. Each record also contains the number of items in the warehouse. The format of each record is

```
FORMAT (I5,2X,I5)
```

   Write a program to print the item number of all items in which the record indicates that there are more than 10 items in the warehouse.

9-7 Application ▪ CAT Scan Database

Biomedical Engineering

In this application, we develop a program to update a database that is used to keep track of the information on CAT scans that have been performed by a hospital. The database is a direct-access file so that information on specific scans can be easily retrieved. The file has the following record format:

Scan ID	Patient ID	Date Mo-Da-Yr	Scan Angle	Number of x-rays	File Reference

The scan ID is a numeric value that can range from 0001 to 9999, and it also serves as the direct-access file key. Patient ID is a numeric value that can range from 1000 to 5999. The date is three two-digit numbers, in the order month, day, year. The scan angle is the integer number of degrees in the CAT scan, where 360° represents a complete circle scan. The number of x-rays is related to the density of the portion of the body being scanned and the resolution desired in the CAT scan; more x-rays are needed for denser organs and for higher resolution images. The number of x-rays is a 4-digit integer. The file reference indicates the location of the original scans in case they are needed for reference; it is a 4-digit character string. The total record length is 25 characters and will appear as RECL = 25 in the OPEN statement.

Scans are often used for follow-up diagnosis or for evaluations related to ongoing research. Therefore, the scans may change location frequently. It is important that the database always contain the current location (file reference) of the scans. Therefore, at the end of each day, the database is updated with any changes in the scan locations. We assume that this update information has been stored in a sequential file, in the order in which the locations were changed. Assume that the last record in the update file contains a patient ID of −999. Write a program to update the scan locations in the master database file.

1. Problem Statement

Update the image locations in the CAT scan database file.

2. Input/Output Description

Input—the direct access database file and the sequential file with the new information

Output—the updated direct access database file

3. Hand Example

Assume that the master database file contains the following information:

Scan ID	Patient ID	Date Mo-Da-Yr	Scan Angle	Number of X-rays	File Reference
108	57	090592	360	500	GW21
109	192	090892	180	650	GA30
111	107	090892	360	2000	HC28
113	679	091192	270	850	JW54

Assume that the location information to be updated is the following:

Scan ID	File Reference
108	GW13
110	GA15
111	HC29

After adding this new information, the database should contain the following information:

Scan ID	Patient ID	Date Mo-Da-Yr	Scan Angle	Number of X-rays	File Reference
108	57	090592	360	500	GW13
109	192	090892	180	650	GA30
111	107	090892	360	2000	HC29
113	679	091192	270	850	JW54

Note that there was one update without a match in the master file. This situation should generate an error message in the program.

4. Algorithm Development

The steps used to solve this problem are straightforward, as shown in the following decomposition and pseudocode. The primary reason that this solution is simple is the power of direct-access file processing.

Decomposition

Read update records and then update the master file.

Pseudocode

```
Update: Read scan ID and location
        If scan ID = -999 then
            more ← false
        else
            more ← true
        While more do
            Read corresponding database record
            If no match then
                Print error message
            else
                Update database record
            Read next scan ID and location
            If scan ID = -999 then
                more ← false
```

The program for performing this update for a direct-access file follows.

FORTRAN Program

```
*-----------------------------------------------------------------------*
      PROGRAM UPDATE
*
*  This program updates the scan location in a database
*  containing information related to CAT scans.
*
      INTEGER SCANID, PATID, DATE, ANGLE, XRAYS, KEY
      LOGICAL MORE
      CHARACTER*4 REF, NEWLOC
*
      DATA MORE /.TRUE./
*
      OPEN (UNIT=10,FILE='CHANGE',ACCESS='SEQUENTIAL',
     +      STATUS='OLD',FORM='FORMATTED')
      OPEN (UNIT=11,FILE='SCANS',ACCESS='DIRECT',
     +      STATUS='OLD',FORM='FORMATTED',RECL=25)
*
      READ (10,5) KEY, NEWLOC
    5 FORMAT (I4,A4)
      IF (KEY.EQ.-999) MORE = .FALSE.
*
   10 IF (MORE) THEN
         READ (11,15,REC=KEY,ERR=20)
     +         SCANID, PATID, DATE, ANGLE, XRAYS, REF
   15    FORMAT (I4,I4,I6,I3,I4,A4)
         WRITE (11,15,REC=KEY) SCANID, PATID, DATE, ANGLE, XRAYS, NEWLOC
   20    IF (KEY.NE.SCANID) PRINT*, 'NO MATCH FOR', KEY
         READ (10,5) KEY, NEWLOC
         IF (KEY.EQ.-999) MORE = .FALSE.
         GO TO 10
      END IF
*
      END
*-----------------------------------------------------------------------*
```

5. Testing

Before you can test this program, you must create the direct-access master file and the formatted sequential update file. A program to build these files from data entered from the terminal follows. The program closes each file after it is built, reopens it as an input file, and prints the data. Generate the files with the initial set of data from the hand example, and then run the update program. After you are comfortable with the steps, develop some new test data.

FORTRAN Program

```
*-----------------------------------------------------------------------------------*
      PROGRAM CREATE
*
*  This program creates a direct file and a formatted sequential
*  file from terminal input data.
*
      INTEGER N, I, SCANID, PATID, DATE, ANGLE, XRAYS,
     +        HOLDID(100), TRAILN
      CHARACTER*4 REF, TRAILR
*
      OPEN (UNIT=9,FILE='SCANS',ACCESS='DIRECT',
     +      STATUS='NEW',FORM='FORMATTED',RECL=25)
      PRINT*, 'ENTER NUMBER OF RECORDS FOR MASTER FILE (MAX OF 100)'
      READ*, N
      DO 10 I=1,N
         PRINT*, 'ENTER SCAN ID, PATIENT ID'
         READ*, SCANID, PATID
         HOLDID(I) = SCANID
         PRINT*, 'ENTER 6-DIGIT DATE MODAYR'
         READ*, DATE
         PRINT*, 'ENTER ANGLE(DEGREES) AND NUMBER OF XRAYS'
         READ*, ANGLE, XRAYS
         PRINT*, 'ENTER 4-CHARACTER LOCATION IN QUOTES'
         READ*, REF
         WRITE (9,5,REC=SCANID) SCANID, PATID, DATE, ANGLE, XRAYS, REF
    5    FORMAT (I4,I4,I6,I3,I4,A4)
   10 CONTINUE
*
      CLOSE (UNIT=9)
      OPEN (UNIT=9,FILE='SCANS',ACCESS='DIRECT',
     +      STATUS='OLD',FORM='FORMATTED',RECL=25)
*
      PRINT*, 'MASTER SCAN FILE'
      DO 15 I=1,N
         READ (9,5,REC=HOLDID(I),ERR=12)
     +         SCANID, PATID, DATE, ANGLE, XRAYS, REF
         PRINT*, SCANID, PATID, DATE, ANGLE, XRAYS, REF
   12    IF (HOLDID(I).NE.SCANID) PRINT*, 'NO RECORD NUMBER', HOLDID(I)
   15 CONTINUE
*
      OPEN (UNIT=10,FILE='CHANGE',ACCESS='SEQUENTIAL',
     +      STATUS='NEW',FORM='FORMATTED')
      PRINT*, 'ENTER NUMBER OF RECORDS FOR UPDATE FILE'
      READ*, N
      DO 30 I=1,N
         PRINT*, 'ENTER SCAN ID'
         READ*, SCANID
         PRINT*, 'ENTER 4-CHARACTER NEW LOCATION IN QUOTES'
         READ*, REF
         WRITE (10,25) SCANID, REF
   25    FORMAT (I4,A4)
   30 CONTINUE
      TRAILN = -999
      TRAILR = 'END'
      WRITE (10,25) TRAILN, TRAILR
*
      CLOSE (UNIT=10)
      OPEN (UNIT=10,FILE='CHANGE',ACCESS='SEQUENTIAL',
     +      STATUS='OLD',FORM='FORMATTED')
*
```

```
      PRINT*, 'UPDATE FILE'
      DO 35 I=1,N
         READ (10,25) SCANID, REF
         PRINT*, SCANID, REF
   35 CONTINUE
*
      END
*----------------------------------------------------------------------*
```

9·8 ■ Inquire Statement

The final statement that we present for working with files is the INQUIRE statement. It has two general forms:

> INQUIRE (FILE=*character expression,inquiry specifier list*)

> INQUIRE (UNIT=*integer expression,inquiry specifier list*)

This executable statement acquires information about a file or a unit number. For example, suppose we are going to allow a user to enter the name of a data file to be used in a program, as we did in the edge detection program in Section 9–4. If the user enters the name of a file that does not exist, the program will terminate with an execution error. If we use the INQUIRE statement, we can determine whether the file exists, and if it does not exist, we can ask the user to enter a different file name. The following statements illustrate this type of interaction with the user:

```
      DONE = .FALSE.
      FOUND = .FALSE.
      PRINT*, 'ENTER FILE NAME OF IMAGE FILE IN QUOTES'
      READ*, FILENM
    5 IF (.NOT.DONE) THEN
         INQUIRE (FILE=FILENM,EXIST=THERE)
         IF (.NOT.THERE) THEN
            PRINT*, 'FILE DOES NOT EXIST'
            PRINT*, 'ENTER NEW FILE NAME OR QUIT IN QUOTES'
            READ*, FILENM
            IF (FILENM.EQ.'QUIT') DONE = .TRUE.
         ELSE
            DONE = .TRUE.
            FOUND = .TRUE.
         END IF
         GO TO 5
      END IF
      IF (FOUND) THEN
         OPEN (UNIT=10,FILE=FILENM,STATUS='OLD')
         .
         .
         .
```

Table 9-1 Inquiry Specifiers

Inquiry Specifier	Variable Type	Value for File Inquiry	Value for Unit Inquiry
ACCESS =	character	'SEQUENTIAL' 'DIRECT'	'SEQUENTIAL' 'DIRECT'
BLANK =	character	'NULL' 'ZERO'	'NULL' 'ZERO'
DIRECT =	character	'YES' 'NO 'UNKNOWN'	—
ERR =	integer	statement number of error routine	statement number of error routine
EXIST =	logical	.TRUE. .FALSE.	.TRUE. .FALSE.
FORM =	character	'FORMATTED' 'UNFORMATTED'	'FORMATTED' 'UNFORMATTED'
FORMATTED =	character	'YES' 'NO' 'UNKNOWN'	—
IOSTAT=	integer	error code	error code
NAME =	character	—	name of the file if it is not a scratch file
NAMED† =	logical	—	.TRUE. .FALSE.
NEXTREC =	integer	next record number in direct-access file	next record number in direct-access file
NUMBER† =	integer	unit number	—
OPENED =	logical	.TRUE. .FALSE.	.TRUE. .FALSE.
RECL =	integer	record length	record length
SEQUENTIAL =	character	'YES' 'NO' 'UNKNOWN'	—
UNFORMATTED =	character	'YES' 'NO' 'UNKNOWN'	—

† These specifiers do not refer to scratch files.

These statements assume that FOUND, DONE, and THERE have been specified to be logical variables and that FILENM has been specified to be a character variable.

The INQUIRE statement is also useful when we are writing a module (function or subroutine) that uses a file and we do not know whether the file has been opened. We will assume that the main program and the modules using the file all use the value 15 for the unit number. The following pair of statements could then be used in a module to determine whether the file had been opened and then to open the file if it was not already open:

```
INQUIRE (UNIT=15,OPENED=AVAIL)
IF (.NOT.AVAIL) OPEN (UNIT=15,FILE='FLIGHT',STATUS='OLD')
```

These statements would assume that AVAIL had been specified to be a logical variable.

Table 9–1 contains a complete list of the inquiry specifiers that can be used with the INQUIRE statement.

Summary

In this chapter we presented a complete discussion of file processing with both sequential and direct files. Data is often used by more than one program; thus, a data file makes the same data easily available to many programs. By carefully choosing the type of file (sequential or direct) and the order of the data in the file, we can handle large amounts of data with simple algorithms and programs.

Debugging Aids

When processing files, a useful subroutine prints the data in the current record in a readable form—you might call this routine SNAP because it gives you a snapshot of a record in the file. When you are debugging a program that uses the file, call the routine every time you want to check the contents of the current record.

Another handy subroutine opens a file and reads through it, printing the key information in each record. This subroutine is useful before and after updating a file to see if the new information has been entered properly.

We also want to emphasize that proper handling of files must occur when one of the files we are using is empty. Using trailer signals helps this situation because a file without data should still have the trailer signal. If you are concerned that a file may not exist, you can use the INQUIRE statement to determine whether or not it exists without causing a program execution error.

Style/Technique Guides

Good documentation is always important when working with data files. The record format and its field descriptions should have the same names in all programs that use the file; for example, if a file contains a stock number, give it the same name in each program that uses it. It is also good to use all the specifications that relate to the file in the OPEN statement; they do not need to be repeated in the other statements that refer to the file, but they should all be included at the beginning in the OPEN statement.

Key Words

direct-access file
external file
father-son update
field
hash code
internal file
key
master file
merge
random access
sequential-access file

Problems

We begin our problem set with modifications to the programs developed earlier in this chapter. Give the decomposition, refined pseudocode or flowchart, and FORTRAN solution for each problem.

Problems 1 – 5 modify the program VOYAGE, given on page 437, which detects edges in a two-dimensional image.

1. Modify the edge-detection program so that it allows the user to specify the symbol used to indicate the edges when the edge image is printed.
2. Modify the edge-detection program so that asterisks are used to outline the edge image when it is printed.
3. Modify the edge-detection program so that it uses the diagonal elements in the computation for the difference. Then instead of using four elements, the computation will use eight elements.
4. Modify the edge-detection program so that it computes the number of points that are interior points and prints the percentage of interior points that are also edge points after printing the edge image.
5. Modify the edge-detection program so that it allows points on the top, bottom, or sides to be edges by using the points on two or three sides for computing the difference and then comparing the difference to one-half or three-fourths of the threshold.

Problems 6 – 10 modify the program MIGRAT, given on page 447 which merged the new whooping crane sightings information with the master data file.

6. Modify the migration program so that it prints a count of the total number of sightings at the end of the report.
7. Modify the migration program so that it prints the maximum number of birds that have been sighted in the current report.
8. Modify the migration program so that it prints a final list of all grid locations of sightings along with the number of sightings in that grid.
9. Modify the migration program so that it tracks only a certain size sighting group. For example, the program could ask the user to enter the size of group of cranes; if the user enters the number 5, then the program prints a report only for the data that included 5 birds in the sightings data.

10. Modify the migration program so that it prints the most sightings during one day in the file. Print this at the end of the report.

Problems 11–15 use the CAT scan database updated in program UPDATE on page 453.

11. Write a subroutine to print the contents of the CAT scan database in a report format.
12. Write a program that stores data from the CAT scan database in arrays (assume a maximum of 200 records in the database) and then prints the information for all CAT scans performed in 1991.
13. Write a program that stores data from the CAT scan database in arrays (assume a maximum of 200 records in the database) and then prints the information for all CAT scans stored in areas with file references that begin with GA.
14. Write a program that stores data from the CAT scan database in arrays (assume a maximum of 200 records in the database) and then prints the information for all CAT scans that used more than 1000 x-rays in the scans.
15. Write a program that computes and prints the percentages of CAT scans with scan angles in the following categories:

Scan Angle Categories (in degrees)
0–90
91–180
181–270
271–360
Over 360

Problems 16–22 use data in a data file called SENSOR that contains maintenance information on mechanical measurement equipment used in a new chemical plant. Each line in the file contains the following information:

Work order number
Identification code for type of measurement device

These values are stored with the following format:

```
FORMAT (I5,2X,I1)
```

The identification code is an integer that represents the following measuring devices:

1. Counter
2. Flowmeter
3. Pressure transducer
4. Thermocouple
5. Pyrometer

The order of the lines in the file corresponds to the order in which the work orders were issued. If a repair involved more than one sensor, more than one line in the file has the same work order number; these lines are consecutive in the file. The following programs are needed by the plant engineers to analyze the reliability of process equipment.

16. Write a program that reads the data from the file SENSOR and prints a report that gives the total number of work orders for counters, flowmeters, and so on. Use the following report form:

```
WORK ORDER SUMMARY
SENSOR              NUMBER OF WORK ORDERS
- - - - - - - - - - - - - - - - - - - - -
COUNTER                     XXXX
FLOWMETER                   XXXX
PRESSURE TRANSDUCER         XXXX
THERMOCOUPLE                XXXX
PYROMETER                   XXXX
```

17. Write a program to print all the work orders for an identification code that is read from the terminal.
18. Write a function called COUNT that reads the data in the file and returns a count of the work orders required for a specified identification code, which is an input argument to the function.
19. Modify the program in problem 16 so that it also prints the total number of work orders.
20. Modify the program in problem 16 so that it includes the following analysis information in the summary report:

```
NUMBER OF SENSORS NEEDING MAINTENANCE               XXXX
NUMBER OF WORK ORDERS WITH ONE SENSOR               XXXX
NUMBER OF WORK ORDERS WITH MULTIPLE SENSORS         XXXX
```

21. Modify the program in problem 16 so that it includes the following summary information in the report:

```
NUMBER OF WORK ORDERS REQUIRING MAINTENANCE
ON BOTH PRESSURE TRANSDUCERS AND PYROMETERS IS   XXXX
```

22. Modify the program in problem 16 so that it prints the work order numbers for all requests for maintenance that include thermocouples. Print four numbers per line using the following format:

```
WORK ORDER NUMBERS FOR THERMOCOUPLE MAINTENANCE
      XXXX   XXXX    XXXX   XXXX
```

Problems 23 – 27 use the data in a direct-access file called TEST that contains the status of tests being performed at a materials testing laboratory. The testing lab offers four types of tests: compression, tensile, shear, and fatigue. The codes for these tests are, respectively, *C*, *T*, *S*, and *F*. Each time a test is completed on a material sample, the information is added to the test status file. The file TEST contains the sample number (integers 1 – 500); the material identification (30 characters); and four characters, which are initially blanks but are updated to *C*, *T*, *S*, and *F* as the material is tested. The format for each record in the file is

```
FORMAT (I3,1X,A30,1X,A4)
```

23. Write a program that reads the information in this file and prints a list of sample numbers for samples that have had the shear test completed. (The tests can occur in any order; thus, the four codes (*C*,*T*,*S*,*F*) can appear in any order in the string of characters.)
24. Write a program that reads the information in this file and prints a testing report. First list all samples that have been through the compression test, then all that have been through the tensile test, and so on. (The tests can occur in any order; thus the four codes (*C*,*T*,*S*,*F*) can appear in any order in the string of characters.) Put appropriate headers at the beginning of each list. If two tests have been completed on a sample, its sample number and identification will appear twice in the report, and so on.
25. Write a program that prints a summary report to give the percentages of materials that have been through each test. Use the following format:

```
SUMMARY OF MATERIAL TESTS
TEST                PERCENTAGE
- - - - - - - - - - - - - - -
COMPRESSION          XXX.X
TENSILE              XXX.X
SHEAR                XXX.X
FATIGUE              XXX.X
```

26. Modify the program in problem 25 so that it also prints the total number of samples in the test file and the total number of tests that have been completed.
27. Modify the program in problem 25 so that it also prints the number of samples that have had one test completed, the number of samples that have had two tests completed, the number of samples that have had three tests completed, and the number of samples that have had all four tests completed.

In problems 28 – 30, develop programs using the five-step design process.

28. Using the direct-access file from Section 9 – 7, write a program that will allow a user to specify a range of dates (using month, day, and year). The program should then print information for all CAT scans that occurred during that period.
29. Using the direct access file from Section 9 – 7, write a program that will allow a user to specify a patient ID. The program should then print information for all CAT scans performed for that patient.
30. Using the direct access file from Section 9 – 7, write a program that will allow a user to indicate a file reference. The program should then print information for all CAT scans stored in that location.

FORTRAN STATEMENT SUMMARY

■ **BACKSPACE** Statement:

BACKSPACE (UNIT=*integer expression,optional file specifiers*)

Examples:

```
BACKSPACE (UNIT=10)

BACKSPACE (UNIT=12,IOSTAT=ERROR)
```

Discussion:

The BACKSPACE statement allows you to back up to the previous record in an input file. When you execute a READ statement following the BACKSPACE statement, you are accessing the same information as the READ statement before the BACKSPACE statement. The file specifiers are discussed in Section 9 – 3.

■ **CLOSE** Statement:

CLOSE (UNIT=*integer expression,optional file specifiers*)

Examples:

```
CLOSE (UNIT=10)

CLOSE (UNIT=15,ERR=99)
```

Discussion:

The CLOSE statement closes a file. Files are automatically closed at the end of a program, so this statement is used primarily when the file is to be closed and reopened again in the same program.

■ **ENDFILE** Statement:

ENDFILE (UNIT=*integer expression,optional file specifiers*)

Example:

```
ENDFILE (UNIT=12)
```

Discussion:

The ENDFILE statement writes an end-of-file record to an output file. The CLOSE and END statements automatically perform this function on most systems.

■ INQUIRE Statement:

`INQUIRE (FILE=`*character expression,inquiry specifier list*`)`

`INQUIRE (UNIT=`*integer expression,inquiry specifier list*`)`

Examples:

```
INQUIRE (FILE='XYDATA',SEQUENTIAL=ANSWER)

INQUIRE (UNIT=12,SEQUENTIAL=ANSWER)
```

Discussion:

The INQUIRE statement has two forms: one to obtain information about a file with a specified name and one to obtain information about a file with a specified unit. The INQUIRY specifiers are listed in Table 9 – 1.

■ OPEN Statement:

`OPEN (UNIT=`*integer expression,*`FILE=`*character expression,*
`STATUS=`*character expression,optional file specifiers*`)`

Examples:

```
OPEN (UNIT=10,FILE='XYDATA',STATUS='OLD')

OPEN (UNIT=15,FILE='EXPER1',ACCESS='DIRECT',STATUS='OLD')
```

Discussion:

The OPEN statement must be used to connect external data files to a program. The UNIT, FILE, and STATUS specifiers are required. Other optional file specifiers may be used to emphasize certain characteristics of the file or to change the default characteristics that are assumed when some file specifiers are omitted.

■ REWIND Statement:

`REWIND (UNIT=`*integer expression,file specifiers*`)`

Examples:

```
REWIND (UNIT=9)

REWIND (UNIT=13,IOSTAT=ERROR,ERR=500)
```

Discussion:

The REWIND statement repositions a sequential file at the first record of the file. Some systems require a REWIND statement after opening a file to begin reading information at the beginning of the file.

10 Numerical Applications

10

APPLICATION

Laser Beam Impact

Light waves from a laser have the same frequency and thus create a beam with one characteristic color. More importantly, the light waves travel in phase, forming a narrow beam that can easily be directed and focused. CO_2 lasers can be used to drill holes in materials such as ceramics, composite materials, and rubber. Medical uses of lasers include repairing detached retinas, sealing leaky blood vessels, vaporizing brain tumors, removing warts and cysts, and performing delicate inner-ear surgery. All of these applications are possible because of the ability to direct and focus the laser energy. This photograph was taken with a scanning electron microscope and shows the impact of a laser beam on brass. (See Section 10-5 for a solution to a problem related to this application.)

Introduction

FORTRAN was specifically designed to perform the numerical computations needed by engineers and scientists. In Chapters 1–9, we presented all the major features of FORTRAN and illustrated them in a variety of applications. In this chapter, we discuss some common numerical techniques used in solving engineering and science problems along with some suggestions for avoiding or minimizing errors that are due to the precision of the computer. The topics that we specifically address are developing a linear model from a set of data values, using matrices to represent engineering data, solving systems of linear equations, and performing numerical integration and differentiation.

10·1 ■ Least-Squares Methods

We often encounter situations in science and engineering when our understanding of a physical process, or our ability to observe or measure it, is limited. The data that we are able to obtain do not occur at points on the curve where we expect them to because of errors in the data, in the theoretical model, or, most often, both. Curve fitting methods such as linear interpolation (which was discussed in Section 5–3 on page 213) assume that the data are correct and the function curve must pass through all the data points. These methods may not be appropriate for data that only approximate the function. In these situations, techniques are needed that are directed more at fitting a particular function to the data in some optimum manner. Therefore, in this section, we assume that the data represent approximate values of a specific function whose form we believe will best fit the data.

The task of selecting a function may or may not be straightforward. Often, we understand the physical process that the data represent and we have a theoretical equation for that process. At other times, the appearance of the plotted data may suggest a certain functional form such as a straight line or a parabola. There may also be times when we must try several different equations before we decide which one best represents the data.

The process of fitting an approximating function to a set of data, such that the resulting curve represents a "best fit," is called regression analysis. We first select an equation whose form we know, but whose coefficients we do not know. Regression is then used to find the combination of coefficients that will minimize some measurement of the errors made in fitting the curve to the data. The most popular means of measuring those errors is the least-squares method. When fitting a curve to a set of data, using the least-squares method, the coefficients of the curve are selected such that the sum of the squared distances between the curve and the data points is minimized. The least-squares method we discuss uses linear regression to fit a linear equation (a straight line) to a set of data.

■ Linear Models

A linear model has the following equation:

$$\begin{aligned} y &= f(x) \\ &= ax + b \end{aligned}$$

Linear regression is used to fit a straight line to a set of data by finding the slope of the line, a, and the y-intercept of the line, b, such that the sum of the squares of the y distances between the line and the data points is minimized. Before we derive the regression equations, we need to define some summation symbols which we will need. The symbol Σ represents a summation of values. Given a set of data points with coordinates $\{(x_1,y_1),(x_2,y_2),\ldots,(x_n,y_n)\}$, we can represent the sum of the x coordinates with the following notation:

$$\sum_{k=1}^{n} x_k = x_1 + x_2 + \cdots + x_n$$

This summation is read as "the sum of x_k as k goes from 1 to n." Similarly, we can express other sums using the notation:

$$\sum_{k=1}^{n} y_k = y_1 + y_2 + \cdots + y_n$$

$$\sum_{k=1}^{n} x_k y_k = x_1 y_1 + x_2 y_2 + \cdots + x_n y_n$$

$$\sum_{k=1}^{n} x_k^2 = x_1^2 + x_2^2 + \cdots + x_n^2$$

$$\sum_{k=1}^{n} b = b + b + \cdots + b = b \cdot n$$

To derive the regression equations, we start by computing the vertical distances between the linear function $f(x)$ and the actual data points. These distances are often referred to as residuals of the data points. Using the figure below, the residuals for two data points are shown:

$$\begin{aligned} d_1 &= y_1 - f(x_1) \\ &= y_1 - (ax_1 + b) \\ &= y_1 - ax_1 - b \\ d_2 &= y_2 - f(x_2) \\ &= y_2 - (ax_2 + b) \\ &= y_2 - ax_2 - b \end{aligned}$$

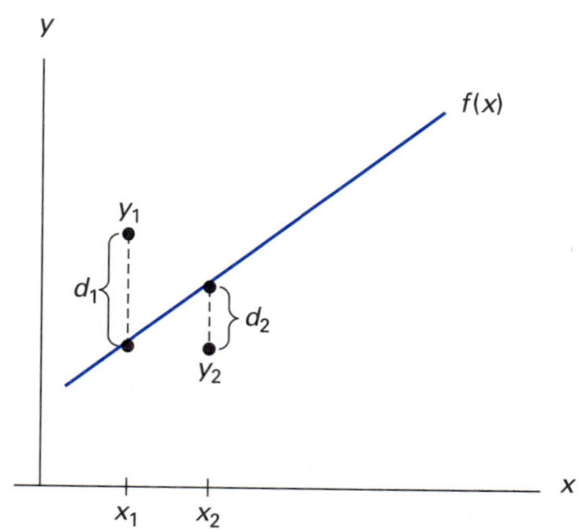

We now wish to minimize the sum of these distances, which represents the total error in fitting the curve to the data points. If we were to simply sum the distances, the positive and negative values would tend to cancel and give us an incorrect measurement of the sum of the errors. To avoid this problem, we first square the distances, or residuals, before summing them. This sum, which is called the error sum, gives us a way to measure the total error, since all the squared distances are positive quantities. The equation for the summation of the squares of the errors, which we shall call E, is then:

$$E = \sum_{k=1}^{n} d_k^2$$
$$= \sum_{k=1}^{n} (y_k - ax_k - b)^2$$

We now apply differential calculus to find the partial derivatives of E with respect to the two unknown coefficients a and b. Since the minimum of a function occurs when its derivative is equal to zero, we set these partial derivatives equal to zero to give us these two equations:

$$\frac{\partial E}{\partial a} = -2 \sum_{k=1}^{n} x_k(y_k - ax_k - b) = 0$$
$$\frac{\partial E}{\partial b} = -2 \sum_{k=1}^{n} (y_k - ax_k - b) = 0$$

These equations are now rearranged to yield two simultaneous equations in the variables a and b:

$$a \sum_{k=1}^{n} x_k^2 + b \sum_{k=1}^{n} x_k = \sum_{k=1}^{n} x_k y_k$$
$$a \sum_{k=1}^{n} x_k + b \cdot n = \sum_{k=1}^{n} y_k$$

Finally, solving these equations for a and b gives:

$$a = \frac{\sum_{k=1}^{n} x_k \sum_{k=1}^{n} y_k - n \sum_{k=1}^{n} x_k y_k}{(\sum_{k=1}^{n} x)^2 - n \sum_{k=1}^{n} x^2} \qquad (10-1)$$

$$b = \frac{\sum_{k=1}^{n} x_k \sum_{k=1}^{n} x_k y_k - \sum_{k=1}^{n} x_k^2 \sum_{k=1}^{n} y_k}{(\sum_{k=1}^{n} x_k)^2 - n \sum_{k=1}^{n} x_k^2} \qquad (10-2)$$

Once the slope a and y-intercept b have been calculated, the equation of the straight line that best fits the data has been determined. If we were to compute the error sum, E, for this line, it would be less than or equal to the error sum for any other straight line we could draw through the data. The error sum, E, also provides a relative measurement of how close the data points are to the line. For example, assume that we have two sets of data that have the same number of data points. Further assume we have determined that the same line provides the best fit, in the least-squares sense, to both sets of data. The set of data that has the smaller error sum will generally lie closer to the line and have less "scatter" in it than the set of data that has the larger error sum. Thus, the error sum can be used to provide a measurement of how well the line fits the data, or possibly how accurately the data were measured.

Another form of the equation for computing b is

$$b = \frac{\sum_{k=1}^{n} y_k - a \cdot \sum_{k=1}^{n} x_k}{n} \qquad (10-3)$$

At first glance, this equation would seem to be preferable to Eq. (10–2) since it is shorter. However, there is a disadvantage to using Eq. (10–3) because it can be less accurate. For example, suppose that we are using only a few digits of accuracy to compute the values of a and b. If we use Eq. (10–3) to compute b, we have already rounded or truncated the answer for a, and we then use that value in the computation of b. If we use Eq. (10–2) to compute b, we are using only the values of the various summations and are likely to get a more accurate answer. When we compute b using a computer, both equations give accurate answers because the computer is using its full accuracy for all the intermediate steps. In the next section, we illustrate an example in which the two equations for b give different answers if a small number of digits of accuracy is used.

■ Polynomial Models

The least-squares method described above can easily be extended to polynomial models of the form:

$$f(x) = a_0 + a_1 x + a_2 x^2 + \cdots + a_n x^n$$

For example, suppose the appearance of the data suggests a good fit can be obtained using a quadratic equation:

$$f(x) = a_0 + a_1 x + a_2 x^2$$

The equation for the sum of the squares of the errors, E, is now

$$E = \sum_{k=1}^{n} (y_k - a_0 - a_1 x_k - a_2 x_k^2)^2$$

Differentiating this equation with respect to a_0, a_1, and a_2 gives us three expressions that can be set to zero in order to find the minimum value of E:

$$\frac{\partial E}{\partial a_0} = -2 \sum_{k=1}^{n} (y_k - a_0 - a_1 x_k - a_2 x_k^2) = 0$$

$$\frac{\partial E}{\partial a_1} = -2 \sum_{k=1}^{n} x_k (y_k - a_0 - a_1 x_k - a_2 x_k^2) = 0$$

$$\frac{\partial E}{\partial a_2} = -2 \sum_{k=1}^{n} x_k^2 (y_k - a_0 - a_1 x_k - a_2 x_k^2) = 0$$

When these equations are rearranged, we have the following set of simultaneous equations in a_0, a_1, and a_2, which we can solve to obtain the coefficients of the best-fit quadratic equation.

$$a_2 \sum_{k=1}^{n} x_k^2 + a_1 \sum_{k=1}^{n} x_k + a_0 n = \sum_{k=1}^{n} y_k$$

$$a_2 \sum_{k=1}^{n} x_k^3 + a_1 \sum_{k=1}^{n} x_k^2 + a_0 \sum_{k=1}^{n} x_k = \sum_{k=1}^{n} x_k y_k$$

$$a_2 \sum_{k=1}^{n} x_k^4 + a_1 \sum_{k=1}^{n} x_k^3 + a_0 \sum_{k=1}^{n} x_k^2 = \sum_{k=1}^{n} x_k^2 y_k$$

In principle, we can use this approach to find the equation of a polynomial of any degree we desire that is the best fit in a least-squares sense. In practice, however, the method becomes unstable as the degree of the polynomial gets larger, because of rounding errors in the computer. If it is necessary to use a high-degree polynomial to fit a set of data, a technique known as orthogonal polynomials can be used, but such techniques are beyond the scope of this chapter.

If the data points are approximated by sums of sine functions, the approximation is called a Fourier series approximation. This technique is commonly used in engineering, but it is also beyond the scope of this chapter. Discussions of Fourier series approximations as well as orthogonal polynomial techniques can be found in most numerical methods texts.

Nonlinear Models

Least-squares curve fitting methods can be applied to virtually any function, but the resulting equations for solving for the coefficients of the function may be nonlinear and, as a result, cannot be solved using the methods for linear simultaneous equations. Occasionally, however, a nonlinear function can be transformed to a linear function that we can solve using our earlier methods. For example, it may be possible to perform an operation on the original nonlinear function that transforms it into a new function that can be plotted as a straight line. Linear regression is then applied to the new function and the similarly transformed data to find a least-squares straight line fit. The slope and y-intercept for this line are then used in the transformation equations for the original function, to obtain the nonlinear equation that best fits the original data. An example of a function that can be linearized is

$$f(x) = bx^a \qquad (10-4)$$

where a and b are constants. If we take the natural logarithm of both sides of this equation, we have

$$\ln f(x) = a \ln x + \ln b \qquad (10-5)$$

We now define the following transformation equations:

$$g(x) = \ln f(x) \qquad (10-6)$$

$$\tilde{b} = \ln b \qquad (10-7)$$

$$\tilde{x} = \ln x \qquad (10-8)$$

$$\tilde{y} = \ln y \qquad (10-9)$$

These transformations, when applied to Eq. (10–5), give

$$g(x) = a\tilde{x} + \tilde{b} \qquad (10-10)$$

which is exactly the same linear equation form we saw earlier. We then proceed exactly as we did earlier to obtain the equations for the slope and y-intercept of the least-squares line, which are

$$a = \frac{(\Sigma_{k=1}^{n} \tilde{x}_k \, \Sigma_{k=1}^{n} \tilde{y}_k - n \, \Sigma_{k=1}^{n} \tilde{x}_k\tilde{y}_k)}{(\Sigma_{k=1}^{n} \tilde{x}_k)^2 - n \, \Sigma_{k=1}^{n} \tilde{x}_k{}^2} \qquad (10-11)$$

$$\tilde{b} = \frac{(\Sigma_{k=1}^{n} \tilde{x}_k \, \Sigma_{k=1}^{n} \tilde{x}_k\tilde{y}_k - \Sigma_{k=1}^{n} \tilde{x}_k{}^2 \, \Sigma_{k=1}^{n} \tilde{y}_k)}{(\Sigma_{k=1}^{n} \tilde{x}_k)^2 - n \, \Sigma_{k=1}^{n} \tilde{x}_k{}^2} \qquad (10-12)$$

The data values x_k and y_k are then transformed using Eqs. (10–8) and (10–9), the various sums are computed, and the results are substituted into Eqs. (10–11) and

(10 – 12) to find a and $\bar{b}$. All that remains is to solve Eq. (10 – 7) for b and substitute into Eq. (10 – 4) to obtain the final nonlinear equation. A final word of caution is necessary if some of the x and y values are non-positive, since the logarithm function does not exist for non-positive values. In this case, additional transformations are used to shift the data so that there will be no non-positive values.

SELF-TEST 10-1

This self-test allows you to check quickly to see if you have remembered the key points from Section 10 – 1. If you have any problems with the exercises, you should reread this section. The solutions are included at the end of the text.

Assume that we have the following three data points collected from an experiment:

X	Y
1.0	2.0
3.0	3.0
4.0	6.0

1. The following two equations have been suggested as good linear approximations:

$$y = x$$
$$y = 1.5x - 1$$

   Sketch the two lines on the same graph and show the locations of the three points relative to the two lines.
2. Using the error sum, determine which line is the better approximation in terms of least-squares.
3. Compute the best linear approximation to these three points using least-squares.
4. Consider the nonlinear function

$$y = be^{ax}$$

   How would you transform it to a linear function?

10·2 Application ■ Accelerometer Model

Mechanical Engineering

One of the most exciting applications of science and engineering is space exploration. Sophisticated sensors and computer equipment aboard manned and unmanned spacecraft have provided a wealth of scientific data as well as the information needed to make decisions during the flights. Collecting data and then using it to develop an equation or model is an important step in analyzing the complex sensor systems.

The guidance and control system for a spacecraft often utilizes a sensor called an accelerometer, which is an electromechanical device that produces an output voltage proportional to the applied acceleration. An accurate model of the response of an accelerometer to known accelerations is needed for system performance studies. Careful tests are performed in an inertial measurement laboratory to obtain data on the accelerometer at several different acceleration levels. The accelerometer test data given in the following hand example clearly show the linear relationship between the input acceleration and the output voltage that is characteristic of an accelerometer. The *x*-axis units are multiples of the acceleration due to gravity, which is approximately 32.2 ft/sec^2 or 9.8 m/sec^2. The *y*-axis units are the measured output voltages of the accelerometer for the various input accelerations. The slope of the straight line that has been drawn through the data is referred to as the scale factor, and the *y*-intercept of the line is referred to as the null bias.

Write a program to determine an accelerometer's scale factor and null bias from a set of data stored in a data file XYDATA. Also tabulate the residuals and compute the error sum. Assume that we do not know how many values are in the file, and it does not contain a trailer signal.

1. Problem Statement

Find the linear equation that best fits a set of data values. Print a report that gives the linear model, residuals, and error sum.

2. Input/Output Statement

Input—a data file XYDATA

Output—a report containing the linear equation, residuals, and error sum

3. Hand Example

A set of eight data values is shown below, along with a graph of the data values and a hand-drawn linear model.

Acceleration	Voltage
−4	−0.593
−2	−0.436
0	0.061
2	0.425
4	0.980
6	1.213
8	1.646
10	2.158

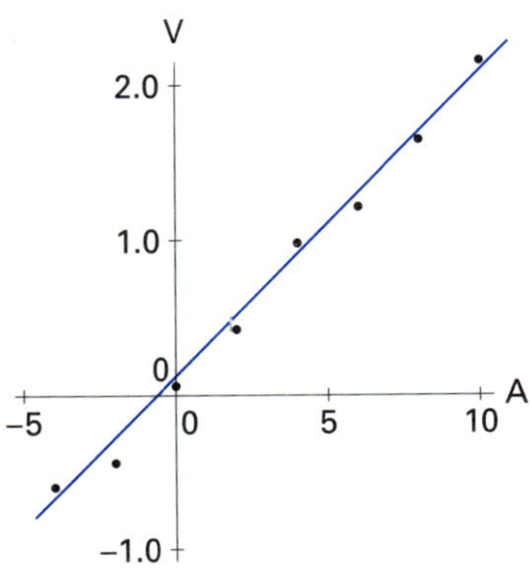

Using linear regression, we now compute by hand the best linear model using only the first three data points. The corresponding sums are:

$$\sum_{k=1}^{3} x_k = -4 + -2 + 0 = -6$$

$$\sum_{k=1}^{3} y_k = -0.593 + -0.436 + 0.061 = -0.968$$

$$\sum_{k=1}^{3} x_k y_k = -4(-0.593) + -2(-0.436) + 0(0.061) = 3.244$$

$$\sum_{k=1}^{3} x_k^2 = (-4)^2 + (-2)^2 + (0)^2 = 20$$

Using the equations to compute a and b (the slope and y-intercept) from the previous section, we determine the following model:

$$y = 0.164x + 0.004$$

Recall that we presented two equations for computing b in the previous section. Using the first equation, the value of b is 0.00433, which we rounded to three decimal places for the computations in this hand example. However, if we use the second equation for b, the value computed is 0.00533. This difference is a result of the extra operations involved when b is computed using a, instead of being computed directly from the various sums. As we mentioned, this difference is generally not significant when using the full accuracy of a computer, but it can be significant in computations that are limited to a few digits of accuracy as in our hand example. Generally speaking, we should use maximum precision for all intermediate calculations and not round off results until the end of the calculation, whether we do them by hand or computer.

We now use the linear equation to compute the estimated y values and the residuals:

```
THE LINEAR EQUATION IS
Y =    0.164 X +    0.004

ORIGINAL    ORIGINAL    ESTIMATED    RESIDUAL
   X           Y            Y

 -4.000      -0.593      -0.652       0.059
 -2.000      -0.436      -0.324      -0.112
  0.000       0.061       0.004       0.057

ERROR SUM =    0.019
```

4. Algorithm Development

The decomposition of this problem solution into general steps is

Decomposition

Read x and y data.
Compute slope and y-intercept.
Compute y estimates and residuals.
Print report.

As we refine the decomposition, we recognize that we need a loop to read the x and y data. Because we are reading each pair of data values from a single line, we can also add the values as we read them to the sums that we are going to need for the calculations. We need to use arrays for the x and y data because the data is needed for the report. If we only wanted the values for the slope and y-intercept of the linear model, we would not need arrays for the x and y data. The individual residuals are used for computing the error sum and are also printed in the report. However, we can compute and print the residual and then square and add it to the sum in the same loop—thus, we do not need an array for the residual values.

Pseudocode

```
Linear: k ← 1
        sumx ← 0
        sumy ← 0
        sumxy ← 0
        sumxx ← 0
        While more data do
            Read x(k), y(k)
            sumx ← sumx + x(k)
            sumy ← sumy + y(k)
            sumxy ← sumxy + x(k) · y(k)
            sumxx ← sumxx + x(k) · x(k)
            k ← k + 1
        n ← k − 1
        Compute slope and y-intercept
        Print slope, y-intercept
        error ← 0
        For k = 1 to n do
            ynew ← slope · x(k) + y-intercept
            res ← y(k) − ynew
            error ← error + res · res
            Print x(k), y(k), ynew, res
        Print error
```

We now convert the pseudocode into FORTRAN.

FORTRAN Program

```
*-----------------------------------------------------------------------*
      PROGRAM LINEAR
*
*  This program computes a linear model for a set of data
*  and then computes the residual sum to evaluate the model.
*
      INTEGER K, N
      REAL X(500), Y(500), SUMX, SUMY, SUMXY, SUMXX,
     +     SLOPE, YINT, YNEW, RES, ERROR
*
      DATA K, SUMX, SUMY, SUMXY, SUMXX, ERROR /1,5*0.0/
*
      OPEN (UNIT=10,FILE='XYDATA',STATUS='OLD')
*
*  Compute sums.
*
    5 READ (10,*,END=50) X(K), Y(K)
         SUMX = SUMX + X(K)
         SUMY = SUMY + Y(K)
         SUMXY = SUMXY + X(K)*Y(K)
         SUMXX = SUMXX + X(K)*X(K)
         K = K + 1
         GO TO 5
*
*  Compute slope and y-intercept.
*
   50 N = K - 1
      SLOPE = (SUMX*SUMY - REAL(N)*SUMXY)/
     +        (SUMX*SUMX - REAL(N)*SUMXX)
      YINT = (SUMX*SUMXY - SUMXX*SUMY)/
     +       (SUMX*SUMX - REAL(N)*SUMXX)
*
*  Print report.
*
      PRINT*, 'THE LINEAR EQUATION IS'
      PRINT 55, SLOPE, YINT
   55 FORMAT (1X,'Y = ',F7.3,' X + ',F7.3)
      PRINT*
      PRINT*,'ORIGINAL   ORIGINAL   ESTIMATED   RESIDUAL'
      PRINT*,'   X          Y           Y               '
      PRINT*
*
      DO 65 K=1,N
         YNEW = SLOPE*X(K) + YINT
         RES = Y(K) - YNEW
         ERROR = ERROR + RES*RES
         PRINT 60, X(K), Y(K), YNEW, RES
   60    FORMAT (1X,F7.3,4X,F7.3,4X,F7.3,5X,F7.3)
   65 CONTINUE
*
      PRINT*
      PRINT 70, ERROR
   70 FORMAT (1X,'ERROR SUM = ',F7.3)
*
      END
*-----------------------------------------------------------------------*
```

Fortran 90

Fortran 90 contains a new intrinsic function for summing the elements of an array. This function could be used to compute the four sums needed in this program.

5. Testing

If we test this program with the data set given earlier in this section, the following report is printed:

```
THE LINEAR EQUATION IS
Y =    0.200 X +    0.080

ORIGINAL    ORIGINAL    ESTIMATED    RESIDUAL
   X           Y            Y

 -4.000      -0.593      -0.722        0.129
 -2.000      -0.436      -0.321       -0.115
  0.000       0.061       0.080       -0.019
  2.000       0.425       0.481       -0.056
  4.000       0.980       0.882        0.098
  6.000       1.213       1.283       -0.070
  8.000       1.646       1.684       -0.038
 10.000       2.158       2.085        0.073

ERROR SUM =    0.055
```

We can check this using hand calculations. Performing the various summations, we get

$$\sum_{k=1}^{8} x_k = 24$$

$$\sum_{k=1}^{8} y_k = 5.454$$

$$\sum_{k=1}^{8} x_k y_k = 50.040$$

$$\sum_{k=1}^{8} x_k^2 = 240$$

We now use Eqs. (10–1) and (10–2) to compute a and b:

$$a = \frac{(24)(5.454) - (8)(50.040)}{(24)^2 - (8)(240)} = 0.2004643$$

$$b = \frac{(24)(50.040) - (240)(5.454)}{(24)^2 - (8)(240)} = 0.0803571$$

Rounding these results to three places and substituting them into the linear equation form gives

$$y = 0.200x + 0.080$$

The error sum is similarly computed by hand using

$$E = \sum_{k=1}^{8} (y_k - ax_k - b)^2$$
$$= 0.0546393$$

which rounds to

$$E = 0.055$$

The following graph contains the original data points plus the linear equation determined by our program to be the best fit for the data.

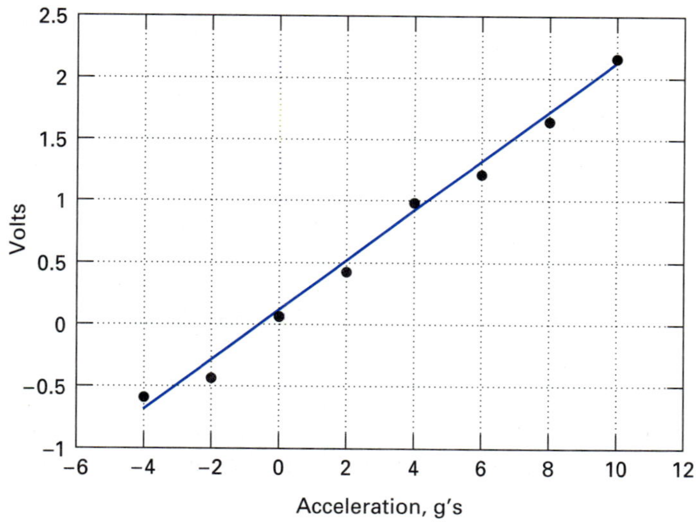

10·3 ■ Matrix Operations

Many engineering and science computations use a matrix or rectangular grid as a convenient way to represent a set of data. Capital letters in boldface are used to refer to entire matrices, and lowercase letters with subscripts are used to refer to individual elements in the matrix. To refer to the entire matrix, we also use a reference to an individual element in brackets with variable subscripts, as in $[a_{i,j}]$. In FORTRAN, a matrix is easily represented with a two-dimensional array. Operations performed with two-dimensional arrays generally require more than a single statement because the operations must be able to access all elements of the array; thus loops are needed. In this section, we define a number of the common operations performed with matrices and develop subprograms to implement them in FORTRAN.

In Chapters 6 and 7, we emphasized the importance of using the same array dimension specification both in the main program and in a subprogram when using two-dimensional arrays. In this chapter we assure correct dimensioning by using an operational size and a dimensional size for two-dimensional arrays. The dimensional size is the number of rows and the number of columns used in the array definition; we use DROWS and DCOLS to specify this dimensional size. The operational size is specified by NR (the number of rows) and NC (the number of columns) and represents the size of the two-dimensional array actually used. (Recall that we must dimension the array to the maximum size that we want to be able to use.)

Example 10-1

Scalar Multiplication

Multiplying each element in a matrix by a scalar is referred to as scalar multiplication. Write a subroutine to multiply a matrix **A** by a scalar s and return the result in a matrix B, as shown in the following matrix notation:

$$[b_{i,j}] \leftarrow [s \cdot a_{i,j}]$$

To illustrate, the elements of the matrix A are multiplied by a scalar value of 4, and the result is a new matrix **B**:

$$A = \begin{bmatrix} 1.0 & 2.2 \\ 3.0 & 4.0 \\ -1.0 & 0.0 \end{bmatrix} \qquad 4A = B = \begin{bmatrix} 4.0 & 8.8 \\ 12.0 & 16.0 \\ -4.0 & 0.0 \end{bmatrix}$$

The operational size of the arrays representing **A** and **B** must be the same, and we assume that their dimensional size is also the same. (If the dimensional sizes are different, two additional arguments are needed for the subroutine.)

Solution

The steps in this solution involve defining a pair of nested loops to access each array element and then multiplying each element of **A** by the scalar:

```
*-----------------------------------------------------------------------*
      SUBROUTINE SCALAR(A,S,B,NR,NC,DROWS,DCOLS)
*
*  This subroutine multiplies an array by a scalar.
*
      INTEGER NR, NC, DROWS, DCOLS, I, J
      REAL A(DROWS,DCOLS), S, B(DROWS,DCOLS)
*
      DO 10 I=1,NR
         DO 5 J=1,NC
            B(I,J) = S*A(I,J)
    5    CONTINUE
   10 CONTINUE
*
      RETURN
      END
*-----------------------------------------------------------------------*
```

Example 10-2

Matrix Addition

Matrix addition can be performed only with matrices of the same size. The result of the addition is another matrix of the same size in which the elements are the sum of the elements in the corresponding positions of the original matrices, as shown in matrix notation:

$$[c_{i,j}] \leftarrow [a_{i,j} + b_{i,j}]$$

To illustrate, matrix **A** is added to matrix **B**, and the result is a new matrix **C**:

$$\mathrm{A} = \begin{bmatrix} 1.0 & 2.2 \\ 3.0 & 4.0 \\ -1.0 & 0.0 \end{bmatrix} \qquad \mathrm{B} = \begin{bmatrix} 4.0 & -3.0 \\ 2.0 & 6.0 \\ -4.0 & 0.5 \end{bmatrix}$$

$$\mathrm{A} + \mathrm{B} = \mathrm{C} = \begin{bmatrix} 5.0 & -0.8 \\ 5.0 & 10.0 \\ -5.0 & 0.5 \end{bmatrix}$$

Write a subroutine called ADDMX with arguments that include the three matrices plus the operational size and dimensional size of the arrays representing the matrices. Again, if the arrays have different dimensional sizes, more subroutine arguments are needed.

Solution

This subroutine is similar to the one for scalar multiplication, but instead of multiplying each element by a number, the corresponding elements of the two input matrices are added:

```
*-----------------------------------------------------------------------*
      SUBROUTINE ADDMX(A,B,C,NR,NC,DROWS,DCOLS)
*
*  This subroutine adds matrices A and B and
*  stores the result in matrix C.
*
      INTEGER NR, NC, DROWS, DCOLS, I, J
      REAL A(DROWS,DCOLS), B(DROWS,DCOLS), C(DROWS,DCOLS)
*
      DO 10 I=1,NR
         DO 5 J=1,NC
            C(I,J) = A(I,J) + B(I,J)
    5    CONTINUE
   10 CONTINUE
*
      RETURN
      END
*-----------------------------------------------------------------------*
```

This subroutine is written so that the matrix that represents the sum is a separate matrix; but, if we want to store the sum in one of the original matrices, we can list it also as the output matrix in the CALL statement, as shown:

```
CALL ADDMX(A,B,B,NR,NC,DROWS,DCOLS)
```

◀

Matrix Subtraction

◀ **Example 10-3**

Matrix subtraction can also be performed only with matrices of the same size. The result of the subtraction is another matrix of the same size in which the elements are the difference of the elements in the corresponding positions of the original matrices, as shown in matrix notation:

$$[c_{i,j}] \leftarrow [a_{i,j} - b_{i,j}]$$

To illustrate, matrix **B** is subtracted from matrix **A**, and the result is a new matrix **C**:

$$\mathbf{A} = \begin{bmatrix} 1.0 & 2.2 \\ 3.0 & 4.0 \\ -1.0 & 0.0 \end{bmatrix} \qquad \mathbf{B} = \begin{bmatrix} 4.0 & -3.0 \\ 2.0 & 6.0 \\ -4.0 & 0.5 \end{bmatrix}$$

$$\mathbf{A} - \mathbf{B} = \mathbf{C} = \begin{bmatrix} -3.0 & 5.2 \\ 1.0 & -2.0 \\ 3.0 & -0.5 \end{bmatrix}$$

Although the order in adding matrices does not matter, the order in subtracting matrices obviously does matter.

Write a subroutine called SUBMX with arguments that include the three matrices plus the operational size and dimensional size of the arrays representing the matrices. Again, if the arrays have different dimensional sizes, more subroutine arguments are needed.

Solution

This subroutine is very similar to the one to add two matrices:

```
*-----------------------------------------------------------------------*
      SUBROUTINE SUBMX(A,B,C,NR,NC,DROWS,DCOLS)
*
*  This subroutine subtracts matrix B from matrix A
*  and stores the result in matrix C.
*
      INTEGER NR, NC, DROWS, DCOLS, I, J
      REAL A(DROWS,DCOLS), B(DROWS,DCOLS), C(DROWS,DCOLS)
*
      DO 10 I=1,NR
         DO 5 J=1,NC
            C(I,J) = A(I,J) - B(I,J)
    5    CONTINUE
   10 CONTINUE
*
      RETURN
      END
*-----------------------------------------------------------------------*
```

As before, this subroutine is written so that the matrix that represents the difference is a separate matrix, but if we want to store the difference in one of the original matrices, we can list it also as the output matrix in the CALL statement.

Fortran 90

In Fortran 90, scalar multiplication and addition and subtraction of matrices can be done with an arithmetic expression in a single assignment statement.

Dot Product

Example 10-4

The dot product is an operation performed with two vectors of the same size. (A vector is a matrix with one column or one row, and is thus easily implemented in a one-dimensional array.) The dot product between two vectors of size N is a number computed by adding the products of the values in corresponding positions in the vectors, as shown in the summation equation:

$$\text{Dot product} \leftarrow \sum_{i=1}^{N} a_i b_i$$

To illustrate, the dot product of vectors **A** and **B** is computed:

$$\mathbf{A} = \begin{bmatrix} 3.0 \\ 1.5 \\ -0.5 \end{bmatrix} \qquad \mathbf{B} = \begin{bmatrix} 1.0 \\ 2.0 \\ 3.0 \end{bmatrix}$$

$$\begin{aligned} \text{Dot product of } \mathbf{A} \text{ and } \mathbf{B} &= \mathbf{A} \cdot \mathbf{B} \\ &= (3.0)(1.0) + (1.5)(2.0) + (-0.5)(3.0) \\ &= 3.0 + 3.0 - 1.5 \\ &= 4.5 \end{aligned}$$

Write a function to compute the dot product of two vectors with a common size N.

Solution

Note that this subprogram is written as a function instead of a subroutine because it returns a single value to the main program. Also, since we are using one-dimensional arrays, we do not have to distinguish between operational size and dimensional size.

```
*-----------------------------------------------------------------------*
      REAL FUNCTION DOT(A,B,N)
*
*  This function computes the dot product of A and B.
*
      INTEGER  N, I
      REAL A(N), B(N)
*
      DOT = 0.0
      DO 10 I=1,N
         DOT = DOT + A(I)*B(I)
   10 CONTINUE
*
      RETURN
      END
*-----------------------------------------------------------------------*
```

Matrix Multiplication

Example 10-5

Matrix multiplication is not computed by multiplying corresponding elements of the matrices. The value in position (i,j) of the product of two matrices is the dot product of row i of the first matrix and column j of the second matrix, as shown in the summation equation:

$$[c_{i,j}] \leftarrow \sum_{k=1}^{N} a_{i,k} b_{k,j}$$

In the equation, i and j are fixed values, and k varies in the summation.

Because dot products require that the vectors have the same number of elements, we must have the same number of elements in each row of the first matrix as we have in each column of the second matrix to compute the product of the two matrices. The product matrix has the same number of rows as the first matrix and the same number of columns as the second matrix. Thus, if **A** and **B** both have 5 rows and 5 columns, their product has 5 rows and 5 columns. If **A** has 3 rows and 2 columns and **B** has 2 rows and 2 columns, their product has 3 rows and 2 columns. To illustrate, consider the following matrices **A** and **B**:

$$\mathbf{A} = \begin{bmatrix} 1.0 & 2.2 \\ 3.0 & 4.0 \\ -1.0 & 0.0 \end{bmatrix} \qquad \mathbf{B} = \begin{bmatrix} 4.0 & -3.0 \\ 2.0 & 6.0 \end{bmatrix}$$

The first element in the product $\mathbf{C} = \mathbf{AB}$ is

$$\begin{aligned} c_{1,1} &= \sum_{k=1}^{N} a_{1,k} b_{k,1} \\ &= a_{1,1} b_{1,1} + a_{1,2} b_{2,1} \\ &= (1.0)(4.0) + (2.2)(2.0) \\ &= 8.4 \end{aligned}$$

Similarly, we can compute the rest of the elements in the product of **A** and **B**:

$$\mathbf{AB} = \mathbf{C} = \begin{bmatrix} 8.4 & 10.2 \\ 20.0 & 15.0 \\ -4.0 & 3.0 \end{bmatrix}$$

In this example, we cannot compute **BA** because **B** does not have the same number of elements in each row as **A** has in each column. But, when both **AB** and **BA** can be computed, **AB** is usually not equal to **BA**.

An easy way to decide if a matrix product exists is to write the sizes of the two matrices side by side. Then if the two inner numbers are the same, the product exists; the size of the product is represented by the two outer numbers. To illustrate, in the example above, the size of **A** is 3×2 and the size of **B** is 2×2. Therefore, if we want to compute **AB**, we look at the sizes:

$$3 \times 2,\ 2 \times 2$$

The two inner numbers are the same (2), so **AB** exists and its size is determined by the two outer numbers, 3×2. If we want to compute **BA** we again look at the sizes:

$$2 \times 2,\ 3 \times 2$$

The two inner numbers are not the same (2,3), so **BA** does not exist.

We now develop a subroutine to multiply two matrices. The arguments of the subroutine must include the two input matrices, the output matrix, and the operational sizes and dimensional sizes of the arrays representing the matrices. An additional logical variable is included in the argument list. This variable will return a value of true if the operational sizes of the arrays are invalid for matrix multiplication.

Solution

```
*-----------------------------------------------------------------------*
      SUBROUTINE MULTMX(A,ANR,ANC,ADROWS,ADCOLS,
     +                  B,BNR,BNC,BDROWS,BDCOLS,
     +                  C,CNR,CNC,CDROWS,CDCOLS,ERROR)
*
*  This subroutine multiplies arrays A and B
*  and stores the product in array C.
*
      INTEGER ANR,ANC,ADROWS,ADCOLS,BNR,BNC,BDROWS,BDCOLS,
     +        CNR,CNC,CDROWS,CDCOLS,I,J,K
      REAL A(ADROWS,ADCOLS),B(BDROWS,BDCOLS),C(CDROWS,CDCOLS)
      LOGICAL ERROR
*
      ERROR = .FALSE.
      IF (ANC.NE.BNR) ERROR = .TRUE.
      IF (ANR.NE.CNR) ERROR = .TRUE.
      IF (BNC.NE.CNC) ERROR = .TRUE.
*
      IF (.NOT.ERROR) THEN
         DO 30 I=1,CNR
            DO 25 J=1,CNC
               C(I,J) = 0.0
               DO 15 K=1,ANC
                  C(I,J) = C(I,J) + A(I,K)*B(K,J)
   15          CONTINUE
   25       CONTINUE
   30    CONTINUE
      END IF
*
      RETURN
      END
*-----------------------------------------------------------------------*
```

Fortran 90

Fortran 90 contains two new intrinsic subprograms for computing the dot product and for multiplying two matrices. The subprograms are named DOT_PRODUCT and MATMUL.

Matrix operations are often used to solve simultaneous linear equations. Systems of simultaneous equations appear in virtually every technical area. They are often used in the stress analysis of mechanical systems, in the analysis of a fluid-flow system, and in the analysis of the current or voltages in an electrical circuit. The design of airplane control systems also requires the solution of systems of simultaneous equations. The data from these analyses are stored in a matrix, and the system of simultaneous equations represented by this matrix is solved to compute the desired result.

SELF-TEST 10-2

This self-test allows you to check quickly to see if you have remembered the key points from Section 10-3. If you have any problems with the exercises, reread this section. The solutions are included at the end of the text.

Compute the following new matrices using A, B, C, and D:

$$A = \begin{bmatrix} 2.0 & 1.0 \\ 0.0 & -1.0 \\ 3.0 & 0.0 \end{bmatrix} \qquad B = \begin{bmatrix} 1.0 & 3.0 \\ -1.0 & 5.0 \end{bmatrix}$$

$$C = \begin{bmatrix} 3.0 & 2.0 \\ -1.0 & -2.0 \\ 0.0 & 2.0 \end{bmatrix} \qquad D = \begin{bmatrix} 1.0 \\ 2.0 \end{bmatrix}$$

1. A + 2C
2. 4C − A
3. 4(C − A)
4. D · D
5. (2D) · (−3D)
6. AB
7. BD
8. CD
9. (CB)D
10. (A + C)D

10-4 ■ Gauss Elimination

Gauss elimination is a method for solving a system of equations. Before we discuss the steps in Gauss elimination, we first review the geometric interpretation of solving a system of equations. Consider a set of three simultaneous equations written in the following form:

$$\begin{aligned} a_{1,1}x + a_{1,2}y + a_{1,3}z &= b_1 \\ a_{2,1}x + a_{2,2}y + a_{2,3}z &= b_2 \\ a_{3,1}x + a_{3,2}y + a_{3,3}z &= b_3 \end{aligned}$$

Let a matrix **A** with three rows and three columns contain the coefficients of the unknown variables, a matrix **X** with three rows and one column contain the variables, and a matrix **B** with three rows and one column contain the constants on the right side of the equations:

$$A = \begin{bmatrix} a_{1,1} & a_{1,2} & a_{1,3} \\ a_{2,1} & a_{2,2} & a_{2,3} \\ a_{3,1} & a_{3,2} & a_{3,3} \end{bmatrix} \quad X = \begin{bmatrix} x \\ y \\ z \end{bmatrix} \quad B = \begin{bmatrix} b_1 \\ b_2 \\ b_3 \end{bmatrix}$$

Thus, the system of equations can be represented in matrix form:

$$AX = B$$

Go through the steps to verify that this matrix equation represents the three simultaneous equations given at the beginning of this section. The solution to this set of simultaneous equations is a unique set of values for x, y, and z that satisfy each of the three equations.

Geometrically, each equation of a set of three simultaneous equations with three unknowns represents a plane. If the three planes intersect in a common point, then the solution of the three simultaneous equations is the set of x, y, and z coordinates of the single point that is common to all three planes, as shown in the diagram below:

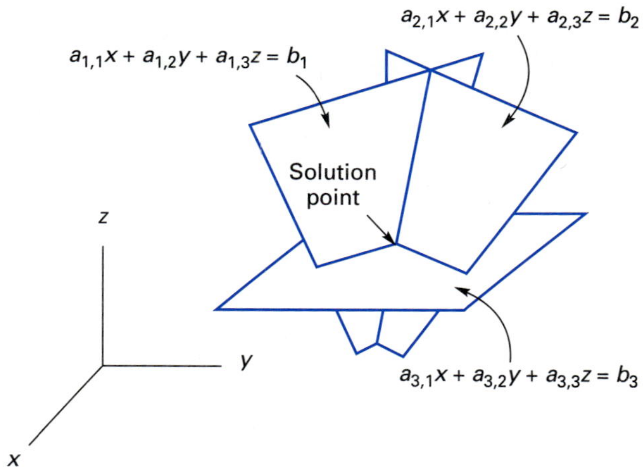

A unique solution does not exist if two or more of the equations represent the same plane. In fact, there are infinitely many solutions to the set of equations in this case:

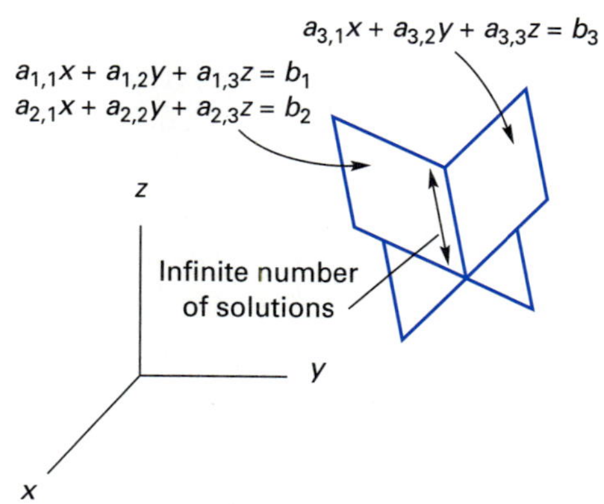

If two or more of the planes are parallel, then the planes do not meet in a single common point and there is no solution to the system of equations:

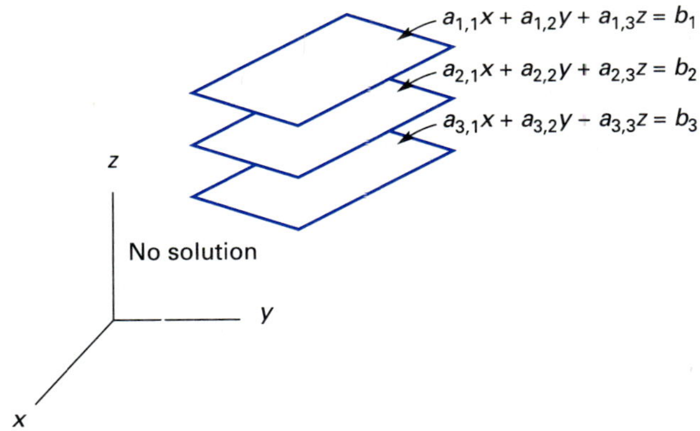

When there is not a unique solution, the system is called a singular system of equations. Conversely, a nonsingular system is one that has a unique solution. In practice, a third possibility occurs when the planes are very nearly the same plane or are very nearly parallel; these systems are called ill-conditioned systems.

The Gauss elimination method solves for the unknowns in a system of simultaneous equations by combining equations. We will first illustrate this method with an example. Consider the following set of equations:

$$\begin{aligned} 2x + 3y - z &= 1 \\ 3x + 5y + 2z &= 8 \\ x - 2y - 3z &= -1 \end{aligned}$$

Gauss elimination begins by using the first equation to eliminate the first variable, $3x$, in the second equation. To do this, we multiply the first equation by $\frac{3}{2}$ (or 1.5) and subtract it from the second equation, as shown:

$$\begin{array}{rl} 3x + 5y + 2z = 8 & \text{second equation} \\ \underline{3x + 4.5y - 1.5z = 1.5} & \text{first equation times 1.5} \\ 0x + 0.5y + 3.5z = 6.5 & \text{difference} \end{array}$$

Thus, our new set of equations is:

$$\begin{aligned} 2x + 3y - z &= 1 \\ 0x + 0.5y + 3.5z &= 6.5 \\ x - 2y - 3z &= -1 \end{aligned}$$

The solution to this new set of equations is also a solution to the original set of equations since the modifications only added equivalent expressions to both sides of an equation or multiplied both sides of an equation by the same value.

We now eliminate the variable x in the third equation by multiplying the first equation by 0.5 and subtracting it from the third equation, as shown:

$$\begin{array}{rl} x - 2y - 3z = -1 & \text{third equation} \\ \underline{x + 1.5y - 0.5z = 0.5} & \text{first equation times 0.5} \\ 0x - 3.5y - 2.5z = -1.5 & \text{difference} \end{array}$$

Our new set of equations is now:

$$\begin{aligned} 2x + \ \ 3y - \quad z &= \ \ 1 \\ 0x + 0.5y + 3.5z &= \ \ 6.5 \\ 0x - 3.5y - 2.5z &= -1.5 \end{aligned}$$

Note that we have now eliminated all terms with x except in the first equation. We now move to the second variable and eliminate it in all equations after the second equation. We accomplish this by multiplying the second equation by -7 and subtracting it from the third equation, which yields

$$\begin{aligned} 2x + \ \ 3y - \quad z &= 1 \\ 0x + 0.5y + 3.5z &= 6.5 \\ 0x + \ \ 0y + \ 22z &= 44 \end{aligned}$$

If we have N equations with N unknowns, we eliminate the first unknown from all but the first equation, we eliminate the second unknown from all but the first and second equations, and so on until the last equation has only one variable.

We now begin the back-substitution process to solve for the unknowns. Using our example data, we know from the last equation that $22z = 44$, or that $z = 2$. Substituting the value of z in the second equation, which is $0.5y + 3.5z = 6.5$, gives $0.5y + 3.5(2) = 6.5$, which results in $y = -1$. We now know the values of y and z and can substitute these values in the first equation to determine the value of x. Since $2x + 3y - z = 1$, then $2x + 3(-1) - (2) = 1$, or $2x = 6$, and finally $x = 3$.

In general, we perform the back-substitution by starting with the last equation, and backing up one equation each step, until we reach the first equation. After performing the back-substitution for each variable, we have the final solution.

To improve accuracy, a process known as "pivoting" is frequently used. In this process, we define a pivot equation and a pivot coefficient. Recall that Gauss elimination begins by using the first equation to eliminate the first variable (x) in all equations after the first equation. For this step, the first equation is the pivot equation and the first coefficient in the pivot equation is the pivot coefficient. We then eliminate the second variable (y) from all equations after the second equation, defining the second equation as the pivot equation and the second coefficient in the pivot equation as the pivot coefficient. This continues until the pivot equation is the last equation and the pivot coefficient is the last coefficient in the pivot equation. If the absolute value of the pivot coefficient is small compared to the corresponding coefficients in the rows below it, then we will have to multiply the pivot coefficient by a large value to perform the elimination step. And if there is a small error in the pivot coefficient from earlier steps, multiplying it by a large value and using it to eliminate the coefficients below can result in large errors. These errors can be greatly reduced if we reorder the set of equations such that the first equation (the pivot equation) is the equation with the largest coefficient (in absolute value) for the first variable (the pivot coefficient). We then eliminate the first variable from the remaining equations. Starting with the second equation, we then reorder the equations such that the second equation has the largest coefficient (in absolute value) for the second variable. We then eliminate the second variable from all equations after the second equation. The reordering and elimination continue in this way until we reach the final equation, which contains only one variable. This process is called "partial pivoting" and usually provides good accuracy. If additional accuracy is needed, "complete pivoting" can be done by similarly exchanging columns. If columns are exchanged, it is important to keep track of the changes in the order of the variables.

The back-substitution process then occurs exactly as discussed previously. If at some time in the reordering we find that all the coefficients for a variable are zero or are very close to zero, then the system is either ill-conditioned or does not have a unique solution.

In the next section we develop a program that uses Gauss elimination to solve a system of simultaneous equations.

10-5 Application ▪ Deformable Mirrors

Optical Engineering

One of the most interesting recent advances in the area of optics has been the development of "deformable" mirrors—mirrors whose surfaces can be reshaped by various techniques to correct for distortions in the optical path between the observer and the object being viewed. As an example, consider an astronomer who is observing the planet Saturn through a telescope, as shown in the following diagram:

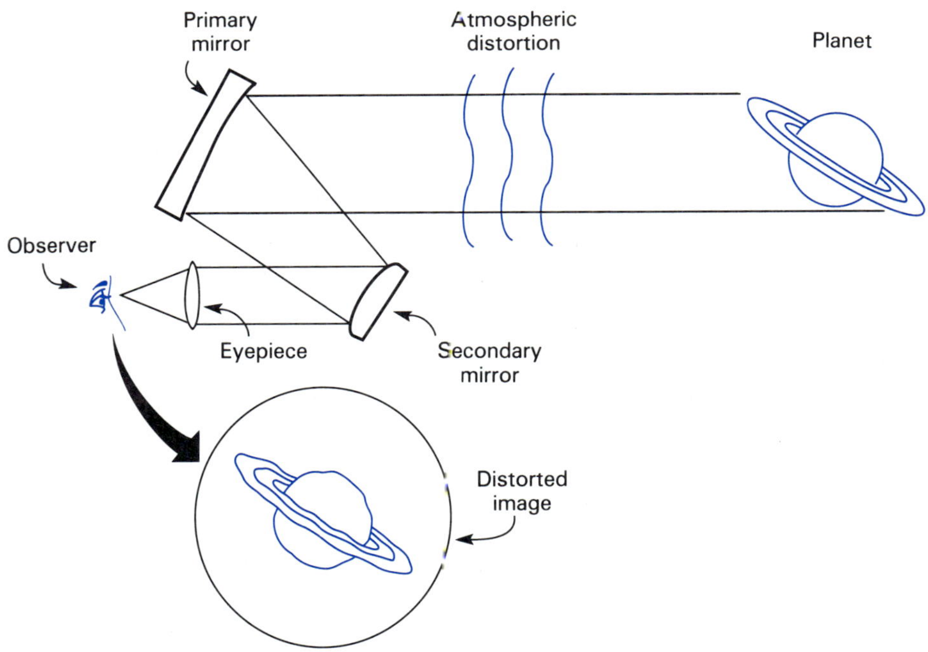

Because of atmospheric distortion caused by turbulence and pressure changes and imperfections in the various optical elements of the telescope, the light rays are bent to various degrees such that the image of Saturn, as perceived by the astronomer, is distorted. The idea behind deformable mirrors, or "adaptive optics" as they are more generally called, is to somehow detect the distortion present and use that information to recontour one or more of the mirrors in the telescope to cancel the distortion, thereby presenting the viewer with an undistorted image.

One way this technique might be implemented is shown in the following diagram, in which a few new optical elements have been added to the previous diagram:

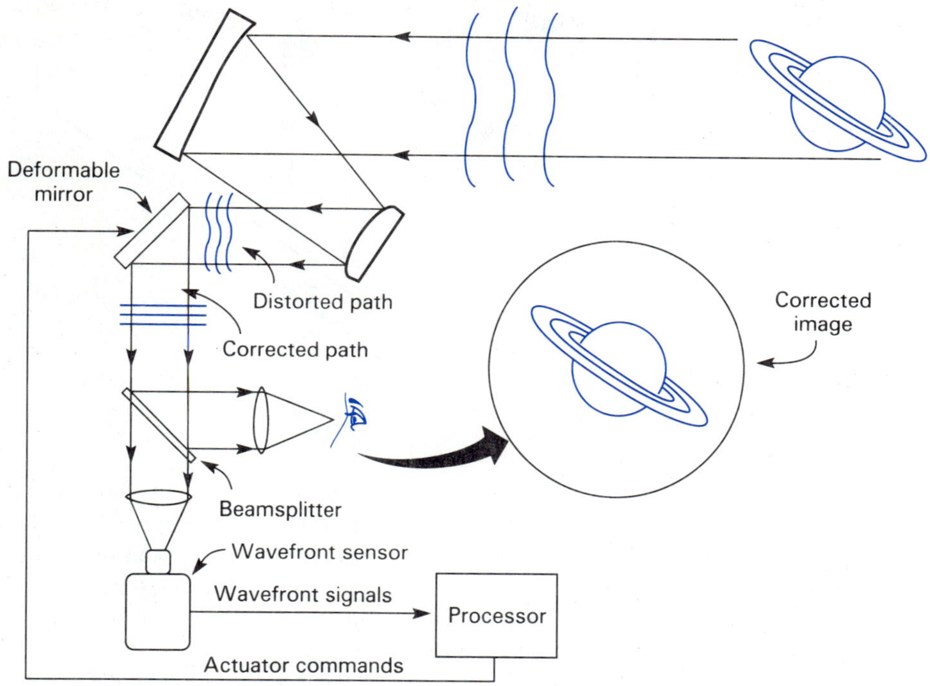

The new elements include a deformable mirror, a beamsplitter that enables a "wavefront sensor" to share the optical path with the observer, and a processor that provides the signals to shape the deformable mirror.

As seen in the diagram, the distorted image is reflected off the deformable mirror and sent to the beamsplitter. The beamsplitter, in turn, sends the image to the observer and the wavefront sensor. The wavefront sensor is a device that measures the distortion in the image. The distortion measurements are sent to a processor, which determines the corrections needed to cancel the distortion and then sends the commands to the deformable mirror to reshape it.

The deformable mirror is one of the more interesting elements of the system. A sketch showing a square mirror having 25 actuators (movable elements) is shown in the following diagram:

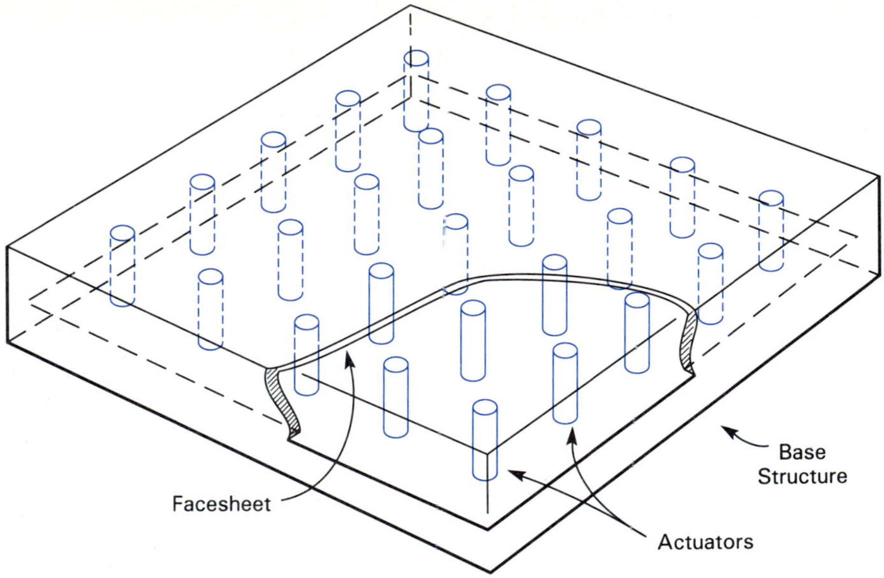

25-Actuator Deformable Mirror

The mirror uses a rigid base structure that supports the actuators. The actuators, along with the mirror's edge, support the relatively thin facesheet that is a highly polished, extremely flat, metal or glass surface. The actuators can expand or contract slightly when a voltage is applied, thereby moving the facesheet. When the actuators are used in unison, they are capable of producing the optical corrections needed to obtain an undistorted image.

The process used to obtain the correct shape for the facesheet of the deformable mirror involves a number of steps, which can be summarized in a system of equations that must be solved simultaneously. The coefficients of the system of equations represent the optical corrections that are needed and how the actuators interact with each other. The unknowns of the system of equations represent the voltages that need to be applied simultaneously to the actuators to produce the desired optical correction. Thus, the problem solution involves the solution of N simultaneous equations if there are N actuators in the mirror. The number of actuators in the deformable mirror in the diagram is 25, and thus a system of 25 equations with 25 unknowns would need to be solved in order to deform it properly.

Write a program to use Gauss elimination to solve a set of linear equations. Assume that the coefficients are contained in a data file named MIRROR. The solution should be written to a data file since it will be the input to the program that controls the actuators.

1. Problem Statement

Write a program that solves a system of simultaneous equations using Gauss elimination.

2. Input/Output Description

Input—a data file containing the number of equations and the coefficients for the system of equations

Output—a data file containing the solution to the system of simultaneous equations

3. Hand Example

Assume that the data file contains the following information:

```
3
2   3  -1   1
3   5   2   8
1  -2  -3  -1
```

Using the reorder and elimination process for each variable gives the following steps: Select the first variable and reorder the equations if necessary:

$$\begin{aligned} 3x + 5y + 2z &= 8 \\ 2x + 3y - z &= 1 \\ x - 2y - 3z &= -1 \end{aligned}$$

We now eliminate the first variable from each of the equations after the first equation:

$$\begin{aligned} 3x + 5y + 2z &= 8 \\ 0x - \tfrac{1}{3}y - \tfrac{7}{3}z &= -\tfrac{13}{3} \\ 0x - \tfrac{11}{3}y - \tfrac{11}{3}z &= -\tfrac{11}{3} \end{aligned}$$

Starting with the second equation, we reorder the equations so that the second equation has the largest absolute value for the second coefficient:

$$\begin{aligned} 3x + 5y + 2z &= 8 \\ 0x - \tfrac{11}{3}y - \tfrac{11}{3}z &= -\tfrac{11}{3} \\ 0x - \tfrac{1}{3}y - \tfrac{7}{3}z &= -\tfrac{13}{3} \end{aligned}$$

We now eliminate the second variable from each equation after the second equation:

$$\begin{aligned} 3x + 5y + 2z &= 8 \\ 0x - \tfrac{11}{3}y - \tfrac{11}{3}z &= -\tfrac{11}{3} \\ 0x + 0y - 2z &= -4 \end{aligned}$$

We are now ready to do the back-substitution. We start with the last equation and solve for z. We then substitute that value in the next-to-last equation. Thus, from the third equation above, we find that z is equal to 2. Then we add $\frac{11}{3}z$ (or $\frac{11}{3} \cdot 2$) to both sides of the second equation.

$$\begin{aligned} 3x + 5y + 2z &= 8 \\ 0x - \tfrac{11}{3}y + 0z &= \tfrac{11}{3} \\ 0x + 0y + 1z &= 2 \end{aligned}$$

We now solve the second-from-the-bottom equation:

$$\begin{aligned} 3x + 5y + 2z &= 8 \\ 0x + 1y + 0z &= -1 \\ 0x + 0y + 1z &= 2 \end{aligned}$$

We are now at the first equation, which we solve to get our final solution.

$$\begin{aligned} 1x + 0y + 0z &= 3 \\ 0x + 1y + 0z &= -1 \\ 0x + 0y + 1z &= 2 \end{aligned}$$

Thus, the final results are

$$\begin{aligned} x &= 3 \\ y &= -1 \\ z &= 2 \end{aligned}$$

4. Algorithm Development

The decomposition for this problem solution is the following:

Decomposition

Read coefficient information from a data file.
Solve system of equations.
Write solution to a data file.

Solving the system of equations requires pivoting, or reordering the equations, if necessary, before each elimination step. The reordering is done by finding the equation with the maximum absolute value for the coefficient of the first unknown and putting that equation first. This equation becomes the pivot equation, and its first coefficient is the pivot coefficient. We then use the pivot equation to eliminate the first unknown in all equations after the pivot equation. To do this, we determine a special factor. This factor is the value that we multiply the pivot equation by to get a new equation that we then subtract from the current row in order to eliminate the term in the pivot column. (Refer to the hand example again if necessary.) This factor is the coefficient in the pivot column in the current row divided by the pivot coefficient.

Finally, we need to consider the back-substitution. We start with the last equation, which now only has the last variable. We solve for this variable and back-substitute it into the next-to-last equation, which can then be solved for the next-to-last variable. This back-substitution process continues until we have solved for all of the variables.

As we combine these ideas into pseudocode, it is clear that we have several independent operations—the reordering step, the elimination step, and the back-substitution. We implement these as subroutines to make our program more readable and easier to debug.

In the computer program, we can perform the steps in solving this system of equations using a matrix of coefficients. We also need the constants from the right side of the equations, but instead of storing the constants in a separate matrix we will use an augmented coefficient matrix that contains the coefficients and the constants. Thus, for the hand example, the augmented matrix is

$$\mathbf{A} = \begin{bmatrix} 2 & 3 & -1 & 1 \\ 3 & 5 & 2 & 8 \\ 1 & -2 & -3 & -1 \end{bmatrix}$$

The algorithm then references elements of this matrix to determine when reordering is needed. The elimination and back-substitution processes also use and modify this matrix, which is implemented in a two-dimensional array. Since this two-dimensional array is used in both the main program and subprograms, we use DROWS and DCOLS as subprogram arguments to specify the dimensional size; the number of equations, N, can be used to specify the operational size, which is N rows and $N+1$ columns.

Pseudocode

```
Gauss: drows ← 25
       dcols ← 26
       Read n and the augmented coefficient array, a
       pivot ← 1
       error ← false
       While pivot < n and no error do
           Call order (a,drows,dcols,n,pivot,error)
           If no error then
               Call elim (a,drows,dcols,n,pivot)
               pivot ← pivot + 1
       If error then
           Print 'NO UNIQUE SOLUTION'
       Else
           Call backsb (a,drows,dcols,n,soln)
           Print 'SOLUTION WRITTEN TO DATA FILE'
           Write n to data file
           Write soln values to data file

Order (a,drows,dcols,n,pivot,error):
       rmax ← pivot
       For row = pivot+1 to n do
           If abs(a(row,pivot)) > abs(a(rmax,pivot)) then
               rmax ← row
       If abs(a(rmax,pivot)) < 0.00001 then
           error ← true
       Else
           If rmax ≠ pivot then
               For k = 1 to n+1 do
                   temp ← a(rmax,k)
                   a(rmax,k) ← a(pivot,k)
                   a(pivot,k) ← temp
       Return
```

Elim (a,drows,dcols,n,pivot):

For row = pivot + 1 to n do

$$\text{factor} \leftarrow \frac{\text{a(row,pivot)}}{\text{a(pivot,pivot)}}$$

a(row,pivot) ← 0.0

For col = pivot + 1 to n + 1 do

a(row,col) ← a(row,col) − a(pivot,col) · factor

Return

Backsb (a,drows,dcols,n,soln);

For row = n to 1 in steps of − 1 do

For col = n to row+1 in steps of − 1 do

a(row,n + 1) ← a(row,n + 1) − soln(col) · a(row,col)

$$\text{soln(row)} \leftarrow \frac{\text{a(row,n+1)}}{\text{a(row,row)}}$$

Print soln, the solution array

The structure chart and FORTRAN program for this solution are the following:

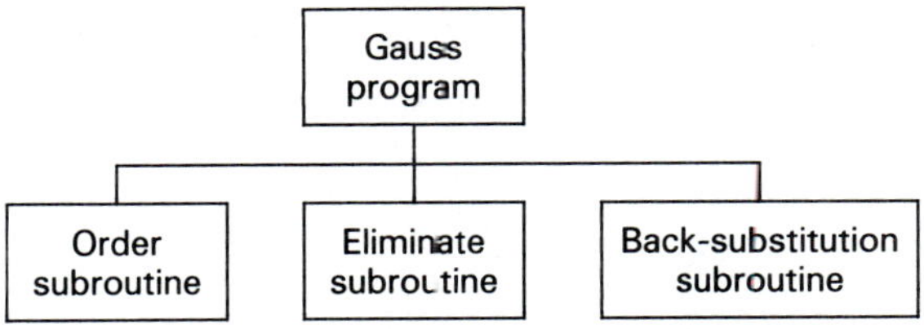

FORTRAN Program

```
*-----------------------------------------------------------------------*
      PROGRAM GAUSS
*
*  This program uses the Gauss elimination method to
*  solve a set of simultaneous equations.
*
      INTEGER DROWS, DCOLS, N, I, J, PIVOT
      REAL A(25,26), SOLN(25)
      LOGICAL ERROR
*
      DROWS = 25
      DCOLS = 26
      OPEN (UNIT=10,FILE='MIRROR',STATUS='OLD')
      READ (10,*) N
      DO 5 I=1,N
         READ (10,*) (A(I,J),J=1,N+1)
    5 CONTINUE
*
      PIVOT = 1
      ERROR = .FALSE.
```

```
   10 IF (PIVOT.LT.N.AND..NOT.ERROR) THEN
         CALL ORDER(A,DROWS,DCOLS,N,PIVOT,ERROR)
         IF (.NOT.ERROR) THEN
            CALL ELIM(A,DROWS,DCOLS,N,PIVOT)
            PIVOT = PIVOT + 1
         END IF
         GO TO 10
      END IF
*
      IF (ERROR) THEN
         PRINT*, 'NO UNIQUE SOLUTION EXISTS'
      ELSE
         CALL BACKSB(A,DROWS,DCOLS,N,SOLN)
         PRINT*, 'SOLUTION WRITTEN TO DATA FILE'
         OPEN (UNIT=11,FILE='ACTUATOR',STATUS='NEW')
         WRITE (11,*) N
         DO 20 I=1,N
            WRITE (11,*) SOLN(I)
   20    CONTINUE
      END IF
*
      END
*-----------------------------------------------------------------------*
      SUBROUTINE ORDER(A,DROWS,DCOLS,N,PIVOT,ERROR)
*
*  This subroutine reorders the equations so that the pivot
*  position in the pivot equation has the maximum absolute value.
*
      INTEGER DROWS, DCOLS, N, ROW, RMAX, PIVOT, K
      REAL A(DROWS,DCOLS), TEMP
      LOGICAL ERROR
*
      RMAX = PIVOT
      DO 10 ROW=PIVOT+1,N
         IF (ABS(A(ROW,PIVOT)).GT.ABS(A(RMAX,PIVOT))) RMAX = ROW
   10 CONTINUE
*
      IF (ABS(A(RMAX,PIVOT)).LT.1.0E-05) THEN
         ERROR = .TRUE.
      ELSE
         IF (RMAX.NE.PIVOT) THEN
            DO 20 K=1,N+1
               TEMP = A(RMAX,K)
               A(RMAX,K) = A(PIVOT,K)
               A(PIVOT,K) = TEMP
   20       CONTINUE
         END IF
      END IF
*
      RETURN
      END
*-----------------------------------------------------------------------*
      SUBROUTINE ELIM(A,DROWS,DCOLS,N,PIVOT)
*
*  This subroutine eliminates the element in the pivot
*  position from rows following the pivot equation.
*
      INTEGER DROWS, DCOLS, N, PIVOT, ROW, COL
      REAL A(DROWS,DCOLS), FACTOR
*
```

```
      DO 10 ROW=PIVOT+1,N
         FACTOR = A(ROW,PIVOT)/A(PIVOT,PIVOT)
         A(ROW,PIVOT) = 0.0
         DO 5 COL=PIVOT+1,N+1
            A(ROW,COL) = A(ROW,COL) - A(PIVOT,COL)*FACTOR
    5    CONTINUE
   10 CONTINUE
*
      RETURN
      END
*-----------------------------------------------------------------------*
      SUBROUTINE BACKSB(A,DROWS,DCOLS,N,SOLN)
*
*  This subroutine performs the back-substitution to
*  determine the solution to the system of equations.
*
      INTEGER DROWS, DCOLS, N, ROW, COL
      REAL A(DROWS,DCOLS), SOLN(DROWS)
*
      DO 20 ROW=N,1,-1
         DO 10 COL=N,ROW+1,-1
            A(ROW,N+1) = A(ROW,N+1) - SOLN(COL)*A(ROW,COL)
   10    CONTINUE
         SOLN(ROW) = A(ROW,N+1)/A(ROW,ROW)
   20 CONTINUE
*
      RETURN
      END
*-----------------------------------------------------------------------*
```

5. Testing

In an algorithm as complicated as this one, you should initially use very simple data, such as that used in the hand example. You should also print the values in the array A as you debug the steps in order to follow the execution of the program. It would be very useful to have a subroutine that would print the values in A in an easily readable form. Then, each time you want to see the values in A, you just insert the following statement in your program:

```
CALL PRINT (A,N)
```

In fact, you would probably want to include it in each loop initially. Then, as you verify that certain loops are working properly, you could remove the subroutine reference from those loops. There are ways to combine some of the steps outlined in this algorithm, but we have chosen not to combine them so that the algorithm will be easier to follow.

We now test the program with a more realistic set of data. The following values represent the contents of a data file for a 25-actuator deformable mirror, and thus there are 25 equations in the system of equations:

```
25
20.00  1.69 -0.49  0.00  0.00  1.69  0.40 -0.10  0.00  0.00
-0.48 -0.10 -0.05  0.00  0.00  0.00  0.01  0.00  0.00  0.00
 0.00  0.00  0.00  0.00  0.00  -20.
 1.81 20.00  1.93 -0.47  0.00  0.28  1.76  0.66 -0.13  0.00
-0.48 -0.17 -0.18 -0.03  0.00  0.00  0.00  0.00  0.00  0.00
 0.00  0.00  0.00  0.00  0.00  -10.
```

```
-0.49  2.00 20.00  1.98 -0.48 -0.30  0.70  1.78  0.71 -0.31
-0.03 -0.21 -0.20 -0.19 -0.06  0.02  0.00 -0.01  0.00  0.00
 0.00  0.00  0.00  0.00  0.01  0.0
 0.01 -0.50  1.90 20.00  2.00  0.00 -0.16  0.72  1.77  0.29
 0.00 -0.05 -0.21 -0.19 -0.50  0.00  0.00 -0.01 -0.01  0.00
 0.00  0.00  0.00  0.01  0.00  10.
 0.00  0.01 -0.47  1.72 20.00  0.00  0.00 -0.11  0.39  1.70
 0.00  0.00 -0.04 -0.10 -0.52  0.00  0.00  0.00 -0.01 -0.02
 0.00  0.00  0.00  0.01  0.00  20.
 2.00  0.32 -0.48  0.00  0.00 20.00  1.78 -0.21 -0.01  0.00
 2.04  0.67 -0.22  0.00  0.00 -0.52 -0.15 -0.05  0.00  0.00
-0.01 -0.01  0.00  0.00  0.00 -20.
 0.79  3.52  1.00 -0.42  0.00  3.49 20.00  2.97 -0.23  0.01
 1.07  3.13  1.10 -0.18  0.00 -0.40 -0.18 -0.20 -0.04 -0.01
-0.01 -0.01 -0.02 -0.01  0.00 -10.
-0.37  0.75  3.40  0.77 -0.38 -0.58  3.02 20.00  2.99 -0.56
-0.47  0.97  2.85  0.96 -0.46 -0.02 -0.18 -0.21 -0.17 -0.03
 0.00  0.00 -0.01 -0.01  0.00  0.0
 0.00 -0.44  1.10  3.55  0.82  0.03 -0.22  3.13 20.00  3.57
 0.03 -0.23  1.21  3.21  0.96 -0.01 -0.08 -0.22 -0.21 -0.42
 0.00 -0.01 -0.03 -0.02 -0.02  10.
 0.00  0.01 -0.50  2.97  2.02  0.00  0.00 -0.20  1.84 20.00
 0.00  0.00 -0.20  0.67  1.99  0.00 -0.01 -0.05 -0.15 -0.50
 0.00  0.00  0.00 -0.01 -0.01  20.
-0.51 -0.30 -0.05  0.00  0.00  2.01  0.72 -0.20  0.00  0.00
20.00  1.76 -0.19  0.00  0.00  2.09  0.70 -0.21  0.00  0.00
-0.48 -0.30 -0.05  0.00  0.00 -20.
-0.43 -0.63 -0.52 -0.07  0.01  0.84  3.27  1.13 -0.24  0.00
 3.72 20.00  3.20 -0.23 -0.02  0.87  3.25  1.06 -0.20  0.02
-0.42 -0.62 -0.53 -0.07  0.00  -10.
-0.10 -0.50 -0.45 -0.47 -0.10 -0.49  1.20  3.19  1.20 -0.50
-0.45  3.16 20.00  3.18 -0.44 -0.48  1.22  3.21  1.23 -0.48
-0.10 -0.48 -0.45 -0.50 -0.08  0.0
 0.00 -0.04 -0.46 -0.57 -0.36  0.00 -0.18  0.99  3.03  0.77
 0.00 -0.16  2.70 20.00  3.55  0.00 -0.20  0.97  3.07  0.76
 0.00 -0.03 -0.47 -0.57 -0.38  10.
 0.00  0.00 -0.03 -0.26 -0.48  0.00  0.00 -0.17  0.66  1.88
 0.00  0.00 -0.18  1.80 20.00  0.00  0.00 -0.18  0.67  1.97
 0.00  0.00 -0.04 -0.28 -0.50  20.
-0.01  0.00  0.01  0.00  0.00 -0.50 -0.15 -0.04  0.00  0.00
 1.88  0.70 -0.20  0.00  0.00 20.00  1.77 -0.19 -0.01  0.00
 2.03  0.30 -0.51  0.00  0.00  -20.
 0.00 -0.02  0.00  0.00  0.00 -0.40 -0.20 -0.21 -0.05  0.00
 1.11  3.04  1.10 -0.19  0.00  3.46 20.00  3.00 -0.18  0.00
 0.78  3.51  1.05 -0.41  0.00  -10.
 0.00  0.01 -0.01  0.00  0.02 -0.04 -0.21 -0.18 -0.18 -0.06
-0.52  0.97  3.00  1.00 -0.47 -0.61  3.08 20.00  3.21 -0.61
-0.39  0.80  3.70  0.81 -0.41  0.0
 0.01  0.00  0.00  0.02  0.00  0.01 -0.08 -0.23 -0.21 -0.42
 0.03 -0.22  1.30  3.22  1.21 -0.02 -0.24  3.14 20.00  3.56
-0.02 -0.42  1.06  3.52  0.80  10.
 0.00  0.00  0.01  0.00  0.01  0.00  0.00 -0.06 -0.15 -0.50
 0.01  0.00 -0.20  0.71  2.10  0.00 -0.03 -0.21  1.82 20.00
 0.00  0.00 -0.50  0.32  2.03  20.
-0.01  0.00  0.02  0.00  0.01  0.00  0.00  0.00  0.00  0.00
-0.58 -0.13 -0.06  0.00  0.00  1.77  0.42 -0.12 -0.04  0.00
20.00  1.71 -0.52  0.00  0.00  -20.
 0.00  0.01  0.00  0.01  0.00  0.01  0.02  0.00  0.00  0.00
-0.50 -0.19 -0.20 -0.05  0.00  0.30  1.81  0.70 -0.16  0.00
 1.97 20.00  2.00 -0.48  0.00  -10.
 0.00  0.00  0.00  0.00  0.00  0.00  0.00  0.01  0.00  0.00
-0.03 -0.17 -0.18 -0.17 -0.03 -0.26  0.70  1.75  0.66 -0.27
```

```
-0.48  1.97 20.00  1.94 -0.46  0.0
 0.00  0.00  0.00  0.00  0.00  0.00  0.00  0.01 -0.01  0.00
 0.00 -0.04 -0.21 -0.20 -0.46  0.00 -0.16  0.69  1.80  0.30
-0.02 -0.51  1.91 20.00  2.02  10.
 0.00  0.00  0.00  0.00  0.00  0.00  0.00  0.00 -0.01  0.01
 0.00  0.00 -0.05 -0.11 -0.48  0.00  0.00 -0.11  0.39  1.70
 0.00 -0.01 -0.51  1.70 20.00  20.
```

After running the program, the data file ACTUATOR is generated, which contains the solution to this set of simultaneous equations:

```
25
-.915546
-.403108
1.971845E-03
.393537
.923172
-.814070
-.167461
-3.078443E-03
.177356
.758083
-.854364
-.269669
-4.713885E-03
.285722
.868225
-.818150
-.170535
-1.285186E-03
.156909
.805012
-.917450
-.394034
1.204488E-03
.391093
.917205
```

10-6 ■ Numerical Integration and Differentiation

The operations of integration and differentiation give engineers and scientists important information about functions or data sets. For example, distance, velocity, and acceleration are all related to each other through integrals (integration) and derivatives (differentiation). Velocity is the integral of acceleration and the derivative of distance with respect to time. The topics of integration and differentiation are covered in detail in calculus courses, but the underlying principles can be explained simply in terms of areas and slopes. The integral of a function over an interval represents the area under the graph of the function; differentiation corresponds to computing the tangents or slopes to the function at specified points. Both these computations can be numerically approximated using FORTRAN.

■ Integration Using the Trapezoidal Rule

In order to use the analytical techniques of calculus to obtain the integral of a function over an interval, we must have an equation for the function. In many engineering and scientific applications, we have data points or measurements from the function, but we do not have an explicit equation. Therefore, we need a method that requires only points of the function to numerically compute the integral. In other applications, we may have an equation that defines the function, but it is difficult or impossible to determine the integral analytically. In this case we would also like to have a method that allows us to compute points or values of the function and then numerically evaluate the integral. The technique that we present in this section is a simple way to numerically estimate the area under a curve, given points on the curve. The technique uses the areas of trapezoids and thus is called integration using the trapezoidal rule.

The integral of the function $f(x)$, evaluated from a to b, is expressed as $\int_a^b f(x)\,dx$ and represents the area under the function $f(x)$ from $x=a$ to $x=b$, as shown in this diagram:

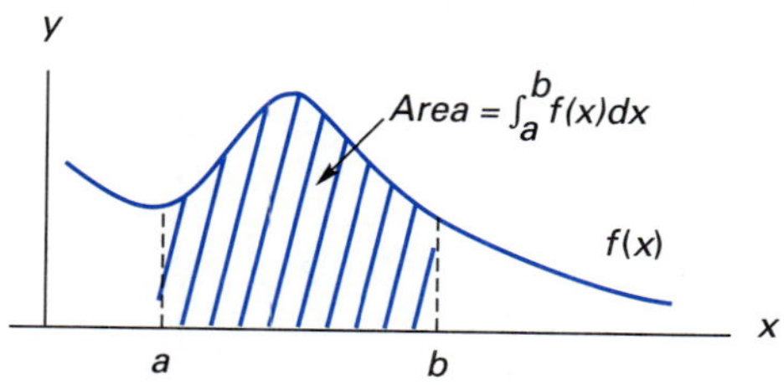

If we are given the function that represents the curve, we can evaluate the function at points spaced along the interval of interest, as shown:

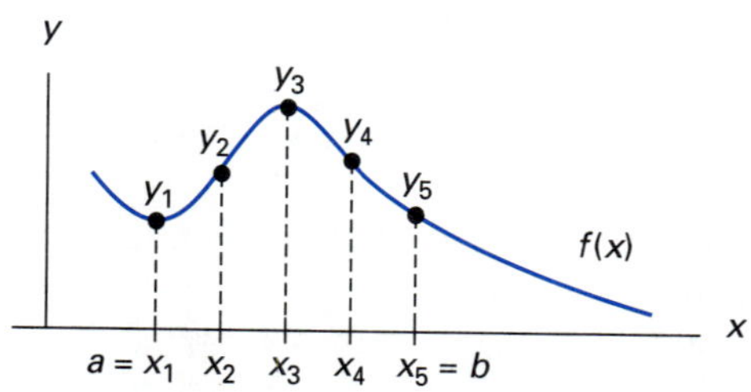

Note that since $y=f(x)$, we can represent $f(x_1)$ as y_1, $f(x_2)$ as y_2, and so on.

If we join the points on the curve with straight line segments, we form a group of trapezoids whose combined areas approximate the area under the curve. The closer the points are together on the curve, the more trapezoids there are in the interval, and thus the more accurate will be our approximation to the integral. In the diagram below, we use five points on the curve to generate four trapezoids, and the sum of the areas of the four trapezoids is then an approximation to the integral of the function between a and b.

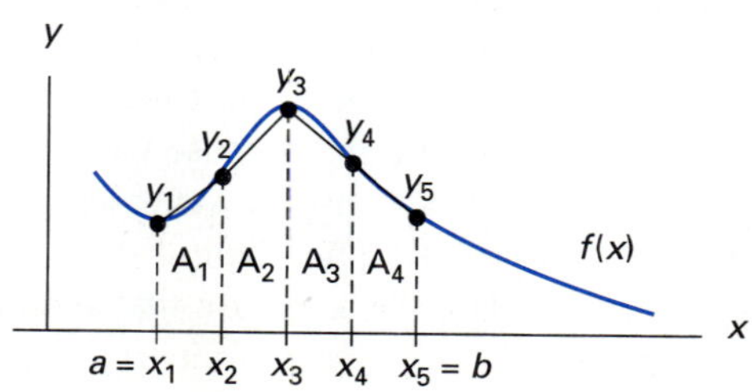

Recall that the area of a trapezoid is equal to one-half times the base times the sum of the two heights (or sides):

$$\text{area} = \tfrac{1}{2} \cdot \text{base} \cdot (\text{height1}+\text{height2})$$

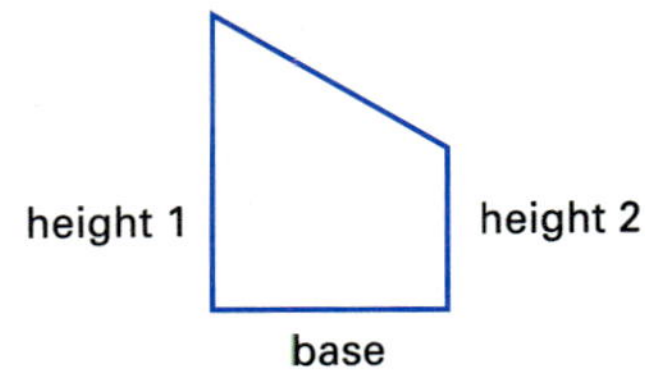

Thus, the area of the first trapezoid, A_1, is computed using the pair of points (x_1,y_1) and (x_2,y_2):

$$A_1 = \tfrac{1}{2} \cdot (x_2 - x_1) \cdot (y_1 + y_2)$$

Since the points on the curve are equally spaced along the x axis in this example, the base of each of the trapezoids is the same value. We can then compute the individual areas of the trapezoids as

$$A_1 = \tfrac{1}{2} \cdot \text{base} \cdot (y_1 + y_2)$$
$$A_2 = \tfrac{1}{2} \cdot \text{base} \cdot (y_2 + y_3)$$
$$A_3 = \tfrac{1}{2} \cdot \text{base} \cdot (y_3 + y_4)$$
$$A_4 = \tfrac{1}{2} \cdot \text{base} \cdot (y_4 + y_5)$$

Thus, the total area between a and b can be approximated by the sum of the areas of the four trapezoids:

$$\int_a^b f(x)dx \approx \frac{\text{base}}{2}((y_1 + y_2) + (y_2 + y_3) + (y_3 + y_4) + (y_4 + y_5))$$
$$\approx \frac{\text{base}}{2}(y_1 + 2y_2 + 2y_3 + 2y_4 + y_5)$$

In general, if the area under a curve is divided into N trapezoids with equal bases, the area can be approximated by the following equation:

$$\int_a^b f(x)dx \approx \frac{\text{base}}{2}(y_1 + 2\sum_{k=2}^{N} y_k + y_{N+1}) \qquad (10-13)$$

This equation is referred to as the trapezoidal rule.

When computing an integral with this numerical technique, we need to remember that the data points on the curve could come from different sources. If we have the equation for the curve, the program can compute the data points that we then use as the heights of the trapezoids; in this case, we can choose the data points to be as close together or as far apart as we wish. Another possibility is that the points are experimentally collected data; in this case, we have a set of x coordinates that represent the trapezoid base values and the y coordinates that represent the heights of the trapezoids. We can still use the trapezoid areas to estimate the integral, but we cannot choose data points that are closer together or farther apart because we do not have a function to evaluate; we only have the available data to use. If the bases of the trapezoids determined by the data points are not of equal value, then we have to add the areas of the trapezoids individually, instead of using the equation that assumes that the bases are equal.

■ Differentiation Using Central Differences

Much of the field of calculus is concerned with the concepts of derivatives and integrals of functions. Derivatives and integrals are closely related, because they reverse or "undo" each other. If we take the derivative of a function, we get a new function. If we then integrate that new function, we get the original function back again, to within a constant. Reversing the order (integral, then derivative) also gives us back the original function.

We saw in the previous discussion that the integral of a function could be described graphically—it was the area under the function curve. The derivative of a function is the rate of change of the function. Like the integral, it can also be described graphically, as shown in the plot below, which contains a function curve $y=f(x)$ and a line L that is tangent to the curve at the point (x_1,y_1). The first derivative of $f(x)$, with respect to x at x_1 is equal to the slope of the tangent line at x_1, which is dy/dx.

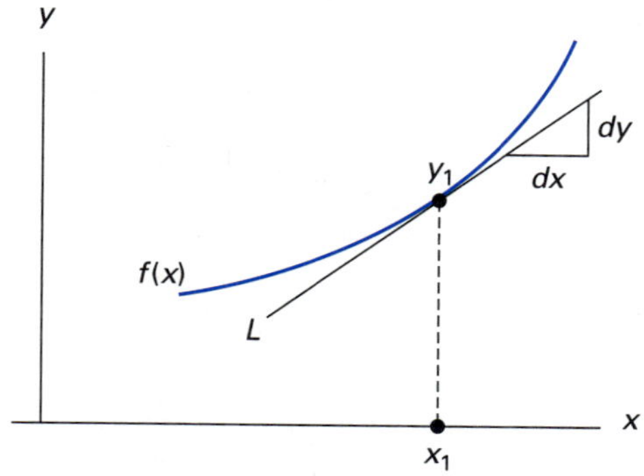

If we calculated the slopes of the tangent lines at many points along the function curve and plotted the resulting values, we would get a new curve that would be the first derivative of $y=f(x)$. Tangent lines to this new curve would represent the derivative of the first derivative, or the second derivative of $y=f(x)$. Third and higher derivatives can be obtained by continuing this process of calculating the slopes of tangent lines to the curve and plotting those values to get the next curve.

When the derivative of a function is difficult or impossible to find mathematically, we can estimate it graphically, and thus numerically, by constructing secant lines between data points for the function and computing their slopes. In the figure below, we show three of the data points from a larger set of data for a function $y=f(x)$.

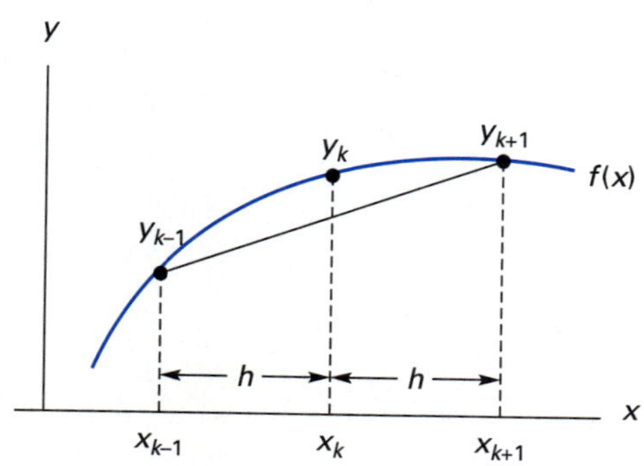

As illustrated in the figure, the first derivative y_k' at x_k can be estimated by computing the slope of the secant line connecting points y_{k-1} and y_{k+1}:

$$y_k' \approx \frac{y_{k+1} - y_{k-1}}{2h} \tag{10-14}$$

Note that as the data points get closer together, our estimate for the derivative at y_k should become more accurate because in the limit, as h approaches zero, the slope of the secant line connecting the data points approaches the slope of the tangent line at y_k.

To compute the second derivative y_k'', which is the rate of change of the slope or of the first derivative at x_k, we apply this method again. In the following figure, we draw secant lines between the adjacent points and compute the slopes of these two lines. We then compute the difference in the slopes of the two lines and divide by the distance between their midpoints. The result is the rate of change of the slope, which is also an estimate of the second derivative of the function at x_k.

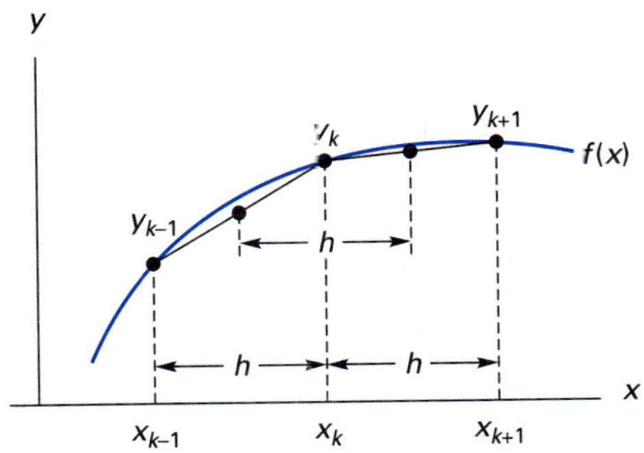

Thus our formula for estimating the second derivative is

$$y_k'' = \frac{(y_{k+1} - y_k)/h - (y_k - y_{k-1})/h}{h}$$

$$= \frac{y_{k+1} - 2y_k + y_{k-1}}{h^2} \tag{10-15}$$

The equations for the first derivative and for the second derivative are examples of "central-difference" expressions because they compute differences using data values on both sides of the point at which we are estimating the derivative. Similar difference expressions can be derived using only points to the left or only points to the right of the point at which we are estimating the derivative; these formulas are called backward-difference and forward-difference expressions, respectively. The central-difference expressions are recommended over the backward- and forward-difference expressions because they are more accurate. Note that we cannot compute derivatives for the first and last points of a set of data using central-difference equations because we do not have function values on both sides of the endpoints. For these points we would use forward- or backward-difference expressions.

Caution should be exercised when using numerical differentiation because it should be used only with accurate data sets. Noise or other sources of inaccuracy in the data can cause large inaccuracies in the estimates of the derivatives. This problem can be seen clearly in the figures below. Each graph shows a set of data that represent the same unknown function $f(x)$. In the left figure the data points are accurate and closely spaced, but in the right figure they are noisy and widely spaced. In the left figure, we see that we can get a reasonably good estimate of the slope of the curve at point B by computing the slope of the secant line which connects points A and C. On the other hand, we see that the same technique applied to the figure on the right does not provide an accurate estimate of the slope at point B. And computing the second derivative, which is the rate of change of the slope of the curve, can introduce even larger errors.

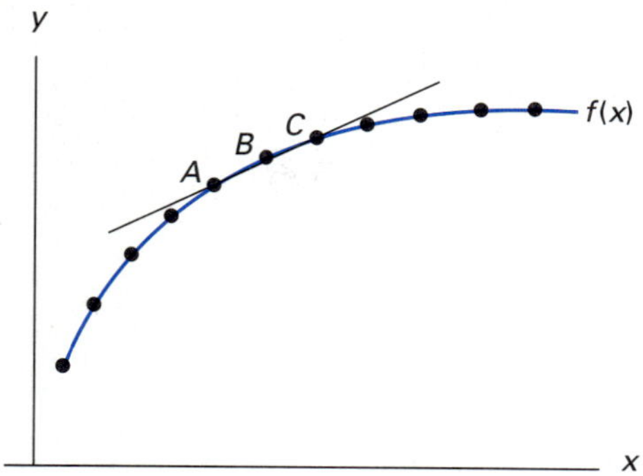

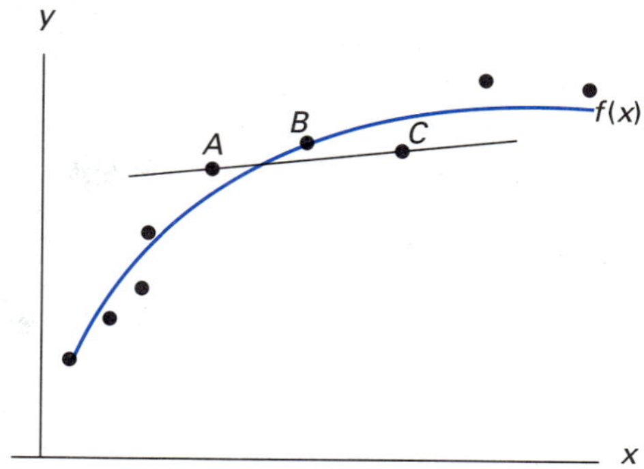

We see, therefore, that numerical differentiation should be used only for data sets that represent the function accurately, and that even then the results should be used with care.

Another technique for estimating derivatives, especially when the data are inaccurate, would be to use the curve fitting techniques. If you fit a least-squares polynomial model to the data, you can then take the derivative of the polynomial using calculus and solve for the derivatives at specific points. This method may give more accurate results, but it requires more computations.

SELF-TEST 10-3

This self-test allows you to check quickly to see if you have remembered the key points from Section 10–6. If you have any problems with the exercises, you should reread this section. The solutions are included at the end of the text.

For Problems 1–4, let the function $f(x)$ be defined by the following equation:

$$f(x) = 3x - 2x^2$$

1. Sketch the function over the interval $[-1,2]$.
2. Use the trapezoidal rule to compute the integral of $f(x)$ from $x=0$ to $x=1$, using two trapezoids.
3. Use the trapezoidal rule to compute the integral of $f(x)$ from $x=0$ to $x=1$, using five trapezoids.
4. The exact value of the integral is 5/6. Compare your answers in problems 2 and 3 to this exact value. Explain the difference between the answers for problems 2 and 3.

Problems 5–7 use the following data that represent time and altitude data from the launch of a weather balloon:

Time (seconds)	Altitude (feet)
0.0	0.0
0.5	50.0
1.0	75.0
1.5	125.0
2.0	175.0

5. Plot this altitude data and sketch the curve it represents.

6. Compute first-derivative values using the central-difference equation derived in this section. Sketch this velocity data.

7. Compute second-derivative values using the central-difference equation derived in this section. Sketch this acceleration data.

10.7 Application ▪ Sounding Rocket Trajectory

Aerospace Engineering

A two-stage sounding rocket is launched to perform high-altitude atmospheric research on the ionosphere. (Sounding rockets probe different levels of the atmosphere.) The first stage of the rocket burns for approximately 35 seconds and accelerates the rocket to a velocity of 1250 meters per second. It then coasts for almost 2 minutes before reaching the lower region of the ionosphere at about 100 kilometers. By then, gravity has slowed the rocket's ascent to about 100 meters per second. The second stage then ignites and accelerates the rocket through the ionosphere and into space.

The rocket carries a scientific package for conducting several measurements on the upper atmosphere. A telemetry system in the rocket's payload section (in the nose of the rocket) transmits the data to a receiver at the launch site. In addition to the scientific data, performance measurements on the rocket itself are transmitted to be monitored by range safety personnel and to be analyzed later by engineers. One of those measurements is the rocket's altitude from the time of launch until the test is completed. The altitude measurements are plotted versus the time of flight in the graph below, which contains data points collected at 10-second intervals along the actual altitude curve.

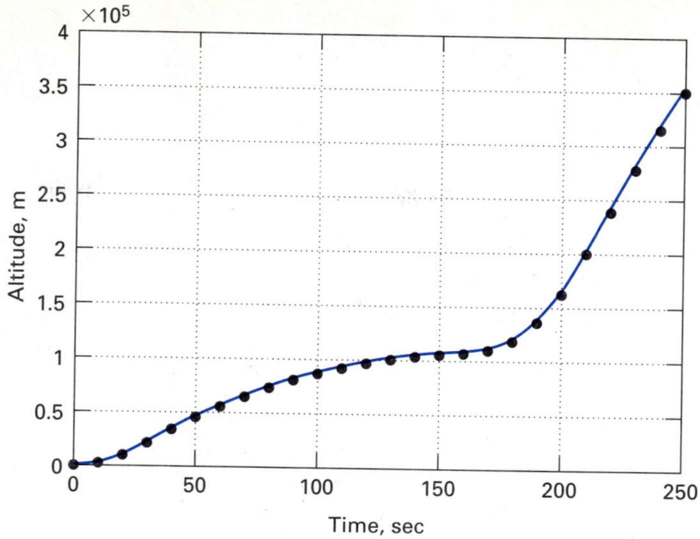

Before the rocket is flown, a simulation program is used to predict the acceleration, velocity, and altitude of the rocket as a function of time. After the actual flight of the rocket, a separate program is needed to differentiate the recorded altitude data, to obtain estimates for (or to reconstruct) the velocity and acceleration for comparison with the simulation results.

Write a program that reads the recorded altitude data from a data file and estimates the corresponding velocity and acceleration information using numerical differentiation. Assume that the first line in the data file contains an integer that specifies the number of data points in the file; a data point consists of a time value and its corresponding altitude value in meters. Use numerical differentiation to compute and store the velocity and acceleration information in data files.

1. Problem Statement

Use numerical differentiation to compute velocity and acceleration data for a sounding rocket using the time and altitude data.

2. Input/Output Description

Input—a data file containing the time and altitude data

Output—two data files; one contains the estimated velocity information and the other contains the estimated acceleration information

3. Hand Example

Assume that the first six values of altitude data are the following:

Time	Altitude
0.0	0.0
1.0	100.0
2.0	250.0
3.0	430.0
4.0	680.0
5.0	980.0

The derivative with respect to time of altitude data in meters gives the velocity in units of meters per second. Since the data is collected at equally spaced intervals in time, we can use Eq. (10–14) from the previous section to perform the computation of the first derivative, with the increment between data points equal to 1.0 second. Thus, the equation for computing the first derivative is

$$y_k' = \frac{y_{k+1} - y_{k-1}}{2h}$$

$$= \frac{y_{k+1} - y_{k-1}}{2.0}$$

The velocity values are

$$\text{velocity at 1.0 sec} = \frac{250 - 0.0}{2.0}$$

$$= 125 \text{ m/sec}$$

$$\text{velocity at 2.0 sec} = 165 \text{ m/sec}$$
$$\text{velocity at 3.0 sec} = 215 \text{ m/sec}$$
$$\text{velocity at 4.0 sec} = 275 \text{ m/sec}$$

We now use Eq. (10–15) to compute the second derivative from the altitude data. This equation is

$$y_k'' = \frac{y_{k+1} - 2y_k + y_{k-1}}{h^2}$$

$$= \frac{y_{k+1} - 2y_k + y_{k-1}}{1.0}$$

The acceleration values are

$$\text{acceleration at 1.0 sec} = \frac{250 - (2)(100) + 0}{1.0}$$

$$= 50 \text{ m/sec}^2$$

$$\text{acceleration at 2.0 sec} = 30 \text{ m/sec}^2$$

$$\text{acceleration at 3.0 sec} = 70 \text{ m/sec}^2$$

$$\text{acceleration at 4.0 sec} = 50 \text{ m/sec}^2$$

4. Algorithm Development

The decomposition of the solution into general steps is the following:

Decomposition

Read altitude data.
Compute and store velocity data.
Compute and store acceleration data.

The most straightforward way to implement the numerical differentiation technique is to store the time and altitude data from the data file in arrays. Then, we use the equations for computing the first and second derivatives to calculate values of velocity and acceleration and store these values in additional arrays. When we write the information in the two output data files, we write the number of points in the first line and follow that with the data points.

We now develop the pseudocode to implement this differentiation technique.

Pseudocode

Numdif: Read the number of altitude points, N
Read the time and altitude data into arrays
$h \leftarrow time(2) - time(1)$
For $k = 2$ to $N - 1$ do

$$vel(k) \leftarrow \frac{alt(k+1) - alt(k-1)}{2\,h}$$

Write time(k), vel(k) to data file

$$acc(k) \leftarrow \frac{alt(k+1) - 2 \cdot alt(k) + alt(k-1)}{h^2}$$

Write time(k), acc(k) to data file

The next step is to convert the pseudocode to FORTRAN.

FORTRAN Program

```
*-----------------------------------------------------------------*
      PROGRAM NUMDIF
*
*  This program uses numerical differentiation to compute the
*  velocity and acceleration data for a sounding rocket.
*
      INTEGER N, K
      REAL TIME(512), ALT(512), H, VEL(512), ACC(512)
*
      OPEN (UNIT=15,FILE='ALTITUDE',STATUS='OLD')
      OPEN (UNIT=16,FILE='VELOCITY',STATUS='NEW')
      OPEN (UNIT=17,FILE='ACCEL',STATUS='NEW')
*
```

```
*  Read time and altitude data.
*
      READ (15,*) N
      DO 10 K=1,N
         READ (15,*) TIME(K), ALT(K)
   10 CONTINUE
*
*  Compute and store velocities and accelerations.
*
      H = TIME(2) - TIME(1)
      WRITE (16,*) N-2
      WRITE (17,*) N-2
*
      DO 20 K=2,N-1
         VEL(K) = (ALT(K+1) - ALT(K-1))/(2.0*H)
         WRITE (16,*) TIME(K), VEL(K)
         ACC(K) = (ALT(K+1) - 2*ALT(K) + ALT(K-1))/(H*H)
         WRITE (17,*) TIME(K), ACC(K)
   20 CONTINUE
*
      END
*----------------------------------------------------------------------*
```

5. Testing

The following data represent time and altitude above sea level for the two-stage rocket discussed at the beginning of this section:

Time	Altitude	Time	Altitude
0.0	6.000000E+01	130.0	1.008788E+05
10.0	2.926538E+03	140.0	1.034222E+05
20.0	1.017024E+04	150.0	1.049857E+05
30.0	2.148626E+04	160.0	1.061926E+05
40.0	3.383508E+04	170.0	1.102465E+05
50.0	4.525083E+04	180.0	1.196263E+05
60.0	5.563449E+04	190.0	1.361064E+05
70.0	6.503796E+04	200.0	1.620957E+05
80.0	7.346143E+04	210.0	1.995064E+05
90.0	8.090491E+04	220.0	2.387758E+05
100.0	8.736838E+04	230.0	2.770653E+05
110.0	9.285185E+04	240.0	3.143748E+05
120.0	9.735532E+04	250.0	3.507043E+05

The next pair of plots contain the actual velocity and acceleration functions along with circles that represent the values computed from the altitude data using numerical differentiation. Note that numerical differentiation does a good job of estimating the velocity and acceleration functions, except at points where the function changes rapidly. Also, from observing the velocity data we can see the rocket's velocity increasing and then slowly decreasing after the first stage of the rocket burns out. When the second stage is fired, the velocity begins to increase again.

From the acceleration plot, you can easily see the accelerations caused by the firing of the first stage and of the second stage. In the intervals after the firings, the acceleration is -9.8 m/sec^2, which is the downward acceleration due to gravity.

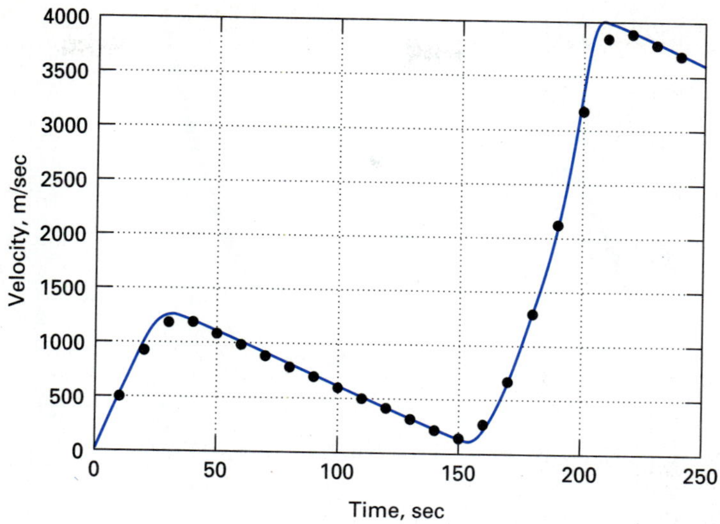

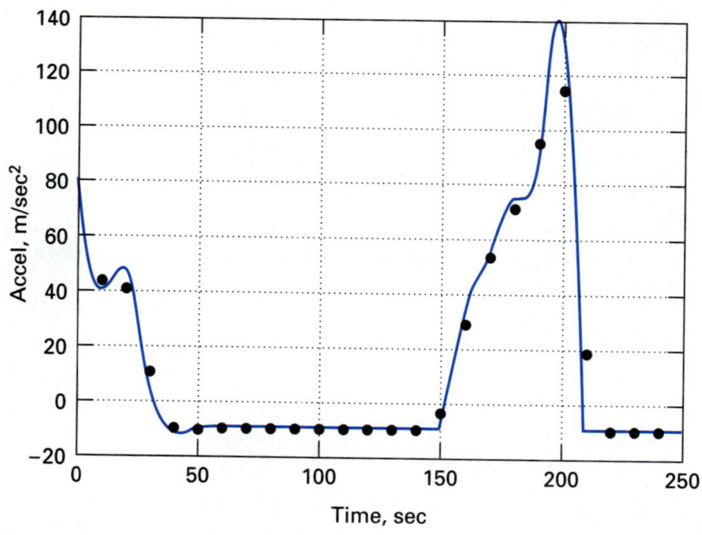

The data in the following two plots provide an interesting comparison to the previous plots. For these plots, the data points are 1 second apart, rather than 10 seconds apart. As you can see, when we use smaller time increments, our numerical estimates for velocity and acceleration become more accurate in the regions where the functions are changing rapidly.

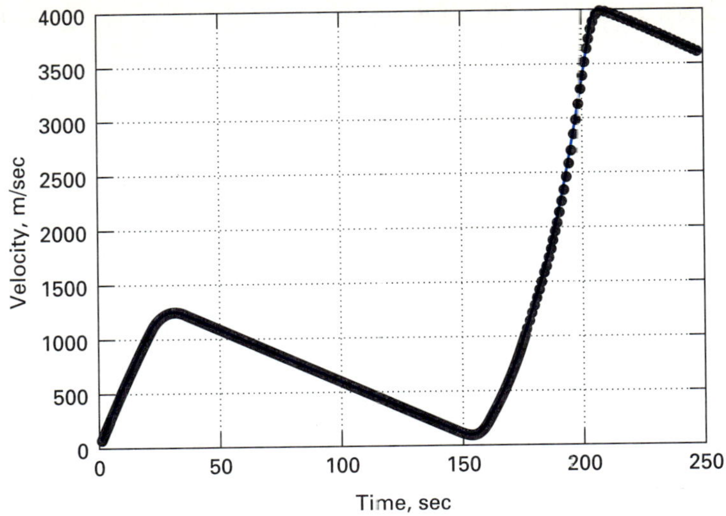

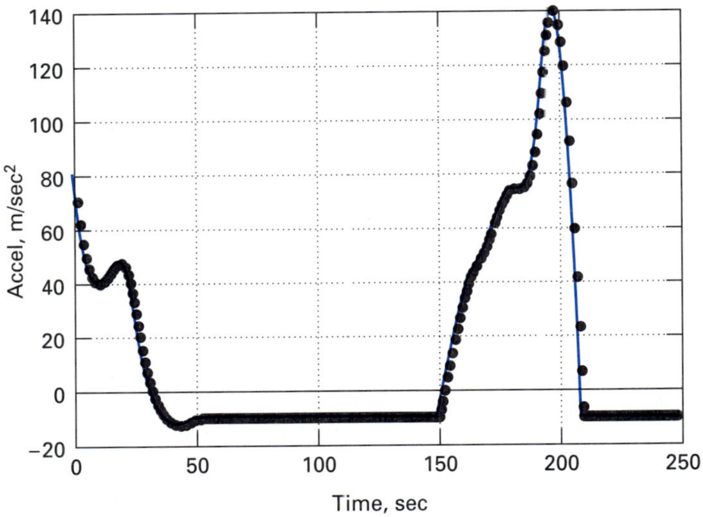

One limitation of the solution presented in this section is caused by the fact that we stored the data in arrays. The program specifies a maximum of 512 points; if more altitude points are needed, the array sizes need to be larger. It is also possible to develop a solution to this problem without using arrays. Since three altitude data points are needed to compute the corresponding velocity and acceleration, we could develop an algorithm that stores three altitude values in memory. After computing the corresponding velocity and acceleration values and writing the new values to data files, we then read a new altitude value to replace one of the three altitude values and repeat the process. This solution is more complicated to develop, but it is not limited by array sizes and is thus a more flexible solution.

Summary

Some of the numerical techniques commonly used by engineers and scientists were introduced in this chapter. A set of data was modeled using a linear equation, and the model was evaluated using a sum of squared error values. A number of matrix operations were implemented in FORTRAN subprograms so that they could easily be added to other programs. The Gauss elimination method was presented for solving a system of simultaneous equations, and the solution was developed using matrix manipulations. Finally, numerical integration using the trapezoidal rule and numerical differentiation using central differences were discussed.

Debugging Aids

To debug least-squares problems, it is very useful to plot the original points and the approximating function. The original points should not necessarily fall on the approximating function, but the function should be a good fit to data points.

When debugging programs with matrices, it is imperative to have a routine that prints the matrices in an easy-to-read format. Then, as we are debugging, we can use statements to call the print routine each time we need to check the contents of the array. Once the program is debugged, the calls to the print routine can be removed. These types of routines are often called snapshot routines, because they give us a snapshot of the situation at the time that the routine is referenced. The Gauss elimination method is a multistep method, and debugging multistep methods can be very difficult. Start by using a very simple hand example that you have worked out ahead of time, and compare your hand solution to the output from the snapshot routine to slowly and carefully debug the process.

The equations for most numerical integration and differentiation techniques are simple, and therefore debugging these routines is usually straightforward. However, some caution must be taken in determining the step size of the small intervals used in these techniques. If the step size is too large in numerical integration, then trapezoids may not provide good approximations to the area under the slope. If the step size is too large in numerical differentiation, then the slope is computed using data points that are not close to the point at which we are estimating the derivative, and thus the result may not be accurate. If the step size is too small in numerical integration or differentiation, truncation and roundoff within the computer can cause errors. Therefore, selecting the proper step size can be an important part of numerical integration or differentiation.

Style/Technique Guides

Numerical applications may often use techniques that are not familiar to all programmers; thus, be sure to document the program and its modules carefully. If certain numerical applications are going to be used frequently, develop a set of modules that apply to the application. For example, if you are using matrices frequently, develop a set of modules to perform the operations that you need, and use this set consistently.

FORTRAN does not have a standard set of numerical approximation functions and subroutines; thus, in this chapter we wrote our own programs and subprograms. However, a number of excellent packages exist that are written in FORTRAN and thus are accessible from a FORTRAN program. These packages include routines to find matrix inverses, to solve differential equations and large systems of simultaneous equations, and to fit curves to a set of data. In general, if a routine exists in a numerical package to perform the operation that you need, it is better to use that routine than to write one yourself because the general routine is written to handle special cases and to perform operations so that precision errors are minimized.

Key Words

Gauss elimination	numerical differentiation
linear model	numerical integration
matrix	residual

Problems

We begin our problem set with modifications to programs developed earlier in this chapter. Give the decomposition, pseudocode or flowchart, and FORTRAN solution for each problem.

Problems 1–5 modify the program LINEAR, given on page 475, which computed a linear model for a set of data.

1. Modify the linear model program so that it prints the point that has the largest residual (in absolute value)—this is the point that deviates most from the approximate straight line.
2. Modify the linear model program so that it computes the residual sum as the sum of the absolute value of the difference between the actual data value for *y* and its estimated value.
3. Modify the linear model program so that it computes the slope and *y*-intercept in a subroutine.
4. Modify the linear model program so that it reads a data file that has a trailer record containing −999, −999 as the coordinates of the data point.
5. Modify the linear model program so that it asks the user to enter an *x* value and then uses the linear equation that has been computed to estimate the corresponding *y* value.

Problems 6–10 modify the program GAUSS, given on page 494, which uses Gauss elimination to solve a set of simultaneous equations.

6. Modify the Gauss elimination program so that the reorder subroutine prints a message specifying which rows were switched.
7. Modify the Gauss elimination program so that it includes a debugging subroutine PRINT that will print the values in the A array in an easily readable form.

8. Modify the Gauss elimination program so that the steps to print the solution are printed in a subroutine rather than in the main program.
9. Modify the Gauss elimination program so that the data are read by a subroutine instead of the main program. The subroutine should ask the user to enter the name of the file and then open the file, read the data, and close the file.
10. Modify the Gauss elimination program so that it writes the solution to the set of simultaneous equations to a data file. The first line of the data file should contain the number of actuators, and each following line should contain the number of the actuator and its corresponding value.

Problems 11–15 modify the program NUMDIF, given on page 507, which computes the velocity and acceleration for a sounding rocket.

11. Modify the differentiation program so that it uses the following forward-difference approximation for the slope:

$$y_k' = \frac{y_{k+1} - y_k}{h}$$

(You will need to modify the equations for both derivatives.)
12. Modify the differentiation program so that it uses the following backward difference approximation for the slope:

$$y_k' = \frac{y_k - y_{k-1}}{h}$$

(You will need to modify the equations for both derivatives.)
13. Modify the differentiation program so that it uses the following central-difference approximation, which does not assume that the step size between points is always the same value:

$$y_k' = \frac{y_{k+1} - y_{k-1}}{x_{k+1} - x_{k-1}}$$

(You will need to modify the equations for both derivatives.)
14. Modify the differentiation program so that it does not use arrays and thus is more flexible. (See the comments at the end of Section 10–6.)
15. Modify the differentiation program so that the output is one file that contains both the velocity and acceleration data. The first line of the file contains the number of data points. The following lines contain three values, the time, the corresponding velocity, and the corresponding acceleration.

In problems 16–24, develop programs and modules using the five-step process.

16. When we transmit communication signals, we are concerned about the power in the signal because the more powerful the signal, the better the transmission that occurs. However, for efficient transmission, we do not want to transmit more signal power than is necessary. Hence, when we have a signal to transmit, we often compute the function that describes the power of the signal with respect to the frequencies within the signal. Before transmitting the sig-

nal, the power of the signal contained in an interval or band between two frequencies is computed; this computation is the integral of the power function between the two frequencies, or the area under the power function curve between the two frequencies. Write a program to compute the power in a specified frequency band given the following equation, which describes the power in a signal with respect to frequency:

$$\begin{aligned} y &= f(x) \\ &= 4e^{-x} \end{aligned}$$

where the units of x are Hz (Hertz, or cycles per second) and the units of y are power per Hz. Use the trapezoidal rule to approximate the power in a band of frequencies, and allow the user to choose both the band of frequencies and the number of trapezoids.

17. Modify the program in problem 16 so that the number of trapezoids is initially set to 10 and the corresponding area is computed. Then, the number of trapezoids is doubled and the area is recomputed. This process continues until the change in the area is less than 0.01.

Problems 18–20 refer to the following algorithm for computing π. The area of a circle with radius 1 is equal to π, and thus the area of a quarter-circle with radius 1 is equal to $\pi/4$. If we compute an estimate of the area of this quarter-circle and multiply that value by 4, we have an estimate for the value of π. To compute the area of the quarter-circle, we sum the area of the subsections of the circle that are approximated by trapezoids, as shown in the following diagram. The values for y_i and y_{i+1} can be computed using the sine and cosine functions. If we assume that the areas of the subsections are added, starting with the subsections on the right, the appropriate equations are

$$\begin{aligned} \text{sub}_i &= 0.5 \cdot dx_i \cdot (y_{i+1} + y_i) \\ x_i &= \cos \theta_i \\ y_i &= \sin \theta i \\ dx_i &= x_i - x_{i+1} \end{aligned}$$

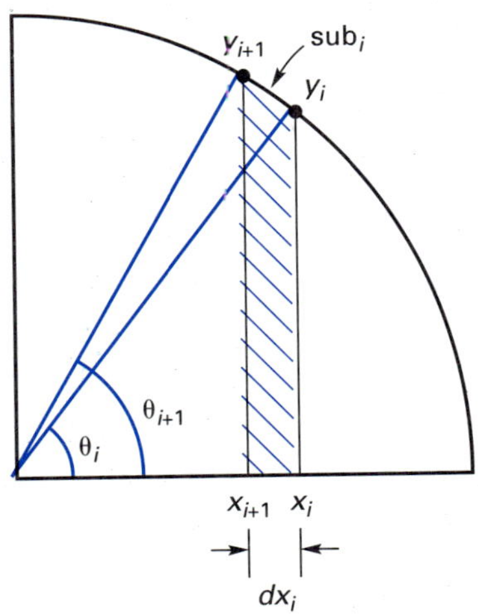

18. Write a program to compute π using the technique just described. Let the number of subsections be entered by the user.

19. Modify the program developed in problem 18 so that the variables and all computations are performed in double precision.

20. Modify the program developed in problem 18 so that the number of subsections is initialized to 100. Print the number of subsections and the estimate of π; then repeat the process increasing the number of subsections by 100. Continue until the number of subsections is equal to 1000.

21. Write a subroutine to compute the transpose of an integer matrix, where a transpose is defined as another matrix that is generated by exchanging the rows and columns of the original matrix. An example of a matrix **A** and its transpose is

$$\mathbf{A} = \begin{bmatrix} 2 & 5 & 1 & 1 \\ 3 & 1 & 0 & 5 \\ 8 & 9 & 9 & 4 \end{bmatrix} \qquad \text{Transpose of } \mathbf{A} = \begin{bmatrix} 2 & 3 & 8 \\ 5 & 1 & 9 \\ 1 & 0 & 9 \\ 1 & 5 & 4 \end{bmatrix}$$

The subroutine would be called with the following statement, where **T** is the transpose of **A**; ANR, ANC, TNR, TNC represent the operational sizes of **A** and **T**; and AROWS, ACOLS, TROWS, TCOLS represent the dimensional sizes of **A** and **T**:

```
CALL TRANSP(A,ANR,ANC,AROWS,ACOLS,T,TNR,TNC,TROWS,TCOLS)
```

22. Write a subroutine that normalizes the values in a matrix **A** to values between 0 and 1 by replacing each value with the following:

$$a_{i,j} \leftarrow \frac{a_{i,j} - \text{minimum}}{\text{maximum} - \text{minimum}}$$

where the minimum is the minimum value in the matrix and the maximum is the maximum value in the matrix. Thus, the maximum value is scaled to 1, the minimum value is scaled to 0, and all values in between are scaled accordingly. Assume that the subroutine is called with the following statement, where NA represents the normalized matrix:

```
CALL NORM(A,NA,NR,NC,DROWS,DCOLS)
```

Also assume that NR and NC represent the operational sizes of both matrices and that DROWS and DCOLS represent the dimensional sizes of both matrices.

23. Write a subroutine that multiplies a coefficient matrix **A** by a solution matrix **X**. The result should be equivalent to the constant matrix **B**. Hence, this subroutine could be used in debugging a program to solve a system of simultaneous equations. Use the following statement to reference the subroutine:

```
CALL CALCB(A,NR,NC,DROWS,DCOLS,X,B)
```

Assume that NR and NC represent the operational size of **A** and that DROWS and DCOLS represent the dimensional size of **A**. NR represents the operational size of both **X** and **B**.

24. Write a subroutine that receives a matrix **A** that contains the coefficients of a system of equations and a solution matrix **X** for the system. Compute and print the value of **AX**. Include as arguments the actual and dimensional sizes of **A**.

11 The New Fortran 90 Standard

11

APPLICATION

Fortran 90

Although it is one of the oldest high-level languages, FORTRAN continues to be one of the most popular because each new standard has kept the strengths of its numerical computations while updating the language. The updating improves current features and adds new features to enhance the computational capabilities, the control structures, and the data structures. Each new standard is upward compatible with the previous standard, so previously written programs continue to execute correctly. However, each new standard adds significant new features, and thus our problem solutions can be more efficient and effective when we take advantage of the new capabilities. With Fortran 90 now an established international standard, the ANSI (American National Standards Institute) technical committee is already looking to the future and the next Fortran standard.

Photo © Alain McLaughlin

Introduction

In this chapter we preview some of the new features of Fortran 90. We begin with the expanded character set and the improved source format of the statements. We then cover some of the new features relative to data objects, control constructs, and procedures. These discussions cover the flexible way that Fortran 90 deals with data types and how that allows us to define new data structures in our programs. Since arrays are such an important data structure in many engineering problem solutions, we devote one section to a discussion of some of the enhancements relative to arrays. Another section covers the expansion of the DO statement and the addition of the CYCLE and EXIT statements. We next discuss some new features related to procedures, which include functions and subroutines. Finally, we discuss pointers, a new data object that allows us to build linked data structures.

11·1 ■ Expanded Character Set and Source Format

Fortran 90 includes several significant additions to its character set. We first discuss this new character set and its implications related to variable names and relational operators. We then present the two allowable source formats for programs.

■ Fortran Character Set

The Fortran character set includes the 26 alphabetic letters, the 10 numeric digits, and the underscore character (_). The set of special characters available has been expanded from 13 characters in FORTRAN 77 to the set of 21 characters shown in Table 11 – 1. These special characters are used for operations and to separate components in a Fortran statement. A character literal can now be enclosed in either single quotes or double quotes.

In addition to the standard character set and the set of special characters, Fortran 90 allows compilers to include additional character sets. These character sets can be used for special purposes and include symbols for mathematics, chemistry, and music. To incorporate additional languages, character sets such as Kanji (Chinese), Greek, Cyrillic (Russian and other Slavic languages), Hindi, Magyar (Hungarian), and Nihongo (Japanese) can be included.

■ Variable Names

The characters that can be included in a name have been expanded from just letters and digits to include the underscore character. In addition, the maximum length has been expanded from 6 characters to 31 characters. These additions allow us to use names that are much more descriptive for not only variables but also programs, functions, and subroutines, as shown in the following list:

```
X_SUM
ROOT_1
ERROR_SUM
LINEAR_REGRESSION
```

Table 11·1 Fortran 90 Special Characters

Character	Character Name
	Blank
=	Equals
+	Plus
−	Minus
*	Asterisk
/	Slash
(	Left parenthesis
)	Right parenthesis
,	Comma
.	Decimal point or period
'	Apostrophe
:	Colon
!	Exclamation point
"	Quotation mark
%	Percent
&	Ampersand
;	Semicolon
<	Less than
>	Greater than
?	Question mark
$	Currency symbol

If the compiler permits lowercase letters, they are equivalent to the uppercase letters except within character string data.

■ Relational Operators

Fortran 90 allows the use of alternative relational operators, as shown in the Table 11–2.

Table 11·2 Relational Operators

Relational Operation	FORTRAN 77	Fortran 90 Addition
Equal	.EQ.	==
Not equal	.NE.	/=
Less than	.LT.	<
Less than or equal	.LE.	<=
Greater than	.GT.	>
Greater than or equal	.GE.	>=

Free and Fixed Source Form

Fortran 90 allows two types of source forms, free form and fixed form. A program must be in one or the other form; it cannot mix the forms in the same program.

In fixed source form, a line can contain no more than 72 characters. Positions 1–5 are reserved for statement labels and position 6 is used to indicate that a line is a continuation of the previous line. Fortran statements must be within positions 7–72. Comment lines are indicated by the letter C or the character * in position 1. Comments can also be indicated by the character !; a comment initiated by the character ! can be on a line by itself or can follow a Fortran statement.

In free source form, a line can contain no more than 132 characters, and there are no restrictions on where a statement may appear in the line. The character & is used at the end of the current line to indicate that the current statement is to be continued on the next line. Comments are indicated by the character ! and can appear on lines by themselves or can follow a Fortran statement.

In both fixed and free format, a semicolon can be used to separate multiple statements on the same line, as in:

```
COUNT = 0;  SUM = 0.0
```

A trailing semicolon is ignored.

INCLUDE Line

Additional source text can be incorporated into a program with the INCLUDE line, which has the form:

`INCLUDE` *character constant*

The character constant is typically a filename. The information in the file is then inserted as part of the source text in the program. The INCLUDE line can occur anywhere within the program and thus could include data definitions, main program statements, or subprograms.

11·2 Intrinsic and Derived Data Types

Fortran 90 contains five intrinsic data types that are defined as part of the language—integer, real, complex, character, and logical. Additional data types can be derived from these data types.

Intrinsic Data Types

Every Fortran 90 compiler must include the five intrinsic data types. In addition, the real data type must include two kinds of values—real values and double-precision values. The real data value is the default for real values. Real data types might also include additional types, such as a data type with more precision than double precision. The character data type must contain at least the Fortran character set, but in addition it may have other character sets as described in Section 11–1.

When one of the intrinsic data types has more than one kind of value, the kind parameter is used to distinguish them. For example, since the real data type includes real values and double-precision values, the kind parameter can be used to distinguish between them; the kind parameter for real values is 0.0 and the kind parameter for double precision is 0.0D0. The kind parameter for integers is 0; the kind parameter for complex numbers is 0.0; the kind parameter for the default character set is 'A'. Additional kind parameters may be defined by a computer system/compiler. Consult the Fortran documentation to determine what additional kinds of data types are available to use in your Fortran 90 programs.

To specify constants that are not default types, the kind parameter is indicated on numeric constants following the underscore character. For example, the constant 1.23_0.0D0 refers to a double-precision value. The kind parameter is indicated on a character constant at the front and is followed by an underscore, as in GREEK_"$\tau\beta\pi$"; note that this constant assumes that the character kind GREEK has been defined for the system being used.

■ Type Declarations

Type declaration statements are used to specify the data type and characteristics, or attributes, of a variable. In Fortran 90, the type statement can include two colons to separate the type from the list of variables. In addition, a variable can be initialized on a type statement as shown in these statements:

```
INTEGER :: M, N, COUNT=0
REAL (KIND (0.0D0) :: SUM
```

■ Derived Data Types

Derived data types can be defined from the intrinsic data types. For example, we might want to define a structure that contains a chemical name and its molecular weight. In FORTRAN 77, the only structure was an array, and array elements had to be the same type; therefore we could not include a chemical name and its molecular weight in the same array. In Fortran 90 programs, we can define structures using combinations of the default data types. An example of a defined data type is the following:

```
TYPE CHEMICAL
   CHARACTER (LEN30) :: NAME
   REAL :: WEIGHT
END TYPE CHEMICAL
```

To define a variable with this type, we use the following statement:

```
TYPE (CHEMICAL) :: AMINO_ACID
```

To reference a component within this structure, the name of the structure is followed by a percent sign, followed by the component name. Therefore, to refer to the weight of the amino acid, we would use the reference AMINO_ACID % WEIGHT.

■ Attributes

Every data object (such as a constant, a variable, or a data structure) has a type associated with it. In addition, there are other characteristics or properties that are used to define data objects. These additional characteristics are called attributes and can be defined on the type declaration statement. In the previous chapters on FORTRAN 77, we discussed the attributes of array size and of parameters. These attributes are shown on these statements:

```
REAL, PARAMETER :: PI = 3.14159
INTEGER, DIMENSION (3,3) :: TEMPERATURE
```

In Appendix B, we discuss some of the less frequently used attributes including SAVE, EXTERNAL, and INTERNAL. Other Fortran 90 attributes include POINTER, TARGET, and INTENT; these attributes are discussed later in this chapter.

11·3 ■ Array Enhancements

Since arrays are an important data structure in engineering problem solutions, we selected some of the new array features to include in this section. We first discuss computations with arrays, in both expressions and function references. We then discuss dynamic array allocation and give an example to show how it can be used.

■ Array Computations

In Fortran 90, array names without subscripts can be used in expressions and assignments. These statements are interpreted element by element. Therefore, consider the following statements, where A, B, and C are arrays:

```
A = 0
B = B + 2.0
C = A + B
```

In the first statement, all elements of A are initialized to zero. In the second statement, all elements of B are incremented by 2.0. In the third statement, A is added elementwise to B and the sum is stored in the array C; this statement assumes that the sizes of A, B, and C are the same.

When an intrinsic function is applied to an array name without a subscript, the intrinsic function is applied to the entire array. Therefore, the following statement will replace all values in the array X with the corresponding absolute values:

```
X = ABS(X)
```

■ New Array Functions

A number of new intrinsic functions that apply specifically to arrays were added to Fortran 90. We list a number of these functions, along with a brief description in Table 11–3.

■ Masked Array Assignment

A mask expression is a logical expression. When we apply a mask to an array, the logical expression is applied to each element of the array, and the corresponding expression is then either true or false. If the expression is true, then a specified

Table 11·3 Intrinsic Functions Involving Arrays

Function	Value Computed
DOT_PRODUCT(A, B)	Dot product of vectors A and B
MATMUL(A,B)	Matrix multiplication AB
MINVAL(A)	Minimum value in array A
MAXVAL(A)	Maximum value in array A
PRODUCT(A)	Product of values in array A
SUM(A)	Sum of values in array A
MAXLOC(A)	Location of maximum value in A
MINLOC(A)	Location of minimum value in A

statement block can be executed; if the expression is false, then a different statement block can be executed. For example, suppose that we want to change all negative values in an array to the value zero and we want to add 2.5 to all other values. We can use the masked array assignment (which uses the new WHERE statement) to perform these steps with the following statements:

```
REAL, DIMENSION(10,5) :: PLATE
...
WHERE (PLATE < 0.0)
   PLATE = 0.0
ELSE WHERE
   PLATE = PLATE + 2.5
END WHERE
```

■ Dynamic Array Allocation

In Fortran 90, we can initially define an array without specifying the size of the array. This is very useful when the size of the array is computed within the program or is read from a data file. In FORTRAN 77, we had to define an array to the maximum possible size that we might need, even though we might actually use only a small fraction of it. In addition to allocating the memory needed for an array during the execution of a program, we can also release or deallocate the memory when we no longer need the array. The statements to allocate or deallocate memory are the following:

ALLOCATE *(array name (size))*

DEALLOCATE *(array name)*

Assume that the first line of a data file contains the number of lines of valid data in the file. The following statements define arrays to store the data and allocate the memory after the number of elements has been determined.

```
INTEGER :: COUNT
REAL, DIMENSION(:), ALLOCATABLE :: X, Y
...
READ (9,*) COUNT
ALLOCATE (X(COUNT), Y(COUNT))
```

We can read the rest of the data from the file into the arrays X and Y.

11-4 ■ Control Statements

Fortran 90 controls the order in which statements within a program are executed using three kinds of control constructs—the IF construct, the CASE construct, and the DO construct. The IF construct is basically the same control structure that is included in FORTRAN 77; the CASE construct is a new control structure; the DO construct is an expanded version of the DO loop. Each of these constructs can contain statement blocks, which are groups of statements treated as a unit.

■ CASE Construct

The CASE construct is useful when we want to execute different blocks of statements depending on the value of an expression. The general form of the CASE construct is the following:

```
SELECT CASE (expression)
CASE (case selector)
     block of statements
CASE (case selector)
     block of statements
...
CASE DEFAULT
     block of statements
END SELECT
```

When the CASE construct is executed, the expression (also called a case expression) is evaluated first. This expression can be integer, character, or logical. The case selectors that follow are then examined to find the first one that contains a value equivalent to the case expression. The corresponding block of statements is then executed, and control transfers to the statement following the END SELECT statement.

A simple example of the CASE statement is the following:

```
SELECT CASE (CODE)
CASE (1,2,7,9)
   SUM = SUM + 1
CASE (5)
   SUM = SUM + 3
END SELECT
```

If the value of code is equal to 1, 2, 7, or 9, then 1 is added to SUM; if code is equal to 5, then 3 is added to SUM.

The case selector in a CASE construct can contain a single value, a list of values, or a range indicator that is of the form `low:`, `:high`, or `low:high`. If the case selector is `low:`, then the corresponding block of statements will be executed if `low` is less than or equal to the expression. If the case selector is `:high`, then the corresponding block of statements will be executed if the expression is less than or equal to `high`. If the case selector is `low:high`, then the corresponding block of statements will be executed if `low` is less than or equal to the expression which is less than or equal to `high`. We illustrate this type of case selector using an example that is first solved using an IF construct and is then solved using the CASE construct.

IF Construct

```
IF (DIST.LE.250) THEN
   TOWER = 1
   NEAR = DIST
ELSE IF (DIST.LE.750) THEN
   TOWER = 2
   NEAR = ABS(DIST - 500)
ELSE
   TOWER = 3
   NEAR = 1000 - DIST
END IF
```

CASE Construct

```
SELECT CASE (DIST)
CASE (:250)
   TOWER = 1
   NEAR = DIST
CASE (:750)
   TOWER = 2
   NEAR = ABS(DIST - 500)
CASE DEFAULT
   TOWER = 3
   NEAR = 1000 - DIST
END SELECT
```

■ DO Construct

The DO statement has been expanded to the following general form:

DO *loop control*
  block of statements
END DO

The loop control includes the counting loop from FORTRAN 77, with statements of the following form:

```
DO 10 K=1,N
```

There are also two additional types of loop control in Fortran 90.

The first new type of loop control has the following form:

DO
  block of statements
END DO

Since the loop is not controlled by an index on the DO statement, an exit must be provided within the block of statements. The EXIT statement is a new statement that transfers control to the statement following the END DO statement.

The second new type of loop control is a While loop and has the following form:

DO WHILE *(logical expression)*
  block of statements
END DO

The logical expression is evaluated, and if it is true, the block of statements is executed. Control then returns to the DO WHILE statement, and the loop continues to be executed as long as the logical expression is true.

The CYCLE statement is another new statement in Fortran 90 that is very useful in developing control constructs. If this statement is executed within a DO loop, the rest of the loop will be skipped and control will be transferred to the beginning of the loop. Note the difference between the CYCLE statement and the EXIT statement. If an EXIT statement is executed within a DO loop, control passes to the statement that follows the DO loop; if a CYCLE statement is executed within a DO loop, control passes back to the DO statement for the next cycle.

The following examples illustrate the two new types of DO statements using program segments that read and sum data values until a negative value is read.

DO Construct

```
SUM = 0
DO
   READ*, X
   IF (X.LT.0) EXIT
   SUM = SUM + X
END DO
```

DO WHILE Construct

```
DONE = .FALSE.
SUM = 0
DO WHILE (.NOT.DONE)
   READ*, X
   IF (X.LT.0) THEN
      DONE = .TRUE.
   ELSE
      SUM = SUM + X
   END IF
END DO
```

The implementation on the left is both shorter and simpler to read. In fact, the DO END DO version of the DO construct can be used to implement both While loops and counting loops.

11·5 ■ Intrinsic and User-Defined Procedures

In Fortran 90, procedures include both functions and subroutines. In addition, a new procedure called a module is defined. We summarize some of the new features of both intrinsic procedures and user-defined procedures in this section.

■ New Intrinsic Procedures

Fortran 90 contains a number of new intrinsic procedures, including inquiry functions that allow you to determine information about a data type. The functions in Table 11–4 return information relative to the type of X (but not relative to the value of X).

Intrinsic subroutines are also included in Fortran 90 and are used to generate random numbers and to obtain the date and time. Additional intrinsic functions are included to perform character string manipulations and bit string manipulations.

Table 11·4 Inquiry Intrinsic Functions

Function	Value Returned
DIGITS(X)	Number of significant digits
EPSILON(X)	Smallest resolution between values
HUGE(X)	Largest value
MAXEXPONENT(X)	Maximum exponent
MINEXPONENT(X)	Minimum exponent
PRECISION(X)	Decimal precision
RADIX(X)	Base
RANGE(X)	Decimal exponent range
TINY(X)	Smallest value

■ Internal and External Procedures

The user-defined functions and subprograms allowed in FORTRAN 77 are external procedures because they are external to the main program and other subprograms. Fortran 90 also allows procedures to be internal to a main program or another subprogram. The advantage of an internal procedure is that it has access to all the data objects in the program or subprogram that contains it; therefore, fewer arguments are needed in the argument lists.

An internal procedure must be preceded by a CONTAINS statement. The internal procedure, or procedures, must then be followed by the END statement for the main program or the subprogram that contains the internal procedures.

In Fortran 90, the FUNCTION statement also includes a RESULT clause that specifies the variable that is to return the function value, as shown in the following statement:

```
FUNCTION F(X)  RESULT (SUM)
```

In FORTRAN 77, the result variable was assumed to be the name of the function.

Attributes can be added to the dummy arguments to clearly indicate which variables are input values, which are output values, and which are both. These attributes are specified with the INTENT attribute and either (IN), (OUT), or (INOUT) in the specification statements.

■ Modules

Fortran 90 adds a new procedure called a module, which provides a means for sharing constants, variables, type definitions, and procedures. A module is not executed directly, but its contents can be used by other program units (main program, functions, subroutines) with the USE statement.

■ Recursive Procedures

Fortran 90 allows a procedure to refer to itself within the procedure. This special type of reference is called recursion. Recursion is a powerful technique that can be especially useful in solving certain types of problems in which the current problem can be defined in terms of a similar smaller problem, and the smaller problem can be defined in terms of a still smaller similar problem, until we finally reach the solution of the smallest problem.

The best way to understand recursion is with an example. A factorial computation occurs frequently in engineering and science applications. Recall that, by definition, n factorial, or $n!$, is computed as

$$n! = n \cdot (n-1) \cdot (n-2) \cdot (n-3) \cdot \cdots \cdot 3 \cdot 2 \cdot 1$$

Thus,

$$6! = 6 \cdot 5 \cdot 4 \cdot 3 \cdot 2 \cdot 1$$

However, note that we could also define 6! in terms of 5!, as

$$6! = 6 \cdot 5!$$

Then 5! could be defined in terms of 4!, as

$$5! = 5 \cdot 4!$$

Thus, a recursion process emerges as we define a factorial in terms of a smaller factorial, and that smaller factorial in terms of a still smaller factorial, until we get to 0!. By definition, 0! is equal to 1. This is a very critical step in recursion. We must eventually get to a stopping point, or recursion cannot be done with the computer. Once we get to the stopping point, we reverse the process by bringing that value back to the step that referenced it, compute a new value there, then back again to the step that referenced that one, and so on until we are back to the original problem. We can look at this process with the following diagram.

6! = 6 • 5!

5! = 5 • 4!

4! = 4 • 3!

3! = 3 • 2!

2! = 2 • 1!

1! = 1 • 0!

0! = 1
We now take the value
for 0! and go back one
step at a time.

1! = 1 • 1 = 1

2! = 2 • 1 = 2

3! = 3 • 2 = 6

4! = 4 • 6 = 24

5! = 5 • 24 = 120

6! = 6 • 120 = 720

Note that the example recursively referenced the factorial function six times.

Fortran 90 allows recursive functions and recursive subroutines. These procedures must include the word RECURSIVE in the procedure heading. It is also necessary to include a RESULT clause that allows the computer to distinguish between the use of the function name as a value and the function name as a reference to the function. A recursive function to compute a factorial is shown here:

```
*-----------------------------------------------------------------------*
      RECURSIVE FUNCTION FACTORIAL(N) RESULT (PRODUCT)
*
*  This function recursively computes N!
*
      INTEGER, INTENT (IN) :: N
      INTEGER :: PRODUCT
*
      IF (N < 0) THEN
         PRODUCT = -1
      ELSE IF (N == 0) THEN
         PRODUCT = 1
      ELSE
         PRODUCT = N*FACTORIAL(N-1)
      END IF
*
      END FUNCTION FACTORIAL
*-----------------------------------------------------------------------*
```

An example of a recursive subroutine is the quicksort algorithm. The quicksort algorithm selects some value, which we will call a pivot value, from the list to be sorted and separates the values into two groups—those larger than the pivot value and those smaller than the pivot value. In doing this separation, the pivot value is placed in its proper position in the list. The values in the two parts, however, are not necessarily in the proper order. We can now take the group of values smaller than the pivot, select a new pivot from this group, and separate it into two groups based on the new pivot. The new pivot value will be placed in its proper position, and we have two new groups—the group of values smaller than the new pivot value and the group of values larger than the new pivot value.

Thus, a recursion process emerges as we define a sort as the separation of a list into two groups, one with values larger than a pivot value and one with values smaller than a pivot value, while the pivot value is positioned in its proper place. Each of these new groups can be separated into two smaller groups, with the new pivot value positioned in its proper place, and so on until we get to a group of two values. This pair of values is switched if necessary to put them in the proper order. This is again a very critical step in recursion. We must eventually get to a stopping point, or recursion cannot be done with the computer. Once we get to the stopping point, we reverse the process by bringing back the sorted pair of values and fitting it into the next larger group. When both halves of that group are together, it is fit into the next larger group, and so on until we are back to the original list, which will now be sorted in the proper order.

Recursive procedures are not commonly used in engineering problem solutions. However, when a problem solution can be defined recursively, the recursive solution is usually the simplest solution.

11·6 ■ Pointer Variables

The inclusion of pointers in Fortran 90 allows us to generate and use a very important class of data structures—linked data structures. Because of the name "pointer," we tend to think of a pointer variable as pointing to another variable. However, a pointer is more general and thus should be considered to be a name that is associated with a data object, which might be a variable, or a data structure, or a subset of a data structure. A pointer can also be considered to be an alias to a data object.

A variable that is to be used as a pointer must be defined with the pointer attribute and must be the same type as the object with which it is to be associated. Similarly, an object aliased by a pointer must be given a target attribute, as in the following statements:

```
REAL, TARGET :: X
REAL, POINTER :: TOP
```

The statement to associate the pointer TOP with X is the following:

```
TOP => X
```

A data object can have multiple pointers associated with it.

Linked Lists

A linked list is similar to an array because it is a group of elements that has an order; there is a first element, a second element, and so on. However, a linked list is different from an array in several ways. First, we do not use a subscript to reference an element in the linked list; instead, we use a pointer variable. Each element in a linked list has a pointer associated with it that points to the next element in the list. The constant nil is typically used to indicate that a pointer is not associated with another variable and thus is used to indicate the end of a linked list, as shown in this diagram of a linked list with four elements.

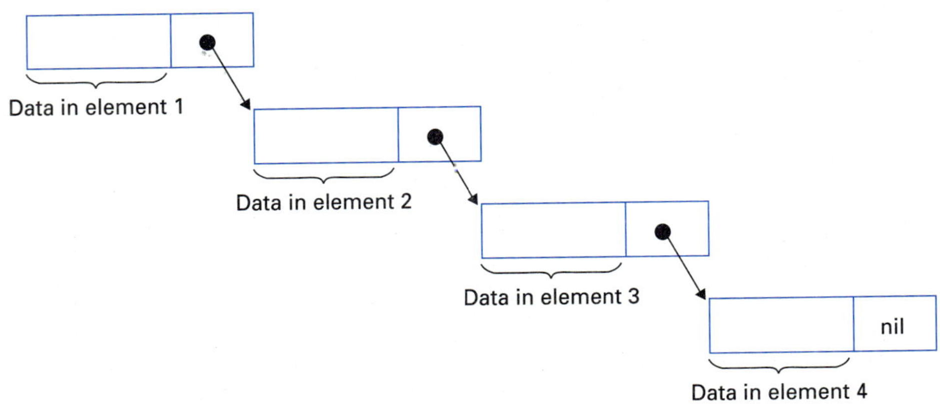

In addition to building and accessing the data in a linked list, we often want to insert new items or delete old items. These types of operations are especially efficient with linked lists. When we remove an item from a linked list, all we have to do is change the previous pointer so that it points to the item following the one we want to delete. These deletion steps are shown in the diagram below, which shows a linked list (that initially contained five elements) before and after the deletion of the third element:

Before deletion of third element:

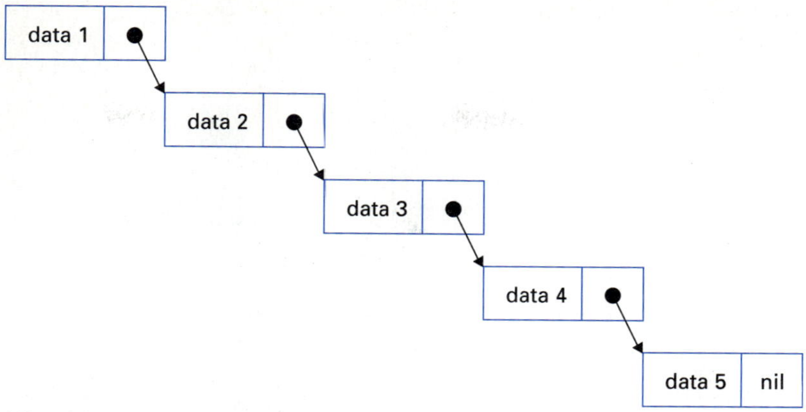

After deletion of third element:

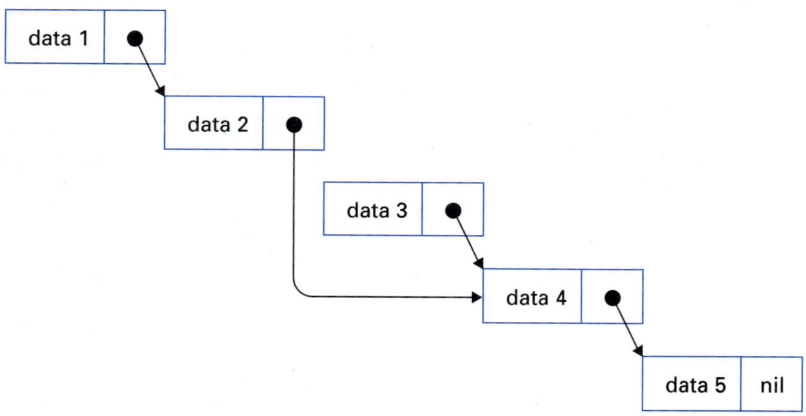

Even though the third element still points to the fourth element, the third element cannot be accessed because there is no pointer to it.

Recall that deleting an item in an array required that we move all the items following the one deleted. If an array is large, these steps can be time consuming. With a linked list, we only had to modify the pointer to the item being deleted.

When we add an item to a linked list, we need to change two pointers. The pointer in the item before the new item has to be changed to point to the new item, and the pointer in the new item needs to point to the item that follows it. The following diagram illustrates these steps for inserting an item between the second and third elements of a linked list.

Before insertion between second and third elements:

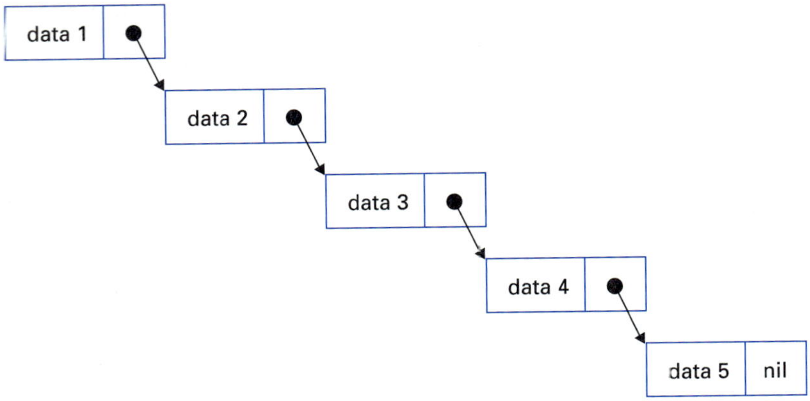

After insertion between second and third elements:

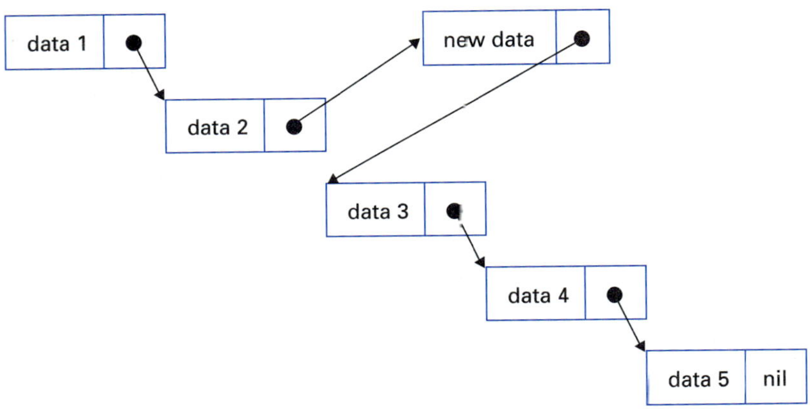

Recall that adding an item to an array required that all the items past the new item be moved one position to make room for the new item. If the array is large, these steps can also be time consuming. With a linked list, we only needed to modify two pointers in order to insert an item.

Both inserting and deleting items in a linked list require that we access the items in the list, beginning with the first item. As we access the items, we need additional pointers to point to the previous item and to the next item. When we find the proper point, we then perform the insertion or deletion. An insertion or deletion is then really a combination of a search through the linked list to find the correct position and then the steps for the insertion or deletion itself.

Developing the insertion and deletion routines here goes beyond the scope of this chapter, which is to preview some of the new components in Fortran 90. However, the key elements in the routines have been discussed and provide the background for developing the routines.

■ Additional Linked Structures

We now briefly introduce five additional linked data structures to demonstrate to you the powerful data structures that can be implemented with pointers.

Circularly Linked List A circularly linked list is generated when the last element in a linked list points to the first element in the list, as shown in the following diagram.

Circularly linked list

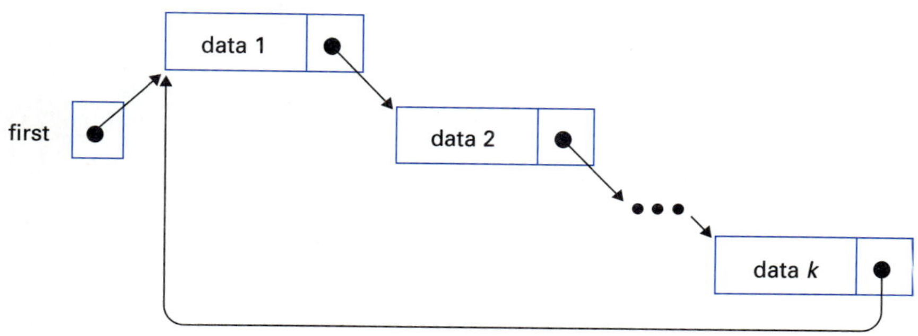

Note that the nil constant is not used with the circularly linked list because there really is not an end to the list. However, in an empty linked list the pointer first will not be allocated. (A new intrinsic function allows you to determine if a pointer has been allocated.)

Doubly Linked List The pointer in a linked list is used to point ahead to the next element. There are applications in which we would like to have the data linked together so that we can move forward or backward in the list. The following diagram shows a linked list with both forward and backward links.

Doubly linked list

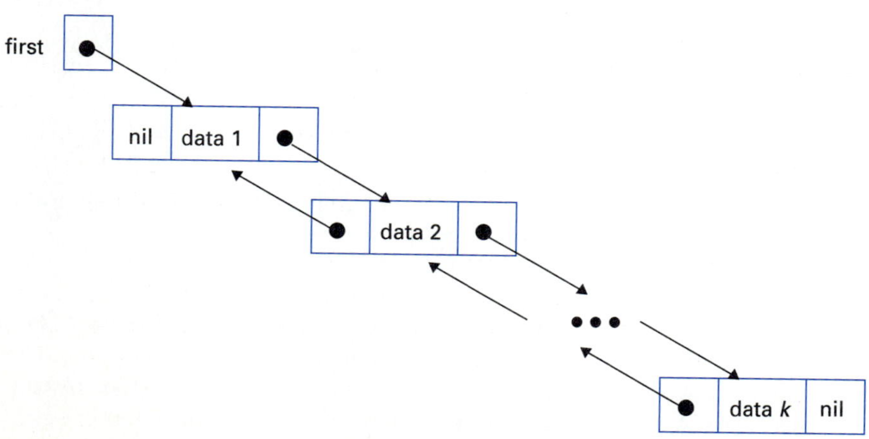

Although there is clearly an advantage to being able to move in either direction in a linked list, the routines for manipulating such a list become longer. For example, each insertion requires changing two forward links and two backward links. We must also be sure that the backward link of the first element in the list and the forward link of the last element are not associated variables.

Stack A stack is one of the most popular linked structures. It is often described in terms of a bucket, as shown in this diagram:

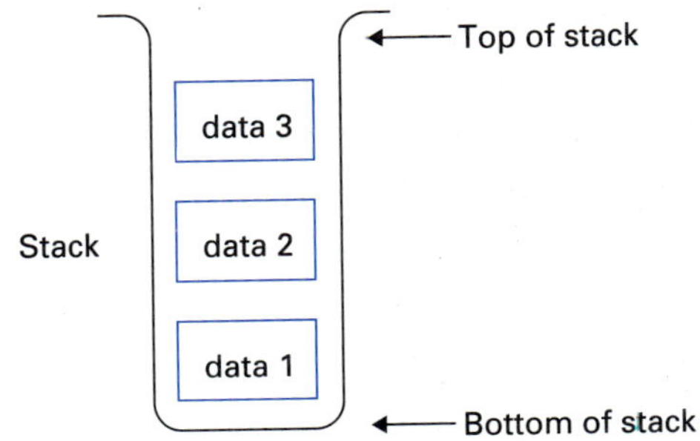

Adding an item to a stack is analogous to dropping it in the bucket. The top item on the stack is always the last item added. When we remove an item from a stack, it is the top item, or the last item that we added. This data structure is called a lifo, or last in first out, structure. The routine for adding items to a stack is often called a push routine, and the routine for removing items from a stack is often called a pop routine.

The routines for handling the push and pop routines must keep track not only of the links between elements in the stack but also of the top and bottom of the stack. The top of the stack is the position for the next insertion. Thus, if the top of the stack and the bottom of the stack point to the same position, the stack is empty. The next diagram shows how the stack is implemented using a linked list.

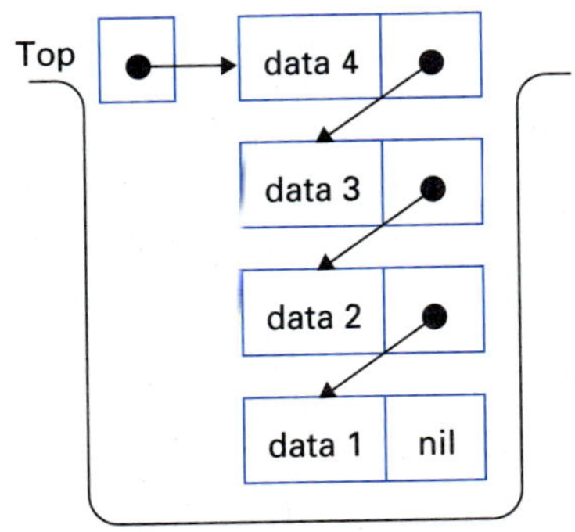

Queue The data structure called a queue is one with which you are very familiar, although you may not have realized that this structure had a name. Every time you stand in line, whether it is at the grocery store, the bank window, or the fast-food restaurant, you are in a queue. A queue is a data structure in which items are added at one end and removed from the other, as shown in the following diagram:

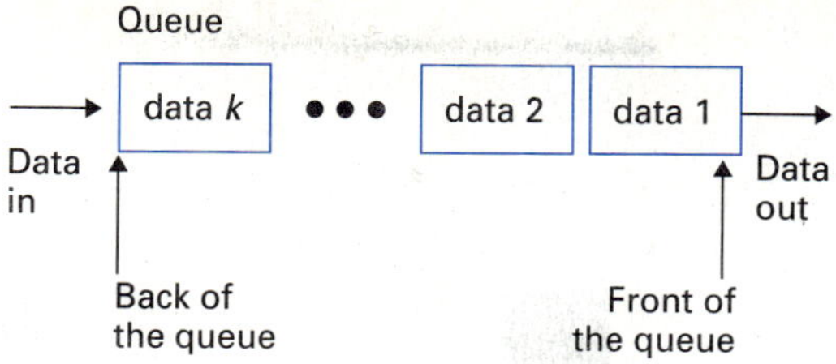

The queue is called a fifo, or first in first out, structure.

The routines for working with a queue must be able to insert at one end of the queue and to delete from the other end. Thus, we need pointers for the front of the queue and for the back (sometimes these positions are called the head and tail of the queue). Obviously, we also need to be able to detect an empty queue. The links within the queue are similar to the regular linked list, but we can only insert at one end and delete from the other. The diagram below shows how a linked list is used to implement the queue:

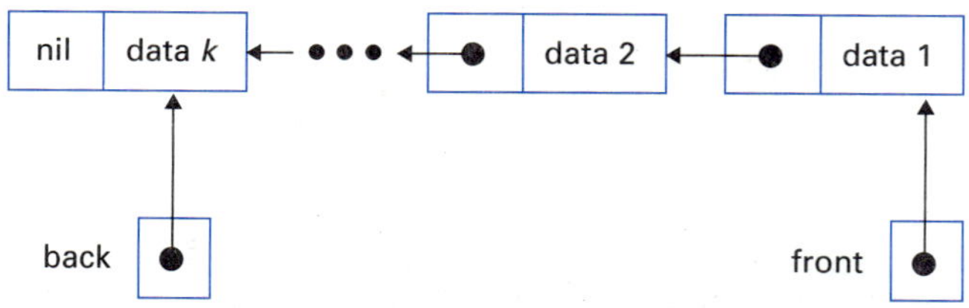

Binary Tree The final linked data structure that we present is a binary tree. A binary tree is a data structure that begins with a single element, often called the root of the tree. This element has a left branch and a right branch. The overall structure of a binary tree is shown in the next diagram:

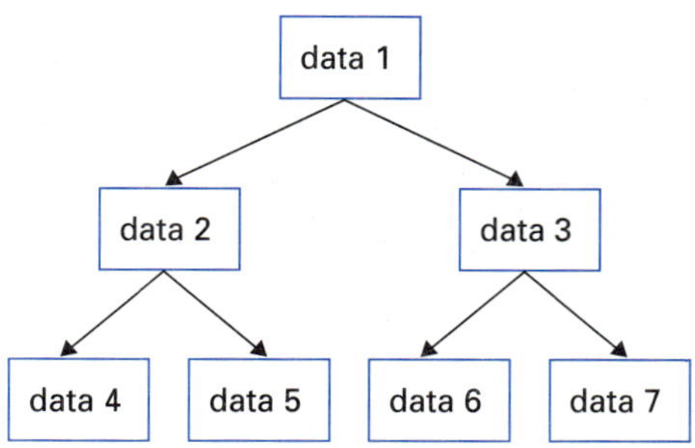

Binary trees are especially useful in certain types of searches. For example, if we assume that the data stored in the tree is ordered, with small values always to the left and larger values always to the right, then the algorithm to determine if a particular value is in the list is very efficient. We first compare the root to the value for which we are searching. The results of the comparison immediately determine which half of the tree is left to search. The comparison in the first branch of the correct half of the tree reduces the search to one-fourth of the tree, and so on. This process can be illustrated with the following tree: Suppose we wish to determine if the number 189 is contained in the tree. We begin with the root element. Since 189 is greater than 157, we know we must search the right branch. The first right branch contains the value 208, which is greater than the number 189. We thus take the left branch at the value 208. The branch value 179 represents the end of the branch, and we now know that the value 189 is not in the tree. If we wanted to insert it in the tree, we are now at the position to perform the insertion.

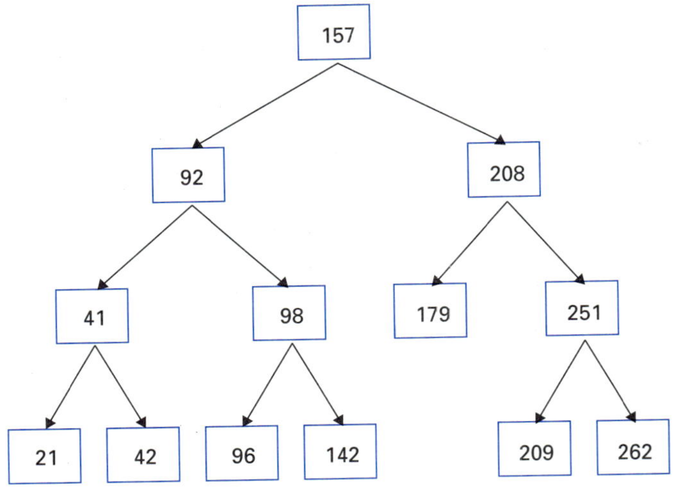

The routines to search a tree and to add and delete elements in the tree require the use of the root position and the left and right links. The implementation of the tree can be performed like this:

This section has introduced you to the more common linked data structures. Many powerful algorithms using these structures can now be implemented in Fortran 90 because of the addition of pointers.

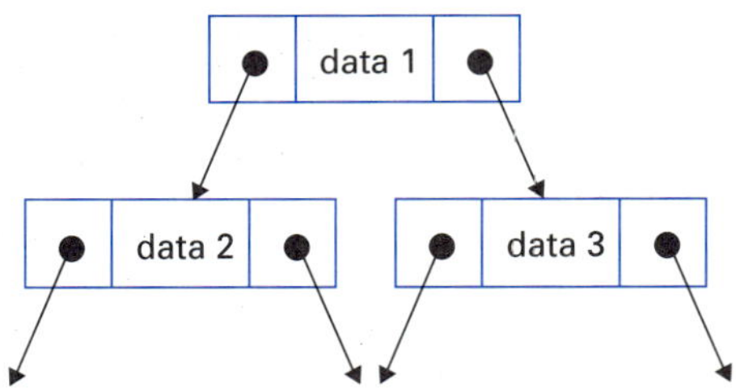

Summary

In one chapter we can only begin to describe the powerful new features in this new standard. Fortran 90 compilers are currently available for some computers, and additional compilers are in development. The additional computational capabilities, the new data structures, and the new control structures will make it even easier to write readable programs to solve many different types of engineering problems. Since the new standard also incorporates the FORTRAN 77 standard, old programs will still execute properly while new programs will be easier to write and simpler to debug. The document that describes the complete language is entitled American National Standard Programming Language Fortran 90, ANSI X3.198-1991. It is identical to ISO/IEC 1539:1991, which is the International Fortran Standard.

Appendix A

FORTRAN 77 Intrinsic Functions

In the following table of intrinsic functions, the names of the arguments specify their type as indicated below:

Argument		Type
X	→	real
CHX	→	character
DX	→	double precision
CX	→	complex, a + b*i*
LX	→	logical
IX	→	integer
GX	→	generic

Function type, the second column of the table of intrinsic functions, specifies the type of value returned by the function.

Generic function names are printed in color. Any type argument that is applicable can be used with generic functions, and the function value returned will be the same type as the input arguments, except for type conversion functions such as REAL and INT.

Function Name	Function Type	Definition
SQRT(X)	Real	$\sqrt{X}$
DSQRT(DX)	Double precision	$\sqrt{DX}$
CSQRT(CX)	Complex	$\sqrt{CX}$
ABS(X)	Real	$\|X\|$
IABS(IX)	Integer	$\|IX\|$
DABS(DX)	Double precision	$\|DX\|$
CABS(CX)	Complex	$\|CX\|$
EXP(X)	Real	e^X
DEXP(DX)	Double precision	e^{DX}
CEXP(CX)	Complex	e^{CX}
LOG(GX)	Same as GX	$\log_e GX$
ALOG(X)	Real	$\log_e X$
DLOG(DX)	Double precision	$\log_e DX$
CLOG(CX)	Complex	$\log_e CX$
LOG10(GX)	Same as GX	$\log_{10} GX$

(Continued)

Function Name	Function Type	Definition
ALOG10(X)	Real	$\log_{10}$ X
DLOG10(DX)	Double precision	$\log_{10}$ DX
REAL(GX)	Real	Convert GX to real value
FLOAT(IX)	Real	Convert IX to real value
SNGL(DX)	Real	Convert DX to single precision
ANINT(X)	Real	Round to nearest whole number
DNINT(DX)	Double precision	Round to nearest whole number
NINT(X)	Integer	Round to nearest integer
IDNINT(DX)	Integer	Round to nearest integer
AINT(X)	Real	Truncate X to whole number
DINT(DX)	Double precision	Truncate DX to whole number
INT(GX)	Integer	Truncate GX to an integer
IFIX(X)	Integer	Truncate X to an integer
IDINT(DX)	Integer	Truncate DX to an integer
SIGN(X, Y)	Real	Transfer sign of Y to |X|
ISIGN(IX, IY)	Integer	Transfer sign of IY to |IX|
DSIGN(DX, DY)	Double precision	Transfer sign of DY to |DX|
MOD(IX, IY)	Integer	Remainder from IX/IY
AMOD(X, Y)	Real	Remainder from X/Y
DMOD(DX, DY)	Double precision	Remainder from DX/DY
DIM(X, Y)	Real	X − (minimum of X and Y)
IDIM(IX, IY)	Integer	IX − (minimum of IX and IY)
DDIM(DX, DY)	Double precision	DX − (minimum of DX and DY)
MAX(GX,GY, . . .)	Same as GX, GY, . . .	Maximum of (GX,GY, . . .)
MAX0(IX,IY, . . .)	Integer	Maximum of (IX,IY, . . .)
AMAX1(X,Y, . . .)	Real	Maximum of (X,Y, . . .)
DMAX1(DX,DY, . . .)	Double precision	Maximum of (DX,DY, . . .)
AMAX0(IX,IY, . . .)	Real	Maximum of (IX,IY, . . .)
MAX1(X,Y, . . .)	Integer	Maximum of (X,Y, . . .)
MIN(GX,GY, . . .)	Same as GX, GY, . . .	Minimum of (GX,GY, . . .)
MIN0(IX,IY, . . .)	Integer	Minimum of (IX,IY, . . .)
AMIN1(X,Y, . . .)	Real	Minimum of (X,Y, . . .)
DMIN1(DX,DY, . . .)	Double precision	Minimum of (DX,DY, . . .)
AMIN0(IX,IY, . . .)	Real	Minimum of (IX,IY, . . .)
MIN1(X,Y, . . .)	Integer	Minimum of (X,Y, . . .)
SIN(X)	Real	Sine of X, assumes radians
DSIN(DX)	Double precision	Sine of DX, assumes radians
CSIN(CX)	Complex	Sine of CX

Appendix B

Additional FORTRAN 77 Topics

This appendix summarizes a number of features of FORTRAN that were not introduced in earlier chapters but that should be included for completeness. We have divided these additional features into specification statements, control statements, subprogram features, and formatting features. Most of these features are from older versions of FORTRAN. In general, the use of these features is discouraged because they make programs more difficult to debug and to understand. For example, the control structures discussed employ multiple branches from a single statement and thus no longer yield structures with one entrance and one exit.

Specification Statements

Two specification statements, and thus nonexecutable statements, are included here. The IMPLICIT statement is used to specify the beginning letters of variable names that are to be associated with a particular type, such as REAL or CHARACTER. The EQUIVALENCE statement allows the sharing of data storage.

IMPLICIT Statement We have discussed six different specification statements: INTEGER, REAL, LOGICAL, CHARACTER, DOUBLE PRECISION, and COMPLEX. Only two of these statements, INTEGER and REAL, have default values. That is, variable names beginning with letters I–N specify integer variables by default, and all other variable names specify real variables by default. The IMPLICIT statement allows us to specify defaults for variables of all types. Its general form is

> `IMPLICIT` *type 1 (default), type 2 (default), . . .*

For instance, if a program contained only integers, you could specify that any variable is an integer with this statement:

```
IMPLICIT INTEGER(A-Z)
```

Or, you might want to specify that the first half of the alphabet represents beginning letters of integer names and the last half represents real names:

```
IMPLICIT INTEGER(A-M), REAL(N-Z)
```

If you are following the convention of beginning all double-precision variable names with the letter D instead of listing all the names in a DOUBLE PRECISION statement, you could use the following:

```
IMPLICIT DOUBLE PRECISION(D)
```

An implicit declaration can be overridden with a specification statement, as shown here:

```
IMPLICIT COMPLEX(C), LOGICAL(L)
CHARACTER*10 CHAR
```

The variable CHAR should be a complex variable according to the IMPLICIT statement, but instead it is defined as a character string by the CHARACTER statement.

If you type all variables used in your programs, as we have recommended and as we have done in our sample programs, the IMPLICIT statement is unnecessary.

EQUIVALENCE Statement The EQUIVALENCE statement, a specification statement that permits data storage to be shared by several variables, has the following general form:

> `EQUIVALENCE` *(variable list 1), (variable list 2), . . .*

The variable list may contain variable names, array names, and character substring names. The EQUIVALENCE statement causes all the names enclosed in a set of parentheses to reference the same storage location. Character variables cannot be equivalenced with noncharacter variables. In fact, it is best to use the same type in all equivalence lists. The entire arrays are involved when array elements are equivalenced, as shown in the next example, because an array is always stored sequentially in memory. Two variables in a common block or in two different common blocks cannot be made equivalent, and two variables in the same array cannot be made equivalent.

Consider the following EQUIVALENCE statement:

```
INTEGER HEIGHT, DIST
REAL A(5), B(9), C(2,2)
EQUIVALENCE (HEIGHT,DIST), (A(1),B(4),C(1,1))
```

The first variable list specifies that HEIGHT and DIST are to occupy the same location that can be referenced by either variable name. The equivalence of storage locations specified by the second variable list is best explained using the following diagram of computer memory:

	B(1)		
	B(2)		
	B(3)		
A(1)	B(4)	C(1,1)	All three variables share the same storage location.
A(2)	B(5)	C(2,1)	
A(3)	B(6)	C(1,2)	
A(4)	B(7)	C(2,2)	
A(5)	B(8)		
	B(9)		

By specifying that A(1) and B(4) share the same location, we also have implicitly specified that A(2) and B(5) share the same location, and so on through A(5) and B(8).

Furthermore, we have equated the location that stores A(1) and B(4) with C(1,1), and hence other implicit equivalences have been specified as shown in the diagram. When using two-dimensional arrays in equivalence statements, it is important to remember that they are stored by columns.

■ Control Statements

The control structures mentioned in this section contain multiple branches and therefore have multiple exits. Because these statements do not follow a one-entrance, one-exit path of execution, we discourage their use. The main reason that multiple branch statements are included in the language is so that programs written in earlier versions can still be used without modifications. (Older versions of FORTRAN did not include all forms of the IF statements that were presented in Chapter 3, and thus multiple branching could not always be avoided.)

ARITHMETIC IF Statement The general form of the arithmetic IF statement is

> IF *(arithmetic expression) label 1, label 2, label 3*

Labels 1, 2, and 3 must be references to executable statements in the program. The arithmetic expression is evaluated and, if it represents a negative value, control passes to the statement referenced by label 1. If the expression represents zero, then control passes to the statement referenced by label 2. Finally, if the expression represents a positive value, control passes to the statement referenced by label 3. In the following arithmetic IF statement, control will pass to statement 10 if A is greater than B, to statement 15 if A is equal to B, and to statement 20 if A is less than B:

```
IF (B - A) 10, 15, 20
```

Thus, the arithmetic IF statement is a three-way branch equivalent to the following statements:

```
IF (arithmetic expression.LT.0.0) GO TO label 1
IF (arithmetic expression.EQ.0.0) GO TO label 2
GO TO label 3
```

Early versions of FORTRAN did not include even the simple IF statement presented in Chapter 3. Hence, all IF statements were written in the form of arithmetic IF statements at that time.

COMPUTED GO TO Statement The general form of the computed GO TO statement is

> GO TO *(label 1, label 2, . . . , label n), integer expression*

Labels 1, 2, . . . , and *n* must be references to executable statements in your program.

The computed GO TO statement is used for a multiway branch of control. For example, if we wish to execute a different set of statements dependent on the rank of a student, we could use the following computed GO TO statement, where RANK = 1 for freshman, 2 for sophomore, 3 for junior, 4 for senior, and 5 for graduate. Assume RANK is an integer variable.

```
INTEGER RANK
.
.
.
GO TO (11, 15, 20, 17, 17), RANK
PRINT*, 'RANK VALUE IN ERROR'
```

If RANK = 1 (representing a freshman), then the computed GO TO statement will be executed as if it were

```
GO TO 11
```

Similar branches would occur for RANK = 2 and RANK = 3. For seniors and graduate students (RANK = 4 and RANK = 5), control will transfer to statement 17, illustrating the fact that the statement labels do not have to be unique. If the value of RANK is such that it does not cause a branch (in this case, less than 1 or greater than 5), control passes to the next statement, which we have used to print an error message.

This type of multiway branch is also sometimes called a CASE statement because it tests a number of cases and then branches depending on the results of the tests. The IF-ELSE IF statement provides a structured way to implement an algorithm that performs different steps depending on a series of tests.

ASSIGNED GO TO Statement The ASSIGN statement and the assigned GO TO statement work together to yield a multibranch structure. The general forms of these two statements are

> `ASSIGN` *integer constant* `TO` *integer variable*

> `GO TO` *integer variable, (label 1, label 2, . . . , label n)*

The assigned GO TO statement looks very similar to the computed GO TO statement, but there are some significant differences.

1. The integer variable referenced in the assigned GO TO must have been initialized with the ASSIGN statement.
2. The integer variable can be used only to store statement references.
3. If the value of the integer variable is not in the list of labels, an execution error occurs.

In the next example, the value 3 has been initially assigned to K. The IF statements may change the value stored in K to either 11 or 20. When the assigned GO TO statement is executed, control will transfer to statement 11 if K = 11, statement 20 if K = 20, or statement 3 if K = 3. Otherwise, an execution error occurs.

```
ASSIGN 3 TO K
.
.
.
IF (A.LT.B) ASSIGN 20 TO K
IF (A.GE.C) ASSIGN 11 TO K
.
.
.
GO TO K, (3, 11, 20)
```

Again, the IF-ELSE IF statement provides a structured alternative to this multiway branch statement.

Subprogram Features

This section discusses additional features of FORTRAN that relate to subprograms. The SAVE, INTRINSIC, and EXTERNAL statements are not frequently used but can be very useful, as pointed out in the following discussions. The ENTRY statement and alternate return point from a subprogram are covered so that the coverage of FORTRAN 77 is complete, but their use is discouraged, again because they do not support a one-entrance, one-exit path of execution that is simple to follow.

SAVE Local variables are those used in a subprogram that are not arguments; thus, they tend to be totals, loop indexes, and counters. The values of these local variables are generally lost when a RETURN statement is executed. A SAVE specification statement will, however, save the values of local variables so they will contain the same values as they did at the end of the previous reference. This nonexecutable statement appears only in the subprogram. The general form of the SAVE statement is

SAVE *variable list*

The values of all local variables will be saved if the list of variables is omitted.

To illustrate the use of the SAVE statement, suppose you wanted to know how many times a subprogram was accessed. The following statements would initialize the counter COUNTR to zero at the beginning of the program and increment COUNTR each time the subprogram was used. Recall that the DATA statement does not reinitialize COUNTR each time the function is used.

```
*-----------------------------------------------------------------------*
      REAL FUNCTION AVE(X,Y)
      .
      .
      .
      INTEGER COUNTR
      SAVE COUNTR
      DATA COUNTR /0/
```

```
      .
      .
      .
      COUNTR = COUNTR + 1
      .
      .
      .
      RETURN
      END
*-----------------------------------------------------------------------*
```

INTRINSIC, EXTERNAL The INTRINSIC and EXTERNAL statements are specification statements used when subprogram names are to be used as arguments in another subprogram. The general forms of these nonexecutable statements are

`INTRINSIC` *subprogram list*

`EXTERNAL` *subprogram list*

These statements appear only in the module that sends the arguments representing the subprogram names. If the argument is an intrinsic function, use the INTRINSIC statement. If the argument is a user-written function or a subroutine, use the EXTERNAL statement.

We reference a subroutine twice in the following statements. In one reference, the subroutine replaces each value in an array with its natural logarithm. The other reference replaces each value in an array with its logarithm, using base 10.

```
*-----------------------------------------------------------------------*
      PROGRAM TEST1
      .
      .
      .
      REAL X(10), TIME(10)
      INTRINSIC ALOG, ALOG10
      .
      .
      .
      CALL COMPUT(X,ALOG)
      .
      .
      .
      CALL COMPUT(TIME,ALOG10)
      .
      .
      .
      END
*-----------------------------------------------------------------------*
      SUBROUTINE COMPUT(R,F)
*
*  This subroutine applies a function to the real
*  array R.
*
      INTEGER I
      REAL R(10)
```

```
*
      DO 10 I=1,10
         R(I) = F(R(I))
   10 CONTINUE
*
      RETURN
      END
*-----------------------------------------------------------------------*
```

ENTRY The ENTRY statement is used to define entry points into a subprogram other than the entry point at the beginning of the subprogram. The general form of the statement is

> **ENTRY** *entry name (argument list)*

The ENTRY statement is placed at the point in the subprogram that is to be an alternative entry. The argument list does not have to be the same as that for the original entry point. The ENTRY statement is nonexecutable and will not affect execution of the subprogram if it is in the statements being executed from a previous entry point.

The following statements illustrate references to a subroutine through two different entry points.

```
*-----------------------------------------------------------------------*
      PROGRAM TEST2
      .
      .
      .
      CALL SUBAA(X)
      .
      .
      .
      CALL SUBAB(X,K)
      .
      .
      .
      END
*-----------------------------------------------------------------------*
      SUBROUTINE SUBAA(T)
      .
      .
      .
      ENTRY SUBAB(T,J)
      .
      .
      .
*
      RETURN
      END
*-----------------------------------------------------------------------*
```

One of the fundamental advantages of structured programming lies in the simplicity of the interface between modules. The use of multiple entry points to a subprogram complicates that linkage; their usage is therefore not generally recommended. If you want to use a portion of a subprogram, define that portion as a subprogram itself. It can then be referenced by other subprograms in addition to the main program, and the simple interface between modules is maintained.

Alternate RETURNS Normally, the execution of a RETURN statement in a subroutine returns control to the first statement following the CALL statement; however, a return point can be specified with an argument in the subroutine. The argument list in the SUBROUTINE statement contains asterisks in the locations of arguments that are the alternate return points. The RETURN statement has this expanded general form:

> **RETURN** *integer expression*

If the value of the integer expression is 1, the return point is the statement number that corresponds to the first asterisk in the argument list. If the value of the integer expression is 2, the return point is the statement number that corresponds to the second asterisk, and so on. The following statements will help clarify this process.

```
*-----------------------------------------------------------------------*
      PROGRAM TEST3
      .
      .
      .
      CALL SUB1(A,B,*20,*50)
      .
      .
      .
   20 PRINT 25, A
      .
      .
      .
   50 COUNT = COUNT + 1
      .
      .
      .
      END
*-----------------------------------------------------------------------*
      SUBROUTINE SUB1(X,Y,*,*)
      .
      .
      .
*
      RETURN I
      END
*-----------------------------------------------------------------------*
```

If the value of I is 1 in the subroutine, then control will return to statement 20. If the value of I is 2, then control returns to statement 50. An execution error occurs if the value of I is not 1 or 2.

Again, multiple return points also complicate the linkage between modules and generally should be avoided. Structured alternatives can be developed using the IF structures.

■ Formatting Features

The formatting features discussed here are rarely used. If you do use them or work with programs that use them, be sure to document their use carefully.

Additional Format Specifications The following FORMAT specifications are not routinely used but occasionally simplify the input and output steps in a program.

Gw.d The G format code is a generalized code to transmit real data. The width w specifies the number of positions in the input or output that are used. Input data can be entered in an F or E format. The real advantage of the G format is in output formats. If the exponent of the data value is negative or larger than d, the output is performed with an Ew.d specification; if the exponent is between 0 and d, the output is performed with an F specification that will print d significant digits followed by four spaces. Thus, very large or small values are automatically printed with an E format, and values of reasonable size are printed with an F format. For example, if the G specification is G10.3, then the value 26.8 is printed as ${}_{bb}26.8_{bbbb}$, and the value 1248.1 is printed as ${}_{b}0.125E_{b}04$.

wH Literal data can be specified in an output format with an H, or Hollerith, specification. The width w specifies the total number of positions in the literal. The literal itself immediately follows the H. The following two formats are equivalent:

```
10 FORMAT (1X,'EXPERIMENT NO. 1')
10 FORMAT (1X,16HEXPERIMENT NO. 1)
```

Specifying literals with apostrophes is easier than using an H format because we do not need to count the characters in the literal; hence, H formats are rarely used.

Lw Logical variables can be read or printed with an L specification. In an input specification, the first nonblank character (in the w characters read) must be T or F; the variable receives the corresponding true or false value. In an output specification, the letter T or F is printed, again corresponding to whether the variable is true or false.

Format Extensions The following FORMAT extensions are not specifications that correspond to a variable; they are modifiers that affect the performance of the specifications already presented.

Ew.dEe and Gw.dEe The addition of Ee to an exponential or generalized format specifies that e positions are to be printed in the exponent. The Ee affects only output specifications.

nP The addition of nP to an F, E, or G format code specifies a scale factor n that is applied to subsequent specifications until another scale factor is encountered. The actual value stored is multiplied by 10**n to give the number read or printed when the scale factor n is in effect. For instance, if the following READ statement is

```
  READ 5, A, B
5 FORMAT (2PF4.1,F5.1)
```

and the data line read is

```
12.1362.4
```

then the value stored in A is 0.121 and the value stored in B is 3.624. Any computations with A and B use the values 0.121 and 3.624.

The output statement

```
      PRINT 10, A,B
   10 FORMAT (1X,F4.1,1X,F5.1)
```

generates the following data line:

```
00.1bbb3.6
```

The scale factor might be useful in applications that use percentages—the input could be in the form XX.X, but the internal values used in calculations and the output would use the form .XXX.

S, SP, and SS These options affect I, F, E, and G specifications during execution of output statements. If a numeric value is negative, the minus sign is printed in the first position to the left of the data value. If the numeric value is positive, the printing of the plus sign is system dependent. If SP precedes a specification, a sign is printed in that value and in all subsequent values, whether the value is positive or negative. If SS precedes a specification, only a minus sign is printed in that value and in all subsequent values. If S precedes a specification, the system designation of producing signs is restored. The following example illustrates the use of the SP modifier. If these statements are executed,

```
      A = 36.2
      PRINT 5, A, A, A
    5 FORMAT (1X,F5.1,1X,SPF5.1,1X,F5.1)
```

the output line is

```
b36.2b+36.2b+36.2
```

BN and BZ The BN and BZ modifiers specify the interpretation of nonleading blanks in numeric data fields during execution of input statements. Normally, leading and nonleading blanks are converted to zeros in numeric input fields. The modifier BN, however, specifies that blanks be considered null characters or ignored in the current and all succeeding specifications. The BZ modifier restores the interpretation of all blanks as zeros in numeric fields. If the data line

```
b21bb21b
```

is read with the statement

```
      READ 15, I, J
   15 FORMAT (I4,BNI4)
```

the value stored in I is 210 and the value stored in J is 21.

Colon A colon terminates the format if there are no more items in the input or output list. The following statements and their corresponding output illustrate the usefulness of this feature:

```
      MAX = 20
      MIN = -5
      PRINT 10, MAX
      PRINT 10, MAX, MIN
   10 FORMAT (1X,'MAX =',I3,:,2X,'MIN =',I3)
```

The output from the first PRINT statement is

```
MAX = 20
```

The output from the second PRINT statement is

```
MAX = 20  MIN = -5
```

Without the colon, the output from the first PRINT statement would be

```
MAX = 20  MIN =
```

Variable Formatting

In input and output statements up to this point, the format identifier has always been a statement number reference. However, this format identifier can also be an integer variable that has been initialized by an ASSIGN statement (defined earlier in this appendix) with the number of the desired FORMAT statement. The format identifier can also be a character constant, character array element, character array, or character expression.

Appendix C

Plotting Data Files with MATLAB and Lotus 1-2-3

In solving engineering problems, it can be very helpful to view a plot of data values related to the problem. These data values may represent the input values that are used by a program, or they may represent the output values computed by a program. In either case, we will assume that the data values have been stored in a data file and that we would like to generate a plot of them. We also assume that the file is an ASCII file; ASCII (American Standard Code for Information Interchange) files are written in a standard format that can be read by most software programs and packages. When you generate a data file with a FORTRAN program, the file is automatically written as an ASCII file. If you generate a data file using a word processor, you must specify that you want the data stored in an ASCII file (also called a text file); otherwise, the data is stored with special characters that are unique to the word processor, and thus you may have difficulty reading the file with other software.

We now present the steps for plotting a data file using MATLAB and using Lotus 1-2-3. In both cases, we are interested in obtaining a simple set of steps for easily generating a graph so that we can visualize the information represented by the data values.

Generating a Data File with a FORTRAN Program

The program listed below is a simple program that generates 101 points of the function:

$$f(t) = 2\,\sin(2\pi t)$$

where t ranges from 0.0 to 1.0 in increments of 0.01 second.

```
*-----------------------------------------------------------------*
      PROGRAM SIGGEN
*
*  This program generates a signal using the sine function.
*
      INTEGER K
      REAL PI, T, F
*
      OPEN (UNIT=15,FILE='SIGNAL',STATUS='NEW')
*
      PI = 3.141593
      DO 10 K=1,101
         T = (K-1)*0.01
         F = 2.0*SIN(2.0*PI*T)
         WRITE (15,*) T, F
   10 CONTINUE
*
      END
*-----------------------------------------------------------------*
```

This program generates a data file containing 101 lines, with each line containing two values. The first value represents the time value and the second value represents the corresponding value of the sine function. The first five function values are

$$f(0.00) = 2\ \sin(2\pi \cdot 0.00) = 0.0000000$$

$$f(0.01) = 2\ \sin(2\pi \cdot 0.01) = 0.1255810$$

$$f(0.02) = 2\ \sin(2\pi \cdot 0.02) = 0.2506665$$

$$f(0.03) = 2\ \sin(2\pi \cdot 0.03) = 0.3747626$$

$$f(0.04) = 2\ \sin(2\pi \cdot 0.04) = 0.4973798$$

The first five lines of the data file then contain the following values:

```
0.00    0.0000000
0.01    0.1255810
0.02    0.2506665
0.03    0.3747626
0.04    0.4973798
```

Plotting the Data File with MATLAB

MATLAB requires that the name of a data file have a file extension; therefore, assume that we have copied the data file SIGNAL to a file named SIGNAL.DAT. The load command can now be used to load the data values from the file into a matrix, or two-dimensional array, with each line in the data file stored as one row in the array:

```
>>load signal.dat;
```

The name of the array containing the data is the same as the name of the data file, but without the extension. If the data file is not in the same directory as the MATLAB program, the full path name should be used with the load command.

The plot command can be used with one or two arguments. To plot the data in the signal array, we specify that the first variable is the first column and that the second variable is the second column:

```
>>plot(signal(:,1),signal(:,2))
```

The plot command should then generate the following graph:

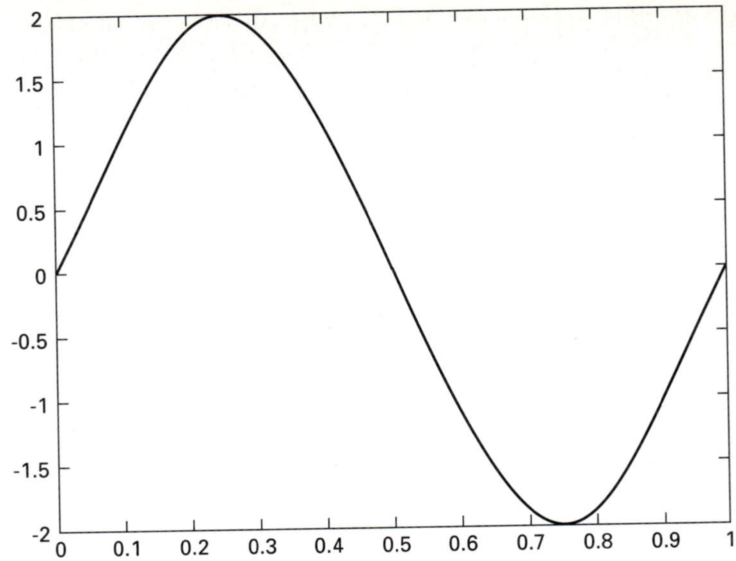

The plot command generates a linear X-Y graph. There are also options that allow you to plot with log-log scales and semilog scales and to generate polar plots, contour plots, 3-D plots, and bar graphs. MATLAB commands can also be used to label or title the graph and to add grid lines.

The easiest way to print the graph on many computers is to generate a screen dump by holding the Shift key down and then pressing the PrtSC key. If you are using a Macintosh, select the print command from the File menu.

Plotting the Data File with Lotus 1-2-3

To plot data values using Lotus 1-2-3, you must first copy (or import) the values into a worksheet. If you have not used a worksheet, refer to a Lotus 1-2-3 manual for more information on using and accessing a worksheet before proceeding with these steps.

Step 1—Use the arrow keys to position the cell pointer to the cell that you want to hold the first data value from the file. Generally, this will be the upper left corner of the worksheet, or address A1.

Step 2—Select the File Import Numbers command, using /FIN. At this point you will be prompted to enter the file name of the ASCII file, with the full path name if the file is not stored in the same directory as the 1-2-3 software. If the file name does not have an extension, 1-2-3 requires that you enter the file name followed by a period. After entering the file name, the data should automatically be stored in the worksheet, as shown in the next worksheet, which contains the values from the SIGNAL data file:

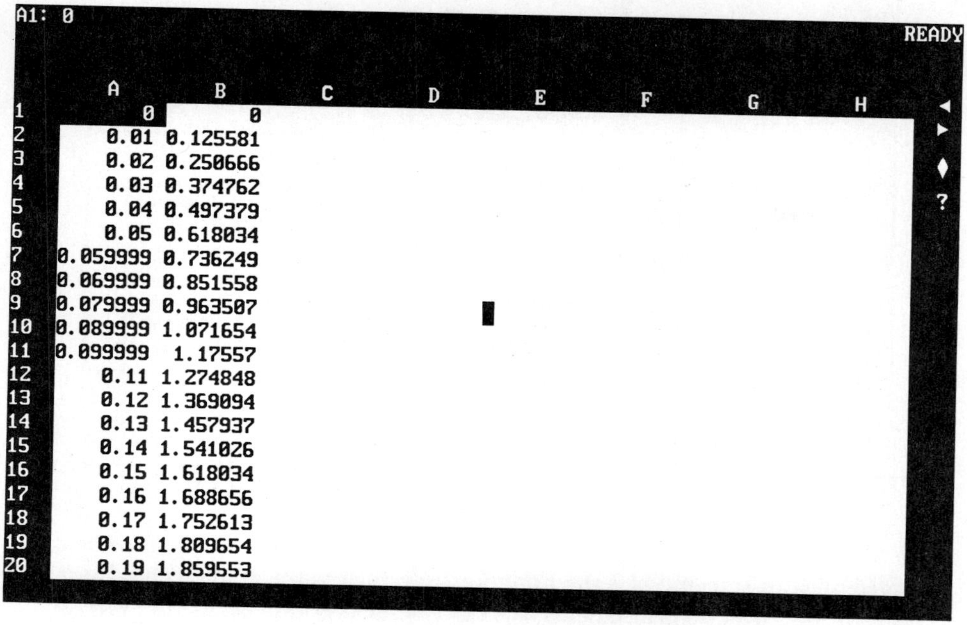

Step 3—To plot the data, select the Graph command using /G. Select the F2(Edit) function key to edit the Graph Settings dialog box. Select an XY plot and give an X range for the x values and an A range for the y values. Using the worksheet containing the SIGNAL data values, the specific keystrokes are:

/G	(Selects the graph command)
F2(Edit) function key	(Allows you to edit settings)
TX	(Selects xy graph type)
RX A1..A101 enter	(Selects x data range)
RA B1..B101 enter	(Selects y data range)
enter	(Saves graph settings)

The dialog box should now contain the following information.

```
─────────────────────────── Graph Settings ───────────────────────────
 ┌Type──────────────┐  ┌Ranges─────────────────┐  ┌Orientation─────┐
 │( ) Line          │  │X: [A1..A101·······]   │  │(*) Vertical    │
 │(*) XY            │  │A: [B1..B101·······]   │  │( ) Horizontal  │
 │( ) Bar           │  │B: [···············]   │  └────────────────┘
 │( ) Stacked bar   │  │C: [···············]   │
 │( ) Pie           │  │D: [···············]   │  ┌Zero line───────┐
 │( ) HLCO          │  │E: [···············]   │  │[x] Y axis      │
 │( ) Mixed         │  │F: [···············]   │  │[x] X axis      │
 └──────────────────┘  └───────────────────────┘  └────────────────┘
 ┌Frame─────────────┐                             ┌Grid lines──────┐
 │[x] Left          │  [x] Margins on             │[ ] Vertical    │
 │[x] Right         │  [ ] Stack Data ranges      │[ ] Horizontal  │
 │[x] Top           │  [ ] 3-D bars               └────────────────┘
 │[x] Bottom        │  [ ] Colors on
 └──────────────────┘
──────────────────────────────────────────────────────────────────────
                  Press F2 (EDIT) to edit settings
```

Step 4—Select the View command. The corresponding graph should now be displayed on your screen. Press the Enter key to return to the graph menu. If you want to add further enhancements, such as titles and grid lines, use the various options available in the dialog boxes. A graph of the data from the SIGNAL file is shown below.

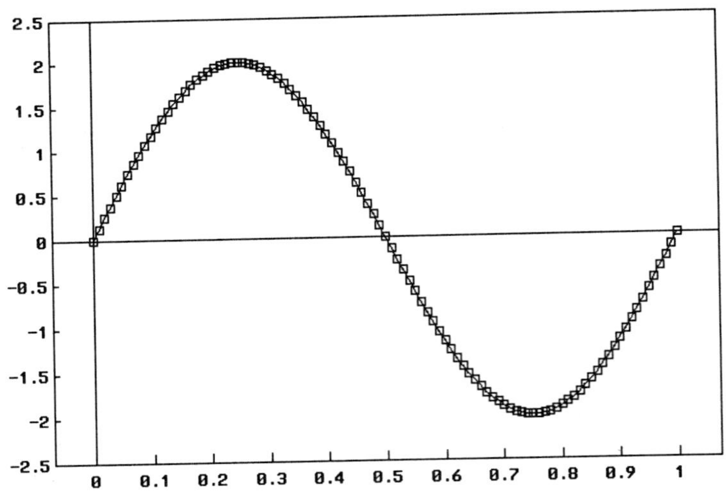

To print a graph, you must first save it as a graph file. The graph file is then printed using the PrintGraph program. Not all printers can print graphics, so you may need to check the printer manual to be sure that the printer connected to your computer can be used to print graphics.

Step 5—Select the Save command to save the file with a .PIC file extension. Select the Quit command to return to the worksheet, and then select the Quit Yes Yes command to exit the 1-2-3 program.

Step 6—To start the PrintGraph program, enter the word *lotus* after the system prompt. An access menu will be displayed. Choose PrintGraph, and then select the Settings Hardware Printer to list the printers installed with your system. Choose the desired printer and press the enter key. Select the Quit command twice to return to the first menu. Then select Image-Select to list the graph files available and to highlight the graph you want to print. (If the graph file is not in the same directory as the 1-2-3 program, you will need to use the Settings Hardware menu to specify the directory containing the graph file.) At this point you can use the F10(GRAPH) function key to view the file to be sure it is the one you want to print. Press the Enter key once to return to the graph menu and again to return to the main menu. Then select the Align Go Page command to print the graph.

Glossary of Key Words

actual argument A function or subroutine argument used in a subprogram reference.

algorithm A stepwise procedure for solving a problem.

argument An expression used in a function or subroutine reference.

arithmetic expression An expression of variables, constants, and arithmetic operations that can be evaluated as a single numerical value.

arithmetic logic unit (ALU) A fundamental computer component that performs all the arithmetic and logic operations.

array A group of variables that share a common name and are specified individually with subscripts.

ascending order An order from lowest to highest.

ASCII code A binary code (American Standard Code for Information Interchange) commonly used by computers to store information.

assembler A program that converts an assembly language program into machine language.

assembly language A programming language that is unique to an individual computer system.

assignment statement A FORTRAN statement that assigns a value to a variable.

binary language Machine language instructions written as sequences of 0's and 1's.

binary search An algorithm that searches an ordered list by continually dividing the array in half as it looks for a specific value.

blank common A single group of storage locations that is accessible to subprograms without being specified as subprogram arguments.

BLOCK DATA subprogram A subprogram that is used to assign initial values to variables in named common using DATA statements.

branch A change in the flow of a program such that the steps are not executed in the sequential order in which they are written.

bubble sort Another name for a multipass sort algorithm that generally requires more than one pass through the list in order to guarantee that the list is sorted into the desired order.

buffer An internal storage area used to store input and output information.

bug An error in a computer program.

carriage control A character used at the beginning of a buffer of printed output that specifies the page spacing desired before the line is printed.

cathode ray tube (CRT) terminal A terminal that uses a video screen for its input and output.

central processing unit (CPU) The combination of the processor unit, the ALU, and the internal memory that forms the basis of a computer.

character string A string or group of characters that contains numerical digits, alphabetical letters, or special characters.

collating sequence The ascending order of characters specified by a particular code.

comment line A statement included in FORTRAN programs to document the program; it is not translated into machine language.

common block A block or group of storage locations that is accessible to subprograms without being specified as subprogram arguments.

compilation The process of converting a program written in a high-level language into machine language.

compiler The program that converts a program written in a high-level language into machine language.

complex value A numerical value that is of the form $a + bi$, where $i = \sqrt{-1}$.

compound logical expression A logical expression formed by combining two single logical expressions with the connector .AND. or .OR.

computer A machine that is designed to perform operations that are specified with a set of program instructions.

computer network A network that links computers so they can communicate with each other.

concatenation An operation that connects two strings together to form one string.

condition An expression that can be evaluated to be true or false.

constant A specific value used in arithmetic or logical expressions.

continuation line A statement used to continue a FORTRAN statement that otherwise would extend past column 72; the continuation statement must contain a nonblank character in column 6 to signify that it is a continuation line.

control structure A structure that controls the order of execution of a series of steps.

conversational computing A method of interacting with the computer in which the computer seems to converse with the user in an English-like manner.

counting loop A loop that is repeated a specific number of times.

data file A file used to store information used by a program or generated by a program.

database management program Programs that allow you to store a large amount of data and then easily retrieve pieces of the data and format it into reports.

debug The process of eliminating bugs or errors from a program.

decomposition The process of dividing a problem solution into a series of smaller problems.

deletion A technique for removing an element from an ordered list.

descending order An order from highest to lowest.

diagnostic A message that describes an error in a program that has been located in either the compilation or execution step.

direct-access file A file whose information can be accessed in nonsequential order.

DO loop An iterative loop specified in FORTRAN with the DO statement.

double-precision value A real value that has been specified to have more precision than the standard real value.

driver A main program written specifically to test a subprogram.

dummy argument An argument used in a function or subroutine statement.

EBCDIC code A binary code (Extended Binary-Coded-Decimal Interchange Code) commonly used by computers to store information.

echo A debugging aid in which the values of variables are printed immediately after they are read.

element A specific storage location in an array.

END option An option that can be used in a READ statement to generate a branch to a specified program statement if the end of the data (or data file) is reached.

executable statement A statement specifying action to be taken in a program that is translated into machine language by the compiler.

execution The process of executing the steps specified by a program.

explicit typing A specification of the type of information to be stored in a variable with a specification statement.

exponential notation A notation for real values that uses the letter E to separate the mantissa and the exponent.

external file A file that is available to a program through an external device such as a disk drive or tape drive.

father-son update A type of file updating that uses a transaction (son) file to update information on the master (father) file.

field A unit of information in a record.

flowchart A graphical diagram used to describe the steps in an algorithm.

formatted I/O The input or output statements that use FORMAT statements to describe the spacing.

FORTRAN character set The set of characters accepted by FORTRAN compilers.

FORTRAN 77 The version of FORTRAN established in 1977.

function A subprogram that returns a single value.

Gauss elimination A technique for solving a system of equations.

generic function A function that returns a value of the same type as its input argument.

hardware The physical components of a computer.

hash code A code used to compute a record number for accessing a direct access file.

high-level language An English-like language that must be converted into machine language before it can be executed.

IF structure A structure that tests a condition and executes a set of steps if the condition is true.

implicit typing The specification of the type of information (real or integer) to be stored in a variable by the beginning letter of the variable name.

implied DO loop A DO loop that can be specified completely on an I/O statement or a DATA statement.

increment value The parameter in a DO loop that specifies the increment to be added to the index each time the loop is executed.

index The variable used as a loop counter in a DO loop.

initial value The parameter in a DO loop that specifies the initial value of the index.

initialize To give an initial value to a variable.

input/output (I/O) The information that a program reads or writes.

insertion A technique for adding an element in an ordered list.

insertion sort A sort that begins at the top of the list, comparing adjacent elements. If an element is out of order, it is continually exchanged with the value above it in the list until it is in its proper place.

integer value A value that contains no fractional portion.

intermediate result A result used in evaluating an expression to get the final result.

internal file A file defined on information stored in the internal memory of the computer.

internal memory A small amount of memory associated with the processing unit and the ALU.

intrinsic function A function included in a compiler library.

iterative loop A loop that is controlled by the value of a variable called the index of the loop or the loop counter.

key An integer used to specify the record number for accessing records in a direct-access file.

left-justified No blanks on the left side.

lexicographic order Dictionary order.

library function A function in a library available to the compiler.

limit value The parameter in a DO loop that specifies the value used to determine completion of the DO loop.

linear model An equation of the form $y=ax+b$ that approximates the relationship between two variables.

list-directed I/O The input or output statements that do not use FORMAT statements to describe the spacing.

literal A character string.

logic error An error in the logic used to define an algorithm.

logical expression An expression of variables, constants, and operations that can be evaluated as a single logical value.

logical operator One of the operators .NOT., .AND., and .OR. that is used with logical expressions.

logical value A value that is either true or false.

loop A group of statements that are executed repeatedly.

low-level language Binary or machine language used to communicate with the computer.

machine language The binary language understood by computers.

main program A complete program that may access functions and subroutines.

master file A file that contains the master information or most accurate information.

matrix A mathematical structure for storing information in a rectangular grid with rows and columns.

memory The storage available for the variables and constants needed in a program.

merge An operation that combines two ordered lists into one ordered list.

microprocessor A CPU that is contained in a single integrated circuit chip which contains thousands of components in an area smaller than your fingernail.

mixed-mode operation An operation between values that are not of the same type.

module A function or a subroutine.

multidimensional array A group of variables that share the same name and whose elements are specified by more than one subscript.

multipass sort A sort algorithm that generally requires more than one pass through the list in order to guarantee that the list is sorted into the desired order.

named common A group of storage locations that is accessible to subprograms by name without being specified as subprogram arguments.

nested function A function argument that is the value of another function.

nested loop A loop that is completely contained within another loop.

nonexecutable statement A statement that affects the way memory is used by a program although it is not converted into machine language by the compiler.

numerical differentiation Numerical techniques for estimating the derivative (or slope) of a function at a specified point.

numerical integration Numerical techniques for estimating the integral of a function (or the area under the graph of the function) over a specified interval.

object program A program in machine-language form.

one-dimensional array A group of variables that share the same name and whose elements are specified by one subscript.

operating system A set of programs that provide the interface between you (the user) and the computer hardware.

overflow An error condition that occurs when the result of an arithmetic operation yields a result that is too large to be stored in the computer's memory.

parameter A value or variable used in the DO statement to specify the DO loop.

processor A fundamental computer component that controls the operation of the other parts of the computer.

program A set of statements that specify a complete algorithm in a computer language.

pseudocode The English-like statements used to describe the steps in an algorithm.

random access A file-access technique in which records can be accessed in any order.

real value A value that may contain a fractional or decimal portion.

record The basic unit of information related to a data file.

relational operator An operator used to compare two arithmetic expressions.

repetition A structure in which steps are repeated, such as in a While loop or a counting loop.

residual A value used to determine the quality of a linear model for a set of data.

right-justified No blanks on the right side.

rounding A technique that approximates a value.

scientific notation A notation for real values that expresses the value as a number between 1 and 10 multiplied by a power of 10.

search algorithm An algorithm that searches a list looking for a specific value.

secondary memory Additional memory that can be used by the processing unit and the ALU.

selection A structure that tests a condition to determine which steps are to be performed next.

selection sort A sort that is based on finding the minimum value and placing it first in the list, finding the next smallest value and placing it second in the list, and so on.

sentinel signal A signal at the end of a data file that indicates that no more data follows.

sequence A structure in which steps are performed one after another, or sequentially.

sequential access file A file whose information can be accessed only in a sequential order.

software The programs used to specify the operations in a computer.

software tool A program that has been written to perform common operations.

sort To put in a specific order.

source program A program in a high-level language form.

specification statement A statement that specifies the nature of the values to be stored in a variable.

spreadsheet program A software tool that allows you to easily work with data that can be displayed in a grid of rows and columns.

statement function A function that can be defined in a single assignment statement that is placed before any executable statement in a program.

statement label A number that appears in columns 1 – 5 of a FORTRAN statement and that can be used by other statements to reference the statement.

stepwise refinement A process for converting a general algorithm to one that is detailed enough to be converted into a computer language.

structure chart A diagram that outlines the module structure of a program.

structured programming Programming with a top-down flow that is easy to follow and modify because of its structure.

subprogram A function or subroutine.

subroutine A subprogram that may return many values, a single value, or no value.

subscript An integer variable or constant used to specify a unique element in an array.

substring A string that is a subset of another string and that maintains the original order of characters.

syntax error An error in a FORTRAN statement.

time-sharing A method of interacting with the computer in which multiple programs are being executed at the same time although the user appears to have the complete attention of the computer.

top-down design Technique for problem solving in which the solution is first decomposed into a set of smaller steps, which are then refined individually in more and more detail until the problem is solved.

trailer signal A signal at the end of a data file that indicates that no more data follows.

truncation A technique that approximates a value by dropping its fractional value and using only the integer portion.

two-dimensional array A group of variables that share the same name and whose elements are specified by two subscripts.

type statement A statement used to specify variable types.

underflow An error condition that occurs when the result of an arithmetic operation yields a result that is too small to be stored in the computer's memory.

update file A file that contains updates to a master file.

user-friendly A term used to describe a program that is easy to use.

user interface The part of the program that interfaces the user to the steps in the program itself. The user interface usually consists of the input and output portion of the program.

variable A memory location referenced with a name whose value can be changed within a program.

variable dimensioning A technique that permits the size of an array in a subprogram to be specified by an argument to the subprogram.

While loop A loop that is executed as long as a specified condition is true.

word processor A program that has been written to help you to enter and format text.

Answers to Self-tests

Self-test 2–1, page 30

1. invalid (decimal point)
2. valid
3. valid
4. invalid (too long)
5. invalid character (__)
6. invalid character (__)
7. invalid characters (parentheses)
8. invalid (starts with a digit)
9. valid
10. invalid character (%)
11. not the same (15.7, 0.00157)
12. not the same (−1.7, 0.17)
13. same
14. not the same (0.005, 0.0000005)
15. not the same (0.899, 8990)
16. not the same (−0.044, 0.044)

Self-test 2–2, page 38

1. Y = 12.5
2. X = 4.1
3. RESULT = −13

Self-test 2–3, page 41

1. `M = SQRT(X**2 + Y**2)`
2. `U = (U + V)/(1.0 + (U*V/C**2))`
3. `Y = YO*EXP(-A*T)*COS(2.0*PI*F*T)`
4. `T = ((5.0/9.0)*(TF - 32.0)) + 273.15`
5. `B = K*(I*D*SIN(THETA))/(R**2)`
6. `S = SQRT(S1**2/N1 + S2**2/N2)`
7. $PE = \dfrac{-G \cdot ME \cdot M}{R}$
8. $DF = E \cdot DA \cdot \cos\theta$
9. $AV = \dfrac{x2 - x1}{T2 - T1}$

10. $CA = \frac{4\pi^2 \cdot R}{T^2}$

11. $DIST = V \cdot TIME + \frac{ACC \cdot TIME^2}{2}$

12. $P = P0 \cdot e^{\frac{-M \cdot G \cdot X \cdot TK}{R}}$

Self-test 2–4, page 57

1. X$_{b}$=$_{bbb}$-27.6$_{b}$DEGREES
2. DISTANCE$_{b}$=$_{bb}$0.287E$_{b}$05$_{bbbbb}$VELOCITY$_{b}$=$_{b}$-2.60

Self-test 2–5, page 74

1. $_{bb}$3.50$_{bbbbbbbbbbbbb}$*******$_{b}$0.0020
2. TIME$_{b}$=$_{bb}$3.50$_{bbbbb}$RESPONSE$_{b}$1$_{b}$=$_{bb}$0.18E+03
TIME$_{b}$=$_{bb}$3.50$_{bbbbb}$RESPONSE$_{b}$2$_{b}$=$_{bb}$0.20E-02
3. EXPERIMENT$_{b}$RESULTS

   TIME$_{bb}$RESPONSE$_{b}$1$_{bb}$RESPONSE$_{b}$2
3.50$_{bbbbb}$178.800$_{bbbbbbb}$0.002
4. XX.XXX$_{b}$XX.XXX$_{b}$XX.XXX$_{b}$XX.XXX
5. XXX.XX
XXX.XX
XXX.XX
XXX.XX
6. X.XX
XX.X
X.XX
XX.X
7. XX.XXXXX.XXX
XX.XXXXX.XXX

Self-test 3–1, page 112

1. false
2. false
3. false
4. true
5. true
6. false
7. false
8. true
9. `IF (TIME.GT.5.0) TIME = TIME + 0.5`
10. `IF (SQRT(POLY).GE.8.0) PRINT*, 'POLY = ', POLY`
11.
```
DIFF = ABS(VOLT1 - VOLT2)
IF (DIFF.LT.6.0) THEN
   PRINT*, 'VOLT1 = ', VOLT1
   PRINT*, 'VOLT2 = ', VOLT2
END IF
```

12.
```
IF (ABS(DEN).LT.0.005) PRINT*, 'DENOMINATOR IS TOO SMALL'
```

13.
```
LNVAL = LOG(X**2)
IF (LNVAL.GE.3.0) THEN
   TIME = 0.0
   SUM = SUM + X
END IF
```

14.
```
IF ((DIST.LT.50.0).OR.(TIME.GT.10.0)) THEN
   TIME = TIME + 1
ELSE
   TIME = TIME + 0.5
END IF
```

15.
```
IF (DIST.GE.50.0) THEN
   TIME = TIME + 2.0
   PRINT*, 'DISTANCE > 50.0'
END IF
```

16.
```
IF (DIST.GT.100.0) THEN
   TIME = TIME + 2.0
ELSE IF (DIST.GT.50.0) THEN
   TIME = TIME + 1.0
ELSE
   TIME = TIME + 0.5
END IF
```

Self-test 3–2, page 140

1. 10 times
2. 9 times
3. 13 times
4. 7 times
5. 9 times
6. 91 times
7. COUNT = 8
8. COUNT = 15
9. COUNT = −16
10. COUNT = 18
11. COUNT = −1

Self-test 3–3, page 151

1. COUNT = 101
2. COUNT = 36
3. COUNT = 10

Self-test 4–1, page 169

1. TIME = 0.0
   TEMP = 86.3
2. TIME = 0.0
   TEMP = 0.5

3. TIME1 = 0.0
   TEMP1 = 86.3
   TIME2 = 0.5
   TEMP2 = 93.5
4. TIME1 = 0.0
   TEMP1 = 86.3
   TIME2 = 0.5
   TEMP2 = 93.5
5. TIME1 = 0.0
   TEMP1 = 0.5
   TIME2 = 1.0
   TEMP2 = 1.5
6. TIME1 = 0.0
   TEMP1 = 0.5
   TIME2 = 86.3
   TEMP2 = 93.5

Self-test 4–2, page 177

1. works
2. works
3. would not work—time must be −99.0
4. would not work—the program will try to read a value for the variable ALT, causing an execution error
5. works

Self-test 4–3, page 188

1. first 3 lines:

```
1906   8.3
1911   6.6
1923   7.2
```

   last 3 lines:

```
1992   6.1
1992   6.9
 -99   0.0
```

2. first 3 lines:

```
  24
1906   8.3
1911   6.6
```

   last 3 lines:

```
1991   6.1
1992   6.1
1992   6.9
```

3. first 3 lines:

```
1906   8.3
1911   6.6
1923   7.2
```

   last 3 lines:

```
1991   6.1
1992   6.1
1992   6.9
```

4. The choice of methods is a personal preference. All three methods are reasonable.

Self-test 5 – 1, page 211

1.
```
M(b1)b=bbb10
M(b2)b=bbbb9
M(b3)b=bbbb8
M(b4)b=bbbb7
M(b5)b=bbbb6
M(b6)b=bbbb5
M(b7)b=bbbb4
M(b8)b=bbbb3
M(b9)b=bbbb2
M(10)b=bbbb1
```

2.
```
bb-3bbb0bbb5bb12bb21bb32bb45bb60
```

3.
```
TIMEbb1b=bb3.00
TIMEbb5b=bb5.00
TIMEbb9b=bb7.00
TIMEb13b=bb9.00
TIMEb17b=b11.00
```

Self-test 5 – 2, page 227

1. Array contents after each switch:

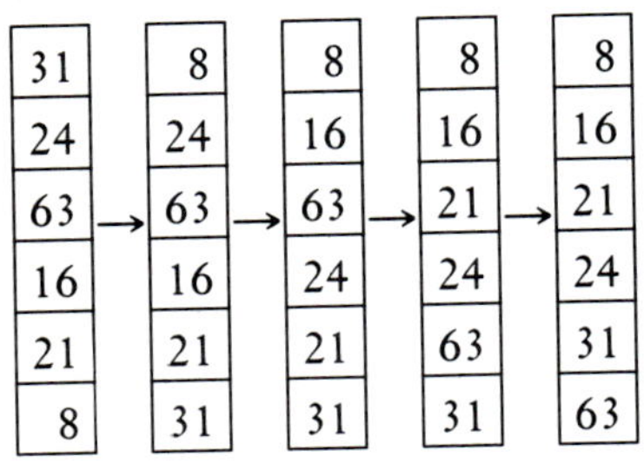

2. Array contents after each switch:

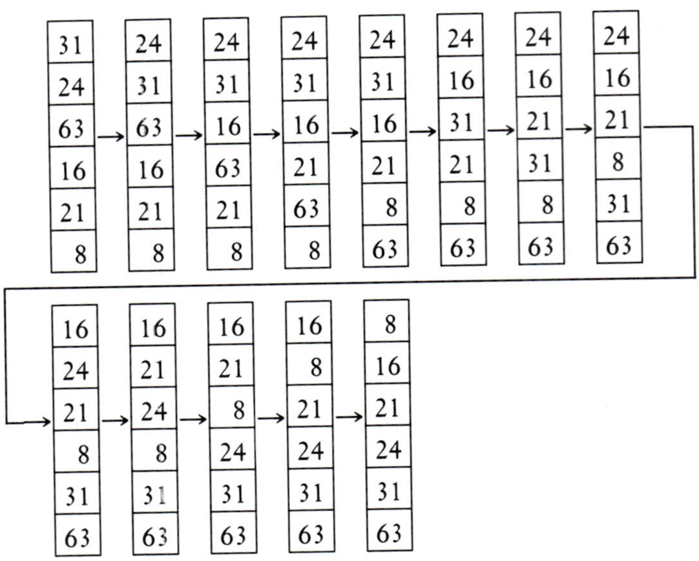

3. Array contents after each switch:

31	24	24	24	16	16	16	16	16	16	16	16	8
24	31	31	16	24	24	24	21	21	21	21	8	16
63	63	16	31	31	31	21	24	24	24	8	21	21
16	16	63	63	63	21	31	31	31	8	24	24	24
21	21	21	21	21	63	63	63	8	31	31	31	31
8	8	8	8	8	8	8	8	63	63	63	63	63

Self-test 5–3, page 238

1.

4	6	8	10
6	8	10	12
8	10	12	14
10	12	14	16
12	14	16	18

```
bbb12bbb14bbb16bbb18
```

2.

1	2	0
2	3	1
3	4	2

```
bbb1bbb2bbb0
bbb2bbb3bbb1
bbb3bbb4bbb2
```

3.

11.5	14.5	17.5
13.0	16.0	19.0

```
b11.5b14.5b17.5
b13.0b16.0b19.0
```

Self-test 6–1, page 265

1. `AREA(SIDE) = SIDE**2`
2. `AREA(SIDE1,SIDE2) = SIDE1*SIDE2`

3. `AREA(BASE,HEIGHT) = BASE*HEIGHT`
4. `AREA(BASE, HT1, HT2) = 0.5*BASE*(HT1 + HT2)`
5. `AREA(BASE,HEIGHT) = 0.5*BASE*HEIGHT`

Self-test 6–2, page 286

1. S = 5.8
2. S = 2.9
3. S = 5.3
4. S = 12.2

Self-test 7–1, page 330

1. ```
   NEW VALUES OF K ARE:
   bbbb1bbbb2bbbb3bbbb0bbbb1
   bbbb2bbbb3bbbb0bbbb1bbbb2
   ```
2. ```
   NEW VALUES OF K ARE:
   bbbb1bbbb2bbbb3bbbb0bbbb1
   bbbb2bbbb3bbbb0bbbb9bbb10
   ```

Self-test 7–2, page 354

1. Since the list at any given time is always in order (the new values are inserted in their proper slots), the final list (after all the insertions have been made) does not depend on the order of the insertions. Intermediate lists (the lists that result after each insertion) will depend on the order of the insertions.
2. The duplicate value is inserted above the existing value.
3. The first value will be inserted in the proper position and then the duplicate value will be inserted above that (assuming that the array is not full).
4. Start with a list that is full and contains 10, 12, 31, and 54. Nothing can be inserted unless a value is deleted. Assume the following insertions and deletions occur:

delete 54	list becomes	10, 12, 31
insert 3	list becomes	3, 10, 12, 31
insert 5	list becomes	3, 5, 10, 12
delete 12	list becomes	3, 5, 10

   Again with the original list, suppose the same steps were taken in the following order:

delete 12	list becomes	10, 31, 54
insert 3	list becomes	3, 10, 31, 54
insert 5	list becomes	3, 5, 10, 31
delete 54	value not in list	3, 5, 10, 31

Self-test 8–1, page 386

1. 'TEN$_b$TOP$_b$ENGINEERING$_b$'
2. 'TEN$_b$TOP$_b$'
3. 'ENGINEERING'

4. 'A'
5. 'ENGINEERING$_b$ACHIEVEMENTS$_{bbb}$'
6. 'TEN$_b$TOP$_b$'
7. 'TEN$_b$TOP$_b$ENGINEERING$_b$ACHIEVEMENTS$_{bbb}$'
8. 'TEN$_b$ACHIEVEMENTS$_{bbb}$'
9. 'TOP$_b$TEN'
10. 'ENGINEERS'$_b$ACHIEVEMENTS$_{bbb}$'
11. LASER$_b$
12. FIBER$_b$
13. CADCAM
14. '''$_{bbb}$
15. $_{bb}$12.4
16. GENETI

Self-test 8–2, page 395

1. 0.75D+00
2. 1.3D+00
3. 1.0D+00/9.0D+00
4. 5.0D+00/6.0D+00
5. −10.5D+00
6. 3.0D+00
7. $_{bbb}$0.78692D-02
8. $_{bbb}$0.787D-02
9. ************

Self-test 8–3, page 407

1. CX = 0.0 + 3.0i
2. CX = −3.0 + 3.0i
3. CX = 2.0 + 1.0i
4. CX = −2.0 + 0.0i
5. CX = 3.5 − 1.5i
6. CX = 1.41421 + 0.0i
7. $_{bb}$2.0+$_b$-1.0$_b$i
8. ($_{bb}$2.00,$_b$-1.00)

Self-test 9–1, page 434

1.

```
*-----------------------------------------------------------------------*
      PROGRAM INDATA
*
*  This program counts the number of records in two data files.
*
      REAL VAL1, VAL2
      INTEGER COUNT1, COUNT2, IOERR1, IOERR2
*
      OPEN (UNIT=11,FILE='DATA1',STATUS='OLD',IOSTAT=IOERR1)
      OPEN (UNIT=12,FILE='DATA2',STATUS='OLD',IOSTAT=IOERR2)
*
      COUNT1 = 0
      COUNT2 = 0
*
      IF (IOERR1.EQ.0) THEN
    5    READ (11,10,END=30) VAL1, VAL2
   10       FORMAT (F6.2,1X,F6.2)
            COUNT1 = COUNT1 + 1
            GO TO 5
   30    PRINT 35, 'DATA1', COUNT1
   35    FORMAT(1X,'THE NUMBER OF RECORDS IN ',A,' IS',I4)
      ELSE
         PRINT*, 'ERROR IN OPENING DATA1'
      END IF
*
      IF (IOERR2.EQ.0) THEN
   40    READ (12,10,END=50) VAL1, VAL2
            COUNT2 = COUNT2 + 1
            GO TO 40
   50    PRINT 35, 'DATA2', COUNT2
      ELSE
         PRINT*, 'ERROR IN OPENING DATA2'
      END IF
*
      END
*-----------------------------------------------------------------------*
```

Self-test 9–2, page 450

1.

```
*-----------------------------------------------------------------------*
      PROGRAM WAREHS
*
*  This program prints the item number of all items from a direct access
*  file in which the record indicates that there are more than 10 items
*  in the warehouse.
*
      INTEGER ITEMNO, ITEMCT, I
*
      OPEN (UNIT=10,FILE='STORES',ACCESS='DIRECT',
     +      STATUS='OLD',RECL=12)
*
      PRINT*, 'ITEM NO.   ITEM COUNT'
*
```

```
      DO 10 I=1,100
         READ (10,20,REC=I) ITEMNO, ITEMCT
   20    FORMAT (I5,2X,I5)
         IF (ITEMCT.GT.10) THEN
            PRINT 30 ITEMNO, ITEMCT
   30       FORMAT (1X,2X,I3,8X,I5)
         END IF
   10 CONTINUE
*
      END
*-----------------------------------------------------------------------*
```

Self-test 10–1, page 471

1.

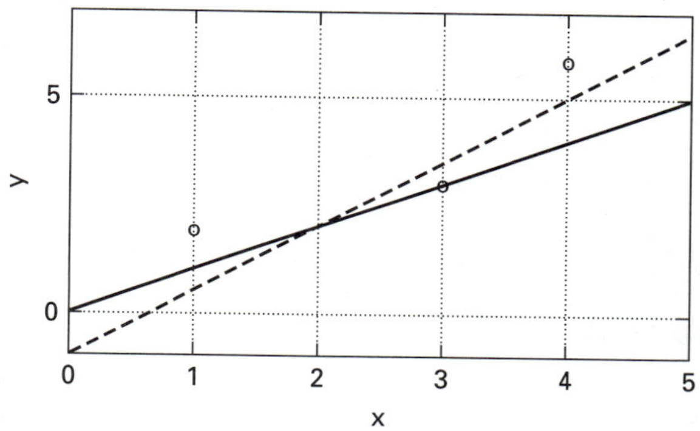

2. Error sum for the first model is 5.0.
   Error sum for the second model is 3.5.
   Therefore, the second model is the better model.
3. $y = 1.2143x + 0.4286$
4. Take the natural logarithm of both sides of the equation:

$$\ln y = \ln b + ax$$

Let $\tilde{y} = \ln y$, and let $\tilde{b} = \ln b$. Then $\tilde{y} = ax + \tilde{b}$.

Self-test 10–2, page 484

1. $\begin{bmatrix} 8 & 5 \\ -2 & -5 \\ 3 & 4 \end{bmatrix}$

2. $\begin{bmatrix} 10 & 7 \\ -4 & -7 \\ -3 & 8 \end{bmatrix}$

3. $\begin{bmatrix} 4 & 4 \\ -4 & -4 \\ -12 & 8 \end{bmatrix}$

4. 5
5. -30

6. $\begin{bmatrix} 1 & 11 \\ 1 & -5 \\ 3 & 9 \end{bmatrix}$

7. $\begin{bmatrix} 7 \\ 9 \end{bmatrix}$

8. $\begin{bmatrix} 7 \\ -5 \\ 4 \end{bmatrix}$

9. $\begin{bmatrix} 39 \\ -25 \\ 18 \end{bmatrix}$

10. $\begin{bmatrix} 11 \\ -7 \\ 7 \end{bmatrix}$

Self-test 10–3, page 503

1.

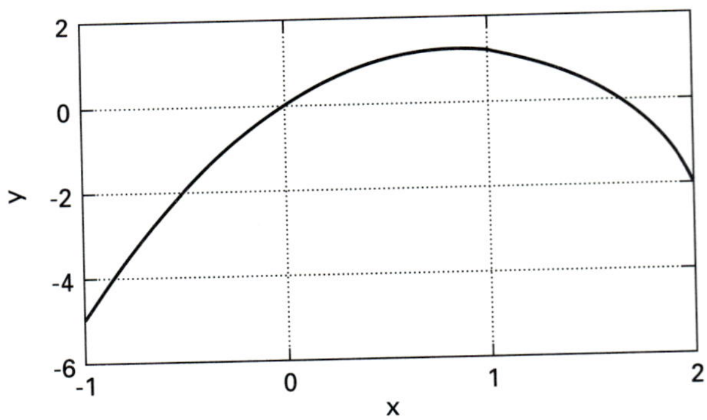

2. 0.75
3. 0.82
4. The exact value is 0.83, to two decimal places. The answer with five trapezoids is more accurate because five trapezoids approximate the area better than two trapezoids.

13.

```
*----------------------------------------------------------------------*
      PROGRAM DATE
*
*  This program estimates the age of an artifact from the
*  proportion of carbon remaining in the artifact.
*
      REAL CARBON, AGE, CENTRY
*
      PRINT*, 'ENTER PROPORTION REMAINING FOR CARBON DATING'
      READ*, CARBON
*
      AGE = (-LOG(CARBON))/0.0001216
      CENTRY = AGE/100.0
*
      PRINT 5, CENTRY
    5 FORMAT (1X,'ESTIMATED AGE OF ARTIFACT IS ',F6.2,'CENTURIES')
*
      END
*----------------------------------------------------------------------*
```

18.

```
*----------------------------------------------------------------------*
      PROGRAM RELY
*
*  This program computes the reliability of instrumentation
*  using a Bernoulli equation.
*
      INTEGER N
      REAL P1, P2, P3, PARALL, SERIES
*
      PRINT*, 'ENTER RELIABILITY OF COMPONENTS 1, 2, 3'
      PRINT*, '(USE PERCENTAGE BETWEEN 0.0 AND 100.0)'
      READ*, P1, P2, P3
*
      PARALL = (P2/100.0 + P3/100.0 -
     +          (P2/100.0)*(P3/100.0))*100.0
      SERIES = (P1/100.0)*(PARALL/100.0)*100.0
*
      PRINT*, 'PERCENT OF THE TIME THAT THE EQUIPMENT'
      PRINT 5, SERIES
    5 FORMAT (1X,'SHOULD WORK WITHOUT FAILURE IS ',F6.2,'%')
*
      END
*----------------------------------------------------------------------*
```

24.

```
*----------------------------------------------------------------------*

      PROGRAM STRIDE
*
*  This program reads the length of a leg, and then
*  computes and prints the time required for a stride.
*
      REAL LEG, PI, G, TIME, LS
      PARAMETER (PI=3.141593, G=32.0)
*
      PRINT*, 'ENTER THE LEG LENGTH IN FEET'
      READ*, LEG
*
```

```
      TIME = PI*SQRT(2.0*LEG/(3.0*G))
      LS = 0.75*LEG
*
      PRINT*
      PRINT 5, TIME
    5 FORMAT (1X,'THE STRIDE TIME IS ',F5.2,' SECONDS')
      PRINT 6, LEG
    6 FORMAT (1X,'FOR A LEG LENGTH OF ',F5.2,' FEET')
      PRINT 7, LS
    7 FORMAT (1X,'THE LENGTH OF A STRIDE IS',F5.2,' FEET')
*
      END
*-----------------------------------------------------------------*
```

30.

```
*-----------------------------------------------------------------*
      PROGRAM CONVRT
*
*  This program converts meters to kilometers to miles.
*
      REAL METERS, KMETER, MILES
*
      PRINT*, 'ENTER METERS'
      READ*, METERS
*
      KMETER = METERS/1000.0
      MILES = KMETER/1.609
*
      PRINT 5, METERS
    5 FORMAT (1X,F8.2,' METERS')
      PRINT 10, KMETER
   10 FORMAT (1X,F8.2,' KILOMETERS')
      PRINT 15, MILES
   15 FORMAT (1X,F8.2,' MILES')
*
      END
*-----------------------------------------------------------------*
```

Chapter 3

3.

```
*-----------------------------------------------------------------*
      PROGRAM PIPE
*
*  This program reads the indices of refraction for two materials
*  forming a light pipe. It also reads the angle of incidence for
*  light striking the pipe, and determines if the light is transmitted.
*
      INTEGER I
      REAL N1, N2, ANGLE, CRTCL
*
      DO 10 I = 1,5
*
         PRINT*, 'ENTER INDEX OF REFRACTION FOR ROD'
         READ*, N1
         PRINT*, 'ENTER INDEX OF REFRACTION FOR SURROUNDING MEDIUM'
         READ*, N2
         PRINT*, 'ENTER ANGLE OF TRANSMISSION OF LIGHT IN DEGREES'
         READ*, ANGLE
*
```

```
         IF (N2.GT.N1) THEN
            PRINT*, 'LIGHT IS NOT TRANSMITTED'
         ELSE
            CRTCL = ASIN(N2/N1)*(180.0/3.141593)
            IF (ANGLE.GT.CRTCL) THEN
               PRINT*, 'LIGHT IS TRANSMITTED'
            ELSE
               PRINT*, 'LIGHT IS NOT TRANSMITTED'
            END IF
         END IF
*
   10 CONTINUE
*
      END
*----------------------------------------------------------------------*
```

10.

```
*----------------------------------------------------------------------*
      PROGRAM ROCKET
*
*  This program simulates a rocket flight.
*
      REAL TIME, HEIGHT, NEWHT
      LOGICAL FIRST
*
      TIME = 0.0
      HEIGHT = 60.0
      FIRST = .TRUE.
*
      PRINT 5
    5 FORMAT (1X,'TIME (SEC.)          HEIGHT (FT.)')
      PRINT*
*
   10 IF (HEIGHT.GT.0.0.AND.TIME.LE.100.0) THEN
*
         NEWHT = 60.0 + 2.13*TIME**2 - 0.0013*TIME**4
     +           + 0.000034*TIME**4.751
         IF (NEWHT.LT.HEIGHT.AND.FIRST) THEN
            PRINT 15, TIME
   15       FORMAT (1X,'ROCKET BEGINS RETURNING AT 'F5.1,' SECONDS')
            FIRST = .FALSE.
         END IF
         HEIGHT = NEWHT
         TIME = TIME + 0.01
         GO TO 10
*


         PRINT*, 'ENTER NEXT SET OF DATA'
         READ*, BATCH, TEMP, PRESSR, DWELL
         GO TO 5
      END IF
*


    5    FORMAT (1X,2X,F3.1,4X,F4.2,3X,F4.1)
         Y = Y + 0.25
   10 CONTINUE
*
      END
*----------------------------------------------------------------------*
```

12.

```
*----------------------------------------------------------------------*
      PROGRAM SEALS
*
*  This program analyzes data on batches of sutures that have not
*  been properly sealed and then prints a report.
*
      INTEGER BATCH, COUNT, REJCTT, REJCTP, REJCTD
      REAL TEMP, PRESSR, DWELL, PERCT, PERCP, PERCD
*
      COUNT = 0
      REJCTT = 0
      REJCTP = 0
      REJCTD = 0
*
      PRINT*, 'ENTER BATCH NUMBER, TEMPERATURE, PRESSURE, DWELL'
      PRINT*, 'FOR BATCHES THAT HAVE BEEN REJECTED'
      PRINT*, '(NEGATIVE BATCH NUMBER TO STOP)'
      READ*, BATCH, TEMP, PRESSR, DWELL
*
    5 IF (BATCH.GE.0) THEN
         IF (TEMP.LT.150.0.OR.TEMP.GT.170.0) REJCTT = REJCTT + 1
         IF (PRESSR.LT.60.0.OR.PRESSR.GT.70.0) REJCTP = REJCTP + 1
         IF (DWELL.LT.2.0.OR.DWELL.GT.2.5) REJCTD = REJCTD + 1
         COUNT = COUNT + 1
         PRINT*, 'ENTER NEXT SET OF DATA'
         READ*, BATCH, TEMP, PRESSR, DWELL
         GO TO 5
      END IF
*
      PERCT = REAL(REJCTT)/REAL(COUNT)*100.0
      PERCP = REAL(REJCTP)/REAL(COUNT)*100.0
      PERCD = REAL(REJCTD)/REAL(COUNT)*100.0
*
      PRINT*
      PRINT*, 'SUMMARY OF BATCH REJECT INFORMATION'
      PRINT*
      PRINT 10, REJCTT, PERCT
   10 FORMAT (1X,I4,' BATCHES OF ',F7.1,
     +        ' % REJECTED DUE TO TEMPERATURE')
      PRINT 15, REJCTP, PERCP
   15 FORMAT (1X,I4,' BATCHES OR ',F7.1,
     +        ' % REJECTED DUE TO PRESSURE')
      PRINT 20, REJCTD, PERCD
   20 FORMAT (1X,I4,' BATCHES OR ',F7.1,
     +        ' % REJECTED DUE TO DWELL')
*
      END
*----------------------------------------------------------------------*
```

17.

```
*----------------------------------------------------------------------*
      PROGRAM TIMBER
*
*  This program computes a reforestation summary for an area
*  which has not been completely harvested.
*
      INTEGER ID, YEAR
      REAL TOTAL, UNCUT, RATE, REFOR
*
      PRINT*, 'ENTER LAND IDENTIFICATION (INTEGER)'
      READ*, ID
      PRINT*, 'ENTER TOTAL NUMBER OF ACRES'
```

```
      READ*, TOTAL
      PRINT*, 'ENTER NUMBER OF ACRES UNCUT'
      READ*, UNCUT
      PRINT*, 'ENTER REFORESTATION RATE'
      READ*, RATE
*
      IF (UNCUT.GT.TOTAL) THEN

         PRINT*, 'UNCUT AREA LARGER THAN ENTIRE AREA'
*
      ELSE
*
         PRINT*
         PRINT*, 'REFORESTATION SUMMARY'
         PRINT*
         PRINT 5, ID
    5    FORMAT (1X,'IDENTIFICATION NUMBER ',I5)
         PRINT 10, TOTAL
   10    FORMAT (1X,'TOTAL ACRES = ',F10.2)
         PRINT 20, UNCUT
   20    FORMAT (1X,'UNCUT ACRES = ',F10.2)
         PRINT 30, RATE
   30    FORMAT (1X,'REFORESTATION RATE = ',F5.3)
         PRINT*
         PRINT*, 'YEAR REFORESTED  TOTAL REFORESTED'
*
         DO 50 YEAR=1,20
            REFOR = UNCUT*RATE
            UNCUT = UNCUT + REFOR
            IF (MOD(YEAR,2).EQ.0) THEN
               PRINT 40, YEAR, REFOR, UNCUT
   40          FORMAT (1X,I3,F11.3,F17.3)
            END IF
   50    CONTINUE
*
      END IF
*
      END
*-----------------------------------------------------------------------*
```

24.

```
*-----------------------------------------------------------------------*

      PROGRAM TABLE
*
*  This program prints a table of values for F where F = XY - 1
*  for a given set of X and Y values.
*
      INTEGER I
      REAL F, X, Y
*
      PRINT*, '   X   ', '   Y   ', '   F   '
      Y = 0.5
      DO 10 I = 1, 9
         X = REAL(I)
         F = X*Y - 1.0
         PRINT 5, X, Y, F
    5    FORMAT (1X,2X,F3.1,4X,F4.2,3X,F4.1)
         Y = Y + 0.25
   10 CONTINUE
*
      END
*-----------------------------------------------------------------------*
```

Chapter 4

3.

```
*-----------------------------------------------------------------------*
      PROGRAM GUSTS
*
*  This program determines the maximum windgust at Stapleton
*  International Airport in December 1990. If the gust occurred
*  on more than one day, the last day is printed.
*
      INTEGER MAXDAY, K, A1, A2, A3, A4, A5, A6, A7, A8, A9, A10, A11,
     +        A12, A13, A14, A15, A16, A17, A18
      REAL MAX, RAIN
*
      OPEN (UNIT=8,FILE='DEC90',STATUS='OLD')
*
      MAX = 0.0
      MAXDAY = 0
*
      DO 10 K=1,31
         READ (8,*) A1, A2, A3, A4, A5, A6, A7, A8, A9, A10, A11,
     +              A12, A13, A14, A15, A16, A17, A18, RAIN
         IF (RAIN.GT.MAX) THEN
            MAX = RAIN
            MAXDAY = K
         END IF
   10 CONTINUE
*
      PRINT 15, MAX, MAXDAY
   15 FORMAT (1X,'MAXIMUM RAINFALL OF ',F6.2,'OCCURRED ON DEC. ',I2)
*
      END
*-----------------------------------------------------------------------*
```

8.

```
*-----------------------------------------------------------------------*
      PROGRAM PATH
*
*  This program determines the critical path information
*  for a project.
*
      INTEGER EVENT, TASK, DAYS, TOTAL, NUMBER, MIN, MAX,
     +        WEEKS, PLUS, SUMTSK, NUMTSK
      LOGICAL DONE
*
      OPEN (UNIT=8,FILE='PROJECT',STATUS='OLD')
*
      TOTAL = 0
      SUMTSK = 0
      NUMTSK = 0
*
      PRINT*, 'PROJECT COMPLETION TIMETABLE'
      PRINT*
      PRINT*, 'EVENT NUMBER     MINIMUM TIME     MAXIMUM TIME'
*
      READ (8,*) EVENT, TASK, DAYS
      NUMBER = EVENT
      MIN = DAYS
      MAX = DAYS
```

```
      IF (EVENT.EQ.99) THEN
         DONE = .TRUE.
      ELSE
         DONE = .FALSE.
      END IF
*
    5 IF (.NOT.DONE) THEN
         IF (EVENT.EQ.NUMBER) THEN
            IF (DAYS.LT.MIN) THEN
               MIN = DAYS
            ELSE IF (DAYS.GT.MAX) THEN
               MAX = DAYS
            END IF
         ELSE
            PRINT 10, NUMBER, MIN, MAX
   10       FORMAT (1X,I2,14X,I3,13X,I3)
            TOTAL = TOTAL + MAX
            NUMBER = EVENT
            MIN = DAYS
            MAX = DAYS
         END IF
         SUMTSK = SUMTSK + DAYS
         NUMTSK = NUMTSK + 1
         READ (8,*) EVENT, TASK, DAYS
         IF (EVENT.EQ.99) DONE = .TRUE.
         GO TO 5
      END IF
*
      PRINT 10, NUMBER, MIN, MAX
      TOTAL = TOTAL + MAX
*
      WEEKS = TOTAL/5
      PLUS = TOTAL - WEEKS*5
      PRINT*
      PRINT 15, TOTAL
   15 FORMAT (1X,'TOTAL PROJECT LENGTH = ',I3,' DAYS')
      PRINT 20, WEEKS, PLUS
   20 FORMAT (1X,'                     = ',I3,' WEEKS',I2,' DAYS')
      PRINT*
      PRINT 25, REAL(SUMTSK)/REAL(NUMTSK)
   25 FORMAT (1X,'AVERAGE NUMBER OF DAYS PER TASK = ',F5.1)
*
      END
*-----------------------------------------------------------------*
```

13.

```
*-----------------------------------------------------------------*
      PROGRAM PULSE
*
*  This program generates a sonar signal.
*
      INTEGER NUMBER, K
      REAL E, PD, FREQ, A, PERIOD, T, PI, TIME, SIGNAL
*
      OPEN (UNIT=10,FILE='SONAR',STATUS='NEW')
*
      PRINT*, 'ENTER TRANSMITTED ENERGY IN JOULES'
      READ*, E
      PRINT*, 'ENTER PULSE DURATION IN SECONDS'
      READ*, PD
      PRINT*, 'ENTER SINUSOID FREQUENCY IN HERTZ'
```

```
      READ*, FREQ
*
      A = SQRT(2.0*E/PD)
      PERIOD = 1.0/FREQ
      T = PERIOD/10.0
      NUMBER = NINT(PD/T)
      PI = 3.141593
*
      DO 10 K=0,NUMBER-1
         TIME = REAL(K)*T
         SIGNAL = A*COS(2.0*PI*FREQ*TIME)
         WRITE (10,*) TIME, SIGNAL
   10 CONTINUE
*
      TIME = -99.0
      SIGNAL = -99.0
      WRITE (10,*) TIME, SIGNAL
*
      END
*-----------------------------------------------------------------------*
```

18.

```
*-----------------------------------------------------------------------*
      PROGRAM TESTS
*
*  This program analyzes pressure data from three chambers.
*
      INTEGER PRESS1, PRESS2, PRESS3, MAX1, MAX2, MAX3, I
*
      OPEN (UNIT=10,FILE='RESULTS',STATUS='OLD')
*
      READ (10,*) MAX1, MAX2, MAX3
      DO 5 I=1,19
         READ (10,*) PRESS1, PRESS2, PRESS3
         IF (PRESS1.GT.MAX1) MAX1 = PRESS1
         IF (PRESS2.GT.MAX2) MAX2 = PRESS2
         IF (PRESS3.GT.MAX3) MAX3 = PRESS3
    5 CONTINUE
*
      PRINT 10, 1, MAX1
      PRINT 10, 2, MAX2
      PRINT 10, 3, MAX3
   10 FORMAT (1X,'MAXIMUM PRESSURE IN CHAMBER ',I1,' = ',I4)
*
      END
*-----------------------------------------------------------------------*
```

Chapter 5

1.

```
*-----------------------------------------------------------------------*
      PROGRAM WIND
*
*  This program reads a file of wind tunnel test data and then
*  uses linear interpolation to compute lift coefficients for
*  additional flight angles.
*
      INTEGER N, K
      REAL A(500), C(500), ALPHA, CL
*
      OPEN (UNIT=10,FILE='LIFT',STATUS='OLD')
*
```

```
      READ (10,*)  N
      DO 5 K=1,N
         READ (10,*)  A(K), C(K)
  5   CONTINUE
*
      PRINT*, 'DATA COVERS ANGLES FROM ',A(1),' TO ',A(N)
      PRINT*, 'ENTER FLIGHT PATH ANGLE IN DEGREES'
      READ*, ALPHA
*
 10   IF (ALPHA .NE. 999.0) THEN
         IF (A(1).LE.ALPHA.AND.ALPHA.LE.A(N)) THEN
*
            IF (ALPHA.EQ.A(1)) THEN
               K = 2
            ELSE
               K = 1
 15            IF (A(K) .LT. ALPHA) THEN
                  K = K + 1
                  GO TO 15
               END IF
            END IF
            CL = C(K-1) + (ALPHA - A(K-1))/(A(K) - A(K-1))
     +                  *(C(K) - C(K-1))
            PRINT  20, ALPHA, CL
 20         FORMAT (1X,'FLIGHT ANGLE = ',F7.2/
     +               1X,'CORRESPONDING COEFFICIENT OF LIFT = ',F7.3)
         ELSE
*
            PRINT*, 'ANGLE OUT OF RANGE FOR DATA FILE'
*
         END IF
*
         PRINT*
         PRINT*, 'ENTER FLIGHT PATH ANGLE IN DEGREES'
         PRINT*, '(999.0 TO QUIT)'
         READ*, ALPHA
         GO TO 10
      END IF
*
      END
*-----------------------------------------------------------------*
```

9.

```
*-----------------------------------------------------------------*
      PROGRAM EARTH
*
*  This program will read a file of earthquake data and sort
*  and print it in ascending order.
*
      INTEGER LOCATE, I, N, J, PTR, LAST, FIRST, K
      REAL QUAKE(200), HOLD, MEDIAN
*
      OPEN (UNIT=9,FILE='MOTION',STATUS='OLD')
*
      READ (9,*) LOCATE
      PRINT 5, LOCATE
    5 FORMAT (1X,'LOCATION NUMBER: ',I5)
*
      I = 1
   10 READ (9,*,END=20) QUAKE(I)
         I = I + 1
         GO TO 10
```

```
*
   20 N = I - 1
      LAST = N
      DO 40 J=1,N-1
         PTR = J
         FIRST = J + 1
         DO 30 K = FIRST, LAST
            IF (QUAKE(K).LT.QUAKE(PTR)) PTR = K
   30    CONTINUE
         HOLD = QUAKE(J)
         QUAKE(J) = QUAKE(PTR)
         QUAKE(PTR) = HOLD
   40 CONTINUE
*
      DO 60 I=1,N
         PRINT 50, I, QUAKE(I)
   50    FORMAT (1X,I3,'.',3X,F6.4)
   60 CONTINUE
*
      IF (MOD(N,2).EQ.1) THEN
         MEDIAN = QUAKE(N/2+1)
      ELSE
         MEDIAN = (QUAKE(N/2) + QUAKE(N/2+1))/2.0
      END IF
      PRINT 65, MEDIAN
   65 FORMAT (1X,'MEDIAN EARTHQUAKE VALUE IS ',F6.4)
*
      END
*-----------------------------------------------------------------------*
```

13.

```
*-----------------------------------------------------------------------*
      PROGRAM PWRPLT
*
*  This program computes and prints a composite report
*  summarizing several weeks of power plant data.
*
      INTEGER POWER(20,7), MIN, TOTAL, COUNT, I, J, N
      REAL AVE
      DATA TOTAL, COUNT /0, 0/
*
      PRINT*, 'ENTER NUMBER OF WEEKS FOR ANALYSIS'
      READ*, N
*
      OPEN (UNIT=12,FILE='PLANT',STATUS='OLD')
      DO 5 I=1,N
        READ (12,*) (POWER(I,J), J=1,7)
    5 CONTINUE
*
      MIN = POWER(1,1)
      DO 15 I=1,N
         DO 10 J=1,7
            TOTAL = TOTAL + POWER(I,J)
            IF (POWER(I,J).LT.MIN) MIN = POWER(I,J)
   10    CONTINUE
   15 CONTINUE
      AVE = REAL(TOTAL)/REAL(N*7)
*
      DO 25 I=1,N
         DO 20 J=1,7
            IF (POWER(I,J).GT.AVE) COUNT = COUNT + 1
   20    CONTINUE
```

```
   25 CONTINUE
*
      PRINT 30
   30 FORMAT (1X,15X,'COMPOSITE INFORMATION')
      PRINT 35, AVE
   35 FORMAT (1X,'AVERAGE DAILY POWER OUTPUT = ',F5.1,' MEGAWATTS')
      PRINT 40, COUNT
   40 FORMAT (1X,'NUMBER OF DAYS WITH GREATER THAN ',
     +        'AVERAGE POWER OUTPUT = ',I2)
      PRINT 45
   45 FORMAT (1X,'DAYS(S) WITH MINIMUM POWER OUTPUT:')
      DO 60 I=1,N
         DO 55 J=1,7
            IF (POWER(I,J).EQ.MIN) PRINT 50, I, J
   50       FORMAT (1X,12X,'WEEK ',I2,'    DAY ',I2)
   55    CONTINUE
   60 CONTINUE
*
      END
*-----------------------------------------------------------------------*
```

19.

```
*-----------------------------------------------------------------------*
      PROGRAM NAVIG
*
*  This program reads the elevation data for a set of land
*  grids and determines the number of peaks in each grid.
*
      INTEGER MAP(100,100), I, J, ID, NROWS, NCOLS, COUNT,
     +        MAX, MIN
*
      PRINT 5
    5 FORMAT (1X,'SUMMARY OF LAND GRID ANALYSIS')
      PRINT 10
   10 FORMAT (1X,'IDENTIFICATION    NUMBER OF POINTS    ',
     +        'NUMBER OF PEAKS')
*
      OPEN (UNIT=15,FILE='ELEVTN',STATUS='OLD')
*
      READ (15,*) ID
   15 IF (ID.NE.99999) THEN
*
         READ (15,*) NROWS,NCOLS
         DO 20 I=1,NROWS
            READ (15,*) (MAP(I,J), J=1,NCOLS)
   20    CONTINUE
*
         COUNT = 0
         DO 30 I=2,NROWS-1
            DO 25 J=2,NCOLS-1
               IF ((MAP(I-1,J).LT.MAP(I,J)).AND.
     +             (MAP(I+1,J).LT.MAP(I,J)).AND.
     +             (MAP(I,J-1).LT.MAP(I,J)).AND.
     +             (MAP(I,J+1).LT.MAP(I,J))) THEN
     +                COUNT = COUNT + 1
               END IF
   25       CONTINUE
   30    CONTINUE
*
         PRINT 35, ID, NROWS*NCOLS, COUNT
   35    FORMAT (1X,I7,10X,I7,10X,I7)
```

```
*
      MAX = MAP(1,1)
      MIN = MAP(1,1)
      DO 45 I=1,NROWS
         DO 40 J=1,NCOLS
            IF (MAP(I,J).GT.MAX) MAX = MAP(I,J)
            IF (MAP(I,J).LT.MIN) MIN = MAP(I,J)
   40    CONTINUE
   45 CONTINUE
      PRINT 50, MAX, MIN
   50 FORMAT (1X,'MAXIMUM ELEVATION = ',I6,5X,
     +        'MINIMUM ELEVATION = ',I6)
      READ (15,*) ID
      GO TO 15
*
      END IF
*
      END
*-----------------------------------------------------------------------*
```

25.

```
*-----------------------------------------------------------------------*
      INTEGER TIME(30)
      ...
      DO 50 I=2,30,2
         PRINT 45, I, TIME(I)
   45    FORMAT (1X,'TIME(',I2,') CONTAINS ',I4,' SECONDS')
   50 CONTINUE
*-----------------------------------------------------------------------*
```

Chapter 6

```
*-----------------------------------------------------------------------*
      PROGRAM TABLE1
*
*  This program generates a temperature conversion table.
*
      INTEGER IN, OUT
      REAL FIRST, CHANGE, LAST, NEXT, NEW, TEMP,
     +     CTOF, KTOF, RTOF, FTOC, FTOK, FTOR, HOLD
*
*  Conversion functions use Fahrenheit as the base
*  temperature unit.
*
      CTOF(TEMP) = 1.8*TEMP + 32.0
      KTOF(TEMP) = CTOF(TEMP - 273.15)
      RTOF(TEMP) = TEMP - 459.67
      FTOC(TEMP) = (TEMP - 32.0)*0.5555556
      FTOK(TEMP) = FTOC(TEMP) + 273.15
      FTOR(TEMP) = TEMP + 459.67
*
      PRINT*, 'CODE TEMPERATURE AS FOLLOWS:'
      PRINT*, '1-FAHRENHEIT'
      PRINT*, '2-CENTIGRADE'
      PRINT*, '3-KELVIN'
      PRINT*, '4-RANKIN'
      PRINT*, 'ENTER CODE FOR TABLE INPUT'
      READ*, IN
      PRINT*, 'ENTER CODE FOR TABLE OUTPUT'
      READ*, OUT
      PRINT*, 'ENTER NUMBER OF DEGREES FOR FIRST LINE: '
```

```
      READ*, FIRST
      PRINT*, 'ENTER CHANGE IN DEGREES BETWEEN LINES: '
      READ*, CHANGE
      PRINT*, 'ENTER NUMBER OF DEGREES FOR LAST LINE: '
      READ*, LAST
*
      PRINT 5
    5 FORMAT (1X,5X,'TEMPERATURE CONVERSION TABLE')
      PRINT 10
   10 FORMAT (1X,'DEGREES, INPUT',10X,'DEGREES, OUTPUT')
*
      NEXT = FIRST
   20 IF (NEXT.LE.LAST) THEN
*
         IF (IN.EQ.1) THEN
            HOLD = NEXT
         ELSE IF (IN.EQ.2) THEN
            HOLD = CTOF(NEXT)
         ELSE IF (IN.EQ.3) THEN
            HOLD = KTOF(NEXT)
         ELSE
            HOLD = RTOF(NEXT)
         END IF
*
         IF (OUT.EQ.1) THEN
            NEW = HOLD
         ELSE IF (OUT.EQ.2) THEN
            NEW = FTOC(HOLD)
         ELSE IF (OUT.EQ.3) THEN
            NEW = FTOK(HOLD)
         ELSE
            NEW = FTOR(HOLD)
         END IF
*
         PRINT 25, NEXT, NEW
   25    FORMAT (1X,F9.2,18X,F9.2)
         NEXT = NEXT + CHANGE
         GO TO 20
*
      END IF
*
      END
*-----------------------------------------------------------------------*
```

7.

```
*-----------------------------------------------------------------------*
      PROGRAM REPORT
*
*  This program generates a report from the daily production
*  information for a set of oil wells.
*
      INTEGER MO, DA, YR, ID, N, I
      REAL OIL(7), TOTAL, AVE, INDAVE, MAX
      DATA N, TOTAL, MAX /0, 0.0, 0/
*
      OPEN (UNIT=12,FILE='WELLS',STATUS='OLD')
      READ (12,*) MO, DA, YR
      PRINT*, 'OIL WELL PRODUCTION'
      PRINT 5, MO, DA, YR
    5 FORMAT (2X,'WEEK OF ',I2,'-',I2,'-',I2)
      PRINT*
```

```
      PRINT*, 'WELL ID       AVERAGE PRODUCTION'
      PRINT*, '              (IN BARRELS)'
*
      READ (12,*) ID, (OIL(I), I=1,7)
   10 IF (ID.NE.99999) THEN
         INDAVE = AVE(OIL,7)
         PRINT 15, ID, INDAVE
   15    FORMAT (1X,I5,9X,F6.2)
         N = N + 1
         TOTAL = TOTAL + INDAVE
         IF (INDAVE.GT.MAX) MAX = INDAVE
         READ (12,*) ID, (OIL(I), I=1,7)
         GO TO 10
      END IF
*
      PRINT*
      PRINT 20, N, TOTAL/REAL(N)
   20 FORMAT (1X,'OVERALL AVERAGE FOR ',I3,' WELLS IS ',F6.2)
      PRINT 25, MAX*7.0
   25 FORMAT (1X,'MAXIMUM WEEKLY PRODUCTION IS ',F8.2)
*
      END
*-----------------------------------------------------------------------*
```

(no changes in function AVE)

```
*-----------------------------------------------------------------------*
```

11.

```
*-----------------------------------------------------------------------*
      PROGRAM ROOTS
*
*  This program determines the roots the interval [-5,5]
*  for a quartic polynomial using an incremental search and
*  bisection method.
*
      INTEGER COUNT, I
      REAL A(0:4), LEFT, RIGHT, MID, F
      LOGICAL DONE
*
      PRINT*, 'ENTER COEFFICIENTS A0, A1, A2, A3, A4'
      READ*, A
*
      PRINT 5, A
    5 FORMAT(/,'POLYNOMIAL:'/,1X,9X,'4'11X,'3',11X,'2'/
     +       1X,4(F7.3,' X + '),F7.3/)
*
      COUNT = 0
      PRINT*, 'ENTER LEFT AND RIGHT INTERVAL POINT'
      READ*, LEFT, RIGHT
      LAST = NINT((RIGHT - 0.25 - LEFT)/0.25) + 1
*
      DO 40 I = 1,LAST
         RIGHT = LEFT + 0.25
*
         IF (ABS(F(A,LEFT)).LT.0.001) THEN
*
            PRINT 15, LEFT, F(A,LEFT)
   15       FORMAT (1X,'ROOT = ',F7.3,3X,'F(ROOT) = ',F7.3)
            COUNT = COUNT + 1
*
         ELSE IF (F(A,LEFT)*F(A,RIGHT).LT.0.0) THEN
*
```

```
            DONE = .FALSE.
            SIZE = RIGHT - LEFT
*
   20       IF (SIZE.GT.0.01.AND..NOT.DONE) THEN
               MID = (LEFT + RIGHT)/2.0
               IF (ABS(F(A,MID)).LT.0.001) THEN
                  DONE = .TRUE.
               ELSE IF (F(A,MID)*F(A,LEFT).LT.0.0) THEN
                  RIGHT = MID
               ELSE
                  LEFT = MID
               END IF
               SIZE = RIGHT - LEFT
               GO TO 20
            END IF
*
            IF (SIZE.GT.0.01) THEN
               ROOT = MID
            ELSE
               ROOT = (LEFT + RIGHT)/2.0
            END IF
*
            PRINT 15, ROOT, F(A,ROOT)
            COUNT = COUNT + 1
*
         END IF
         LEFT = LEFT + 0.25
   40 CONTINUE
*
      IF (ABS(F(A,LEFT)).LT.0.001) THEN
         PRINT 15, LEFT, F(A,LEFT)
         COUNT = COUNT + 1
      END IF
      IF (COUNT.EQ.0) THEN
         PRINT*, 'NO ROOTS IN INTERVAL [-5,5]'
      END IF
*
      END
*-----------------------------------------------------------------------*
      REAL FUNCTION F(A,X)
*
*  This function evaluates a quartic polynomial at X.
*
      REAL A(0:4), X
*
      F = A(0)*X**4 + A(1)*X**3 + A(2)*X**2 + A(3)*X + A(4)
*
      RETURN
      END
*-----------------------------------------------------------------------*
```

30.

```
*-----------------------------------------------------------------------*
      INTEGER FUNCTION INVERT(NUM)
*
*  This function reverses the digits in a two-digit number.

      INTEGER NUM, DIGIT1, DIGIT2
*
      DIGIT1 = NUM/10
      DIGIT2 = MOD(NUM,10)
```

```
      INVERT = DIGIT2*10 + DIGIT1
*
      RETURN
      END
*-----------------------------------------------------------------*
```

Chapter 7

3.

```
*-----------------------------------------------------------------*
      PROGRAM SIGGEN
*
*  This program generates a signal composed of a sine wave
*  plus random noise.
*
      INTEGER SEED, I, N
      REAL PI, T, NOISE, X
      DATA PI, T /3.141593, 0.0/
*
      PRINT*, 'ENTER A POSITIVE INTEGER SEED: '
      READ*, SEED
      OPEN (UNIT=15,FILE='SIGNAL',STATUS='NEW')
*
      PRINT*, 'ENTER NUMBER OF DATA POINTS TO GENERATE'
      READ*, N
*
      DO 10 I=1,N
         CALL RANDOM (SEED, NOISE)
         X = 2*SIN(2*PI*T) + NOISE
         WRITE (15,*) T, X
         T = T + 0.01
   10 CONTINUE
*
      END
*-----------------------------------------------------------------*
```

(no changes in subroutine RANDOM)

```
*-----------------------------------------------------------------*
```

8.

```
*-----------------------------------------------------------------*
      PROGRAM STREAM
*
*  This program computes the maximum oxygen deficit for a group
*  of wastewater discharge streams.
*
      INTEGER N, J, NUM
      REAL DAYS, QD, QS, BODD, BODS, TMIX, KR, DOXYGN,
     +     DEFMAX, DEFDAY
*
      OPEN (UNIT=10,FILE='STREAMS',STATUS='OLD')
      PRINT*, 'ENTER TIME PERIOD FOR STREAM ANALYSIS IN DAYS'
      READ*, DAYS
      PRINT*, 'ENTER NUMBER OF ANALYSES PER DAY (INTEGER)'
      READ*, NUM
      PRINT*
      PRINT*, 'OXYGEN DEFICIT ANALYSIS OF WASTEWATER DISCHARGE STREAMS')
      PRINT*
*
      READ (10,*) N
      DO 30 J=1,N
```

```
      READ (10,*) QD, QS, BODD, BODS, TMIX, KR, DOXYGN
      CALL CALC(NUM,QD,QS,BODD,BODS,TMIX,KR,DOXYGN,
     +          DAYS,DEFMAX,DEFDAY)
      PRINT 10, J, DEFMAX
 10   FORMAT (1X,'STREAM ',I3,':',' MAXIMUM DEFICIT = ',F6.3)
      PRINT 20, DEFDAY
 20   FORMAT (1X,12X,'OCCURRED AT DAY ',F3.1)
      PRINT*
 30 CONTINUE
*
    END
*-------------------------------------------------------------------*
    SUBROUTINE CALC(NUM,QD,QS,BODD,BODS,TMIX,KR,DOXYGN,
   +                DAYS,DEFMAX,DEFDAY)
*
*  This subroutine calculates the maximum oxygen deficit for a
*  stream along with the day that it occurred.
*
    INTEGER STEPS, J, NUM
    REAL QD, QS, BODD, BODS, TMIX, KR, DOXYGN,
   +     FSMIX, KD, BODMIX, DEFCT, INCR,
   +     DAYS, DEFMAX, DEFDAY, T, TEMP1, TEMP2, TEMP3
*
    BODMIX = ((BODS*QS) + (BODD*QD))/(QS + QD)
    FSMIX = BODMIX*(0.02*TMIX + 0.6)/0.68
    KD = 0.1*(1.047**(TMIX - 20.0))
*
    DEFMAX = 0.0
    DEFDAY = 0.0
    STEPS = INT(DAYS)*NUM
    INCR = 1.0/REAL(NUM)
*
    DO 10 J=1,STEPS
       T = REAL(J)*INCR
       TEMP1 = (KD*FSMIX)/(KR - KD)
       TEMP2 = 10.0**(-KD*T) - 10.0**(-KR*T)
       TEMP3 = DOXYGN*(10.0**(-KR*T))
       DEFCT = (TEMP1*TEMP2) + TEMP3
       IF (J.EQ.1.OR.DEFCT.GT.DEFMAX) THEN
          DEFMAX = DEFCT
          DEFDAY = T
       END IF
 10 CONTINUE
*
    RETURN
    END
*-------------------------------------------------------------------*
```

12.

```
*-------------------------------------------------------------------*
    PROGRAM UPDATE
*
*  This program updates a composite materials information list by
*  adding new composite materials along with their warehouse locations.
*
    INTEGER LIMIT, J, ID(500), LOC(500), COUNT, NEWID, NEWLOC
    LOGICAL DONE
*
    PARAMETER (LIMIT=500)
*
    OPEN (UNIT=8,FILE='COMPIN',STATUS='OLD')
*
```

```
      DONE = .FALSE.
      J = 1
    5 IF (.NOT.DONE) THEN
         READ (8,*) ID(J), LOC(J)
         IF (ID(J).EQ.99999) THEN
            DONE = .TRUE.
         ELSE
            J = J + 1
         END IF
         GO TO 5
      END IF
      COUNT = J
      DONE = .FALSE.
*
   10 IF (.NOT.DONE) THEN
         PRINT*, 'ENTER NEW ID AND LOCATION NUMBER'
         PRINT*, '(NEGATIVE VALUES TO QUIT)'
         READ*, NEWID, NEWLOC
         IF (NEWID.GE.0) THEN
            IF (COUNT.EQ.LIMIT) THEN
               PRINT*, 'LIST IS FULL'
            ELSE
               CALL INSERT(LIMIT,NEWID,NEWLOC,COUNT,ID,LOC)
            END IF
         ELSE
            DONE = .TRUE.
         END IF
         GO TO 10
      END IF
*
      OPEN (UNIT=9,FILE='COMPOUT',STATUS='NEW')
*
      DO 15 J=1,COUNT
         WRITE (9,*) ID(J), LOC(J)
   15 CONTINUE
      PRINT 20, COUNT
   20 FORMAT (1X,'THE NUMBER OF COMPOSITE MATERIALS IS ',I4)
*
      END
*-----------------------------------------------------------------------*
      SUBROUTINE INSERT (LIMIT,NEWID,NEWLOC,COUNT,ID,LOC)
*
*  This subroutine inserts an element in an ordered list.
*
      INTEGER LIMIT, NEWID, NEWLOC, COUNT, ID(LIMIT), LOC(LIMIT), J, K
      LOGICAL DONE
*
      DONE = .FALSE.
      J = 1
    5 IF (.NOT.DONE) THEN
         IF (ID(J).LT.NEWID) THEN
            J = J + 1
         ELSE
            DONE = .TRUE.
         END IF
         GO TO 5
      END IF
*
      IF (ID(J).EQ.NEWID) THEN
         PRINT*, 'ID ALREADY IN FILE'
      ELSE
         COUNT = COUNT + 1
```

```
         DO 10 K=COUNT,J+1,-1
            ID(K) = ID(K-1)
            LOC(K) = LOC(K-1)
   10    CONTINUE
         ID(J) = NEWID
         LOC(J) = NEWLOC
      END IF
*
      RETURN
      END
*-------------------------------------------------------------------*
```

24.

```
*-------------------------------------------------------------------*
      SUBROUTINE GREAT(Z,W)
*
*  This subroutine moves corresponding values of Z into W
*  unless the value is less than the average of all values
*  in Z. In these cases the average value of Z is used in W.
*
      INTEGER I, J
      REAL Z(5,4), W(5,4), SUM, AVE
*
      SUM = 0.0
      DO 10 I=1,5
         DO 5 J=1,4
            SUM = SUM + Z(I,J)
    5    CONTINUE
   10 CONTINUE
      AVE = SUM/20.0
      DO 20 I=1,5
         DO 15 J=1,4
            IF (Z(I,J).LE.AVE) THEN
               W(I,J) = Z(I,J)
            ELSE
               W(I,J) = AVE
            END IF
   15    CONTINUE
   20 CONTINUE
*
      RETURN
      END
*-------------------------------------------------------------------*
```

Chapter 8

4.

```
*-------------------------------------------------------------------*
      PROGRAM WEIGHT
*
*  This program reads character strings containing amino acids
*  from large protein molecules, and computes the molecular weights.
*

      INTEGER K, MW(20), N, J, BLNK, NCHAR, AMNUM, SUM, START, AMWT,
     +        COUNT
      CHARACTER*3 REF(20)
      CHARACTER*150 PROTN
      LOGICAL ERROR
*
```

```
      OPEN (UNIT=9,FILE='AMINO',STATUS='OLD')
      DO 10 K=1,20
         READ(9,*) REF(K), MW(K)
   10 CONTINUE
*
      OPEN (UNIT=10,FILE='PROTEIN',STATUS='OLD')
      READ(10,*) N
*
      DO 30 J=1,N
*
         READ(10,*) PROTN
         BLNK = INDEX(PROTN,' ')
         NCHAR = BLNK - 1
         AMNUM = NCHAR/3
         SUM = 0
*
         IF (MOD(NCHAR,3).NE.0) THEN
*
            PRINT*, 'LENGTH ERROR IN PROTEIN ', J
            PRINT*, PROTN(:BLNK)
            PRINT*
*
         ELSE
*
            ERROR = .FALSE.
            COUNT = 0
            DO 20 K=1,AMNUM
               START = (K-1)*3 + 1
               CALL MWT(REF,MW,PROTN(START:START+2),AMWT)
               IF (AMWT.NE.0) THEN
                  SUM = SUM + AMWT
                  COUNT = COUNT + 1
               ELSE
                  PRINT*, 'ERROR IN AMINO ', K, ' PROTEIN ', J
                  ERROR = .TRUE.
               END IF
   20       CONTINUE
            IF (.NOT.ERROR) THEN
               PRINT 15, PROTN(:BLNK), SUM
   15          FORMAT (1X,'PROTEIN: ',A/1X,'MOLECULAR WEIGHT:',I8/)
               PRINT 25, COUNT
   25          FORMAT (1X,'NUMBER OF AMINO ACIDS IS ',I4/)
            ELSE
               PRINT*, PROTN(:BLNK)
               PRINT*
            END IF
*
         END IF
*
   30 CONTINUE
*
      END
*-----------------------------------------------------------------------*
      SUBROUTINE MWT(REF,MW,STRING,WEIGHT)
*
*  This subroutine receives arrays containing the character references
*  and molecular weights for amino acids. It uses these arrays to
*  determine if an input string is an amino acid and, if so, returns
*  the molecular weight of the amino acid; otherwise zero is returned.
*
      INTEGER MW(20), WEIGHT, K
      CHARACTER*3 REF(20), STRING
*
      WEIGHT = 0
```

```
      DO 10 K=1,20
         IF (STRING.EQ.REF(K)) WEIGHT = MW(K)
   10 CONTINUE
*
      RETURN
      END
*-----------------------------------------------------------------------*
```

7.

```
*-----------------------------------------------------------------------*
      PROGRAM TEMP
*
*  This program initializes the temperatures in a metal plate
*  and determines the equilibrium temperatures based on a
*  tolerance value.
*
      INTEGER NROW, NCOL, I, J
      LOGICAL EQUILB
      DOUBLE PRECISION OLD(10,10), NEW(10,10), TOLNC,
     +                 TOP, BOT, LEFT, RIGHT
*
      PRINT*, 'ENTER TEMPERATURE GRID SIZE:'
      PRINT*, 'ROWS, COLUMNS (MAXIMUM 10,10) '
      READ*, NROW, NCOL
      PRINT*, 'ENTER ISOTHERMAL EDGE TEMPERATURES:'
      PRINT*, 'TOP, BOTTOM, LEFT, RIGHT '
      READ*, TOP, BOT, LEFT, RIGHT
      PRINT*, 'ENTER EQUILIBRIUM TOLERANCE VALUE: '
      READ*, TOLNC
*
*  INITIALIZE TEMPERATURE ARRAY
*
      CALL FIRST(NEW,NROW,NCOL,TOP,BOT,LEFT,RIGHT)
      CALL MOVE(OLD,NEW,NROW,NCOL)
*
*  PRINT INITIAL TEMPERATURE ARRAY
*
      PRINT*
      PRINT*, 'INITIAL TEMPERATURES'
      PRINT*
      CALL PRINT(OLD,NROW,NCOL)
*
*  UPDATE TEMPERATURES UNTIL EQUILIBRIUM
*
      EQUILB = .FALSE.
   20 IF (.NOT.EQUILB) THEN
         EQUILB = .TRUE.
         DO 30 I=2,NROW-1
            DO 25 J=2,NCOL-1
               NEW(I,J) = (OLD(I-1,J) + OLD(I+1,J) +
     +                     OLD(I,J-1) + OLD(I,J+1))/4.0+00
               IF (DABS(NEW(I,J) - OLD(I,J)).GT.TOLNC)
     +            EQUILB = .FALSE.
   25       CONTINUE
   30    CONTINUE
         CALL MOVE(OLD,NEW,NROW,NCOL)
         GO TO 20
      END IF
*
* PRINT EQUILIBRIUM TEMPERATURE ARRAY
*
      PRINT*
      PRINT*, 'EQUILIBRIUM TEMPERATURES'
```

```
      PRINT*
      CALL PRINT(OLD,NROW,NCOL)
*
      END
*-----------------------------------------------------------------------*
```

(no changes in subroutine PRINT)

```
*-----------------------------------------------------------------------*
```

(no changes in subroutine MOVE)

```
*-----------------------------------------------------------------------*
      SUBROUTINE FIRST(NEW,NROW,NCOL,TOP,BOT,LEFT,RIGHT)
*
*  This subroutine initializes the temperature array.
*
      INTEGER NROW, NCOL, I, J
      DOUBLE PRECISION NEW(10,10), TOP, BOT, LEFT, RIGHT
*
      DO 5 J=1,NCOL
         NEW(1,J) = TOP
         NEW(NROW,J) = BOT
    5 CONTINUE
      DO 15 I=2,NROW-1
         NEW(I,1) = LEFT
         DO 10 J=2,NCOL-1
            NEW(I,J) = 0.0D+00
   10    CONTINUE
         NEW(I,NCOL) = RIGHT
   15 CONTINUE
*
      RETURN
      END
*-----------------------------------------------------------------------*
```

13.

```
*-----------------------------------------------------------------------*
      PROGRAM ELECT1
*
*      This program determines the magnitude and phase of an RC
*      circuit on a sine wave.
*
      REAL R, MC, C, W, MAGN, PHASE
      COMPLEX I, HW
*
      I = (0.0, 1.0)
*
      PRINT*, 'ENTER RESISTANCE IN OHMS'
      READ*, R
      PRINT*, 'ENTER CAPACITANCE IN MICROFARADS'
      READ*, MC
      PRINT*, 'ENTER THE SINE FREQUENCY IN RADIANS PER SEC'
      READ*, W
*
      C = MC*1.0E-06
      HW = (I*W*R*C)/(1.0 + I*W*R*C)
      MAGN = CABS(HW)
      PHASE = ATAN(AIMAG(HW)/REAL(HW))
*
      PRINT 5, MAGN, PHASE
    5 FORMAT (1X,'MAGNITUDE EFFECT:',F5.2,3X,
     +        'PHASE EFFECT:', F5.2)
*
      END
*-----------------------------------------------------------------------*
```

17.

```
*----------------------------------------------------------------------*
      SUBROUTINE CNDNS(IN,OUT)
*
*  This subroutine removes all groups of multiple blanks
*  from IN and stores in OUT.
*
      INTEGER I, K
      CHARACTER*50 IN, OUT
*
      OUT = ' '
      K = 1
      DO 10 I=1,49
         IF (IN(I:I).NE.' ') THEN
            OUT(K:K) = IN(I:I)
            K = K + 1
         ELSE
            IF (IN(I+1:I+1).NE.' ') THEN
               OUT(K:K) = IN(I:I)
               K = K + 1
            END IF
         END IF
   10 CONTINUE
      OUT(K:K) = IN(50:50)
*
      RETURN
      END
*----------------------------------------------------------------------*
```

Chapter 9

2.

```
*----------------------------------------------------------------------*
      PROGRAM VOYAGE
*
*  This program detects edges in a two-dimensional image.
*
      INTEGER I, J, IMAGE(40,50), ID, NR, NC, NEWID
      REAL LIMIT
      CHARACTER FILENM*6, EDGE(40)*50, LINE*50
      LOGICAL DONE
*
      DO 3 I=1,50
         LINE(I:I) = '*'
    3 CONTINUE
      PRINT*, 'ENTER NAME OF IMAGE FILE ENCLOSED IN QUOTES'
      READ*, FILENM
      OPEN (UNIT=8,FILE=FILENM,STATUS='OLD')
*
      PRINT*
      PRINT*,'IMAGES IN THIS FILE'
      READ(8,*) ID, NR, NC
    5 IF (ID.NE.9999) THEN
         PRINT 10, ID,NR,NC
   10    FORMAT (1X,'ID = ',I4,' SIZE = (',I2,',',I2,')')
         DO 20 I=1,NR
            READ(8,15)  IMAGE(I,1)
   15       FORMAT (50I1)
   20    CONTINUE
         READ(8,*) ID, NR, NC
         GO TO 5
      END IF
```

```
*
      PRINT*
      PRINT*, 'ENTER ID OF IMAGE TO BE ANALYZED'
      READ*, NEWID
      PRINT*, 'ENTER THRESHOLD FOR EDGE DETECTION'
      READ*, LIMIT
*
      REWIND (UNIT=8)
      READ(8,*) ID, NR, NC
      DONE = .FALSE.
   25 IF (.NOT.DONE) THEN
         IF (ID.EQ.NEWID) THEN
            DO 30 I=1,NR
               READ (8,15) (IMAGE(I,J),J=1,NC)
   30       CONTINUE
            CALL CONVERT(LIMIT,IMAGE,EDGE,NR,NC)
            PRINT*
            PRINT 35, LIMIT
   35       FORMAT (1X,'THRESHOLD VALUE = ',F5.2)
            PRINT 40, LINE(1:NC)
            DO 45 I=1,NR
               PRINT 40, EDGE(I)(1:NC)
   40          FORMAT (1X,'*',A,'*')
   45       CONTINUE
            PRINT 40, LINE(1:NC)
            DONE = .TRUE.
         ELSE IF (ID.EQ.9999) THEN
            DONE = .TRUE.
            PRINT*, 'IMAGE NOT FOUND'
         ELSE
            DO 50 I=1,NR
               READ(8,15) IMAGE(I,1)
   50       CONTINUE
            READ(8,*) ID, NR, NC
         END IF
         GO TO 25
      END IF
*
      END
*-----------------------------------------------------------------------*
```

(no changes in subroutine CONVRT)

```
*-----------------------------------------------------------------------*
```

10.

```
*-----------------------------------------------------------------------*
      PROGRAM MIGRAT
*
*  This program merges new sighting information into the master
*  file of migration information on whooping cranes.
*
      INTEGER M,D,Y,T,MO,DA,YR,TIME,GRID1,GRID2,BIRDS,
     +        SMO,SDA,SYR,STIME,SGRID1,SGRID2,SBIRDS,
     +        CMO,CDA,CYR,CTIME,CGRID1,CGRID2,CBIRDS,COUNT,
     +        MAXCT,HOLDM,HOLDD
      DOUBLE PRECISION DATE, CDATE, SDATE
      LOGICAL DONE
*
      DATE(M,D,Y,T) = DBLE(REAL(Y)*1.0D08) +
     +                DBLE(REAL(M)*1.0D06) +
     +                DBLE(REAL(D)*1.0D04) +
     +                DBLE(REAL(T))
*
```

```
      OPEN (UNIT=10,FILE='SIGHTS',STATUS='OLD')
      OPEN (UNIT=11,FILE='CRANES',STATUS='OLD')
      OPEN (UNIT=12,FILE='TEMP',STATUS='NEW')
*
      READ (10,5) SMO,SDA,SYR,STIME,SGRID1,SGRID2,SBIRDS
    5 FORMAT (3I2,1X,I4,1X,2I2,1X,I4)
      READ (11,5) CMO,CDA,CYR,CTIME,CGRID1,CGRID2,CBIRDS
      SDATE = DATE(SMO,SDA,SYR,STIME)
      CDATE = DATE(CMO,CDA,CYR,CTIME)
      IF (SMO.EQ.99.AND.CMO.EQ.99) THEN
         DONE = .TRUE.
      ELSE
         DONE = .FALSE.
      END IF
*
   10 IF (.NOT.DONE) THEN
         IF (CDATE.LT.SDATE) THEN
            WRITE (12,5) CMO,CDA,CYR,CTIME,CGRID1,CGRID2,CBIRDS
            READ (11,5) CMO,CDA,CYR,CTIME,CGRID1,CGRID2,CBIRDS
            CDATE = DATE(CMO,CDA,CYR,CTIME)
         ELSE
            WRITE (12,5) SMO,SDA,SYR,STIME,SGRID1,SGRID2,SBIRDS
            READ (10,5) SMO,SDA,SYR,STIME,SGRID1,SGRID2,SBIRDS
            SDATE = DATE(SMO,SDA,SYR,STIME)
         END IF
         IF (SMO.EQ.99.AND.CMO.EQ.99) DONE = .TRUE.
         GO TO 10
      END IF
      WRITE (12,5) SMO,SDA,SYR,STIME,SGRID1,SGRID2,SBIRDS
      CLOSE (UNIT=11,STATUS='DELETE')
      CLOSE (UNIT=12)
*
      OPEN (UNIT=11,FILE='CRANES',STATUS='NEW')
      OPEN (UNIT=12,FILE='TEMP',STATUS='OLD')
      PRINT*, 'WHOOPING CRANE MIGRATION'
      PRINT*
      PRINT*, 'CURRENT SIGHTINGS'
      PRINT*
*
      HOLDM = 0
      HOLDD = 0
      COUNT = 0
      MAXCT = 0
   15 READ (12,5,END=35) MO,DA,YR,TIME,GRID1,GRID2,BIRDS
      IF (MO.NE.99) THEN
         PRINT 20, MO,DA,YR,TIME
   20    FORMAT (1X,I2,'-',I2,'-',I2,4X,I4)
         PRINT 25, GRID1,GRID2
   25    FORMAT (1X,5X,'GRID LOCATION:  ',2I3)
         PRINT 30, BIRDS
   30    FORMAT (1X,5X,'NUMBER OF BIRDS',1X,I5)
         IF (MO.EQ.HOLDM.AND.DA.EQ.HOLDD) THEN
            COUNT = COUNT + 1
         ELSE
            IF (COUNT.GT.MAXCT) MAXCT = COUNT
               COUNT = 1
               HOLDM = MO
               HOLDD = DA
            END IF
         END IF
         WRITE (11,5) MO,DA,YR,TIME,GRID1,GRID2,BIRDS
         GO TO 15
*
```

```
   35 PRINT 40, MAXCT
   40 FORMAT (1X,'MAXIMUM NUMBER OF SIGHTINGS IN ONE DAY = ',I4)
*
   50 STOP
      END
*-----------------------------------------------------------------------*
```

12.

```
*-----------------------------------------------------------------------*
      PROGRAM UPDATE
*
*  This program updates the scan location in a database
*  containing information related to CAT scans.
*
      INTEGER SCANID(200), PATID(200), DATE(200), ANGLE(200),
     +        XRAYS(200), KEY, I
      LOGICAL MORE
      CHARACTER*4 REF(200), NEWLOC
*
      DATA MORE /.TRUE./
*
      OPEN (UNIT=10,FILE='CHANGE',ACCESS='SEQUENTIAL',
     +      STATUS='OLD',FORM='FORMATTED')
      OPEN (UNIT=11,FILE='SCANS',ACCESS='DIRECT',
     +      STATUS='OLD',FORM='FORMATTED',RECL=25)
*
      READ (10,5) KEY, NEWLOC
    5 FORMAT (I4,A4)
      IF (KEY.EQ.-999) MORE = .FALSE.
*
      I = 1
   10 IF (MORE) THEN
         READ (11,15,REC=KEY,ERR=20)
     +         SCANID(I), PATID(I), DATE(I), ANGLE(I), XRAYS(I), REF(I)
   15    FORMAT (I4,I4,I6,I3,I4,A4)
         WRITE (11,15,REC=KEY) SCANID(I), PATID(I), DATE(I), ANGLE(I),
     +                         XRAYS(I), NEWLOC
         REF(I) = NEWLOC
   20    IF (KEY.NE.SCANID) PRINT*, 'NO MATCH FOR', KEY
         READ (10,5) KEY, NEWLOC
         IF (KEY.EQ.-999) THEN
            MORE = .FALSE.
         ELSE
            I = I + 1
         END IF
         GO TO 10
      END IF
*
      COUNT = I
      PRINT*, 'INFORMATION FOR CAT SCANS PERFORMED IN 1991'
      PRINT*, 'SCAN ID    ANGLE  XRAYS   REF'
      DO 30 I=1,COUNT
         IF (DATE(I).EQ.1991) THEN
            PRINT 35 SCANID(I), ANGLE(I), XRAYS(I), REF(I)
   35       FORMAT (1X,I4,1X,I4,2X,I6,2X,I4,2X,A4)
         END IF
   30 CONTINUE
*
      END
*-----------------------------------------------------------------------*
```

17.

```
*-----------------------------------------------------------------------*
      PROGRAM PLANT
*
*  This program prints the work orders for specified pieces
*  of equipment.
*
      INTEGER TYPE, ORDER, CODE
      LOGICAL DONE
*
      OPEN (UNIT=8,FILE='SENSOR',STATUS='OLD')
      DONE = .FALSE.
    5 IF (.NOT.DONE) THEN
         PRINT*, 'ENTER SENSOR TYPE (1 THROUGH 5)'
         PRINT*, 'OR ENTER 9 TO QUIT'
         READ*, TYPE
         IF (TYPE.NE.9) THEN
            PRINT*
            PRINT*, 'WORK ORDERS:'
            REWIND (UNIT=8)
   10       READ (8,15,END=20) ORDER, CODE
   15          FORMAT (I5,2X,I1)
               IF (CODE.EQ.TYPE) PRINT*, ORDER
               GO TO 10
   20       PRINT*,'END OF FILE REACHED'
         ELSE
            DONE = .TRUE.
         END IF
         GO TO 5
      END IF
*
      END
*-----------------------------------------------------------------------*
```

Chapter 10

1.

```
*-----------------------------------------------------------------------*
      PROGRAM LINEAR
*
*  This program computes a linear model for XY data and then
*  computes the residual sum to evaluate the model.
*
      INTEGER I, N
      REAL X(500),Y(500),SLOPE,YINT,YNEW,RES,
     +     SUMX,SUMY,SUMXY,SUMXX,SUMRES,DEVX,DEVY,MAXDEV
*
      DATA I,SUMX,SUMY,SUMXY, SUMXX, SUMRES /1,5*0.0/
*
      OPEN (UNIT=10,FILE='XYDATA',STATUS='OLD')
    5 READ (10,*,END=50) X(I), Y(I)
         SUMX = SUMX + X(I)
         SUMY = SUMY + Y(I)
         SUMXY = SUMXY + X(I)*Y(I)
         SUMXX = SUMXX + X(I)*X(I)
         I = I + 1
         GO TO 5
*
   50 N = I - 1
      SLOPE = (SUMX*SUMY - REAL(N)*SUMXY)/
     +        (SUMX*SUMX - REAL(N)*SUMXX)
```

```
      YINT = (SUMY - SLOPE*SUMX)/REAL(N)
*
      PRINT*, 'THE LINEAR EQUATION IS'
      PRINT 55, SLOPE, YINT
   55 FORMAT (1X,'Y = ',F6.2,' X + ',F6.2)
      PRINT*
      PRINT*, 'ORIGINAL    ORIGINAL    ESTIMATED    RESIDUAL'
      PRINT*, '   X           Y            Y                 '
      PRINT*
*
      DO 65 I=1,N
         YNEW = SLOPE*X(I) + YINT
         RES = Y(I) - YNEW
         SUMRES = SUMRES + RES*RES
         PRINT 60, X(I), Y(I), YNEW, RES
   60    FORMAT (1X,F6.2,6X,F6.2,6X,F6.2,7X,F6.2)
         IF (I.EQ.1) THEN
            MAXDEV = ABS(RES)
            DEVX = X(I)
            DEVY = Y(I)
         ELSE
            IF (MAXDEV.LT.ABS(RES)) THEN
               MAXDEV = ABS(RES)
               DEVX = X(I)
               DEVY = Y(I)
            END IF
         END IF
   65 CONTINUE
*
      PRINT*
      PRINT 70, SUMRES
   70 FORMAT (1X, 'RESIDUAL SUM = ', F6.2)
      PRINT 75, DEVX, DEVY
   75 FORMAT (1X,'POINT (',F6.2,',',F6.2,') DEVIATES THE MOST',
     +        ' FROM THE LINE')
*
      END
*----------------------------------------------------------------------*
```

6.

```
*----------------------------------------------------------------------*
```

(no changes in main program GAUSS

```
*----------------------------------------------------------------------*
      SUBROUTINE ORDER(A,N,PIVOT,ERROR)
*
*  This subroutine reorders the equations so that the pivot
*  position in the pivot equation has the maximum absolute value.
*
      INTEGER N, ROW, RMAX, PIVOT, K
      REAL A(25,26), TEMP
      LOGICAL ERROR
*
      RMAX = PIVOT
      DO 10 ROW=PIVOT+1,N
         IF (ABS(A(ROW,PIVOT)).GT.ABS(A(RMAX,PIVOT))) RMAX = ROW
   10 CONTINUE
*
      IF (ABS(A(RMAX,PIVOT)).LT.1.0E-05) THEN
         ERROR = .TRUE.
      ELSE
         IF (RMAX.NE.PIVOT) THEN
            DO 20 K=1,N+1
```

```
                TEMP = A(RMAX,K)
                A(RMAX,K) = A(PIVOT,K)
                A(PIVOT,K) = TEMP
   20       CONTINUE
            PRINT 25, PIVOT, RMAX
   25       FORMAT (1X,'ROWS INTERCHANGED:',I3,2X,I3)
         END IF
      END IF
*
      RETURN
      END
*-----------------------------------------------------------------------*
```

(no changes in subroutine ELIM)

```
*-----------------------------------------------------------------------*
```

(no changes in subroutine BACKSB)

```
*-----------------------------------------------------------------------*
```

12.

```
*-----------------------------------------------------------------------*
      PROGRAM NUMDIF
*
*  This program uses numerical differentiation to compute the
*  velocity and acceleration data for a sounding rocket.
*
      INTEGER N, K
      REAL TIME(512), ALT(512), H, VEL(512), ACC(512)
*
      OPEN (UNIT=15,FILE='ALTITUDE',STATUS='OLD')
      OPEN (UNIT=16,FILE='VELOCITY',STATUS='NEW')
      OPEN (UNIT=17,FILE='ACCEL',STATUS='NEW')
*
*  Read time and altitude data.
*
      READ (15,*) N
      DO 10 K=1,N
         READ (15,*) TIME(K), ALT(K)
   10 CONTINUE
*
*  Compute and store velocities and accelerations.
*
      H = TIME(2) - TIME(1)
      WRITE (16,*) N-1
      WRITE (17,*) N-2
*
      DO 20 K=2,N
         VEL(K) = (ALT(K) - ALT(K-1))/H
         WRITE (16,*) TIME(K), VEL(K)
         IF (K.NE.2) THEN
            ACC(K) = (ALT(K) - 2*ALT(K-1) + ALT(K-2))/(H*H)
            WRITE (17,*) TIME(K), ACC(K)
         END IF
   20 CONTINUE
*
      END
*-----------------------------------------------------------------------*
```

21.

```
*-----------------------------------------------------------------------*
      SUBROUTINE TRANSP(A,AROW,ACOL,T,TROW,TCOL)
*
*  This subroutine transposes matrix A into matrix T.
```

```
*
      INTEGER AROW, ACOL, A(AROW,ACOL), TROW, TCOL,
     +        T(TROW,TCOL), I, J
*
      DO 10 I=1,AROW
         DO 5 J=1,ACOL
            T(J,I) = A(I,J)
    5    CONTINUE
   10 CONTINUE
*
      RETURN
      END
*-----------------------------------------------------------------------*
```

Index

All Fortran 90 references are shown in color.

A

B

C

D

E

F

G

H

I

J

K

L

P

Q

R

S

T

U

V

W

X